Microsoft® SQL Server® 2008

R2 ANALYTICS & DATA VISUALIZATION

About the Authors

Doug Harts is a services executive at Microsoft currently helping U.S. Federal agencies implement Microsoft technology roadmaps. As a former chief technology officer of the Microsoft Gold development partner that published the market's first SQL Server web-based ad hoc report tool, which co-launched with Reporting Services in 2000, Doug has been involved in business intelligence research and design with Microsoft-Redmond and commercial and public organizations around the world. As a current member of the Microsoft Business Intelligence Field Advisory Council, Doug contributes to the design and development of business intelligence technology in the SharePoint Cloud environment. Doug is the author of the McGraw-Hill book *Microsoft Office 2007 Business Intelligence* and can be found with other business intelligence community members at www.OfficeBIcentral.com.

Jim Dugan is a solutions architect in the Microsoft healthcare and benefits team at Microsoft Federal. Jim has been in the information technology field for over 25 years and with Microsoft for 14 of those years. Jim has contributed to many large-scale projects for commercial, federal, and humanitarian efforts. He previously served as technical director of Microsoft's Technology and Innovation Center in Reston, Virginia. He resides with his wife and three kids in Arlington, Virginia, and he can be found with other business intelligence community people at www.OfficeBIcentral.com.

Tricia Wilcox Almas is a technical architect for Business Intelligence Solutions for MicroLink, LLC, a Microsoft Gold Partner. Tricia has been developing solutions and managing IT projects for over 25 years and has extensive experience helping non-profit and government organizations get the most out of their IT investments. Tricia enjoys building data warehouses and cubes, and delivering reporting and performance management solutions for her clients. In her rare leisure time, she assists with fundraising events for Challenger Little League and Special Olympics, and enjoys time with her husband of 25 years and two teenage sons.

About the Technical Editor

Sean Boon is a senior program manager at Microsoft currently working on reporting services specializing in data visualization. In his ten years at Microsoft, Sean has contributed to the design and development of several Microsoft business intelligence products, including the SQL Server Accelerator for Business Intelligence, Excel and Excel Services, the Microsoft chart control that ships as part of the .NET framework, and the Silverlight toolkit. Sean enjoys interacting with customers to help them get the most out of their investments in Microsoft BI and delivering sessions at industry conferences like TechED, the Microsoft Business Intelligence Conference, and SQLPASS. You can find Sean on the reporting services MSDN Forums and on Twitter with the username "seanboon."

Microsoft® SQL Server® 2008

R2 ANALYTICS & DATA VISUALIZATION

Doug Harts

Jim Dugan

Tricia Wilcox Almas

New York Chicago San Francisco Lisbon
London Madrid Mexico City Milan
New Delhi San Juan Seoul Singapore
Sydney Toronto

The McGraw·Hill Companies

Cataloging-in-Publication Data is on file with the Library of Congress

McGraw-Hill books are available at special quantity discounts to use as premiums and sales promotions, or for use in corporate training programs. To contact a representative, please e-mail us at bulksales@mcgraw-hill.com.

Microsoft® SQL Server® 2008 R2 Analytics & Data Visualization

1234567890 WFR WFR 109876543210

ISBN 978-0-07-160143-6
MHID 0-07-160143-0

Sponsoring Editor
Wendy Rinaldi

Editorial Supervisor
Janet Walden

Project Editor
Emilia Thiuri, Fortuitous Publishing Services

Acquisitions Coordinator
Joya Anthony

Technical Editor
Sean Boon

Copy Editor
Bob Campbell

Proofreader
Paul Tyler

Indexer
Jack Lewis

Production Supervisor
George Anderson

Composition
Glyph International

Illustration
Glyph International

Art Director, Cover
Jeff Weeks

Cover Designer
Jeff Weeks

This book is dedicated to Bill Baker, who in many ways has been the "Father of Microsoft Business Intelligence." For the formative decade that started with SQL Server 2000, Bill was the guiding force behind the creation of Analysis Services, Integration Services, and Reporting Services, which comprise the foundation of Microsoft Business Intelligence today. During those years Bill was also a mentor to members of the Microsoft BI Community around the world, reaching out from Redmond with encouragement to anyone that needed support regardless of the size or significance of those he helped. We are fortunate to have been influenced by Bill's leadership. We trust this book is another step toward Bill Baker's vision of "BI for the masses."

Contents at a Glance

Contents

Foreword

What is needed is a new approach, one that complements existing business intelligence and data warehouse investments with powerful desktop tools. At Microsoft, we call this approach "Managed Self-Service." It does not replace the data warehouse but instead enables the desktop user to perform analytics using corporate data from their strategic system, but also from other more ad hoc sources, without having to request every new feature from an already-stressed IT department. Yet, because this solution is built on our productivity, data, and collaboration platforms—Excel, SQL Server, and SharePoint—IT still has insight and oversight of the users' activities. IT, in other words, consists of providers and enablers, rather than a production bottleneck.

This new development is the latest in a long line of business intelligence innovations from Microsoft. Since we released SQL Server 7.0, way back in 1997, we have been at the forefront of delivering business intelligence and data warehousing to all businesses that need it. Over the years, we have met expert practitioners in the field and seen them flourish on the Microsoft data platform. Among them have been the authors of this book: Doug Harts, Jim Dugan, and Tricia Almas.

As experts in "traditional" business intelligence, the authors are well placed to understand how these new technologies work with your existing investments. As seasoned practitioners, they know very well the business problems that can be addressed. Most importantly, as expert communicators they are able to walk you through numerous examples of how to build solutions. Whether you need to explore collaborative BI with SharePoint, or rich visualizations with Reporting Services and Report Builder, or scalable desktop data mash-ups with PowerPivot, or advanced analytics with Data Mining, or indeed any number of powerful features, you'll find this book has something for you.

I think you'll find *Microsoft SQL Server 2008 R2 Analytics & Data Visualization* to be an excellent companion as you make your desk "a tool for supplying the answers quickly."

—*Donald Farmer,* Principal Program Manager,
SQL Server BI Management,
Microsoft Corporation
June 2010

Acknowledgments

I would like to acknowledge my friends, Mark Turner, Joan Barrow, and Steve Dvoranchik, who continue to listen to my enthusiasm for business intelligence topics in the Microsoft world of reporting technology. I also would like to acknowledge SD, who, in particular, has stayed the course with me in this authoring experience, and has proven to be the support I needed the most, exactly when I needed her the most. Working with Tricia and Jim has been a wonderful experience, and the information technology world is lucky to have them as participants. And we all agree that our editor, Wendy Rinaldi, is "the best in the business"—she shares our excitement with the business intelligence theme that resonates with customers everywhere.

—Doug Harts

I would like to acknowledge my God, my family and friends, who have put up with so much. For Karla, James, Maryann, and Paige for dealing with time away and for inspiring me every day. To my late parents, James and Judy Dugan, we miss you very much. Thank you to my in-laws, Carl and Donada Moore, for all of their love, time, and sacrifice. In addition, I would like to thank my brother and sister in Christ Jim Gowler and Dr. Rebecca Crainsmith for blessing my family's life so greatly. I would also like to thank Doug Harts for inviting me to join him on this journey.

—Jim Dugan

I would like to thank my family and friends for supporting my dreams, and to all those business intelligence practitioners before me who blazed the trail and provided wonderful guidance and encouragement. Thanks to our editor, Wendy Rinaldi, for her advice, support, and encouragement when challenges looked like Everest. A special thanks to my friend Don Murdoch, who is always willing to help me with computer problems and networking challenges, and never gives me grief about my deficiencies.

—Tricia Wilcox Almas

Introduction

This book is written for the "information worker" businessperson who already uses Microsoft Office applications such as Excel, Word, or Visio to accomplish his or her daily work. Today, information workers most often work in the collaboration environment of SharePoint, where their spreadsheets and documents are saved and shared, along with SQL Server Data Visualizations such as dashboards and reports, for everyone to view and utilize.

It is this large class of information workers who can now design and share world-class reports and data visualizations using the techniques described in this book. The new SQL Server business intelligence tools from Microsoft take reporting out of the realm of database professionals and place "reporting with graphics" in the hands of all levels of employees in support of real-world work processes.

Information technology professionals are also finding an increasing need to understand the tools presented in this book, as Microsoft Reporting Services in general becomes pervasively more integrated within line-of-business applications. These applications range from generic Microsoft Project Servers to line-of-business case management systems that are often based on Microsoft's XRM case-management/workflow server. And while these applications are often delivered with embedded Microsoft Reporting Services reports, those reports can be enhanced and expanded with a working knowledge of the concepts discussed in this book.

The examples in this book require the use of Reporting Services "Report Builder" version 3.0, which is bundled with SQL Server 2008 version R2—and is available at no additional charge to users of SQL Server. The new PowerPivot product from Microsoft is also discussed/explored in this book and requires Excel 2010 on the user's desktop. However, it should be noted that the chapters in the book do not describe server operating system configuration, or code examples in any detail—it is assumed that the users and consumers of this book have access to SQL Server 2008 R2 and SharePoint 2007 (or SharePoint 2010).

One of the first things that can help with understanding the concepts of SQL Server Data Visualization is to understand how different tools of the SQL Server technology relate to each other, and the roles they play in business intelligence analytics. Each tool has its own unique design interface, but every SQL Server BI component produces charts, gauges, grids, or maps for reporting, analysis, and measurement that are viewable in the browser or within a SharePoint portal. The following "Microsoft BI Matrix" illustration shows the SQL Server Data Visualization components, and how they fit into the roles of reporting, analysis, and measurement.

The Tools in the Book

The Microsoft Business Intelligence Matrix illustration shows a graphical depiction of the Office and SQL Server tools available in the 2010 Office-SharePoint environment. Some of the tools such as Excel 2010 can be installed on individual user desktops in a stand-alone fashion, and can be used with or without the other Office or SharePoint 2010 tools. Report Builder is delivered as part of SQL Server 2008 R2 and can be used as a stand-alone client report design application or as an Internet Information Services (IIS)–connected report designer that can re-use previously constructed report components, such as charts and maps, that are stored on a Reporting Services "Report Server" that resides on IIS.

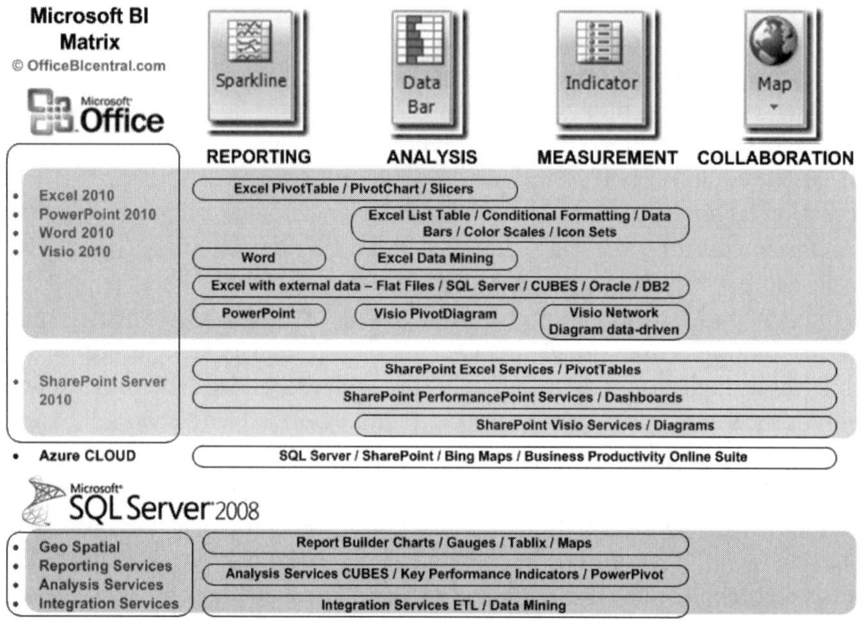

As the Microsoft BI Matrix illustration shows, the business intelligence tools can be viewed in terms of reporting, analysis, measurement, and collaboration roles. For the purposes of this book we will focus on reporting, analysis, and measurement (using the acronym RAM) by designing reports, charts, maps, and gauges with the SQL Server Report Builder. Data Mining is also explored using a unique combination of Excel 2010 and SQL Server Analysis Services, and the new PowerPivot tool, which is presented as the most recent entrant to the Data Mining family of tools.

Further explanation and examples in support of the many working pieces of the Microsoft BI Matrix are available on the following web site:

www.officebicentral.com

Also available on this website are the datasets, report files, and associated content that have been used to write this book and are presented for you to use in your own exploration of the business intelligence concepts herein. This website also offers blogs and commentary regarding the ever-changing world of Microsoft Business Intelligence and is frequented by everyone from beginning report designers to Microsoft experts. Have fun!

The Purpose of the Book

SQL Server 2008 R2 "Data Visualization" raises the bar for that added sizzle in the presentation of business intelligence reports. We will learn how to combine charts, gauges, maps, and sparklines into analytical presentations that can be used as either a report or a dashboard and take you to the next step of making data presentations consistent and polished—a concept that is reinforced with the "BI Tips" sprinkled throughout the chapters.

The chapters on data mining and PowerPivot extend the reporting concepts into analysis that relies on Excel 2010 for the end-user working environment. This is significant when we realize that Excel is, and will likely continue to be, the most widely used report-analysis tool around the world.

Finally the color insert shows various examples of the eye-catching reports, charts, maps, and gauges that can be created with Report Builder 3.0. All of these examples can be created with the Report Builder tool and do not require any special server configurations or code customizations. In a nutshell, this means that with the tools available today you can enjoy self-service business intelligence in a flash!

The Chapters of the Book

Every chapter can be read or referenced in a stand-alone manner because all of the basic and advanced steps are contained in each chapter—they do not have to be read in any particular order. This is meant to serve today's information technology workers who often need a quick working example to get them started on their own business intelligence solution. Also, the figures are designed and captioned to help you scan the pages and find areas of interest using the figures as a graphical guide.

Chapter 1: Charts in SQL Server Reporting Services 2008

This chapter shows how to create reports using the graph types in SQL Server Reporting Services (SSRS) 2008 R2. The combination of multiple chart types in one presentation, 3-D capabilities, and the detailed configuration of axis and data-series labels is becoming more important as the amount and complexity of data increase. Complex data requires a more carefully designed report to tell the data story, and the report must be intuitive to business users that understand the context of the operation or process being presented.

We'll examine the relationship between data types and chart types, and explore the enhanced reporting capabilities of SSRS by creating reports in the Business Intelligence Design Studio (BIDS—also known as Visual Studio Report Designer) and in Report Builder 3.0. Report Designer and Report Builder have both received major usability enhancements, and the new features make report authoring easier and more powerful. We will do an in-depth exploration of the available properties for charts and chart properties that can change the appearance of a chart.

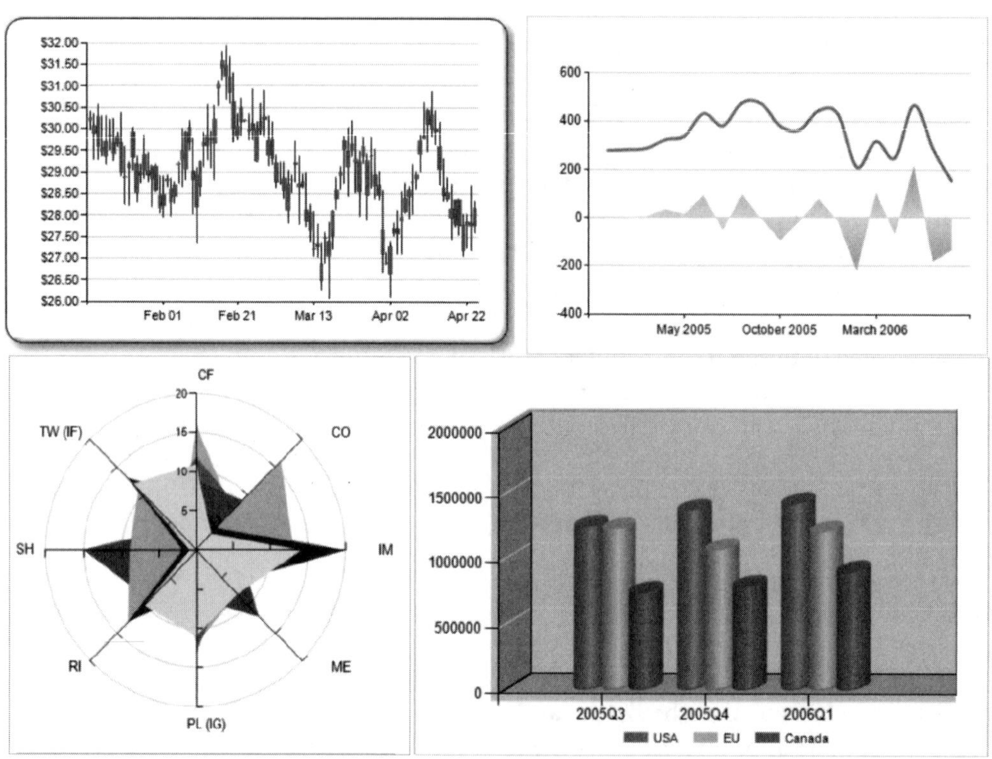

Chapter 2: Gauges in SQL Server Reporting Services 2008

This chapter shows how to create reports using the gauge graph types in SQL Server Reporting Services (SSRS) 2008 R2. Gauges are a new graphic element in SSRS, and it should be noted that gauges provide a presentation and perception of data to end users that is different from charts. This chapter presents a wide range of possibilities for using gauges in report and dashboard displays, and the techniques for configuring the gauges to get the best possible representation of the data.

There are many components to a gauge, including its scale, ranges, and graphic composition. All of these elements are explored in depth so that the report author can create the best gauge display for the information to be conveyed.

Gauges are a special visual data representation that displays a single value. The objective of using gauges for reporting is to make the metric values obvious—and they provide good visualizations for key performance indicators (KPIs) and specialized metrics such as calculated measures. Gauges can show data points compared to a goal or target value where the presentation of comparison values is an important part of the overall gauge meaning—in reports, dashboards, and scorecards, all of which are discussed in this chapter.

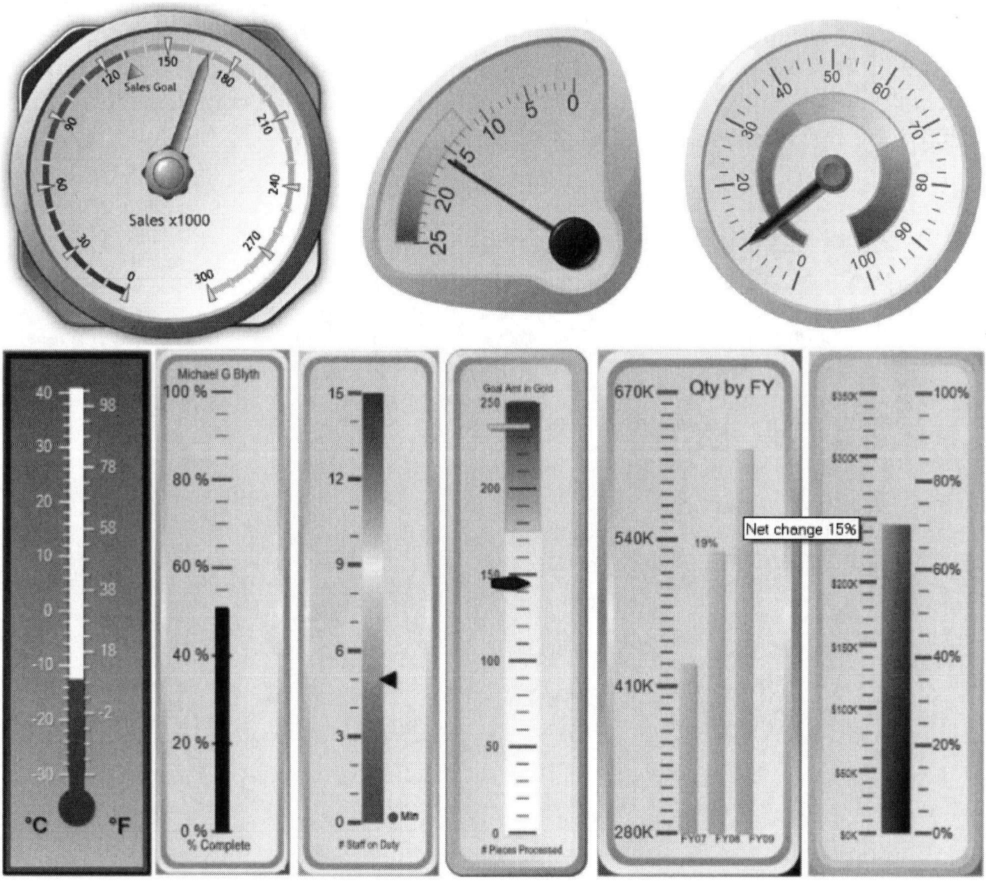

Chapter 3: SQL Server 2008 R2 Map Reports

This chapter shows how to create reports using the map designer in SQL Server Reporting Services (SSRS) 2008 R2. Maps are a new part of Microsoft SSRS, and the designer makes it reasonable, for the first time in the history of map design tools, for everyday report designers to work with map spatial layouts. And this uniquely user-friendly capability is continued with the capability to easily associate analytical data, such as sales by state, with a map spatial layout, such as U.S. states.

We'll explore the various "layers" of a map design, and show how to add colors that can be coordinated with charts, as well as bubble (circles) that can show relative data values by the size of the bubble. There can be many components to a map report, but they all start with a "geo-layer," one of several that for common maps based on the U.S. or world are provided as part of the Report Builder map design process.

Maps can provide an immediate visualization of data that is understood by everyone, since we all are aware of the common topology of the world in which we live—and we so often think of reporting by the geographic boundaries such as counties, states, and countries. It is noted in the chapter that maps are not meant to contain highly detailed data, but they can be combined with charts and matrix-grids that complement the map with row-by-row information.

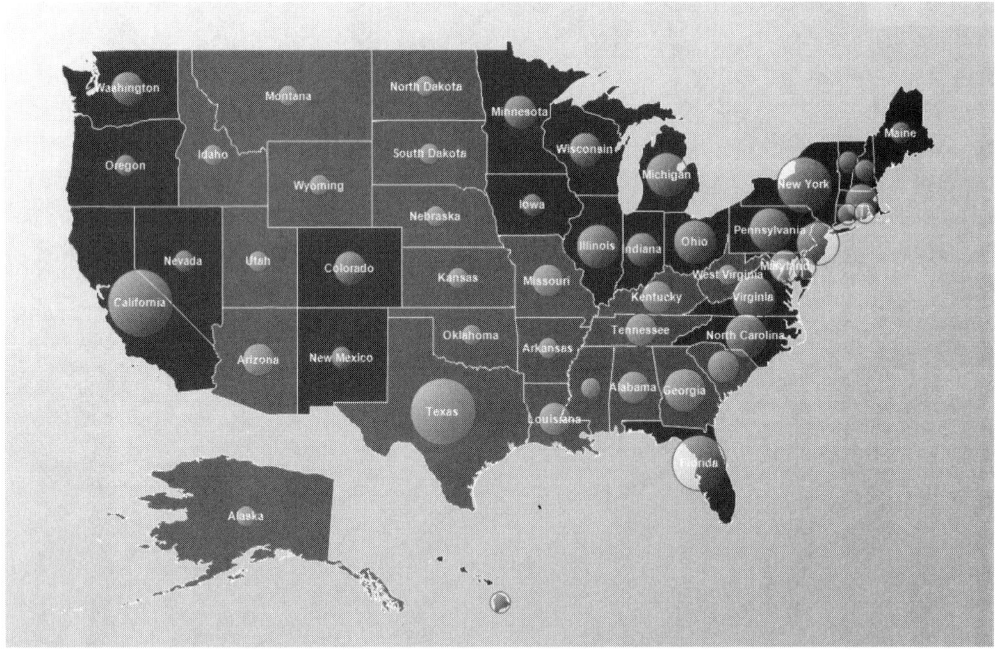

Chapter 4: Data Visualization Delivery

This chapter shows how to deliver the reports using SQL Server Reporting Services (SSRS) 2008 R2 and SharePoint 2007. This topic of information delivery is all about getting the charts, gauges, maps, and other reporting results into the hands of your end users—and we examine the different ways to present data and report examples to an audience.

Microsoft has a rich product portfolio with many integration possibilities, but we will focus on SQL Server Reporting Services (SSRS), Microsoft Office SharePoint Server (MOSS), and PerformancePoint Server (PPS). These are the main platforms for presenting reports, dashboard pages, and collaboration sites—all necessary ingredients for great business intelligence.

There are many ways to deliver reports, and each method has its own options, benefits, and challenges. There are several considerations that determine the best infrastructure to support reporting distribution—and each organization has a unique information culture that is ready to receive the reports based upon technology, processes, people, and leadership strategy. Finding the best way to deliver information requires consideration of each of these factors.

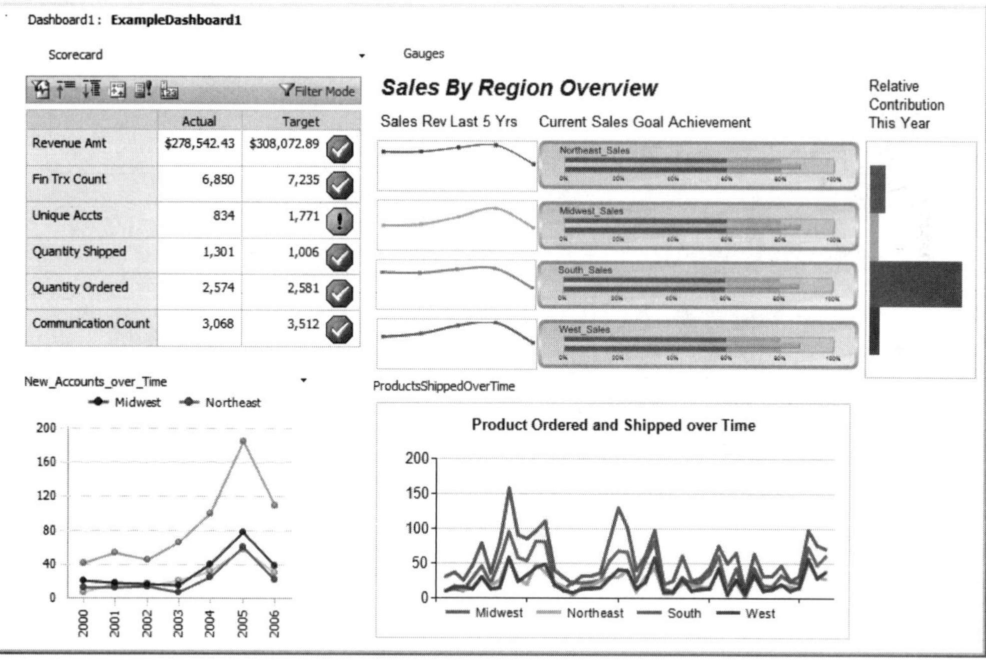

Chapter 5: Microsoft and the Cloud

This chapter uses SQL Server geo-spatial features to provide an overview of a new and exciting technology called "the cloud." The chapter helps clarify some of the terminology and the products available from Microsoft (including Azure, SQL Azure, Office Web Applications, BPOS, and "Project Dallas," just to name a few). The main goal is to demonstrate how you can use this technology inside of your own applications and how you can migrate data from SQL Server 2008 R2 into the cloud, and vice versa. We also discuss how to use Report Builder 3.0 to create a geo-spatial report directly from the cloud, and we describe an innovative database sharing application called "Project Dallas."

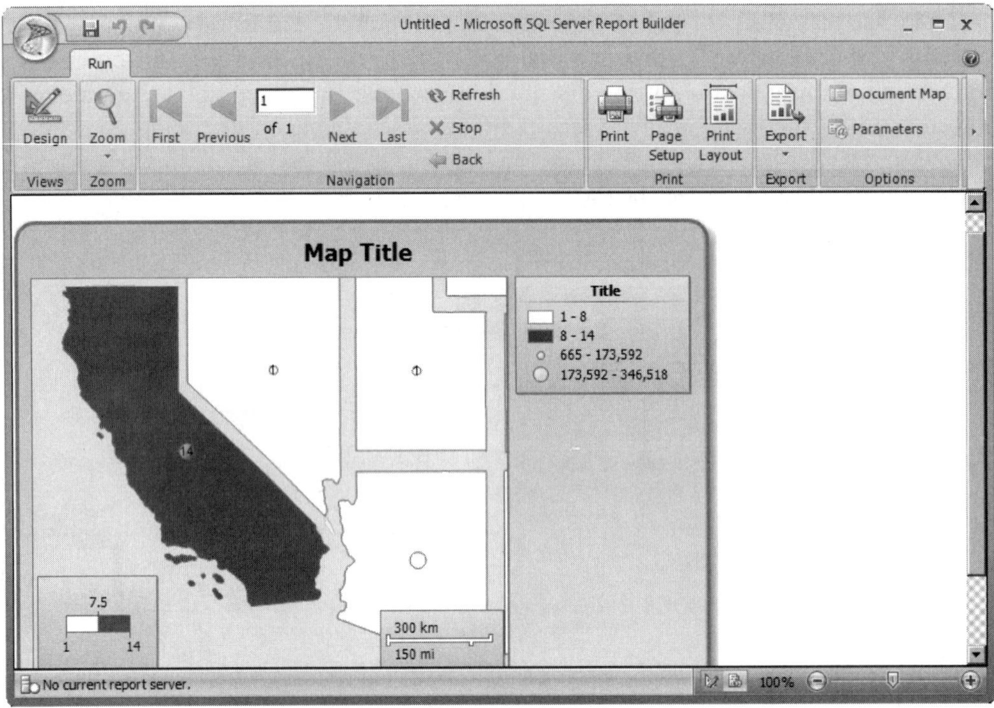

Chapter 6: Data Mining: Real-World Techniques

This chapter shows how to accomplish "heavy lifting" analysis with SQL Server Reporting Services (SSRS) 2008 R2 and SQL Server Analysis Services (SSAS) 2008 R2. And yet, everything presented in this chapter can be done by a business user with Excel 2010 and a network connection to a SQL Server Analysis Services server!

Data mining is an ever expanding field, which historically has required specialized tools and knowledge. It is used for a wide variety of tasks, ranging from fraud analysis to trend-spotting in sales data. This chapter gives an overview of Microsoft SQL Server Data Mining and shows how you can use familiar tools to get started. Frankly, the goal of the chapter is to show you how easy it is to find significant data elements in huge datascts, and display them with understandable Excel 2010 graphics.

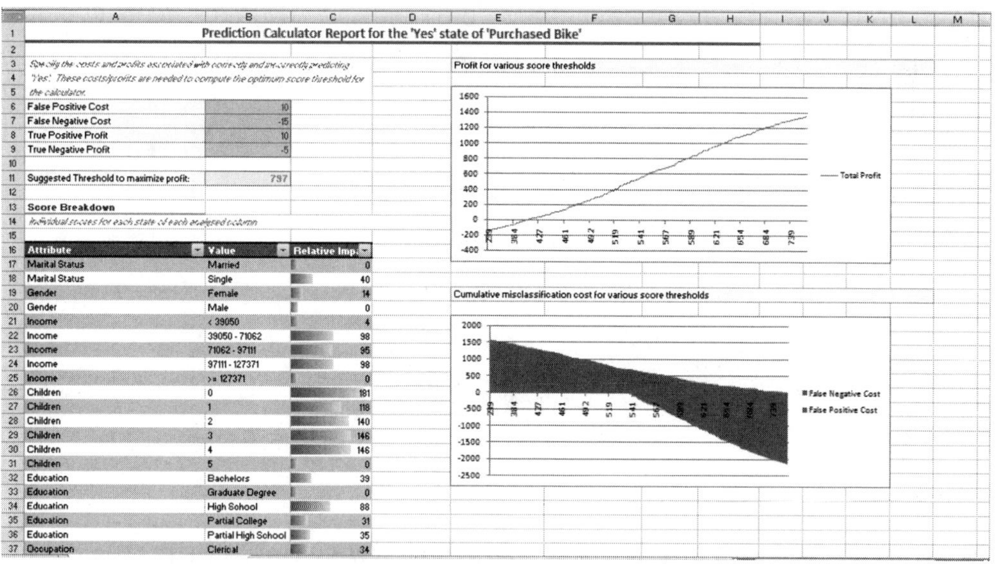

False Positive Cost	10
False Negative Cost	-15
True Positive Profit	10
True Negative Profit	-5
Suggested Threshold to maximize profit:	737

Attribute	Value	Relative Imp.
Marital Status	Married	0
Marital Status	Single	40
Gender	Female	14
Gender	Male	0
Income	< 39050	4
Income	39050 - 71062	98
Income	71062 - 97111	95
Income	97111 - 127371	98
Income	>= 127371	0
Children	0	181
Children	1	118
Children	2	140
Children	3	146
Children	4	146
Children	5	0
Education	Bachelors	39
Education	Graduate Degree	0
Education	High School	88
Education	Partial College	31
Education	Partial High School	35
Occupation	Clerical	34

Chapter 7: Microsoft PowerPivot

This chapter shows how to leverage the amazingly powerful PowerPivot tool that comes with SQL Server 2008 R2 licensing. PowerPivot is an Excel 2010 "add-in" that requires the user to have Excel 2010 on his or her client desktop, and that requires a network connection to a SQL Server 2008 R2 Analysis Services (OLAP) engine.

PowerPivot is unique in that it uses an "in-memory" analysis application running as an Excel 2010 desktop "add-in." This in-memory application also uses on-the-fly compression algorithms that allow it to handle, no kidding, millions of rows of data on a modern 2–4GB RAM desktop computer!

PowerPivot is part of a new set of technologies that is being released with Office 2010 and SQL Server 2008 R2. These tools know how to work with SharePoint 2010 out of the box so that everyone can save and share PowerPivot results centrally. PowerPivot allows you to perform self-service analytics without having to involve your IT department.

We'll explain how to import data into an in-memory structure (achieving a 10–12 × compression ratio). We'll also cover several techniques for delivering some incredible visualizations with very little effort and stunning speed.

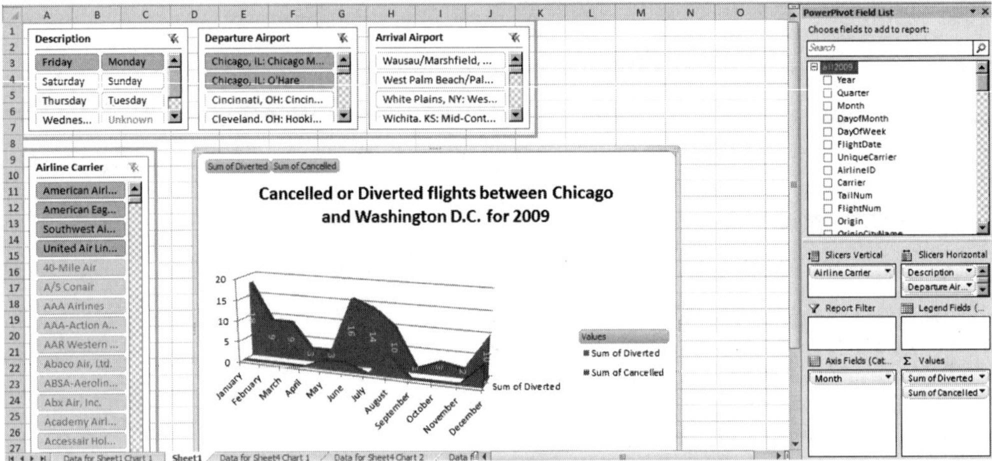

Chapter 8: SQL Server 2008 R2 Analytic Design Techniques

This chapter shows how to polish reports using SQL Server Reporting Services (SSRS) 2008 R2. It's incredibly important to take that extra step and coordinate the components of a good report so that others can make use of it, both as end users visually interpreting the data story and as designers expanding on the basis of existing reports.

We'll cover how to methodically go through the data components, the report components, and the labeling of everything contained in the report presentation. Frankly, the report is not done until these parts are consistent enough to be understood by others proficient in the toolset—and homogenous enough to become part of the narrative documentation that is part of real-world production reporting.

And finally, great attention is paid to the way visual components of a report can work together. There is nothing more frustrating for an end user than a report presentation that has to be explained by a technical design person, and that looks different from the report presentations done by others in the same organization. So the real goal of all this is to acquire the discipline needed to create consistently documented reporting that carries a certain organizational "look and feel" that conforms to design specifications in support of a particular organization's business processes.

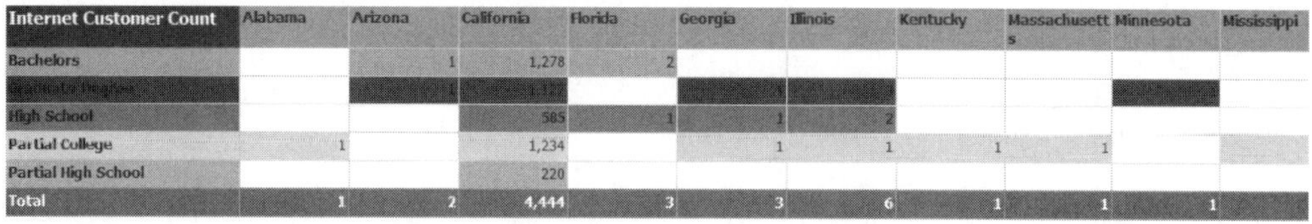

Internet Customer Count	Alabama	Arizona	California	Florida	Georgia	Illinois	Kentucky	Massachusetts	Minnesota	Mississippi
Bachelors		1	1,278	2						
Graduate Degree		1	[illegible]		[illegible]	[illegible]			[illegible]	
High School			585	1	1	2				
Partial College	1		1,234		1	1	1	1		
Partial High School			220							
Total	1	2	4,444	3	3	6	1	1	1	

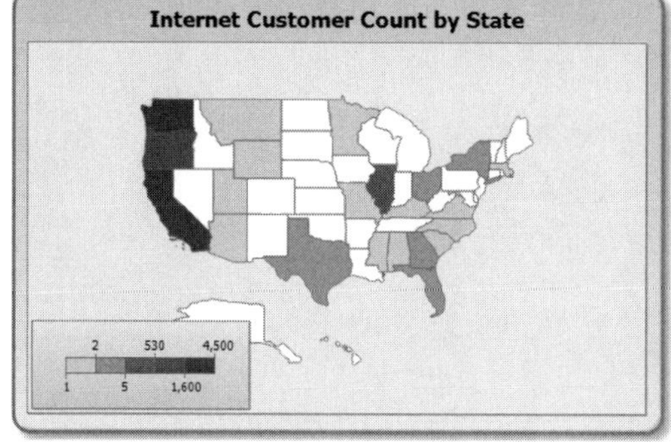

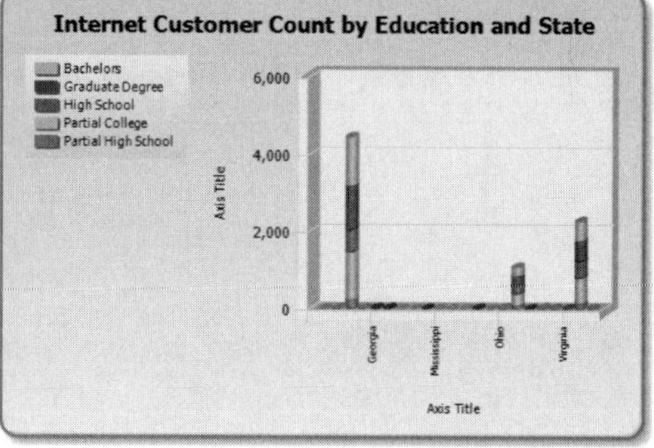

Chapter 1

Charts in SQL Server Reporting Services 2008

In This Chapter

- Determining the Appropriate Chart for the Type of Data Being Displayed
- New Graph Types and Features Available in SSRS 2008
- What to Watch Out for When Upgrading from SSRS 2005
- Step-by-Step Creation of an SSRS Chart Report Using the Report Designer
- In-Depth Examination of Chart Properties
- Advanced Topics, Including Calculated Fields, Visibility Expressions, and Combination Charts
- Wrap-Up

This chapter shows how to create reports using the graph types in SQL Server Reporting Services (SSRS) 2008 R2 to achieve greater information insight and absorption. Most of the examples in this chapter are from the AdventureWorks Report Samples, or are custom created based on that data source. Data visualizations are becoming more important as the amount and complexity of data increase. The more complex the story to tell, the more intuitive the visualizations must be.

Microsoft has improved the charting capabilities inherent in SSRS, and using these graphics appropriately can enhance enlightenment and engagement. The challenge is to select the correct chart type for the type of information being conveyed, and to make sure there is enough contextual information to support decision making. For the report designer, knowing the audience, the story, and the desired outcome will affect the choices made in creating a visual report. SSRS chart reports will be explored in depth to provide an understanding of what is possible. We will show step-wise directions for some reports, but there are so many varieties now that in-depth step-wise directions for all of them would take too much space. We have tried to present the logic and patterns of where the property settings are located, so you can apply the same process when you are creating the other chart types.

For a business intelligence practitioner, creating visual communication of complex data has always been a challenge. Excel has had basic charting for some time, but to use Excel usually required data downloads and a limitation on the amount of data that could be represented. Other business intelligence (BI) tools with great visualization capability are expensive and hard to implement. Microsoft has taken a huge step forward in making the charting tools more accessible and less expensive, making better reporting and "BI for everyone" truly within reach of most organizations. Improved Reporting Services charting and gauge features, rolling PerformancePoint Server into Microsoft Office SharePoint Server and making the design of these visual reports more accessible through improvements to Report Designer and Report Builder, have made Microsoft Business Intelligence a preferred product suite for solution designers.

Examples of the following topics will be provided in this chapter:

- Determining the appropriate graphic for the type of data being displayed
- New graph types and features available in SSRS 2008
- What to watch out for when upgrading from SSRS 2005
- Step-by-step creation of an SSRS chart report using Report Designer
- In-depth examination of chart properties
- Advanced topics, including calculated fields, visibility expressions, and combination charts

BEST REFERENCE

For the AdventureWorks sample databases and report samples, go to: www.codeplex.com/site/search?projectSearchText=SQL%202008%20Adventureworks.

For further information on SQL Server Reporting Services, go to http://msdn.microsoft.com/en-us/sqlserver/cc511478.aspx.

For best practices in information visualization, *see http://www.perceptualedge.com and take the fun and informative graphic design IQ test (www.perceptualedge.com/files/GraphDesignIQ.html).*

For help in understanding MDX for OLAP data sources, see Fast Track to MDX, *by Whitehorn, Zare, and Pasumansky (Springer, 2006).*

Determining the Appropriate Chart for the Type of Data Being Displayed

The objective of using charts, gauges, and visual displays for reporting is to uncover the relationships and patterns in the data and make them more obvious and apparent. Images are the quickest way to support insight, and are more memorable than trying to discern meaning from columns of numbers. Many times it is not the number itself that is important; it is the trend it is a part of, or the relationship between it and the entire group of numbers that is important. These characteristics are much more evident when displayed graphically.

BI TIP

Remember your audience—busy managers and executives require bottom-line information. Charts make that possible by summarizing data and displaying trends that allow people to compare data elements over time.

Here are common guidelines for report authors in choosing appropriate visual elements to clarify and expose data characteristics. One of our heroes, Mr. Stephen Few, an accepted authority on information visualization, has identified seven common relationships in business data. It is much easier to choose the graph type when the report author has a good understanding of the industry, the line of business data, and the reporting objectives. Understanding these data relationships will help to determine the appropriate chart type for a report. Common data relationships are summarized here for reference (taken from a whitepaper by Stephen Few et al., "Effectively Communicating Numbers: Selecting the Best Means and Manner of Display," *Perceptual Edge*, October 2005):

Time series relationship: A series of data points taken at equal intervals of time, for example annual sales for the last five years. This is one of the most used business intelligence chart types. Seeing patterns over time helps business decision makers determine trends and business cycles.

Sales Over Time

120 100 80 60 40 20 0

1983 1988 1993 1998

Ranking relationship: When values are sequenced by size, like Top 10 Products. Bar charts show this type of relation quite well.

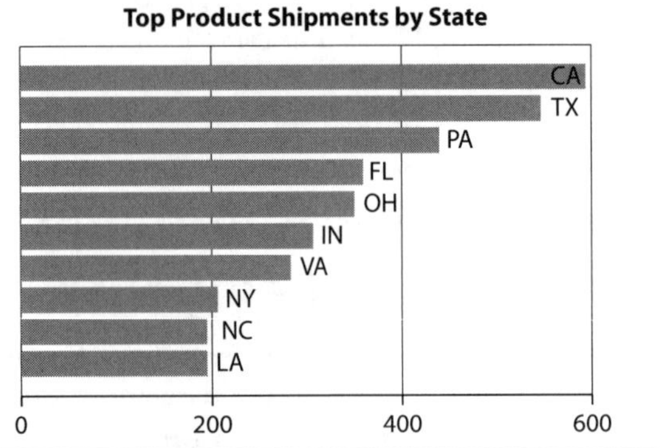

Part-to-whole relationship: When measures are a portion of a total, for example Salary as part of Total Compensation. Commonly displayed using Pie charts.

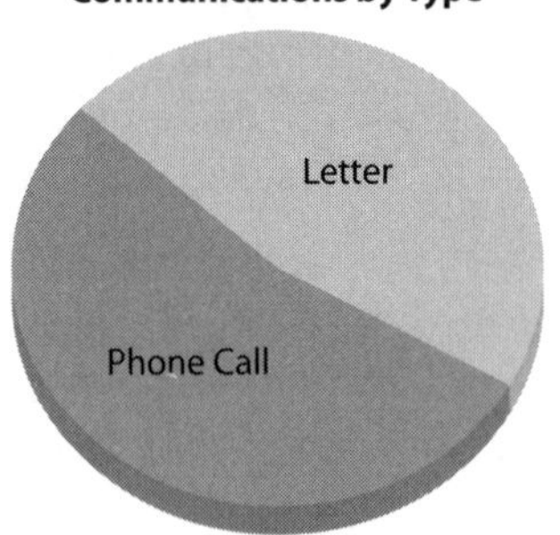

Deviation relationship: When values are compared to a reference value, like actual expense to budget amount. Or to show variation of values for a time period. This is also useful for showing KPI actual vs. target.

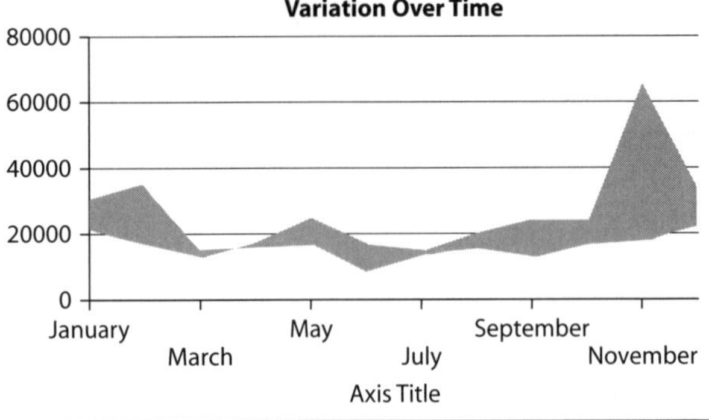

Distribution relationship: When a set of values is displayed across their entire range, this is especially useful for measuring process efficiency, like number of days to complete a workflow. Scatterplot, Histogram, or Pareto charts show this type of information best.

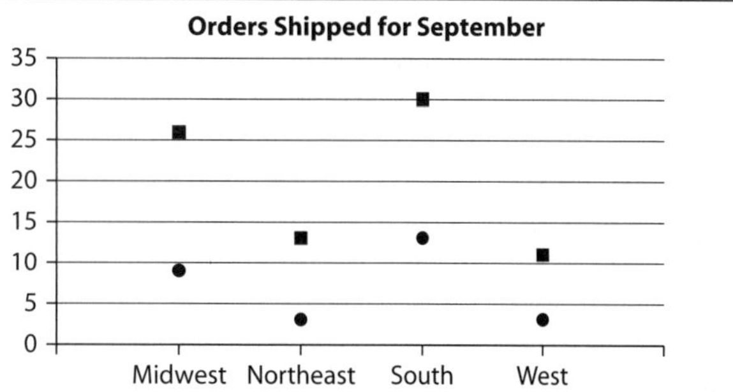

Correlation relationship: When pairs of values, each measuring a different characteristic about an entity, are displayed to reveal a relationship between them, for example the correlation between the price of an item and the number of units sold, or average transaction amount by club level. Scatter or line graphs display this kind of data best, depending upon how many data points are in the dataset.

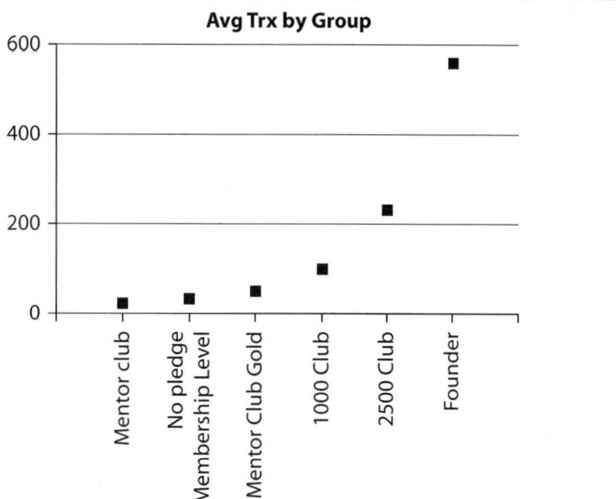

Nominal comparison relationship: Useful for displaying comparisons between values that have little relationship to each other—like geographical regions.

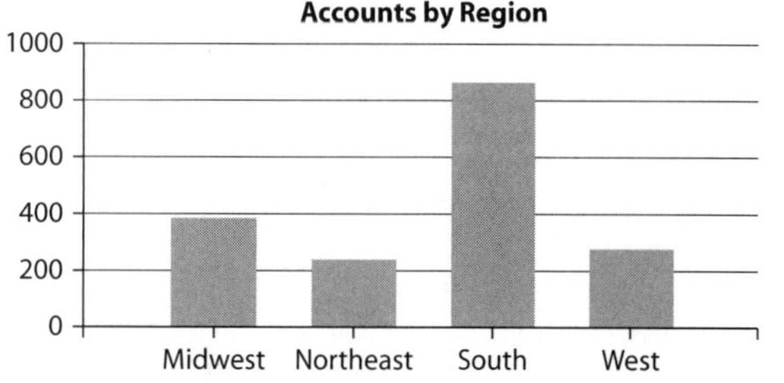

For a more in-depth and complete discussion, please refer to Stephen Few, *Information Dashboard Design: Effective Visual Communication of Data* (O'Reilly Media, 2006).

Choosing a Chart Type

The goal is to choose a chart type that communicates the required data most effectively and efficiently. Each chart type has unique characteristics for dataset display. Reports will be easier to read when the visualizations are suited to the data. The following table summarizes chart type–data type relationships that affect the suitability of a chart to the particular dataset. Use this to help decide which chart type to use when crafting a report.

Chart Type	Time Series	Ranking	Part-to-Whole	Deviation	Distribution	Correlation	Nominal Comparison
Area	✓				✓		
Bar		✓					✓
Column	✓		✓		✓		✓
Line	✓			✓		✓	
Shape			✓		✓		
Polar			✓		✓		✓
Range	✓			✓		✓	
Scatter			✓	✓	✓	✓	

New Graph Types and Features Available in SSRS 2008

SSRS has expanded the choices of chart types available with the latest release, much beyond the original pie, bar, or line charts of previous versions. The incorporation of the Dundas Chart code base has improved this version of Reporting Services by a giant leap since the 2005 version. Most chart types now also have flat and three-dimensional versions. It is important to contemplate how the report will be rendered and displayed, as some media may distort or mangle three-dimensional images. Here are the choices available and some practical applications.

Figure 1-1 shows the Select Chart Type dialog box that displays your chart type choices. We will explore creating most of these graph types later in this chapter.

These are the range of choices you have now for presenting data visually in Reporting Services.

- **Column** Series, stacked, 100% stacked, clustered, 3-D series, 3-D stacked, 3-D 100% stacked, 3-D clustered (rectangle, cylinder). This is probably the most common graph type.
- **Line** Line, smooth line, stepped line, 3-D line, line with markets, smooth line with markers.

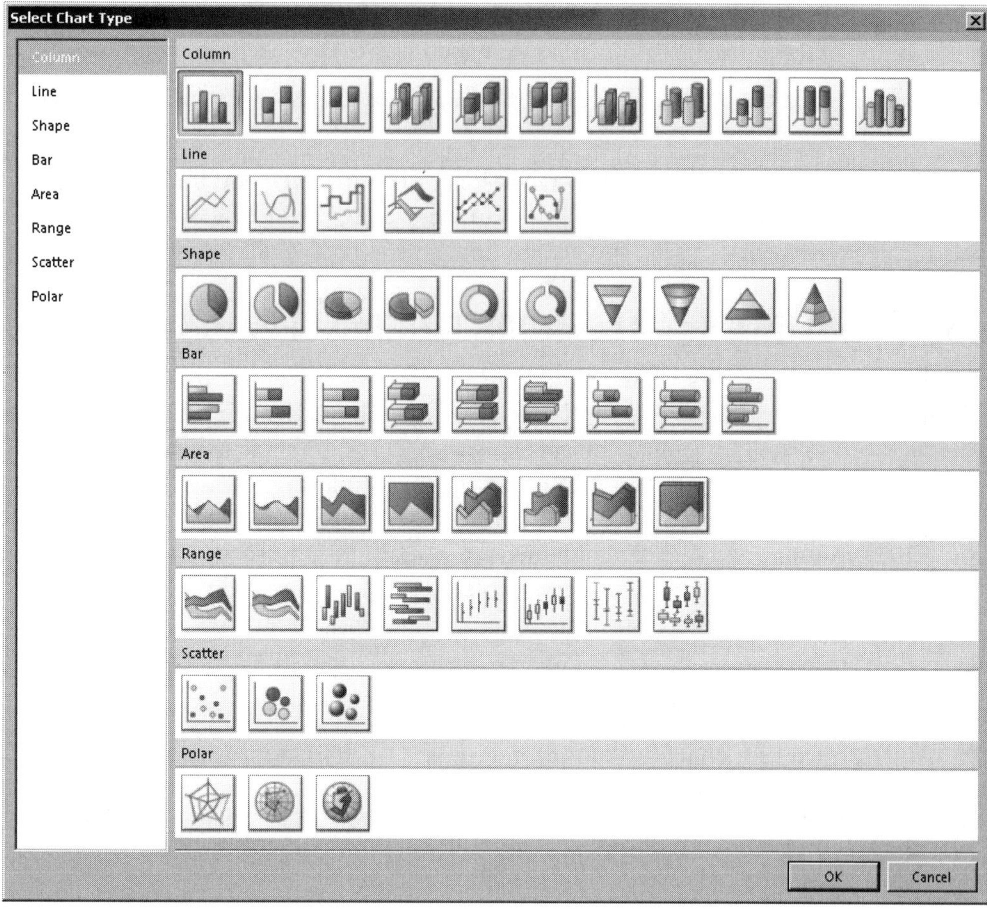

Figure 1-1 *Reporting Services chart types from SSRS 2008 Report Designer*

- **Shape** Pie, exploded pie, 3-D pie, 3-D exploded pie, doughnut, exploded doughnut, funnel, 3-D funnel, pyramid, 3-D pyramid. Funnel is good for showing values for one entity as it changes stages, for example, a sales pipeline report, or a workflow status report.
- **Bar** Bar, stacked bar, 100% stacked bar, 3-D bar, 3-D stacked bar, 3-D 100% stacked bar, 3-D clustered bar (rectangle, cylinder). This is very useful for displaying ranking reports.
- **Area** Area, smooth area, stacked area, 100% stacked area, 3-D area, 3-D smooth area, 3-D stacked area, 3-D 100% stacked area.

- **Range** Range, smooth range, range column, range bar, stock (high-low-open-close), candlestick, error bar, box plot. These are a good way to visualize price range over time.
- **Scatter** Scatter, bubble, 3-D bubble. 3-D bubble charts are useful for displaying multidimensional data.
- **Polar** Polar, radar (kiviat), 3-D radar. Polar diagrams are good for displaying multiple attributes for an entity. For example, we use the radar graph type to find the gaps between datasets, and also to find gaps in team skills for a project team.

New Reporting Services 2008 R2 Chart Features

In addition to all these new chart types, there are some significant new chart features that improve overall visual display and graph functionality, and are available for all chart types. Figure 1-2 shows two chart objects in one chart container, with multiple legends, multiple value axes, calculated series, and a variety of formatting settings used.

- **Chart containers** A chart container can contain multiple chart areas. This allows design of multiple, complementary graphs to explain complex information, and makes it easier to align two charts along a single axis, as shown in Figure 1-2.
- **Multiple titles and legends** Add elements as needed, and move them around the chart areas for best placement option.
- **Multiple axes for charts** Add secondary axes to charts to clarify multiple data series, as shown in Figure 1-2.
- **Custom palettes** Create color schemes to support corporate branding.

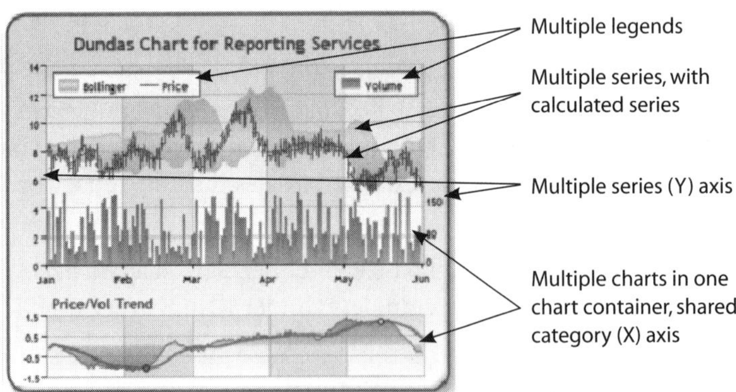

Figure 1-2 *An example of several new chart features in SSRS 2008*

- **Calculated series** Easily add new series to charts without writing expressions, as shown in Figure 1-2. Functions available include: Mean, Moving Average, Bollinger Bands, Standard Deviation, and many common statistical calculations.
- **Large data volumes** Better support for graphic display based on large datasets like data warehouse or data mart sources.
- **Scale breaks** Break the scale of an axis in order to show a variety of values, including outliers.
- **Label rotation** Make graph labels easier to read.
- **Background strip lines** Make graphs more visually appealing and easier to read by including alternate shading in the chart background, as shown in Figure 1-2.
- **Empty point options** Several options to make sparse data easier to graph. Choose an average value or 0, for example.

What to Watch Out for When Upgrading from SSRS 2005

The best approach will be to create new chart-based reports using SQL Server Reporting Services 2008, because there are so many new chart types and features available. However, there are upgrade paths for most SSRS 2005 Reports to the new SSRS 2008 platform, but there are some caveats, as outlined here. Data sources upgrade without incident.

- 2008 Report Designers only support authoring 2008 RDL. In other words, you cannot use SSRS 2008 Report Designer to create SSRS 2005 reports. There is no save as previous version option.
- When you upgrade a report from SSRS 2005 to 2008, the unit of upgrade is the entire report. SSRS 2008 can, however, execute reports created with SSRS 2005.
- SSRS 2005 Reports with native charts will upgrade to SSRS 2008 Reports with native charts. SSRS 2005 Reports that contain Dundas charts and/or gauges (with no unsupported features) will upgrade to SSRS 2008 Reports with native charts and gauges.
- Reports with Dundas unsupported features will not upgrade, and will need to execute as SSRS 2005 Reports. Here is a brief listing of the unsupported features:
    - **Charts** Annotations, custom code, custom legend items
    - **Gauges** Numeric and state indicators, custom code, images
    - **Map and Calendar controls** All unsupported

Step-by-Step Creation of an SRS Chart Report Using the Report Designer

Let's get started on the journey by creating some new reports! There are several steps that must be completed before you actually get to add the chart to the report. Hang with us as we prepare for creating reports by choosing our design tool and getting the Visual Studio solution file created.

There are two report design tools included with SSRS 2008.

- **Report Designer** is a component of Business Intelligence Development Studio (BIDS—Visual Studio shell), and Report Builder, which requires a report model. BIDS is created for the professional report developer or power user, who has a good understanding of database access, query creation, and report formatting.
- **Report Builder** is a vastly improved report creation tool that has a more "Office-like" interface, utilizing the menu ribbon metaphor. Report Builder uses Report Models that predefine the data connection strings, database, tables, and relationships available to the report author. This greatly simplifies the report creation experience, but it also limits the complexity of the dataset one can create.

Fortunately, the graphic elements discussed here are available in both report design tools! For this chapter, we will be using Report Designer; Report Builder will be shown in Chapter 2.

To get started with Report Designer, you need to know that there are two options when creating a new report project:

- **Report Server Project Wizard** Presents dialog boxes and prompts you through creating the report in a logical way by defining the data source first, then the query, then placing you into the design surface. This is the best way to start for beginners, but it cannot create a chart-only report.
- **Report Server Project** This option creates the project solution file, with folders for Data Source items (*.rds Report Data Source files) and Report items (*.rdl Report Definition Language files). If you have existing report items, like shared data sources, that you want to use or edit, choose this selection.

Even though we have created hundreds of reports, we sometimes find the wizard convenient for creating something new. The only drawback is that you cannot use the wizard to create a *chart-only* report. So for this example, use Report Server Project. We will be using the AdventureWorks samples for many of the reports in this chapter; you can download them from the link mentioned on the first chapter page! This way you can see how they have been created without the stress of starting from scratch.

Open the Business Intelligence Development Studio (BIDS)—it is usually found in the SQL Server 2008 Program group on the Start menu.

1. Click the New Project button as shown in Figure 1-3; select the Report Server Project template from the dialog box.
2. Give the report project a meaningful name.
3. Click OK to create the solution file and close the dialog box.

The Report Designer user interface will appear. If you have used Visual Studio before, it will look familiar. Let's review the different areas of the interface and prepare for creating reports.

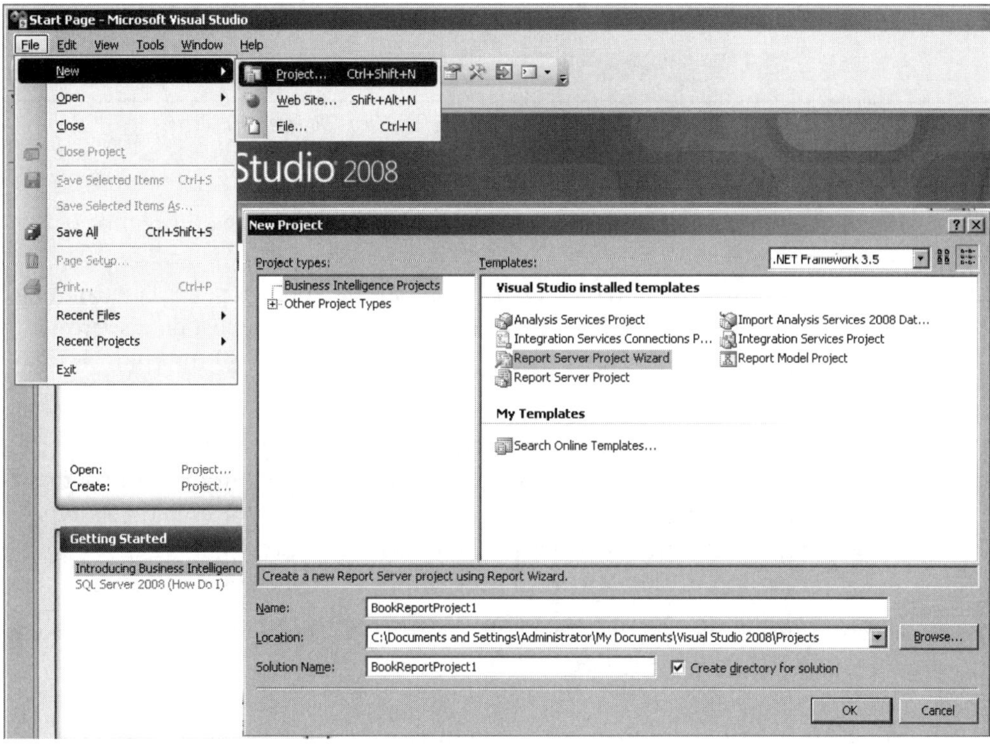

Figure 1-3 *Business Intelligence Development Studio 2008 New Project—Report Server Project*

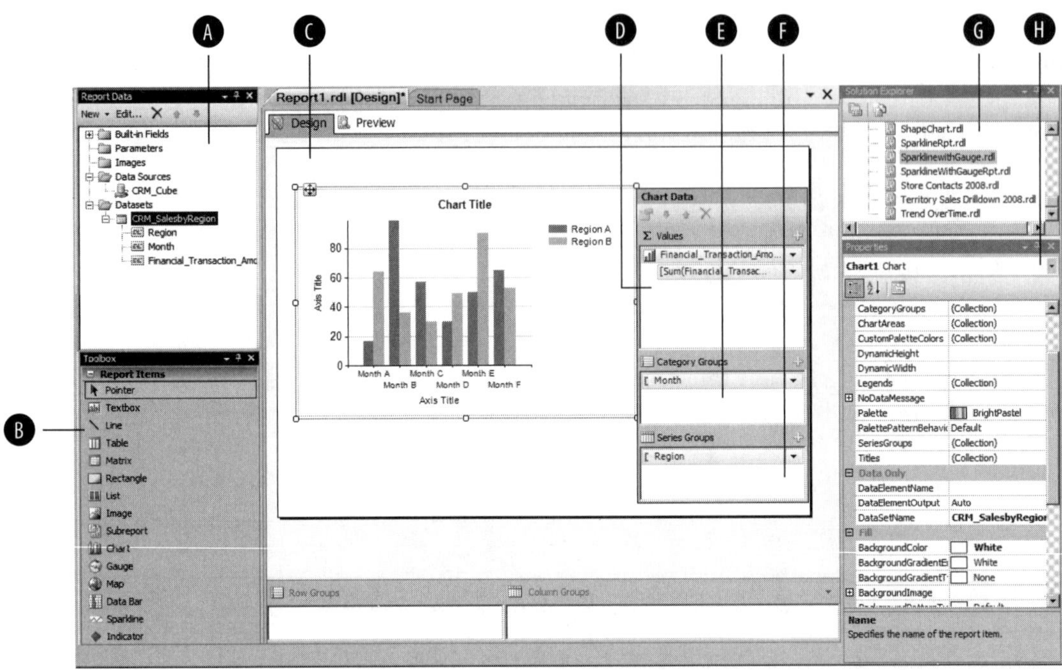

Figure 1-4 *Report Designer interface overview—the many areas of the Report Designer user interface*

The Report Designer interface has three main pane areas as shown in Figure 1-4.

- In the left column are the Report Data pane and the Toolbox pane (labeled A and B in the figure). The Report Data pane is where you create report data sources, datasets, parameters, and images. The Toolbox pane contains all the controls that can be dragged onto the report design surface.
- The Solution Explorer pane and Properties pane are usually located along the right column (G and H). The Solution Explorer pane shows all the data sources and report items for this reporting solution project. Folders for each object type (data sources, reports) are visible even when they are empty. Right-click the folder to get a context menu. The Properties pane shows all the details for a selected item.
- The center area is referred to as the design surface (C) and is where all the elements come together to create a report.

Also, for chart reports, there are three design surface areas for adding data to the report:

- In the Chart Data area that becomes visible when you right-click the design surface: values or measures can be dragged and dropped into the Values area (D), the Category Groups area (E) is the area to drop category fields (or dimensions) for the X axis, and the Series Groups area (F) is the place to drop series fields (or dimensions) for the Y axis.

You will see the solution name at the top of the Solution Explorer pane.

1. To get started with this report, create the data source. Right-click the Shared Data Sources folder and select New Data Source from the context menu as shown in Figure 1-5. As a best practice, give it a meaningful name, not the default Data Source 1.

BI TIP

A best practice for data source naming is to use ServerName_DatabaseName, *for example, LocalHost_AdventureWorksDW2008. If the data source is shared, it will be apparent to all report authors what this data source actually provides.*

2. Select the source type from the drop-down list under Type. Available choices are: Microsoft SQL Server, Microsoft SQL Server Analysis Services, Report Server Model, Oracle, SAP, XML, ODBC.
3. Type in the connection string in the proper format (shown in Figure 1-5) or click the Edit button and fill in the dialog box with the Server name, select a database name from the drop-down list, and click the Test Connection button at the bottom.

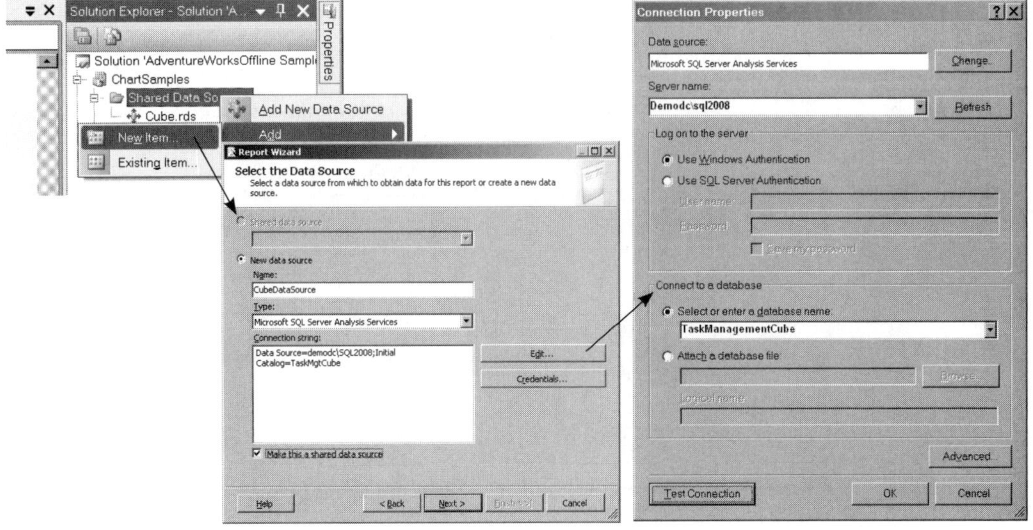

Figure 1-5 *Add a New Data Source, Shared Data Source Properties, and Connection Properties*

4. Click the OK button to close this dialog box and OK in the Shared Data Source Properties dialog box. The new data source will appear in the Data Sources folder.

BI TIP

*If you have several main data sources that get regularly reused, create the Shared Data Source, and then save the *.rds file to a known location (file share or SharePoint Library). Instead of re-creating the same data source in new report projects, use the Add Existing Item choice from the Data Sources context menu, and import your saved data source definition. Benefit: All reports based on the data source will be consistent. See more about this topic in Chapter 5.*

Add a new report item using the same procedure as adding a new data source.

1. Right-click the Reports folder in the Solution Explorer pane, and from the context menu, choose New Item as shown in Figure 1-6.
2. Select Report from the Templates pane of the dialog box.
3. Give the report a meaningful and descriptive name; it is okay to include spaces in the report name (but beware that spaces will pad the report URL with %20 if you are working in Report Server SharePoint integrated mode).
4. Click the Add button at the bottom of the dialog box.
5. The new named report shows in the Reports folder of the Solution Explorer pane, and the design surface displays.

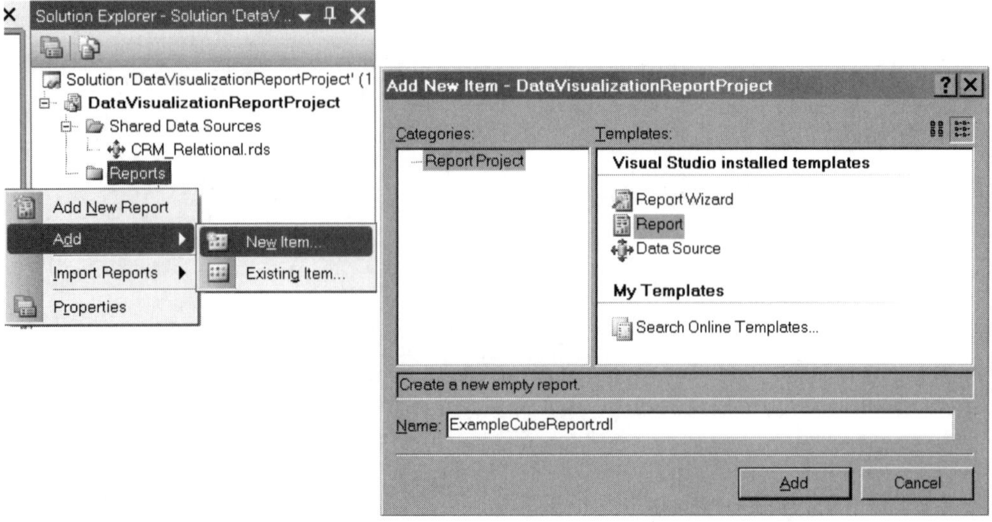

Figure 1-6 *Reports context menu—Add New Report Item*

By creating Shared Data Sources, you make them available for all reports that are created within the report project. When creating the report items' data source, dataset, and parameters, SSRS 2008 Report Designer behaves differently from the 2005 version. Instead of having a tab at the top of the design surface for the data, there is a side pane, like a toolbox. It is this side pane location where you create individual report data sources, create datasets, and specify parameters.

1. Choose Data Source from the New drop-down menu in the Report Data pane, as shown in Figure 1-7.
2. In the Data Source Properties dialog box, give the data source a meaningful name. Select the radio button for an existing Shared Data Source, and choose from the drop-down list. Click OK.
3. Now choose Dataset from the drop-down menu.
4. Enter a Dataset name.

BI TIP

If your report will have multiple datasets, make sure the name accurately reflects the collection of data. For example, AccountingMonthlySummary_April indicates the type and interval/time-frame of the data source.

5. If confident of your skills in SQL (relational data sources) and/or MDX (OLAP data sources), type your query into the query window. The alternative is to click the Query Designer button, located near the bottom of the Dataset Properties dialog box.
6. The Query Designer appears for the data type defined. Since we have chosen an OLAP data source, the MDX Query Designer appears as shown in Figure 1-8.
7. Select the Measures and Dimensions from the Metadata pane and drag them into the pivot table to select them for the dataset query. Drag dimensions into the top pane to use them as filters.
8. When satisfied you have the proper dataset, click OK to finish.

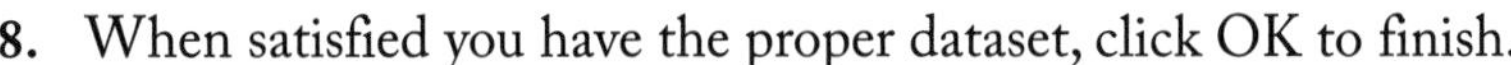

BI TIP

Putting filters in the query reduces the amount of data returned to the result set, generally improving query performance, since they are applied as the query is processed. Filters specified in the report properties are applied after the query has processed and thus do not improve data-source query performance.

The Query Designer Toolbar

To understand the features of MDX Query Designer, get familiar with the toolbar. It is a little different from the toolbar you will find in SQL Server Management Studio.

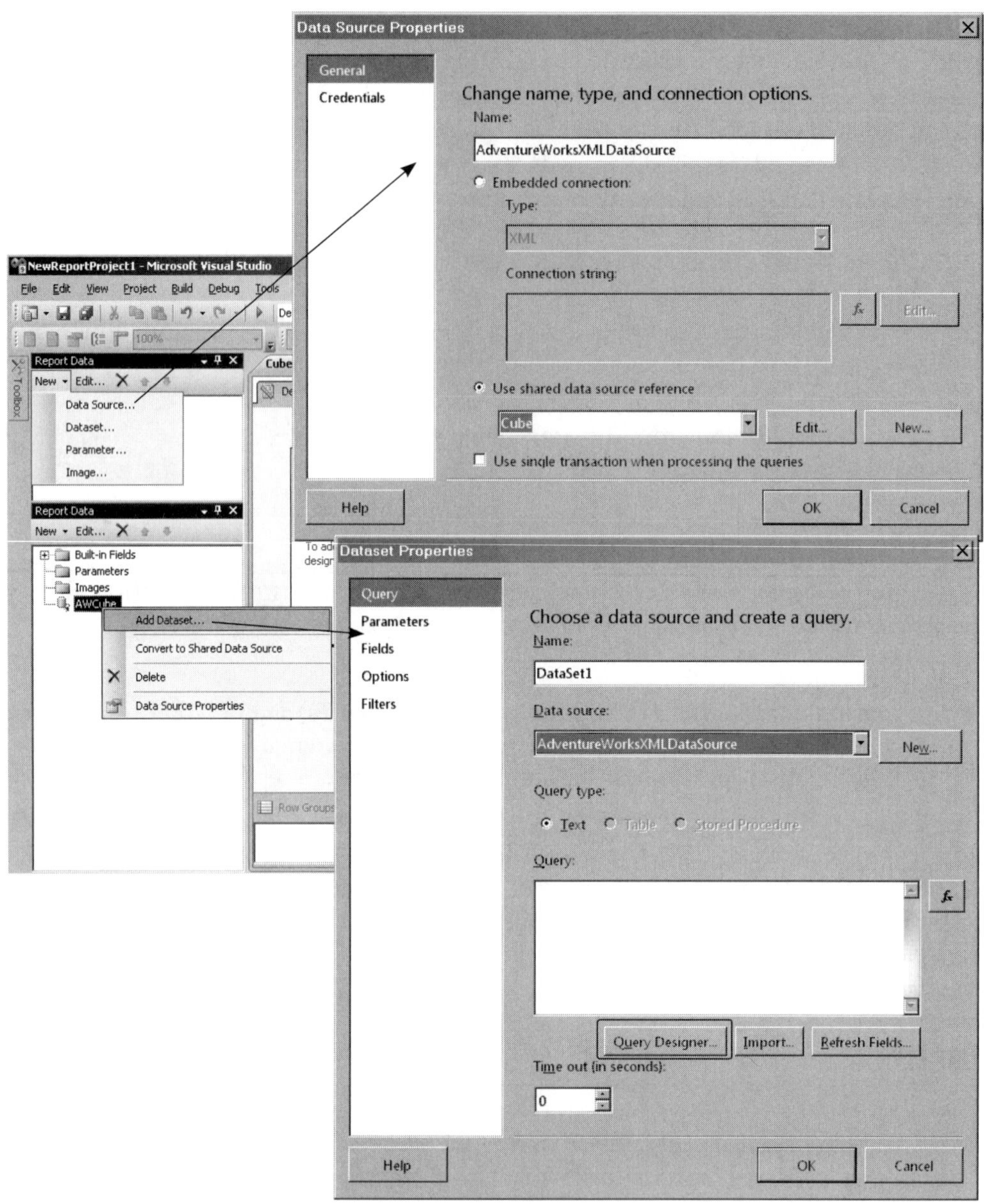

Figure 1-7 *Report Data pane in Report Designer 2008—Report Data Sources and Datasets*

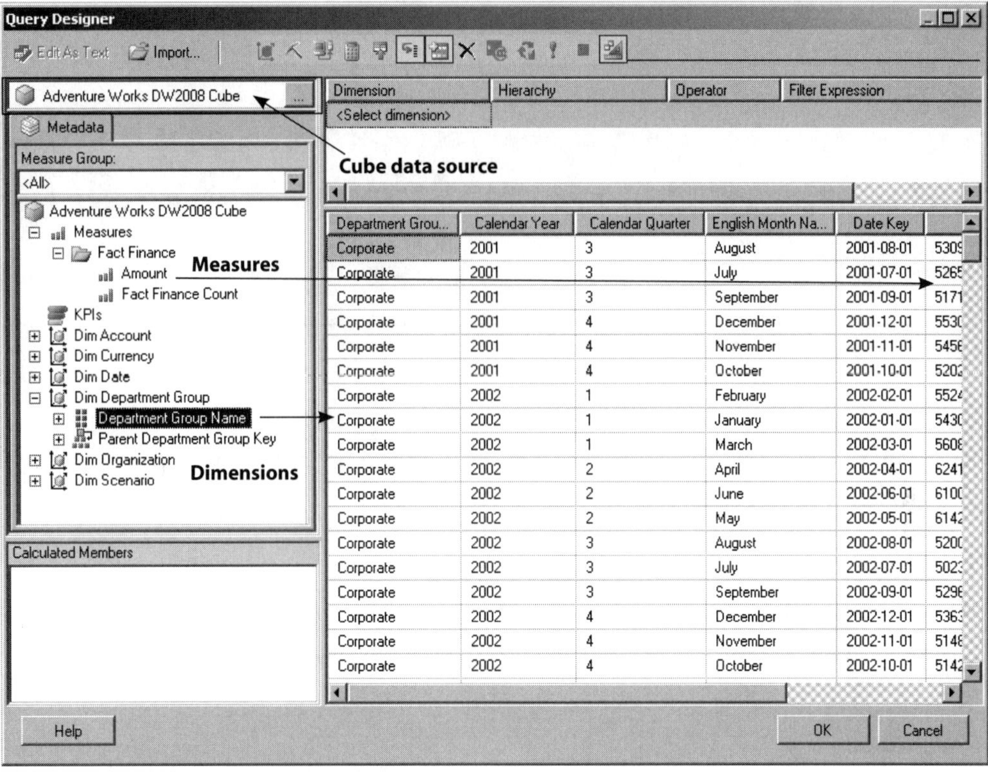

Figure 1-8 *Report Designer MDX Query Designer*

Working with OLAP or Cube data sources makes query creation so much easier because you don't have to specify any table joins—the cube takes care of all the work of specifying relationships for you!

Thinking dimensionally will really open the door to the kind of visualizations that can be used to convey important information without resorting to columns of numbers. Dimensional data makes it much easier to see part-to-whole relationships because parent-child hierarchies are easily created and quite common in most cubes. The whole idea of being able to "drill down" and "drill across" lends itself well to using charts to help the report audience absorb the insight from their data.

The Query Designer toolbar in Figure 1-9 shows the range of ways you can interact with the data source. The Edit As Text button (which is grayed out in Figure 1-9)

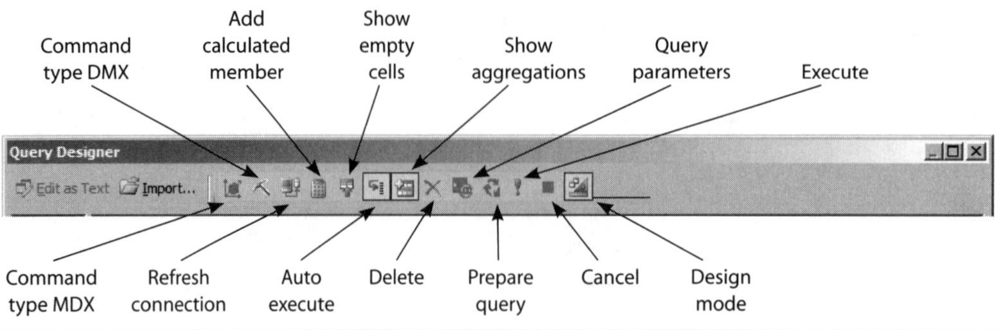

Figure 1-9 *Query Designer toolbar detail*

allows you to edit a *.txt file as an MDX query. The Import button will open a *.sql or *.txt file. The other buttons included on the toolbar are

- **Command Type MDX** Creates a Multidimensional Expression language query.
- **Command Type DMX** Creates a Data Mining Expression language query.
- **Refresh Connection** Refreshes the connection to the server and database.
- **Add Calculated Member** Gives the ability to define members based on formulas.
- **Show Empty Cells** Shows all results, including nulls.
- **Auto Execute** Runs query continuously, without the specific execute command.
- **Show Aggregations** Shows data results with hierarchies rolled up.
- **Delete** Deletes the query or selected item.
- **Query Parameters** Allows the specification of query parameters.
- **Prepare Query** If Auto Execute is toggled off, prepares the query for submission to the data source.
- **Execute** Runs the query.
- **Cancel** Cancels processing of an executing query.
- **Design Mode** Toggles between the pivot table interface and the MDX pane, as shown in Figure 1-10.

If you are interested in the Multidimensional Expression language query, click the Design Mode button, as shown in Figure 1-10, and it will display the MDX for the query.

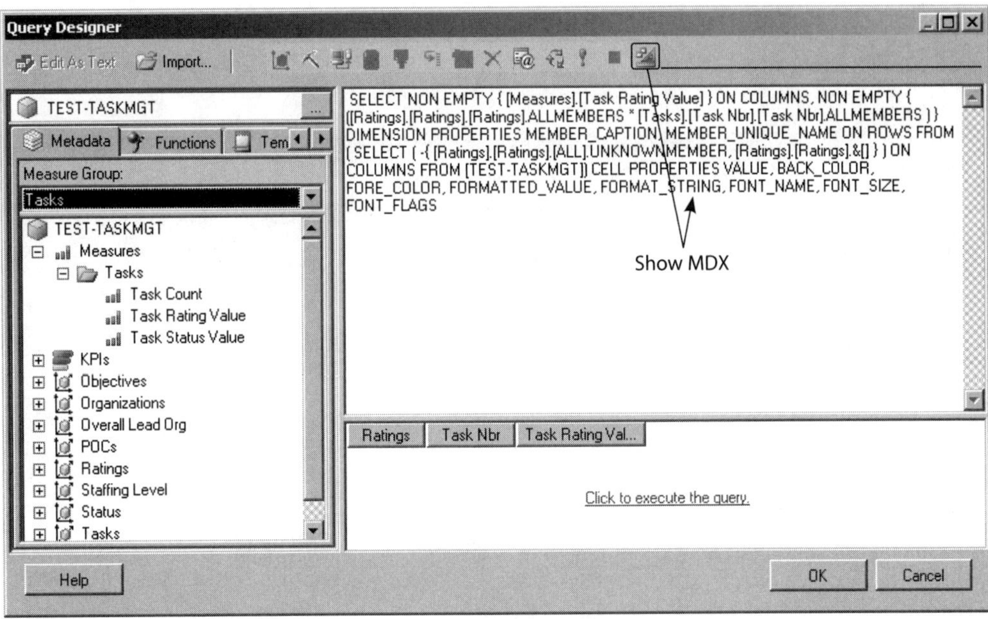

Figure 1-10 *Report Designer Query Designer—Show MDX display*

Beware: Query Designer–generated MDX is not the most optimized code, although is a good place to start if you are just learning MDX because it will show you basic query structure, how to construct calculated measures, how to specify filters, etc.

Adding a Chart to a Report

It is time to add the chart to the report. Choose the chart type that best clarifies the report data. For the Trend Over Time example, a Bar, Line or Area graph is most suitable, according to the Choosing a Chart Type table presented earlier in this chapter. Area is the choice for this initial report.

To create a chart within a report, display the design surface in Business Intelligence Development Studio (BIDS).

1. Drag the Chart item from the Toolbox pane to the design surface area for the chart, as shown in Figure 1-11.
2. The Select Chart Type dialog box will appear. Choose the Area chart type.
3. Once selected, the chart type will display on the design surface with the Chart Data box to drop data fields onto: data (measure) fields, category fields, and series fields as shown in Figure 1-12.

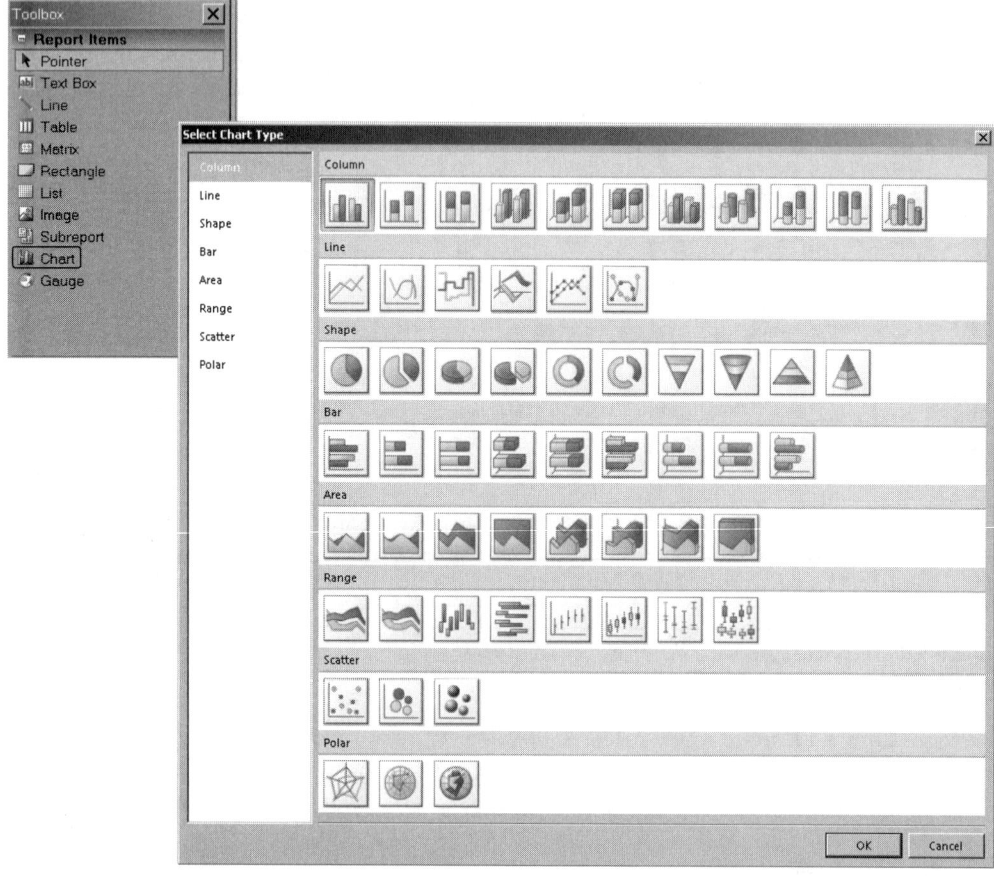

Figure 1-11 *Report Designer Toolbox—Select Chart Type*

4. Drag the fields from the Report Data pane onto the drop area—drag the measure field to the Values area (data fields), drag the series dimension to the Series Groups area (Y axis), and drag the category dimension to the Category Groups area (X axis).
5. Let's finish this example by clicking the Chart Title and typing in something descriptive. Keep in mind the business terms your audience is familiar with and the purpose of the report.
6. Preview the report by clicking the tab at the top of the design surface.

The report should render and display an area chart of amount and count by calendar year.

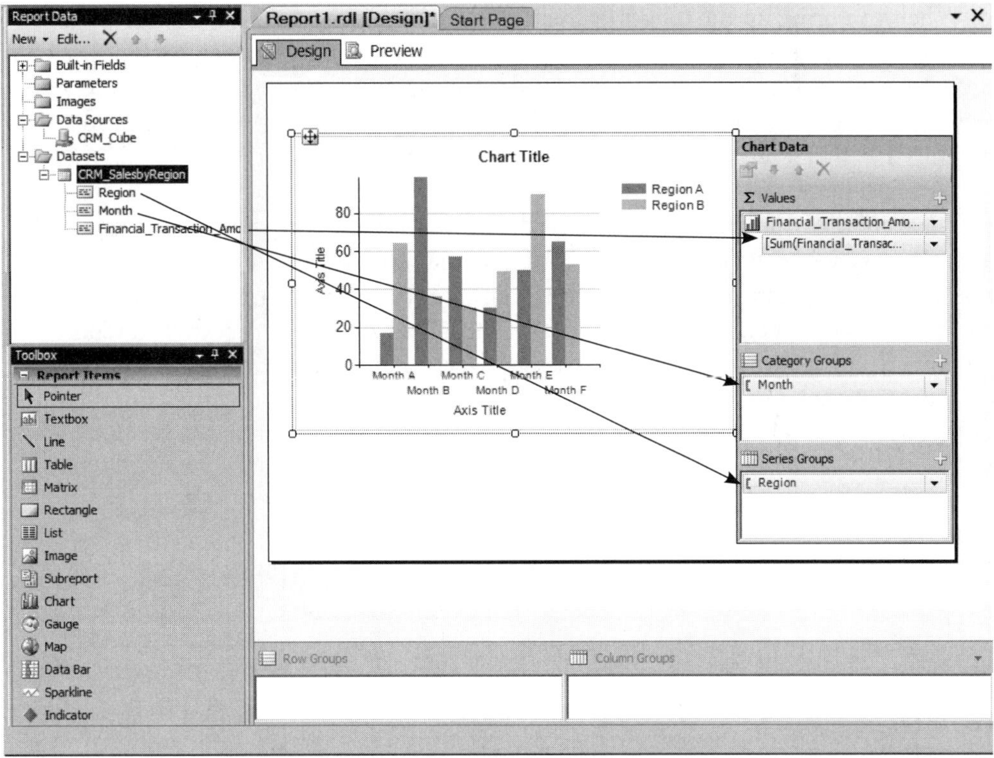

Figure 1-12 *Report Designer Design pane with drop areas exposed—drag data fields to desired location*

BI TIP

Report Titles and Chart Titles should not be identical but should provide context. Remember that a good report tells a story (general title), and the charts help illuminate the plot (specific titles)!

In-Depth Examination of Chart Properties

Once you have the basic chart report created, polish it by setting all the properties to make it look outstanding! Since the report can be printed from the Preview tab, there is no reason to deploy a report until the design and formatting are complete. Formatting of the axis, chart area, and data series are accomplished by setting the various properties. Right-click any axis, and the shortcut menu will appear. Axis formatting and chart area formatting are similar, but not identical, as the axis properties include scale and scale interval.

When you bring up the Chart Formatting context menu, there are slight variations, depending on where on the chart you right-clicked. Figure 1-13 shows each of the property context menus that are possible, depending where on the design surface you right-click. Do not be overwhelmed by this variety. It is a little hard to learn how it is organized at first, but once you understand the logic behind what is displayed, it will become familiar and navigable.

There are ten main areas on the report design surface: the category (X) and value (Y) axes, the data series at the top of the chart area, the series groups at the right side of the chart area, the category groups at the bottom of the chart area, the chart itself, the chart area or container, the title text box, the legend area, the report body, and report properties. The Chart submenu is consistent for each of the variations, and on the Chart submenu, you can navigate back to Chart, Chart Area, or Series properties from here.

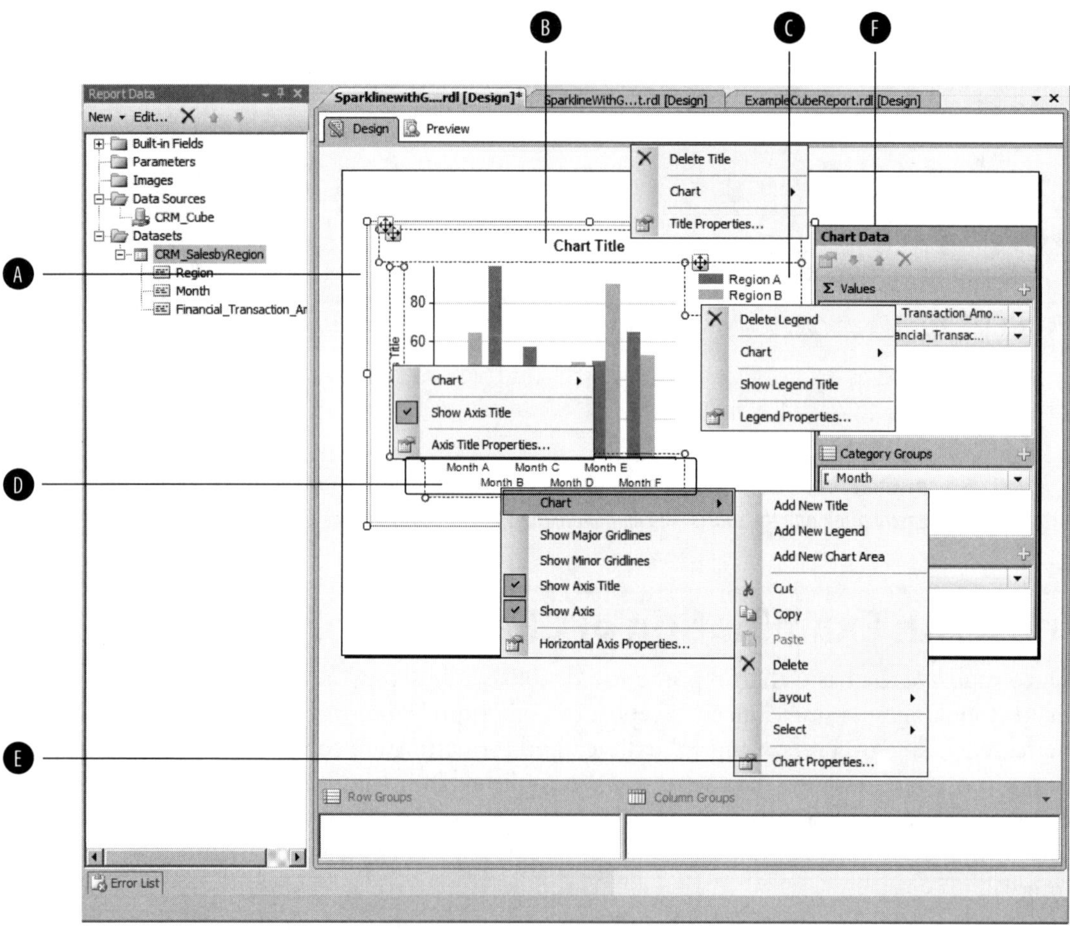

Figure 1-13 *Chart Properties dialog*

Depending on where you right-click in the design surface, the appropriate context menu will appear. As shown in Figure 1-13:

- **A.** Right-click the Axis Title for the Axis Title Properties context menu—set text, alignment, font, font size, style, color, and effects.
- **B.** Right-click Chart Title, and the Title Properties context menu appears. Set the Title text, position, docking, visibility, actions, font, font size, color, style, effects, fill, border, and shadow properties.
- **C.** Right-click the Legend, and the Legend Properties context menu appears. Set Legend text, position, docking, visibility, actions, font, font size, color, style, effects, fill, border, and shadow properties.
- **D.** Right-click an axis, and the Axis Properties context menu appears. Set the axis type, range, interval, direction, interlacing, axis labels, label font, font size, color, effects, number format, major and minor tick marks, and line style.
- **E.** If you select the Chart submenu from any of the context menus, there are choices for inserting a new Title, Legend, or Chart area. Select an area, and the Layout submenu allows you to align, resize, or re-order an object, or select Chart Properties to access the dialog boxes with even more settings.
- **F.** The Chart Data box is the interface for dragging the data elements from the dataset to the report design surface. The Chart Data box has three areas—the top is the Values area for measures, the Category Groups area for data elements used for the category or X axis, and the Series Groups area for data elements used for the data series or Y axis.

Setting all these properties properly will give your chart a polished look.

Using Visibility Properties to Enhance the Report

The visibility option shows up in each category and gives tremendous control over the display or suppression of display based on a condition. Use the Expression Builder dialog to create the criteria to evaluate in order to display any particular chart item. The next section gives an example of using visibility settings to control display.

Figure 1-14 shows the Series Properties and Expression dialog boxes where you set visibility. To set this visibility property,

1. Right-click the data series or series group of interest.
2. Choose the Visibility pane, and click the third radio button, labeled "Show or hide based on an expression."
3. Then click the *fx* (function) button next to the text box. This example shows the Expression dialog box populated with an expression formula to display the data series *only* if there are more than 12 members in the series. This example uses the IIF common function.

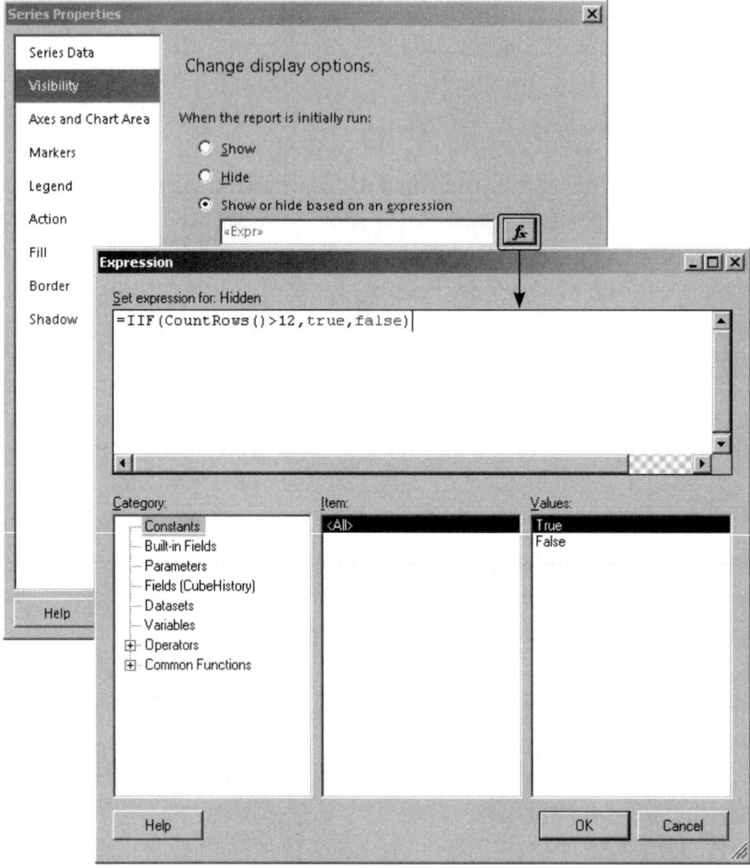

Figure 1-14 *Series Properties dialog and Expression dialog*

This is a very powerful feature and can be used to customize chart reports for particular users.

BI TIP

There is an excellent summary of useful expressions on the MSDN web site here: http://msdn.microsoft.com/en-us/library/ms157328.aspx.

Set the Report Header and Footer

To give your report a bit more polish, especially if it will be routinely printed, set the report headers and footers. Be consistent in the content you include in your headers and footers, and your style will soon become recognizable.

To set the report headers and footers,

1. Right-click any empty space on the report design surface. Under Insert in the context menu, there are choices for Page Header and Page Footer. Click each choice to add it to the report.
2. Now there will be Header and Footer Areas (zones) on your design surface, as shown in A of Figure 1-15.

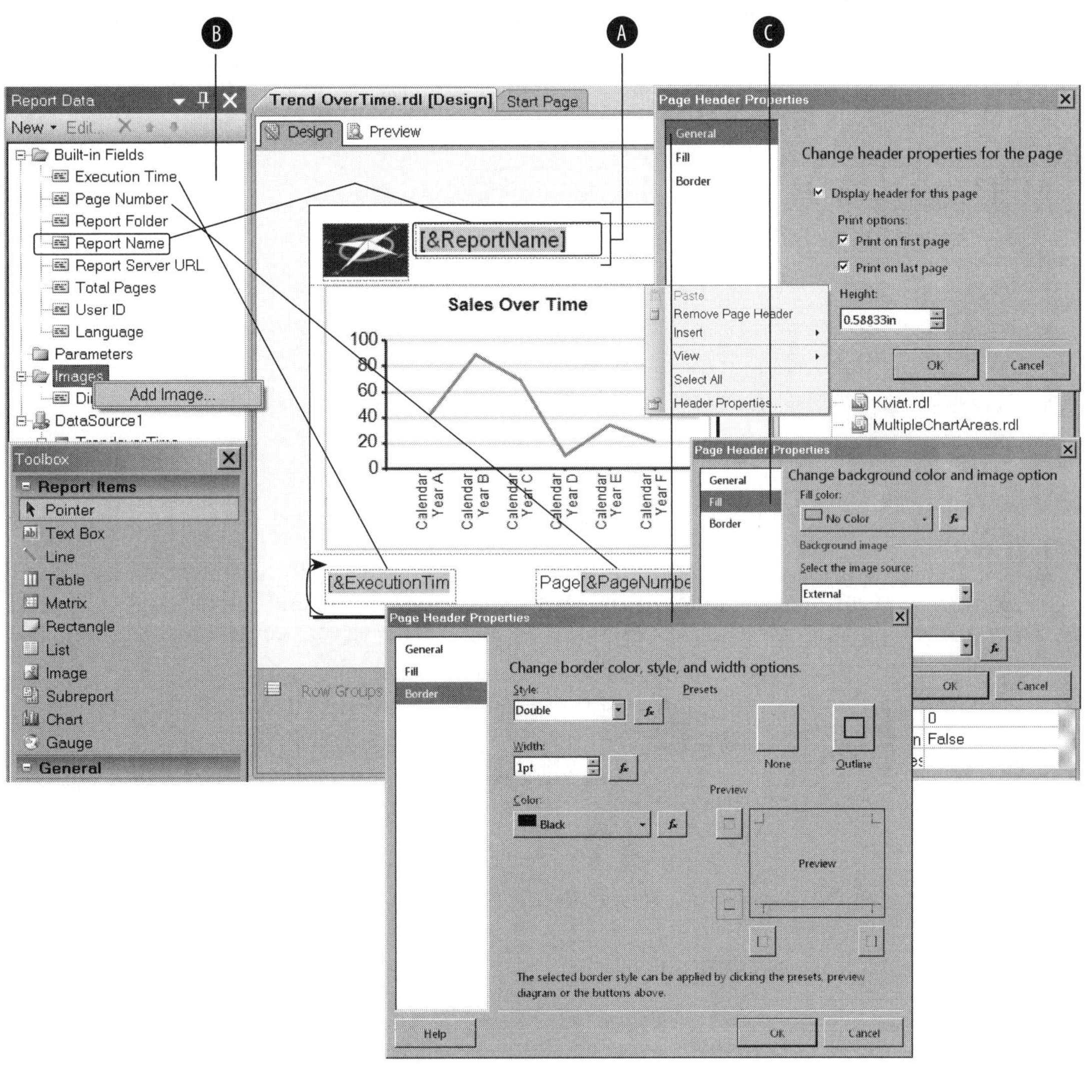

Figure 1-15 *Report header and footer in the design surface. Use the built-in fields to easily add common elements to the report.*

3. Choose Built-in Fields and drag them on the header and footer areas, as shown in B. (This capability represents an improvement over SSRS 2005.)
4. Format the fields by selecting them and then adjusting font, font size, and font color. These settings are found under the Header Properties as shown in C.

Setting all these properties does take a little time, but the results are worth it! The result is a much nicer report display, as shown in Figure 1-16.

Now that the data has been identified and all properties set, preview the report by clicking the Preview tab. After a moment of rendering, the report preview will display, showing how it will look when deployed. There are some minor differences in display, but this is pretty WYSIWYG compared to previous versions of Report Designer. Also, realize that there is a Print Preview button as well, so you can see how it will display on screen and how it will display on paper.

BI TIP

Review these items for report presentation:

- *Look at the margins and make sure there is ample space for an expanding chart or table.*
- *Will the report be mainly viewed online or printed? If it will be printed, pay attention to page breaks and font size (online displays can always be zoomed).*
- *Make sure the page orientation is correct for what is displayed. It may be better to use Landscape for some chart types.*

To set these and other Report Properties,

1. Click the Report menu item as shown in Figure 1-17. Report Properties include: page units (centimeters or inches), paper size and orientation, and margins, as well as custom Code, References to other objects, and Variables that control report behavior.

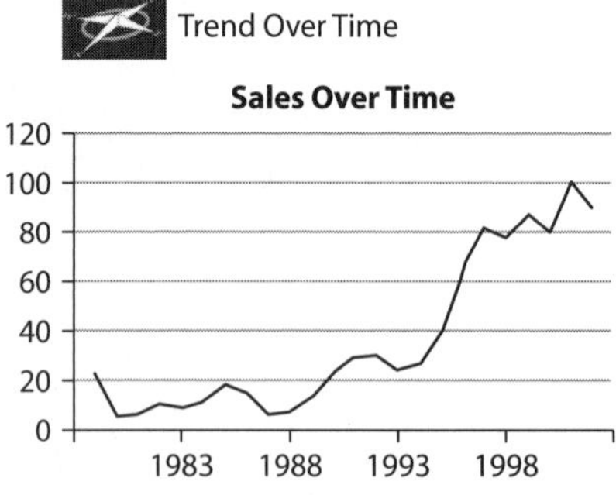

Figure 1-16 *Chart Report with Logo image, headers, and footers*

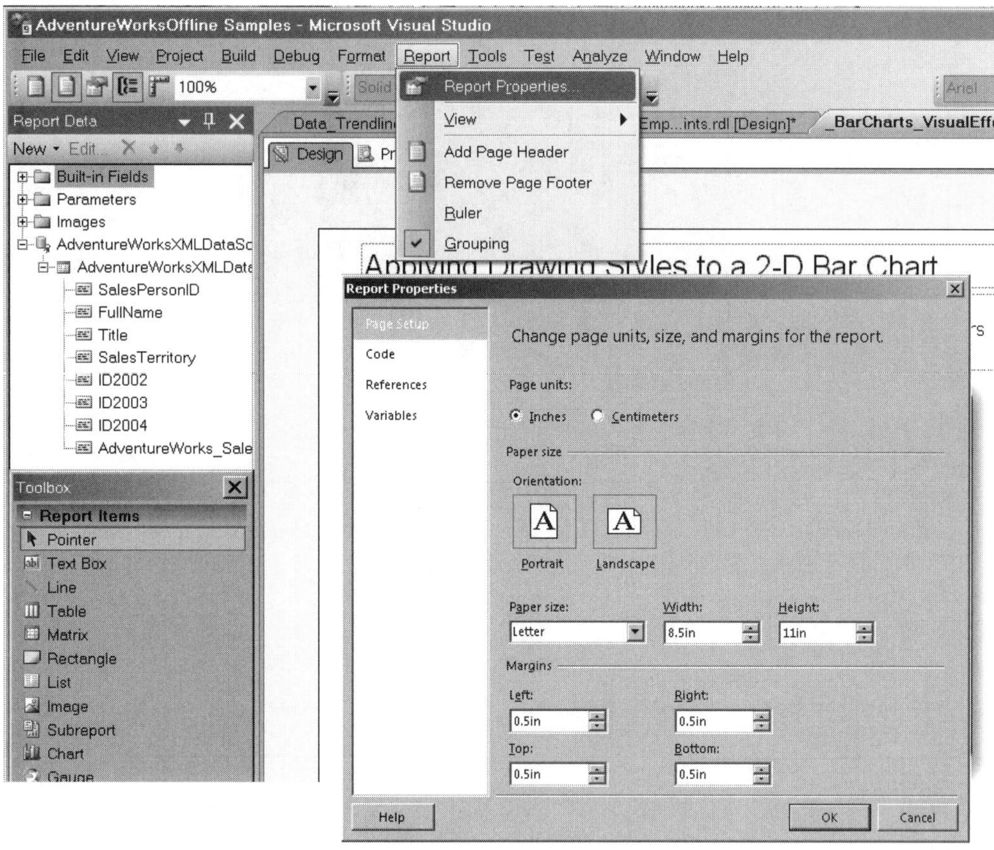

Figure 1-17 *Report Properties dialog*

Now that all these properties have been set, preview the report one more time. Looks good, ready to deploy! Deployment and report delivery options will be explored in-depth in Chapter 5. See the Report as rendered in Figure 1-18.

In reviewing the preview as shown in Figure 1-18 for Amount and Count over Time, it is plain to see the relationship between the two data series, but we gain no insight into the micro-trends that are occurring in the data. The table gives detail about the amount by department, but that isn't displayed in the chart. Because year was chosen for the category axis, monthly fluctuations are not apparent. A different visualization may be better at illuminating the actual relationships that are invisible here.

Compare this to the next display, shown in Figure 1-19. By changing the chart type to Line, and adding the Department Group data element as Data Series, and adding more detail on the category (date) axis, we make it much easier to discern that

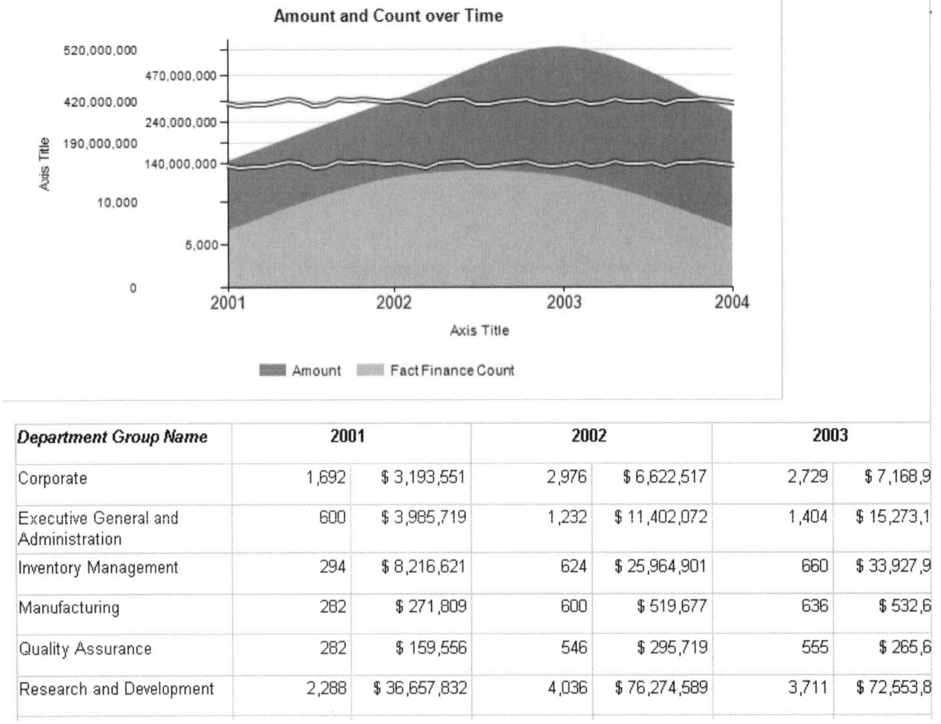

Department Group Name	2001		2002		2003	
Corporate	1,692	$ 3,193,551	2,976	$ 6,622,517	2,729	$ 7,168,9
Executive General and Administration	600	$ 3,985,719	1,232	$ 11,402,072	1,404	$ 15,273,1
Inventory Management	294	$ 8,216,621	624	$ 25,964,901	660	$ 33,927,9
Manufacturing	282	$ 271,809	600	$ 519,677	636	$ 532,6
Quality Assurance	282	$ 159,556	546	$ 295,719	555	$ 265,6
Research and Development	2,288	$ 36,657,832	4,036	$ 76,274,589	3,711	$ 72,553,8

Figure 1-18 *Report Preview—Area chart*

Sales and Marketing consistently spent the most money! They outpaced the other departments so much, even with more detail, it is hard to discern their trends.

So even though changing the chart type did show more detail, it still doesn't have the impact it could if it had a better visualization. This type of data is the perfect candidate for a Sparkline report. Sparklines were first introduced by Edward R. Tufte, professor emeritus from Yale University.

Sparkline Reports

The latest version of Report Builder and Reporting Services includes several new chart types that support the display of small multiple charts. These are the Sparkline, Databar, and Indicator. Exploring these features in Report Builder will be covered in Chapter 2.

You can also create a *sparkline* report in Report Designer. Thank you to Sean Boon for his inspiring blog post on sparklines: http://blogs.msdn.com/seanboon/archive/2008/10/10/how-to-build-sparkline-reports-in-sql-server-reporting-services.aspx. These work great with Matrix/Tablix grids but do not work with Table grids. Sparkline reports have some

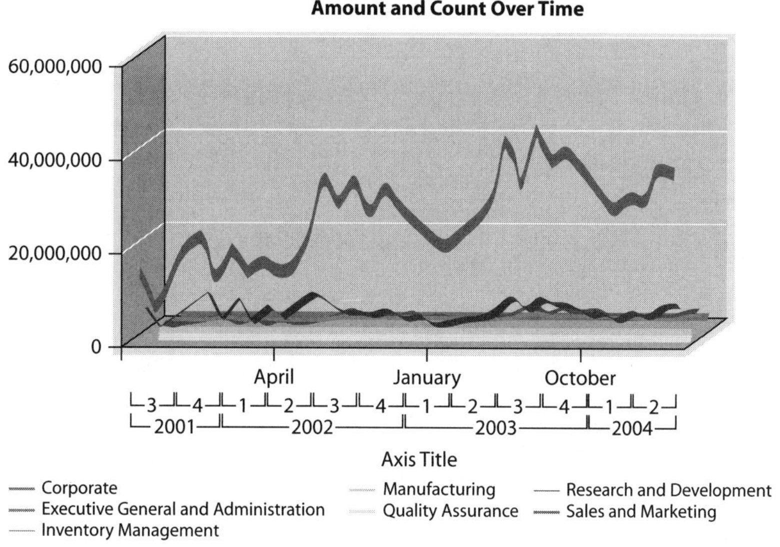

Figure 1-19 *Line chart with Time Dimension and By Division (more details than previous chart)*

unique characteristics and don't have axes values, so make sure the dataset has consistent category and value axes. They are good at displaying relative micro-trends, but not for comparison of actual values between the groups. The most recent version of SQL Server Reporting Services includes three new chart types that weren't in earlier versions: Sparkline, Databar, and Indicators. These three chart types support visualizations that weren't available previously. The Sparkline and Databar chart types support the small multiple formats described by Edward R. Tufte in his seminal work, *The Visual Display of Quantitative Information, Second Edition* (Graphics Press, 2001).

Sparkline reports are very good at displaying trends over time in a small enough format that multiple series or categories of information can be compared. To create a Sparkline report, the steps are basically the same whether you are in SQL Server Business Intelligence Design Studio (BIDS) or in Report Builder. For this example, use BIDS where the process for creating a sparkline or databar has been improved dramatically.

In BIDS, create a new report so that you can start with a clear design surface.

1. Right-click the design surface (upper-left star) and choose Insert and then Sparkline, as shown in Figure 1-20. Alternately, you can click-drag the Sparkline report object from the Toolbox onto the design surface.
2. Right-click within the chart area, and in the Chart Data box, choose the desired report data elements for Values, Category Groups, and Series Groups by clicking the plus sign and choosing the desired data element from the drop-down list provided.

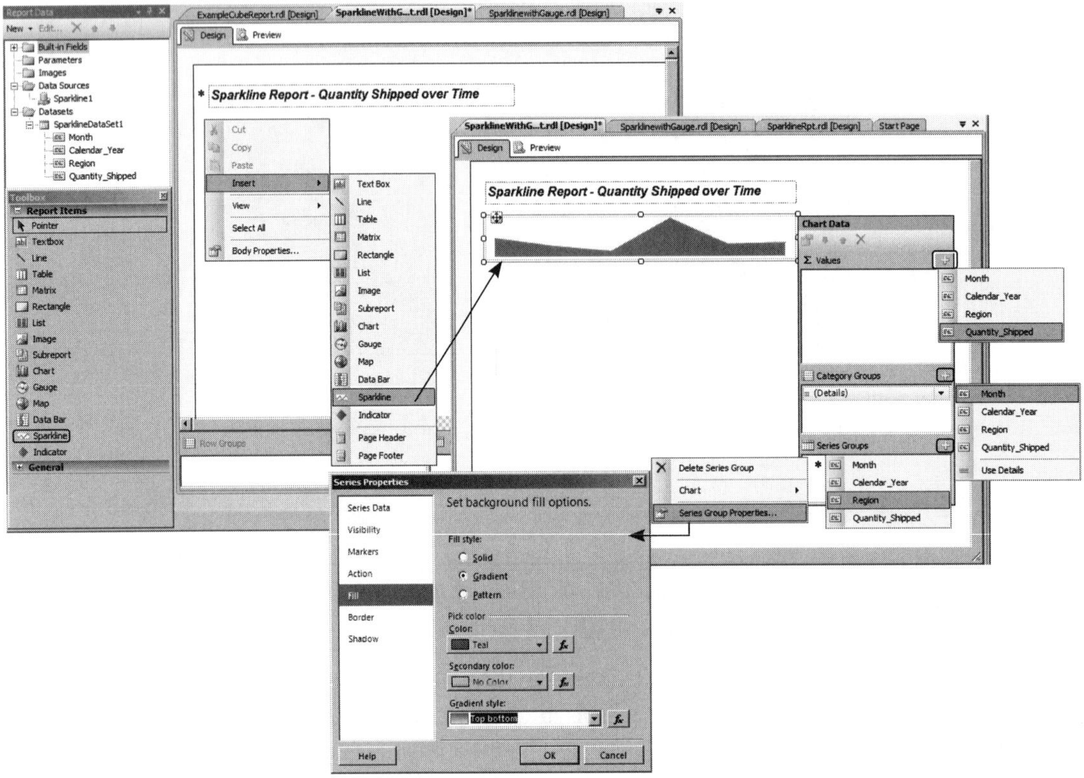

Figure 1-20 *Preparing for a sparkline*

3. Nice color formatting will make the trend lines more evident. Once the data has been selected, right-click in the Series Group area (red star), and select the Fill pane from the Series Properties dialog box, as shown at the bottom of Figure 1-20.
4. Under Fill Style, select Gradient. Under Pick Color, choose a dark color as the primary color, then white or a lighter hue of the same color for the secondary color. Then, most important, choose the Gradient Style from the drop-down list. The default is solid, so if you forget this choice, the effect won't display. Choose the Top Bottom selection for a nice fade effect.

Now that the chart is prepared, it is time to get it into a tablix/matrix and add some context. Figure 1-21 shows the process you go through and the tablix properties to set to make the sparkline report succeed.

1. Back on the design surface, choose a matrix report item from the Toolbox pane and drag it onto the design surface of the report as shown in Step A of Figure 1-21.
2. Now, drag the existing chart item into the data area of the matrix (Step B).

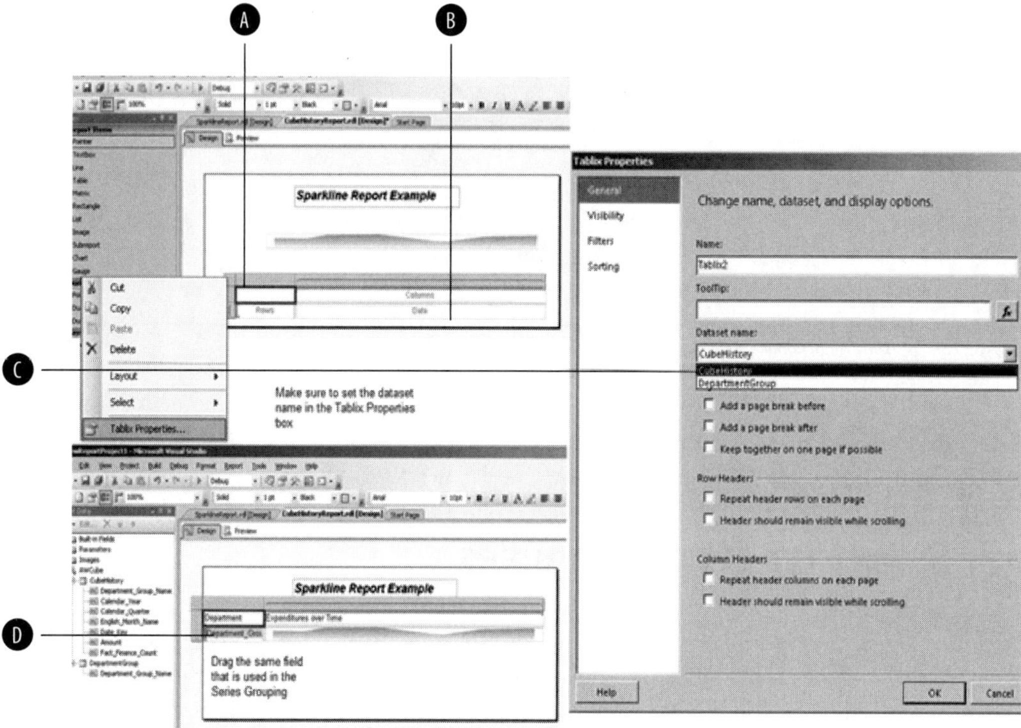

Figure 1-21 *Sparkline report—creating the tablix*

3. Right-click on the Tablix and choose Tablix Properties; in the General pane, set the Dataset Name equal to the dataset used to create the chart (Step C).
4. Add the same field as used in the chart series group to the matrix on the same row as the chart item (Step D).
5. Save, then preview.

Sparklines are called "high-density" reports because a lot of information is displayed in very little space. As you can see in the report preview shown in Figure 1-22, the spending trends of each department group are shown over the entire timeline, allowing a quick comparison of cycles between departments.

Compared to our previous chart types, it cannot be determined which department spends the most, but it can be determined that Executive General and Administration, and Inventory Management have the same cycles; Corporate is pretty flat and consistent throughout the time frame; and that Quality Assurance, and Research and Development seem to have some, but not all, spending patterns in common. With this display it is easy to see that Sales and Marketing has a very set spending pattern that escalates as

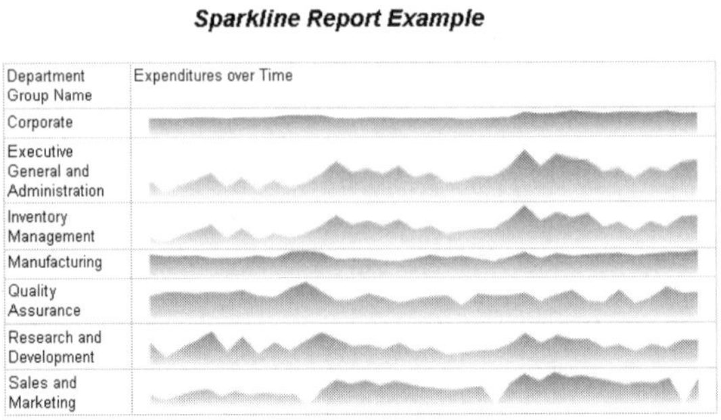

Sparkline Report Example

Department Group Name	Expenditures over Time
Corporate	
Executive General and Administration	
Inventory Management	
Manufacturing	
Quality Assurance	
Research and Development	
Sales and Marketing	

Figure 1-22 *Sparkline report preview*

the year goes on. This is an example of gaining insight by choosing the best visualization to suit the purpose!

Basic Report Types and Examples

Let's compare some other examples, and then build some more reports. This example is from the AdventureWorks report samples, the Product Line Sales Report. It is nicely formatted and includes both table and graphic elements, but notice how difficult it is to compare actual values as Pie Slices in the bottom section, Top Stores. The first example, Figure 1-23, is as published, with a Pie chart to compare five very close values.

Although the report author did not violate the rule of thumb of no more than ten pie slices, because the values are so similar it is hard to determine exactly which had the largest sales by looking at the chart. Compare this chart to the next one, Figure 1-24, with our changes. By changing the Pie chart to a Bar chart, and sorting from largest sales amount to smallest, it is entirely perceptible which store had the largest sales amount. Though it uses fewer colors, it is much easier to discern that the Totes and Baskets Company edged out Excellent Riding Supplies in annual sales. Although the pie looks nice, it just doesn't convey the useful information apparent in the Bar chart. Changing the chart type is easy, as is sorting if you know where to find the properties.

Change the Chart Type and Sort Values

To change the appearance of the chart and the order in which the values are displayed, do the following:

1. On the design surface right-click within the chart area, and select Change Chart Type from the context menu as displayed in Figure 1-24. (Note: if you click in a blank area, you will not get the same context menu.)
2. The Chart Type dialog box will appear with all your choices. Select the desired chart type and click OK.

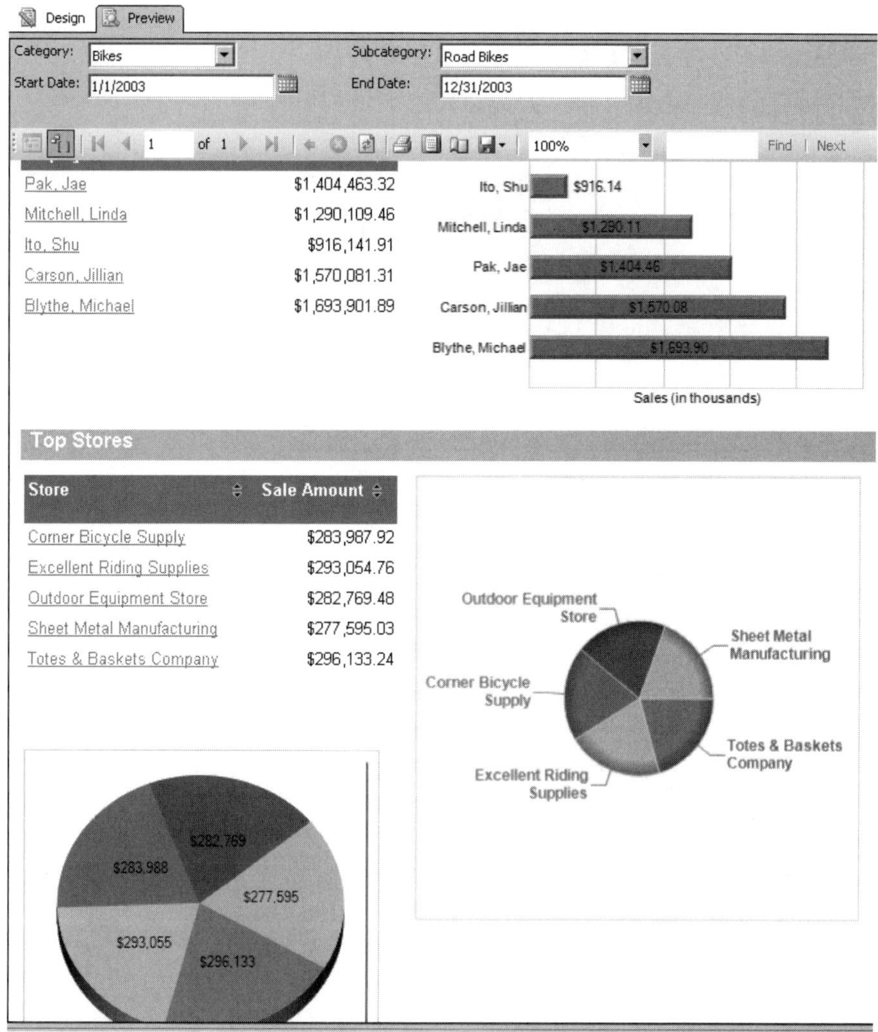

Figure 1-23 *AdventureWorks Product Line Sales 1*

3. To sort the values, right-click the category group field in the category drop zone, and select Category Group Properties as shown in Step A of Figure 1-25.
4. Select Sorting from the Explorer pane (Step B).
5. Add a Sort Item by clicking the Add button (Step C).
6. In the Sort By column, choose the field from the drop-down (Step D).
7. Select Order as ascending (A to Z) or descending (Z to A) (Step E).
8. Click OK to close the dialog box and apply changes (Step F).

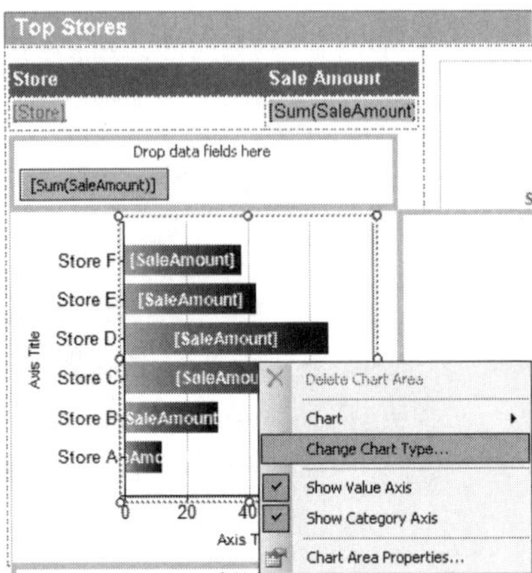

Figure 1-24 *Change the chart type*

With some minor changes we have improved the ability of the report to convey the important information—the ranking of the top five Stores, their annual sales amounts, and most important, how they compare to each other—something that was hard to detect from viewing the Pie chart. Figure 1-26 shows a report with parameters.

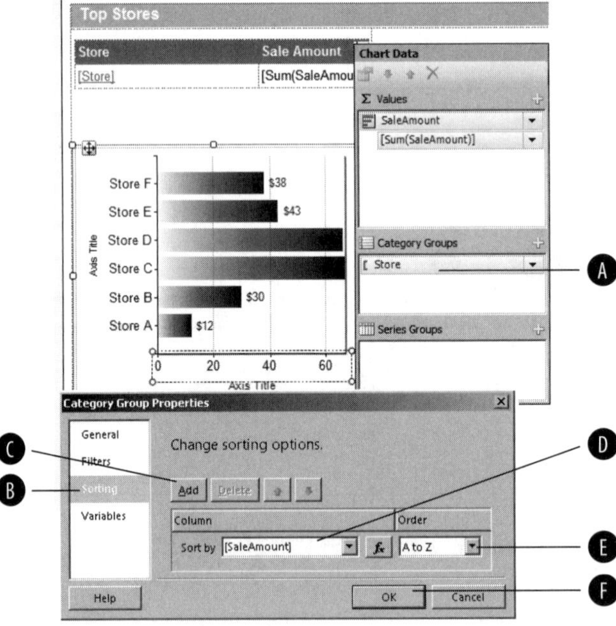

Figure 1-25 *Category Group Properties—sorting the category group*

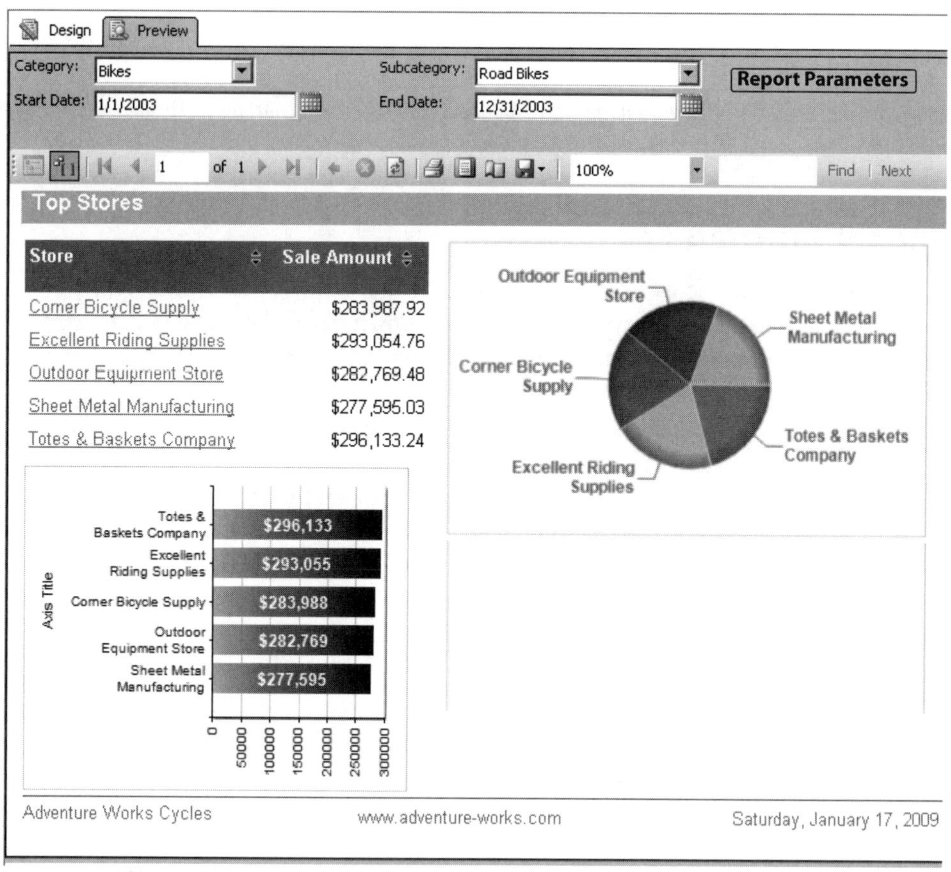

Figure 1-26 *AdventureWorks Product Line Sales 2—two types of charts with parameters*

Parameters can be used to reduce the scope of the dataset returned, which allows the user to narrow in on more specific information.

By providing decision makers with the ability to absorb information visually, the attention factor is improved. By providing the ability to drill down on the dimensional information by using parameters, insight can be personalized for audience preferences and curiosities. A personnel manager may want the same report, but parameterized by sales territory and associate. The logistics manager may want to see the same information geographically, to improve shipping routes and carriers. The marketing manager may want to see it by DMA or Claritas Cluster. If your organization has a data warehouse or master data management solution, you have just hit a goldmine!

BI TIP

Remember your audience—they want the most insight at a glance that the chart report can deliver. If it leaves them with questions, you have missed an important piece of data or description that needs to be included.

Report Parameters

Report parameters give the user the ability to choose the values for information filters. Like the examples named, each type of user has their own particular circle of concern and circle of influence (as our friend Stephen Covey has noted). When working with large data sources, like a data warehouse, invest the time to optimize your queries and build in good parameters to help your stakeholders get more out of the available reporting tools. If you have talked to them and gathered good report requirements, the report can be designed to deliver summary as well as detailed information. Many times they may want to drill to detail from a chart report. Seeing the patterns change visually as a representation of the underlying data is a powerful analysis tool. You can achieve this result by using report parameters.

Another AdventureWorks sample report that displays a lot of charting capability is the Employee Sales Report. Parameters limit the dataset being displayed by filtering for one (or several) of all values in an attribute dimension. By intelligent use of parameters, a report can be personalized to show information for only one individual or area of interest. Report parameters are used to limit the data to use in a report, to connect related reports together, and to vary report presentation. Using parameters can improve report performance because it limits the amount of data retrieved from the query.

Figure 1-27 has charts to show individual sales by month for a period of three years, a chart to display selected months' sales by category, and an order summary table, with drill-down to individual order detail items. The parameters of Report Month, Report Year, and Employee control what data is retrieved and displayed.

Let's look at the details of how this report is personalized. The three parameters allow the user to choose what time frame and employee to display the information for. Parameters to control values in the dataset and other conditions are available in the Report Data pane. Creating a new parameter involves some forethought. For this report example, the report has three report areas, based on different datasets, but all using the same set of report parameters.

In Report Designer you only have to create those parameters once, and reuse them for each dataset, making it easier to achieve consistency between the parts of the whole report. Make report parameters in two steps: create the report query with parameters, specify the details. If you create the parameters in this way, Report Designer will automatically link the query parameters to report parameters of the same name. When specifying query parameters in the SQL query *WHERE* clause, use the @ sign to distinguish them, as shown in Figure 1-28.

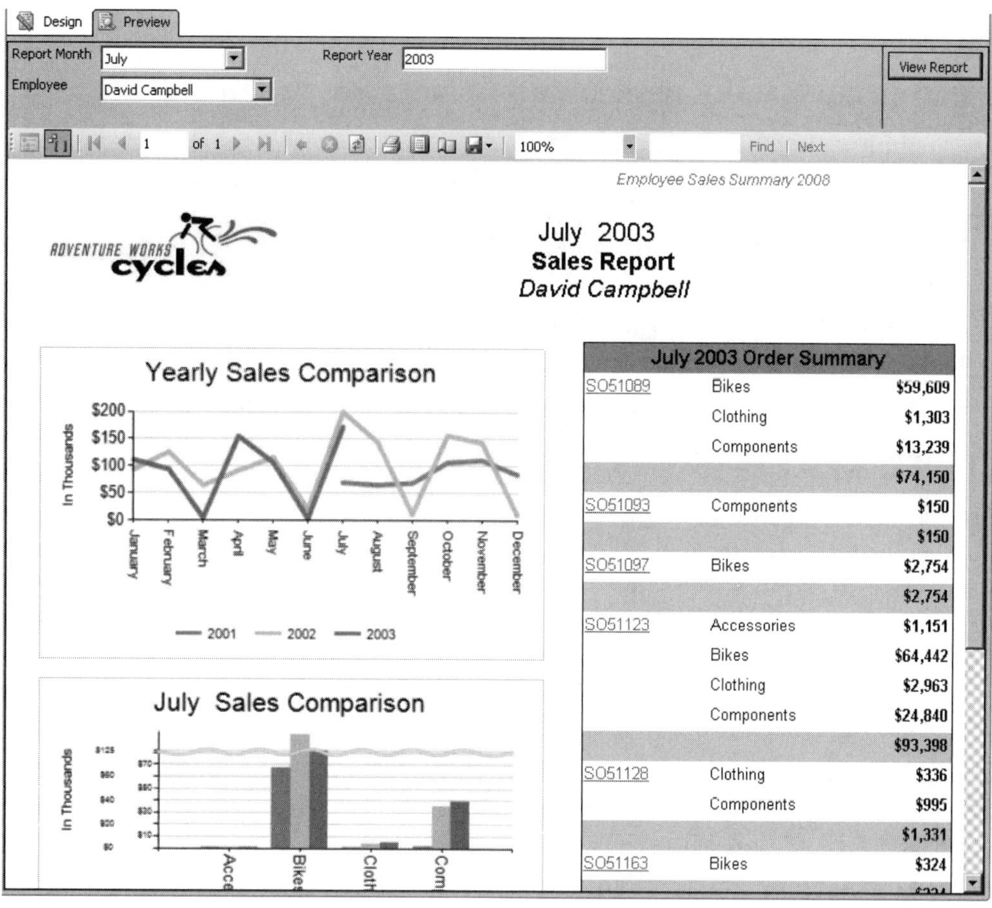

Figure 1-27 *AdventureWorks Employee Sales Report—personalize reporting through parameters*

Create a New Query Parameter

It's easy to create a new query parameter, since just about everything is wizard driven in Report Designer. To add a new query parameter, do the following:

1. On the dataset of interest, right-click and select Dataset Properties from the context menu as shown in Step A of Figure 1-28.
2. In the Dataset Properties dialog box, type the SQL query into the query pane, using the @ sign to distinguish query parameter names, like the example shown in Step B. If you format your query properly, the tool will add your parameters to the dialog box automatically.
3. To edit an existing parameter, choose Parameters from the Dataset Properties dialog (Step C).
4. Click the OK button to close and save your changes.

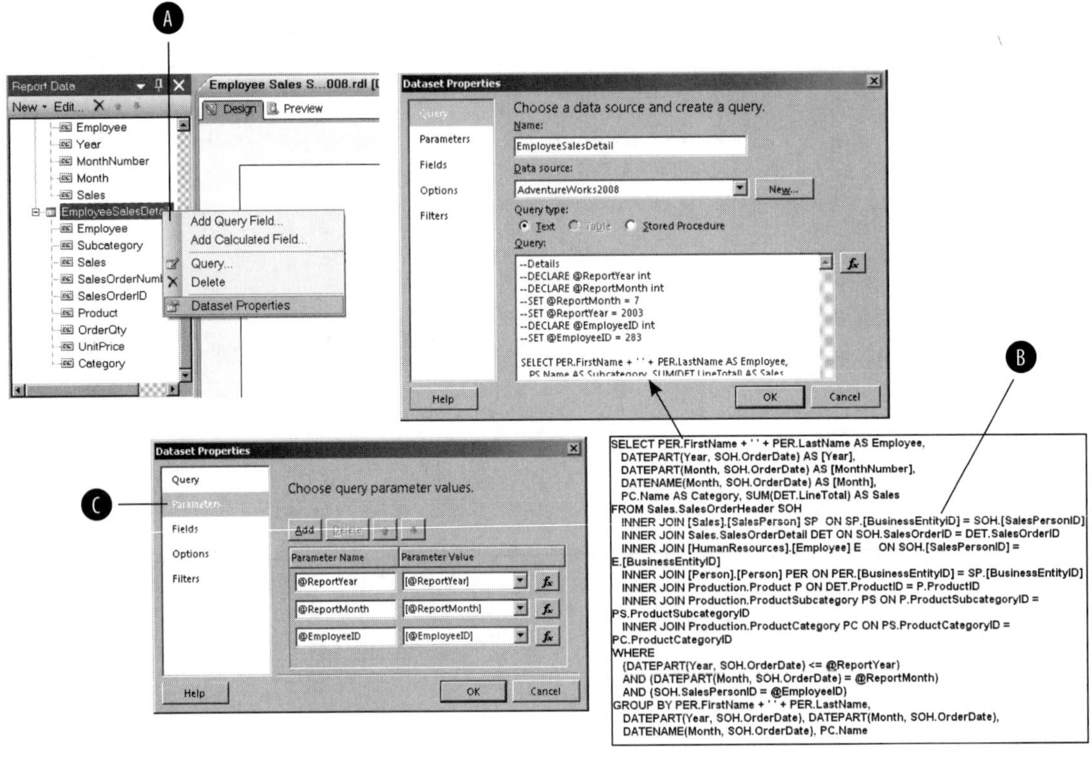

Figure 1-28 *Query Parameters example—use the @ sign to distinguish parameter names*

If you want to use parameters to filter all report items, then make sure the parameter names you use in the queries all match. For example, if you use @ReportYear for one query, don't use @Report_Year for the others because that would create a new parameter. Consistent naming will help you avoid that problem.

Report Parameters are created automatically when you create the query parameters. You can view Report Parameters to see how they are applied to each area.

1. As shown in A of Figure 1-29, right-click one of the Parameters listed in the Report Data pane, and choose Parameter Properties from the context menu.
2. The dialog will display the basic information on the General pane. Make sure the data type matches the intended value type, as pointed out at B.
3. The choice of Visible, Hidden, and Internal parameters is also on this pane, giving the report author flexibility in presetting values and connecting to subreports. Remember that if a report parameter is hidden, it must receive its value from a source other than the user interface (a default setting or main report if it is a subreport).
4. The Available Values pane is where the important details are collected. Options for Available Values include: None (user types in free-form), Specify Values

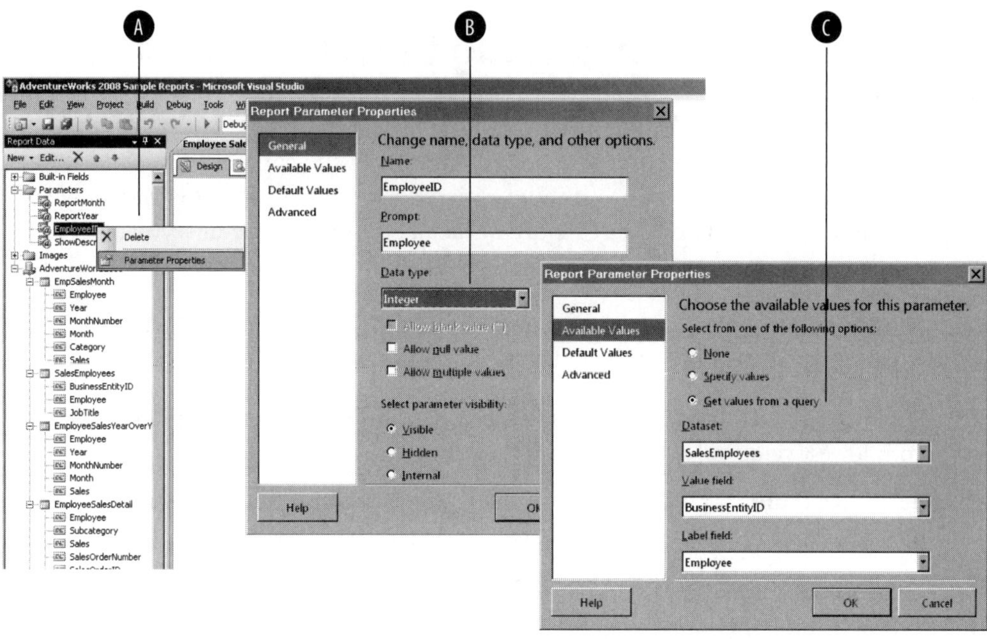

Figure 1-29 *Report Parameters dialogs*

(report author types in a list of choices) or Get Values From A Query (select dataset, value field, and label field), as shown in this example at C. Using a dataset to return available parameter values is a best practice.

5. On the Default Values pane setting default values for all report parameters will allow the report to execute when selected, instead of waiting for the user to input them. Defaults can always be overridden by choosing new values through the user interface, unless the parameters are hidden.
6. Click OK to save all changes and close the dialog box.

BI TIP

For parameters based on a single or multiple values from a database column that is included in the dataset, it is a best practice to create a separate query, for each parameter, to retrieve those values (using Select Distinct*). If you use the same fields from within the dataset as the Value Field and Label Field, duplicate values will show (for example, John, John, John). Providing the parameter choices through a separate query will improve report processing and allow the parameter list to be unique choices as opposed to showing multiple instances of the same value.*

The smart use of parameters can greatly improve the functionality and personalization of a report. Some parameters may be at the report level as well, and not used by any particular query or dataset. Report parameters can be used to control the conditional display of items based on a value obtained at runtime, like userid or date.

Advanced Topics, Including Calculated Fields, Visibility Expressions, and Combination Charts

Many times the dataset for the report is representative of the company's business but lacks adequate comparative data. Without writing complicated code, it is very easy to add calculated fields to many Chart reports. Calculated series come in several varieties out of the box:

- **Mean** The sum of a group divided by the number of items, this means average in layman's terms.
- **Median** For a group of numbers the median is found by arranging all the numbers from lowest value to highest value and selecting the middle one.
- **Bollinger Bands** Developed for stock trading analysis, this series shows the high and low limits based on previous values and standard deviations.
- **Moving Average** Here the calculation of the average moves with time periods.
- **Exponential Moving Average** A moving average where weighting factors are applied and the weight for each older data point decreases exponentially. This gives more weight to the more recent values.
- **Triangular Moving Average** Similar to the Exponential Moving Average, this uses a triangular number.
- **Weighted Moving Average** This is a moving average where weighting factors are applied based on age of the value.
- **MACD (Moving Average Convergence/Divergence)** This shows the difference between a fast and slow exponential moving average. Used mostly for stock and commodity trading analysis.
- **Detrended Price Oscillator** A calculation that attempts to eliminate the long-term trends, leaving short-term trends on which to act.
- **Relative Strength Index** This is a financial technical analysis oscillator showing price strength by comparing upward and downward close-to-close movements. Very similar to the MACD.
- **Standard Deviation** Of a collection of numbers, this is a measure of the dispersion of the numbers from their mean value.
- **TRIX (Triple Exponential)** A triple-smoothed exponential moving average, this is used mostly for stock and commodity trading analysis.

Examples of Calculated Series

The Trend Line example report shown in Figure 1-30 shows several new features that can add rich context and improve readability to your graphic reports. This sample contains the sales data by date, the calculated series *moving average,* and Strip Lines on the chart background for emphasis on the time period: Quarters.

Calculated series can only be added to charts that do *not* have multiple series. This is logical, because if you had multiple series, which of the multiple data points per time period would be inputs to the calculated series? However, you can add more than one calculated series to a chart.

BI TIP

Use trend lines for charts where no discernable pattern is evident (the trend line can effectively overlay a visible pattern on top of the series data) or where you want to emphasize the trend over time.

1. Start with the simple chart, Sales Amount over Time. On the design surface, right-click the data field that is in the data fields drop zone, as shown in Step A of Figure 1-31.
2. Select Add Calculated Series from the context menu (Step B). If you have any fields dropped in the Series drop zone, the Add Calculated Series menu item does not appear.
3. The Calculated Series Properties dialog box will appear, where you see the variety of choices.

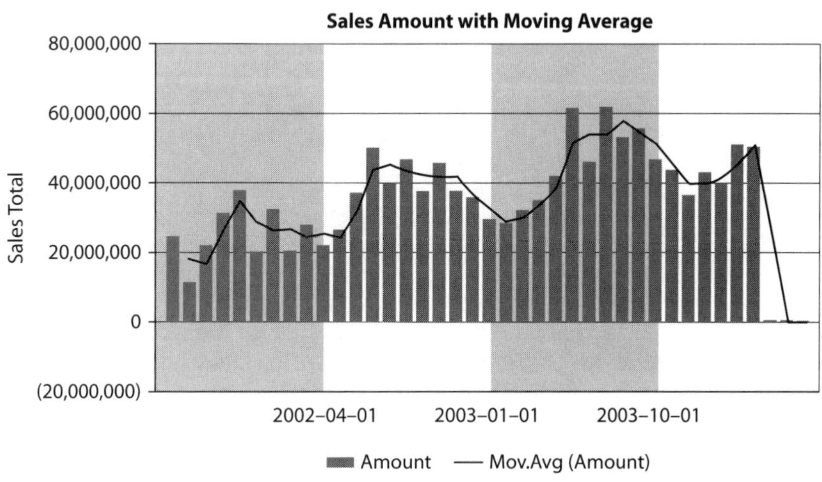

Figure 1-30 *Trend Line report example—shows the Moving Average calculated field on the report*

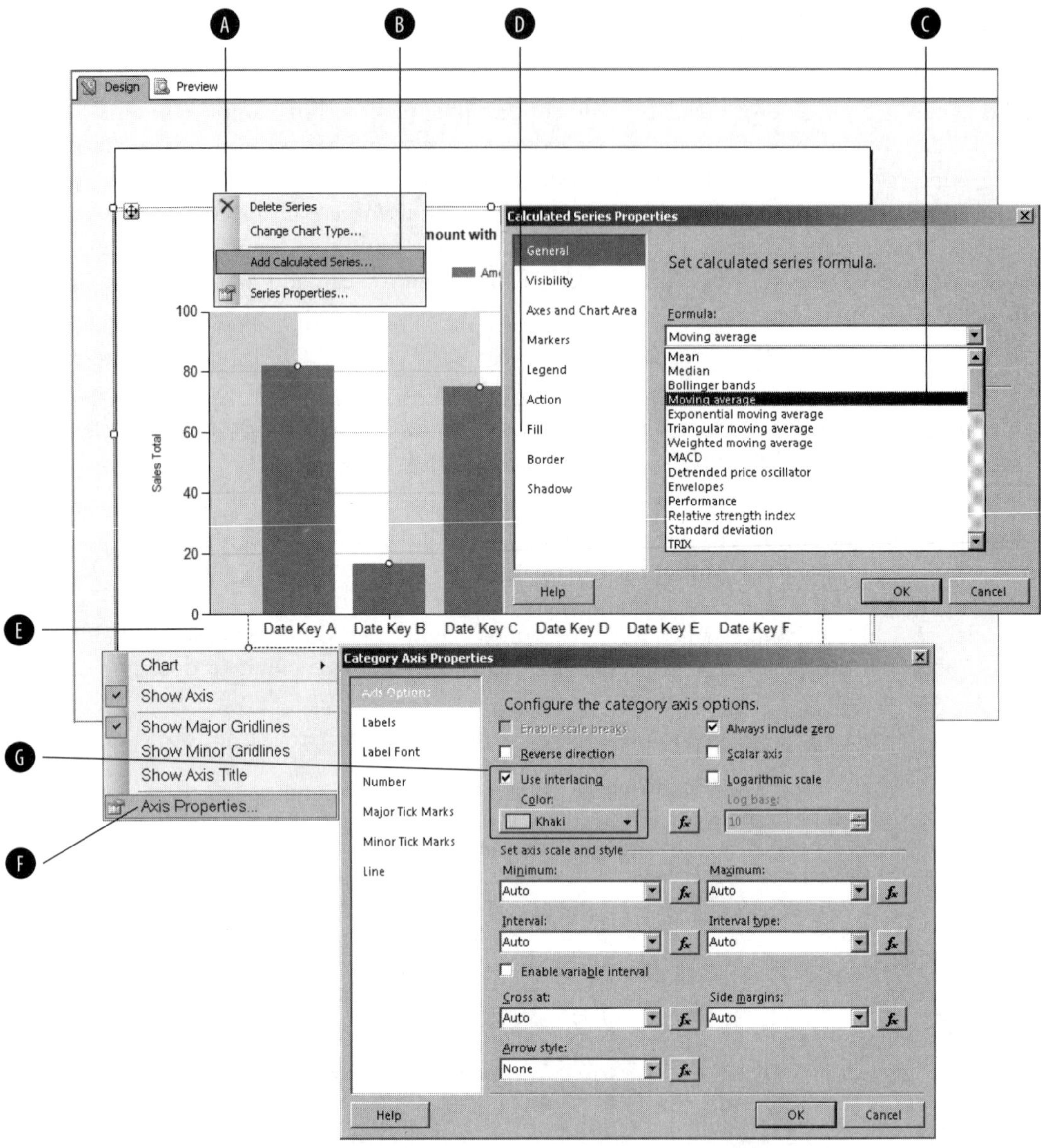

Figure 1-31 *Trend Line Report Example—Design pane showing Calculated Series Properties and Category Axis Properties*

4. On the General pane, select the Formula to use for the calculated series. For this example, Moving Average (Step C).
5. If the formula chosen takes parameters, fields for those show up under the Formula text box.

6. Click Fill in the Explorer pane and choose a bright or bold color for the calculated series to make it stand out (Step D).
7. Click the OK button at the bottom of the dialog box to apply settings.

Adding Strip Lines, aka Interlacing

For the last formatting option on this report, add the Strip Lines by selecting the Category Axis Properties.

1. Right-click the category (X) axis inside the boundary lines as shown in Step E of Figure 1-31, then select Axis Properties from the context menu (Step F).
2. Strip Lines are actually called Interlacing, so tick the check box for Use Interlacing and pick a color to alternate with the Chart Area background color selected (Step G).
3. Strip lines can be added to either axis, so if vertical strip lines are desired to highlight time series or a distinction between categories, then add them to the category axis. If horizontal strip lines are desired to help discriminate the difference between values on the Y axis, configure them in the Value Axis Properties. Do not use strip lines on both axes or you will end up with a checkerboard!
4. Click the OK button at the bottom of the dialog box to save settings.

The trend lines from the calculated series and Strip Lines enhance the readability of the chart and allow the viewer to instantly discriminate any pattern in the data.

Multiple Series (Y) Axis

Another improvement is the ability to have two Y axes to clarify datasets that have different scalar values. This allows the display of relationships between two distinct measures, items that trend or don't trend as expected. For example, the count of transactions and the value of transactions. If the average transaction amount is quite high, it may be hard to display on one axis scale, even with an axis scale break. Figure 1-32 shows a Trend chart with 2 value (Y) axes, and you can see the relationship between the two data series quite distinctly.

In order to create a chart with two value (Y) axes, create a chart report with at least two data series.

1. First, define each series by dragging the data field from the dataset pane onto the top data drop zone, as shown in Figure 1-33.
2. Right-click the series to change as shown in Step A of Figure 1-33.
3. Select Change Chart Type from the context menu (Step B). When this selection is chosen for one particular data series, it only changes the chart type for that series. The Select Chart Type dialog box will display with all your chart type choices. Select Line chart and click OK to apply the setting.

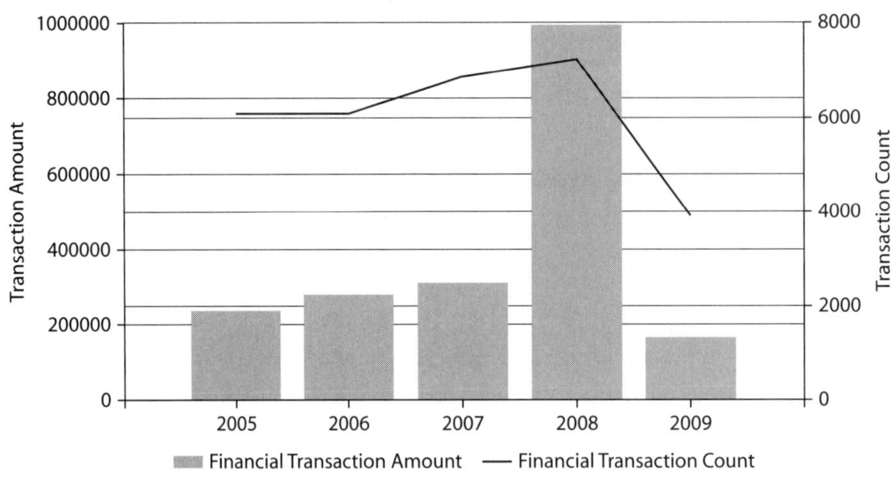

Figure 1-32 *Trend chart with two Value (Y) axes*

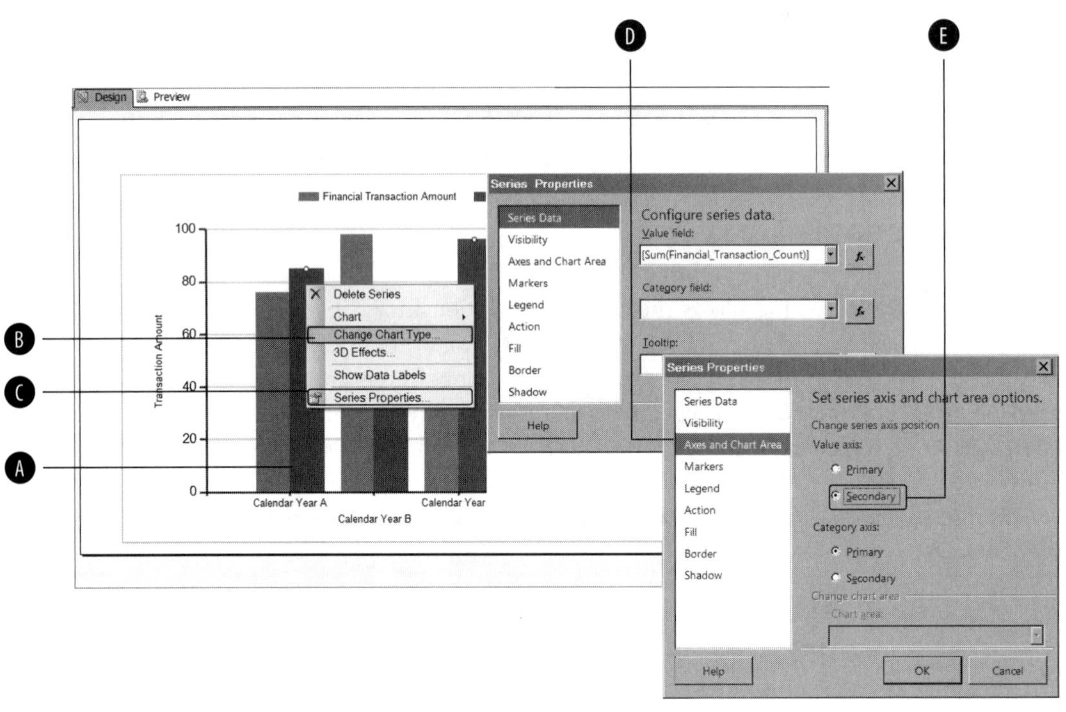

Figure 1-33 *Trend Chart—Change Chart Type*

4. In order to set the secondary axis, right-click the data series, then select Series Properties (Step C).
5. Choose Axes and Chart Area from the Explorer pane.
6. From the Series Properties dialog box, choose Axes and Chart Area from the list (Step D).
7. Under the Value Axis: selection, click the Secondary radio button (Step E). The system will examine the dataset and automatically scale the axis based on that series.
8. Click OK to save and apply changes.

Range Chart Types and Examples

Range charts show multiple values for each x-axis interval. The recognizable example is the high-low-open-close chart originally created to show stock price volatility. Range charts are good for displaying data that has multiple measurements to compare per period. Let's examine some more examples, and discover the details that give them appeal.

Box Plot Charts

The *Box Plot* chart type consists of box symbols that show the distribution of data within one or more datasets. The majority distribution is contained inside the rectangle, and whisker lines show the upper and lower limits. The chart takes values for x,y, high whisker, low whisker, high box, low box, mean, and median.

Box Plot charts are range charts and are appropriate for showing data that has an associated range of values that have a normal distribution pattern. This supports easily identifying outliers. Figure 1-34 shows a Box Plot chart in design mode, so the layout of data fields can be seen. The Y axis is the measure axis—how many units, dollars, people? The X axis is the category of information—like date for a time series chart—or it could be product category, territory, or department as a slicer dimension in the chart. This chart type would be a good visualization for data like highly volatile inventory where you need to see how the various values change over time, especially if using JIT stock replenishment.

Candlestick Charts

Candlestick charts are another range chart type traditionally used for showing Stock High-Low-Open-Closed values. Candlestick charts, like the one in Figure 1-35, are a variation of the Stock chart where the size of the line is determined by the high and low values, and the size of the candlestick or bar is determined by the open and close values. This chart type is also appropriate for any product or service that has volatile pricing or even volatile inventory levels. The bars on the Candlestick chart can be configured to vary based on whether the values are upward trending or downward trending for the observation period (daily). These colors are defined using the Price Up Color and Price Down Color properties.

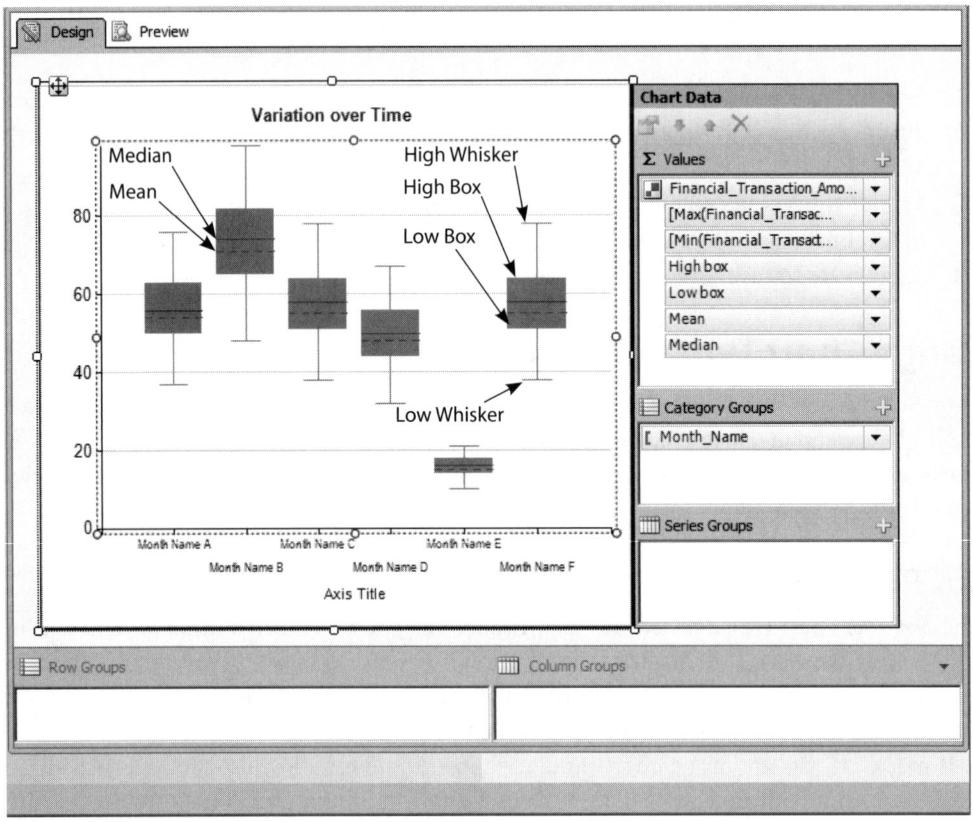

Figure 1-34 *Box Plot chart—in design mode with drop zones exposed*

Different chart series properties will be available depending on the chart type. *Range* charts display price up color and price down color under both the General and Data Point groups. Figure 1-36 shows property settings for Range charts, including the labels—high, low, open, close. Varying these attributes gives the report author remarkable abilities to customize the display and alter the look of the same report types with alternate datasets.

The standard range chart type is the *Stock* chart. It is a very similar visualization to the Candlestick chart, but with less decoration. Stock charts have other applications beside stock price display. Think of using this type of range chart for displaying call center data or help desk data where there are peak times, lull times, and a variation in the number of operators handling calls.

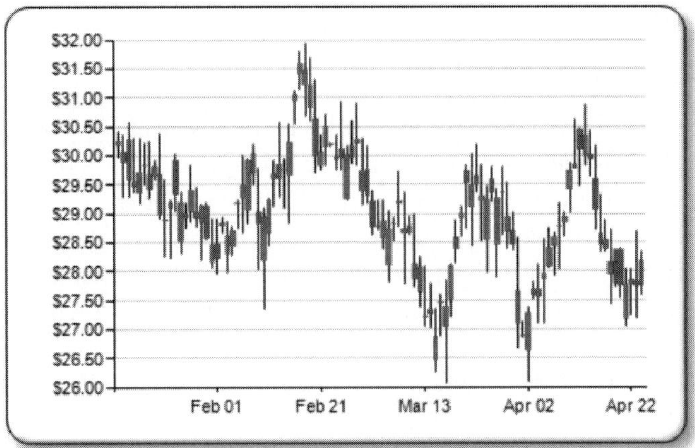

Figure 1-35 *Candlestick chart*

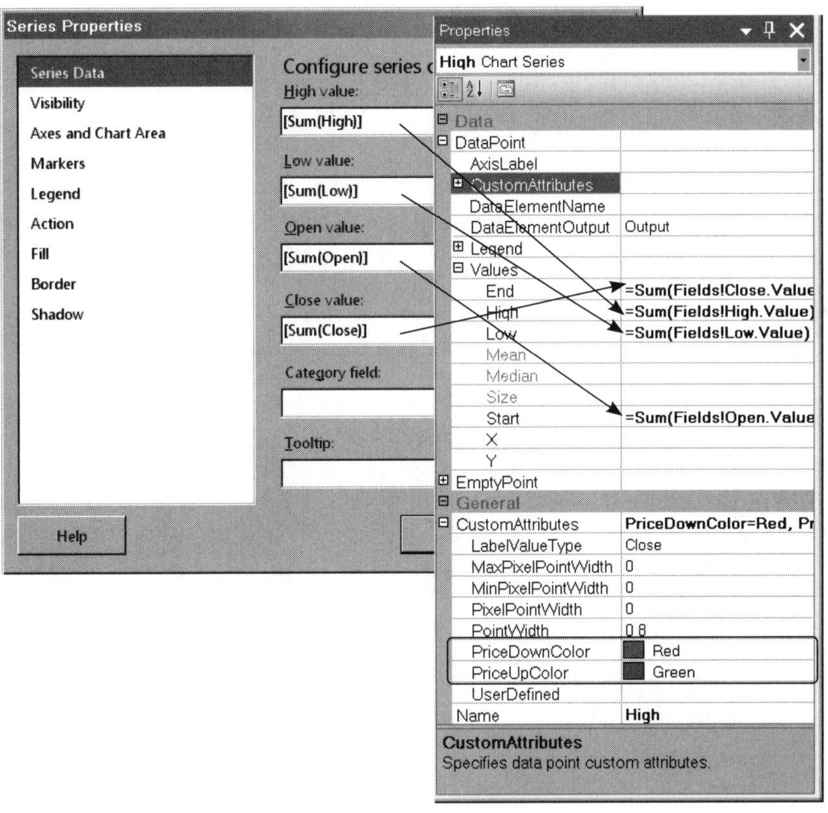

Figure 1-36 *Series properties for Range chart type*

Shape Charts: Pyramids, Funnels, Pies, Doughnuts, Collected Pie

Another chart type with interesting possibilities is the *Shape* chart. Pies, Doughnuts, and other shapes like funnels and pyramids are good visualizations to illuminate data where the percentage of the whole is the motivating factor, or the desire is to display values in a process—like a sales pipeline or workflow status.

Other interesting and useful chart types can help to illuminate other data patterns. A new addition to the Chart choices, Shape charts are useful for seeing an item that has multiple statuses.

The *Pyramid* chart is a type of Shape chart that behaves like a Pie chart—all series values add up to 100 percent, and it does not use a categorical axis.

1. Pyramid series properties include the drawing style (square base or round base), the rotation angle, and the point gap. Here is the same chart with the Rotation Angle set to –10 and the point gap set to 2. It is shown as A and B in Figure 1-37.
2. Funnel Chart series properties include Drawing Style (square or circular base), Rotation Angle, Label Alignment and Label Style, Minimum Point Height, Neck Height and Neck Width, Label Placement, Point Gap, and Funnel Style (Yls Height, Yls Width), as shown as C and D in Figure 1-37.

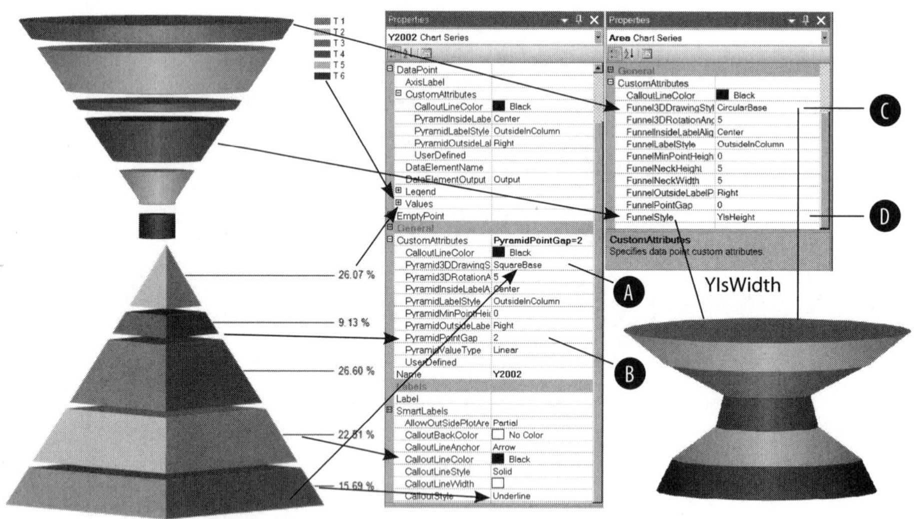

Figure 1-37 *A Variety of Shape chart examples. They show part-to-whole relationships, vary the gap, use YlsHeight or YlsWidth, show a Circular or Square base, add Labels and Callouts.*

3. The odd shape is a Funnel Chart (same data) displayed with Funnel Style Yls Width, no point gap, and rotation set to +5.
4. The Funnel uses the same data as the Pyramid. A Funnel chart is good for displaying things like the number of sales prospects by status—with the largest group at the top and the smallest, signed contract group at the bottom. Or for the number of items at a particular stage of workflow. The funnel shape naturally connotes movement through a process or filter.

Pie and *Doughnut* charts are the most common Shape charts, and they have special properties as well. Pie and Doughnut charts are very succinct presentations of part-to-whole data relationships. They are most appropriate when the number of slices is less than ten, and where the boundaries are easily recognizable. Pie charts have fallen out of favor with many statisticians and information visualization gurus because of their lack of specificity and the fact that sometimes it is very difficult to determine which slice is actually the largest slice of the pie or doughnut.

BI TIP

If the Pie has more than ten slices, or all the slice values are very similar, consider using a Bar chart instead to make part-to-whole relationships clearer.

The fact remains that Pie charts are very recognizable and accepted in the business community, and if labeled properly, they can present information in a way that is clearly and instantly recognizable and understood. Below are several examples of Doughnut and Pie charts. The addition of the Dundas code base into Reporting Services has greatly improved the control and design of these charts, and given them a much more appealing visual quality for presentations.

Doughnut charts are merely Pie charts with a doughnut hole in the middle. The size of the doughnut hole can have significance as well. The Doughnut Radius setting controls the amount of space in the doughnut hole. The smaller the number, the larger the doughnut hole; the larger the number, the smaller the hole. A doughnut radius of 100 means a solid middle—a Pie chart. There are two drawing styles for Pie and Doughnut charts, SoftEdge and Concave, as shown in Figure 1-38. Use of these drawing styles can make these charts more eye-catching.

To set these properties, set the drawing style to increase the visual impact of your chart when you are using Pie and Doughnut charts. These drawing effects are applied using the series properties, as shown in Figure 1-39. The soft edge or concave drawing style, similar to bevel or emboss effects, can give the chart a polished and professional look, enhancing presentation quality. For Doughnut charts, set the Doughnut Radius through Series Properties, as shown in Figure 1-39.

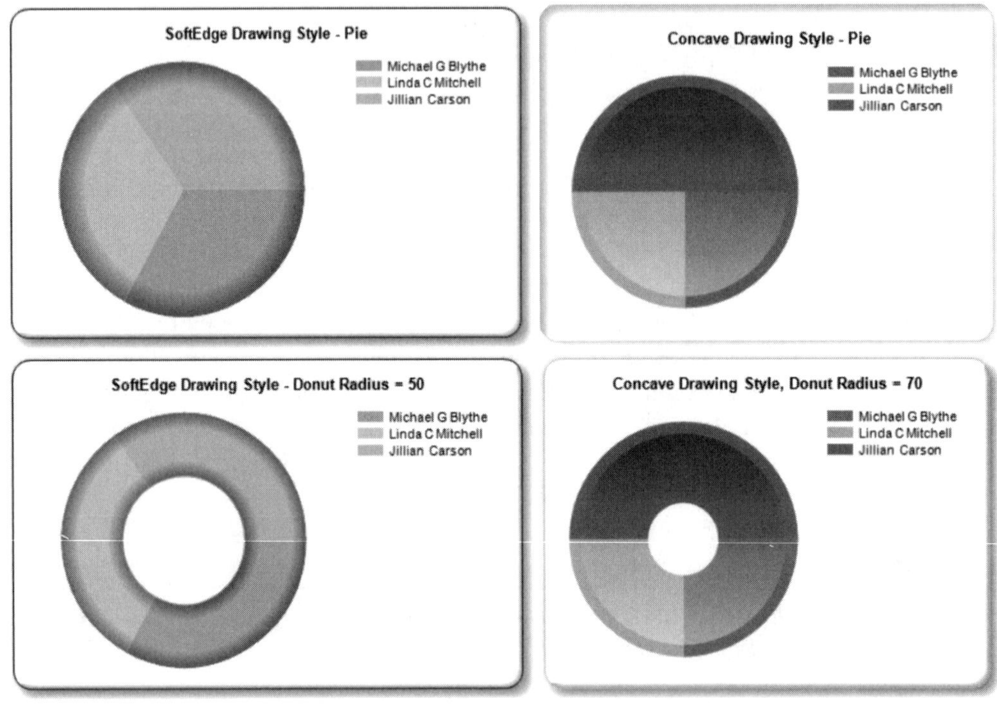

Figure 1-38 *Doughnut chart examples*

Another technique that can be used with Pie and Doughnut Charts and is worth exploring is the *Collected Pie.* As shown in Figure 1-40, if a Pie chart is going to have so many slices that it is hard to determine their value, or there will be label collision, a group of the smaller pieces can be aggregated and optionally exploded into an ancillary Collected Pie to better display the details. The other choice is to combine the small slices into one slice, called the *Single Slice.*

As shown in the first example in Figure 1-40, many small pie slices are collected into a single slice labeled "Other." In the second example, the "Other" slice is exploded into the ancillary pie chart next to the main Pie chart.

The properties to set this type of display are under Chart Series, General, Custom Properties. As shown in Figure 1-41, the series of properties for this option include

- **CollectedStyle** Either Single Slice or Collected Pie
- **CollectedThreshold** The percentage value that is the limit for full pie slices. For example, if the CollectedThreshold = 5, then any slice that is less than 5 percent of the total will be accumulated into the Collected Pie
- **CollectedThresholdUsePercent** Always true if CollectedStyle = Collected Pie

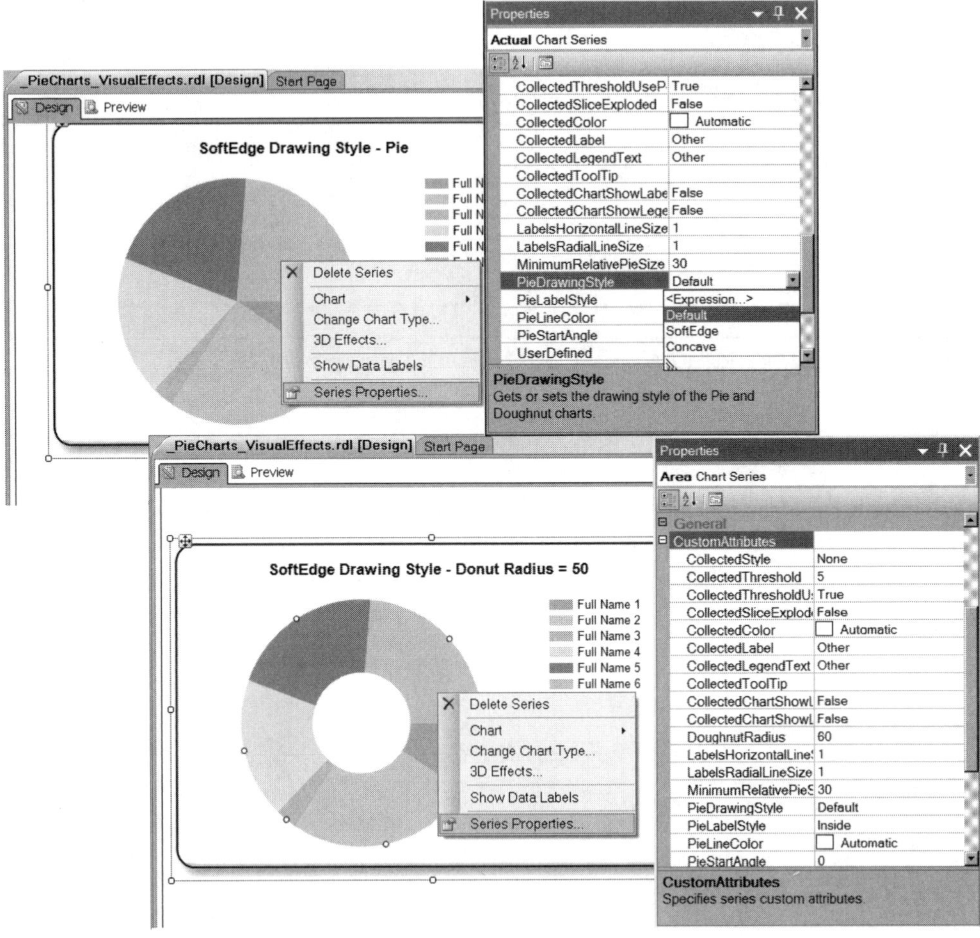

Figure 1-39 *Pie Drawing Style Property and Doughnut Radius Property—both accessed from the Series Properties context menu*

- **CollectedSliceExploded** Only applies to the Single Slice CollectedStyle
- **CollectedColor** Only applies to the Single Slice CollectedStyle
- **CollectedLabel** Defaults to Other, but any descriptive text is allowed
- **CollectedLegendText** What to call the CollectedPie or Single Slice in the Legend
- **CollectedToolTip** Enables displaying ToolTips for the CollectedPie
- **CollectedChartShowLabels** Enables displaying the data labels on the CollectedPie
- **CollectedChartShowLegend** Enables the display of a legend for the CollectedPie

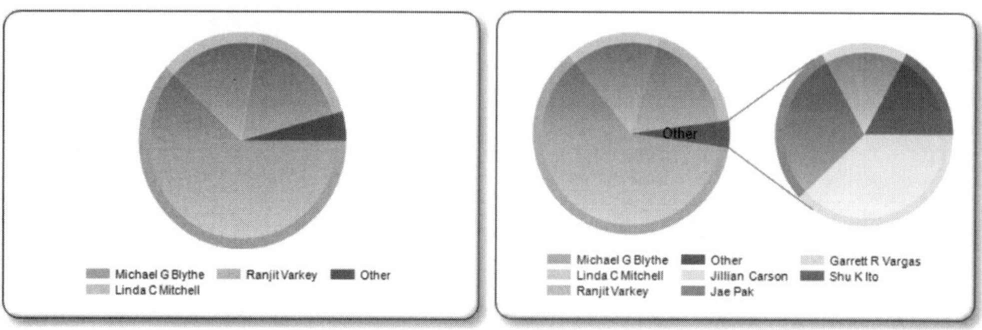

Figure 1-40 *Collected and Exploded Pie chart examples—ways to handle many small slices*

To change the data labels,

1. First right-click the pie data series and choose Show Data Labels from the context menu, as shown in Step A of Figure 1-41.
2. The data labels will display. Right-click within the label boundary (Step B).

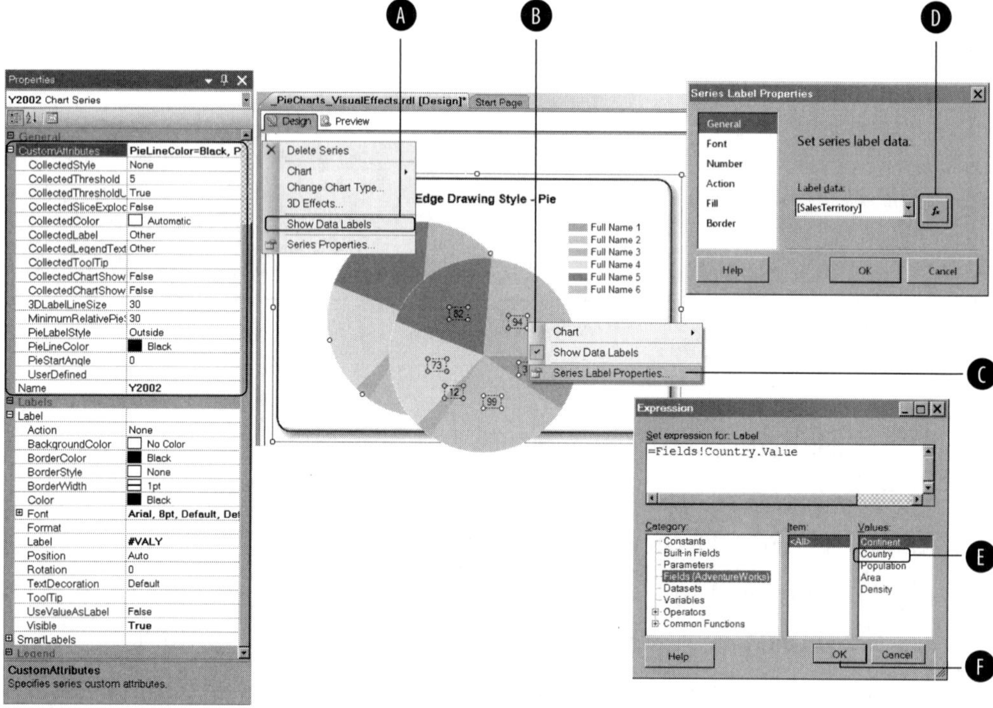

Figure 1-41 *Pie data label properties and customization*

3. Select Series Label Properties from the context menu (Step C).
4. On the General pane, click the Function button (Step D), next to the Label Data drop-down list.
5. The Expression dialog box will appear, and you can choose or create a fitting label.
6. To choose a field from the dataset, under Category select Fields, and then pick the field you want from the Values column (Step E).
7. Save and apply changes by clicking OK (Step F).

Handling Missing Data and Statistical Formula Support

How charts handle the display of missing data or empty points can greatly impact how the chart is rendered, and how useful the visualization is. Sometimes it is appropriate to have the empty value, but when you want a smoother data visualization, SSRS 2008 R2 now has several options for handling missing data points, and the charting options make it easy to identify data that are placeholders. The example in Figure 1-42 shows a data table with missing data points. The RowCounter could just as easily be a time series where measurements are missing and a trend is still expected.

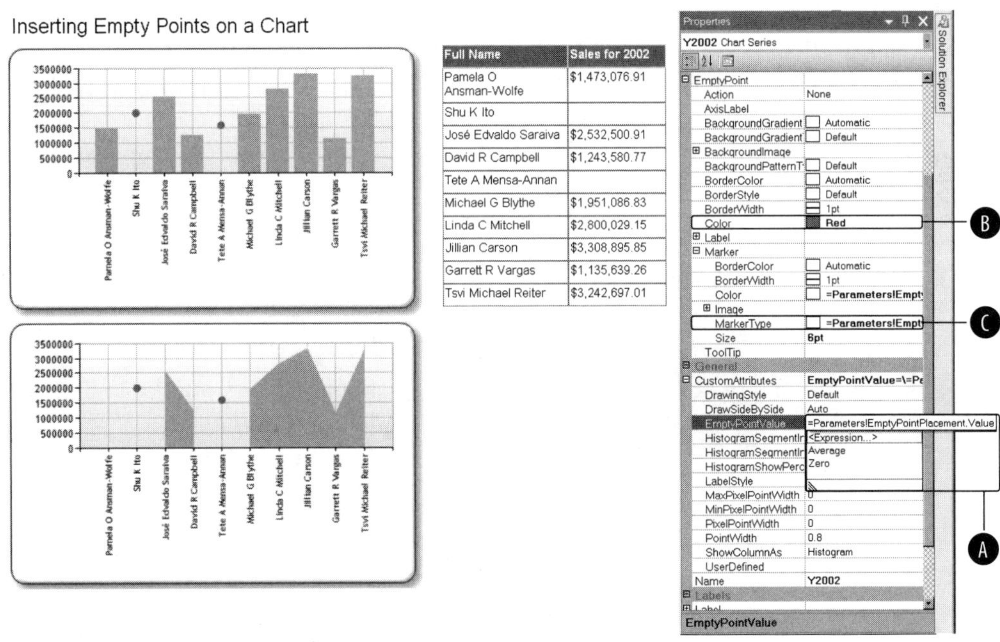

Full Name	Sales for 2002
Pamela O Ansman-Wolfe	$1,473,076.91
Shu K Ito	
José Edvaldo Saraiva	$2,532,500.91
David R Campbell	$1,243,580.77
Tete A Mensa-Annan	
Michael G Blythe	$1,951,086.83
Linda C Mitchell	$2,800,029.15
Jillian Carson	$3,308,895.85
Garrett R Vargas	$1,135,639.26
Tsvi Michael Reiter	$3,242,697.01

Figure 1-42 *Showing empty points for missing data*

To set the handling for empty points, go to the Chart Series Properties box.

1. As shown in Step A of Figure 1-42, in the Custom Attributes section of the General group, set the EmptyPointValue setting to 0 if you want to display empty points. Other options are Average or a custom expression.
2. Change the color of the marker (Step B) and line for EmptyPoints under the Data group of the Series Properties.
3. Play with the color and marker type (Step C) until a suitable representation is found. Remember that color should not be the only distinguishing factor; best practices suggest altering the shape of the marker as well as the color to distinguish dissimilar data points.

Line Charts, Special Charts, and More on Calculated Series

The *Step Line* chart, like the one shown in Figure 1-43, is good for showing data points over time where a smooth line averages the data values too much and would mislead the audience from the true information being displayed. The Step Line uses only vertical and horizontal lines to connect the data points. This type of chart may be very useful for understanding inventory levels, sales volumes, number of pieces by status, or any data type that has discrete values that should not be smoothed. This example shows a calculated series using Moving Average as a reference point. If you wanted to show ranges along with the Step Line, the Bollinger Bands or Envelopes type of calculated series makes for a very interesting display.

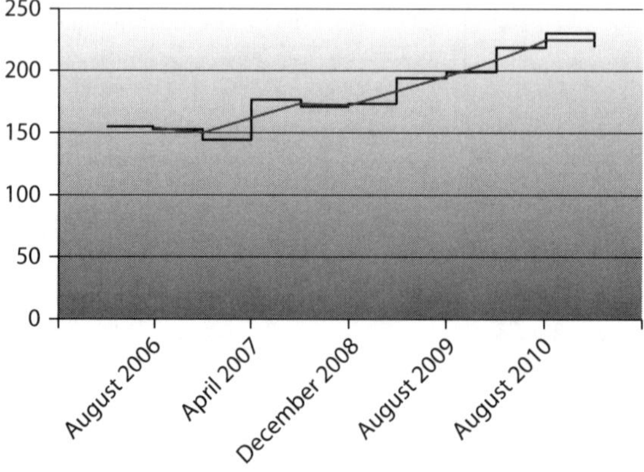

Figure 1-43 *Step Line chart*

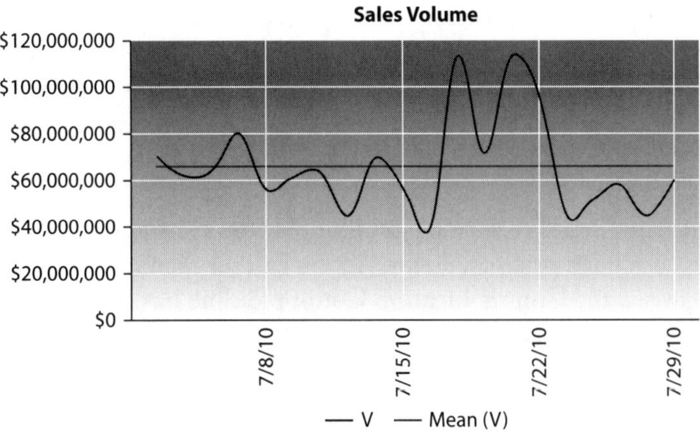

Figure 1-44 *Smooth Line chart—large variations are apparent*

The *Smooth Line* chart, like the one in Figure 1-44, presents the data in a way that looks like a wave. It minimizes the display of small variations, but large differences look dramatic, like the increase that happened right after 7/15.

Here are more examples of charts that display multiple series with financial and statistical calculations. *Bollinger Bands,* like that shown in Figure 1-45, show the values and a range of variance calculated based on adjacent values.

Bollinger Bands show a range of the amount of variance as calculated over a number of periods. The smaller the area between upper and lower borders, the smaller the amount of variance. Like in Figure 1-45, this visualization can be especially useful

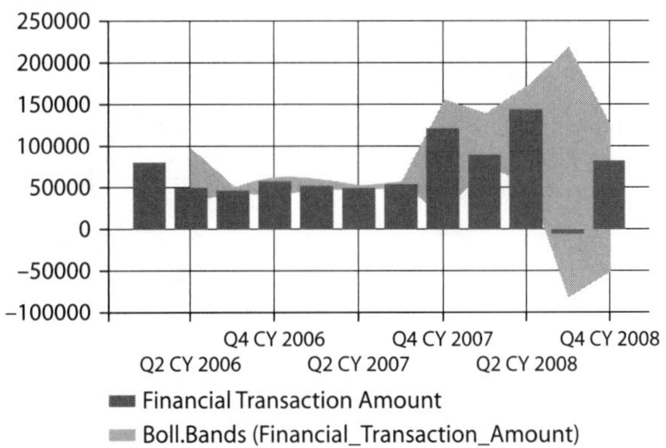

Figure 1-45 *Calculated series—Bollinger Bands*

for helping to spot periods of relatively little variance over larger trends. In looking at this example, it is very apparent that for a full year from Q2 2006 until Q2 2007, the financial transaction amounts were relatively stable. Then they spiked, came down, spiked, dropped off, then spiked again. The Bollinger Band (behind the bars) really points out the variance of the changes that occurred in the volatile period between Q4 2007 and Q4 2008.

Another calculated series that helps to highlight upward and downward movement of trends is the detrended price oscillator. As you can see from the example shown in Figure 1-46, when the Communication Count plot line has a negative slope, the calculated series shows below the 0 line.

In Figure 1-46, the calculated series shown at bottom really helps your eyes focus on the upward and downward movement of the data as displayed by the trend line at top.

Two special chart types that prove very useful are the *Pareto* chart and the *Histogram* chart. The Pareto chart is composed of a Column chart, descending-sorted by value, and a Line chart that shows the accumulated percentage of the items in the series. You only add the data series for the columns; the accumulated percentage series is calculated for you, as is all formatting for the secondary Y axis by the report chart property settings. As shown in Figure 1-47, regular column charts can be turned into Pareto charts by changing the ShowColumnAs property from Normal to Pareto.

To create a Pareto chart, start by creating a regular Column chart. Then change these properties to accomplish the change to a Pareto chart:

1. To change the normal Column chart into a Pareto chart, choose the ShowColumnAs = Pareto under the Custom Attributes section of the General group, as shown in Figure 1-47.

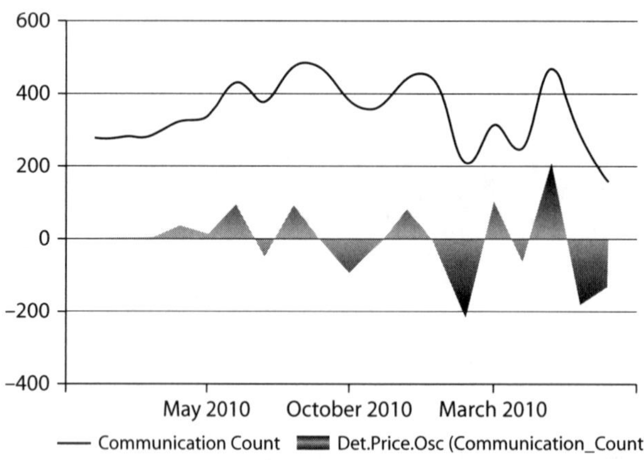

Figure 1-46 *The calculated series—detrended price oscillator makes downward trends more apparent.*

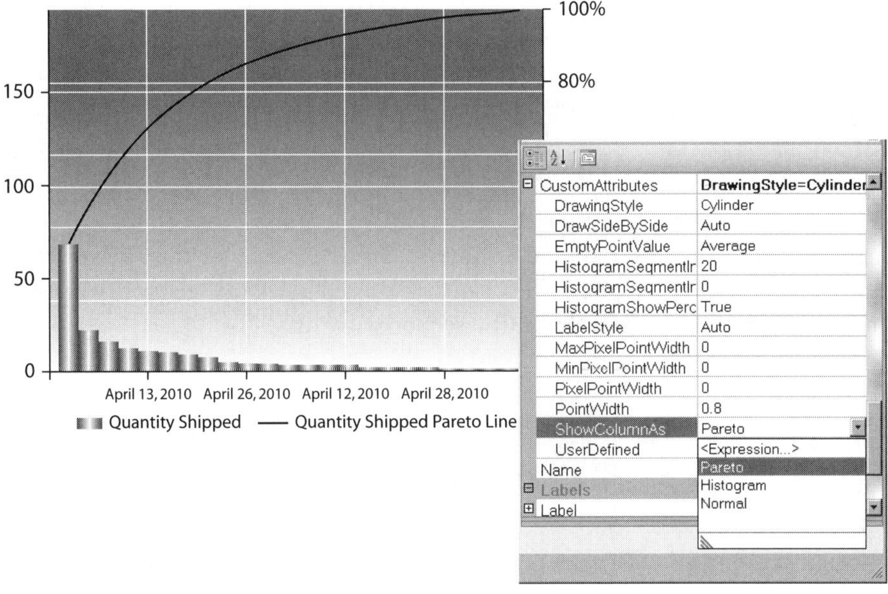

Figure 1-47 *Pareto Chart example*

2. In order to get the data series to sort descending, set the Sorting options on the Category Group Properties. Bring this up by right-clicking the Category Group data field, as shown in Figure 1-48.
3. In the Category Group Properties box, click Sorting in the Explorer pane, and then click Add.
4. Choose the column to sort by, and ascending or descending sort order. Click OK to close the dialog box.

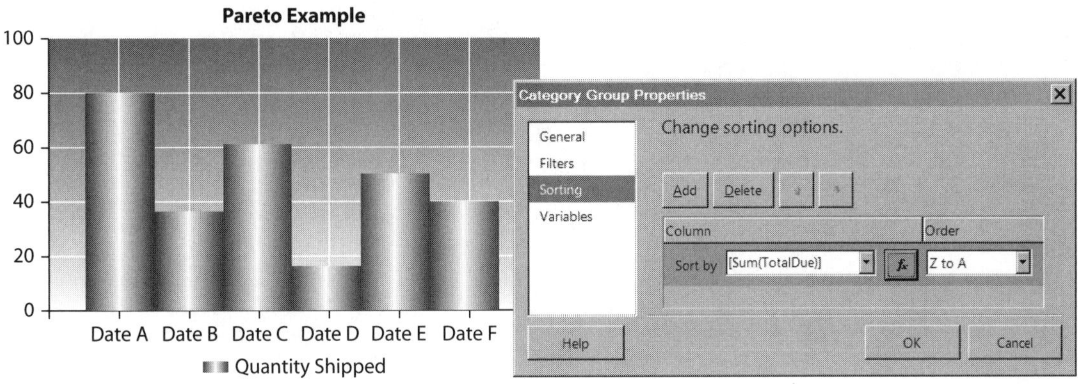

Figure 1-48 *Category Group Properties—Sorting*

As shown in Figure 1-48, the Category Group Properties box is where you can set filters, sort the category values, and apply variables or other general settings.

The other special chart of note is the Histogram chart. Histograms show data distributions by value grouping. This is extremely useful if you want to know totals or counts by value range, for example, how many (count) payments were between $50–$100, $101–$150, or $151–$200; or how many orders were for 1–5 pieces, 6–10, 11–15, etc. Many times, knowing the value for the group and ranking the groups is more insightful than knowing the individual values. The input table for this type of chart is the number of values by category. The resulting graph shows the frequency distribution by value group, and the percentage on the secondary Y axis.

BI TIP

BI charts like the histogram are particularly effective once the end users become familiar with this type of visualization. Then they can gain keen insight at a glance!

Figure 1-49 shows a Histogram chart and the data series Properties pane associated with this type of chart.

In a Histogram chart, like in Figure 1-49, the discrete values for each group are displayed with their real value on one value (Y) axis and in this example the percent of total on the second value (Y) axis, because in the Properties pane the HistogramShowPercentOnSecondaryYAxis is set to "True."

One thing to note is that, although the Pareto chart type supports enhanced drawing styles (Embossed, Cylinder), the Histogram chart does not! So make sure your other chart formatting is a little flashier.

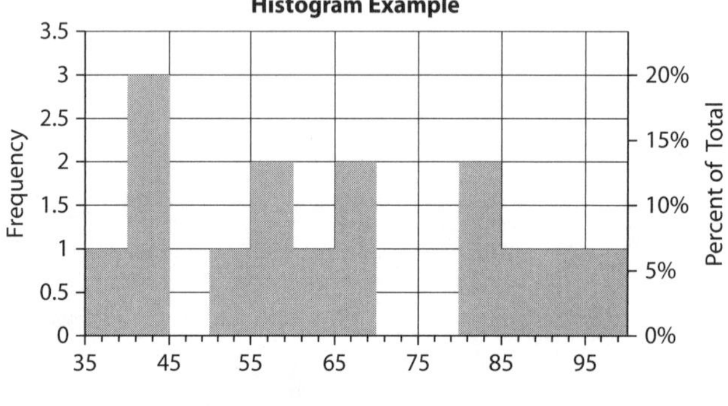

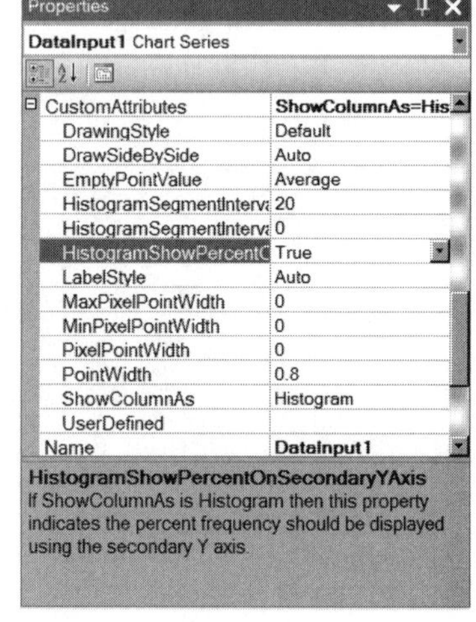

Figure 1-49 *Histogram Chart example*

BI TIP

If you want your information delivery to satisfy the end users, here are three simple steps:

- *Gather good requirements that include interviews with intended report consumers.*
- *Be creative in your presentation with appealing charts that are easily understood.*
- *Train end users and stakeholders to understand what is being presented to them with brief introductory sessions that explain the new reports to consumers.*

Range charts are good at showing a range of values by category and can plot more than one series at a time. As shown in Figure 1-50, the *Range Column* chart shows the individual ranges per category, in this example time period, as columns. It is an interesting display and helps the report viewer to instantly understand and gain insight from the discrete fluctuations that occur by date. It is very evident that the amount of price volatility for MOT on the days between 8/1 and 8/5 was much greater than at any other time of the month displayed.

Comparing the two Range charts in Figure 1-50, note that each example is using the same sample data. Depending on which type you choose, different facts are emphasized. For example, in the range column chart on the left, the variation in price in MOT between 8/1 and 8/5 is emphasized, but the small daily variations that spike upward in HGL are de-emphasized and almost lost amid the larger MOT columns. In the Range chart on the right, those facts are more evident. Choosing the right visualization must support what it is you are trying to convey about the data.

Another available chart type is a *Point* chart. Point charts show each data point as a discrete marker. This can be a very significant display for certain types of data, because outliers are usually easy to spot, and trends can be correlated if warranted. The Point chart in Figure 1-51 shows two series of experiments. The trend for Experiment A seems very straightforward, but is it significant? If the category axis represents test subjects, then maybe the trend is not significant, and the Point chart is a better choice than showing a Line chart of the same data that would make the observation points look like a trend.

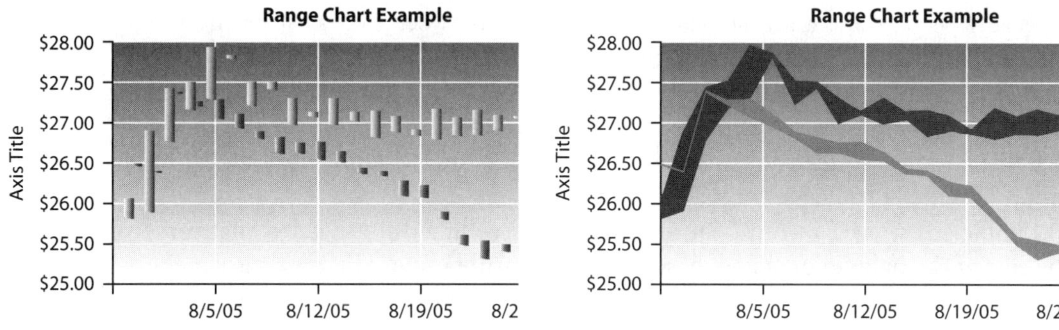

Figure 1-50 *Range Column chart and Range Area chart*

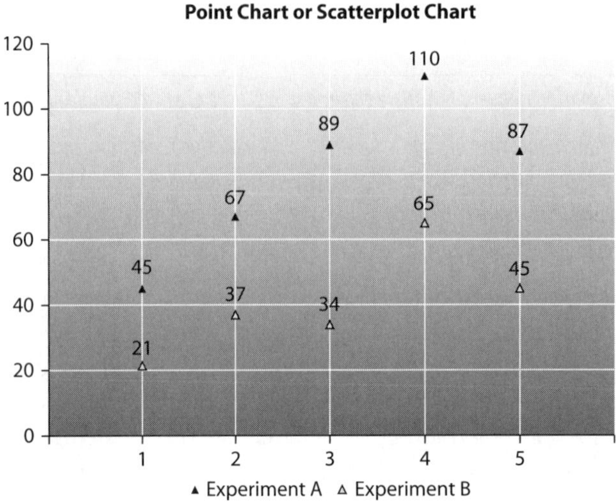

Figure 1-51 *Point Chart example*

Point charts, like the example in Figure 1-51, are good graphic displays for certain data relationships, but they must be well labeled. Don't make the audience guess at context; label the data series and both the category (X) axis and the value (Y) axis to make sure the exact meaning of the display is understood.

Another variation of a Point chart is called the Scatterplot. *Scatterplot* charts usually show many data points and can help illuminate the relationship between two variables. They may be further enhanced by adding a calculated series to help illuminate the trends hiding in the points. These charts are very good for many data points (1,000s) and suitable for statistical, scientific, or engineering data analysis. Series markers can be varied, like the example shown in Figure 1-52, and changing both the shape and the color will make the series easier to distinguish for regular as well as color-blind viewers.

Scatterplot charts like Figure 1-52 are good for showing multidimensional data, especially where there is an established relationship between the variables and the measure, for example membership club level and average transaction size.

Bubble charts are another interesting way to display data relationships that may get lost without the proper visualization. Figure 1-53 shows an example of a Bubble chart that displays three dimensions—the sum of the amount, the number of items in the group, and the percentage of total.

Bubble charts, as shown in Figure 1-53, are three-dimensional charts that vary the size of the bubble (or shape) based on the measure value. The Y axis is generally another measure, and the category scale is the descriptive dimension. Add labels to

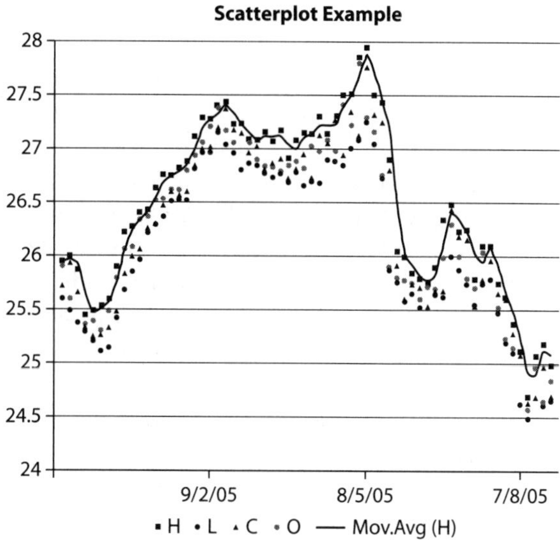

Figure 1-52 *Scatterplot chart with calculated series*

clarify the view. Bubble charts are wonderful for displaying dimensional data. We have used them to display the relative value of a group of donors based on loyalty program membership and length of program membership. To change the shape used for the bubble, change the Marker Type in the Series Properties, as shown in Figure 1-53 in the Properties pane.

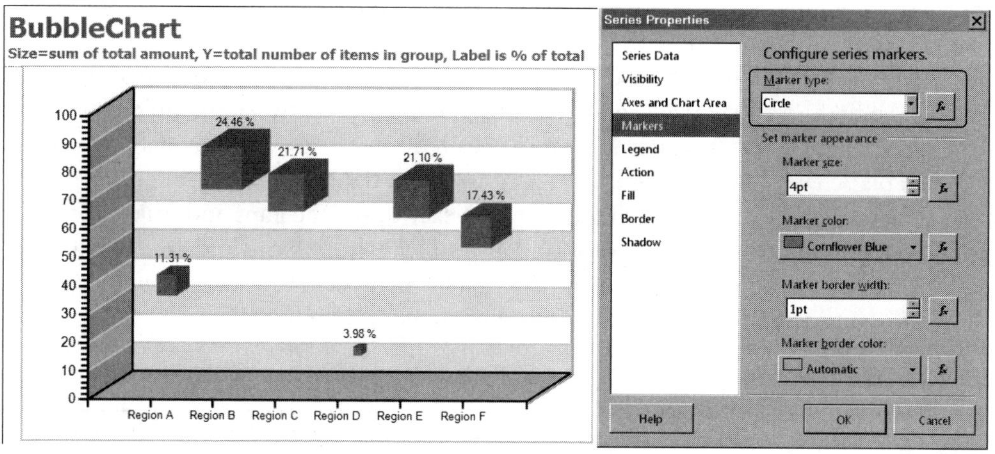

Figure 1-53 *Bubble chart example*

Area, Polar, and Radar Charts

Area charts come in several varieties, each with its own advantages. *Area, Stacked Area,* and *100% Stacked Area* are the choices; then add 3-D options to get the full range of options. Area charts are good for displaying continuous data; this makes them (and Line charts) the best choice for displaying time series data. Area charts have the visual advantage over Line charts for conveying the volume of the measure being displayed.

Stacked Area charts show the proportion each series contributes to the whole amount. The 100% Stacked Area type shows the proportion that each series contributes to 100 percent of the whole. Use the semitransparent color palette on Area charts to allow all series to be recognized. The examples in Figure 1-54 show the varieties of area charts. Do not dismiss them as too simple to get the point across. Seeing the volume of a measure shown as area can be a powerful visualization for comparison.

Using the transparent color palette for Area charts, like the examples shown in Figure 1-54, allows multiple data series to be displayed without losing the distinction between them. In the examples in Figure 1-54, the emphasis in the Regular Area chart is the difference between the two data series. In the Stacked Area chart, it is the combination of the two series that is emphasized. In the 100% Stacked Area chart, it is the ratio between the two series, not the total amount, that is emphasized. Choose your chart type carefully to focus the display on the important characteristics.

Polar charts display a data series as a set of points on a 360° circle, or polygon, instead of a linear chart. You can use the Polar chart, which is a form of Area chart, or the Radar chart, which just plots the points on the 360° axis. Usually, the center of the circle = 0, and the outermost ring is the largest value. The data series can be displayed as lines, markers, or area. Radar charts, also known as spider charts or kiviat diagrams, are useful for comparing multiple series of category data. Radar charts are also good for scenarios like web traffic by hour, where the visual maps to our image of a clock. Months or days of the week work well too. If the data is just random categories, it's probably not a good option. We find Radar charts useful for helping to find gaps between multiple sets of data, for example, finding the skills gap in a project team by overlaying all members' test scores.

The Polar chart shown in Figure 1-55 shows seven data series overlaid onto a circular axis. Because of the layering effect, it is easy to see the gaps and spikes for each layer at each measurement point, and also to see who has the highest value at each measurement point. Even though this display may seem unusual, it has merit and should be considered for comparing multiple datasets.

BI TIP

One caveat for Polar/Radar charts is that they cannot be combined with any other chart type in the same chart container, although other charts can be placed in their own chart containers on the same report!

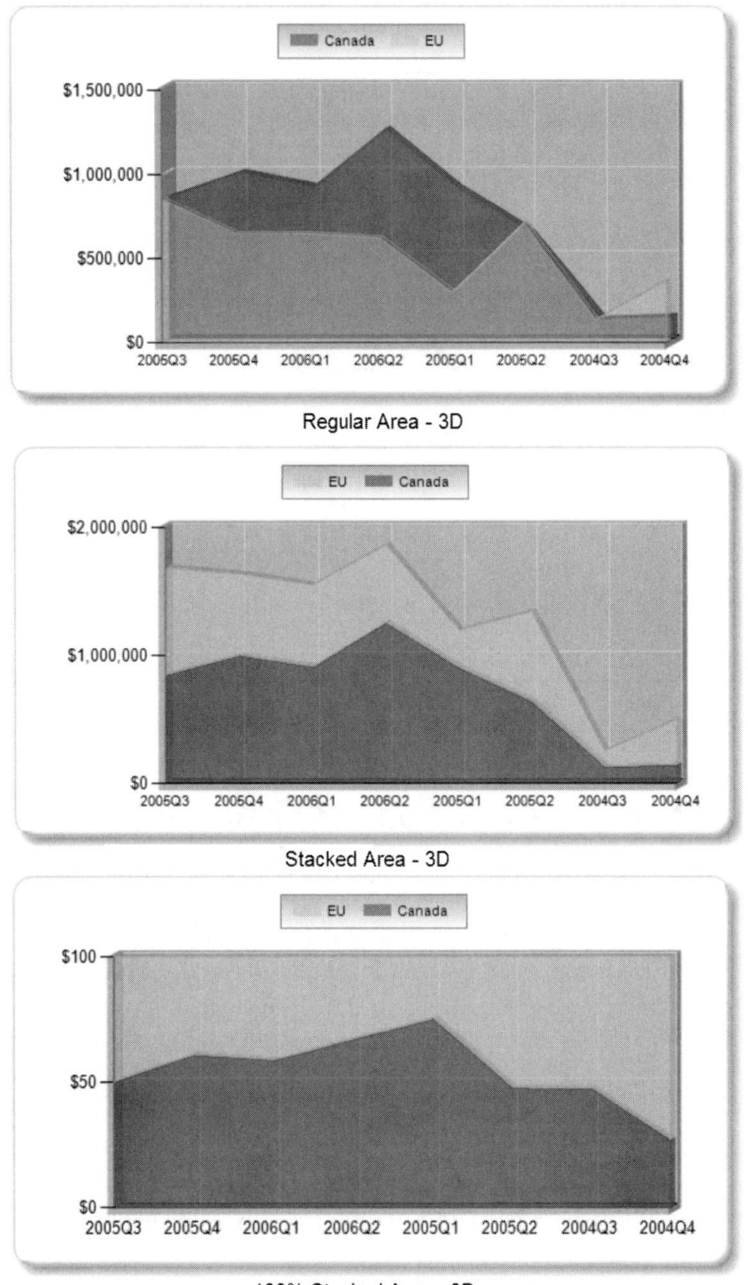

Figure 1-54 *Area chart examples—using the transparent color palette*

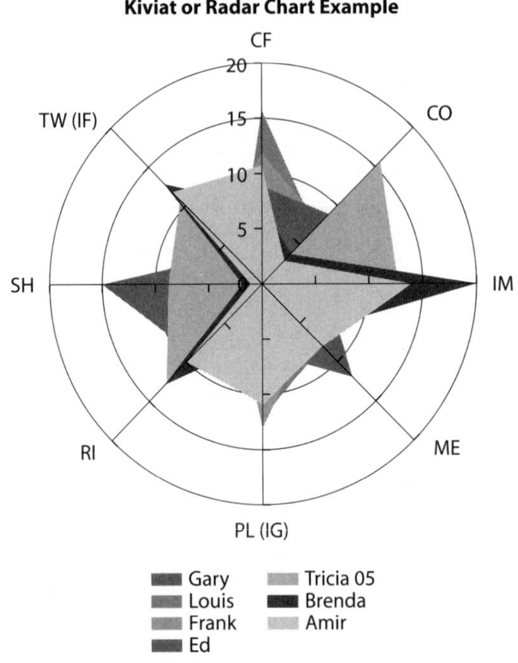

Figure 1-55 *Polar chart example—find gaps by overlaying the series*

Multiple Chart Areas and Series Groupings

To display multiple charts based on the same series and category, use Multiple Chart Areas. This new feature allows a more consistent view of data, no matter what the visualization. Some chart types are not allowed as multiple chart items (Range, Scatter, and Polar). Since there is more control over legends and title areas, combining chart items into a chart area can ease the display and maintenance of chart reports. The main benefit of combining charts into the same chart container is for axis alignment. There are several tricks to making multiple charts work correctly, and part of it is the properties! An example of multiple chart areas within on chart container is shown in Figure 1-56.

In the multiple chart areas scenario, there are many options for combining the chart types. Think through the message you are trying to convey with the graphic display, and choose the most appropriate chart types to represent the data characteristics that need emphasis.

Create the chart in the normal way, choosing the primary chart type you would like to display first. It can always be changed later, but it flows easier if you make good choices to start with.

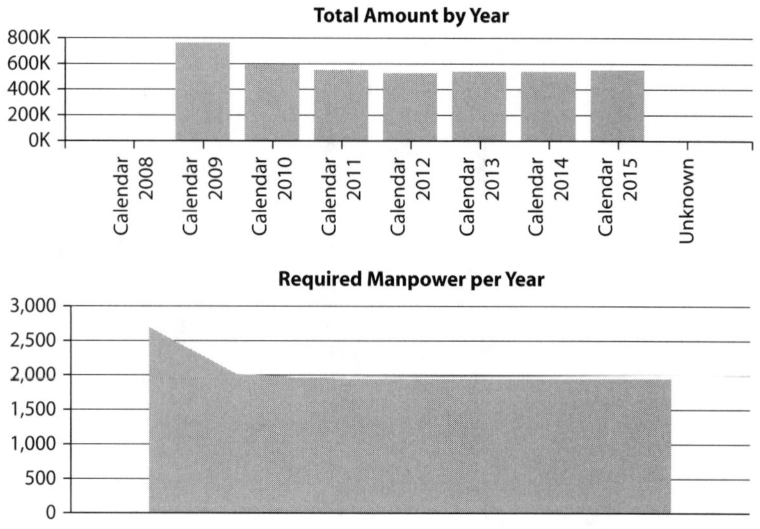

Figure 1-56 *Multiple chart areas—X-Axis Alignment*

To put multiple charts into the same container,

1. In the Design pane, right-click inside the chart area, and select Add New Chart Item from the context menu, as shown in Figure 1-57.
2. This will insert an empty chart item into the chart area.
3. Now for the trick. Each Chart Item requires its own data field. Drag another data item into the data fields drop zone.
4. Right-click the data field and select Series Properties, as shown in Figure 1-58.
5. In the Series Properties dialog box, select the Axes And Chart Area pane. In the lower part of the dialog box, click the drop-down list for Chart Area, and select Area1.
6. Once the new chart displays in the secondary chart area, right-click the chart series, and select Change Chart Type from the context menu.
7. Select the chart type desired from the Select Chart Type dialog box that pops open.
8. Set other properties as desired.
9. After all the settings have been determined, click somewhere in the Design pane to close all the dialog boxes, and then click the Preview tab.

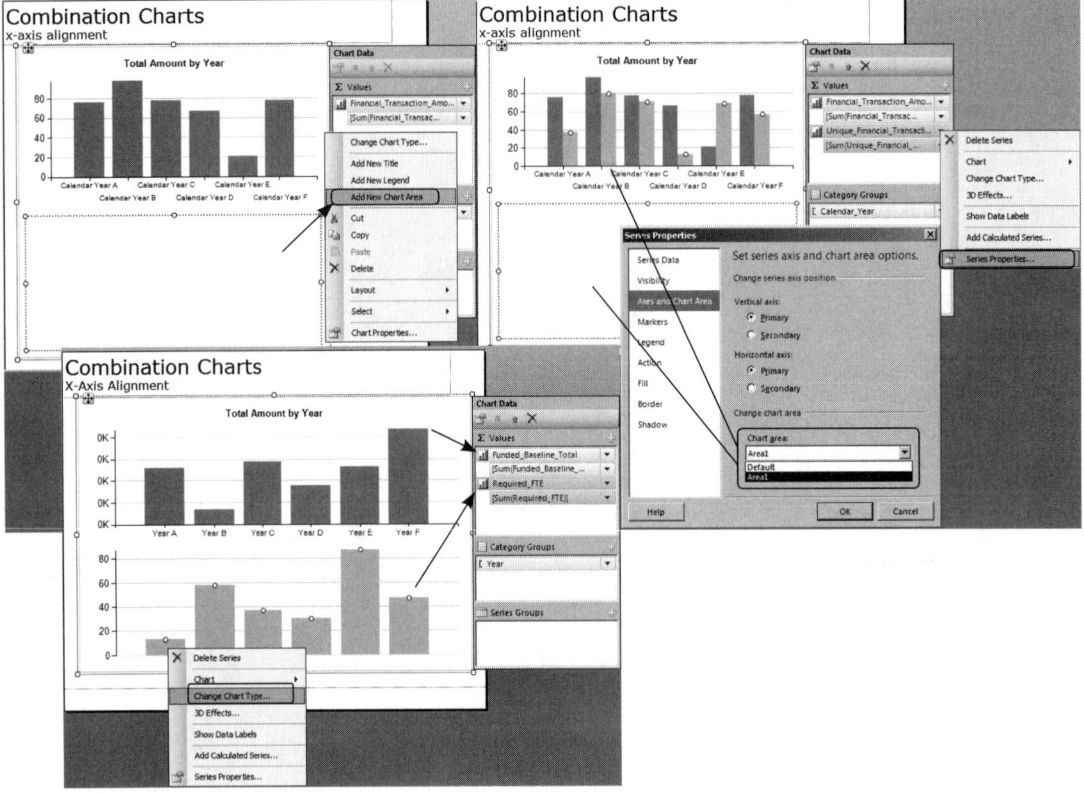

Figure 1-57 *Adding a new chart area*

To manage the various chart areas, use the ChartArea Collection Editor:

1. Navigate to the Collection Editor by going to Chart Properties (not Chart Area Properties as you may suspect), as shown in Figure 1-58.
2. If you want to remove a chart area, either right-click the Chart Area and select Delete, or add and remove chart areas through the ChartArea Collection Editor.

The ChartArea Collection Editor, which is hidden behind the ellipses button in the Chart Properties pane, is where you control the settings for the individual chart areas in a multichart report. As shown in Figure 1-58, set the properties for each Chart Area through this dialog box.

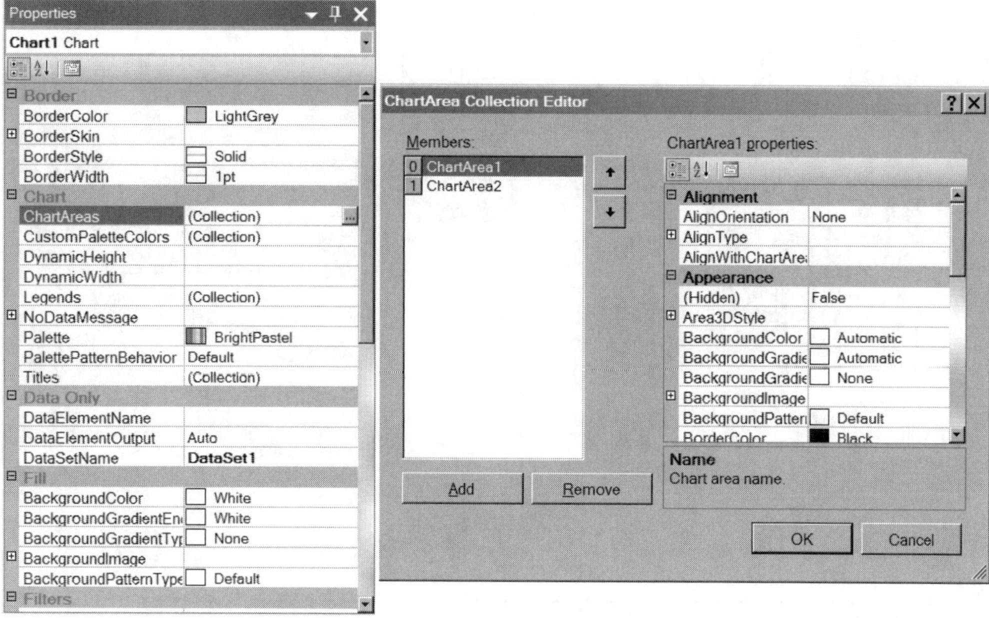

Figure 1-58 *ChartArea Collection Editor*

Series Data Grouping

Whether you have multiple charts together or an individual chart, grouping the data series will make the chart more understandable to the report viewer. To set the data series grouping,

1. Right-click the data series in the Series Drop Zone on the report design surface as shown in Step A of Figure 1-59.
2. Choose Series Group Properties from the context menu (Step B).
3. In the Series Group Properties dialog box, on the General pane, click Add (Step C).
4. Select an attribute field from the drop-down list (Step D) or click the *fx* button and create an expression.
5. Filtering, Sorting, and other variables can also be set in this dialog box.
6. Click OK (Step E) to save and apply changes.

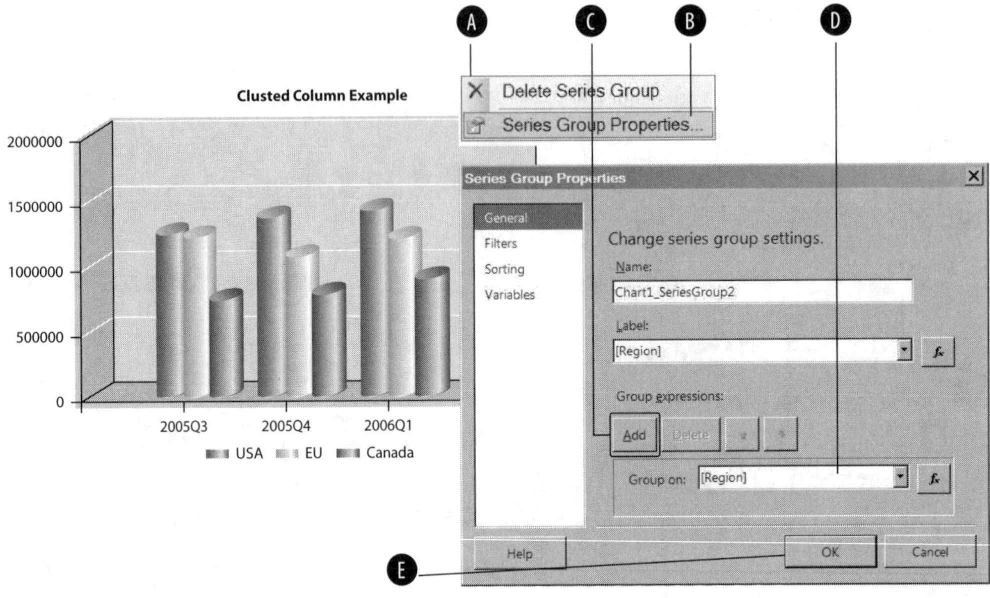

Figure 1-59 *Clustered Column example*

Grouping the data series, like the example in Figure 1-60, makes the data more understandable to the report viewer. It makes sense to group the data by time period, and adding the regional series group makes it clear how the values are changing over time in the various regions.

Formatting Charts for Presentation

The final steps to polishing the chart for display is to set all the eye-appealing properties to make sure there is enough information conveyed without overwhelming the presentation. Border, titles, data labels, legends, axis labels, and backgrounds all help to make the chart more visually attractive.

Borders

Borders give definition and eye-appeal to charts. Use them to draw attention to the chart and distinguish it from other report elements. There are a myriad of choices for Borders, and given the fill, pattern, and line width options, the combination of features is endless.

BI TIP

Best practice suggests that one style be adopted as a standard to give all charts from one report author (or report-creating department) the same look and feel. This results in a consistent look and feel to an organization's reports that helps consumers interpret different reports quickly—because the reports follow a similar presentation pattern.

There is a variety of border types, like those shown in Figure 1-60. Line, Embossed, Raised, Sunken, Frame, and Frame with Title are shown in the examples. If that isn't enough, you can always use the Expression Builder to create a custom border!

Titles

Chart Titles are the main piece of metadata conveying meaning to the report audience. Naming the chart with logical descriptions will help provide the proper context for interpreting the information displayed. Chart Titles can now contain expressions, making it easy to customize the title based on report parameters or userid. Besides the main Chart Title, Axes Titles and additional titles can be added to the chart area. If the axis value isn't crystal clear, it may be useful to specify an Axis Title. Figure 1-61 shows

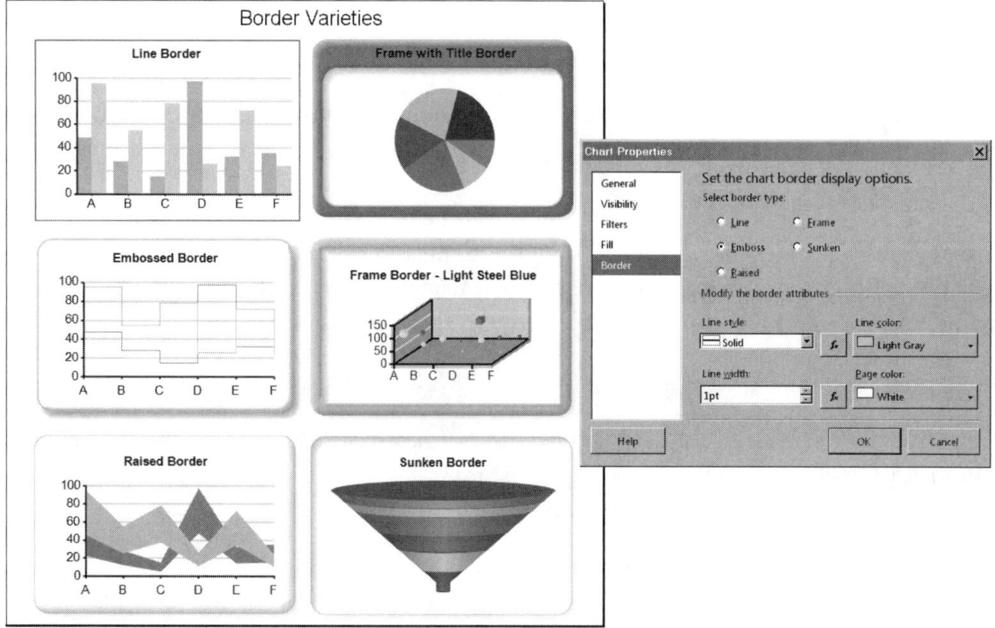

Figure 1-60 *Chart Borders—A variety of chart borders are available, including Embossed, Frame, Line, and Sunken.*

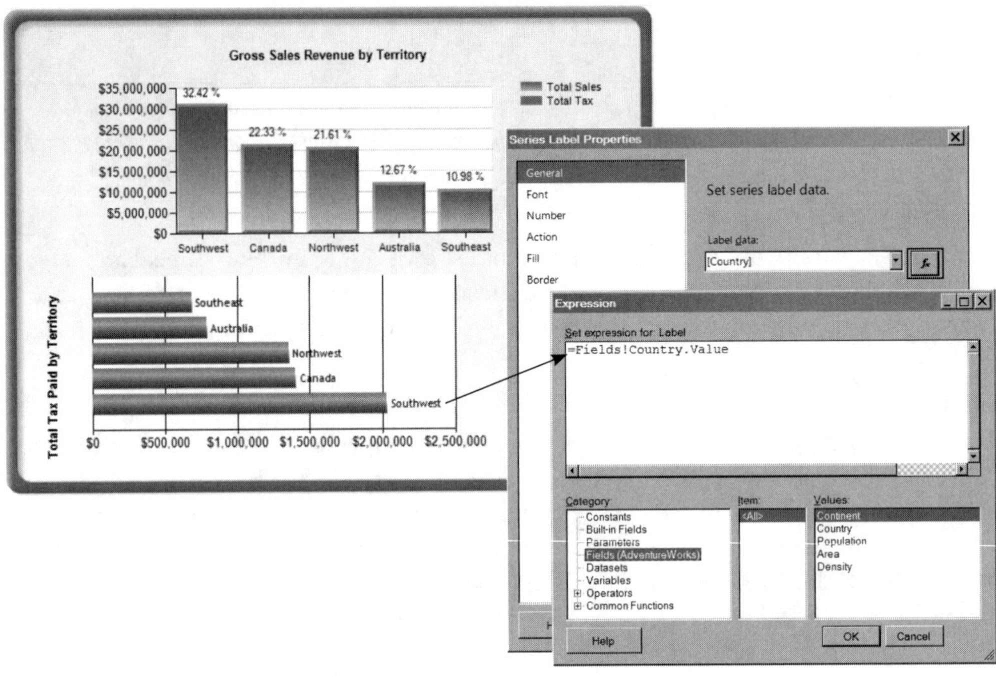

Figure 1-61 *Formatted chart—Border, Titles, and Data Labels*

formatted chart reports with a Border, two Titles, and various data labels. The Bar chart displayed has data labels based on an expression to display the Y-axis value, eliminating the need for Y-axis titles.

In Figure 1-61, this example shows how to set the data labels by navigating to the Series Label Properties dialog box, then choosing the Expression Builder from the General pane. Click the *fx* button, and build your data labels using the constants, built-in fields, data fields, and common functions available through the Expression Builder.

BI TIP

Be forewarned, Axis Titles take space from the chart area, so if space is tight and an Axis Title will not add clarity, skip it and save the space for the chart.

Data Labels

Use data labels to add more metadata to the chart. Do not use labels to repeat information already apparent. For example, in Figure 1-61 in the top chart, data labels display the percent of total for each column, so in that view the report viewer is getting four pieces of information: the value measurement, the region it is for, the percentage of the total that it represents, and how that element compares to its peers. In the second chart, data labels display the region the measurement is for, to avoid using a legend when there is only one data series.

Legends

Legends are the table of contents for the chart. If the chart has more than one or two data series, or more than two categories, a legend can help to elucidate all the pieces. Legends have many of the same format properties as chart areas—font, visibility, fill, border, patterns, shadows. In addition, placement in the chart area is very flexible and customizable.

Figure 1-62 shows the Legend Properties dialog box and the Legend Properties pane. There are many settings you can use to customize the display and make it visually appealing. Adding a gradient background fill or a border around the legend will give it emphasis. Consider this if the chart contains data that may be overlooked or misunderstood.

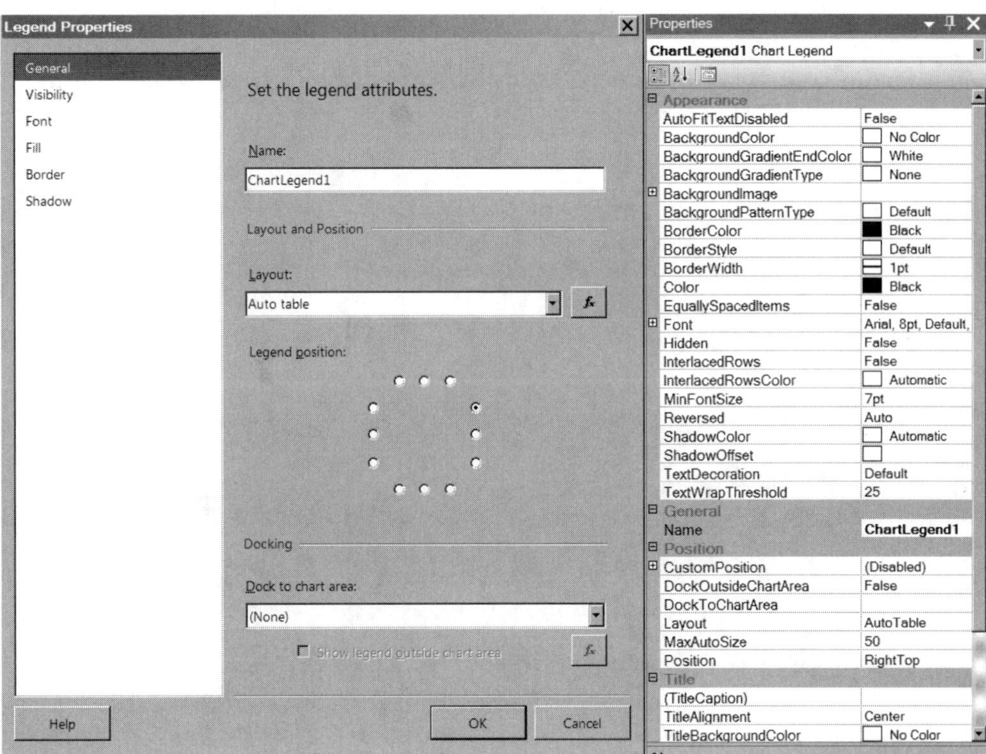

Figure 1-62 *Chart Legend Properties*

Axes

When preparing a chart for presentation, axis formatting can have a huge impact. Depending on the measures and categories used, making it easier to distinguish between value intervals will enhance the quick impact the chart will invoke. Ensure that number formatting is set and consistently used. There is an option for using thousands of dollars; using it will simplify the display, but make sure to label it correctly to avoid confusion. Both the value axis (Y) and the category axis (X) have the same properties available. As shown in Figure 1-63, items that are controlled in the Axes Properties are

- **Gridlines (major and minor) and Tick Marks** The default is black 1 pt lines, but using a dark gray or a complementary color can improve visual appeal and reduce a stark first impression. The only place to alter the properties for Gridlines and Tickmarks is in the Properties pane, shown to the right of the dialog box in Figure 1-63.
- **Stripping (aka Interlacing—alternating color intervals)** We have shown examples of both horizontal and vertical strips. In the Properties dialog box, it is called Interlacing. For time series charts, consider using subtle vertical strips to help make trends over time more recognizable. For Column charts that have multiple series and a large Y scale, consider horizontal strips to help report viewers easily comprehend the magnitude between measures.

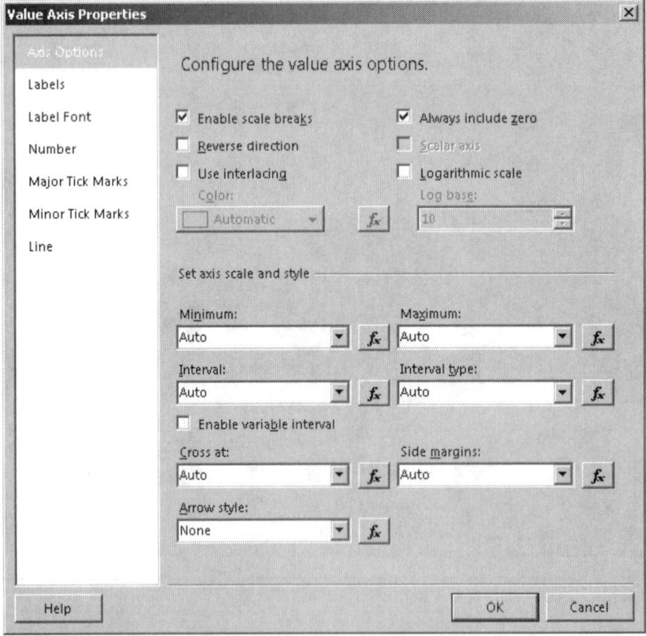

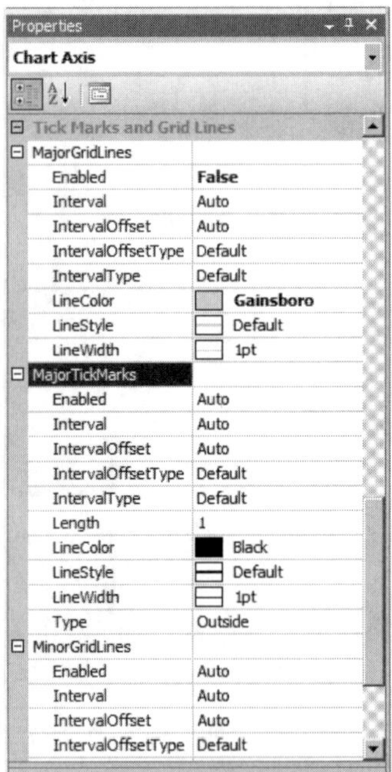

Figure 1-63 *Axis Properties*

- **Scale** Most scales are linear, but options abound for scalar and logarithmic scales. The option of including zero or setting where the X and Y axes cross gives you many options for controlling the display. If that isn't enough, there are always scale breaks so that outliers don't distort the majority of the values. Interval and Interval Type allow control over time series in a whole new way, giving the report author the ability to specify years down to milliseconds!
- **Labels** Labels can be rotated or offset using interlacing; label fonts can be autoscaled based on space available; text wrapping can be enabled or turned off altogether.
- **Line format** A variety of width and line format options are available.

Data Series

Formatting the data series will make the values pop out. This has been covered extensively under each example type, but here is the full spectrum of property settings for data series. Figure 1-64 shows all the dialog boxes for setting Series Properties—Series Data, Visibility, Axes and Chart Area, Legend, Action, Fill, Border, and Shadow panes. Use these settings to achieve control over the visualization and make it outstanding!

Chart Background

When putting all these formatting options together, do not neglect the chart background. Choosing a solid color, pattern, or background image will help enhance the chart display. Using complementary colors coordinated with the Border and Chart Item backgrounds will give the report a polished and professional look. Make sure that there is enough contrast between the data series and the chart background color, so the data values do not get lost in the display.

Differences Between Dundas Controls and Native Microsoft Charts

Since Microsoft has purchased and integrated the Dundas code base for Charts, the main differentiator between the two products is the user interface of the Dundas application. Dundas Charting for Reporting Services has a slick interface and easy presentation of all the property settings in a very developer-friendly dialog box. While working on this chapter, we found ourselves searching the Microsoft Properties looking for the right place to set certain configuration items, but they are all there. That is about the only difference now between the two products. Figure 1-65 shows a couple of examples of the Dundas Chart for Reporting Services interface.

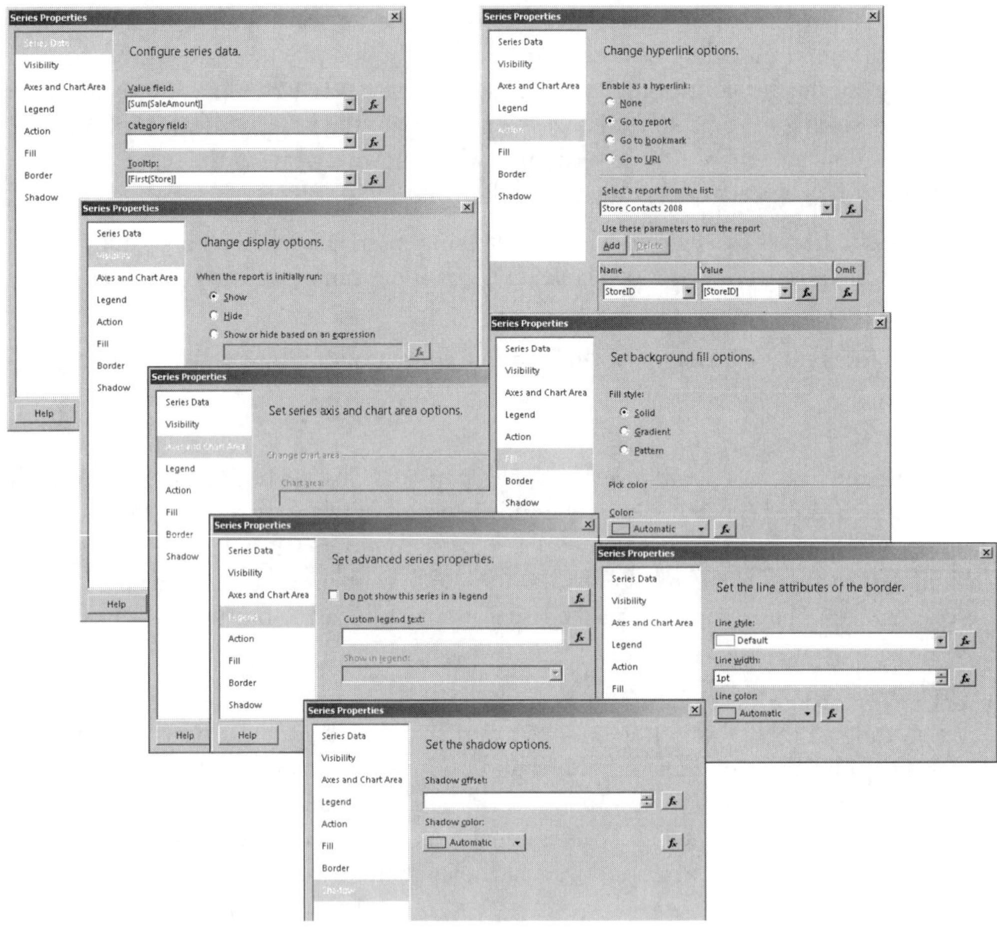

Figure 1-64 *Data Series Properties*

Wrap-Up

We have covered much material in this chapter, from data visualization principles to examples of all the different chart types available now through SSRS 2008. Here are some closing thoughts:

- Make sure you have good report requirements to work with—talk to your intended audience and determine what they are expecting to see. Just because they didn't ask for a chart doesn't mean it wouldn't be helpful to improve understanding!

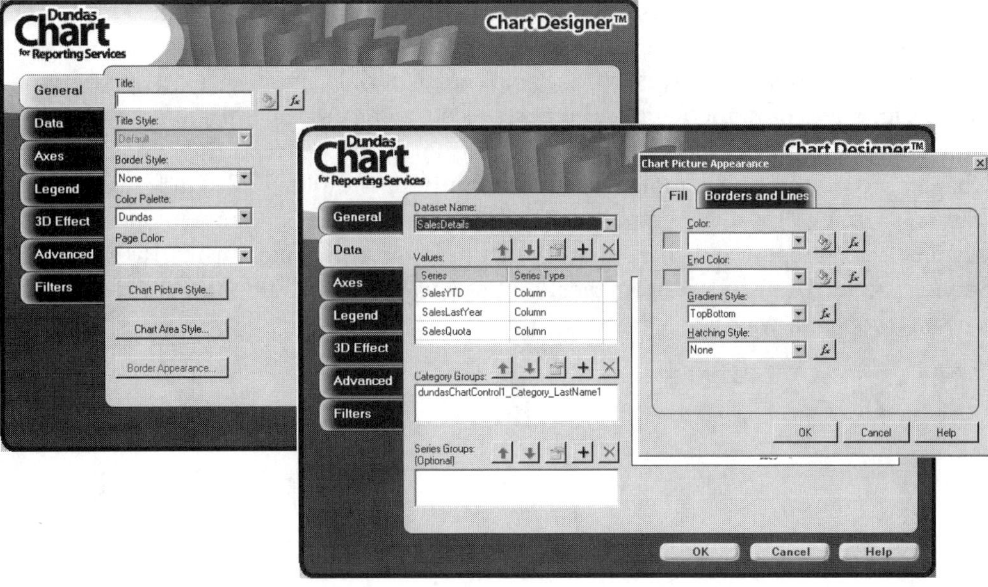

Figure 1-65 *Dundas Chart Designer—the user interface for setting many of the same properties using the Dundas Chart for Reporting Services product*

- Choose the appropriate chart type for the type of data that will be displayed. If unsure, review the data relationships and chart types matrix in the earlier section "Determining the Appropriate Chart for the Type of Data Being Displayed."
- Use appropriate naming and labels to enhance user understanding of the data being displayed.
- Use parameters to make your report scalable and customizable.
- Make sure you set all the properties to give your chart report a polished look.
- Use a consistent color scheme and logo image to make all reports look uniform and recognizable as your product.

This version of Reporting Services incorporates wonderful new functionality. The precision of control over property settings is an enormous enhancement over the previous version. We are so excited about having all these new visualizations to get the point across to report audiences. This will make huge improvements in comprehension of the report recipients, leading to increased action and better engagement with the business.

Using the appropriate charts can make business intelligence a reality and empower managers and executives to gain a greater understanding of their organization, market, sales, finances, human resources, product mix, etc. Multiple small, well-designed charts can replace pages of numeric tabular reports—conveying as much meaning in a much more efficient manner. The next chapter is on gauges, another reporting visualization. Chapter 3 is on the new mapping capabilities in Report Builder 3.0. This great new feature is going to make geographically-based information much more understandable. Chapter 4 is on report and chart delivery methods and will explore using Reporting Services, SharePoint, and PerformancePoint as a way to distribute these wonderful new tools in a coherent way.

Chapter 2

Gauges in SQL Server Reporting Services 2008

In This Chapter

- Determining the Appropriate Gauge for the Type of Data Being Displayed
- Report Creation Tools in SQL Server 2008
- Creating the Bullet Graph Gauge
- Linear Gauge Varieties
- Radial Gauge Details
- Interesting Component Behaviors
- The Gauge Panel and Multiple Gauge Items
- Using Gauges in Reports and Dashboards
- Wrap-Up

This chapter shows how to create gauge reports using SQL Server Reporting Services (SSRS) to achieve greater information insight and absorption. Data visualizations are becoming more important as the amount and complexity of data increase. Gauges have the ability to display data compared to a metric in order to clarify data values. There are many components to a gauge, including its scale, ranges, and graphic composition. A gauge graphic representation is perceived differently than a chart. The goal of this chapter is to present the wide range of possibilities for using gauges appropriately in report and dashboard displays, and to show the techniques for configuring the gauges to get the best possible representation of the data.

BI TIP

Gauges imply boundaries—the data must fall within certain bounds in order to be displayed on the gauge scale. The maximum and minimum scale values are easy to see on a gauge. Also, the value displayed on a gauge is easily perceived as a measure of progress by the human eye.

For example, time series data just isn't displayed well using a gauge; a line or area chart is much more effective for representing this type of data, as shown in Figure 2-1. Charts highlight trends, patterns, and exceptions in the data, and time series analysis is critically concerned with these situations.

Gauges, on the other hand, display one point-in-time measurement as compared to a target, a previous value, or both, with perhaps some qualitative reference (like red/amber/green) to help give context. Most of us are familiar with gauge displays from our automobiles, especially the radiator red zone or the gas gauge red zone, and the reaction to this information that has been programmed into us: Respond, take action. Get coolant, get gas. We can use this instinctual reaction to help us use gauges as effective communicators of critical information to decision makers. So when designing a new dashboard, ask the stakeholder, what information is it that causes you to act? How do you know when it's good or bad? What are the boundaries for that measurement? How do you want to be informed when the gauge is in the red zone—color, alert notification, flashing indicator, sound?

Figure 2-1 *Series data displayed in a line chart*

As you begin to put the storyboard together, consider the types of charts and gauges to use to best convey all the necessary information needed for decision making and action. Many business intelligence authorities discount gauges because they take more space than a simple indicator, but combined with other dashboard elements like charts and numerical grids, gauges can be used to effectively convey important measurement information. We will explore these topics in order to fully examine how gauges can be created in Reporting Services:

- Determining the appropriate gauge for the data
- Creating the gauge graphics and setting gauge properties
- Properties of radial and linear gauges
- Special uses for gauges—displaying metrics, KPIs, and target values
- Combining gauges with charts and other report elements for maximum impact

BEST REFERENCE

For further research on SQL Server Reporting Services, go to http://msdn.microsoft.com/en-us/sqlserver/cc511478.aspx.

To download the AdventureWorks sample database, cube, and reports, visit CodePlex at http://msftdbprodsamples.codeplex.com/.

For examples of different gauge visualizations, visit Dundas at www.dundas.com/Gallery/Flash/Gauge/.

Determining the Appropriate Gauge for the Type of Data Being Displayed

The gauge is a visual data representation that displays a single value. The objective of using gauges for reporting is to make the metric values obvious. Gauges are good visualizations for key performance indicators (KPIs) and metrics (calculated measures) because gauges can show data points compared to a goal or target value. Presenting comparison values is an important part of giving the gauge meaning. Use gauges to display business intelligence and performance management information, like KPIs on dashboards and in scorecards. You can also place a gauge within a report table or matrix to illustrate data values and complement textual descriptions. We will show an example of that at the end of this chapter.

BI TIP

Here are rules of thumb for determining which type of gauge to use, radial or linear, for an information display:

- *Consider the amount and shape of the space available in the report or on the dashboard to display the gauge. If you are displaying gauges on a dashboard, space constraints may dictate which type will fit better into the overall display.*
- *Determine the amount of visual appeal necessary to convey the appropriate information impact. Some gauges are more eye attracting; use shapes, impact colors, and expressions to vary properties.*
- *Ensure you meet audience expectations. If a report audience has become accustomed to seeing particular metrics displayed in a radial gauge, they may have a hard time adjusting to a change in that display style. Determine the ground rules, develop a consistent pattern, and educate your audience about what they are seeing. Generous use of labels and contextual information will help them absorb the meaning behind the numbers.*
- *Generous use of labels and contextual information will help the report audience absorb the meaning behind the numbers.*

Think about a car dashboard—the speedometer is probably displayed as a radial gauge or meter, and the temperature gauge may be displayed as a horizontal linear gauge. Although some visualization professionals have little use for the gauge type of display, we can think of one application where they are entirely appropriate: the Operational Business Intelligence Dashboard. We will show some examples of this later in this chapter.

Displaying gauges is very flexible, and you have many options for connections between gauges. In SSRS Report Designer or Report Builder gauges are like charts; you can have multiple gauges inside a gauge panel just as you can have multiple charts within a chart container. The multiple gauges within one gauge panel can display comparisons between fields in your dataset.

Reporting Services has many gauge choices, and each one has options galore! They are broken into two major groups, Radial and Linear. The following tables display each of the Radial and Linear gauge styles for reference. Radial gauges have four general types:

360° (Full Circle), also known as full round: This gauge type has the maximum sweep range available.	
Full Circle with Mini-Gauge: Use this style to display a secondary metric along with the initial measure. Make sure to place the mini-gauge where it can be seen!	

180° (Half Circle, North and South): This is a familiar representation, and quite adaptable for dashboards.

90° (Quarter Circle, Northeast, Northwest, Southeast, Southwest): This radial gauge type has the smallest sweep range and display area.

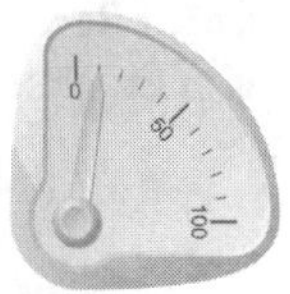

Meter: The meter is like the horizontal linear gauge but supports using a needle pointer.

The number of degrees indicates how large the sweep range is on the gauge; for example, a 90° gauge displays a quarter pie shape with a sweep range of 90°.

Linear gauges can have vertical or horizontal scales; the choices for linear include:

Single Range (horizontal or vertical): These linear gauges are the most commonly used and support multiple scales, pointers, and ranges.

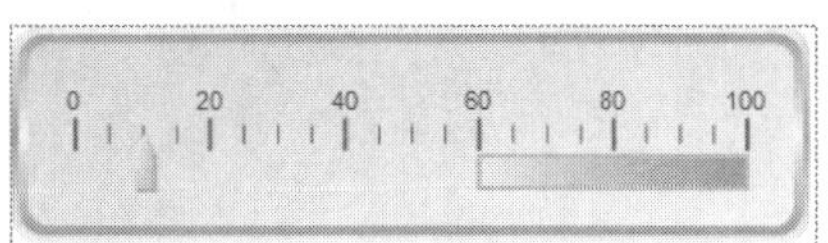

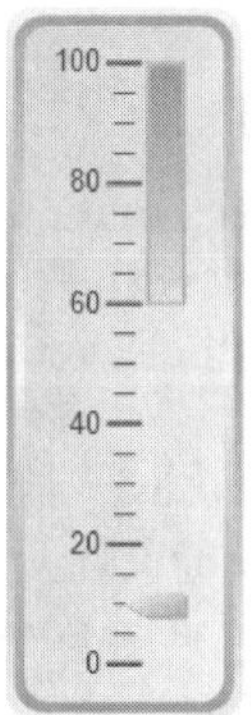

Logarithmic: This is similar to the horizontal linear gauge, with a specialized scale for logarithmic values.

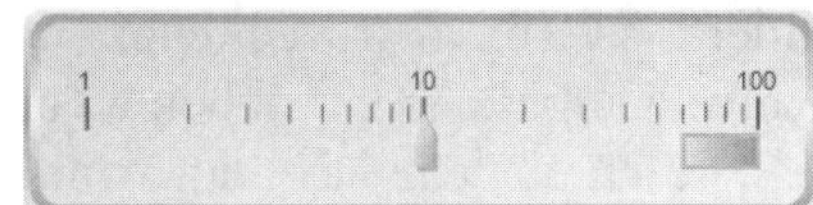

Bullet Graph: This is the most appealing and understandable linear gauge choice. It is used in an example under "Creating the Bullet Graph Gauge" later in this chapter.

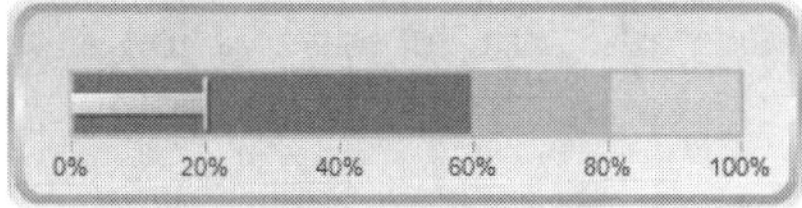

Multiple Bar Pointers: This choice allows the display of multiple measurements for easy comparison.
Two Scales: Compare the metric value against two scales; one may be a percentage.
Multiple Color Ranges: Ranges are available on all gauges; this one is preformatted for ease of use.

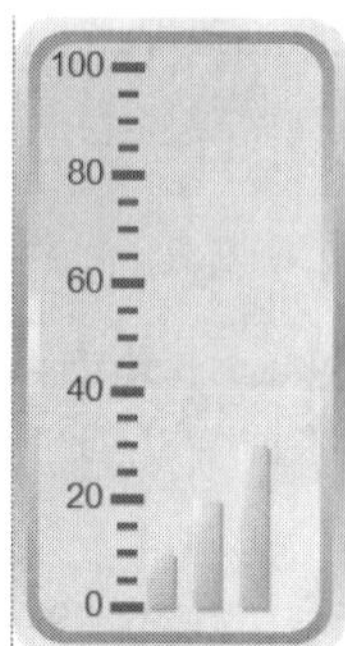

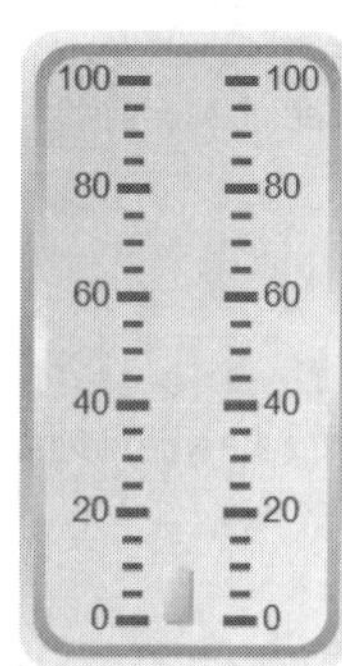

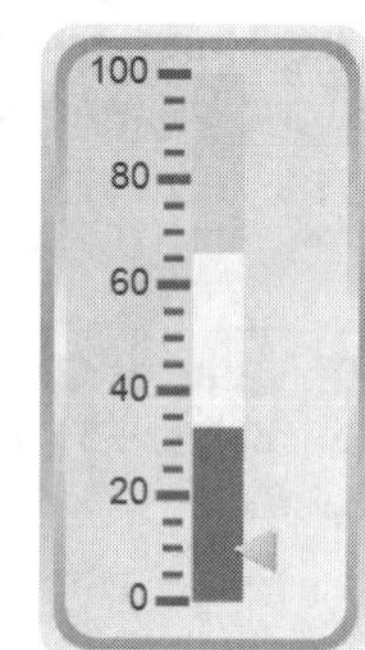

Thermometer: Traditional display with bulb or flask end.
Thermometer with Two Scales (Fahrenheit/Celsius): This type has the two scales preconfigured for ease of use.

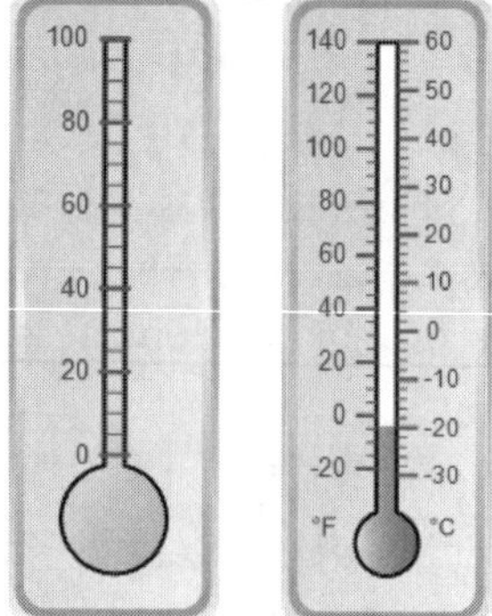

Report Creation Tools in SQL Server 2008

SQL Server Reporting Services (SSRS) is a mature product with several report creation tools. Two report design tools are included with SSRS 2008: Report Designer is for the software developer; Report Builder is for the savvy end user.

- **Report Designer** is a component of Business Intelligence Development Studio (BIDS) and uses the Visual Studio shell. BIDS is created for the professional report developer or power user, who has a good understanding of database access, query creation, and report formatting.
- **Report Builder** is a vastly improved report creation tool that has a more "Office-like" interface, utilizing the menu ribbon metaphor. Report Builder can use report models, which predefine the data connection strings, database, tables, and relationships available to the report author; or embedded or shared data sources. This greatly simplifies the report creation experience and gives flexibility over the dataset one can create.

Fortunately, the graphic elements discussed here are available in both report design tools! In this chapter we use both Report Designer and Report Builder so that the differences in the user interface can be explored.

The choice between using Report Designer and Report Builder 3.0 is getting tougher. Here are some considerations:

BIDS requires an application installation from SQL Server Client Tools. It has a sophisticated display and many options.	Report Builder 3.0 is a click-once run application that downloads from Report Manager. It has a clean, well-organized display with few options.
BIDS allows the creation of multiple reports in one project/solution file.	Report Builder 3.0 works on one report at a time.
BIDS supports complex queries, multiple data sources, report parameters, and filters.	Report Builder 3.0 also supports complex queries, multiple data sources, report parameters, and filters.
BIDS also has other project types that can link into Team Foundation Server, Visual Source Safe, and other development tools.	Report Builder 3.0 is a stand-alone application that doesn't connect to any other development tools or infrastructure.
BIDS was designed for developers.	Report Builder 3.0 was designed for savvy end users.
BIDS can be used to construct specialized report models.	Report Builder 3.0 cannot be used to create report models. They can be used only as data sources.

Report Builder 3.0 is part of the upcoming technical refresh for SQL Server 2008 R2. It is a vast improvement over previous versions of Report Builder, and we may just switch our allegiance from Report Designer as the tool of choice!

BI TIP

If you like Report Builder 3.0, you already have a report model for a data source, and your report doesn't need version control (outside of SharePoint) or integration with other reports, then use it! You will quickly come to appreciate the features and functionality of this vastly improved application.

Now that you have a basic understanding of what styles of gauges are available, and the report creation tools available through SQL Server 2008, we can get started.

Creating an SSRS Report Designer Report

Let's get started on the journey by creating some new reports! There are several steps that must be completed before you actually get to add the gauge to the report. Hang with us as we prepare for creating reports by choosing our design tool and getting the

Visual Studio solution file created. To get started with Report Designer, you need to know that there are two options when creating a new report project:

- **Report Server Project Wizard** Presents dialog boxes and prompts you through creating the report in a logical way by first defining the data source, then designing the query, and then placing you into the design surface. This is the best way to start for beginners, but it cannot create a chart-only report.
- **Report Server Project** This option creates the project solution file, with folders for Data Source items (*.rds Report Data Source files) and Report items (*.rdl Report Definition Language files). If you have existing report items, like shared data sources, that you want to use or edit, choose this selection.

The only drawback to using the Report Wizard is that you cannot use the wizard to create a *gauge-only* report. So for this example, use Report Server Project. We will be using the AdventureWorks samples for many of the reports in this chapter; you can download them from the link listed in Best Reference! This way, you can see how they have been created without the stress of starting from scratch.

Figure 2-2 shows the SSRS Business Intelligence Design Studio (BIDS) user interface and the New Project dialog box that you will see when you start the application.

1. Open the Business Intelligence Development Studio (BIDS)—it is usually found in the SQL Server 2008 Program Group on the Start menu.
2. Click the New Project button as shown in Figure 2-2; select the Report Server Project template from the dialog box.
3. Give the report project a meaningful name.
4. Click OK to create the solution file and close the dialog box.

The Report Designer user interface will appear. If you have used Visual Studio before, it will look familiar. Let's review the different areas of the interface and prepare for creating reports.

The Report Designer interface has three main pane areas as shown in Figure 2-3.

- The Solution Explorer pane and Properties pane are usually located along the right column (G and H). The Solution Explorer pane shows all the data sources and report items for this reporting solution project. Folders for each object type (data sources, reports) are visible even when they are empty. Right-click the folder to get a context menu. The Properties pane shows all the details for a selected item.
- In the left column are the Report Data pane and the Toolbox pane (A and B). The Report Data pane is where you create report data sources, datasets, parameters,

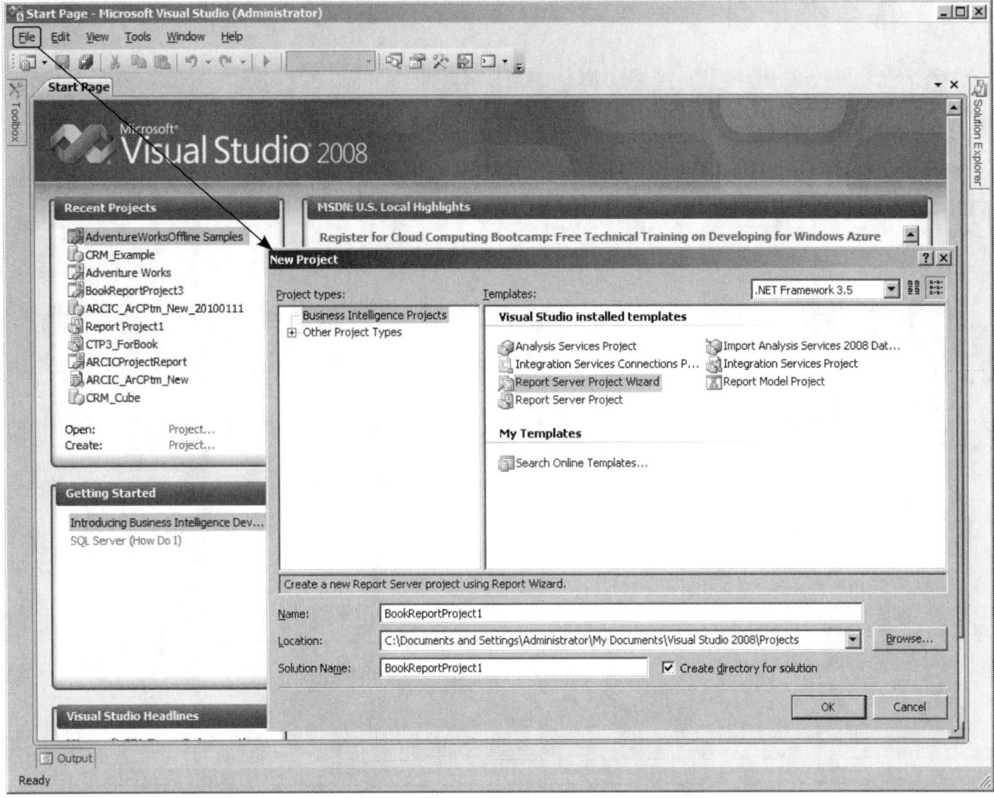

Figure 2-2 *Business Intelligence Development Studio 2008 New Project—Report Server Project*

and images. The Toolbox pane contains all the controls that can be dragged onto the report design surface.

- The center area, referred to as the design surface (C), is where all the elements come together to create a report.

Also, for chart reports, there are three design surface areas for adding data to the report:

- The Chart Data area organizes how the data are displayed. Data Fields (D) is the area to drop measurement data fields. Category Groups (E) is the area to drop category fields (or dimensions)—the X axis.
- Series Groups (F) is the area to drop series fields (or dimensions)—the Y axis.

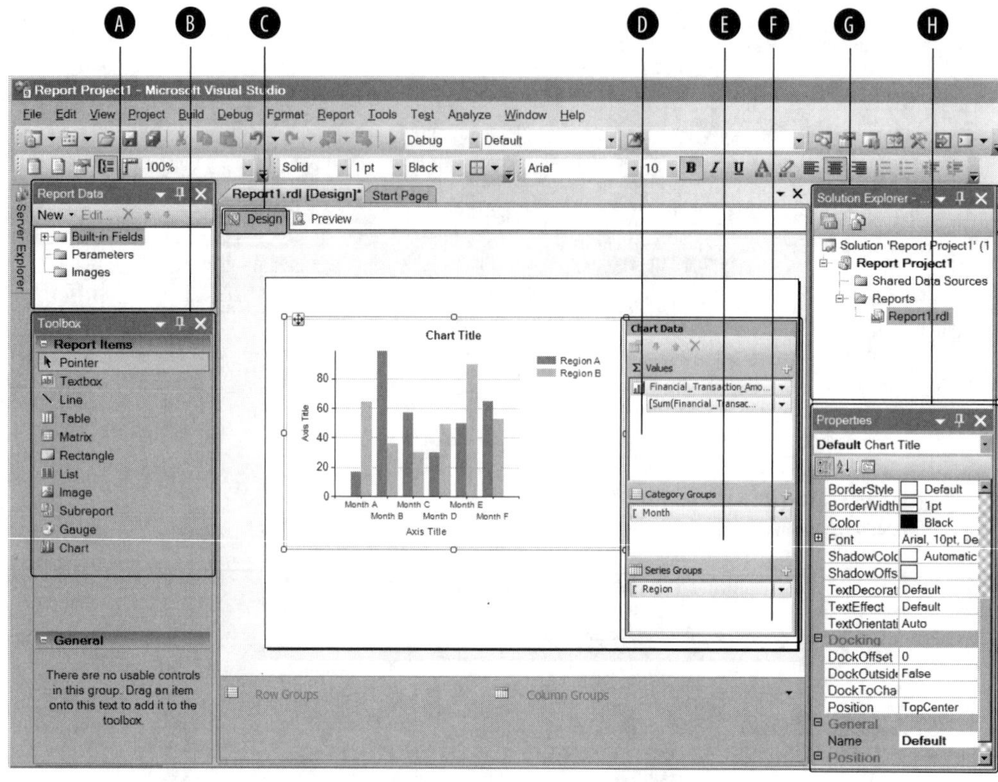

Figure 2-3 *Report Designer interface overview—the many areas of the Report Designer user interface*

You will see the solution name at the top of the Solution Explorer pane.

1. To get started with this report, create the data source. Right-click the Shared Data Sources folder and select New Data Source from the context menu as shown in Figure 2-4. As a best practice, give it a meaningful name, not the default Data Source 1.
2. Select the source type from the drop-down list under Type. Available choices are: Microsoft SQL Server, Microsoft SQL Server Analysis Services, Report Server Model, Oracle, SAP, XML, ODBC.
3. Type in the connection string in the proper format (data source=*server_name*; initial catalog=*database_name*) or click the Edit button and fill in the dialog box with the Server name, select a database name from the drop-down list, and click the Test Connection button at the bottom.
4. Click OK to close this dialog box. Click OK in the Shared Data Source Properties dialog box and the new data source will appear in the Data Sources folder.

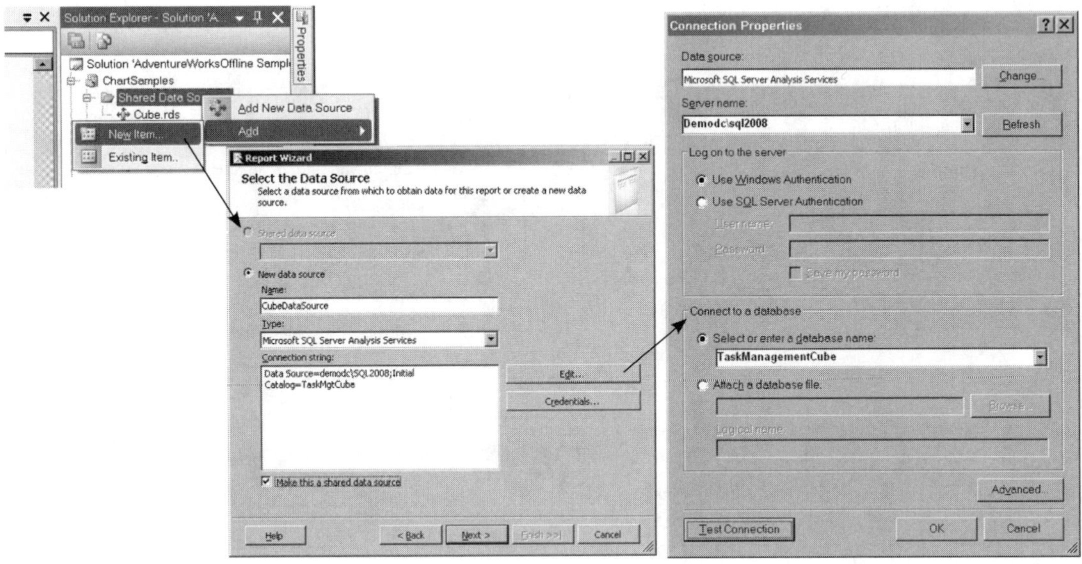

Figure 2-4 *Add a New Data Source, Shared Data Source Properties, and Connection Properties*

Add a new report item using the same procedure as adding a new data source.

1. Right-click the Reports folder in the Solution Explorer pane, and from the context menu, choose New Item as shown in Figure 2-5.
2. Select Report from the Templates pane of the dialog box.
3. Give the report a meaningful and descriptive name; it is okay to include spaces in the report name (but beware that spaces will pad the report URL with %20 if you are working in Report Server SharePoint integrated mode).
4. Click the Add button at the bottom of the dialog box.
5. The new named report shows in the Reports folder of the Solution Explorer pane, and the design surface displays.

By creating shared data sources, you make them available for all reports that are created within the report project. When creating the report items' data source, dataset, and parameters, SSRS 2008 Report Designer behaves differently from the 2005 version. Instead of having a tab at the top of the design surface for the data, there is a side pane, like the Toolbox. It is this side pane location where you create individual report data sources, create datasets, and specify parameters.

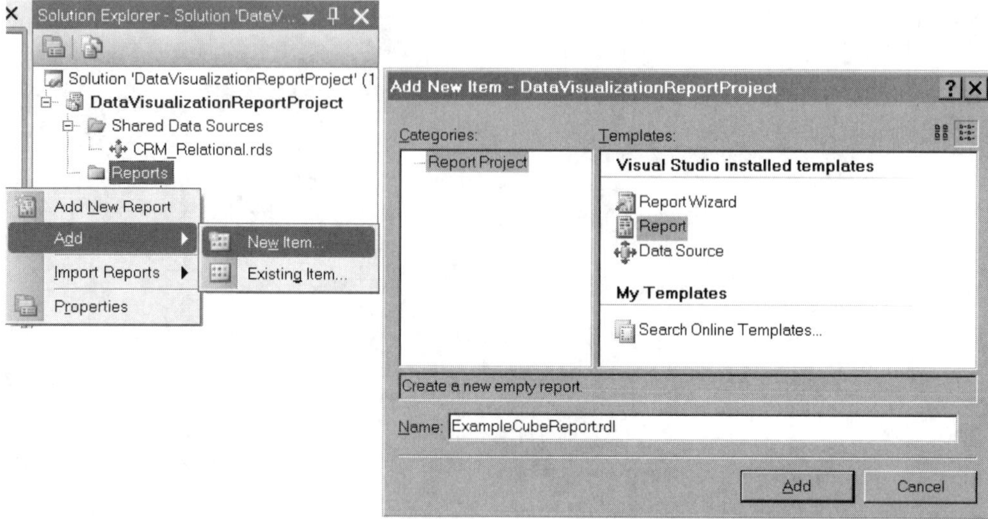

Figure 2-5 *Reports context menu—Add New Report Item*

BI TIP

In practice, most reports use an embedded data source with authorization credentials contained in the report definition—however, it makes sense in an organizational setting to take time and create standard "shared" data sources that can be used by other report design personnel.

1. Choose Data Source from the New drop-down menu in the Report Data pane, as shown in Figure 2-6.
2. In the Data Source Properties dialog box, give the data source a meaningful name. Select the radio button for an existing shared data source, and choose from the drop-down list. Click OK.
3. Now choose Dataset from the drop-down menu.
4. Enter a dataset name.
5. If confident of your skills in SQL (relational data sources) and/or MDX (OLAP data sources), type your query into the query window. The alternative is to click the Query Designer button, located near the bottom of the Dataset Properties dialog box.
6. The Query Designer appears for the data type defined. Since we have chosen an OLAP data source, the MDX Query Designer appears as shown in Figure 2-7.
7. Select the Measures and Dimensions from the Metadata pane and drag them into the pivot table to select them for the dataset query. Drag dimensions into the top panc to use them as filters.
8. When satisfied you have the proper dataset, click OK to finish.

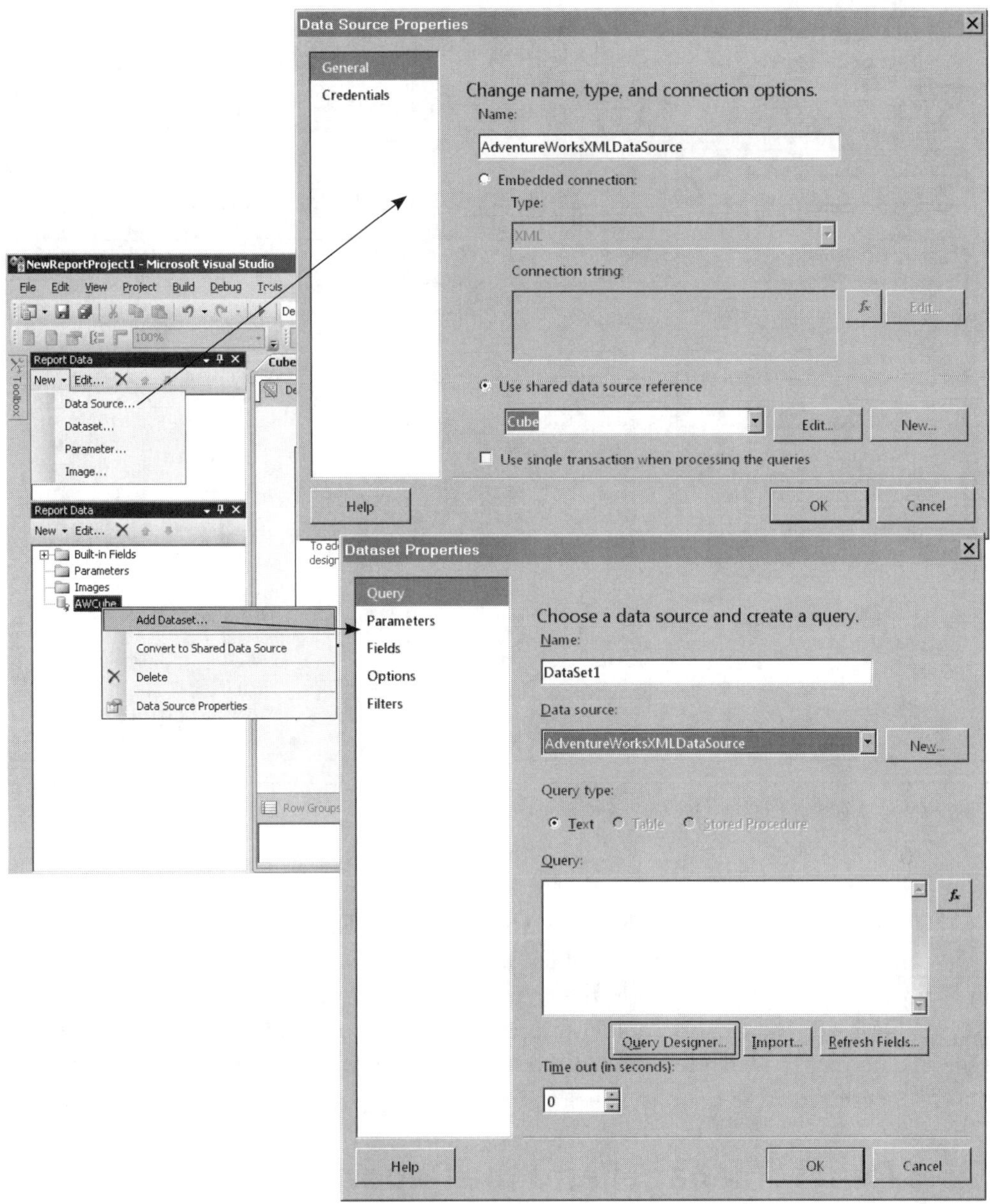

Figure 2-6 *Report Data pane in Report Designer 2008—report data sources and datasets*

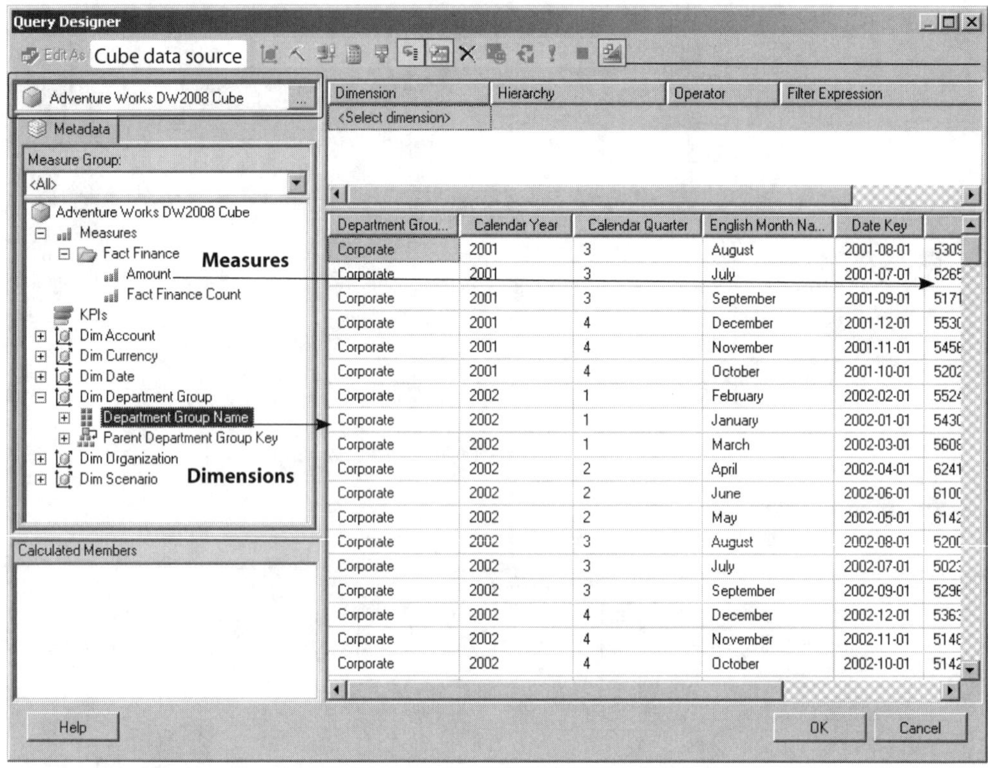

Figure 2-7 *Report Designer MDX Query Designer*

You now have a report and dataset to work with in SSRS Report Designer.

We promised a peek at Report Builder 3.0, so in this chapter we will build a report in Report Builder 3.0. Fortunately, the chart and gauge controls work the same in both Report Designer and Report Builder. Property pane sections and properties are the same. So no matter which report creation tool you are using, you will have a similar design experience.

SSRS Report Manager and the Report Builder 3.0 Interface

Report Builder is a click-once downloaded browser-based application and can be launched from a SharePoint Portal Report Center site, from a locally installed copy, or from SQL Server Report Manager.

BI TIP

Use Report Builder when you have an "SSRS report model" and a straightforward report request. You will be amazed at how quickly you can generate a well-formatted, visually appealing report that combines different display elements to communicate the message!

This example shows SQL Server Report Manager in native mode, which is a self-contained web site. SharePoint integrated mode of Reporting Services will be covered in the next chapter. The home page for Report Manager has two views: List view and Details view, shown in Figure 2-8. The List view has icons, object names, and descriptions. The Details view also allows editing, moving, and deleting the objects.

Report Manager has the same basic functionality as previous versions, but a vastly improved user interface and several improved features, including the ability to add Charts, Gauges, and Maps to ad hoc reports. Previous versions of Report Builder required a report model to use as a data source. Report Builder 3.0 can use report models, shared data sources, or an embedded data source for a new report.

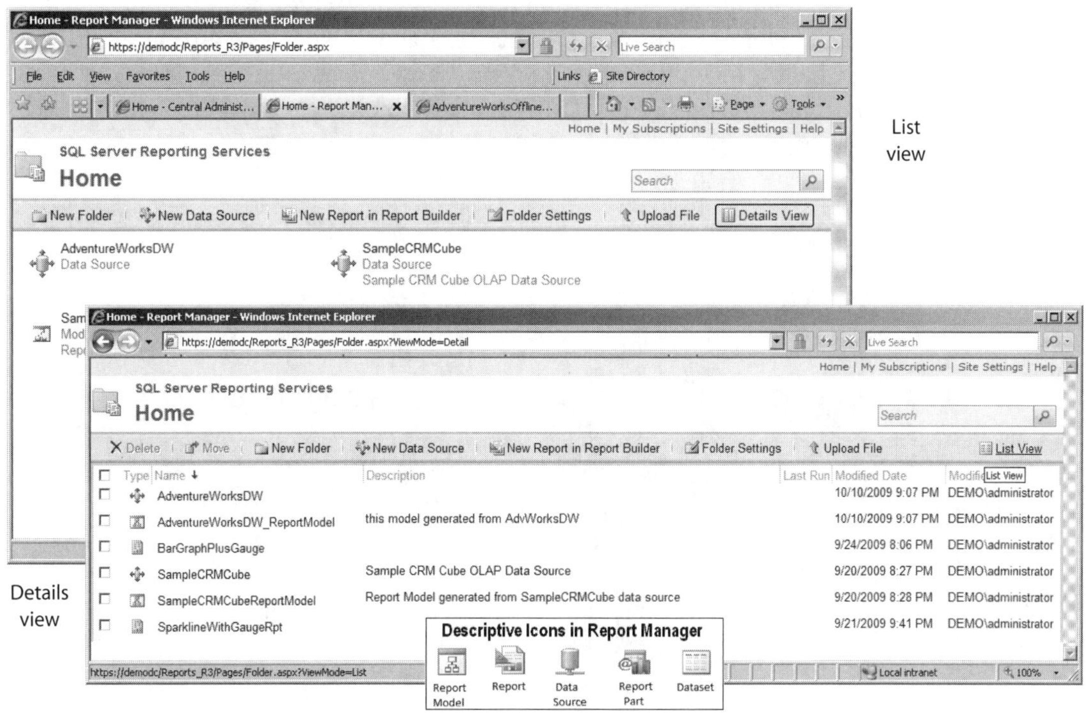

Figure 2-8 *SQL Report Manager Home*

Data sources specify which server and database to use for reports; they are generally in the form of a connection string:

```
data source = SQLServerName; initial catalog = MyDatabaseName.
```

BEST REFERENCE

For connection string formats: www.connectionstrings.com/

Understanding Report Models

Report models are based on the data model of the database (the tables and relationships between them). Report models are sometimes visualized as entity relationship diagrams, or ERDs. Figure 2-9 shows an example entity relationship diagram. This type of diagram is useful for understanding the way data is stored and how it is related. The diagram shows the tables that hold the data; the lines between the tables represent the relationships between the tables and express how the data is related.

For example, in the diagram in Figure 2-9, the FactLabor table is the main or Fact table, which holds the data we are most interested in and want to measure (in this case we measure labor hours by employee); all the other tables in this example diagram (DimTablename) are called dimension tables and hold descriptive information about the data in the FactLabor table. In this example, the FactLabor table has an attribute called CompanyKey, which is linked to (related to) the DimCompany table through that table's CompanyKey. Similarly, the FactLabor table EmployeeKey attribute is the link to the DimEmployee table.

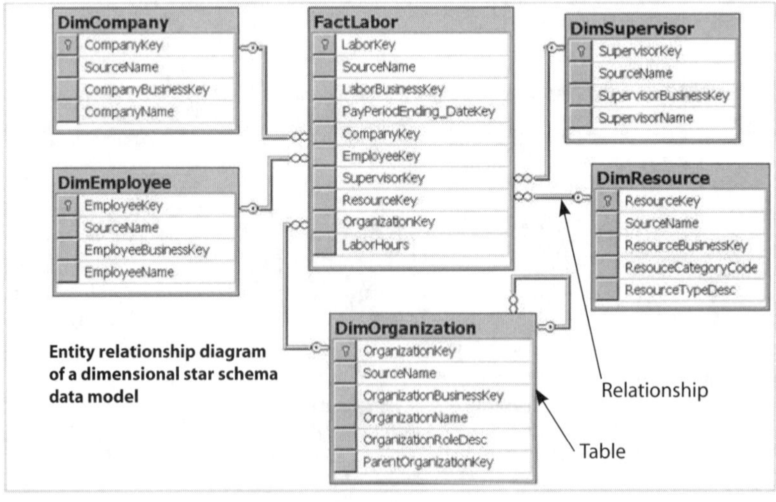

Figure 2-9 *Example of an entity relationship diagram*

One other relationship of note in Figure 2-9 is on the DimOrganization table, where there is a relationship from this table to itself (aka a fishhook). The structure of the DimOrganization table represents the organizational structure for the company that uses this database. The organizational structure is hierarchical—meaning that there is the C-Suite at the top of the organizational pyramid, which breaks down into lines of business, which splits into divisions, which are made up of departments, which decompose into offices. We would call this a parent-child relationship, where the top or upper level is the parent of the subordinate level. The DimOrganization table has an attribute named ParentOrganizationKey, which is the OrganizationKey for the parent. We structure the data this way so that we can roll up or aggregate the data at the various levels of the organization, and so we can determine responsibility and span of control.

Figure 2-9 shows an example of an entity relationship diagram of a dimensionally modeled database. Dimensional designs are optimized for reporting. We provide this data model detail so that you will understand what is going on behind the scenes when you are using a report model to create a report.

Report models predefine the relationships in the data, saving the report author from having to specify complex joins. So in Report Builder, you are presented with a list of Entities and Columns you can choose from, and the framework understands how the data are related. It is also easier to create a report model from an existing data source in Report Manager. In order to create a new report model from an existing data source, navigate to the Report Manager site, either in native (stand-alone) mode or SharePoint integrated mode; both types of implementation support this feature. For our example, we are showing screenshots from native mode.

BI TIP

If you want specialized report models that only display certain views of the data, they can be constructed in Business Intelligence Development Studio (BIDS) where a more sophisticated set of options are available to the report designer.

Create a Report Model

Now that you understand some of the basics behind Report Manager and Report Builder, including the role of the report model, it is time to create one for use. To create a Report Builder report, we'll first create a report model. To create a new report model from an existing data source in Report Manager, follow this procedure:

1. In Report Manager, click the Details View button in the toolbar.
2. Select a data source to work with by double-clicking it, for this case, the data source labeled AdventureWorksDW.

3. The Data Source Details screen will display all the data source connection information, as shown in Figure 2-10. Click the Generate Model button in the toolbar.
4. The Generate Report Model screen will display, allowing entry of Name and Description. When you've entered these, click OK to complete the process.
5. Once the report model is generated, the Report Model Properties screen will display as shown in Figure 2-11, allowing update to any properties that weren't set during initiation.
6. Click the Apply button on any of the screens to save changes.
7. Report models have a variety of properties, just like all the other SQL objects we have been examining. Figure 2-11 shows that the report model has panes of information for: general Properties, Data Sources, Dependent Items (reports created which use this report model), Clickthrough, Model Item Security, and Security.

The Report Model Properties are organized into several screenfuls or panes of information:

- The Properties pane has the Name, Description, and visibility properties, as well as created by, create date, modified by, and modified date metadata for this report model.

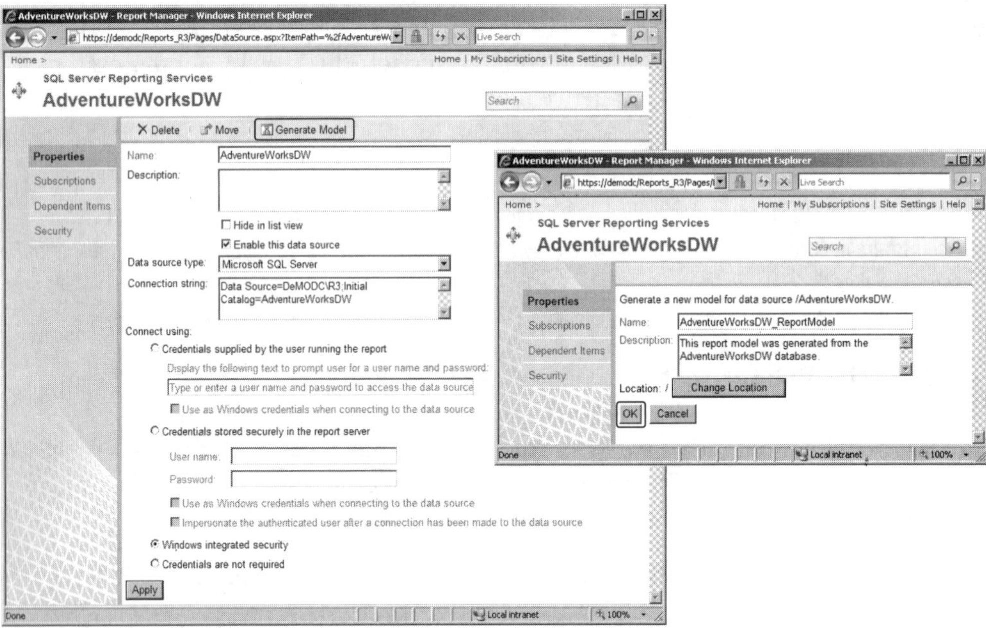

Figure 2-10 *Generate a report model from a data source*

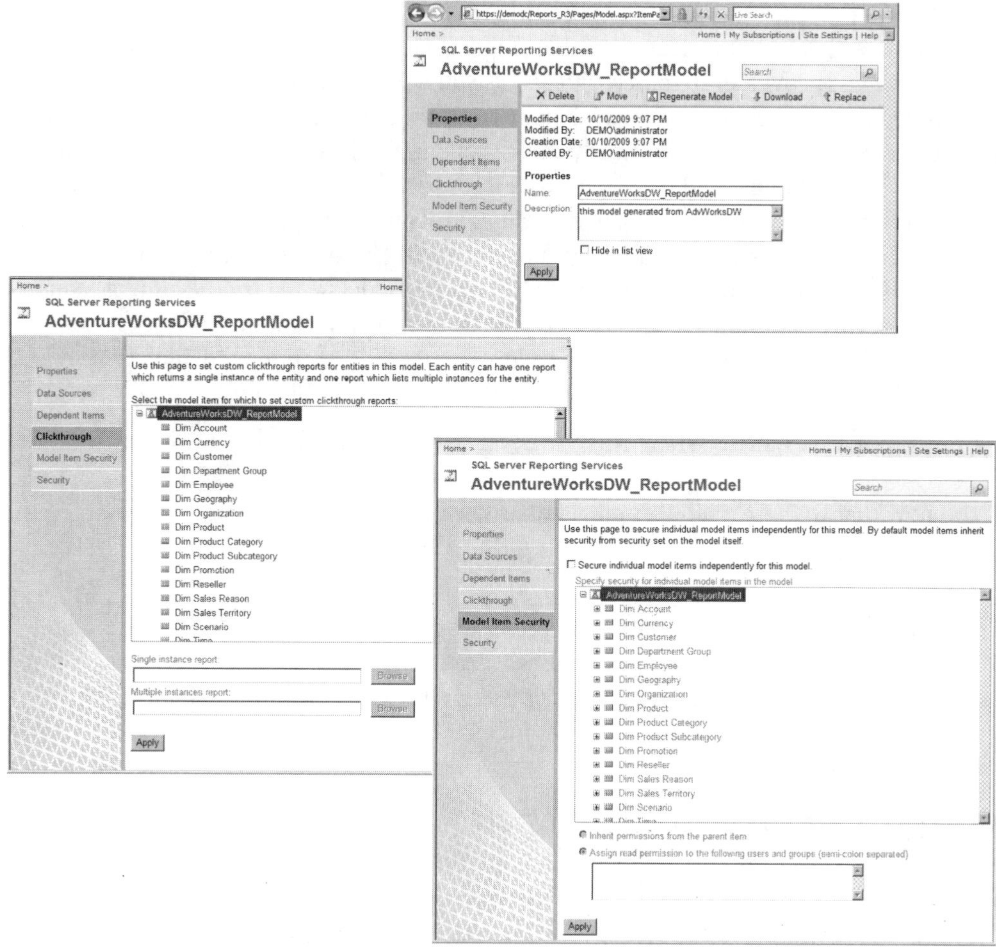

Figure 2-11 *Report Model Properties*

- The Data Source pane contains the link to the data source stored in Report Manager.
- Dependent Items lists all the reports that use this report model as a source.
- As shown in Figure 2-11, the Clickthrough pane allows the definition of one individual instance detail listing report and one multiple instance detail report for each entity in the report model. Why is this useful? Perhaps you want to set a data filter, like on Geography/Region, but you can't remember exactly how the region name is formatted. Using the Clickthrough report for the DimGeography table would provide a list of all the regions.

- Another nice feature is found on the Model Item Security pane. Each Report Manager item can be secured—folder, report, data source, report model, image item, etc. The Model Item Security allows you to secure individual model items independently, or to inherit permissions from the parent item. This would allow you to restrict access to secure, sensitive, or confidential information, but still allow the report model to be used by all who have authority. For example, in our report model example of labor information, maybe the DimEmployee table has access restricted to the Human Resources department. When creating reports, the HR department can use the DimEmployee table found in the report model to display the employee name, along with labor hours. If the same report were created by another report creator outside the HR department, that employee could only retrieve the EmployeeKey attribute of the FactLabor table, not the name or additional information.
- The Security pane is where the role-level security is set for the entire report model.

So now that we have a report model created, we can create a Report Builder 3.0 report.

BI TIP

Report models are reusable definition files that simplify the report creation process by shielding the end user from having to specify data source connection strings and data model particulars, like SQL joins. Build multiple report models from one data source to expose different slices of information and provide broad access to information by your savvy end users.

Create a Report Builder 3.0 Report

As referred to earlier, Report Builder is an application that must be launched from Report Manager or SharePoint. Our example is using Report Manager.

To launch Report Builder in Report Manager, bring up the SSRS Report Manager home page, then:

1. Click the New Report In Report Builder button on the toolbar in Report Manager, as shown in Figure 2-12.
2. The Report Builder click-once application will launch, and the Report Builder user interface will display.

Figure 2-12 shows how Report Builder will open in a new browser-based application window. Let's review the design interface before constructing the report. It is very similar to BIDS, with the look and feel of the PerformancePoint Dashboard Designer. Figure 2-13 dissects the user interface for Report Builder 3.0:

- Figure 2-13 shows the Shortcut menu at the top is reminiscent of the Office Quick Access Toolbar, but it is not configurable—what you see is what you get (A).

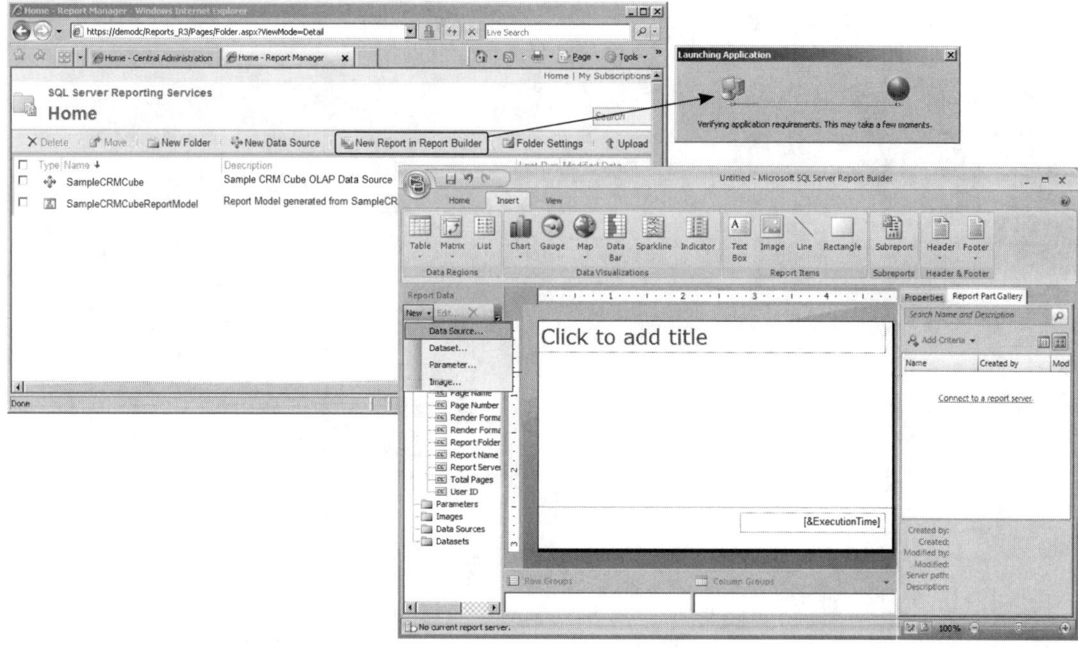

Figure 2-12 *Report Manager and New Report Builder report*

- The main file menu is hidden in the Report Builder logo (B), which when examined up close resembles the SQL Server "potato chip" icon. The Options menu is also found here. There are four ribbon menus; those are examined next.

- The Insert Menu shows the data region, data visualization, and other report items that are available, including the Gauge component (C).
- The Report Data pane is on the left side (D) and contains the data source connection, the dataset queries, report parameters, and any images used on the report.
- The middle pane is the report design surface (E), which are displays for row groups and column groups.
- The right side is the Properties pane (F).
- At the bottom are the Design Mode vs. Run Mode indicator (enlarged at G), the server connection display (H), and the Zoom slider control (lower right corner).

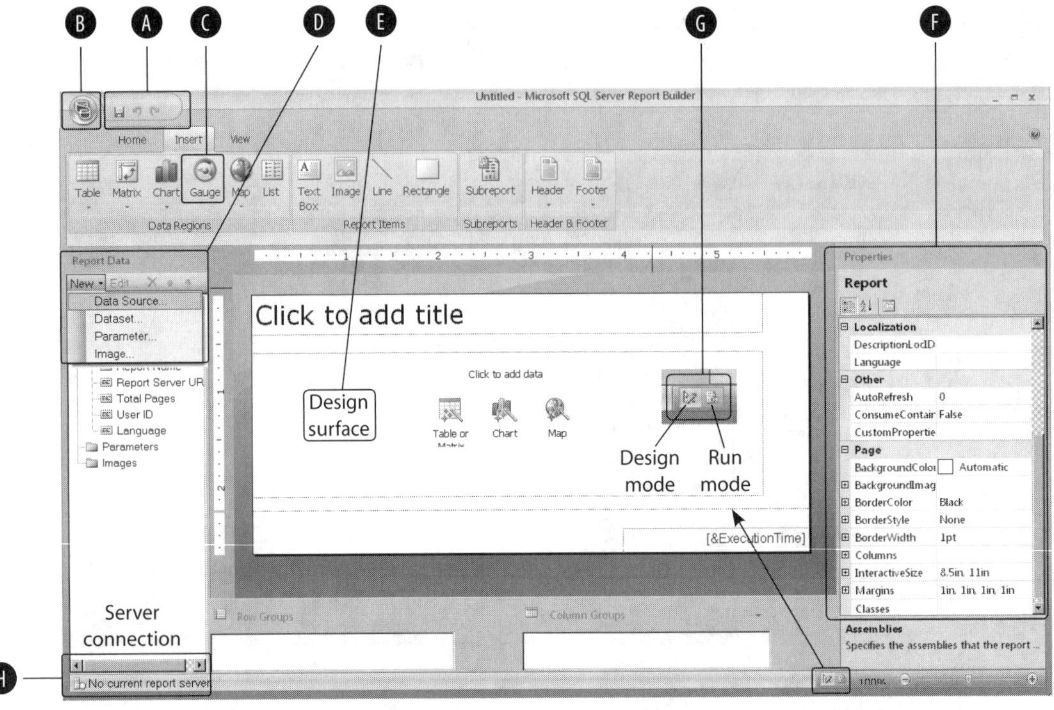

Figure 2-13 *Report Builder 3.0 report design interface*

To create a new report using Report Builder, follow this sequence of activities:

1. Choose a Report Model as the data source. Create a Dataset from the Report Model.
2. Decide which Data Region Control to use.
3. Drag the Gauge Control onto the design surface.
4. Set properties for each of the data regions and components through the Properties pane.
5. Preview the report by clicking the Run button on the Home ribbon menu. The mode will be displayed as an icon at the bottom right of window.

Even though the information displayed is very similar to BIDS, the user interface for Report Builder is friendlier and more Office-like, and less intimidating to report authors who are not software developers.

BI TIP

Most users will find the Report Builder to be their tool of choice. And, it's universally available—the user simply "clicks once" on a link provided by a SQL Server administrator, to download the Report Builder to the user's client machine.

Report Builder Menus

There are four ribbon menus available in Report Builder 3.0: Home, Insert, View, and Run. Here are the structures of the ribbon bar menus that you will find in Report Builder 3.0.

Figure 2-14 shows the Home menu for Report Builder; it toggles with the Run menu. The Home menu has several sections:

- Run or Design View toggle.
- The Clipboard section has Cut, Copy, and Paste buttons; under the Font section are controls for Font name, size, decoration, color, and shrink and grow.
- The Paragraph section has properties for vertical and horizontal alignment, indent, and bulleted or numbered lists.
- The Border section includes line thickness and line style, shading, line color, and custom border properties.
- The Number section has a drop-down for Type (Default, Number, Currency, Date, Time, Percentage, Scientific, Custom); a button to display placeholders or sample data; preset buttons for Currency, Percentage, and Commas; and buttons for decimal places.
- The Layout section has buttons for Merge (tablix) cells, Split cells, and Align (use to align multiple selected items). The submenu for alignment is: Bring To Front, Send To Back, Align [Left, Center, Right], Align [Top, Middle, Bottom].

Figure 2-15 shows the Report Builder Insert ribbon menu. The Insert menu is composed of these elements:

- The Data Regions section has controls to insert: Table, Matrix, and List.
- The Data Visualizations sections has the first-class visual objects: Chart, Gauge, Map, Data Bar, Sparkline, and Indicator.

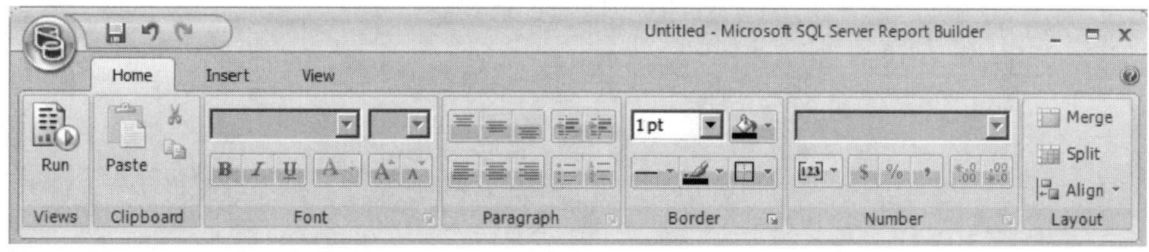

Figure 2-14 *Report Builder Home menu*

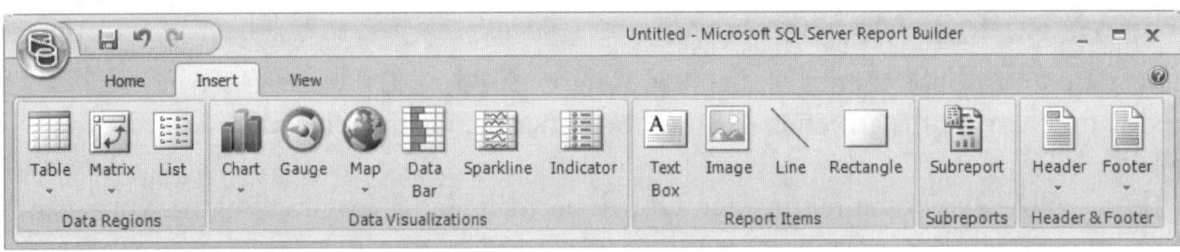

Figure 2-15 *Report Builder Insert ribbon menu*

- Report Items include: Text Box, Image, Line, and Rectangle.
- Subreports—click this button to insert a subreport and configure its connection with the parent report.
- The Header & Footer section has toggle buttons to turn the header area and footer area on and off.

Figure 2-16 displays the Report Builder View ribbon menu. This is where the display options are set.

- Show/Hide: Report Data, Grouping, Properties (pane), Ruler, and the new Report Part Gallery.

Figure 2-17 shows the Run menu, which toggles with the Home menu. The Run menu displays when you click the Run button on the Home menu to preview your report; it has the following elements:

- Design View is a toggle.
- The Zoom section has the typical choices: Page Width, Whole Page, 500%, 200%, 150%, 100%, 75%, 50%, and 25%.

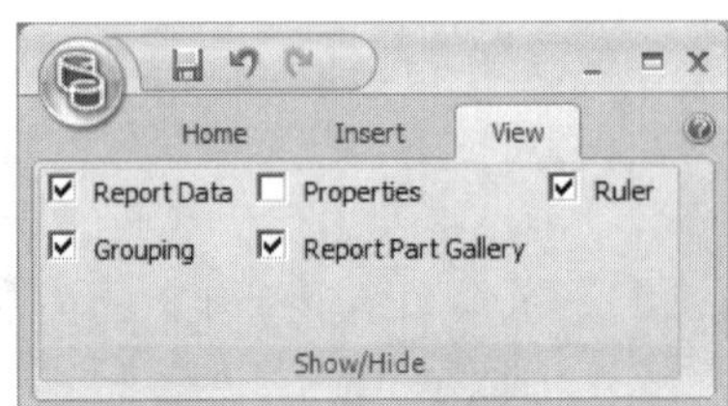

Figure 2-16 *Report Builder View ribbon menu*

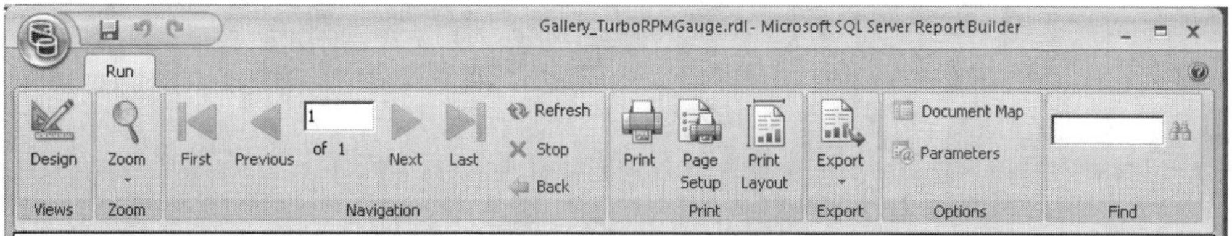

Figure 2-17 *Report Builder Run menu*

- The Navigation section has buttons for First, Previous, Page number, Next, Last, Refresh (view), Stop (processing), and Back.
- The Print section has buttons for Print, Page Setup, and Print Layout.
- Export options include exporting the report to: XML file with report data, CSV (comma delimited), TIFF file, Acrobat (PDF) file, MHTML (web archive), Excel, and Word.
- The Options section has toggle buttons to display or hide the Document Map and Parameters.
- The Find section will find in the report the character string typed into the text box.

Now, when you select Gauge from the Insert menu of Report Builder 3.0, the Select Gauge Type dialog box will appear, exactly as it does in BIDS. Next we will examine the variety of gauge types that can be used to create better reports.

Selecting a Gauge Type

When inserting a gauge into either Report Builder 3.0 or BIDS Report Designer, the Select Gauge Type dialog box will appear, presenting all the choices for gauge varieties. They are broken into two distinct groups—Radial and Linear. Once selected, a gauge cannot be changed from one type to the other.

BI TIP

A gauge can be configured to display a different radial gauge type if it was originally a radial gauge, or a different linear display if it was originally a linear gauge—but radial cannot be changed to linear, and linear cannot be changed to radial.

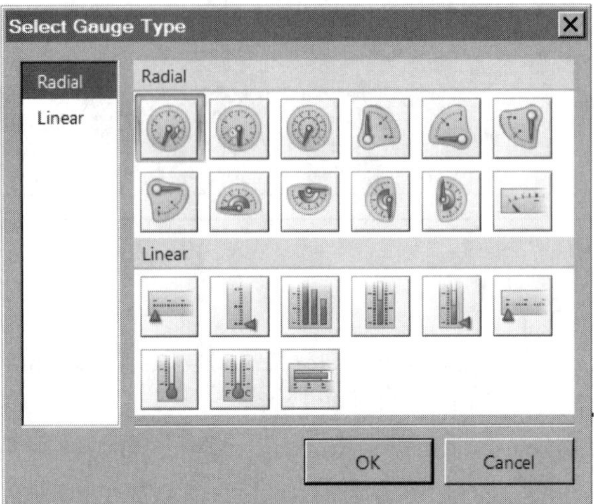

Figure 2-18 *Reporting Services gauge types—choose carefully because the gauge type cannot be changed once selected.*

Gauge types in the Select Gauge Type dialog box, as shown in Figure 2-18, are created by using a combination of gauge properties. Once you have chosen, you cannot change the gauge type the same way you change a chart type. To change the gauge type, you must remove the gauge from the gauge panel and re-add it to the design surface.

Radial gauges have at least one scale and one pointer, and may optionally have ranges and multiple scales. The most familiar example of using two scales is the Thermometer with one pointer to display both Fahrenheit and Celsius temperature measurements inside one gauge. Another use for multiple scales may be to show one value in two different currencies, or absolute and relative values, like actual score and relative rank. The scale can be configured to start at 0 or a value of your choosing, and have any interval desired.

Pointers identify the value being displayed, and there are three types of pointers: needle, marker, and bar. Needle pointers are only available on radial gauges. Marker and bar are available on both radial and linear gauges.

A linear gauge has a different orientation than a radial gauge, but it functions the same and can be integrated into tabular or matrix reports to show progress meters. Examples at the end of this chapter show how to accomplish integrated reports!

Radial Gauge Overview

Let's start with radial gauges and explore all the different configuration items that can be adjusted to provide a unique display. Semicircular (180°) and quarter-round (90°) vary only by how large the scale sweep is, so they are appropriate for measures that have defined boundaries. Figure 2-19 shows a basic radial gauge and delineates its components.

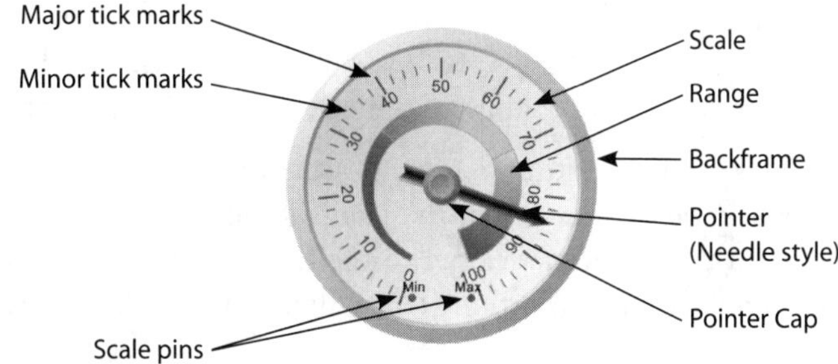

Figure 2-19 *Radial gauge components*

A radial gauge is made up of the following items, and as you may have guessed, there are properties for many of the components. Figure 2-19 labels each of these components, and they are further detailed next. The examples in this chapter will go through the setting of these properties with various values to display the different effects that can be achieved. Each of these gauge components is detailed here.

The gauge frame (BackFrame in the property settings side panel) is the outer shell that surrounds the gauge itself. There is also a gauge panel frame (BackFrame) that you can configure in the same way. It has several properties:

- **Frame Shape** Set the style of the frame surrounding the gauge. Choices are: circular, rectangular, rounded rectangular, default, autoshape, custom circular, custom semicircular, custom quarter-circular. Or you can import a custom frame image.
- **Frame Style** Choose none, edged, simple, or custom. This setting can give the frame the appearance of being raised from the page.
- **Frame Color** Select from palette or custom, and choose gradient or pattern fill styles.

Other gauge properties include

- **Glass Effect** Choose none, simple, or custom. This gives the gauge the appearance of being under glass, like a speedometer. The Glass effect can be set on either the gauge panel backframe, the gauge backframe, or both. Be careful when you set this, because if you choose both, the gauge will appear to be dim under two layers of glass.
- **Scale(s) and Scale Label** Set the sweep angle in degrees, the minimum and maximum values, the interval, the radius of the scale (how much distance between frame and scale), and the width of the scale.

- **Scale Pins** Choose whether to have minimum and maximum pins, their color and shape, and their distance from the scale. Scale pins can be used to show minimum, maximum, or boundary values that are significant in relationship to the gauge scale.
- **Major Tick Marks** This setting determines the interval, how long, how bold, and what shape the tick marks are in the gauge scale. If you are using a radial gauge, think about the difference between the minimum and maximum values and what level of granularity is important. This will also help you decide which sweep distance is needed as well.
- **Minor Tick Marks** This setting controls how long, how bold, and what shape the minor tick marks are, or if they are displayed at all.

BI TIP

Tick marks are an important design component for giving a gauge context. The range of values, the interval between the marks, and the labels you apply will impact the gauge display, and it may become too cluttered. When formatting minor tick marks, ensure that they are smaller and lighter in color than the major tick marks. If the display looks too cluttered, increase the interval value of the major tick marks and decide if minor tick marks are even necessary to the display.

Radial Gauge Elements

Now that you can identify all the parts to the radial gauge, let's discuss some of the important elements and how they are used to convey the meaning of the displayed data.

- **Pointer Type** This setting governs the type of pointer used on the gauge; it can be set to needle, marker, or bar. Needle is only available on radial gauges. If the needle type is selected, there are various needle styles to choose from: Triangular, Rectangular, Tapered with Tail, Tapered, Arrow with Tail, Arrow, Stealth Arrow, Stealth Arrow with Tail, Tapered with Stealth Arrow, Stealth Arrow with Wide Tail, Tapered with Rounded Points. If the marker type is selected, these are the marker style choices: Rectangle, Triangle, Circle, Diamond, Trapezoid, Star, Wedge, Pentagon. And if the bar type is chosen, you can have it start at zero or at scale start. Choose a pointer type that will complement the type of data. If you are showing % complete, then a bar pointer style might be better; if you are displaying a rate, like miles per hour (mph), then a needle style will convey the context better.
- **Pointer Cap** The pointer cap is the button in the middle of the gauge that the pointer extends from. You only need a pointer cap when the Pointer style is needle. The style choices for pointer caps are: Rounded Dark, Rounded, Rounded Light, Rounded with Additional Top, Rounded with Wide Indentation, Rounded

with Indentation, Flattened with Indentation, Flattened with Wide Indentation, and Rounded Glossy with Indentation. Other pointer cap properties include the Fill Color, Fill Gradient, Reflection, and Width. You can also upload a custom image to use for the pointer cap.

- **Ranges** Ranges are color bars that can be situated inside or outside of the scale and indicate zones for data comparison. When talking about KPIs and Performance Metrics, we usually think of the stoplight colors for ranges—Green (good values), Amber (something amiss), and Red (danger zone)—although those are constructs of our own making, and certainly open to challenge. When creating ranges on a radial gauge, there are many properties and options to get just the visual effect you desire. Ranges have border color, fill color, fill gradient, shadow, start width, end width, distance from scale, and placement settings. Ranges can also have actions, in range bar pointer color, in range label color, and in range tick mark color. ToolTips help differentiate values within a particular range.
- **Gauge Label** This is the basic title for the gauge, like a chart title.
- **Border** The border is the very outer delineation of the gauge container. Border options include Line Style, Line Width, and Color.

Figure 2-20 shows a gauge with many properties set, just to give an idea of how much the display can be altered from the original example (Figure 2-19). The border has been selected as semicircular, the gauge frame is simple, the color was changed slightly from before. The ranges were located outside the scale. The pointer cap was enlarged and has a black border, and the needle became the arrow with a more conspicuous pattern.

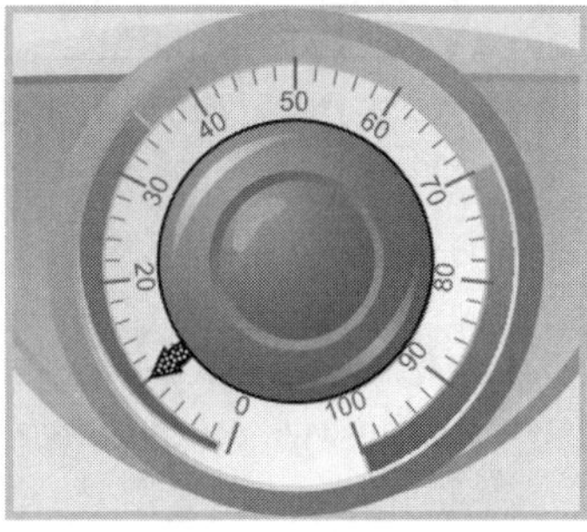

Figure 2-20 *Example radial gauge with all properties set*

Linear Gauge Overview

Linear gauges display their values along either a horizontal or vertical axis, and you can change the orientation through the Gauge Properties dialog box. Linear gauges are more space efficient than radial gauges and can be integrated into tablix reports to show comparison values. Linear gauges can have multiple scales and multiple ranges, like radial gauges.

The value indicator options for linear gauges are a little different from radial gauges, though; they are Marker, Bar, or Thermometer. The thermometer pointer has settings for bulb offset, bulb size, and thermometer style—standard (round) or flask. If you choose the thermometer, the start is always the filled bulb. If you choose the bar pointer, you can choose where on the scale the bar starts and how long it is. If the marker pointer is chosen, the choices for marker shapes are Rectangle, Triangle, Circle, Diamond, Trapezoid, Star, Wedge, and Pentagon.

Selecting the properties for a gauge must reflect the characteristics of the measure being displayed. If the boundary values for the metric as derived are very large, then a gauge probably isn't the best visualization tool. However, to use the driver's dashboard analogy, if the intention of the dashboard is to allow the user to monitor the value of certain operational measures as a gas gauge, a temperature gauge, an RPM gauge, or a voltage gauge does for a driver, then these visualizations could be quite helpful.

BI TIP

Use a linear gauge when you only have the measure and don't have previous amount or goal values to compare against. Use a Bullet Graph gauge when you have the measure, and a goal and/or previous values, and qualitative boundaries with which to create ranges (Warning, Caution, Favorable).

Creating the Bullet Graph Gauge

Let's create a report and add a linear gauge to it. Creating a new report in SSRS was covered previously in this chapter. We will use the Bullet Graph gauge as our linear gauge example, setting all the properties for the linear gauge. Later, we will turn our attention to the radial gauges.

BI TIP

Bullet Graphs were developed by Mr. Stephen Few, noted author. The specification for Bullet Graphs, and how to best use them, can be found at this web location: www.perceptualedge.com/articles/misc/Bullet_Graph_Design_Spec.pdf.

Gauges are now first-class Toolbox items in BIDS, and the icon for the gauge control is found right under the control for a chart. To add a gauge to a report, click and drag the gauge control from the Toolbox and onto the report design surface, as shown in Figure 2-21.

Once you drag the gauge control from the Toolbox onto the report design surface, the Select Gauge Type dialog box will appear, presenting your choices for gauge type as shown in Figure 2-21.

BI TIP

As mentioned, choose carefully, because the gauge type cannot be changed once it is selected. If you have to change the gauge type, you must delete the existing one and select a new type.

For this example, choose the linear gauge type of Bullet Graph, which is the last icon under Linear Gauges shown circled in Figure 2-21. Select the Bullet Graph gauge and click the OK button at the bottom of the Select Gauge Type dialog box. The Bullet Graph gauge will now appear on your SSRS report design surface, as shown in Figure 2-22.

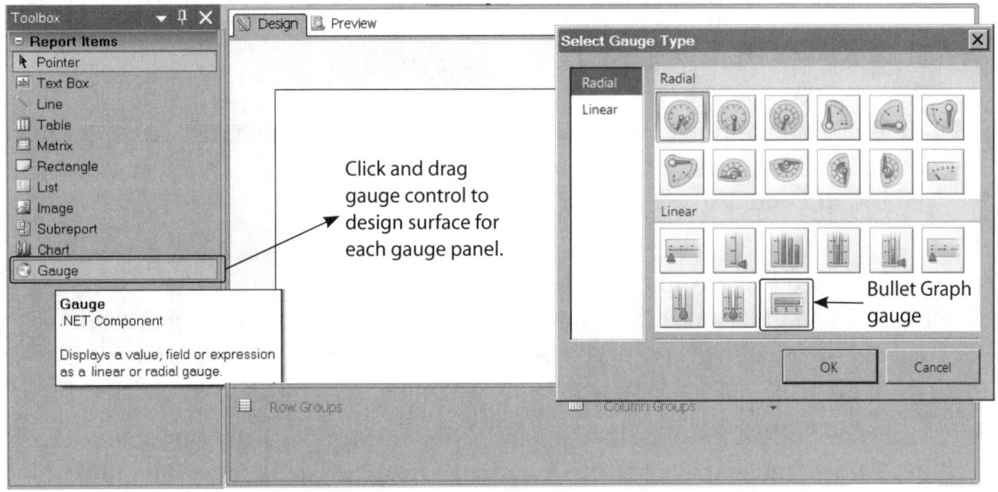

Figure 2-21 *Gauge control in BIDS Toolbox*

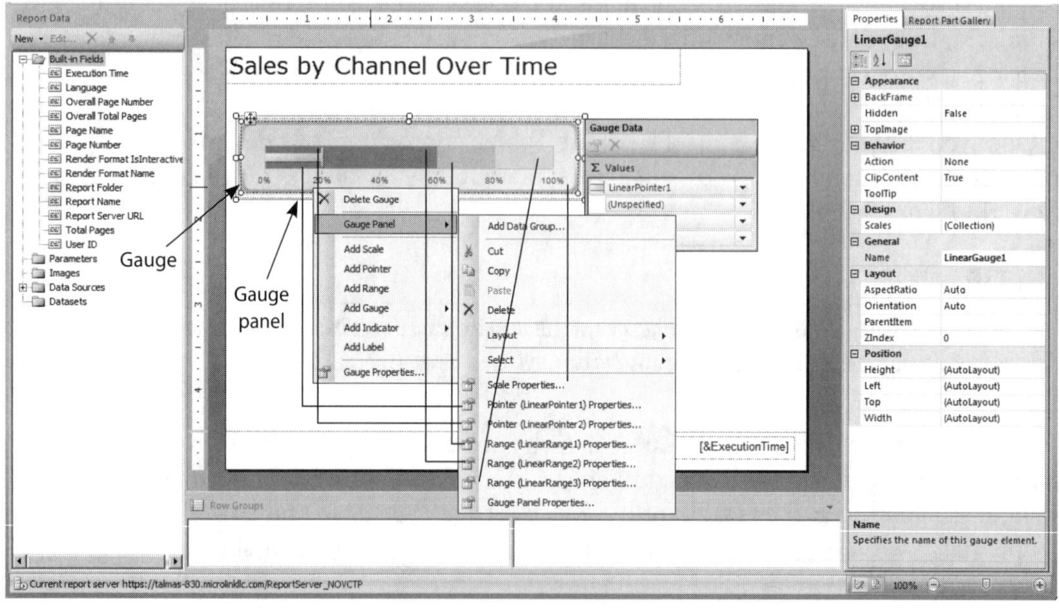

Figure 2-22 *Bullet Graph gauge—predefined pointers and ranges*

Let's dissect this representation for a moment, because it is a little different from the other linear gauges. To display the gauge as in Figure 2-22, click inside the gauge panel to activate the design surface and display the data drop zone.

- The Bullet Graph gauge design template has a data drop zone with two measure areas predefined. Those measures relate to Linear Pointer 1, the longer, narrower bar; and Linear Point 2, the shorter, wider end bar.
- The Bullet Graph gauge also has three ranges predefined. The three ranges can be related to the Red / Amber / Green ratings given to most KPIs. Here the ranges are shown in gradients of a single color, which is much more distinguishable for those with visual impairment like color blindness. Color intensity variation is easy to comprehend and translates easily into grayscale for printing.
- Also in Figure 2-22, notice that right-clicking inside the gauge panel will bring up a context menu that gives many options for adding components and setting various properties.
- Clicking the Gauge submenu as shown in Figure 2-22 gives access to scale, pointer, range and gauge panel properties dialog boxes, as well as selecting the body of the report, or ordering items via the Layout submenu.

As shown in the example in Figure 2-22, a dataset was defined from the AdventureWorks cube. Gauges are best at displaying metric measurements. Using a SQL Server Analysis Services data source makes available the predefined calculated measures and KPIs that are stored in the cube. Using an SSAS KPI gives you the added advantage of being able to pull in predefined goal values, saving the report creator from having to embed that logic in the report.

BI TIP

Business rules about data, including any formulas or calculations, must be clearly documented for each gauge display—to ensure that data quality standards have been practiced. Reviewing this documentation with stakeholders is essential to gaining their agreement and adoption of the solution.

Setting the Pointer Properties

Before we delve into setting all the properties to make this gauge display what we want, let's review the purpose of the pointer and the scale. There is a relationship between the two, especially if you are using a bar pointer type.

BI TIP

Just as in column and bar graphs, in order to make the relative value between values consistent, your scale must the start at 0. If your scale does not start at 0 because of space limitations, then choose a different pointer type to accurately reflect the data relationship. When our eyes compare bars or columns, we evaluate the length of the line and compare it to other members in the set. If the scale does not start at 0, the increment between values is distorted. Avoid issues like these and make your reports more readable.

The pointer is the measure display mechanism, and as such, it is the pointer that gets bound to the data value. Figure 2-23 shows the pointer and scale of a linear gauge for your reference.

BI TIP

Remember that one pointer can display only one value, so think about what type of value you want to display—a percentage of a goal amount or the raw value (like dollars or quantities).

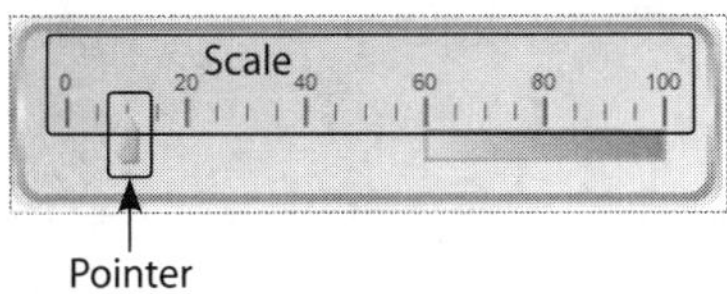

Figure 2-23 *Linear gauge pointer and scale*

The scale or scales are the units of measure—and have minimum and maximum values that are displayed in intervals that support the granularity of the display desired. If the values are large and the variability is low, then starting the scale at 0 will most likely not support a good visualization of the measurement, because the interval will have to be too large, and variations will be compressed. The example shown in Figure 2-23 has only one scale, but remember that gauges can have multiple scales, giving you many options. Consider having the raw value on the primary scale and a percentage value on a secondary scale to bring more illumination of the metric. An alternate scenario may be U.S. Dollars on one scale and Euros on the secondary scale, to show relative values.

Now, let's set the properties to make the Bullet Graph gauge visually stimulating.

Linear Gauge Design Surface and Component Areas

Before we configure the pointer properties, there are a few things to note when working on the design surface of a gauge report. Depending on where in the gauge panel you click, a different context menu will appear (just as when we were working with charts). Figure 2-24 shows these component areas within the design surface and the context menu that appears for that area. As shown in Figure 2-24, on the design surface if you

- Right-click the pointer graphic or the data field for the point (A); the Pointer Properties context menu will appear.
- Click the data field, a list of available data fields will appear for selection (B).
- Right-click a range or within the gauge body; the Range Properties context menu will display (C).
- Right-click the scale or near the bottom of the gauge body; the Scale Properties context menu will appear (D).
- Right-click the gauge background, not on a specific component; you get the Gauge context menu (E).

Setting Pointer Properties

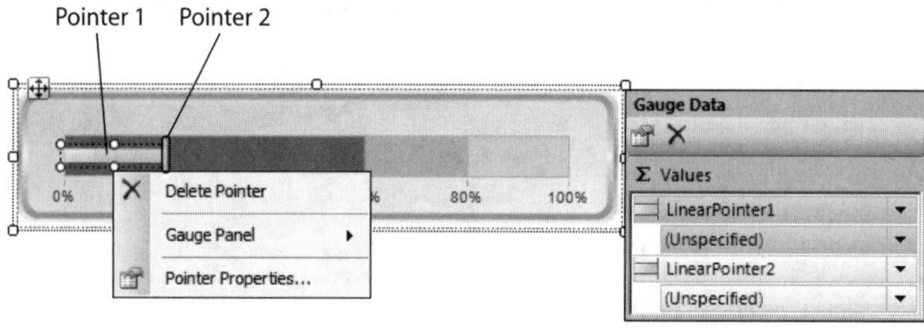

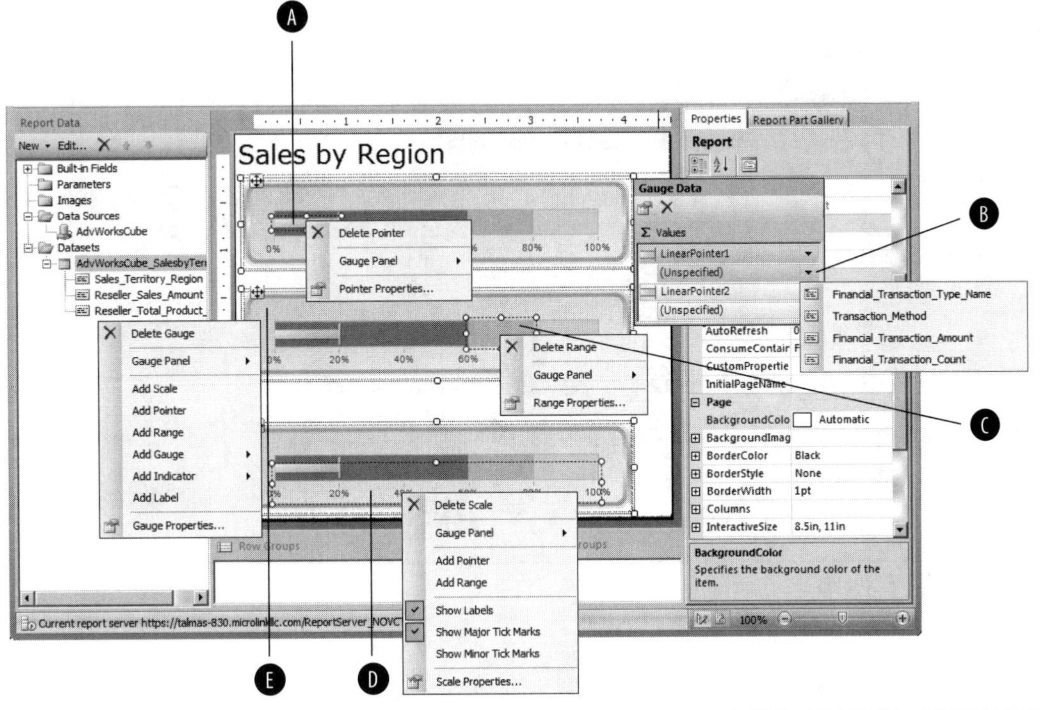

Figure 2-24 *Design surface with Pointer, Range, Data, and Scale zones displayed*

Since the pointer is the component that displays the measurement, let's start there. To configure the pointer properties, first assign the data values for the Linear Pointer 1 and Linear Pointer 2 of the Bullet Graph gauge.

1. Determine if you will use raw values or calculated measures for your data points.
2. Click the dataset shortcut as displayed in Figure 2-24, or drag the desired data element from the dataset in the Report Data pane on the Linear Pointer data drop zone.
3. Set Linear Pointer 1 to your measurement value.
4. Set Linear Pointer 2 to the goal value.
5. Right-click the Pointer zone and the Pointer context menu will appear. Select Pointer Properties to open the dialog box.
6. The Linear Pointer Properties dialog box relates to the Properties pane shown at the left of the design surface as illustrated in Figure 2-25.

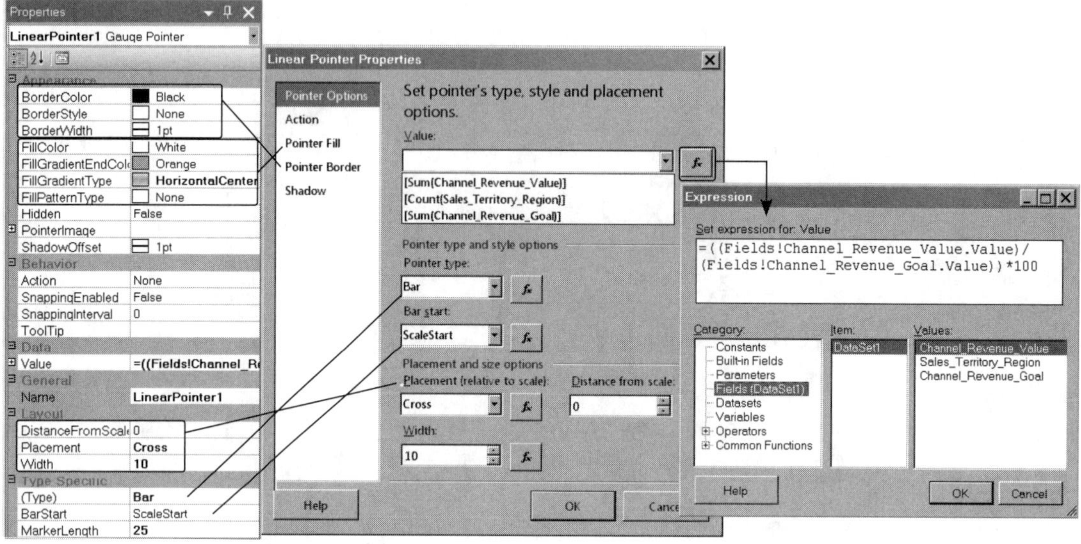

Figure 2-25 *Linear Pointer Properties*

The first order of business is to create the expression for our metric value, as we have determined to use the percentage scale to show value relative to goal.

1. To create the value expression, click the *f*x button to the right of the Value selection box on the Pointer Options pane.
2. You can type the formula into the text box, or add the fields by double-clicking them from the Fields (DataSet) Values list, as shown in Figure 2-25. In the example, the formula is (measurement amount / goal amount) * 100 to give us the percentage of goal achieved. The actual formula shown is

```
=(Fields!Channel_Revenue_Value.Value)/(Fields!Channel_Revenue
_Goal.Value) * 100)
```

3. Set the value for Pointer 2 in the same way. For a percentage expression, goal value / goal value will equal 100 percent. For Pointer 2, the Pointer Type is Marker (instead of Bar), and you may want to choose a different color to distinguish it from the measurement.
4. Once the value of the pointer is set, set the pointer type. For the Bullet Chart gauge, the default is Bar, which is probably best. (Other choices are Marker or Thermometer. If you choose Thermometer, it will be formatted with a bulb at the end.) This is shown in Figure 2-25.
5. The Bar Start box defaults to ScaleStart; the other options are Zero or custom expression.

6. The Pointer Placement and Size options determine where the scale appears relative to the measurement. The options are Cross (across the entire width of the pointer), Inside, or Outside. Distance From Scale sets the gap between the scale and the pointer. The Width property is the width of the pointer bar itself.
7. Set the Pointer Fill colors, gradient, or other patterns on the Pointer Fill pane.
8. Set the Pointer Border, Style, and Width on the Pointer Border pane. Setting Shadows is another option. We will explore the use of Actions in a later example.

The pointer on the linear gauge is the object that displays the value being represented in the gauge. The properties for the distance of the pointer from the scale, its placement (inside, outside, cross), and its width will control how the pointer looks relative to the scale. The choice of color for the pointer is important; to improve contrast, choose a dark color pointer against a light background. The reverse (light pointer and dark background) is acceptable also, but check it in grayscale to ensure there is enough contrast. Now that all the pointer properties are set as referenced in Figure 2-25, let's turn our attention to the scale that will display our measurements.

Setting the Scale Properties

Scale properties allow you to control the display and behavior of the gauge scale. This is where the range of numbers and their meaning are set.

BI TIP

This is the point where knowing your data is very important. When setting the scale range, ensure that the values displayed will fall between the minimum and maximum scale values. If they don't, the gauge cannot provide an adequate visualization. Consider changing the scale values or type to accommodate all measurements—maybe a change from absolute values to a percentage scale will solve the challenge.

Right-click the scale area, and the Scale Properties context menu will appear, as shown in Figure 2-26.

1. Choose the Scale Properties submenu at the bottom of the context menu, as shown in Figure 2-26.
2. The Linear Scale Properties dialog box will display, shown in Figure 2-27. There are panes for General, Action, Layout, Labels, Font, Number, Major Tick Marks, Minor Tick Marks, Fill, Border, and Shadow.
3. On the General pane, set the value options. We have chosen a percentage scale for our example, so examine the data to determine if you need to be able to display more than 100 percent. If your measures are exceeding their goals, then showing by how much will be important! If you have chosen a scale that is not percentage based, you need to specify the minimum and maximum values for the scale. If the KPI goal is closer to 0, click the Reverse Scale Direction check box.

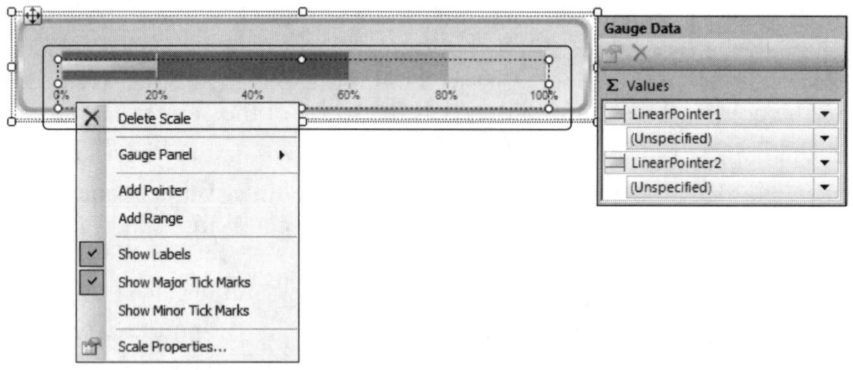

Figure 2-26 *Bullet Graph gauge Scale context menu*

4. The Interval is the amount between major tick marks. For example, if the scale is 0 to 100 with an interval of 20, it will display major tick marks for 0, 20, 40, 60, 80, and 100. If you leave Interval set to Auto, SSRS will calculate the amount between minimum and maximum values and calculate an equidistant number of intervals to display. The Interval Offset is the amount to skip before displaying the first label.
5. Scale Multiplier is a neat feature if you are displaying values that are very large (e.g., >100,000). To reduce the number of label collisions, specify a multiplier (in decimal format) to apply to the scale values. For example, to display an amount in thousands, the multiplier would be 0.001. This calculation is applied only to the labels, not to the pointer values themselves. If you do use a Scale Multiplier, make sure to label it appropriately so that the report audience can understand what they are viewing.

The other two very important panes in this dialog box are the Number pane and the Major Tick Marks pane.

1. On the Number pane, choose the numerical category desired. Custom Expression is always an option by clicking the *fx* button next to the Custom Format text box.
2. On the Major Tick Marks pane, choose the Major Tick Mark Shape. The default is Rectangle, but Triangle, Circle, Diamond, Trapezoid, Star, Wedge, and Pentagon are also available.
3. The property that is hidden by the drop-down list in Figure 2-27 is the Major Tick Mark Placement setting. The choices are Cross, Inside, and Outside. Cross means that the scale will go across the entire gauge body, Inside means the scale will appear at the bottom, and Outside means the scale will appear on the top of the gauge body.

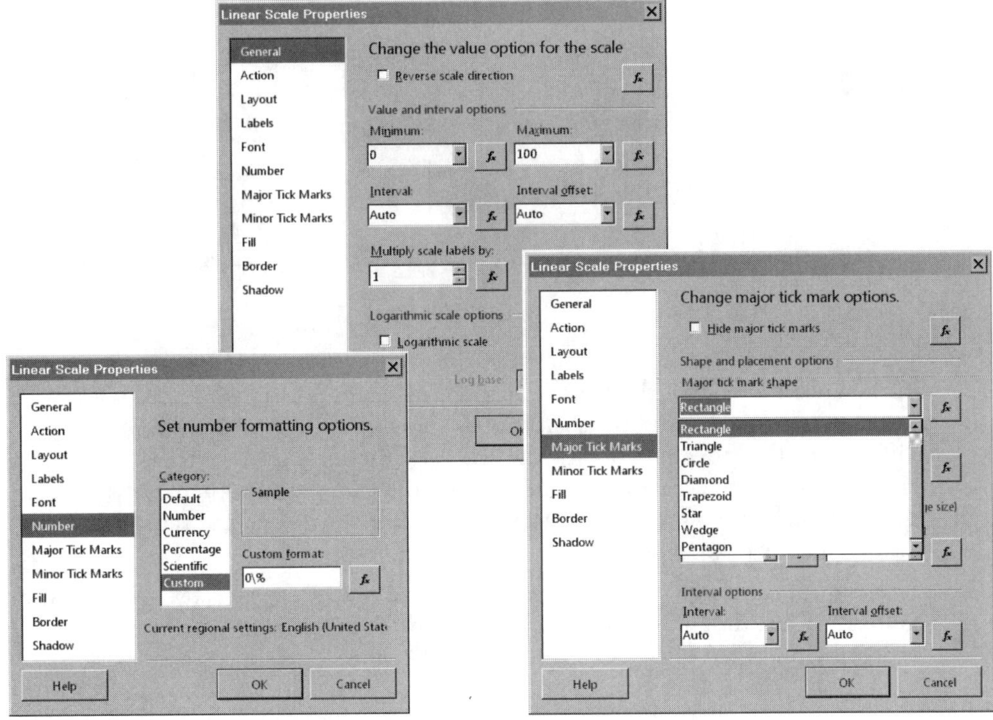

Figure 2-27 *Linear Scale Properties dialogs for General, Number, and Major Tick Marks*

4. The next property (also hidden by the drop-down list in Figure 2-27) is the Width and Length of the Major Tick Mark as percentage of gauge scale.
5. The last property on this pane is the Interval options—Major Tick Mark Interval and Interval Offset. These work the same as the scale Interval and Interval Offset.

There are many property settings available on the gauge scale. Setting the scale properties suitably will enhance the display of the gauge and ensure that your report audience understands the true value of what the gauge is displaying.

Creating a Range

To enhance how the gauge value is perceived, apply ranges to the gauge scale. Ranges are the color bands that sit behind the pointer or next to the scale. Ranges can be correlated with Metric or KPI boundary values (Red, Amber, Green, or Warning, Caution, Favorable).

1. To create or edit a range, right-click the gauge body or existing range, and select Range Properties from the context menu, as shown at the top of Figure 2-28.

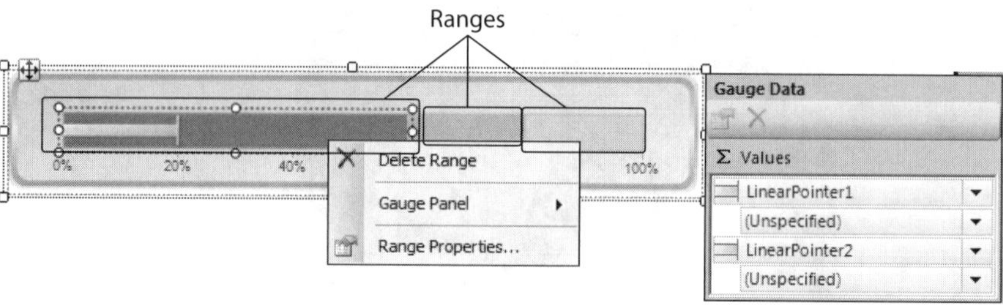

Figure 2-28 *Linear gauge ranges and context menu*

2. On the General pane of the Linear Scale Range Properties dialog box, select the range starting and ending positions, as shown in Figure 2-29. Remember to use values that are aligned with the scale—if the scale is in percent, then use percent values. If the scale is currency or numerical, use values that are within the displayed range. If you have boundary values selected in your dataset, click the *fx* button, and create an expression to use those values.
3. Placement of the range relative to the scale is the next property setting. The choices are Inside, Outside, and Cross. Inside means between the scale and the pointer. Cross is behind the pointer. Outside is on the opposite side from the scale.

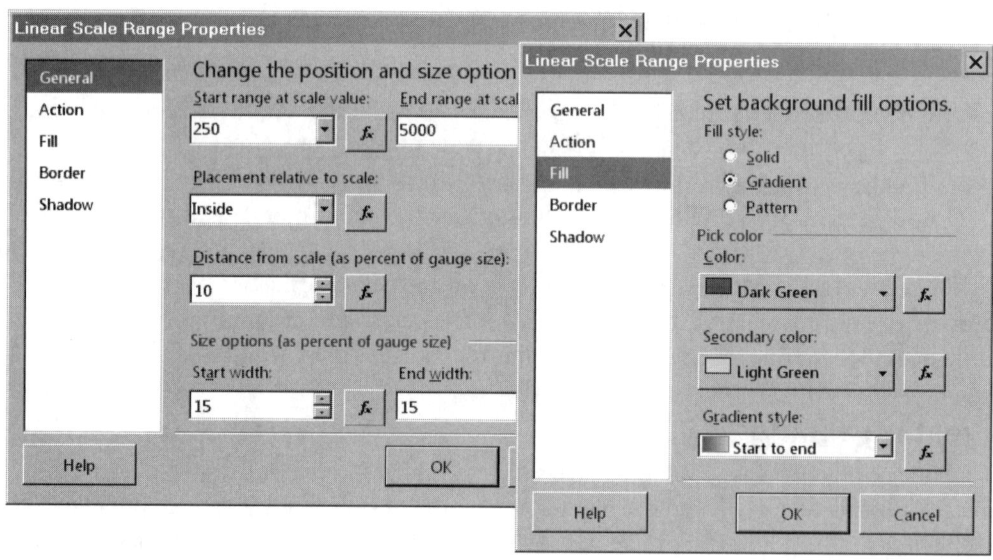

Figure 2-29 *Linear Scale Range Properties—sizing and color options*

4. The Distance From Scale property will move the range around inside the gauge body. Likewise, the setting different Size options for start width and end width will make the range more trapezoidal and less rectangular.
5. On the Fill pane, set the properties to control solid, gradient, or pattern fill, and pick colors.
6. Add additional ranges to each gauge as desired. Try not to overlap the ranges, or the display may get mangled.
7. When all desired properties have been set, click the OK button at the bottom of the dialog box, as shown in Figure 2-29.

Now that all these properties have been set, we have a functional, visually appealing Bullet Chart gauge, what will display our KPIs in relationship to the predefined Warning, Caution, and Favorable ranges.

Setting Gauge Filters

The next thing to explain is how to get each geographic region mapped to a particular gauge. Gauge filters can be applied to data at the gauge panel level to restrict the information that is displayed.

BI TIP

When working with gauges, note that a gauge panel (no matter how many individual gauges are within the one gauge panel) can only be associated with one dataset. If you are going to display multiple gauges within one gauge panel, ensure that all data elements you need are included in that dataset. To display information from multiple datasets, create multiple gauge panels or data regions on the report.

Since we want to display gauges that will be filtered individually, we will create multiple gauge panels to display the data for each of four geographical regions (members of the Sales Territory dimension).

In order to get the multiple gauges, you have a choice. You can copy and paste your already formatted gauge (using CTRL-C and CTRL-V on the design surface), and customize the copies, or repeat the procedure demonstrated previously, and click and drag three more gauge panels onto the design surface and configure each one from scratch. Either way, Figure 2-30 shows an example of how the result will look. The reason for this is that data grouping doesn't work on gauges like it does on graphs, tables, or matrix reports.

Figure 2-30 shows the Report Designer design surface with the four separate gauge panels on it. Each Bullet Graph gauge goes into its own gauge panel, because we want to apply individual filters to each gauge display. Data grouping on a table or matrix will cause

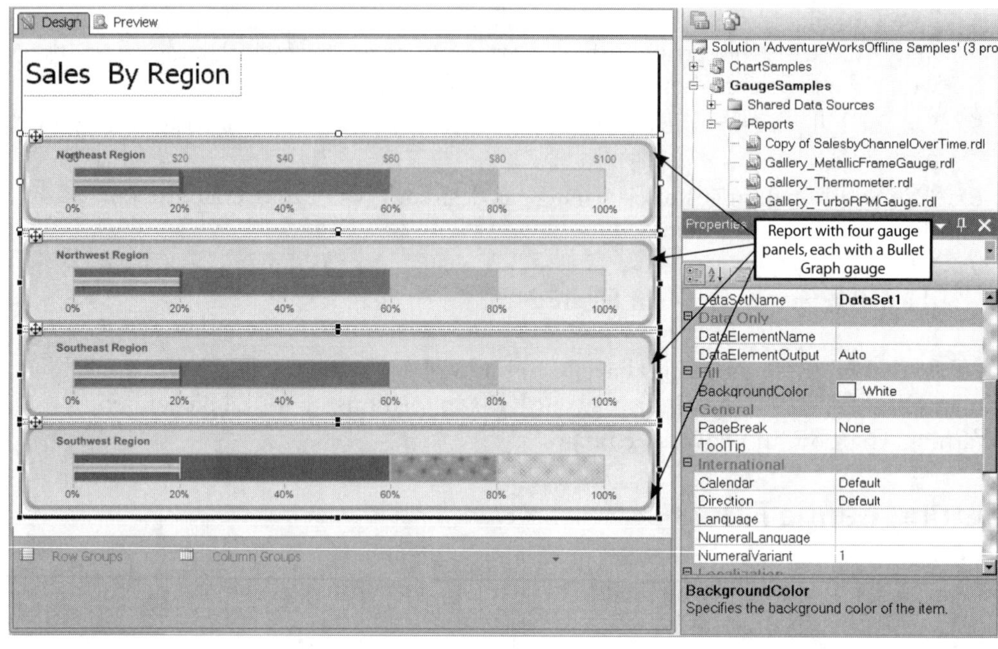

Figure 2-30 *Report design surface with four gauge panels and four filters*

additional rows to display for each group member. Remember that gauge pointers can display only one value. If you apply data grouping to data on a gauge, it will return the last member of the group for the measure to be displayed. That behavior may be appropriate if you are using time series data and you want the gauge to display the most recent value.

For this example, to control what is displayed, use four different gauge panels with the same dataset, and use a filter on each gauge to control which value is displayed. This will ensure that each of the dimension members can be displayed precisely. To set the filter properties,

1. To filter data on a gauge display, right-click the gauge body, and select Gauge from the context menu, then Data Group Properties from the submenu, as shown in Figure 2-31. You will need to repeat this procedure for each gauge related to a specific dimension member.
2. On the Filters pane of the Gauge Panel Group Properties dialog box, click the Add button to open up the text boxes for editing.
3. In the Expression text box, the drop-down will show a list of available dataset fields that can be chosen. If you need to, click the *fx* button and create an expression for your filter. The Datatype text box next to the Expression text box will change to indicate the type of field it is if you choose from the list. If you create a complex expression, you may have to select a datatype here.

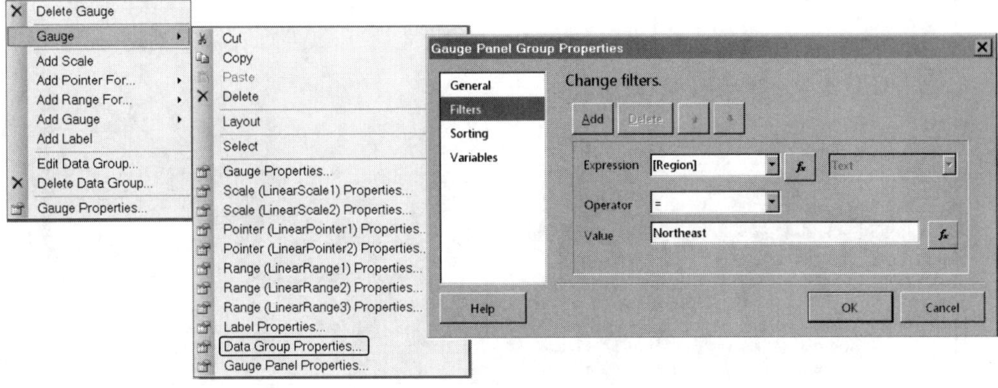

Figure 2-31 *Gauge panel—Data Group Properties—setting filters*

4. The operator button selects the comparison method to use between your expression and the value. The available choices are: =, < >, Like, >, >=,<. <=, Top N, Bottom N, Top %, Bottom %, In (list), Between (range).
5. In the Value text box type in a value, or use the *f*x Expression Editor to create one. If you are filtering on a specific dimension member (as in the example), ensure that you spell the value exactly as it appears in the dimension. Notice there is no drop-down to select the value. So if it is Northeast in the dimension, typing in North East will not match the dimension member and the gauge will return no results because a match could not be made.
6. When finished, click the OK button at the bottom of the dialog box.

Now that the filter is set, the gauge will display the value for only that dimension member, or expression value. This allows us to use the same dataset and still get what we want, a gauge mapped to only one geographic region.

Bullet Graph Gauge Summary

Now that you know all the secrets behind this gauge, let's take a look at the finished product. Figure 2-32 shows the gauges as they have been configured in our example, except for the color variations for the Southwest Region. Here is the recap:

- There is one gauge for each dimension member, in this case Geographic Region.
- The gauge displays the sales amount as a percentage of goal amount.
- Each gauge is labeled to indicate which region it is for.
- The goal amount is indicated by the vertical bar at the 100% mark on the scale.

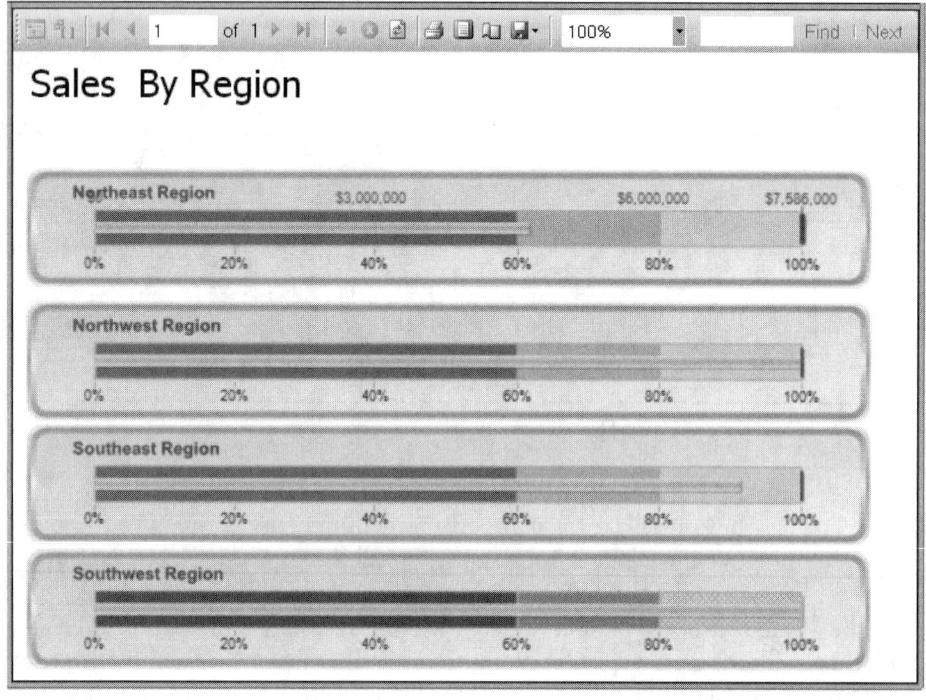

Figure 2-32 *Bullet Graph gauges for each Geographic Region*

- The actual sales amount is represented by the horizontal bar spanning across the middle of each gauge.
- The ranges display the Warning, Caution, and Favorable ranges for the percentage of goal.

So it is easy to see from examining the display in Figure 2-32 that the Northwest Region and Southwest Region met their sales goal. The Southeast Region made approximately 90 percent of their goal amount, and the Northeast Region struggled to achieve around 60 percent of their goal. The Northeast Region gauge also has a secondary scale that correlates the percentage to a dollar amount, to give the viewer a better understanding of the magnitude of the display.

Now that we have walked through setting most of the basic properties for a linear gauge, let's turn our attention to the variety of linear gauge types and their uses.

Linear Gauge Varieties

There are several varieties of linear gauges, and with the assortment of property settings available, you can achieve quite an array of linear gauge displays. The available linear gauge types are: Horizontal, Vertical, Multiple Bar Pointers, Two Scales, Three Color Ranges, Logarithmic, Thermometer, Thermometer Fahrenheit/Celsius, and Bullet Graph, as shown in Figure 2-33.

Choosing a gauge type can be complicated, unless the data you want to display has a distinctive characteristic that makes one type inherently more suitable, for example the Logarithmic type. If the gauge will be incorporated into a dashboard display, there may be design guidelines that will make your choices easier. If there are no guidelines, collaborate with your colleagues and come up with some basic design principles, and then stick to them. It may be as simple as a rule of thumb that states all gauges that display currency will use a vertical linear gauge; numeric, non-currency displays will use a horizontal linear gauge; and metrics that display a KPI, rate, or ratio will use radial gauges.

Any gauge that displays a metric measured against a goal will have ranges. A little consistency will go a long way to making your dashboards, graphs, and gauges appealing and understandable. Many times, space considerations will be the overwhelming factor for gauge type selection; other times it may be visual appeal. It is important to have guidelines to refer to, but make sure they are flexible enough to apply to many different use case scenarios and space allocation challenges.

Figure 2-34 shows the variety available for vertical linear gauges. Pointer styles, scales, color ranges, and other decoration can change the look of similar gauges. From left to right,

- The Thermometer-style vertical gauge shows two scales—Celsius and Fahrenheit. The bulb at the bottom can be round or flask shaped. Besides traditional temperature display, this gauge visualization is used routinely by non-profit organizations to show amount of funds collected compared to a goal (think of United Way).
- The second vertical gauge in Figure 2-34 is a simple linear gauge with a bar pointer style which crosses the scale, no ranges, and one scale, which is labeled Percent Complete.

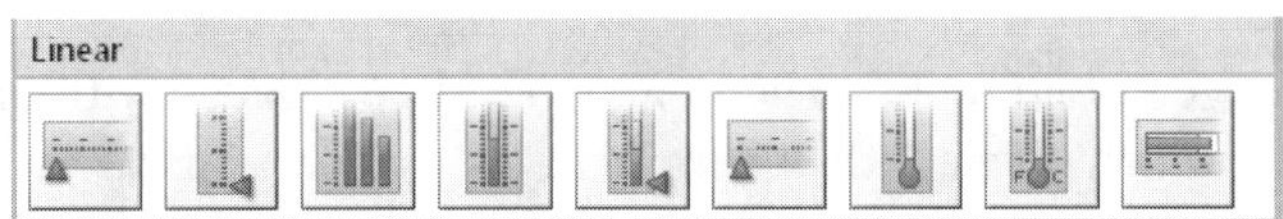

Figure 2-33 *Linear gauge types*

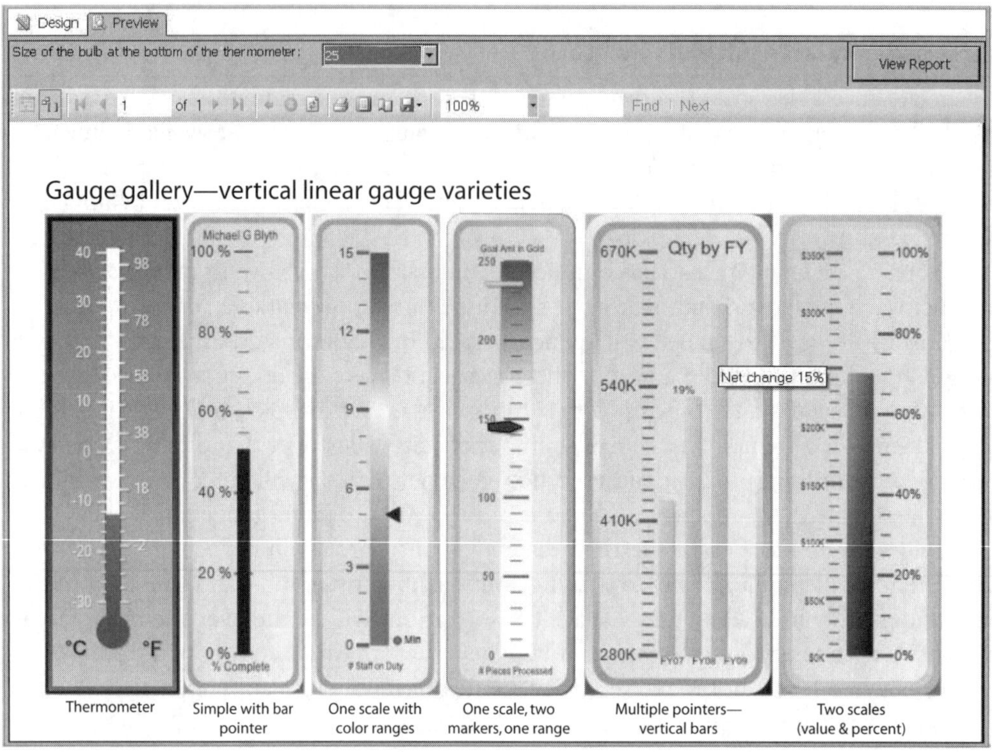

Figure 2-34 *The variety of vertical linear gauges*

- The third vertical gauge has one scale, which shows # Staff on Duty, color ranges outside the scale to help distinguish troublesome values, a minimum value pin (shown immediately above the 0), and a marker-style pointer with a triangular shape, which sits outside the scale and outside the ranges.
- The fourth gauge has one scale that shows values (labeled # of pieces processed), a pentagon-shaped marker-style pointer that crosses the scale, one color range that shows a goal range, and a second rectangular-shaped marker pointer that displays the goal amount that crosses the scale. Remember that the values for both pointers must be in the same dataset.
- The fifth gauge in Figure 2-34 shows a vertical linear gauge with multiple bar pointers, which displays the quantity in thousands by fiscal year for three consecutive years. The scale does not start at zero.
- The last vertical linear gauge shown has two scales—one showing currency in thousands and the other displaying percentage. It has a bar-style pointer, which is positioned outside of the value scale and inside of the percentage scale. Both scales start at zero.

As you can see in Figure 2-34, varying the pointer style, adjusting one or multiple scales, and adding pointers for additional values can greatly change the way a simple vertical linear gauge looks.

BI TIP

Linear gauges are very space efficient, much more so than radial gauges. Vertical linear gauges are good for displaying multiple related measures side by side. Horizontal linear gauges are easy to integrate into tablix reports to show progress or metrics.

Gauge Labels

Let's look at some of the details of customizing linear gauges, starting with labels. In Figure 2-34, only the last gauge didn't have at least one label on it. Labels give context to the display and help the viewer understand what is being represented. Labels can be hard-coded text or expressions based on data elements or functions. You can add multiple labels to a gauge, and they are managed in a collection. To add a label to a gauge,

1. On the design surface, right-click anywhere inside the gauge panel and select Add Label from the context menu, as shown in Figure 2-35.
2. Instead of a dialog box appearing, a text box will appear in your gauge somewhere near the geometric middle. The Properties pane will change to display the Gauge Label settings.

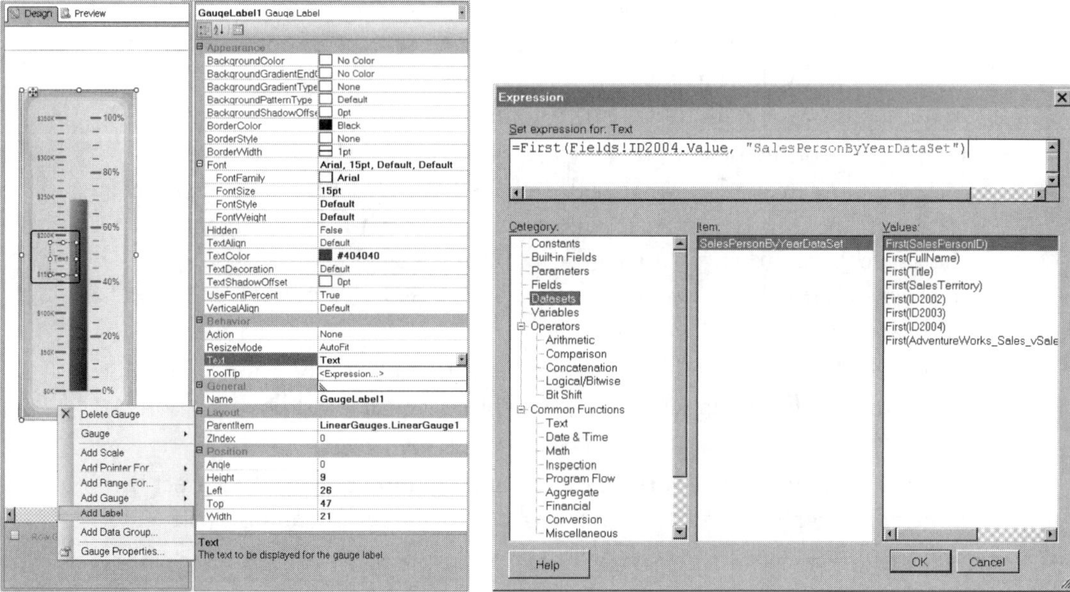

Figure 2-35 *Gauge Label Properties and Expression dialog*

3. Under the Behavior section is the Text property. You may type in a value for a hard-coded label, or click the drop-down and select Expression to bring up the Expression dialog box, as shown in Figure 2-35.
4. To add a label based on the data, select the Datasets category. The Item column will display the dataset name, and the available data elements or fields will display in the Values column. To select a value, double-click it, and it will appear in the top Set Expression For text box. Alternatively, you can type in a field name or formula directly.
5. When finished entering your expression, click the OK button at the bottom of the dialog box. The expression will display in the Text property in the Gauge Label Property pane, but in the text box itself it will only display <<expr>>, denoting an expression. If you have typed in plain text, the label text will display.
6. The property directly under Text is ToolTip. It has the same attributes—type text directly into the property or set an expression. The ToolTip will display when the cursor hovers over the label. An example ToolTip is shown on the fifth gauge—the multiple vertical bars—in Figure 2-34.
7. Setting the position of the text box is a bit of a challenge, and unfortunately, you cannot link or connect the label with a particular gauge component—like the pointer, *except for scale pin labels* (which are covered in the next section). There are several properties, all in the Position section of the Properties pane, as shown in Figure 2-35.
   - Angle is the angle at which the label text will display—empty (default) is horizontal, 90° makes the text vertically aligned, but you can choose any angle that works.
   - Height is the height of the label text box. The larger the number, the taller the text box. My experimentation revealed you need at least a 5 for a single line of text. If the text will wrap, increase this number until it displays properly. If you rotate the text, you will need a larger number for height.
   - Left is the coordinate from the left side of the gauge. The coordinates are measured in percent. The smaller the number, the closer the label text box is to the left margin. The larger the number, the closer it is to the right side of the gauge. If you resize your gauge after setting a label position, you may need to check and re-adjust, since these settings are based on a percentage of the size of the gauge.
   - Top is the distance from the top of the gauge; the smaller the number, the closer it is to the top. For example, 5 here would place the label text box very close to the top; a 90 would place it at the bottom of the gauge.
   - Width is the measurement from the left margin outward and will affect the number of characters that can be displayed. The larger the number, the wider the label text box.

- In the Appearance section of the Properties pane, there are several other settings that affect formatting of the label text box. Font is defined here, as well as Text Align (Default, General, Left, Center, Right); Vertical Align (Default, Top, Middle, Bottom); and Text Color, Text Decoration, and Text Shadow. The Use Font Percent is an important setting—it determines whether the text is autosized based on the size of the gauge, or whether the text will use the point size specified in the Font property. This property defaults to True; if it is set to False, be sure to check the rendering of the gauges to ensure the text size is appropriate to the size of the gauge.

Including labels on the gauge will make them more understandable to the report audience and will provide important contextual information that is not displayed by the gauge value. ToolTips can answer common questions that may arise when viewing the gauge. ToolTips can be set for many of the properties (scale, pointer, range).

Scale Number Formatting

Another nugget we want to share is the formatting of the gauge scale. We walked through how to adjust the main properties of the scale, but there are some nuances that are not obvious but will improve the display. One of those items is formatting the scale label to include an indicator that the scale is displaying values in thousands. When you set the number property for the scale, you have the choice of displaying the number in thousands, but there is no visual clue that indicates that on the number. Alternatively, you could add a label to inform your audience, but as just shown, you cannot link a label to a specific gauge component. Altering the number format string to add a *K* to the end of the number is a good way to solve this problem. There is no way to set this through the Gauge Scale Properties dialog box. Figure 2-36 shows where in the Gauge Scale Properties pane the setting is located, in the Labels and Tick Marks section, under Label Style, called Format String. The first part of the string is the display format for positive numbers (currency, the number, use ",", and zero decimal places); the second part (after the semicolon) is the format string for negative numbers. So for the example shown, negative numbers will appear in parentheses.

Almost all other properties for the scale can be set through the Gauge Scale Properties pane, and in some cases, this is the only place you can set them. An example of that is the scale pins.

Gauge Scale Pins

Scale pins are demarcation points for the maximum and minimum values allowable on the gauge scale; they prevent the pointer from showing a larger or smaller value, respectively. Scale pins can be

Scale pins

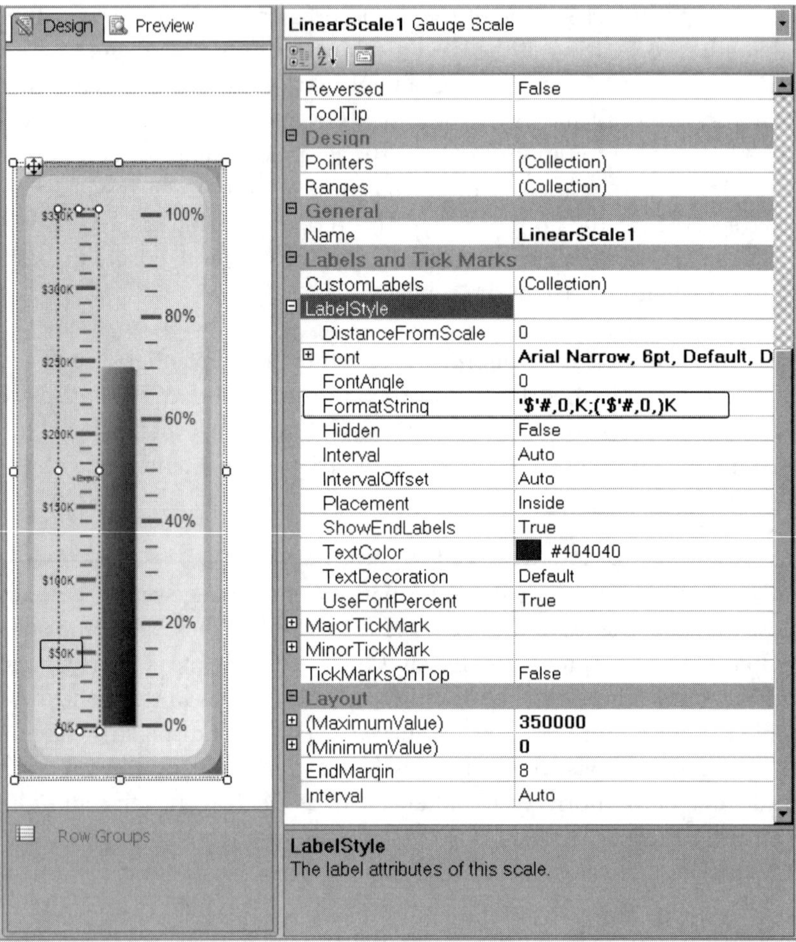

Figure 2-36 *Scale Number Format Properties*

one of a variety of shapes (the same choices as for the marker shape). The illustration shows an example of minimum and maximum scale pins, shown directly next to the range minimum and maximum values. On this gauge the color ranges are placed inside the scale, and the needle-style pointer crosses the scale. It makes sense then that the placement of both the pin and the pin label will be inside and cross the scale, respectively.

Let's review some of the available properties that are shown under the Scale Pins section in Figure 2-37:

- The Distance From Scale property sets the coordinate for the pin shape. This number is the offset of the tick mark from its normal position. The insight here is that a scale pin is just a specialized tick mark.
- The Enable property must be set to True to display the scale pin; it resolves whether the position for the scale pin is enabled.

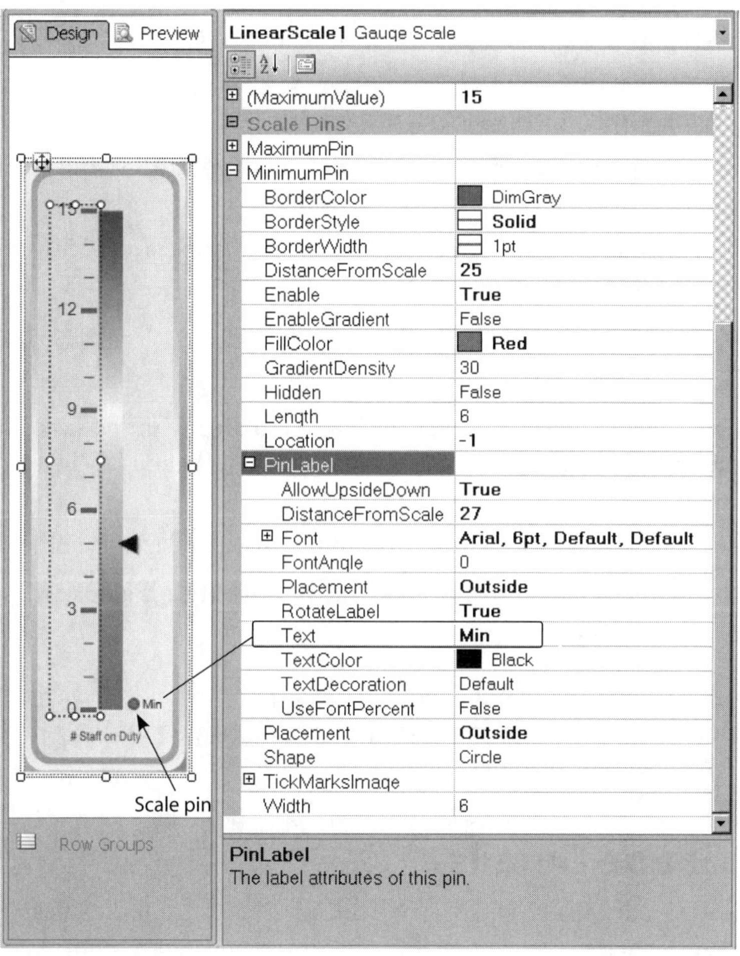

Figure 2-37 *Scale Pins properties*

- The Hidden property must be set to False. This setting determines whether or not to show the specialized tick mark.
- Length applies to the scale pin shape.
- Location (Minimum Pin) governs the location of the position (in degrees or percent), relative to zero on the scale. Negative numbers here put the location farther up the scale; positive numbers place the scale pin farther below zero on the scale.
- Placement is set to Outside, which establishes the position relative to the scale.
- Shape is set to Circle; the shape choices are the same as those for marker pointers (None, Rectangle, Triangle, Circle, Diamond, Star, Trapezoid, Pentagon, and Wedge).
- Tick Marks Image allows the import of a custom picture file to use as the scale pin image.
- Width is the width of the scale pin image.
- The Pin Label properties are inserted in the middle of the list and control the display of the label associated with a scale pin.
    - Allow Upside Down is connected to the Font Angle. In order to rotate the font more than 90°, this must be set to True.
    - Font Angle is the amount to rotate the pin label.
    - Placement is the placement of the pin label relative to the scale.
    - Rotate Label controls whether the label is rotated with the scale. If it is set to True and the entire gauge scale was rotated 90°, the pin label would be rotated as well.
    - Text is the actual text to display. It can be a hard-coded value or an Expression.
    - Use Font Percent controls whether the pin label text is autosized when the gauge is resized.

The use of scale pins can help the report audience understand the gauge scale and boundary values for the metric being displayed. Scale pins prevent the pointer from pointing to a number outside of its range.

Radial Gauge Details

Now let's create a radial gauge and discover the differences from the linear gauge properties. Radial gauges come in four varieties: full round, half round, quarter round, and meter. The smaller half round and quarter round gauges have a smaller scale sweep, so take this into consideration when choosing—if you have metrics that have a smaller possible range of values, then half or quarter round may be the right choice. Also keep in mind that the gauge scale does not have to begin at zero; just make sure to clearly label it so that the report audience can interpret the display correctly. The Meter radial gauge looks very similar to the Horizontal linear gauge, but it supports the needle style of pointer, as well as marker and bar. The Meter radial gauge is particularly suited to metrics that are displaying a rate (e.g., pieces per hour), because of the built-in perception and familiarity with this type of gauge.

Create a Radial Gauge

To create a radial gauge, drag another gauge control onto the design surface of the report. As you can see in Figure 2-38, the radial gauge comes preconfigured with a range and the scale set from 1 to 100. The only data value on the gauge is for the pointer, so we will use the other data elements for setting other properties. For this example, we are using the AdventureWorks Cube and have selected the Channel Revenue KPI, which has actual amount, goal amount, status, and trend measurements. The Geographic Region will be our slicing dimension.

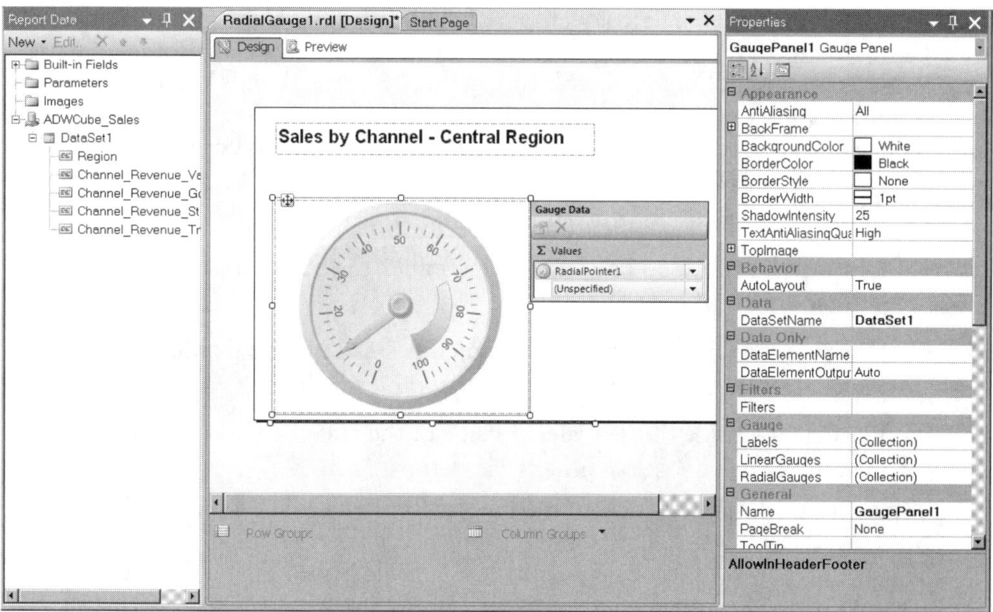

Figure 2-38 *New radial gauge—showing default range and scale*

The report design surface in Figure 2-38 shows a gauge panel with one full-circle radial gauge in it. The Properties pane is displaying the Gauge Panel properties, and you can see that the dataset is connected to the gauge at this level. Just like the linear gauges, radial gauges display the measurement value through the pointer. A pointer can display only one value. You can have multiple pointers in one radial gauge, but be careful with this configuration, as it can be quite confusing if not well labeled.

Setting the Radial Gauge Pointer Properties

To configure this gauge to display the channel revenue amounts and goals, start by setting the properties for the pointer.

1. Drag the Channel_Revenue_Value field from the Report Data pane onto the drop data fields area of the design surface where it shows RadialPointer1.
2. Click the data field to make the RadialGaugePointer1 Gauge Pointer Properties pane display.
3. Change the Fill Color from the default Orange, and choose a FillGradient or FillPattern if desired. If you are going to use colored ranges, choose a color for your pointer that is not similar so that it will stand out against the background.
4. Set the color for the PointerCap in this same Properties pane. Choose a color that is the same as or similar to the pointer unless you want a clear distinction between the two elements. There are a plethora of choices for the Cap Style (Rounded Dark, Rounded, Rounded Light, Rounded with Additional Top, Rounded with Wide Indentation, Flattened with Indentation, Flattened with Wide Indentation, Rounded Glossy with Indentation, Rounded with Indentation). Find a style that is appealing, then stick with it to achieve design consistency. For this example, use Rounded Glossy with Indentation.
5. Other properties to set for the pointer include Layout settings:
   - Distance from Scale—the larger the number, the farther the end of the pointer is from the scale.
   - Width is the distance across the pointer. A small number configures a thin, pin-like shape; a larger number displays a thicker shape.
   - Placement (Inside of the scale, Outside of the scale, or Cross the scale) is relevant if you choose a pointer style that isn't a needle.
6. Type-specific properties include the Pointer Type (Needle, Marker, or Bar), Bar Start, Marker Length, Marker Style (None, Rectangle, Triangle, Circle, Diamond, Trapezoid, Star, Wedge, or Pentagon), and Needle Style (Triangular, Rectangular, Tapered with Tail, Tapered, Arrow with Tail, Arrow, Stealth Arrow with Tail, Stealth Arrow, Tapered with Stealth Arrow, Stealth Arrow with Wide Tail, and Tapered with Rounded Pointer). For this example, use Needle Style, Triangular Shape.

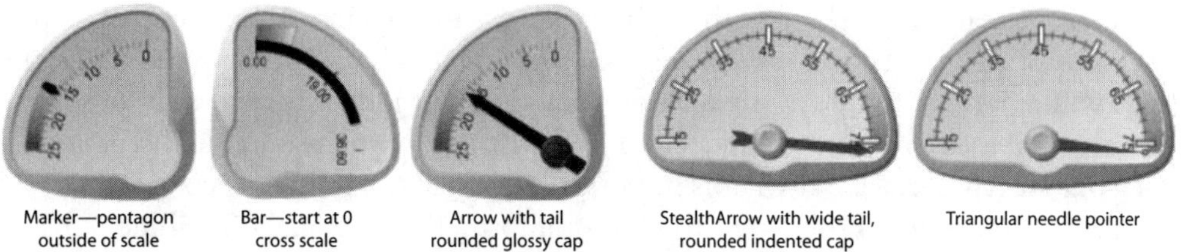

Figure 2-39 *Gauge pointer styles—marker, bar, and various needle styles*

Whew, that's a lot of choices. Let's look at some of the basic choices of pointer type, shown in Figure 2-39. There is an array of choices for pointer styles, and there are variations within each type as well.

- The first example shown in Figure 2-39 is the marker pointer type. This can be one of several shapes (enumerated previously) but is basically a floating shape that indicates the gauge value. This example shows the pentagon shape positioned at the outside of the scale.
- The bar pointer type shows a continuous bar that ends at the gauge value. The example in Figure 2-39 shows the bar position crossing the scale. The bar pointer type is most often associated with Thermometer types of gauge displays.
- The third example is a needle-type Arrow with Tail pointer. The difference between an Arrow and a Stealth Arrow is the angle of the back of the arrowhead.

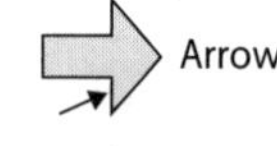

- The fourth display is a needle-type Stealth Arrow with Wide Tail.
- The last image shows a needle-type Triangular pointer.

You can achieve a wide variety of displays by varying the many settings associated with the pointer, like width, length, color, and pattern.

BI TIP

Remember that your audience will appreciate a consistent visual pattern; to achieve that, find a set of gauge properties that is appealing, and use them consistently for all gauges you create. This will make your work recognizable and valued.

The scale, that design element the pointer is measured against, is our next topic. In order to properly set the scale properties, you must be familiar with the type of data the gauge will represent. Basic knowledge of several different industries and their business processes and measurement techniques will allow you to have meaningful discussions with your stakeholders about what is important for them to know to keep the organization on course. Providing this kind of information and analysis will help foster the knowledge needed for effectively managing the organization.

Setting the Radial Gauge Scale Properties

To set the scale properties, determine the value the gauge will display and how you want to represent it. Will this gauge display an actual value or a percentage of a goal amount? This must be determined before the scale can be set appropriately. For our example, two scales will be used—the Primary Scale will display actual dollar value, the Secondary Scale will display percentage of goal. There is one important property that cannot be set from the Properties pane—the number type. So to begin with we will use the Radial Scale Properties dialog box to set this attribute:

1. Right-click the existing gauge scale (Primary) and choose Scale Properties from the context menu, as shown in Figure 2-40.

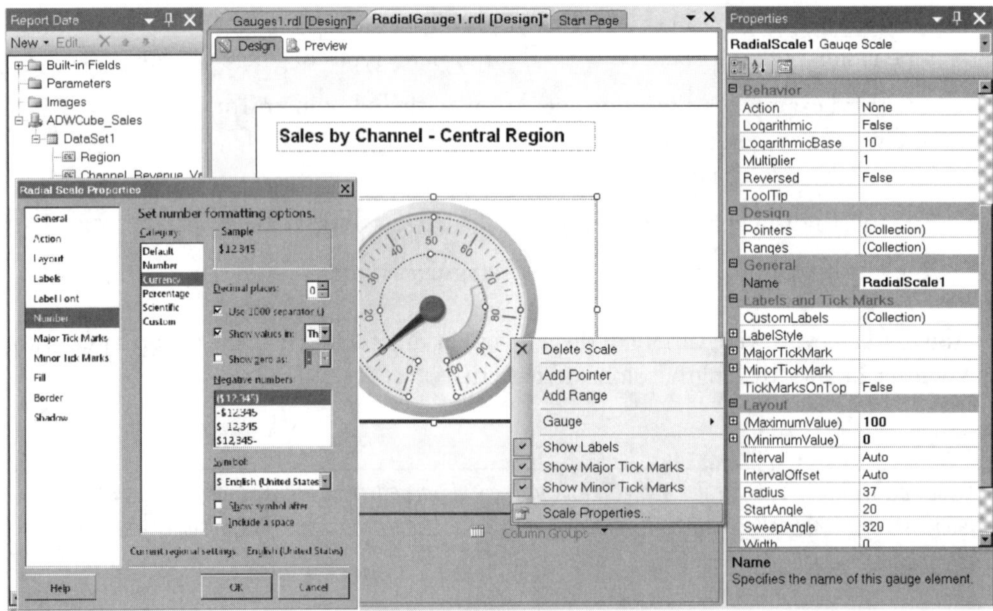

Figure 2-40 *Radial Gauge Scale Properties—Number Formatting*

2. Choose the Number pane of the dialog box, shown in Figure 2-40. The Primary Scale will display the actual channel revenue amount, so choose Currency as the number format. With large numbers, decimal places are rarely useful. Using the thousands separator will make the numbers more readable, and if the numbers are very large (millions), then displaying them in Thousands will make the labels smaller. There are also choices for how zero and negative numbers are displayed.
3. Click the OK button at the bottom of the dialog box to save changes. We will set the other properties through the Properties pane.

BI TIP

All properties can be set through the dialog boxes or through the Properties pane—although some are exclusive to one display or the other (these are pointed out). When working in the Properties pane, if you change a value, then tab or click to another property, the changed value will be saved. In the dialog boxes, you must click OK before the changes are made. For this reason, it is easier to make changes and test the display by simply making changes using the Properties pane.

4. Click the scale in the design surface again to activate that area and make the Radial Scale Properties pane display.
5. The Maximum and Minimum values displayed, Interval, Start Angle, and Sweep Angle are all found under the Layout section of the Properties pane. For this example, we have entered the following expression for the Maximum Value:

```
Sum(Fields!Channel_Revenue_Goal.Value, "DataSet1")
```

This will make the Channel Revenue Goal Amount the maximum value on the scale. For the Minimum Value, use this formula:

```
=Sum(Fields!Channel_Revenue_Goal.Value, "DataSet1")*.5
```

This will allow us to set the ranges for Warning, Caution, and Favorable based on percent of goal.

BI TIP

If the primary scale will display large numbers, change the Minimum value from the default 0 to a formula that calculates a reasonable "base" value for the display. Problems occur when beginning the scale at 0 when the value has very large numbers: tick marks become compressed and the variation between values is hard to distinguish. If you know the data, you may be tempted to enter a fixed number into the Max or Min value fields. But what if your values change wildly from year to year or quarter to quarter? Then manual updates would be necessary to change those values and republish the gauge—thus it's better to use a formula that uses the query results to set the scale.

6. Leave the Interval and Interval Offset properties set to Auto. You can attempt to calculate these yourself, but you probably won't do a better job than the application. And again, if hard-coded values are used, they must be updated when the data changes.
7. Also in the Layout section are the Radius, Start Angle, and Sweep Angle properties. Radius determines how large the scale is inside the frame. Start Angle determines where on the circular (or partial circular) gauge the scale begins, with 0 being due south. The default is 20. Sweep Angle determines how large a range the scale covers, with 360° being a full circle; the default is 320.
8. The next property to set is the Major Tick Marks. The defaults are DimGray rectangular marks that cross the scale, with a length of 10 and a width of 2. Change the border or fill color, length, width, placement, and shape to suit your design standards. For this example, we will use the defaults.
9. Also under the Layout section of the Properties pane is a property named Width. This actually refers to the width of the scale bar itself. All other properties for the scale bar are under the Appearance section. A scale bar is shown in Figure 2-41.
10. And finally, there are two properties that are not included in the dialog boxes: Maximum Pin and Minimum Pin. Scale pins may sit outside of the scale, have a different shape, and prevent the pointer from exceeding the Pin values. For example, if you set a Minimum Pin of 5, the pin will appear before the scale and if there is no data, the pointer will rest against it instead of pointing straight down. A Minimum Pin is shown in Figure 2-41.

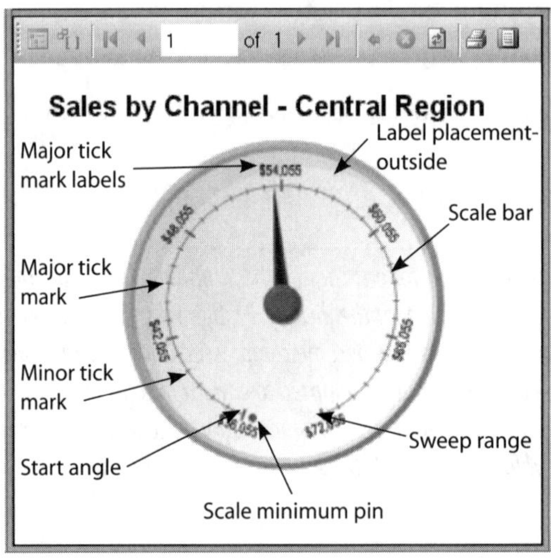

Figure 2-41 *Radial Gauge Scale Properties*

Now that we have the Primary Scale properties set, let us add another scale to show the percentage of goal achieved.

Creating a Secondary Scale

Secondary scales use the same pointer but have a different range of values. This allows you to make comparisons and gain qualitative insight into the measure displayed. To create a secondary scale for this gauge, return to the report design surface.

1. Right-click the gauge panel and select Add Scale from the context menu.
2. Another scale will be placed inside the existing one, and the Gauge Scale Properties pane will display.
3. Right-click the scale area and select Scale Properties from the context menu; then select the Numbers pane.
4. Set the number category as Percentage, Decimal Places to 0.
5. Click the General pane to set the scale minimum and maximum values.
6. Since there is only one pointer, the Secondary Scale needs to be aligned with the Primary Scale in order to display the correct values. Remember that the Primary Scale Maximum value equals the Channel Revenue Goal Amount and the Minimum value was equal to 50 percent of the goal amount. So for the Secondary Scale, the Maximum value should be 1 (equal to 100 percent). The Minimum value was set to 50 percent of the goal value, so on the Secondary Scale the Minimum should be set to 0.5 (which equals 50 percent). Setting the scale in this way ensures that the numerical value and the percentage value indicated by the pointer will be aligned.
7. Click the Minor Tick Marks pane, and click the Hide Minor Tick Marks check box. Then click the OK button at the bottom of the dialog box to save all the settings.

Now our radial gauge has two scales, the primary scale indicates the actual dollar amount of channel revenue, and the secondary scale shows the percentage of revenue goal that amount represents. Let's add one more visual component to help identify the Warning, Caution, and Favorable ratings of these values—the scale ranges.

Adding Scale Ranges to Radial Gauges

Scale ranges are the color bars that are inside, across, or outside of a scale range. They generally connote a rating associated with the value being displayed. If the organization is using Balanced Scorecard methodology or has developed key performance indicators (KPIs) or critical success factor (CSF) metrics, then generally, goal amounts and other boundary values are established when defining these metrics. If that is not the case, then using normative values may assist management with determining what the actual boundaries should be.

This example will use these boundaries:

- **Warning** Less than 75 percent of goal amount
- **Caution** Between 75 percent and 90 percent of goal amount
- **Favorable** 90 percent of goal amount or better

To add a range to a scale, return to the report design surface. Each range needs to be added individually, so repeat this process for each range you wish to add to the gauge.

1. As shown in Figure 2-42, right-click the scale you would like to add a range to. To have the ranges display between the Primary and Secondary Scales, there is a choice to make. The ranges could be placed in the inside position of the Primary Scale, or in the outside position on the Secondary Scale. Because the boundary values to use for the range start and end values are based on a percentage of goal amount, it makes more sense to choose the Secondary Scale, which is based on goal amount and has a percentage number format.
2. Click Add Range from the context menu. The Radial Scale Range Properties dialog box will display, as illustrated in Figure 2-43. Start by adding the warning range.
3. In the General pane, enter the values that correspond to the minimum and maximum values for this range, in this example, 0.5 and 0.75 respectively. Set Placement Relative To Scale to Outside. Start Width and End Width control how much dimensional flare the range has.

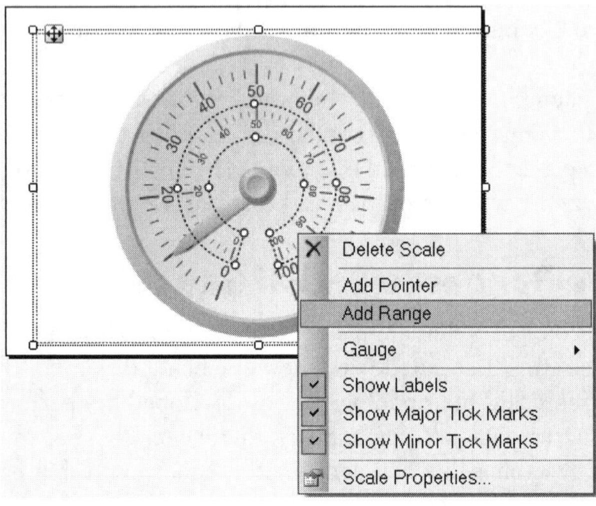

Figure 2-42 *Add Range From Scale context menu*

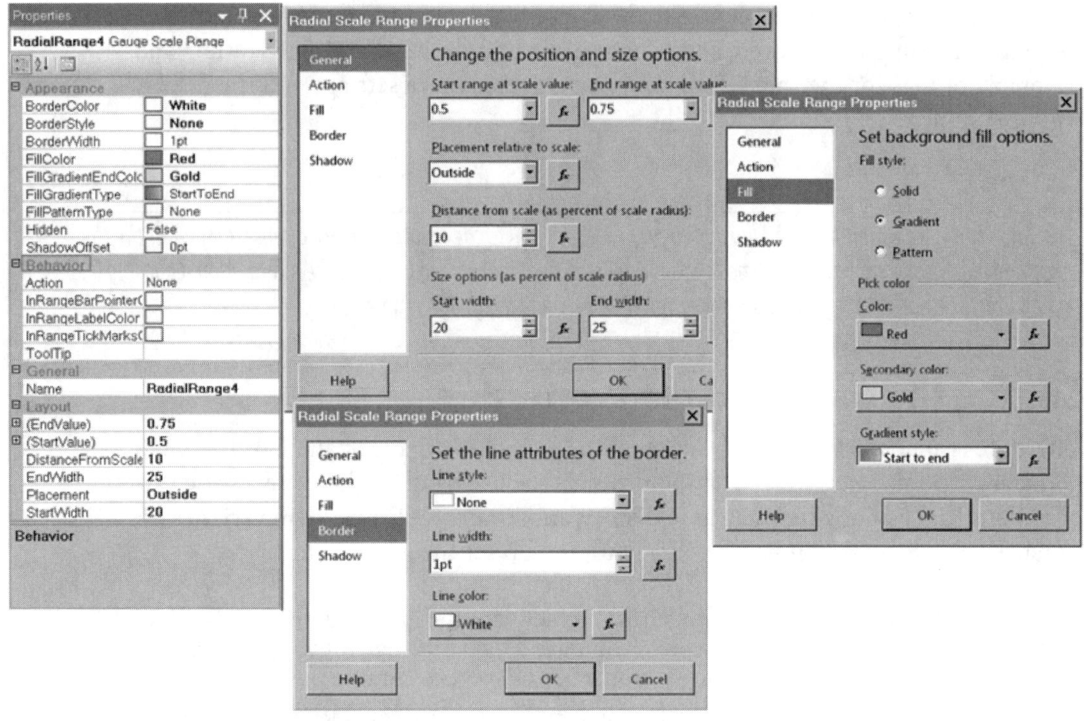

Figure 2-43 *Range Properties pane and dialogs*

4. Click the Fill pane, select Solid, Gradient, or Pattern Fill Style, and set the colors for the range. This is the Warning range, so choose Gradient style, begin with Red and end with Gold, and set the Gradient Pattern to Start To End, as shown in Figure 2-43.
5. Choose the Border pane. To lessen the demarcation between ranges, set the Line Style to None.
6. Click the OK button at the bottom of the dialog box to save changes.
7. Repeat the preceding procedure for each range to add.

You can also set most of these properties by changing the values in the Gauge Scale Range Properties pane as well. The Fill options are under the Appearance section, as are the Border settings. The General options are under the Layout section of the Properties pane. If you want to test different settings, change them in the Properties pane, and when you tab out of the text box, it will save the setting. This is generally easier and quicker than opening and saving through the Properties dialog boxes.

So now the radial gauge is configured—it has two scales, one for values and one for percentage of goal achieved, and it has ranges to indicate Warning, Caution, and Favorable ratings for the value displayed. Just a couple more settings and the display will be complete.

BI TIP

Always set the scale minimum and maximum properties—it gives the report audience a context for what they are viewing. Displaying a scale with no labels is not helpful when trying to interpret the information. Choosing the correct scale and setting its properties correctly will elevate the gauge's value!

Setting the Gauge Frame Properties

There are two borders that can be applied to gauges—the gauge panel border (outer boundary) and the gauge frame, also known as the backframe. There are a wide variety of options for customizing the frame display, and if none of the built-in varieties are suitable, you can always import an image to use! To set the gauge frame,

1. Click the gauge on the design surface to activate the area and display the Radial Gauge Properties pane, as shown in Figure 2-44. Alternatively, right-click the gauge and select use the Gauge Properties dialog box, Frame pane.
2. In the Frame Shape Property, choose a style that suits your design objectives. Beside the standard choices, there are about 15 different custom choices available. The example uses Custom Circular 9.

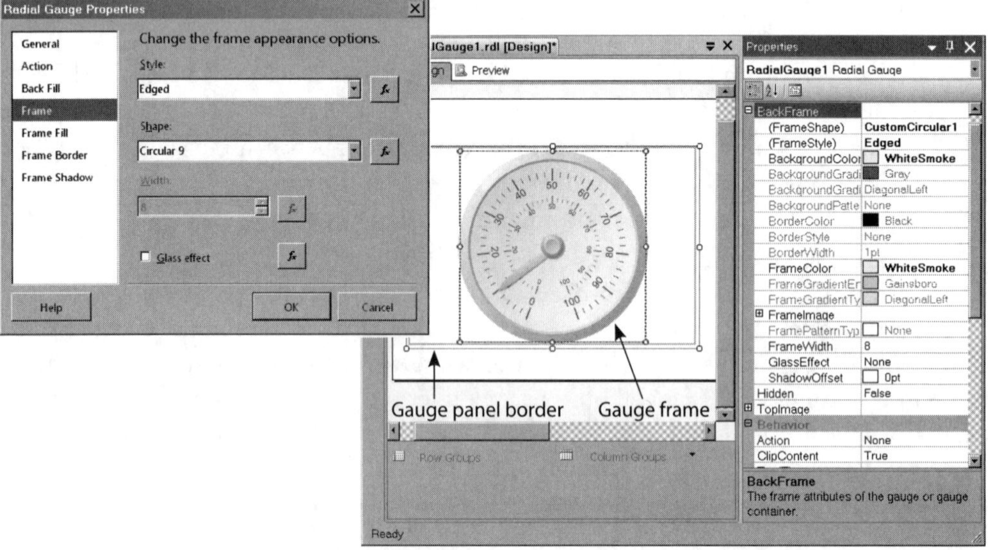

Figure 2-44 *Gauge panel border and gauge frame*

3. Background color can also be changed, but Background Gradient End Color, Background Gradient Type, and Background Gradient Pattern Type are fixed. If you are going to use the Glass effect, make sure your background color is light, or it will be hard to read.
4. If the metallic silver finish isn't acceptable, choose the Frame Color. The Frame Gradient End Color and Frame Gradient Type are fixed.
5. Another option is the Glass effect. When chosen, it makes the gauge appear as if it is under glass by darkening the display and adding reflection highlights. Simple Glass Effect and No Glass Effect both are shown in Figure 2-45.

Setting an appealing backframe will give the gauge a more polished look. Choose gauge panel borders carefully. Depending on how the gauge will be displayed, the border could be unnecessary. Remember, keep the focus on the gauge, not the surrounding embellishments.

Now that we have all the properties set, time to see the finished product. Figure 2-45 shows the resulting gauges with the following attributes:

- A Pointer that is a Triangular Needle style in a dark color, with flat indented cap in a lighter shade
- A Primary Scale showing Channel Revenue Amount in $K, with scale bar, major and minor tick marks
- A Secondary Scale showing Channel Revenue as percentage of goal, with only major tick marks
- Scales that start at 20° and have a 320° sweep range
- Ranges that display gradient colors from Red, Amber, and Green to show boundaries of Warning, Caution, and Favorable revenue goal ratings
- A Minimum scale pin that shows as a red dot before the scale begins
- A gauge background color in a light pastel color
- A gauge frame that is Custom Circular 9 in a medium primary color
- No Glass Effect and Simple Glass Effect
- Gauge panel border in a light neutral hue

As you can see in Figure 2-45, varying only one property setting (Glass effect) can have a large impact on the display of the gauge. The Glass effect can make the gauge more difficult to read, so make sure your design elements have high contrast.

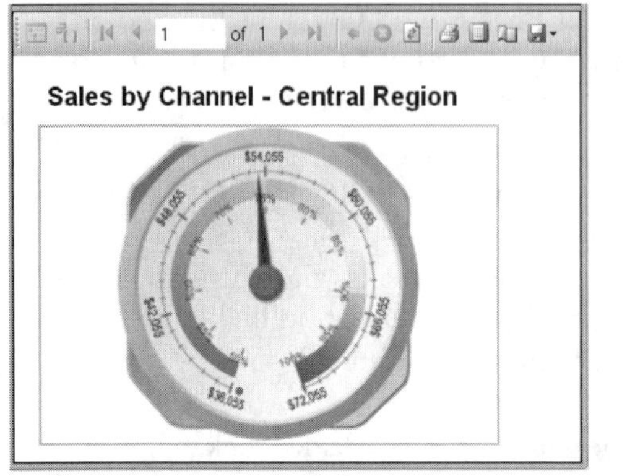

No Glass Effect

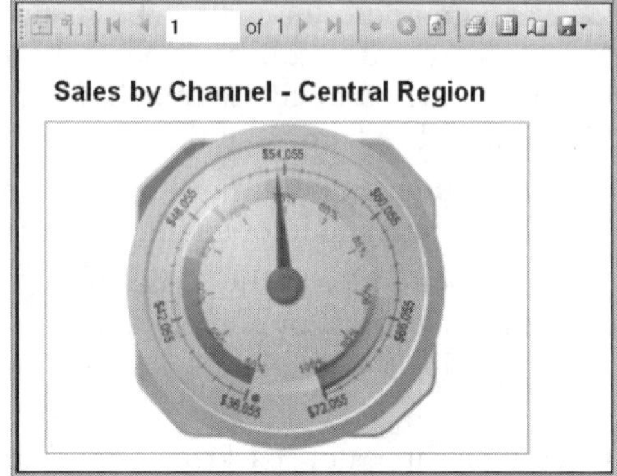

Simple Glass Effect

Figure 2-45 *Configured gauge with all properties set—Showing Glass Effect and No Glass Effect*

Gauge Pointers and Formulas for Data Display

Since gauge pointers can only display one value, there are several properties found in the Gauge Pointer Properties, Data Section that can allow you to manipulate the data without changing the report query. These can be particularly useful and save having to write complex queries to obtain the required results. For example, you may want your gauge to display maximum sales order by salesperson by fiscal year. Just return the whole dataset and use the MAX formula to retrieve the value sought.

Variance is another formula that should get a lot of use in gauges. Consider a gauge displaying response times to a call center. Measuring against established Service Level Agreements (SLAs) is useful, but what if you found that the variance was very broad? It may prompt you to investigate the cause of the variance, and thus improve overall call center performance. Here are the various formulas available for gauge data values.

- **Average** The gauge will calculate the average data value from a dataset and apply it to the pointer.
- **Linear** The gauge will calculate a data value using the formula Value * Multiplier + Addend ($f(x) = x * m + a$), and apply it to the pointer.
- **Max** The gauge will calculate the maximum data value from a dataset and apply it to the pointer.
- **Min** The gauge will calculate the minimum data value from a dataset and apply it to the pointer.

- **Median** The gauge will calculate the median data value from a dataset and apply it to the pointer.
- **OpenClose** The gauge will determine the open and close data values from a dataset and apply the values to either dynamic pointers or a range's minimum and maximum values.
- **Percentile** The gauge control will calculate percentile data values from a dataset and apply the set of values to either dynamic pointers or a range's minimum and maximum values. The MinPercent and MaxPercent can be specified in the Value Properties settings.
- **Variance** The gauge will calculate the variance data value from a dataset and apply it to the pointer or range value.

Interesting Component Behaviors

There are several properties that add interest but are seldom used. The first is called *snapping behavior.* The snapping behavior is when the pointer must point (snap) to a tick mark instead of the exact place on the scale that represents its value. When setting Pointer Properties, look under the Behavior section for Action, Snapping Enabled, Snapping Interval, and ToolTip. These properties are available on either radial or linear gauges.

Consider this example: a scale from 1 to 20, where the major tick marks are in intervals of 5 and the minor tick marks represent 1. If snapping is enabled, and the snapping interval set to 0 or 1, a value of 13.5 would point to the minor tick mark that represents 14—the next higher value, instead of pointing to the space between the tick marks 13 and 14. If the snapping interval was set to 5, the pointer would always point to a major tick mark; in this case, given the value of 13.5, the pointer would point at the major tick mark for 15. You may be asking, why would you want to do this? If the value being displayed is highly variable by small amounts, and that minor variance is inconsequential to how the information is used for decision making, then snapping behavior will smooth out the negligible changes that may appear and simply be annoying.

Another interesting behavior is found for Scale Ranges; it is the In Range variations that can be set for Bar Pointer Color, Label Color, and Tick Marks Color. This only works with bar-type pointers but is available on both linear and radial gauges. Remember that viewers with visual impairments like color blindness may not be able to distinguish the subtle differences, so label well to give context to the display. Figure 2-46 shows an example of a linear gauge with a bar pointer that has color variation based on in-range values. Notice that the range itself has the Hidden property set to True. It seems redundant to have a Color Range showing when the bar pointer is going to display that color.

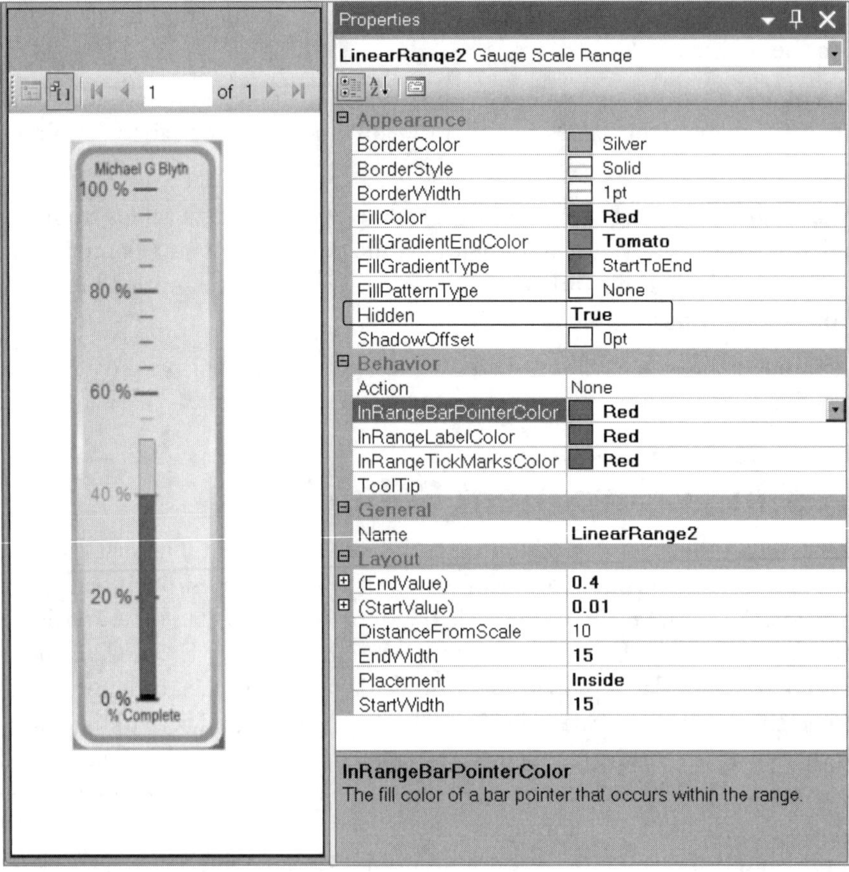

Figure 2-46 *In Range Bar Pointer behavior*

The In Range Bar Pointer variation is an interesting addition to gauge style, and this feature may be very useful in space-constrained dashboards.

The Gauge Panel and Multiple Gauge Items

The *gauge panel* is the container item that can hold one or many gauges for a display. The gauge panel is the object that is connected to the dataset, so all objects that are contained within the gauge panel will share that dataset. We presented an example earlier in the chapter that used separate gauge panels so that specific data filters could be applied to each individual gauge. Now let's explore the opposite condition: all gauges share the same dataset and can display comparisons found within it. That doesn't mean that all gauges within one gauge panel will display the same thing!

BI TIP

When working with creating gauges and performance management display metrics, formulate several related questions in your data query so that you will have a robust resulting dataset. That will give you maximum flexibility in developing the gauge metric display with multiple gauges.

Putting Multiple Gauges into the Gauge Panel

The earlier example of the Bullet Graph linear gauges shows multiple gauge panels all using the same data source. Now let's have an example of several gauges all within the same gauge panel. Keeping all items together in one gauge panel will have less overhead and will keep all items synchronized with changes in the source data. In order to add a gauge to a gauge panel,

1. On the design surface, click the gauge to give it focus. Right-click inside the gauge boundary, and select Add Gauge from the context menu, as shown in Figure 2-47.

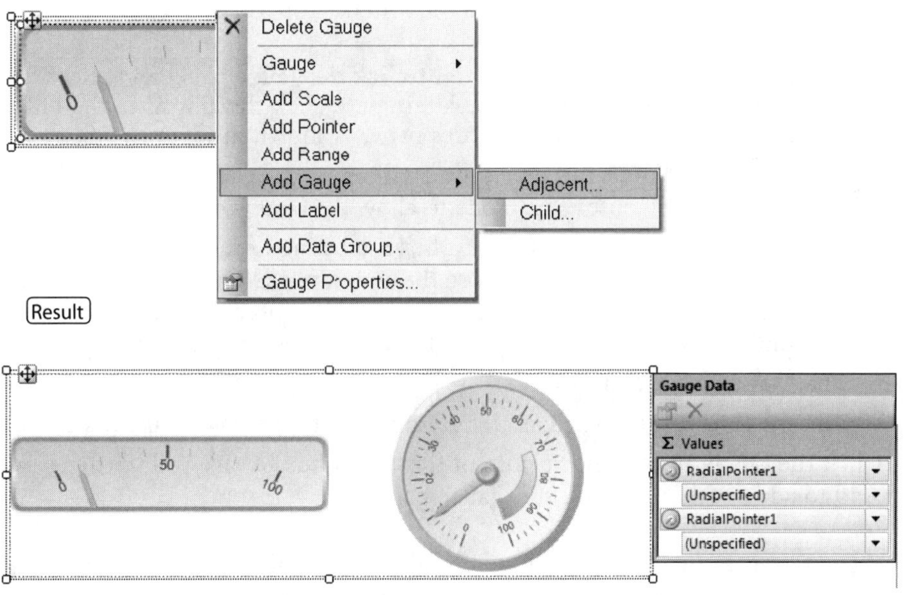

Figure 2-47 *Add Gauge to Gauge Panel context menu*

2. There is a choice between adding an Adjacent Gauge or a Child Gauge. Adjacent items share the dataset and other gauge panel properties, including the space allotted. Child items are subordinate to the initial gauge and are shown as smaller items within the first gauge control, like the radial gauge with Mini-Gauge option in the Gauge Types dialog box.
3. For this example, choose Adjacent.
4. The Gauge Type selection box will appear and you can choose which gauge type you want, radial or linear.
5. Once selected, the new gauge will display alongside the initial gauge in the same gauge panel, as shown in Figure 2-47.
6. Notice that the drop data zone now has two pointer placeholders. Each pointer has its own data binding. Drag a data element from the Dataset pane onto each Pointer placeholder.

Then each gauge will have to be configured normally—set the scale minimum and maximum, format the pointer, add ranges if desired. You can set the filter for all gauges within the gauge panel. So, for example, if you wanted to create a display with several gauges sliced by a dimension (for instance, Geography), create one gauge panel with all gauges for that region, then add a data group filter to each of the gauge panels. Figure 2-48 displays the sequence to get to the Filters Property dialog box:

1. On the design surface of the report, right-click the gauge panel and select Add; Data Group from the context menu. Alternately, click the ellipsis in the Filters Property on the Gauge Panel Properties pane, as shown in Figure 2-48.
2. The Gauge Panel Properties dialog box will appear. To add a filter, click Add; the detail section will enter edit mode to allow data entry of the filter.
3. The drop-down for the Expression text box is a listing of the dataset fields, and the choice for a custom expression. Choose the geographical dimension of interest, in this case Region. The Data Type text box will display the metadata for the expression field. When creating a new field, you must set the data type.
4. Set the Operator to equal (=).
5. Type in the exact text to match; in this example Northeast is what appears in the data.
6. Click the OK button at the bottom of the dialog box to save your changes or click Add to add another filter for this gauge panel.

Use data filters on the gauge panel to keep all gauges within the panel displaying consistent information. Filters are managed as collections because there can be many filters for each gauge panel. Labels and gauges are also managed as collections, because they too have a one-to-many relationship.

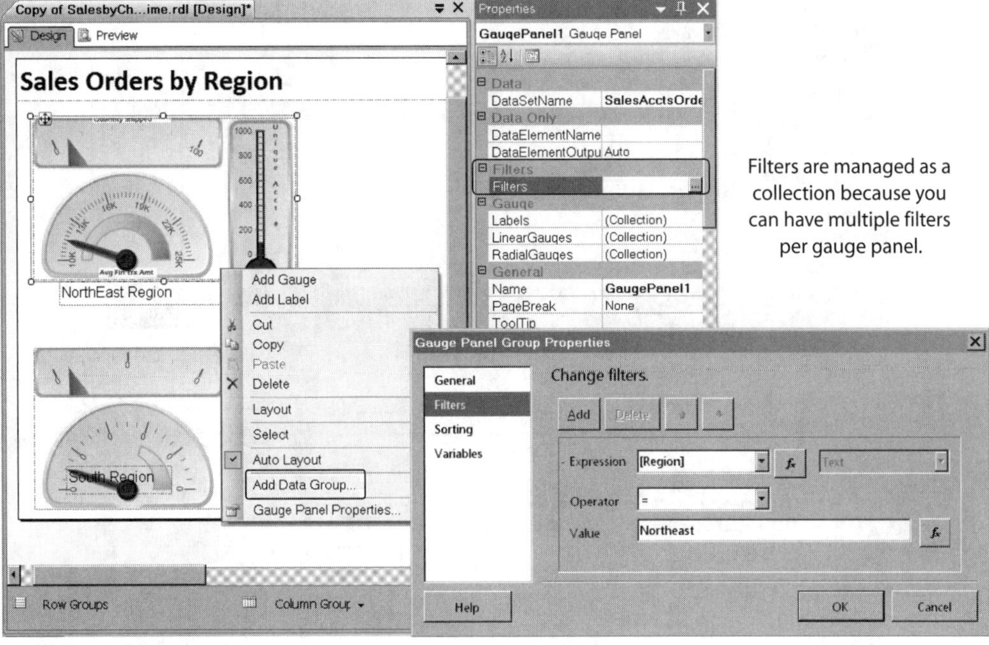

Figure 2-48 *Gauge panel—data group filter properties*

Using Gauges in Reports and Dashboards

Adding gauges to reports and dashboards can be an effective way to add emphasis to the numbers that are important. Gauges can be combined with numerical matrix reports or graphic matrix reports like the Sparkline report. They can also be effectively combined with other graphic components into a dashboard display. Delivery of charts and gauges using various display methods is the topic of Chapter 3, but one example will be shown here.

Let's use the Sparkline report created in Chapter 1 as the basis for this report example. As you may recall, the Sparkline report is a high-density report that is well suited to displaying relative comparisons.

Adding a Gauge to the Sparkline Report

Open the Sparkline report in Report Builder, and navigate to the design surface.

1. To add a new column to the Sparkline report, right-click inside the tablix, and choose Insert Column | Right from the context menu, as shown in Figure 2-49.

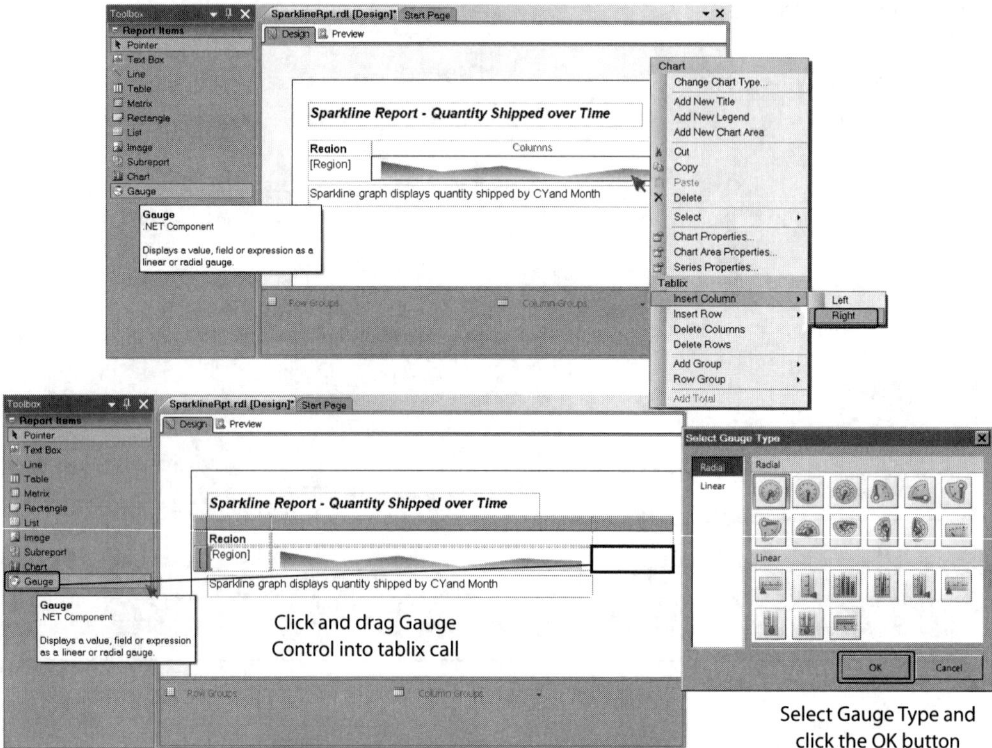

Figure 2-49 *Sparkline report modifications*

2. Once the new column has been created, click inside the new cell. Then click the Gauge control from the Toolbox and drag it into the tablix cell. The Select Gauge Type dialog box will appear.
3. The new gauge control will now appear in the tablix cell.

After making these modifications to the Sparkline report, the process of setting all the properties for the gauge commences. Use a radial gauge for this part of the report. Because the gauge will exist inside the tablix control, there are some operations that are not supported.

BI TIP

You cannot use aggregate functions, row count, or running total expressions for any gauge property when it is embedded in a tablix. That is because of the data scope of the tablix control and the interaction between the tablix and the gauge. This means, for example, that you cannot use the Min and Max functions to set the scale minimum and maximum values. So get familiar with your data before you set the scale properties.

Now that the gauge is on the design surface of the Sparkline report, it needs to be configured. The procedure and properties are the same, whether you are in Report Designer or Report Builder 3.0.

1. Click the gauge until the data drop zone is displayed. Choose Quantity_Shipped from the field list, as shown in Figure 2-50.
2. Click the gauge panel, and select Gauge Panel Properties from the Context menu.
3. In the Gauge Panel Properties dialog box, click Filters in the navigation pane, click Add, and add a Filter for Calendar Year = 2010. We don't need to set a filter for the geographic region, because that is taken care of by the tablix row group. Click the OK button at the bottom of the dialog box to save changes and return to the design surface.
4. Click the Gauge Scale until it becomes the focus, and the Gauge Scale Properties pane displays next to the design surface.
5. In the Gauge Scale Properties pane, in the Layout section, set the maximum value to 600, and the minimum value to 100.
6. Also in the Layout section, set the Start Angle to 40 and the Sweep Angle to 260.
7. If you would like scale pins, set those properties in the Scale Pins section.
8. Preview to make sure the display looks as expected. Make note of spacing considerations and proportion between the two graphic elements on the report. Ensure that context and measurement are clearly labeled and understandable.

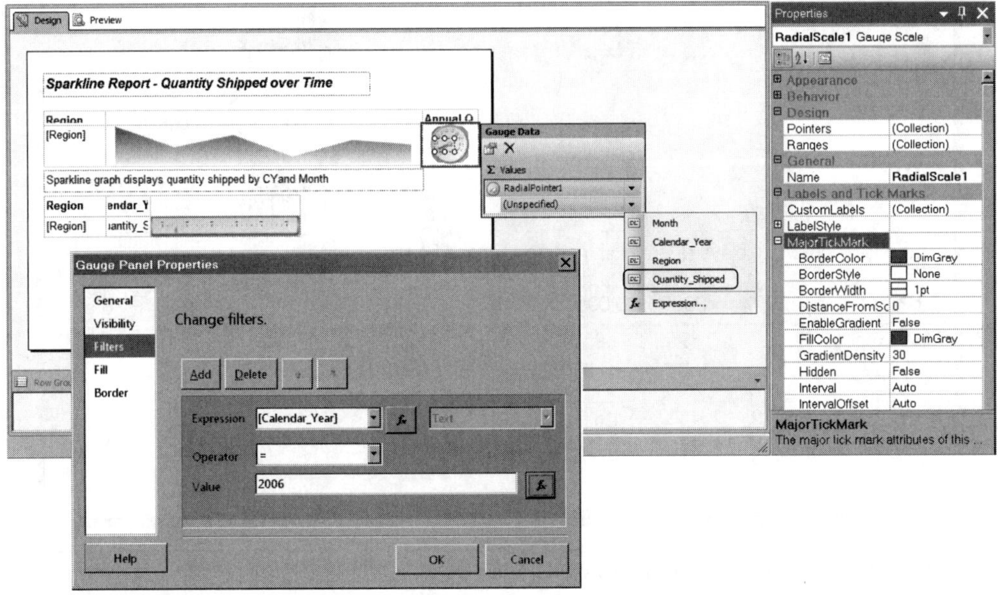

Figure 2-50 *Sparkline report—configure gauge properties*

Now preview the report and admire the results of your efforts, as shown in Figure 2-51. The Sparkline report now displays the quantity shipped over time by geographic region in a Sparkline chart, and it displays the calendar year 2006 quantity shipped by region in the radial gauge. We set the Calendar Year filter explicitly. The grouping by geographic region is controlled by the row grouping on the tablix, which restricts the data passed to the gauge. The table at the bottom of the report shows the data, along with a horizontal linear gauge that uses in-range pointer colors.

There are multiple ways to use the gauge on a dashboard, specifically in a Microsoft Office SharePoint Portal environment. Chapter 4 on visualization delivery will go into more depth on delivery methods for these reporting services objects.

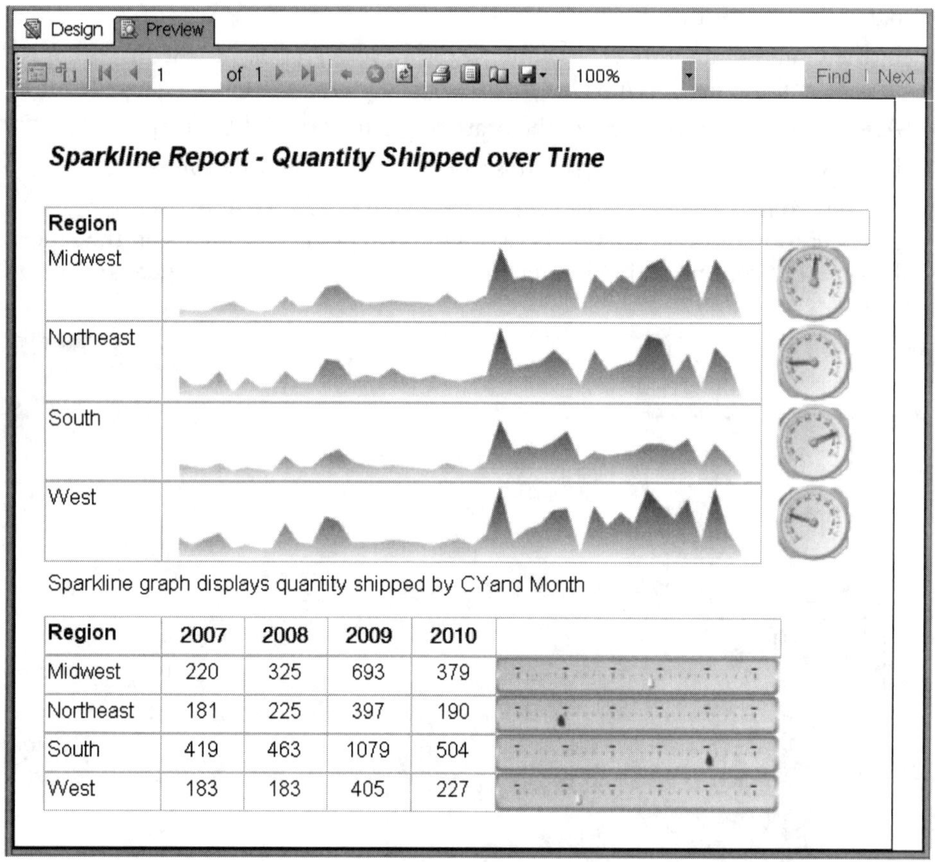

Region	2007	2008	2009	2010
Midwest	220	325	693	379
Northeast	181	225	397	190
South	419	463	1079	504
West	183	183	405	227

Figure 2-51 *Sparkline report with gauge example*

Wrap-Up

This chapter has been all about gauges, starting with determining the appropriate gauge for your information delivery needs. Use your knowledge of the subject matter and the report audience to determine the appropriate gauge type and style to use.

We walked through creating a new report in Report Builder 3.0. This exciting new report creation environment will allow end users with data savvy to create sophisticated-looking reports easily. The new ribbon menu interface makes this design environment mimic the Microsoft Office application experience, and also resembles Microsoft PerformancePoint's Dashboard Designer. Report Builder now fully supports using graphs, gauges, and maps as report objects. Once our report was created, we needed to select a gauge type to use. An overview of radial and linear gauges exposed all the property items that, when configured, produce a gauge.

The first example shows how to create a Bullet Chart gauge to display a measure, a goal amount, and the color ranges for Warning, Caution, and Favorable ratings. We examined pointer properties, scale properties, color ranges, and gauge filters. Learning how to configure these properties for the Bullet Graph gauge is a good overview into the other linear gauge types that are available, and the differences between them. We also looked at labels and ToolTips, scale number formatting, and scale pins.

Then we took a deep dive into a radial gauge, and for a second example, we built a 360° radial gauge. We delved into the nuances of the pointer types and properties for radial gauges, and the variations in scale properties that are available, including creating a secondary scale and controlling the color ranges that appear between the scales. We looked as some ways to change radial gauges from one size to another (like from 360 to 180) by altering certain property settings.

There are some interesting features on gauges that we explored, including in-range marker pointer behaviors, data formulas, and snapping behavior. These are exciting features, because they give the report designer more control over how the visualization represents the data; using them, you can give your gauges variety and make your images pop.

Finally, we have explored the many ways to put gauges into a report, as stand-alone items or as adjacent and child gauges within one gauge panel. There are many possibilities with the features that are available in this version of SSRS. Gauges and charts are important elements of good reports and dashboards, and we showed an example of incorporating a gauge into the Sparkline report created in Chapter 1. Chapter 4 will go into much greater detail about delivering charts and gauges in reports and dashboards using Reporting Services, SharePoint, and PerformancePoint.

Chapter 3

SQL Server 2008 R2 Map Reports

In This Chapter

- Report Builder Maps: A New Feature with SQL Server Reporting Services
- Designing a Basic U.S. Map from Report Builder Spatial Data
- Adding Analytical Color to the Map Report
- Fixing Some Common Map Report Data Source Errors
- Modifying the Map Geography Display Elements
- Adding Color Points to the Map Report
- Designing a Simple World Map from SQL Server Spatial Data
- Modifying the Map Geography Viewport
- Adding Charts to the Map Report
- Adding a Tooltip and Custom Point with Action to the Map Report
- Wrap-Up

We start this chapter with an immediate example shown below, the "Election Map" for the 2008 Presidential Election. End users intuitively pick up on the distribution of Red and Blue states—and the relative size of the bubbles showing Number of Electoral Votes. Also, the parts of the United States that tend to be Red (Republican) or Blue (Democrat) give us a visual grasp of geographic areas of strength for our major political parties.

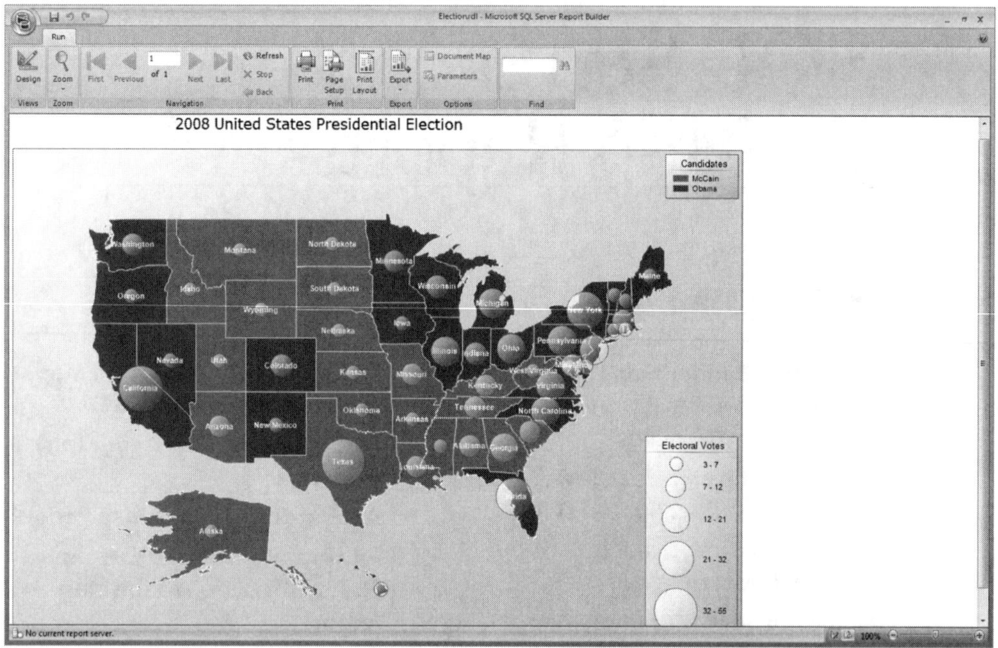

This is why people use a map. The same data could be displayed in a table or matrix (rows and columns)—but it would not be nearly as informative because only a map can convey a sense of analysis against real-world geography. Maps complement the way we see our world and allow us to match analytical data to countries-states-provinces. The Election Map example proves the effectiveness of this "geo-display" mechanism because almost everyone recognizes it and understands the visualization of state-by-state political and cultural characteristics.

Report Builder Maps: A New Feature with SQL Server Reporting Services

SQL Server has long had the three main building blocks of its business intelligence platform: Integration Services, Analysis Services, and Reporting Services. And since the year 2000 (and SQL Server 2000), Microsoft has been remarkably consistent in continuing to build out these three "pillars" of the SQL Server business intelligence capabilities. SQL Server 2005 saw a rewrite of these capabilities (especially Integration Services—to become a truly world-class extraction, transformation, and loading ["ETL"] tool set), and the addition of the Report Builder to the Reporting Services tool set, which already included the Report Designer.

BI TIP

The SQL Server Report Designer uses Microsoft's Visual Studio integrated design environment (or IDE) with a rich feature set to create sophisticated reports, whereas the SQL Server Report Builder uses its own relatively simple Office 2007–like (ribbon menu) design user interface to create reports.

With SQL Server 2008 R2, which releases to market in 2010 as a "business intelligence refresh" improvement for the SQL Server 2008 platform, Microsoft has significantly enhanced the Report Builder—by acquiring the world-class Dundas Map technology, and integrating it natively into SQL Server Reporting Services 2008 R2. Furthermore, Microsoft added support for Bing Maps and SQL Server spatial data types!

This means that SQL Server customers can now make use of Microsoft's leading-edge map reporting software—wholly within the SQL Server Reporting Services Report Builder tool set, with no cost other than SQL Server itself. Note that Microsoft's internal product name for SQL Server 2008 R2 was Kilimanjaro, in case you see references to the product by this name in articles and blogs.

This chapter will focus on the map capabilities of Report Builder 3.0, whereas other chapters in this book will explore the "table and matrix" (which combine to form a "tablix") capabilities. Figure 3-1 shows the map report design screen for the new Report Builder 3.0.

A. **Ribbon menu** This is the main menu for the Report Builder, with Office 2007–like menu tabs and groups of menu options.

B. **Report Elements** This pane provides a Visual Studio–like tree view of all the pieces of a report, including fields, parameters, and data sources.

C. **Row and Column Groups** These panes provide design areas to arrange data elements into rows and columns when creating a table or matrix report.

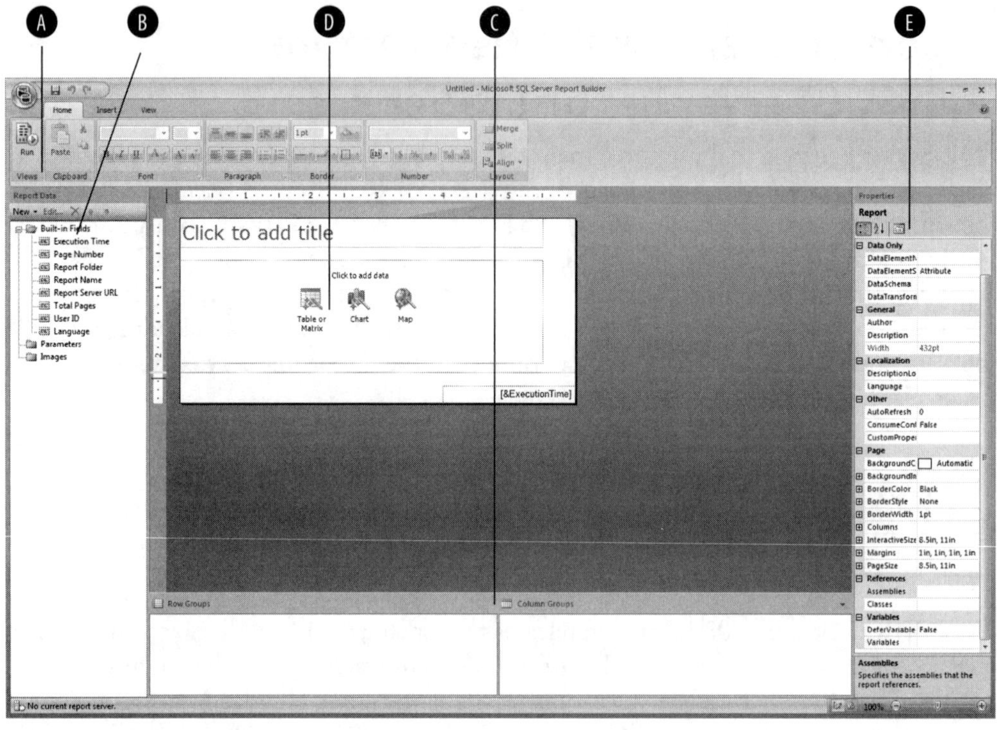

Figure 3-1 *SQL Server 2008 R2 Report Builder design screen: a .NET Windows application*

D. **Report Wizard** These icons start the wizard process for designing tablix, chart, or map report components (which can be combined into a single report).

E. **Report Element Properties** This pane provides a Visual Studio–like tree view of detailed properties of report elements or components.

Note in the Report Builder design screen, the report-map components can be edited by right-clicking the component in the central design pane, to display a drop-down menu of choices. Alternatively, the components can be edited by exploring the right-side Properties tree-view pane, to display very detailed and editable properties of all report elements.

The SQL Server Report Builder comes with 51 "embedded" maps that can be used for the geo-display Polygon layer—a U.S. map and 50 state maps that function as templates on which to display geospatial data. Alternatively, a map layer can be created in Report Builder from SQL Server 2008 geospatial data or by connecting to an ESRI shape file.

At this early point in the chapter, a brief description of spatial data is in order. This chapter will use the following two types of spatial data:

1. **Report-embedded spatial data** This is a self-contained XML format of geo-data that can be used to display a predefined map, such as the United States map we use in this chapter for our first working map example. It's easy because the "embedded" United States map comes with the SQL Server 2008 R2 Report Builder, and so we can use it for U.S. and state displays without having to go out and find geo-data from an outside source. Figure 3-2 shows an example of the contents of a Report Builder embedded format from the Report Definition File for a report.
2. **SQL Server geographic data column** This is a SQL Server 2008 spatial data type that can contain point, line, and polygon data. The polygon is of most interest to us, since the second working example in this chapter will use multiple polygons—actually one polygon per country—to display a World Map with Countries. Figure 3-3 shows an example of a SQL Server geographic data element that contains polygon definitions in the ShapeData column. Note the ShapeData rows also contain country names that can be used to "match" to analytical data, on a country-by-country basis, as you'll see later in the chapter.

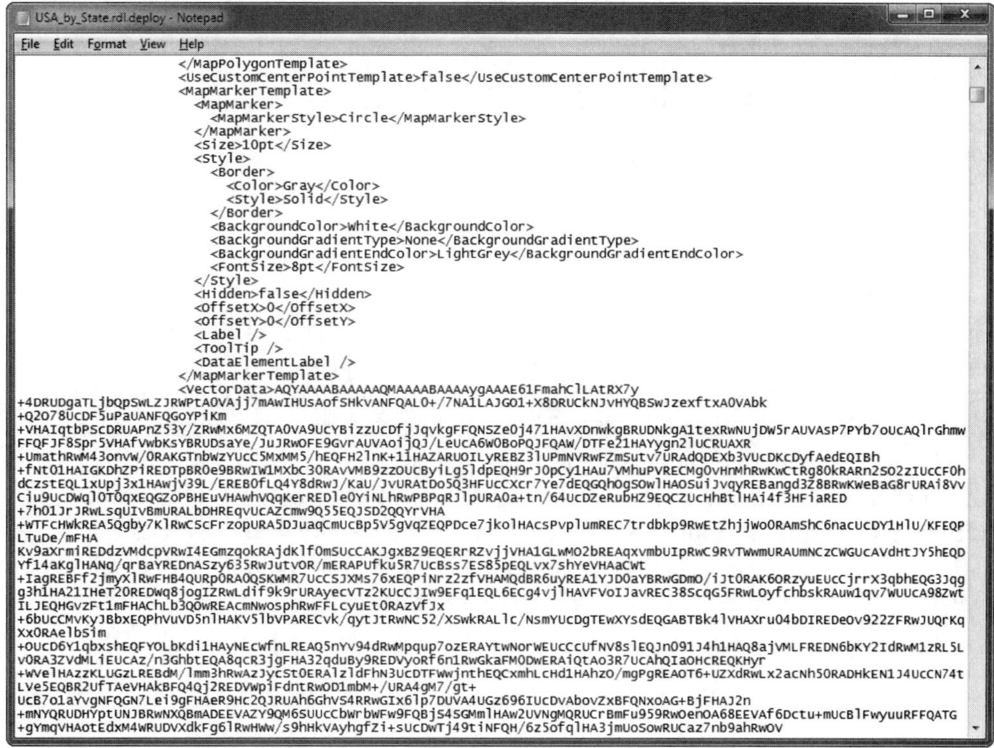

Figure 3-2 *Example of a SQL Server 2008 Report Builder embedded spatial dataset*

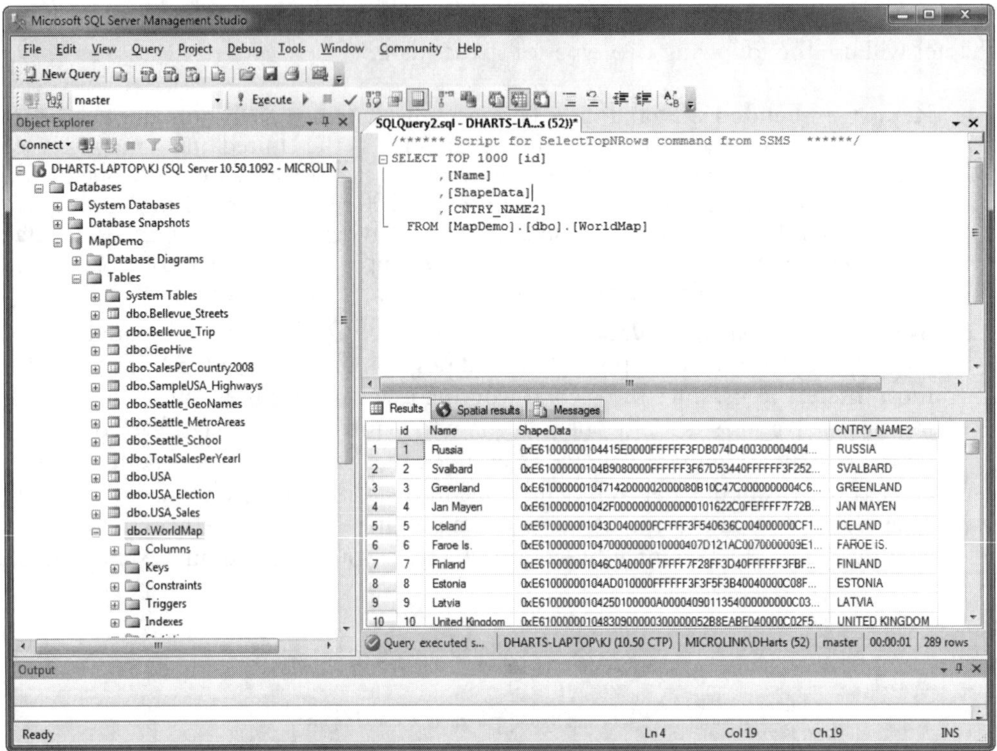

Figure 3-3 *Example of a SQL Server 2008 geographic data element*

For completeness of discussion, an ESRI shape file is a format that is commonly available from government web sites. SQL Server 2008 R2 Report Builder can use these shape files as a source of spatial data, as shown in Figure 3-4 where you see Report Builder opening a shape file (with an overlay of what the shape file looks like when opened in Notepad). Shape "files" are actually made up of at least three files: a .SHP file that contains the geo-point, -line, and -polygon data, a .SHX file that contains index data to the .SHP file contents for speed of access and calculation, and a .DBF file that holds attribute information about the geo-data in the .SHP file.

The polygon concept makes sense with a map that is used in a report to display analytical data, such as population per state, or sales per country—where we wish to

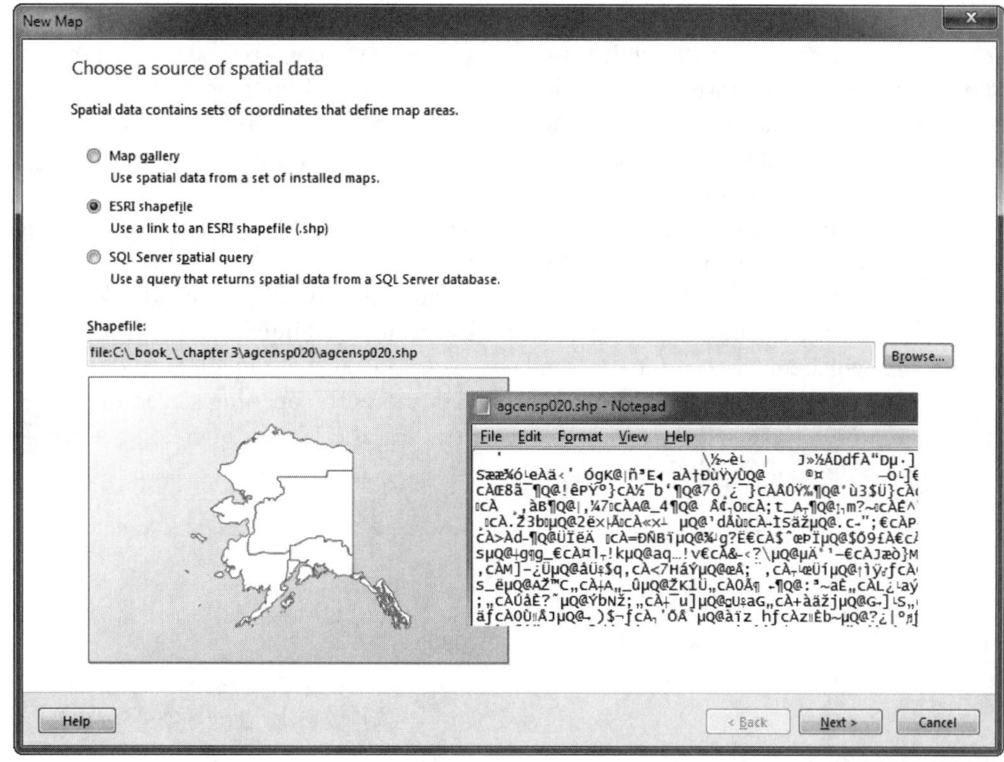

Figure 3-4 *Example of a SQL Server 2008 shape file*

use a color scale to visually show relative levels of population or sales from state to state or country to country on the map. The Report Builder map technology does the job of matching analytical data to spatial data, on a polygon-by-polygon basis. This will become clear as we go through the working example in this chapter.

BI TIP

Every map report starts with a geospatial display layer; which can be a tile layer *that draws its geo-display from an online connection to Bing Maps (Microsoft has renamed Virtual Earth to Bing Maps) or can be a* polygon layer *that draws its geo-display from a report-embedded map (does not require an online connection), or a SQL Server geo-data source, or an ESRI shape file.*

The "wizard" approach to designing maps is normally recommended by the Microsoft product team, since it walks the user through the map/data-source/visualization process to produce a map that conveys information to the consumer of the report-map display. Note that map reports are designed within the broader context of "business intelligence" where we strive to create data visualizations that place information in a display that provides some analytical value.

Table 3-1 shows the important types of maps that you'll look at in this chapter, using the Map Wizard method of creating map reports.

So let's get started with the Report Builder, version 3.0. Initially, we are going to use the Map Wizard because the wizard walks us through the building blocks of a map report, which are easier to understand when we look at them in a logical design process with step-by-step menu actions. Figure 3-5 shows the opening screen in the SQL Server 2008 Report Builder, where we are starting the process of creating a simple United States map of population data.

Wizard Graphic	Map Style	Description
	Basic map	A map that displays polygons as areas; for example, states in the United States. The colors are varied by choosing a palette of predefined colors.
	Color Analytical map	A map that displays polygons as areas; for example, states in the United States. The colors are varied by choosing a color range to represent ranges of analytical data; for example, population by state.
	Bubble map	A map that displays polygons as areas; for example, states in the United States. The analytical data is represented by bubbles that can be varied both by color ranges and size ranges.

Table 3-1 *Report Builder "Wizard" Map Style Choices*

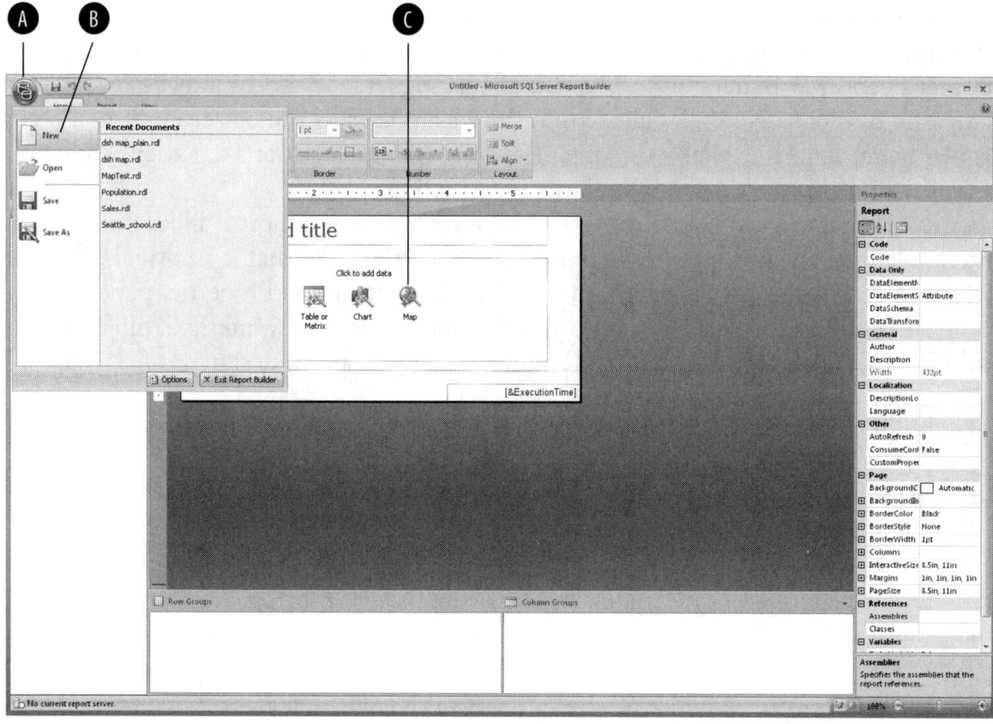

Figure 3-5 *Report Builder: starting a new map*

Designing a Basic U.S. Map from Report Builder Spatial Data

This section will discuss the creation/design of a simple map report, using the Report Builder Map Wizard. We will choose a map layer with spatial data, associate the spatial data with analytical data, and render a simple default display of associated analytical values with a color range for visualization of population data in a U.S. map.

In Figure 3-5 we are simply creating a new report, which will be a map report in the Report Designer. These steps are the same as with other Microsoft Office business intelligence design tools for reports and charting.

1. Click the Office Menu button in the upper-left corner of the Report Designer screen (Step A).
2. Choose New to start a new report (Step B).
3. Click the Map Wizard icon in the central report design pane (Step C).

In Figure 3-5 we are using the Report Builder Wizard icon to start the process of designing a new map report. Microsoft put a lot of work into making this wizard process a good way to demystify the work of creating a map that combines geo-data with analytical data. Note that all steps in the wizard process can be accomplished with regular menu actions as well—the wizard just ties the menu actions together in a logical sequence of dialog boxes that contain the menu actions.

Also worth noting is that all the elements of maps in the Report Builder design interface are accessible through the right-side Properties pane that is a normal part of Microsoft integrated design environments. The elements in the Properties pane have complete configuration details available as well through a tree-view interface. In Figure 3-6 we continue the process of using the Report Builder Wizard to design our first map.

1. In the Source Of Spatial Data dialog box, choose the Map Gallery option button (Step A), which provides embedded map data-display choices.
2. In the Source Of Spatial Data dialog box, select the USA By State Inset map (Step B), which provides an easy-to-view display of U.S. states, including Alaska and Hawaii.
3. In the Map Options dialog box, click Next to accept the default map display choices (Step C).

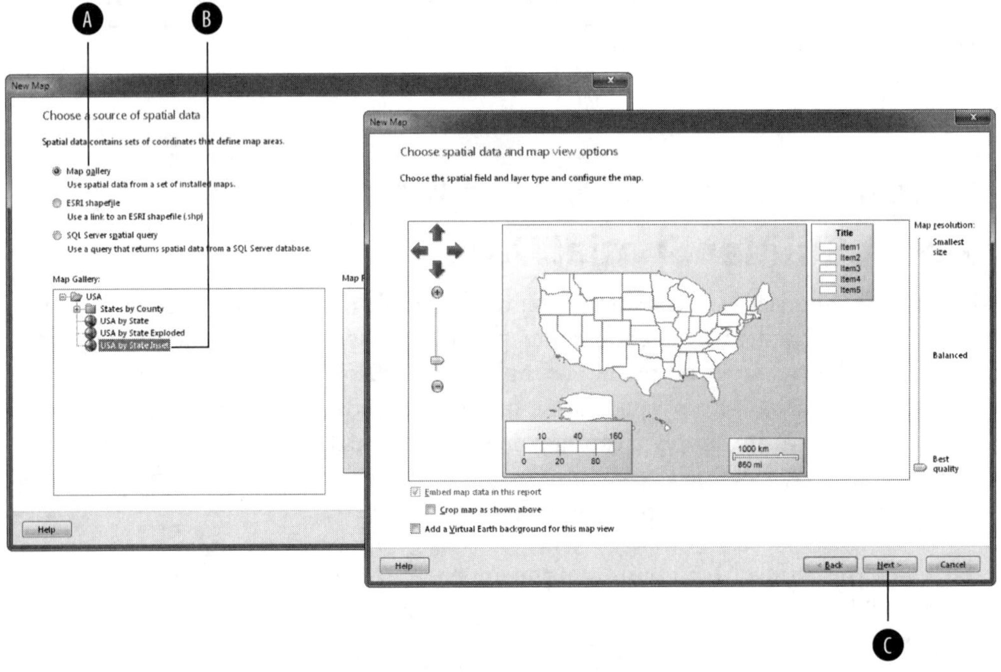

Figure 3-6 *Report Builder: choosing a source of spatial data, and map options*

Note in Figure 3-6, with the Spatial Data dialog box, Report Builder is giving us a quick way to get a default map display in place. There are endless variations on map spatial-data sources that can be discussed, but in this case we're using the Report Builder's built-in U.S.A. map choices so that we don't have to figure out how to connect to a source of spatial data to produce a geo-display.

The States By County choice would open up a tree view of the 50 states, with county boundaries within each state. This is obviously an easy way to create a State geo-display, to which we can subsequently match analytical data to show relative data levels on a county-by-county basis. In Figure 3-7 we continue the process of creating a simple U.S. map.

1. In the Map Visualization dialog box, choose the Color Analytical Map (Step A), which helps us create a map with color-coded polygons of relative data value ranges.
2. In the Connection To Data Source dialog box, select New (Step B) to create a new data source connection for the map's analytical data.

Note in Figure 3-7, with the Map Visualization dialog box—the two interesting choices are Color Analytical Map or Bubble Map. You'll see later in this chapter that it

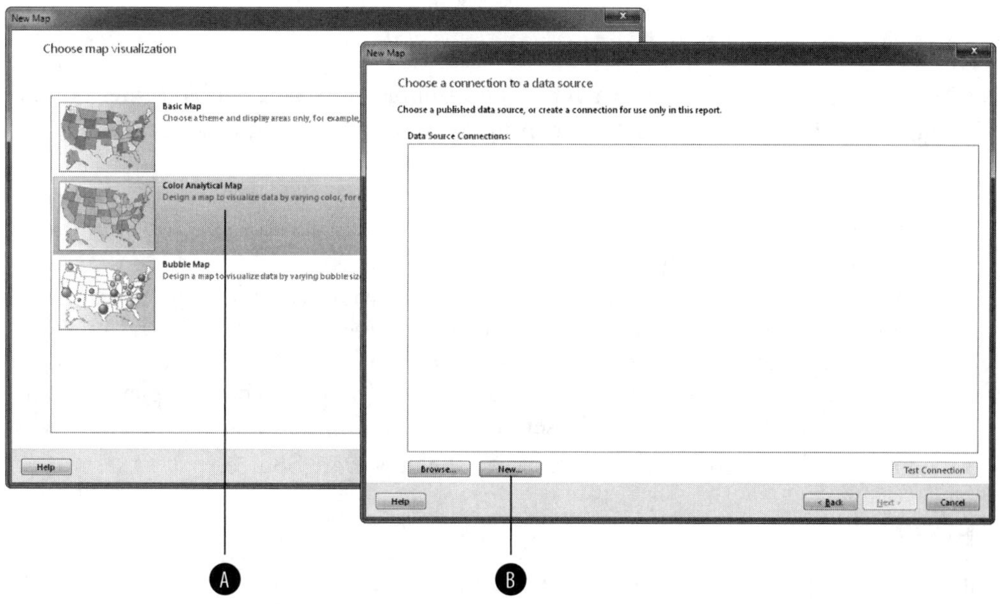

Figure 3-7 *Report Builder: choosing the map visualization, and connecting to an analytical data source*

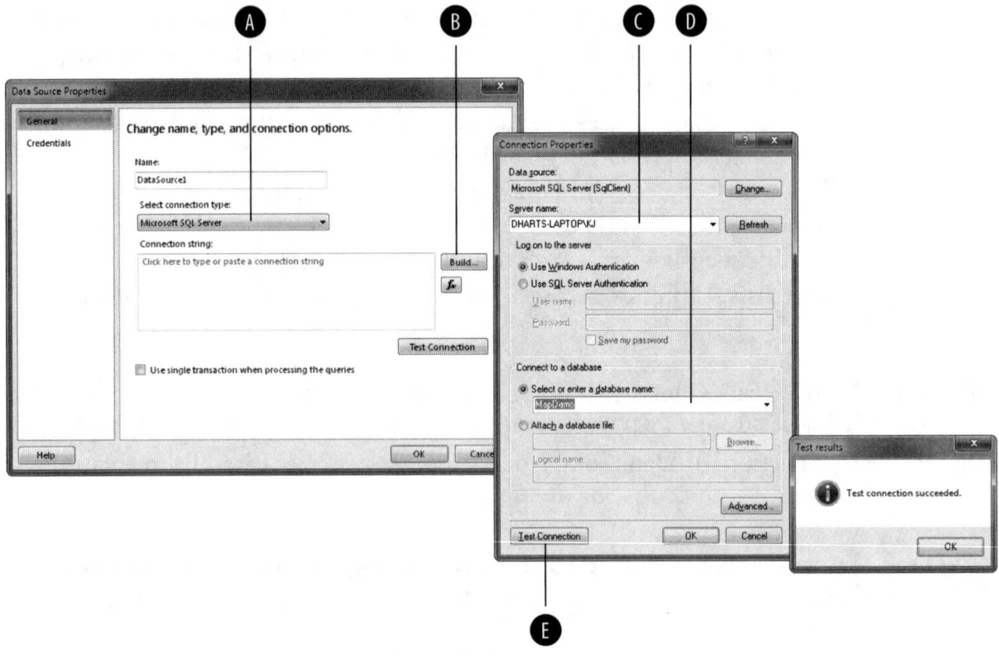

Figure 3-8 *Report Builder: connecting to a data source and choosing Connection Properties*

is easy to change between Color Analytical and Bubble, or to add bubble center points to an analytical map. In Figure 3-8 we continue our process of configuring the data source for analytical data.

1. In the Data Source Properties dialog box, select the Microsoft SQL Server drop-down menu choice (Step A), and click Build (Step B).
2. In the Connection Properties dialog box, choose your available SQL Server in the Server Name drop-down (Step C, which browses for existing SQL Servers both locally and on your network) and select Map Demo for the data source in the "Select or enter a database name" drop-down (Step D, which displays existing databases on the SQL Server chosen in the preceding step).
3. Click Test Connection (Step E) to verify the new Data Source.

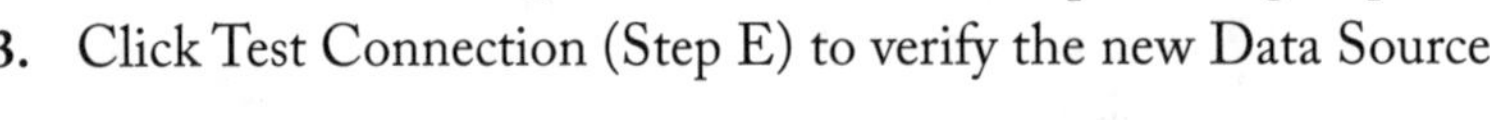

BI TIP

It's rather satisfying to see the Microsoft SQL Server Data Source Connection Wizard following the tried-and-true logic that we've come to expect with Microsoft reporting applications. And with SQL Server 2008, these data sources can bring in SQL Server spatial data types to build a visual map!

However, with our current example, we're just going with the easier route of relying on a built-in (or embedded) map that we chose when starting this Report Builder Wizard example. Figure 3-9 shows how we choose the new data source for the map and design a simple query.

1. In the Choose A Connection To A Data Source dialog box, select the new Data Source (Step A, which we've simply left labeled as "DataSource1").
2. In the Design A Query dialog box, click the USA plus sign (Step B) to expand the data schema.
3 In the Design A Query dialog box, check the Name (Step C) and POP1997 (Step D) data elements.
4. Click Next (Step E) to continue.

Note the nice layout in the Design A Query dialog box, where we don't have to write SQL syntax or create a join to retrieve data. In our simple example, we're just pulling in a couple of fields that we'll use to match to the spatial data, and to display relative

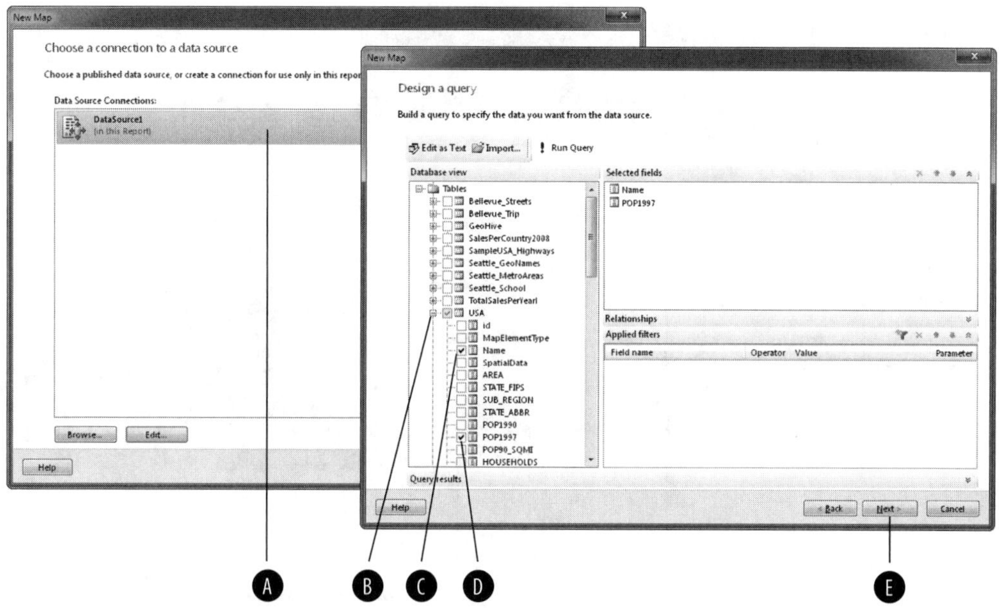

Figure 3-9 *Report Builder: choosing an analytical data source and designing the query*

population values as analytical data. Figure 3-10 shows how we "match" the spatial and analytical data elements.

1. In the Specify The Match Fields For Spatial And Analytical Data dialog box, check the Match Fields check box on the "STATENAME" row (Step A, STATENAME is in the Spatial Dataset Fields column).
2. Select Name from the drop-down in the Analytical Dataset Fields column (Step B); click Next to continue.
3. In the Theme dialog box, select "[Sum(Fields1997)]" from the Field To Visualize drop-down (Step C).
4. In the Theme dialog box, select Light-Dark in the Color Rule drop-down (Step D).
5. In the Theme dialog box, click Finish (Step E) to return to the report design screen.

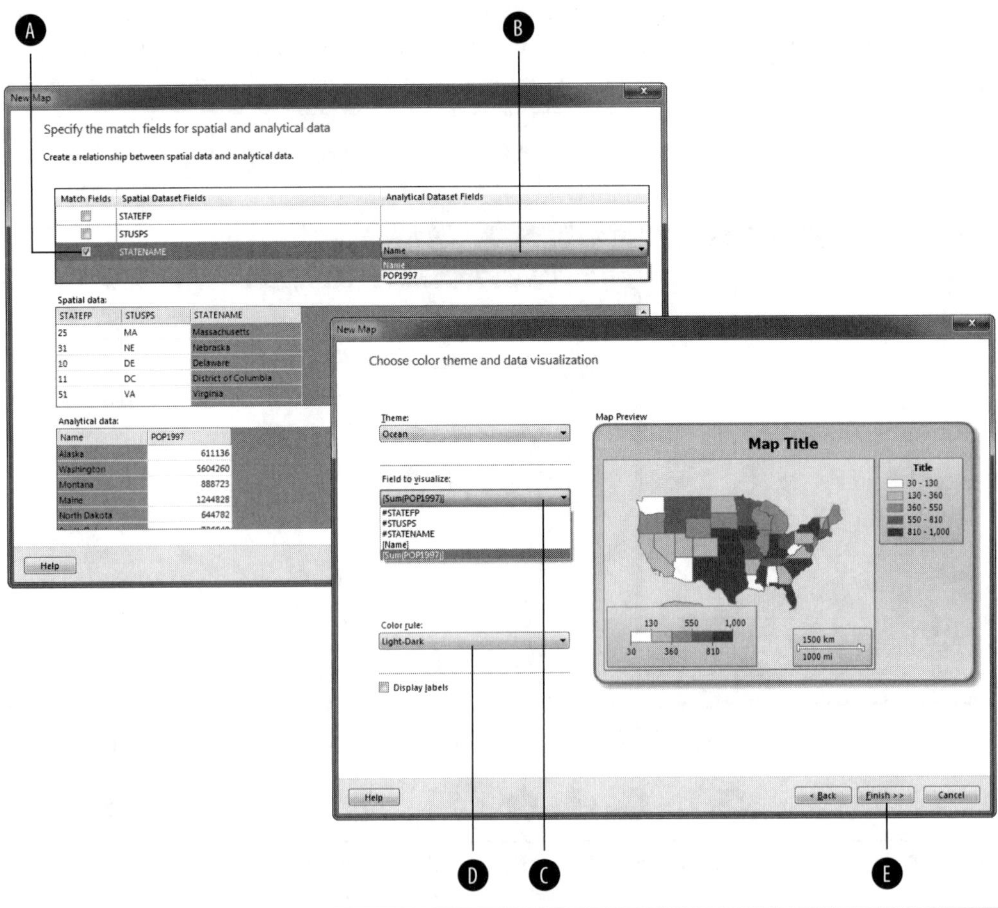

Figure 3-10 *Report Builder: matching spatial and analytical data, and choosing a theme and analytical data value*

The steps in Figure 3-10 show where Microsoft really adds value with the "wizard" approach to building a map report. Since "STATENAME" is part of the embedded map we decided to use at the beginning of the map wizard steps, the wizard provides an easy-to-understand Matching Analytical Data Source dialog box that helps us connect the Name field from the analytical dataset. The Report Builder map will then use this STATENAME-to-Name match to display the "[Sum(Fields1997)]" values in each State subpolygon within the U.S. map!

Note the wizard feature in Figure 3-10 that automatically previews the data from the spatial and analytical datasets. StateName and Name are highlighted, respectively, in the Spatial Data and Analytical Data preview grids—which makes for a nice intuitive way to select the right fields.

So let's review; we need to be able to match a spatial data field to an analytical data field so that the associated analytical value fields can display color-coded information for each spatial data field on the map. Frankly, the other important point to understand about the maps is that they can have multiple layers that simply overlay each other.

BI TIP

The key to the Microsoft Report Builder map display is the ability to match a spatial data field to an analytical data field. Then, any analytical values that are associated with the analytical data fields within the analytical dataset can be displayed in the matching spatial fields on a geo-map!

Figure 3-11 shows the simple map that we've designed, rendered in the Report Builder Preview mode. It's worth noting that we're able to run and preview the Report Builder reports, without ever having installed a SQL Server Reporting Services (SSRS) server, nor an Internet Information Services (IIS) server. This is because the Report Builder is a .NET client application that, when chosen from the SSRS Report Manager menu, exhibits a single-click download behavior that installs the Report Builder 3.0 to the client machine. Also, the SSRS server has an installation of Report Builder 3.0 as part of the SSRS server installation (which can be accessed from Start Programs | Microsoft SQL Server 2008 Report Builder | Report Builder 3.0).

Other chapters in this book discuss the deployment of reports in general, to the Reporting Services Report Manager and other destinations.

1. Click the Run icon on the left end of the Report Builder top menu (Step A).
2. Click the Design icon on the left end of the Render top menu (Step B), to return to the Design screen.

Note in Figure 3-11 that the rendered map automatically has a Color Scale and a Legend with the analytical visualization data divided into five value ranges, by default. We'll explore in later sections how to change these map elements to improve our map report. The default map also has a Distance Scale.

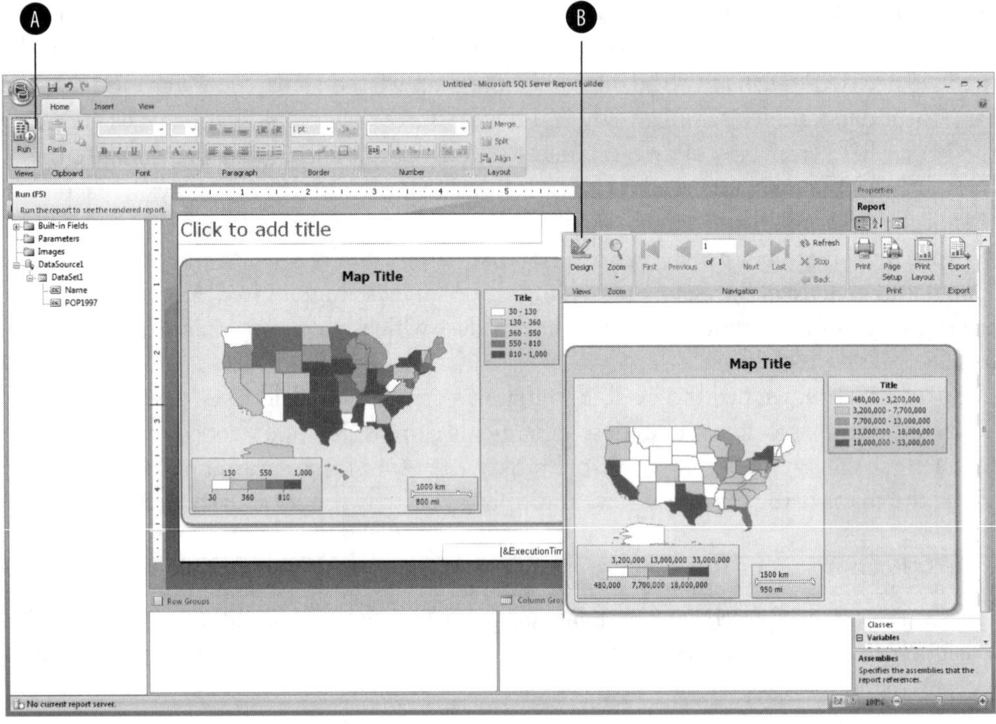

Figure 3-11 *Report Builder: running the Map report*

Adding Analytical Color to the Map Report

This section will explore the enhancement of the map's polygon color rule. We'll change the map Distribution, which arranges the colors of analytical value display across the map polygons, which are states in our working example. The goal is both to achieve a visually pleasing color map effect for the consumer of the map and to accurately convey the low-high analytical values by color.

At this point it's worth taking a look at the ribbon menu at the top of the Report Builder. This menu user interface has been a standard of Microsoft applications since Office 2007, which introduced the ribbon menu organization of menu options. Figure 3-12 shows the three menu groups of the ribbon menu for the Report Builder, where similar menu actions are gathered into groups within the ribbon menu tabs.

A. The Office button is where file-level menu actions are found, including File Open and File Save / Save As.

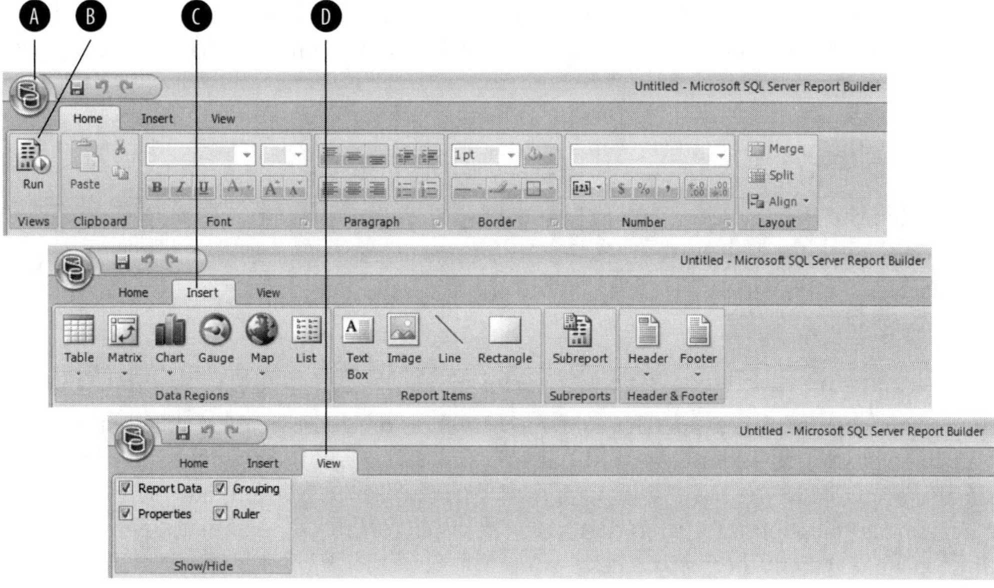

Figure 3-12 *Report Builder ribbon menu*

B. The Run icon to render a report is found on the Home tab—and this is where the common formatting options are located, including Font and Paragraph options.

C. Icons on the Insert tab allow us to insert table, matrix, chart, gauge, map, and list elements into the report being designed. They also include the Subreport menu icon, which supports the embedding of subreports into the report being designed.

D. The View tab simply holds miscellaneous options to Show/Hide report elements in the map report.

Experience has shown that expert users often bypass parts of the ribbon menu, in favor of accessing report elements through the Table Or Matrix, Chart, and Map Wizard icons in the central part of the design interface pane—and then configuring the report element properties through the right-side Properties pane in the Report Builder user interface. Users that are new to the Report Builder design interface are usually happy with the Report Builder ribbon menu, since it does a good job of grouping similar menu actions together into logical menu tabs.

Picking up again with our report design process, Figure 3-13 shows how we click the map to access the Map Layers pop-up menu, where we will enhance the color display of the map's analytical values.

1. Click the map itself, in the central design pane (Step A). Click the map again to cause the Map Layers pop-up menu to display.
2. Click the PolygonLayer1 item in the Map Layers pop-up menu (Step B), or right-click the PolygonLayer1 item.
3. Select the Polygon Color Rule menu choice in the PolygonLayer1 pop-up menu (Step C).

In Figure 3-13 we're starting to work with the map layer properties. You'll find there are many detailed properties that you can learn to use in creating exactly the map visualization desired—and note all the map elements and all the element properties are also available in the right-side pane of Properties, which is a standard part of the Microsoft application integrated design environment (IDE). The pop-up menus simply provide a convenient means to access groups of properties for the map elements.

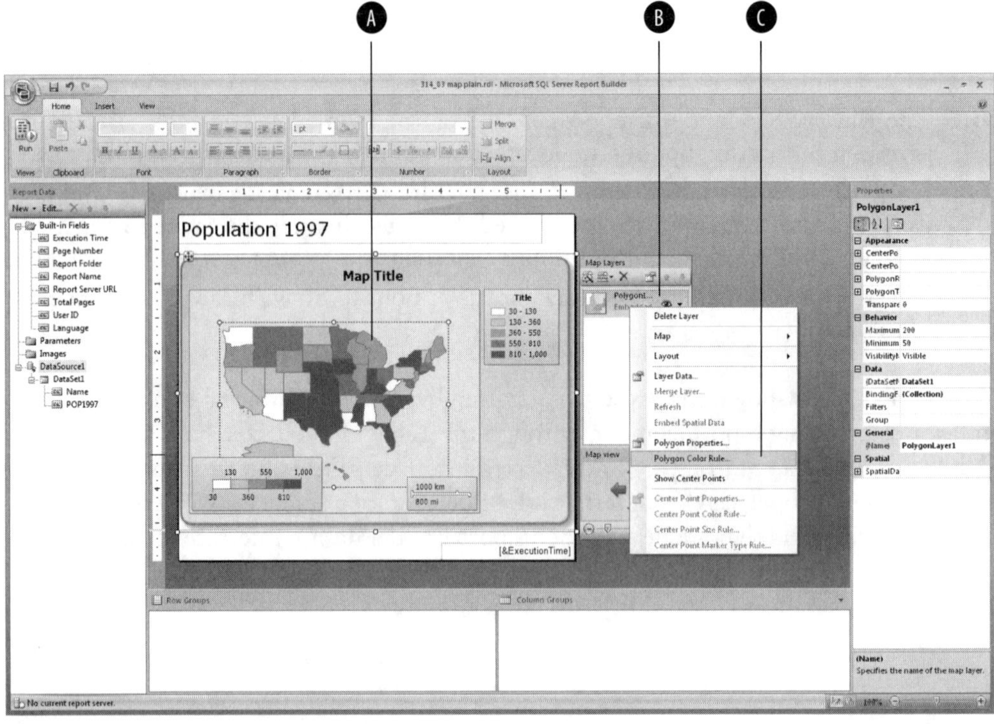

Figure 3-13 *Report Builder: Polygon layer*

BI TIP

The current map layer we're working with is by definition a polygon, which, mathematically, is a multiline enclosure (boundary) made up of many lines to create a smooth visual outline. The U.S. map is actually a combination of state polygons.

Figure 3-14 shows how we can enhance the map's color scheme to create a more interesting visualization of population by state.

1. In the Map Color Rules Properties | General dialog box, choose the "Visualize data by using color ranges" option button (Step A).
2. In the Map Color Rules Properties | General dialog box, select Red for the Start Color (Step B), select Yellow for the Middle Color (Step C), and select Green for the End Color (Step D).
3. In the Map Color Rules Properties | Distribution dialog box, select Optimal for "Change distribution options to divide data into subranges" (Step E) and select 10 for the Number Of Subranges (Step F).

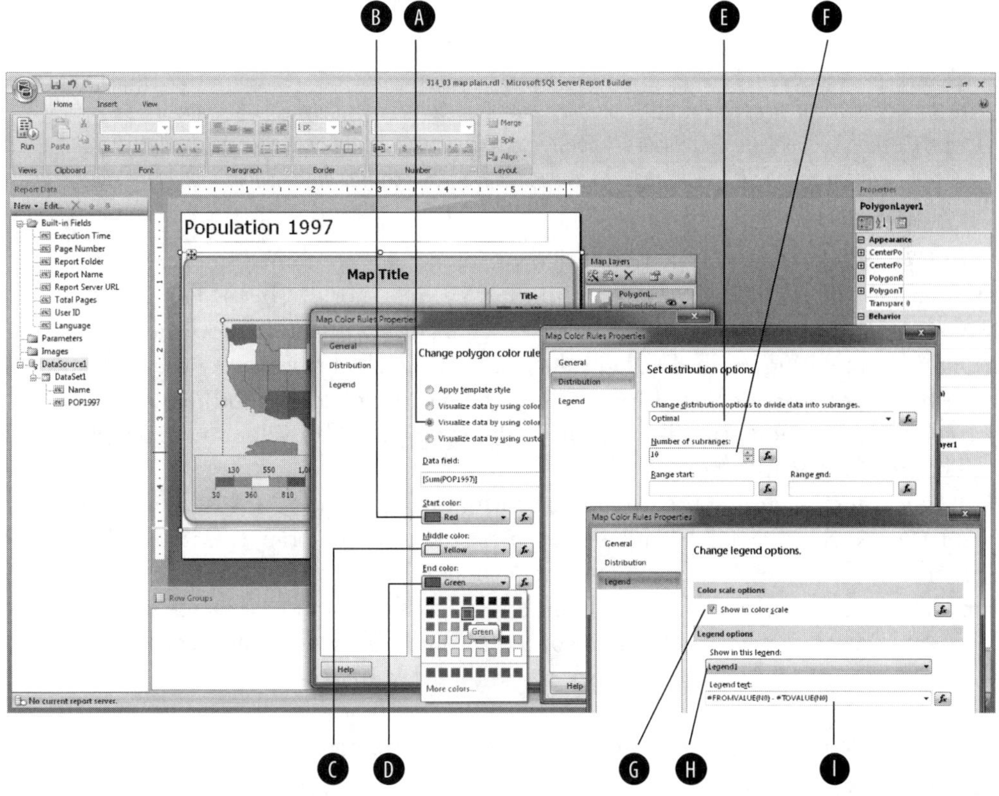

Figure 3-14 *Report Builder: Polygon Color rule*

4. In the Map Color Rules Properties | Legend dialog box, check the Show In Color Scale check box (Step G), select Legend1 in the Show In This legend drop-down (Step H), and choose "#FROMVALUE{NO} - #TOVALUE{NO}" in the Legend Text drop-down (Step I).

In Figure 3-14 we're really jumping into the analytic data visualization configuration. The following choices are available to determine the value subrange distribution method:

- The Optimal distribution option, which we chose for the color range because it provides an even variety of colors across the map populations by state
- EqualInterval, which would distribute the data colors across equal value intervals, regardless of how many states wind up at the low or high end of the display spectrum
- EqualDistribution (also known as the Quantiles distribution method in statistics) to force an equal number of states in each range of the value distribution—which would have been misleading, since it would look like an even distribution of population by subrange across the states of the U.S., which is not the case
- Custom to dictate our own desired subranges of data for the visualization

BI TIP

For the map distribution option, which determines how the colors of the analytical values are spread across the map, Optimal usually provides the best result because it's a cross between the EqualInterval and EqualDistribution options. It's pleasing to the eye and conveys an accurate data visualization in the context of a geo-display.

In Figure 3-15 we chose the Red-Yellow-Green color combination because we'd like to associate a high population value with the pleasing color of Green. This is pretty important, because consumers of the map visualization will automatically associate negative connotations with the Red value (indicating a bad result or a problem), and a positive connotation with the Green value, which can indicate a good result. Choose the color combination carefully, to provide the "first glance" of value to the people that will be viewing the map report!

A quick note regarding the legend text formatting in Figure 3-14 is in order at this point. Our working report legend will be displaying the value ranges with labels in a "From value–To value" format. The format syntax is actually a .NET format string that supports many variations of text and numeric presentation (and for which online help is available through www.msdn.microsoft.com). The following excerpts explain our working example of .NET Format Strings in the Map Legend:

- **#FROMVALUE{NO}** Analytical range beginning value with no decimal places
- **#TOVALUE{NO}** Analytical range ending value with no decimal places

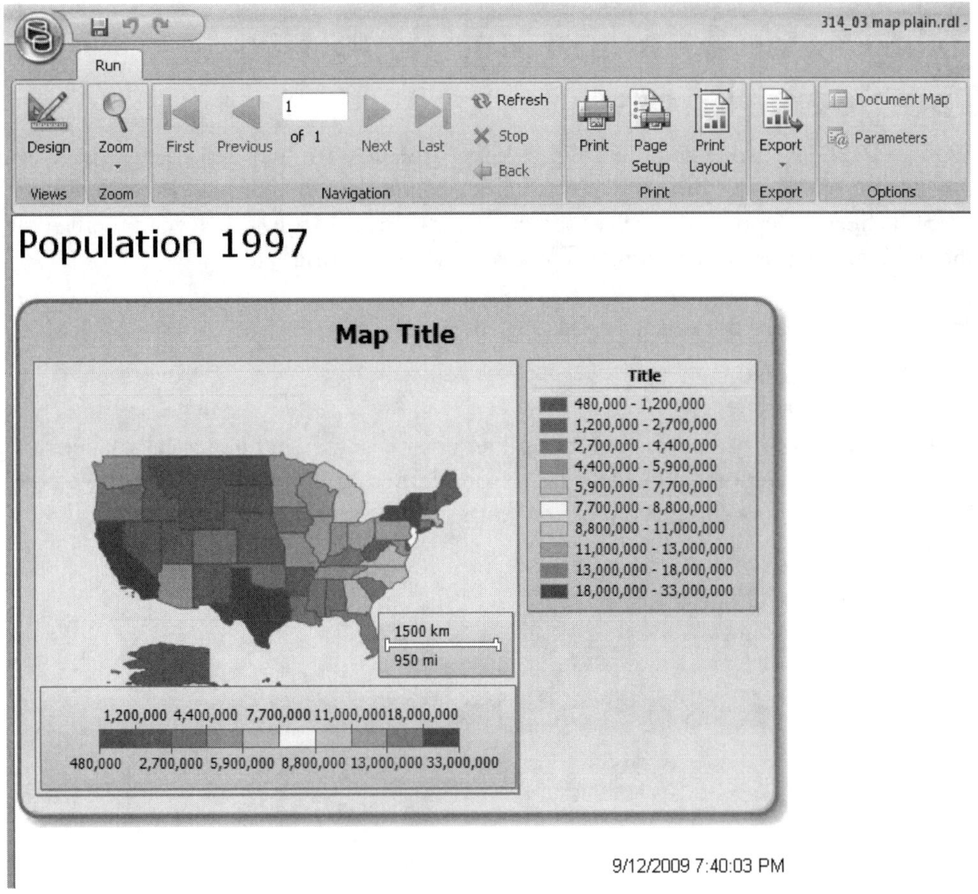

Figure 3-15 *Report Builder: rendering the map*

- **#FROMVALUE{C0}** Analytical range beginning value as Currency with no decimal places
- **#FROMVALUE{C2}** Analytical range beginning value as Currency with two decimal places

In Figure 3-15 you see the rendered report result. We have quite a bit of work to do in enhancing this simple map report, but it's clear the map's analytic values are being displayed in a much more compelling visualization as we work with the Polygon Color rule.

In the next section we'll take a brief detour in our discussion, to look at a common error message that map report designers may run into—and we'll show how to fix the data connection error.

Fixing Some Common Map Report Data Source Errors

Figure 3-16 shows two errors that might easily come up with map reports that have been copied from one Report Builder client machine to another, or that have been deployed to a SQL Server Reporting Services server that is different from the development server where the map report was designed. The two messages in brief are

- "The server was not found . . ."
- "The login failed . . ."

The Microsoft SQL Server Report Builder error is somewhat generically labeled "Failed to preview report." This data source problem is common and can be solved by reconfiguring the data source connection to the SQL Server spatial data and analytical data sources.

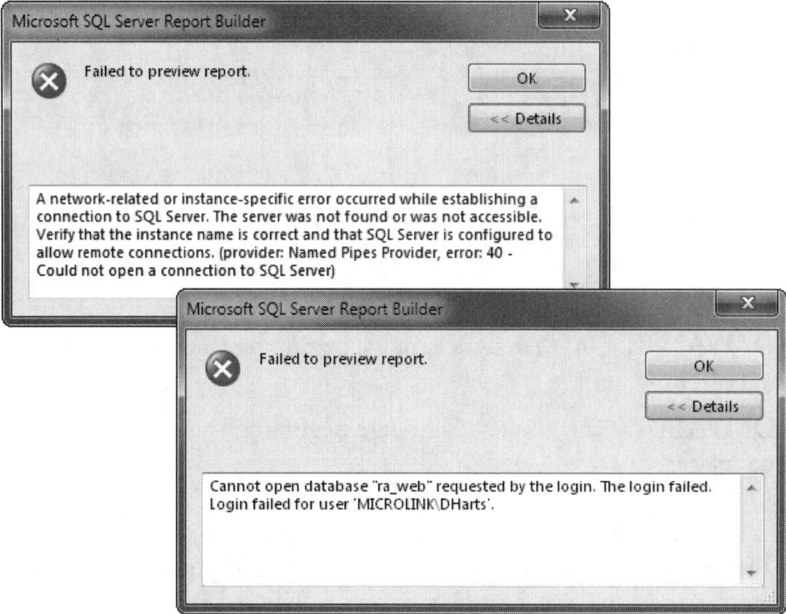

Figure 3-16 *Report Builder: viewing a common error, "Failed to preview report"*

Jumping ahead to Figure 3-17, we see that the SQL Server data source configuration is actually quite straightforward. We need to choose or re-select the server, and refresh or re-enter the login ID and password.

1. Right-click the DataSource icon in the tree view of map report elements, on the left-side pane (Step A).
2. Select the Data Source Properties choice on the pop-up menu (Step B).
3. In the Data Source Properties dialog box | General pane, choose the "Use a connection embedded in my report" option button (Step C), select Microsoft SQL Server for the Select Connection Type (Step D), and click Build to configure the data connection (Step E).
4. In the Connection Properties dialog box, enter a period (.) in the Server Name drop-down (Step F)—which automatically finds the LOCAL SQL Server—or find the desired SQL Server in the drop-down.

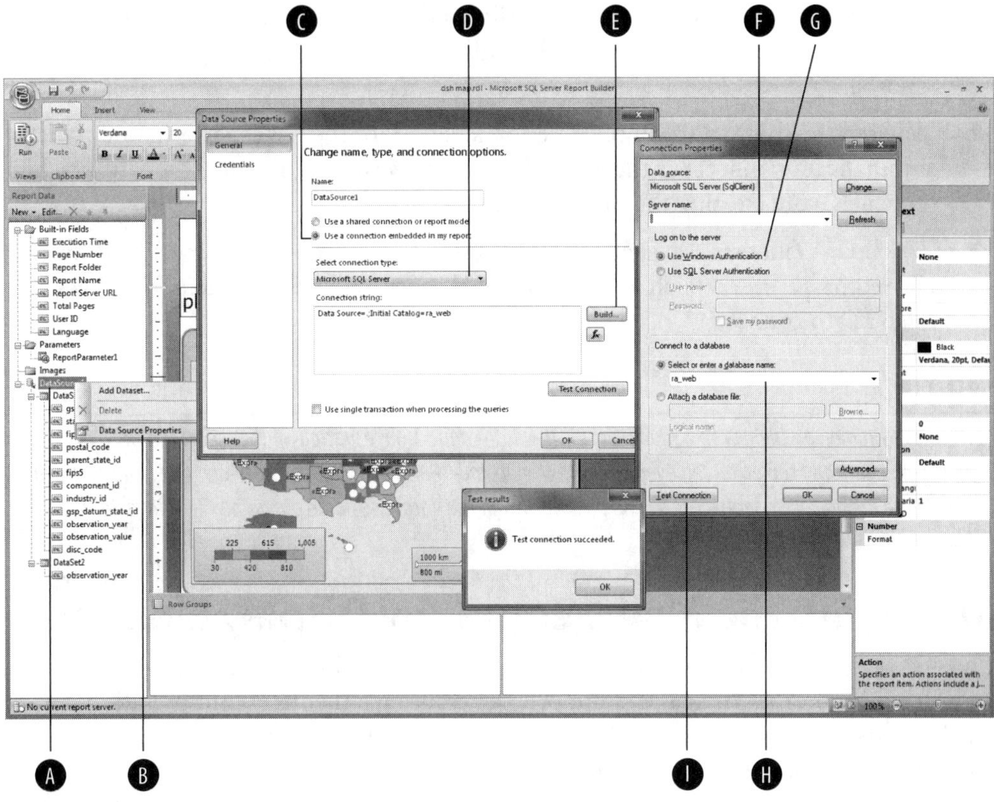

Figure 3-17 *Report Builder: connection error fix*

5. In the Connection Properties dialog box, choose Use Windows Authentication or Use SQL Server Authentication (Step G) and enter a valid SQL Server User Name and Password.
6. In the Connection Properties dialog box, choose the Select Or Enter A Database Name option button, and choose or type the desired database name (Step H, "ra_web" in our working example).
7. Click the Test Connection button (Step I) to display (we hope) Test Connection Succeeded! And click OK to save the changes to the data connection.

Okay, so what did we accomplish with these steps? Frankly, we took a quick tour of the most common configuration elements that allow data, both spatial and analytical, to flow together in the map report. It's worth noting a couple of points about the steps we see with Figure 3-17:

- We are using an embedded data connection (in our report), which is easier for our working example—as compared to a shared data connection that would already have been configured and deployed to a Reporting Services server for use by many reports.
- We used the shortcut of simply entering a period for the SQL Server name, which automatically connects to the local SQL Server we're working on (the same machine on which we're creating the map report).
- We chose Windows Authentication because it's easier than recalling a SQL Server ID and password—which assumes the SQL Server allows our client Windows login ID to connect.

BI TIP

The most common problem with a map report is the data connection, especially if the report has been developed on one machine and copied or deployed to another machine—and the solution is usually to use common sense to validate the database server, the ID and password, and the database name providing the source data.

Modifying the Map Geography Display Elements

This section will explore the enhancement of the map's color scale, distance scale, and legend. The legend in particular is important because it's the main interpretation device for this working map in terms of actual data values. The map itself displays relative population analytic values across the spatial boundaries of states, but it does not have the population values themselves displaying on top of each state—which would be difficult to read across all 50 states.

In Figure 3-18 we continue to modify the map display by configuring some simple elements that are nonetheless important to the user who is visually interpreting the spatial and analytic visualization of data values in a color-code relative manner across the map polygons (states in our working example).

1. Right-click the Color Scale display element in the map (Step A), and click Show Color Scale (Step B) to uncheck it and remove it from the map display.
2. Right-click the Distance Scale display element in the map (Step C), and click Show Distance Scale (Step D) to uncheck it and remove it from the map display.
3. Right-click the Legend display element in the map (Step E), and select the Legend Properties menu choice in the pop-up menu (Step F).
4. In the Map Legend Properties dialog box | General pane, choose the lower-right option button on the Position ring of option buttons (Step G).
5. Click OK (Step H) to save the changes.

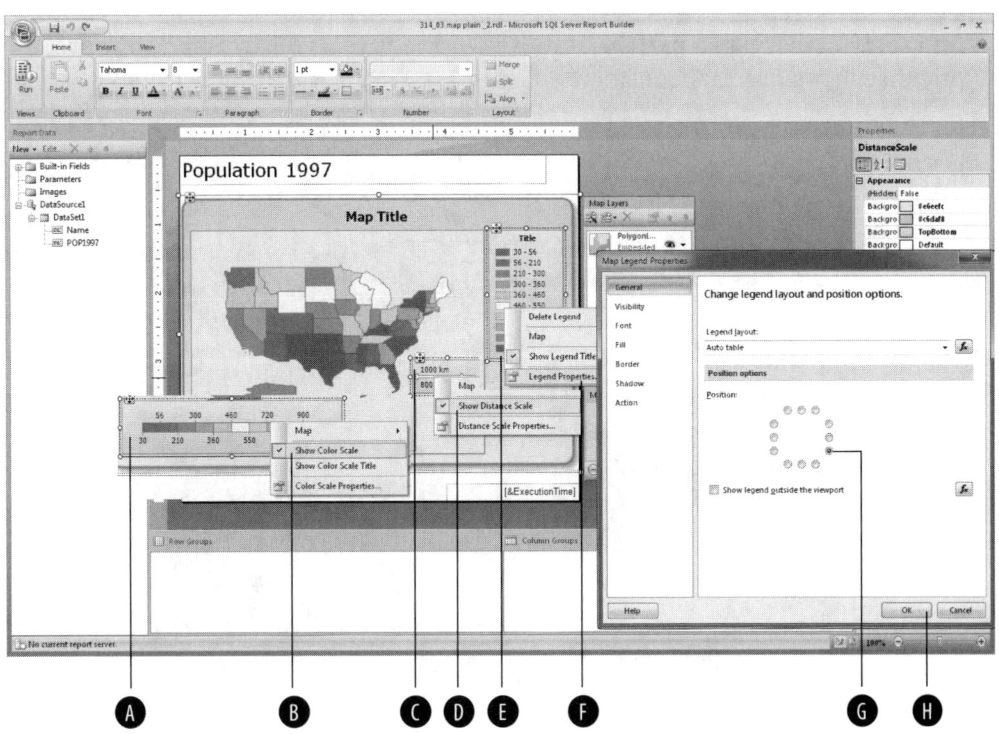

Figure 3-18 *Report Builder: configuring the legend, distance scale, and color scale*

The steps we show in Figure 3-18 are actually pretty important in that we have decided to display *fewer* elements in the map display. This is because the color scale and the distance scale were not providing any more information to the map consumer than the map itself—which is simply visualizing the relative population levels in a color-coded manner state by state. The only element besides the map itself that really helps interpret the population data is the legend, which we repositioned to achieve a straightforward presentation of relative population levels.

It's certainly worth considering the idea that we can add more analytical value to the map, but that should be done carefully, since we want to avoid creating a map report display that is a blur of data that's confusing to the end user.

BI TIP

Generally, fewer elements on a map display are better than more. This is because the user of the map report is busy interpreting the analytical data we've visualized against the spatial geo-data display—and does not need the distraction of trying to interpret multiple analytical data values at the same time, against the background of the geography background.

In Figure 3-19 you see the rendered report result. We have more enhancements that we will apply to this map report, but at this point we have a visually compelling geo-display that shows relative population values by state in an easy-to-understand manner.

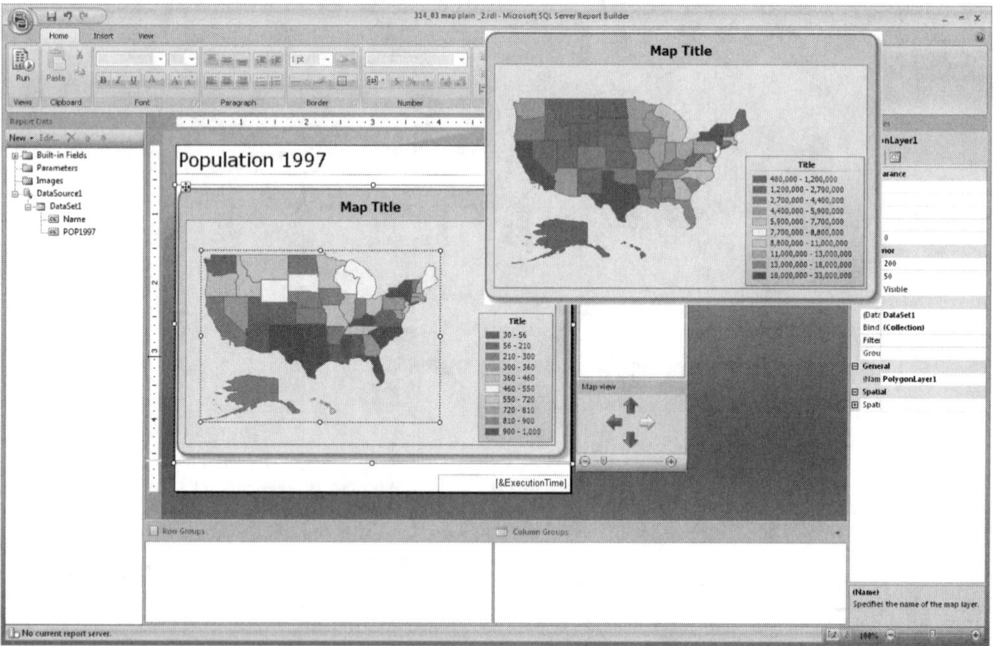

Figure 3-19 *Report Builder: revised rendering of map*

In Figure 3-20 we note the Legend "From-To" Values formatting might be something we'd like to change in the map display. This is accomplished through the Polygon Color rule, Data field—where we use the Formula Editor to achieve custom results as shown in Figure 3-20.

1. Click the map itself, in the central design pane (Step A). Click the map again to cause the Map Layers pop-up menu to display.
2. Click the PolygonLayer1 item in the Map Layers pop-up menu (Step B, or right-click the PolygonLayer1 item).
3. Select the Polygon Color Rule menu choice in the PolygonLayer1 pop-up menu (Step C).
4. In the Map Color Rules Properties dialog box | General pane, click the *fx* icon for the Data Field drop-down (Step D), to display the Expression dialog box.

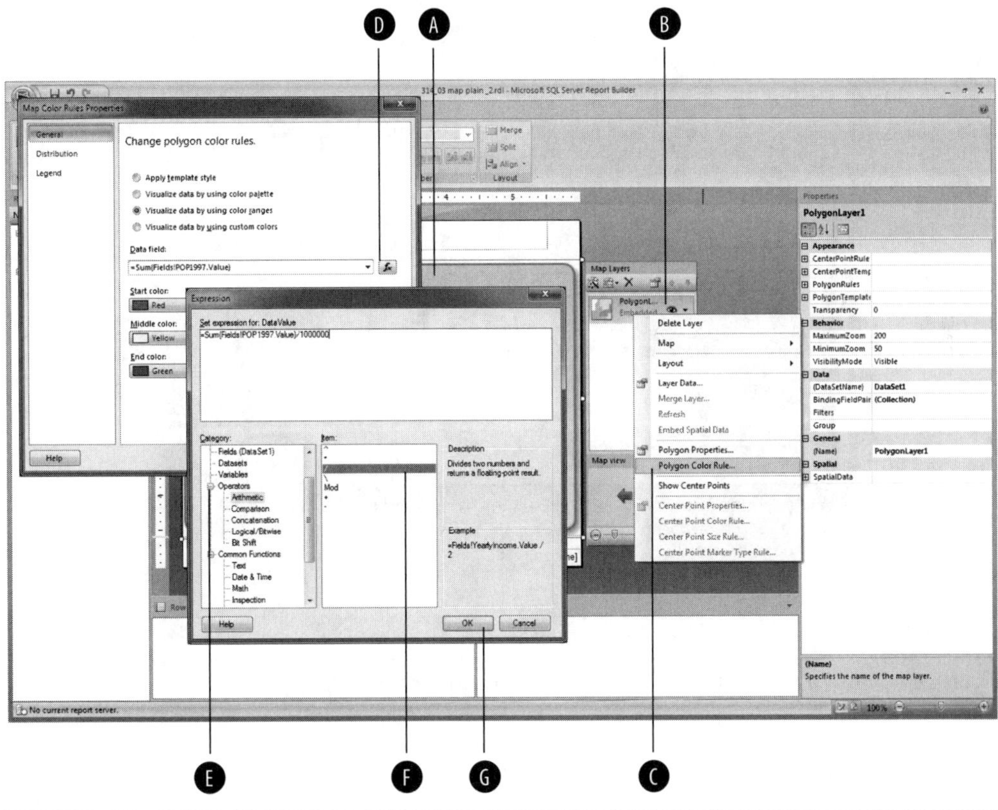

Figure 3-20 *Report Builder: Polygon Color rule | Data field*

5. Click the + button to expand the Operators node of the tree view in the Category pane (Step E), and select the / division operator in the Item pane (Step F).
6. Click OK (Step G) to save the formula.

In Figure 3-21 we see the rendered result, where the State Population ranges are expressed in millions—which is certainly a quicker way to visualize the relative approximate levels of population by state!

Now that we have an understandable display of population data by state, with an easy-to-read legend that does not get in the way of the map itself, we'll explore the concept of *color points* in the following section—which is another way of conveying analytical values on the map report.

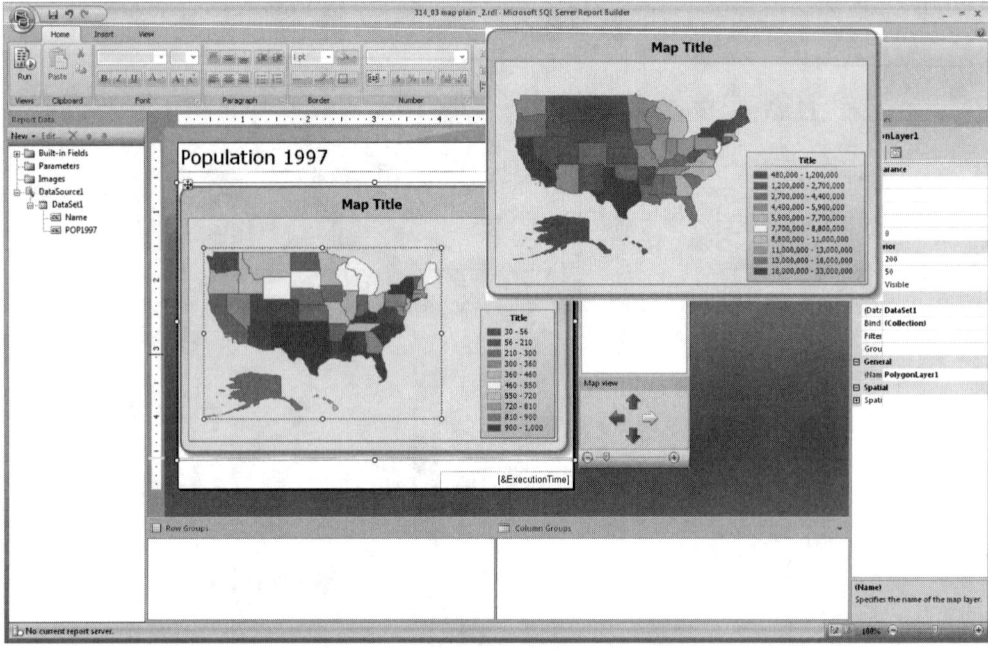

Figure 3-21 *Report Builder: rendering of map with revised legend value formatting*

Adding Color Points to the Map Report

This section will explore the use of the map's color points for the relative display of data on a state-by-state basis, instead of color-coded subregions. The result is quite visually different, and actually shows relative population values by both color point size and color! When used carefully, the color point display is generally easier to understand with many subregions because it avoids the visual clutter of subregion color scales all right next to each other.

In other words, the color-coded subregions that we used in the previous map display showed 50 states, which is a lot to look at. The color point version appears to the eye to have less to look at, and it's easier to see a pattern of population across the United States.

Figure 3-22 shows how we use the concept of a color "template" to remove the multi-coloring of subregions on a map.

1. Click the map itself, in the central design pane (Step A). Click the map again to cause the Map Layers pop-up menu to display.

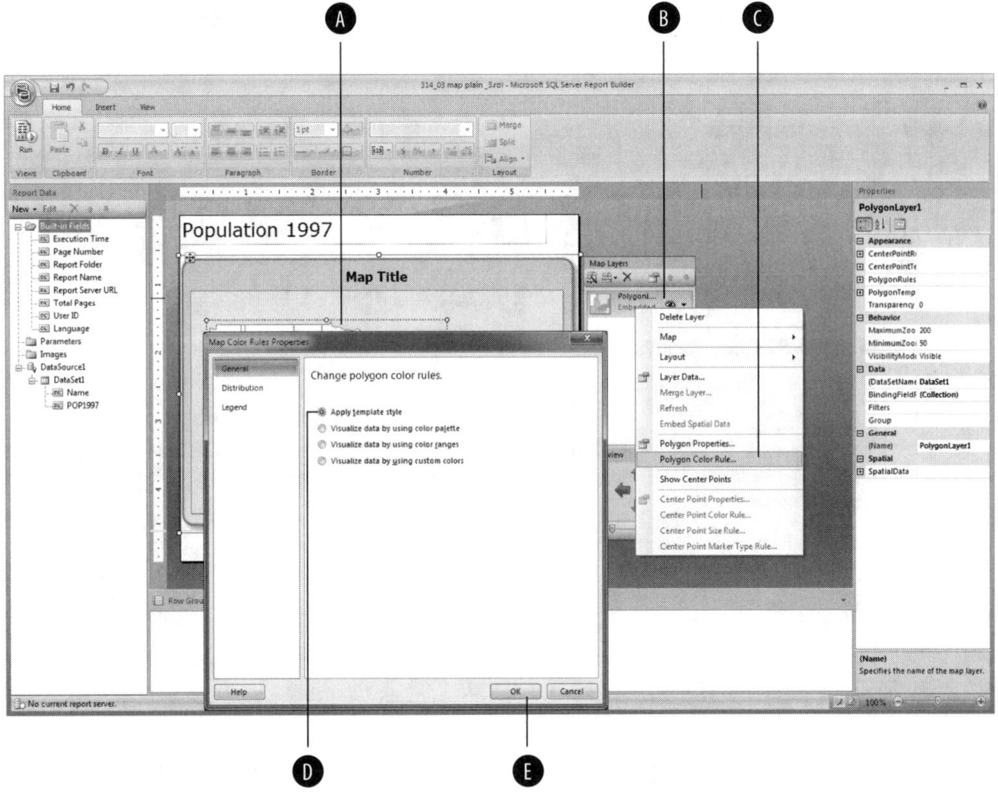

Figure 3-22 *Report Builder: changing the Polygon Color Rule template*

2. Click the PolygonLayer1 item in the Map Layers pop-up menu (Step B, or right-click the PolygonLayer1 item).
3. Select the Polygon Color Rule menu choice in the PolygonLayer1 pop-up menu (Step C).
4. In the Map Color Rules Properties dialog box | General pane, choose Apply Template Style (Step D) for a plain map without color-coded subregions.
5. Click OK (Step E) to save changes.

In Figure 3-23 we jump into the configuration of "Center Points," which adds an element of data visualization to the map that can be configured to really enhance the underlying region and subregion geographic display.

1. Click the map itself, in the central design pane (Step A). Click the map again to cause the Map Layers pop-up menu to display.
2. Click the PolygonLayer1 item in the Map Layers pop-up menu (Step B, or right-click the PolygonLayer1 item).

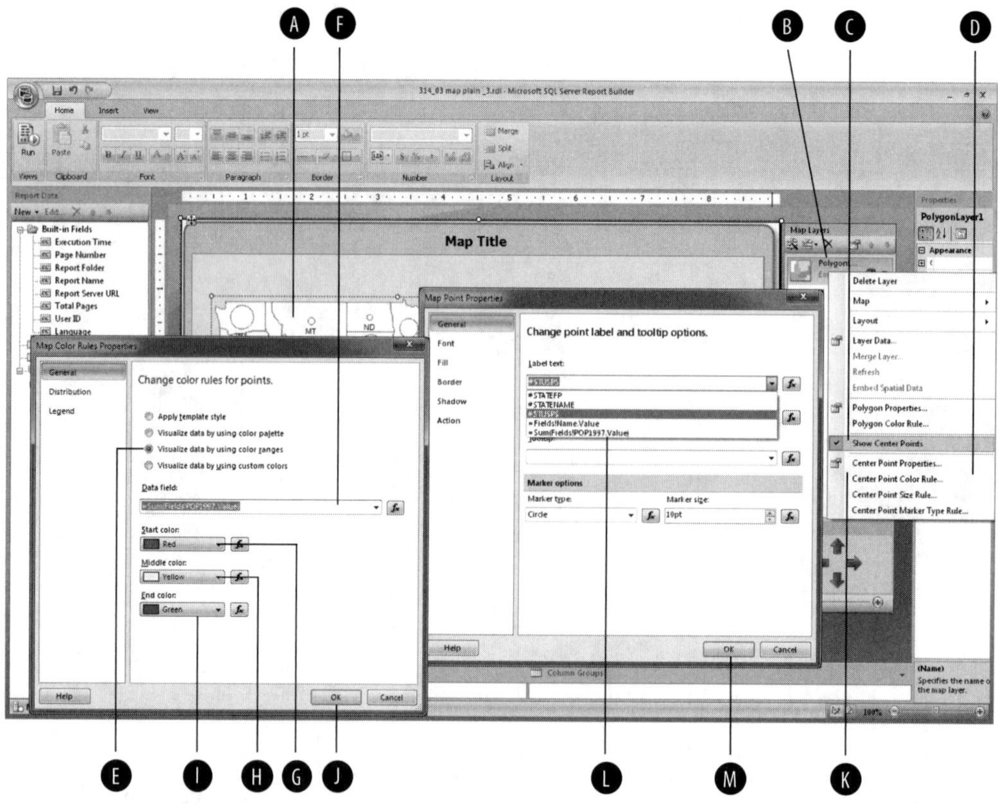

Figure 3-23 *Report Builder: polygon and center point properties*

3. Click the Show Center Points menu check box in the PolygonLayer1 pop-up menu (Step C), to enable the Center Point menu choices.
4. Click the Center Point Color Rule item in the PolygonLayer1 pop-up menu (Step D) to display the Map Color Rules Properties dialog box.
5. In the Map Color Rules Properties dialog box | General pane, select the "Visualize data by using color ranges" option button (Step E).
6. In the Map Color Rules Properties dialog box | General pane, choose "=Sum(Fields!POP1997.Value)" in the Data Field drop-down (Step F).
7. In the Map Color Rules Properties dialog box | General pane, choose Red for the Start Color (Step G), Yellow for the Middle Color (Step H), and Green for the End Color (Step I).
8. Click OK (Step J) to save changes.
9. Now, going back to the PolygonLayer1 pop-up menu, click the Center Point Properties item (Step K), to display the Map Point Properties dialog box.
10. In the Map Point Properties dialog box | General pane, select the "#STUSPS" choice in the Label Text drop-down menu (Step L) for the short-state abbreviation labels used by the U.S. Postal Service.
11. Click OK (Step M) to save changes.

BI TIP

Generally, fewer methods of value display on a map are better than more. This is because the user of the map report is typically not able to interpret more than one relative display at a time against the spatial geo-data display—and thus we are showing relative color points instead of relative color-coded subregions (choose one or the other, but not both).

In Figure 3-24 we continue the process of refining our simple Color Point map report. To achieve a very straightforward presentation, we'll adjust the size of the color points to associate with the population analytical value (we already adjusted the color of the color points to associate with the population analytical value). And we'll eliminate the legend so that the consumer of the report is led to see the range of population values across the geography of U.S. states.

1. Click the map itself, in the central design pane (Step A). Click the map again to cause the Map Layers pop-up menu to display.
2. Click the PolygonLayer1 item in the Map Layers pop-up menu (Step B, or right-click the PolygonLayer1 item).
3. Click the Center Point Size Rule item in the PolygonLayer1 pop-up menu (Step C), to display the Map Layer Size Rules Properties dialog box.
4. In the Map Layer Size Rules Properties dialog box | General pane, select the "Visualize data by using size" option button (Step D).

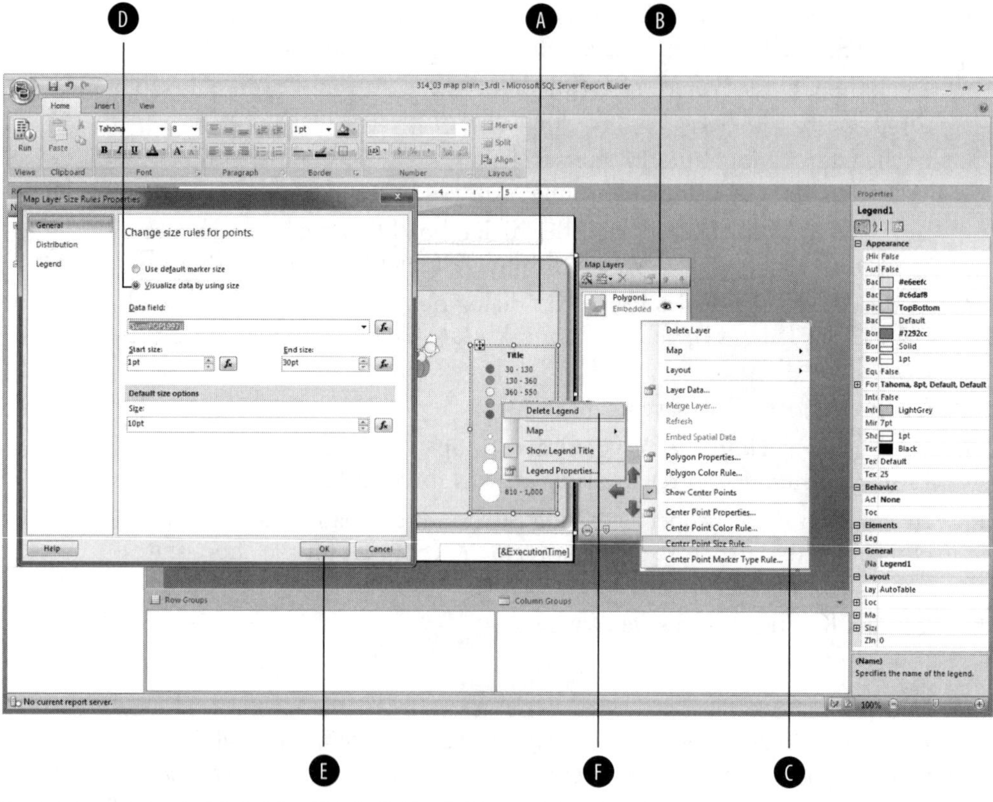

Figure 3-24 *Report Builder: polygon and center point size properties*

5. Click OK (Step E) to save changes.
6. Right-click over the map legend, and click the Delete Legend choice on the pop-up menu (Step F).

In Figure 3-25 you see the rendered report result. We have more enhancements that we will apply to this map report, but at this point we have a visually compelling geo-display that shows relative population values by state in an easy-to-understand manner as the user's eye sweeps across the U.S. display from left to right. Furthermore, we can see, by both color and size, the relative population by state from west to east—and it's not too much information for the human eye!

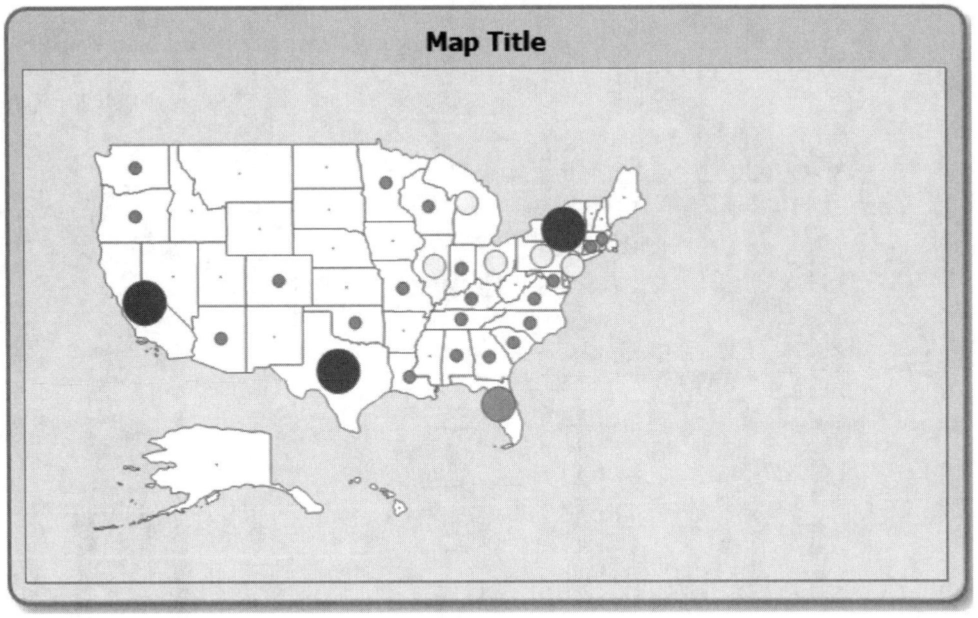

Figure 3-25 *Report Builder: rendering map with center points, color, and size*

For what it's worth, we'll put the map polygon colors back into the report—just to see what it looks like. Figure 3-26 shows how easy it is to put the relative color range, which simply overlays the existing display.

1. Click the map itself, in the central design pane (Step A). Click the map again to cause the Map Layers pop-up menu to display.
2. Click the PolygonLayer1 item in the Map Layers pop-up menu (Step B, or right-click the PolygonLayer1 item).
3. Click the Polygon Color Rule item in the PolygonLayer1 pop-up menu (Step C), to display the Map Color Rules Properties dialog box.
4. In the Map Color Rules Properties dialog box | General pane, select the "Visualize data by using color ranges" option button (Step D).
5. In the Map Color Rules Properties dialog box | General pane, choose "[Sum(POP1997)]" in the Data Field drop-down box (Step E).
6. In the Map Color Rules Properties dialog box | General pane, choose Red for the Start Color (Step F), Yellow for the Middle Color (Step G), and Green for the End Color (Step H).
7. Click OK (Step I) to save changes.

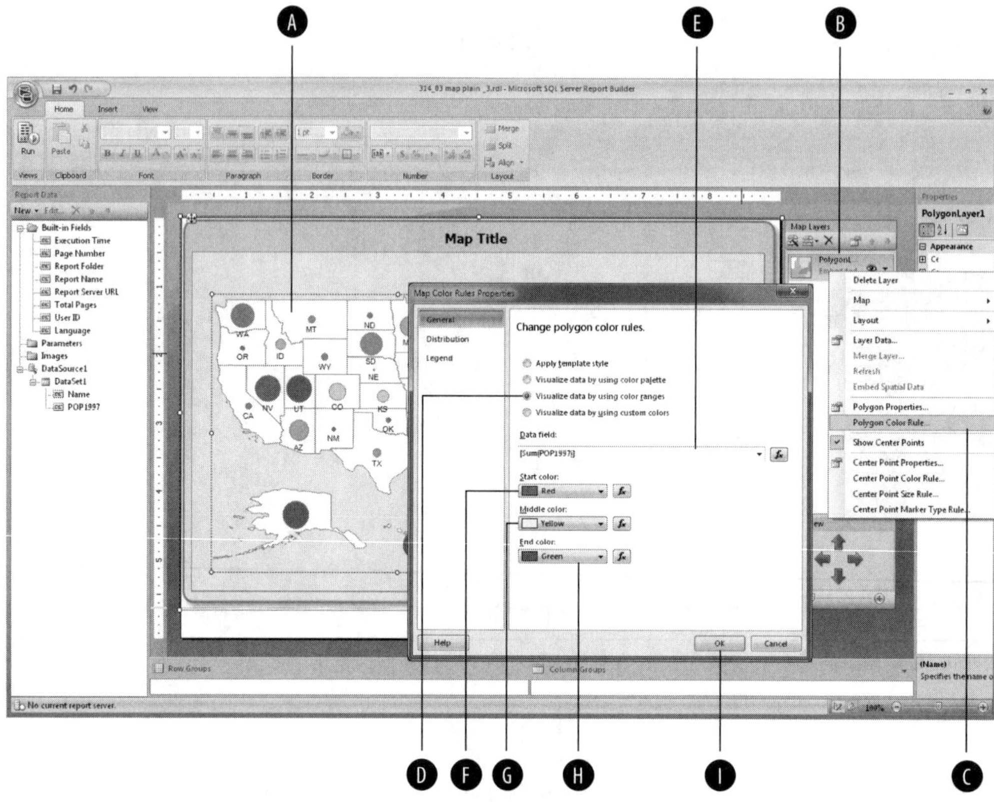

Figure 3-26 *Report Builder: configuration of the Polygon Color rule*

Figure 3-27 shows the newly rendered map report, with both Points and Polygons using the same color range—and with both drawing from the analytical population value. Note that Report Builder automatically presents the choice of SUM of the population value, in both the Color Point and the Color Polygon dialog box drop-down menus. This is typical of the helpful features of the Report Builder that allow us to concentrate on designing the map display without having to worry too much about the data values (or summing of data values) coming in from the datasets configured earlier in the map design process.

Before we leave this simple U.S. map, we'll look at one handy tool that allows us to affix a marker anywhere we wish on the map, with a custom label. This could have many uses, from adding a home office location, to the location of important areas on

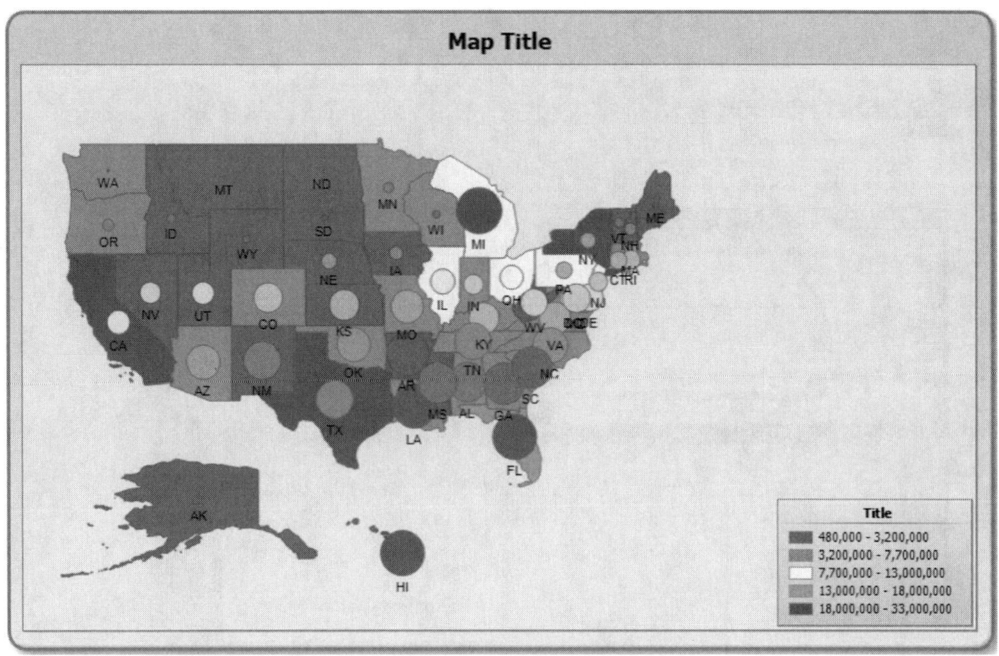

Figure 3-27 *Report Builder: map with polygon colors and point colors*

the map that might not be data-driven. Figure 3-28 shows the steps we take to add this Point layer.

1. Click the map itself, in the central design pane (Step A). Click the map again to cause the Map Layers pop-up menu to display.
2. Click the Add Layer icon in the top of the Map Layers pop-up menu (Step B).
3. Select the Point Layer choice in the Add Layer pop-up menu (Step C), to create a PointLayer1 item in the Map Layer list pane.
4. Right-click over the newly added PointLayer1 item in the Map Layer list pane, and choose the Add Point menu option on the pop-up menu (Step D).
5. As the mouse pointer changes to mouse cross-hairs, move the mouse cross-hairs to the desired custom point location on the map (Step E) and click.
6. Right-click over the newly added Point location on the map, and select the Embedded Point Properties choice on the pop-up menu (Step F), to display the Map Embedded Point Properties dialog box.

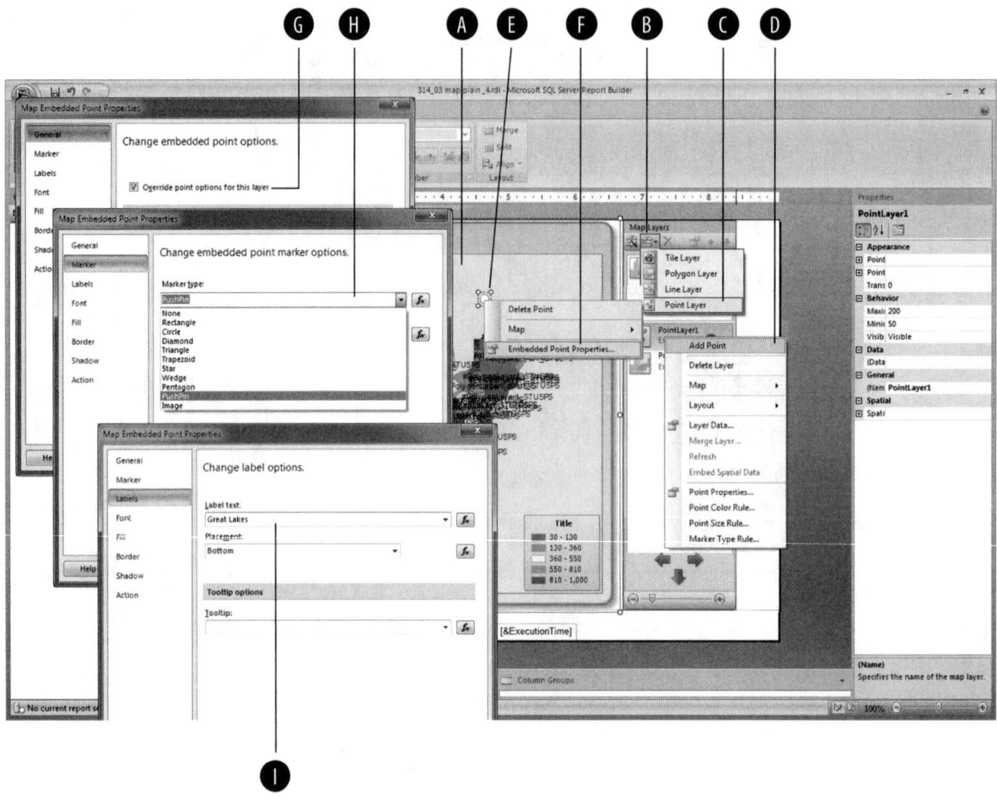

Figure 3-28 *Report Builder: adding a Point layer, and a manually located marker*

7. In the Map Embedded Point Properties dialog box | General pane, check the "Override point options for this layer" check box (Step G), to display menu options for the Point layer in the left-side menu pane.
8. In the Map Embedded Point Properties dialog box | Marker pane, select the PushPin choice in the Marker Type drop-down (Step H).
9. In the Map Embedded Point Properties dialog box | Labels pane, type **Great Lakes** in the Label Text drop-down box (Step I).
10. Click OK to save the Point Layer and Label configuration.

The steps for Figure 3-28 are somewhat lengthy, but the feature of the Report Builder that we see in this process is amazing. We've actually placed a point, manually with the mouse, on a data-driven spatial-analytical map. The point is not data-driven but has a marker type and label text that we manually enter.

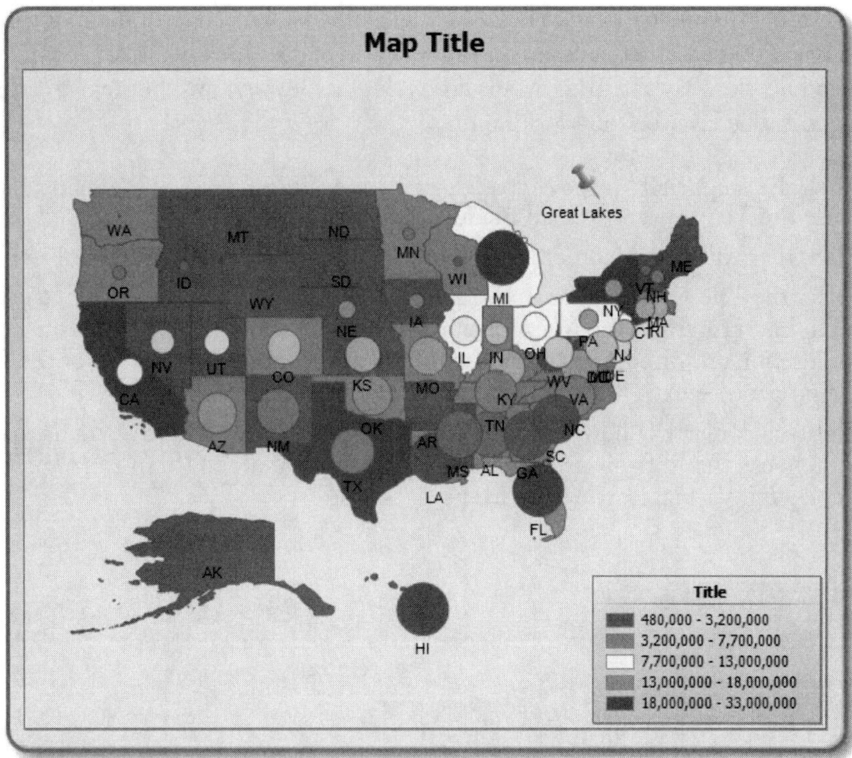

Figure 3-29 *Report Builder: map with point layer and manual point label*

BI TIP

Maps in Report Builder are "multilayer," meaning we can add or overlay spatial displays, analytical values that correspond to the spatial displays, and even points that do not come from any data source (but are instead manually placed and labeled).

Figure 3-29 shows the rendered result, where we have placed a PushPin Marker approximately over the water of the Great Lakes, and labeled it as such. In reality, one could place as many points on this Point layer as desired—and in fact, the points can be either manually created as we did in our working example, or driven from spatial data for the Point layer.

To finish the discussion of map layers, we'll also add a Tile layer to the map, which requires a working Internet connection to render a real-world geo-display Virtual Earth layer (also known today as a Bing Maps layer). Figure 3-30 shows the steps to add, and to debug, the Tile layer on our working map.

1. Click the map itself, in the central design pane (Step A). Click the map again to cause the Map Layers pop-up menu to display.
2. Click the Add Layer icon in the top of the Map Layers pop-up menu (Step B).
3. Select the Tile Layer choice in the Add Layer pop-up menu (Step C), to create a TileLayer1 item in the Map Layers list pane, and note the "The remote name could not be resolved: 'dev.virtualearth.net'" error message at the top of the central design pane—next, connect your computer to the Internet!
4. Right-click over the newly added TileLayer1 item in the Map Layers list pane, and choose the Refresh menu option on the pop-up menu (Step D), to properly display the Virtual Earth/Bing Maps visualization.

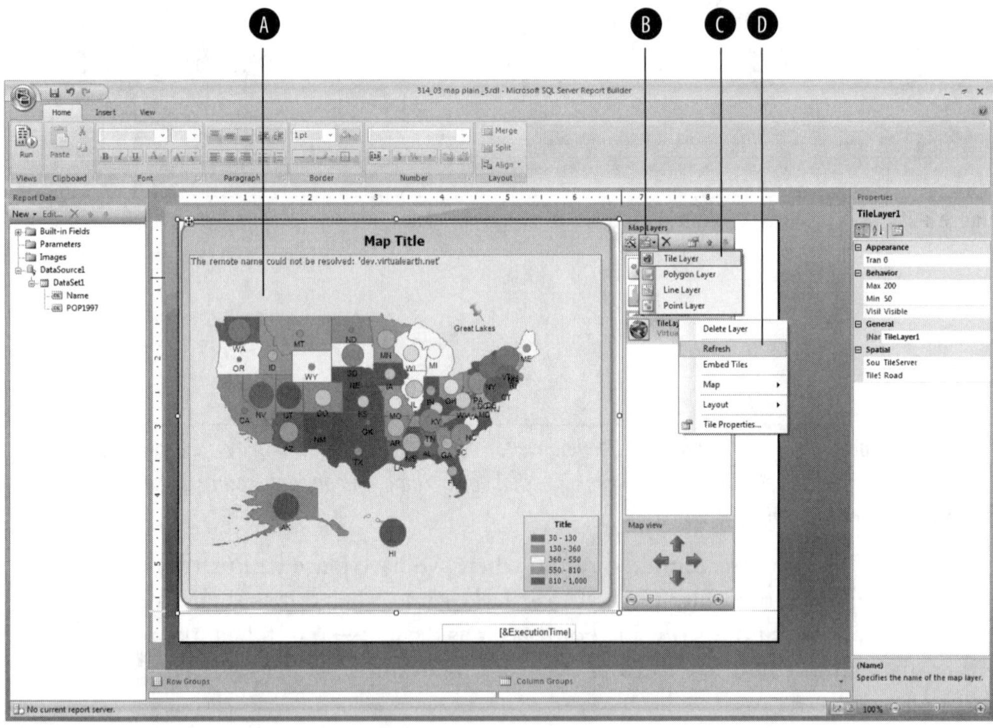

Figure 3-30 *Report Builder: adding a Tile layer, without an Internet connection*

Note in Figure 3-30 we started the steps *without* a working Internet connection—this was done on purpose to show the resulting error message "The remote name could not be resolved: 'dev.virtualearth.net'" at the top of the central design pane. We then connected to the Internet and used the Refresh menu option to display the Virtual Earth real-world background.

Figure 3-31 shows the rendered result with the Tile layer. Although our working example is now getting overly busy with layers and information, it does serve to explain the multilayer concept at work throughout this chapter.

Now that we have dealt with a map constructed from embedded geo-data (the U.S. map choice in the Report Builder Map Wizard), we'll try our hand in the next section at creating a map from spatial data (geo-data) that is drawn from a SQL Server datasct. The process will be remarkably the same, dealing with map spatial and analytical data, and then with the polygon color-coded display.

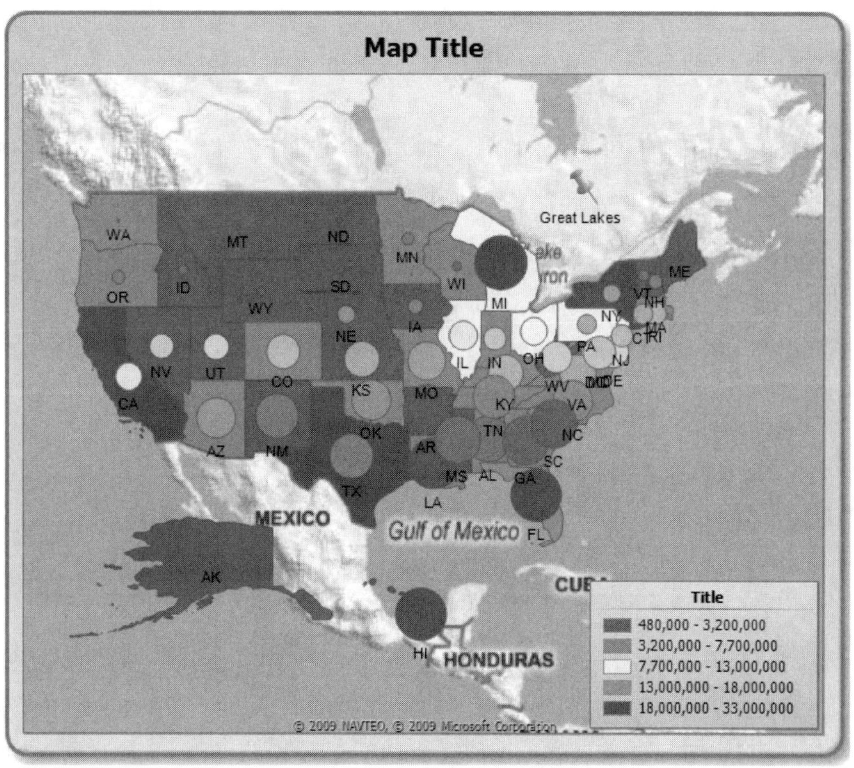

Figure 3-31 *Report Builder: map with Tile layer—with a working Internet connection*

Note, however, that Figure 3-31 is displaying Alaska and Hawaii on top of Mexico. This is because the Bing Maps layer is showing through—and in Figure 3-32 we alter the display by making the Bing Maps layer transparent.

1. Click the map itself, in the central design pane (Step A). Click the map again to cause the Map Layers pop-up menu to display.
2. Select the Tile Layer choice in the Add Layer pop-up menu (Step B), to display the Map Tile Layer Properties dialog box.
3. Click the Visibility tab in the dialog box (Step C), and choose the Hide option button (Step D).
4. Click OK to save this configuration.

Now we see in Figure 3-32 a rendered map that more clearly shows the analytical story on an state-by-state basis, without any underlying geographic layer. It's great that Report Builder has the capability to layer-in real-world geography with Bing Maps—but in this case we're just creating a straightforward data-display map of U.S. states.

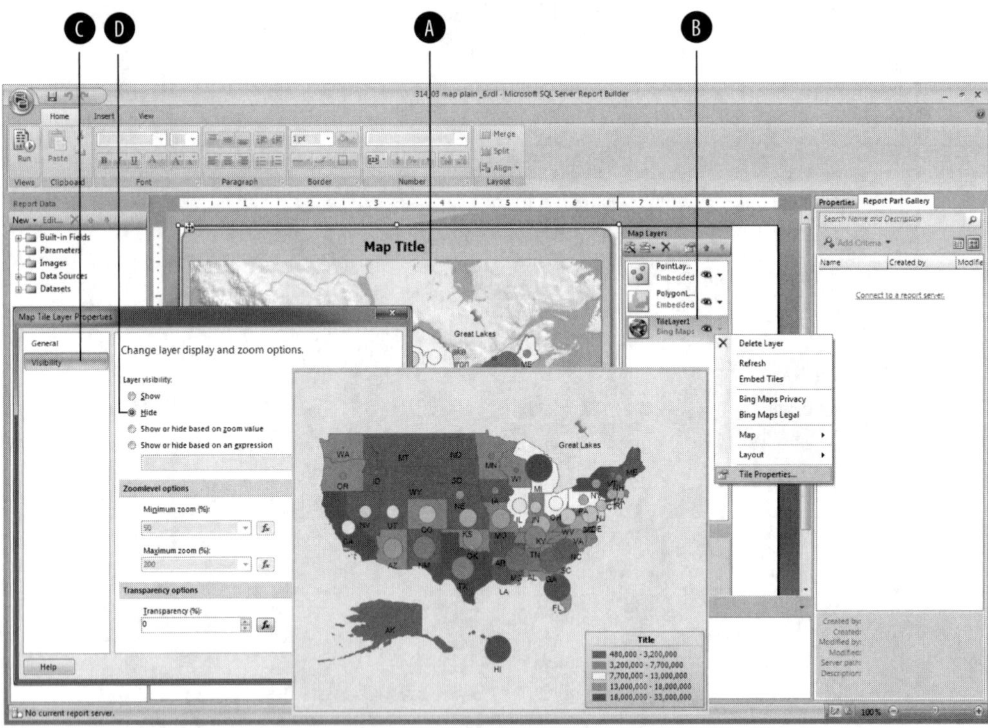

Figure 3-32 *Report Builder: map with Bing Maps layer—transparent*

Designing a Simple World Map from SQL Server Spatial Data

This section will explore the construction of a map geo-display from scratch—drawing on spatial data types from SQL Server 2008. We'll see the interesting technology at work in SQL Server with Polygon information in a spatial data field that can be interpreted by the Report Builder Map Designer, to produce a geo-display of the world. The result is amazing, when we realize we don't have to be spatial data experts to create a good map with analytical data value.

BI TIP

Spatial data types in SQL Server support two kinds of mapping: geography, where we're interested in real-world country-state-province displays (or layers), and geometry, where we're interested in flat-space displays such as buildings on an office campus and floor plans within the buildings.

Figure 3-33 starts our world map design process, in this case without using the Report Builder Map Wizard.

1. Click the Insert tab on the Report Builder top ribbon menu itself (Step A).
2. Click the Map icon on the Data Regions menu group (Step B).
3. Choose Insert Map on the drop-down menu (Step C).

Note how different the initial map report display is in Figure 3-33—we have only a grid that roughly resembles a map with latitude and longitude coordinate grid lines. In the following figures we'll be taking a nuts-and-bolts approach to designing a map report—and not using the wizard that could be started by clicking the Map icon in the Click To Add Data pane, on the central report design screen. We're doing this to gain an understanding of the components that make up a map report.

BI TIP

Remember, a map is basically a geo-layer of spatial data polygons that are used to visually depict areas of the real world—with an overlay of analytical data values that can be associated, value by value, with the areas of the real world. The other thing to keep in mind is that this association of data is accomplished with analytical data values and must have, on a row-by-row basis, data values that can provide a link between a geo-area and an analytical value being displayed.

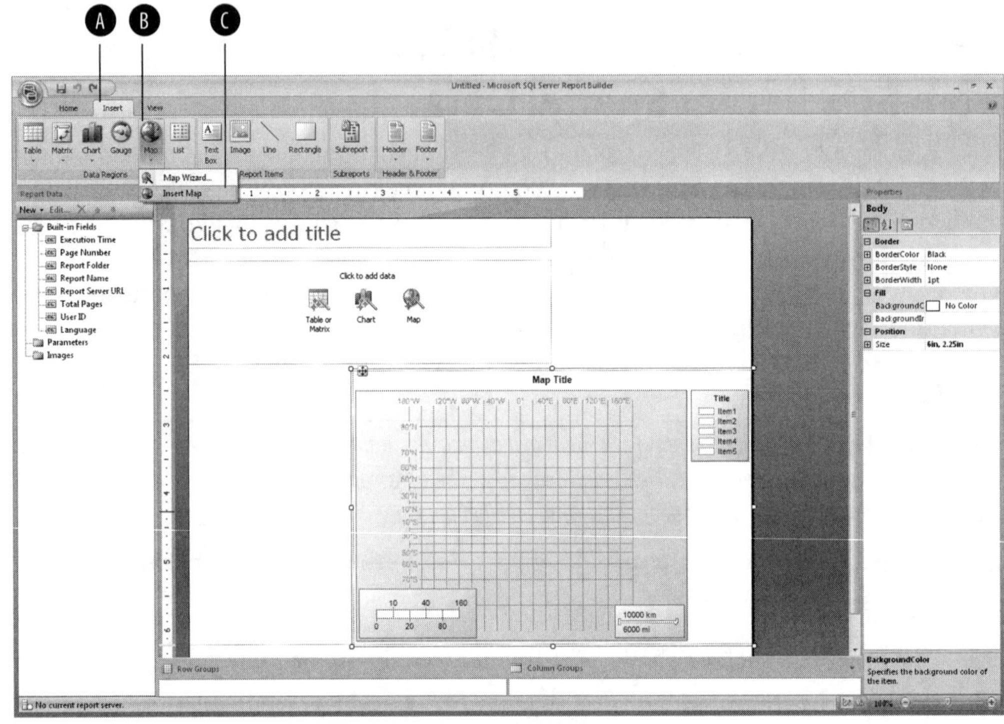

Figure 3-33 *Report Builder: creating a new map from a spatial data source*

In Figure 3-34 we see the next step in our process of manually building a map, where we define a data source connection without using the Map Wizard.

1. Click New (Step A) and choose Data Source on the upper-left Report Data menu (Step B).
2. On the Data Source Properties dialog box | General pane, choose the "Use a connection embedded in my report" option button (Step C), select Microsoft SQL Server in the Select Connection Type drop-down menu (Step D), and click Build (Step E) to display the Connection Properties dialog box for the following steps.
3. Click the Server Name drop-down menu (Step F), and choose the SQL Server desired from the list of available SQL Servers (note, you can simply type a period in the drop-down menu to quickly establish a connection to your Local SQL Server).
4. Choose Use Windows Authentication (Step G) to use your domain ID and Password for the SQL Server database, or choose Use SQL Server Authentication if you have an ID and Password for the SQL Server database.

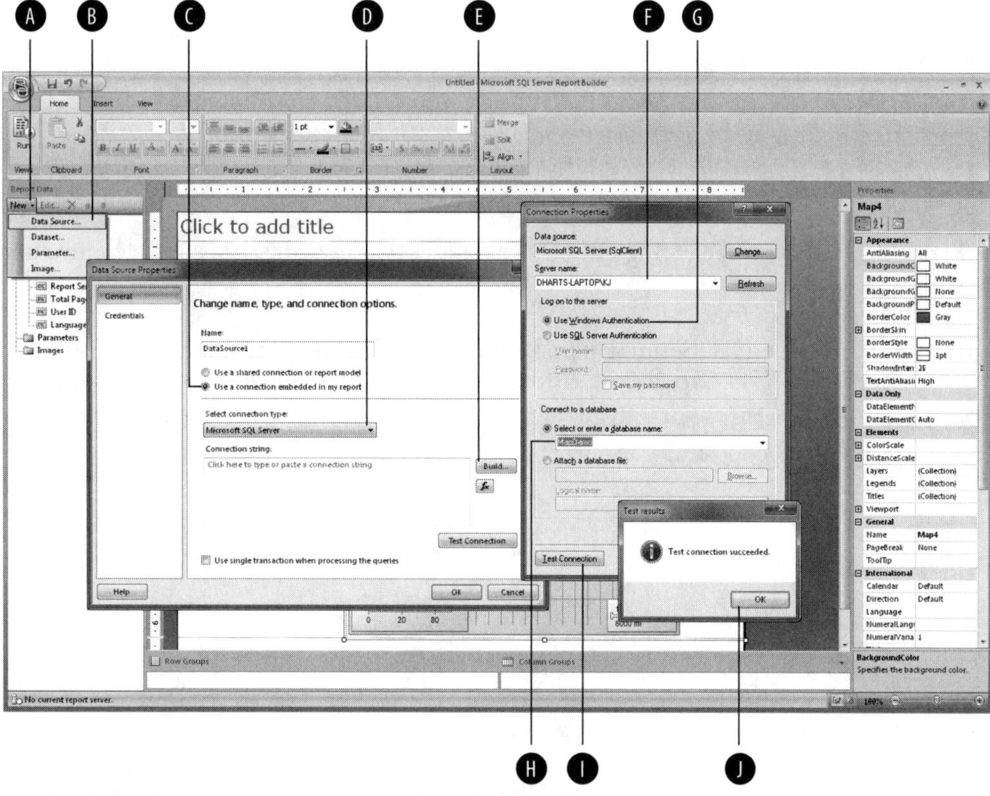

Figure 3-34 *Report Builder: creating a new data source for spatial and analytical data*

5. Choose the "Select or enter a database name" option button on the Connect To A Database sub-pane, and choose MapDemo (Step H) from the list of available databases.
6. Click Test Connection (Step I) to verify that the Connection Properties are valid.
7. Click OK (Step J) to continue and save changes.

The SQL Server connection that we've configured, both for the first U.S. map report and for this world map report, is easy to set up. In fact, report designers working with SQL Server Report Builder often use SQL Server Integration Services (SSIS) to dynamically import data from other types of databases and data sources to a SQL Server database just because it's so much easier to work with analytical data when it's on the SQL Server platform.

BI TIP

Once the map report (or any report, for that matter) data source is established to provide a connection to SQL Server, or Oracle, or any valid data repository, then data source(s) must be configured to draw rows and columns of data from the data source. This is the most challenging part of report design, since the visual design tools are pretty much "what you see is what you get" and readily understood.

Figure 3-35 displays the configuration of a dataset that uses the data source connection to SQL Server.

1. Right-click the DataSource1 item in the report designer left-pane tree of report elements (Step A), and choose Add Dataset from the pop-up menu (Step B).
2. In the Dataset Properties dialog box | Query pane, leaving the DataSet1 default name in place, choose DataSource1 in the Data Source drop-down menu (Step C).

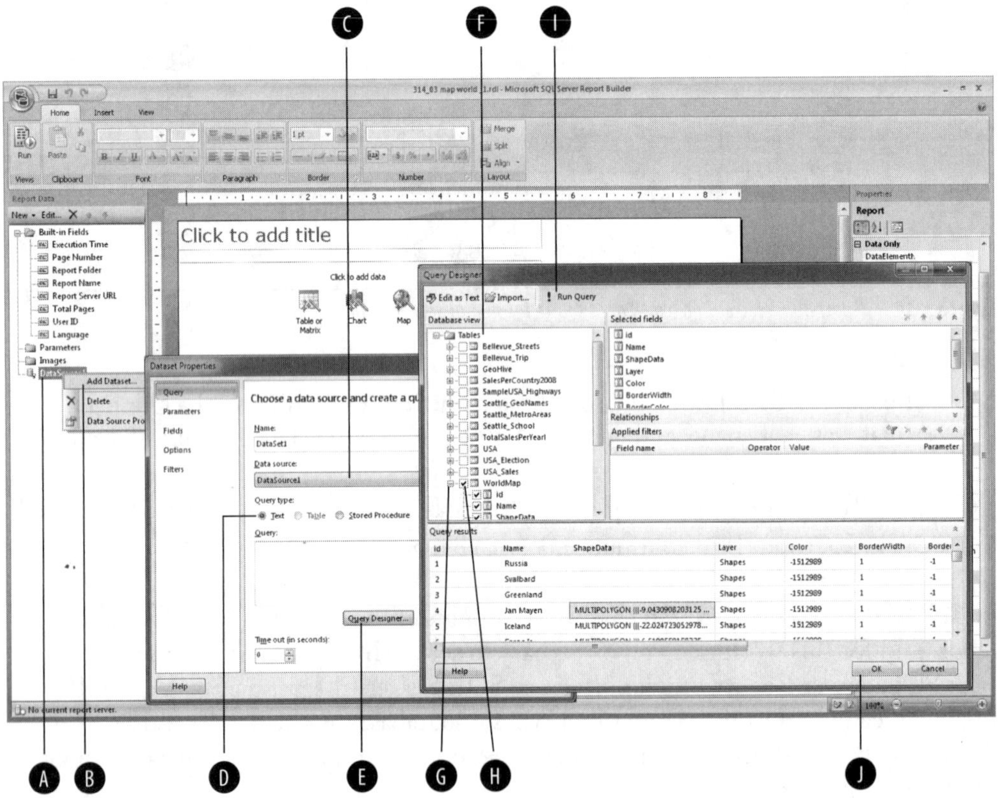

Figure 3-35 *Report Builder: creating a new dataset for spatial data*

3. In the Dataset Properties dialog box | Query pane, choose Text for the Query Type (Step D), and click Query Designer (Step E) to display the Query Designer dialog box.
4. In the Query Designer dialog box, click the + button on the Tables node in the Database view tree (Step F) to display the Data Source tables available.
5. In the Query Designer dialog box, click the + button on the WorldMap node in the Database View tree (Step G) to expand and display the data elements of the WorldMap table.
6. In the Query Designer dialog box, click the check box on the WorldMap node in the Database view (Step H) to select all the Spatial Data elements for the Selected Fields right-side pane.
7. In the Query Designer dialog box, click the Run Query menu button at the top of the dialog box (Step I) to test-run this spatial data query.
8. Click OK (Step J) to save the query.

The steps we followed with Figure 3-35 are notable, in that we chose a spatial dataset from a SQL Server data repository—which has built-in spatial data types! This means that SQL Server 2008 has special data types that are especially for holding geo-data. In running the query for Figure 3-35, we displayed the results of this spatial dataset in the Query Results pane—and we can see that the Shape Data field contains polygon data that the Report Builder Map features will use to draw a map that is made up of the polygons.

BI TIP

The simplest way to understand spatial data is to realize it contains geographic coordinates for real-world locations, much like the GPS coordinates with which we are familiar. The SQL Server Spatial Data type can contain a single point coordinate, or a set of coordinates that represents a line, or a set of coordinates that represents a polygon (which can represent the boundary of a country, for example).

In Figure 3-36 we accomplish the more common task of creating an analytical dataset—which will be used to add analytical display information to the spatial dataset.

1. Right-click the DataSource1 item in the report designer left-pane tree of report elements (Step A), and choose Add Dataset from the pop-up menu (Step B).
2. In the Dataset Properties dialog box | Query pane, leaving the DataSet2 default name in place, choose DataSource1 in the Data Source drop-down menu (Step C).
3. In the Dataset Properties dialog box | Query pane, choose Text for the Query Type (Step D), and click Query Designer (Step E) to display the Query Designer dialog box.

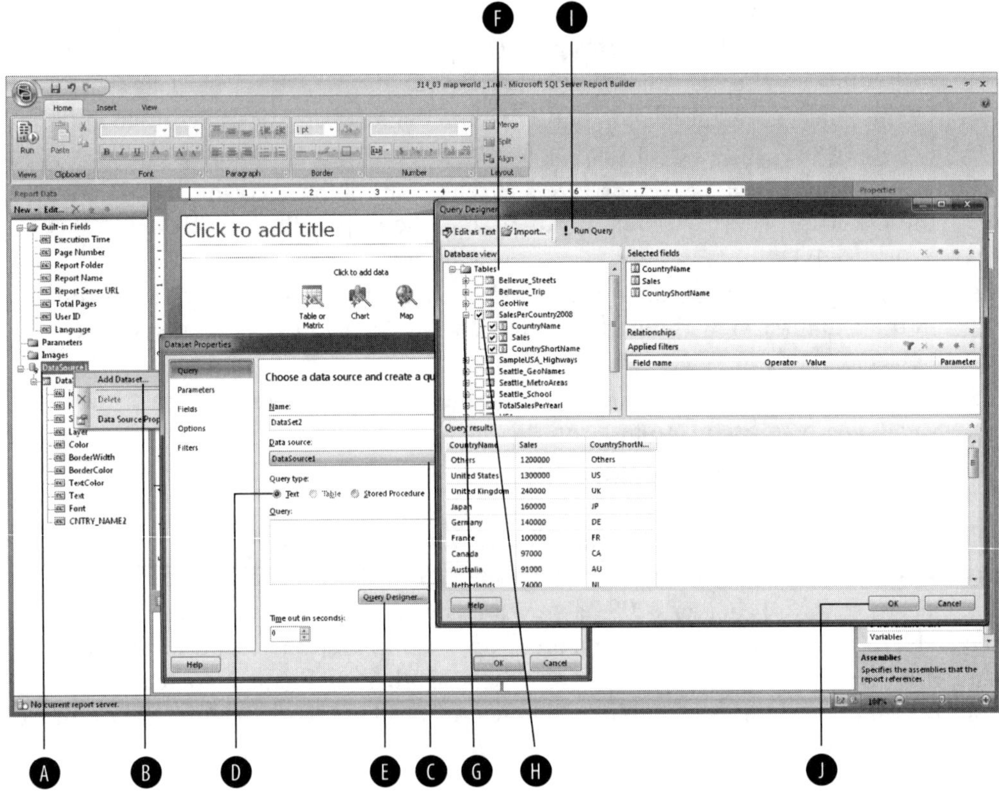

Figure 3-36 *Report Builder: creating a new dataset for analytical data*

4. In the Query Designer dialog box, click the + button on the Tables node in the Database View tree (Step F) to display the Data Source tables available.
5. In the Query Designer dialog box, click the + button on the SalesPerCountry2008 node in the Database View tree (Step G) to expand and display the data elements of the SalesPerCountry2008 table.
6. In the Query Designer dialog box, click the check box on the SalesPerCountry2008 node in the Database View (Step H) to select all the analytical data elements for the Selected Fields right-side pane.
7. In the Query Designer dialog box, click the Run Query menu button at the top of the dialog box (Step I) to test-run this analytical data query.
8. Click OK (Step J) to save the query.

Note in Figure 3-36 that we queried the spatial data field CountryName with contents such as "United States and "United Kingdom." Back in Figure 3-35 we queried the analytical data field Name with contents such as "Russia" and "Svalbard." We will use these fields to match the spatial and analytical datasets for display in the map report!

BI TIP

Once we have spatial data for a map report, the matching of spatial data to analytical data is usually straightforward. A commonsense look at the data will often show fairly obvious connections between spatial and analytical datasets, such as CountryName and Country, for example.

Figure 3-37 continues our map design process, with the addition of a Polygon layer to the map, which will hold and display the spatial data in a world map.

1. Click the map itself, in the central design pane (Step A). Click the map again to cause the Map Layers pop-up menu to display.
2. Click the Add Layer icon in the Map Layers pop-up menu (Step B).
3. Choose the Polygon Layer choice in the drop-down menu (Step C).

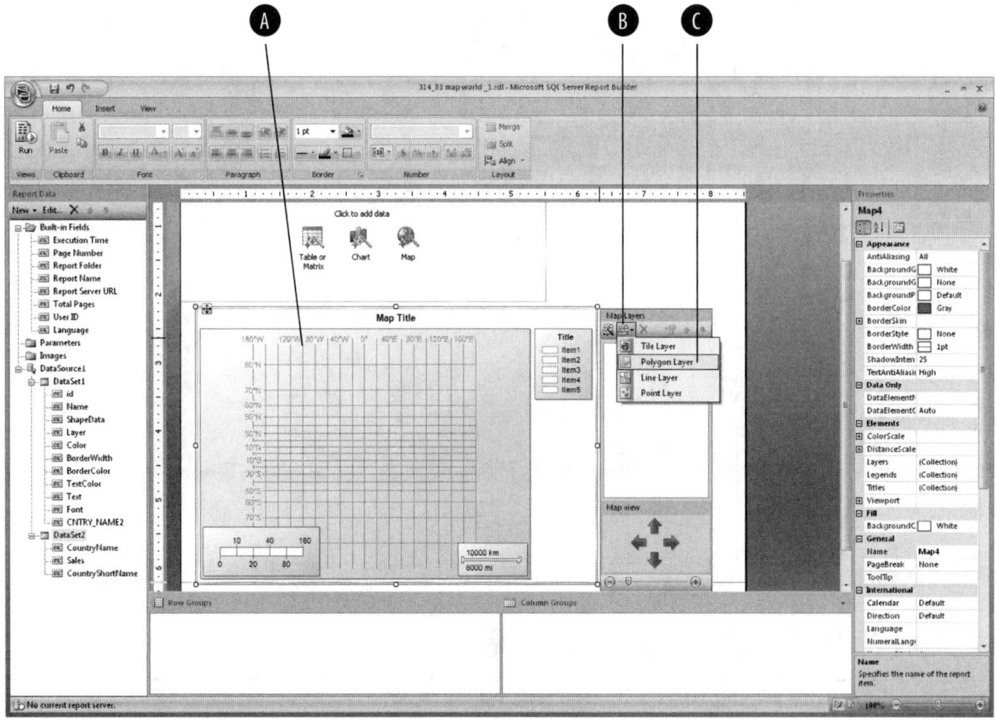

Figure 3-37 *Report Builder: creating a new Polygon layer*

In Figure 3-37 we still don't have a geo-display that looks like a map—we're just adding a Polygon layer to hold the map. Figure 3-38 shows the next steps in this process as we add the spatial data to this Polygon layer of the map.

1. Click the map itself, in the central design pane (Step A). Click the map again to cause the Map Layers pop-up menu to display.
2. Click the PolygonLayer1 choice in the Map Layers pop-up menu (Step B), and choose Layer Data in the Polygon pop-up menu (Step C).
3. In the Map Polygon Layer Properties dialog box | General pane, choose the Spatial Field In A Dataset option button (Step D).
4. In the Map Polygon Layer Properties dialog box | General pane, choose DataSet1 (Step E, which is the default name we used when configuring the spatial dataset) in the Dataset Name drop-down menu.

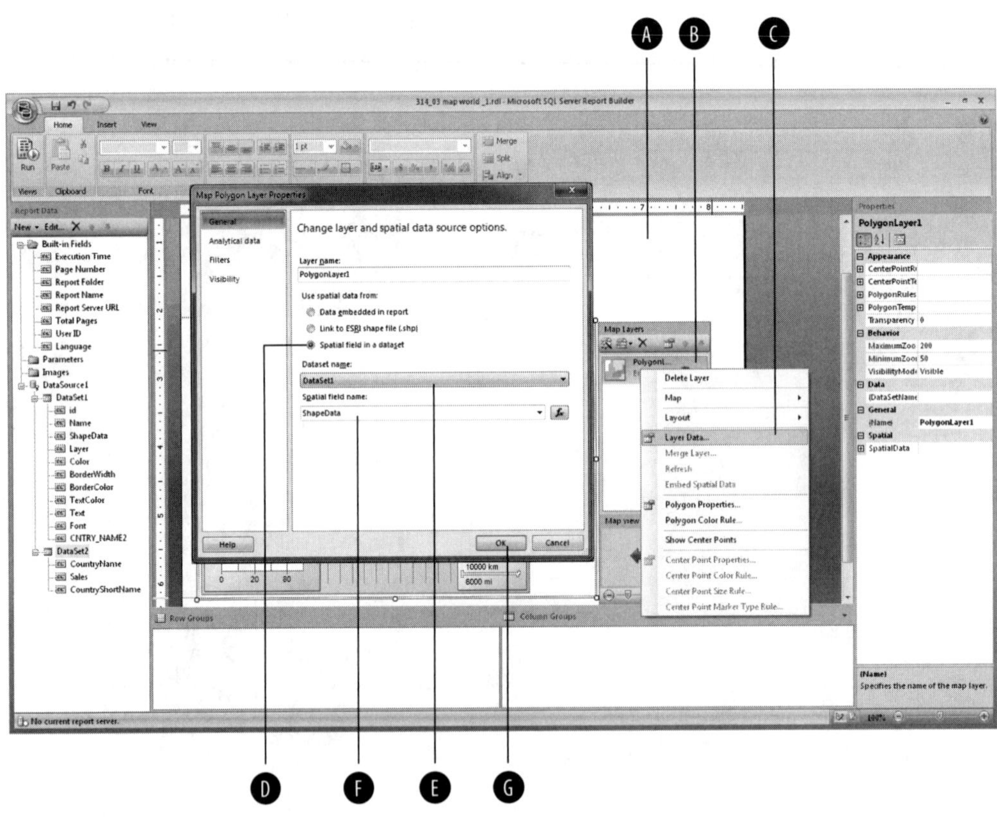

Figure 3-38 *Report Builder: associating spatial data to the Polygon layer*

5. In the Map Polygon Layer Properties dialog box | General pane, choose ShapeData in the Spatial Field Name drop-down menu (Step F).
6. Click OK (Step G) to save the configuration.

Wow, in Figure 3-38 we found the spatial dataset field of ShapeData—which is the same ShapeData field we displayed when configuring the spatial dataset query previously in Figure 3-34! The Report Builder map design features have the built-in ability to interpret the polygon data we saw in the ShapeData field and turn it into a map. This is part of the magic of the Microsoft Report Builder Map technology that makes it reasonable for report designers to create a map report without having to know much about spatial data technology in general.

In Figure 3-39, the association of spatial and analytical data is configured. This is the same process we followed in the first U.S. map we designed earlier in the chapter.

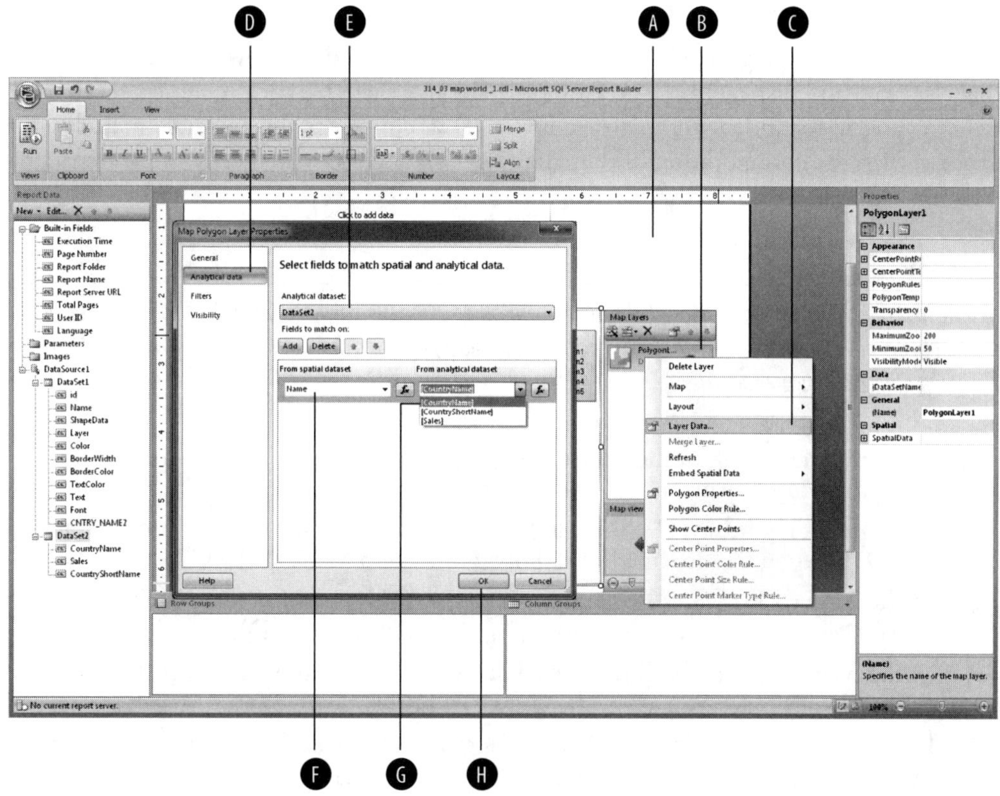

Figure 3-39 *Report Builder: associating analytical data to the Polygon layer, and matching the analytical data to the spatial data*

1. Click the map itself, in the central design pane (Step A). Click the map again to cause the Map Layers pop-up menu to display.
2. Click the PolygonLayer1 choice in the Map Layers pop-up menu (Step B), and choose Layer Data in the Polygon pop-up menu (Step C).
3. In the Map Polygon Layer Properties dialog box, click the Analytical Data choice in the left-side navigation pane (Step D).
4. In the Map Polygon Layer Properties dialog box | Analytical Data pane, choose DataSet2 (Step E, which is the default name we used when configuring the analytical dataset) in the Analytical Dataset drop-down menu.
5. In the Map Polygon Layer Properties dialog box | Analytical Data pane, choose Name in the From Spatial Dataset drop-down menu (Step F).
6. In the Map Polygon Layer Properties dialog box | Analytical Data pane, choose CountryName in the From Analytical Dataset drop-down menu (Step G).
7. Click OK (Step H) to save the configuration.

It's nice to see in Figure 3-39 that the dialog boxes and drop-down menu choices make sense—and display the Spatial Name field and the Analytical CountryName field in an easy-to-understand manner. Figure 3-40 continues this intuitive map design process, with the configuration of the Analytical Data color-scheme, by implementing a Polygon Color rule.

BI TIP

Note that the analytical data color visualization is configured using the Polygon Color rule. This is because we want to display analytical values (or SUMs of analytical values) in colors that vary by sub-polygon—which in the working example are countries.

1. Click the map itself, in the central design pane (Step A). Click the map again to cause the Map Layers pop-up menu to display.
2. Click the PolygonLayer1 choice in the Map Layers pop-up menu (Step B), and choose Polygon Color Rule in the Polygon pop-up menu (Step C).
3. In the Map Color Rules Properties dialog box | General pane, choose the "Visualize data by using color ranges" option button (Step D).
4. In the Map Color Rules Properties dialog box | General pane, select the "=Sum(Fields!Sales.Value)" in the Data Field drop-down menu (Step E).
5. In the Map Color Rules Properties dialog box | General pane, choose Red for the Start Color (Step F), Yellow for the Middle Color (Step G), and Green for the End Color (Step H).
6. Click OK (Step I) to save the configuration.

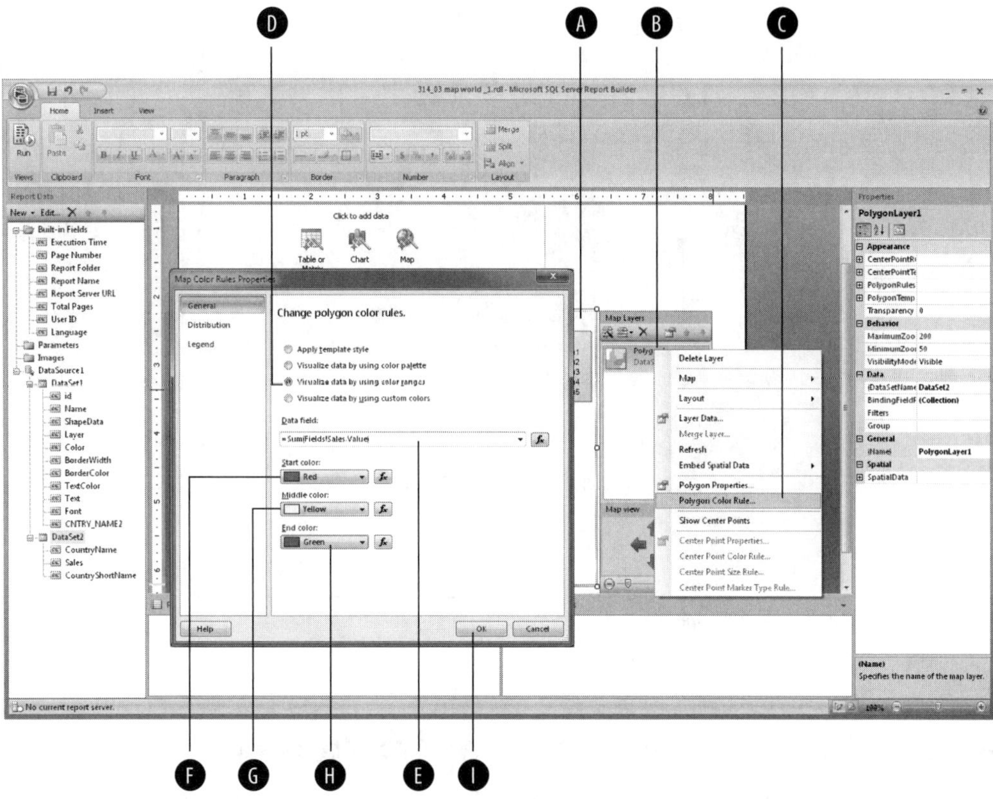

Figure 3-40 *Report Builder: choosing the analytical data element display, and the Polygon Color rule display*

Figure 3-41 shows the newly rendered map report, with countries showing the SUM of sales by Country—which was easy to implement since the Map Report Designer automatically provided a Sum(Fields!Sales.Value) in the Data Field drop-down menu. We are using the familiar "red is bad and green is good" color range, which accurately portrays the higher sales numbers in the "good" color of green.

The map display in Figure 3-41 is rather flat, however, and we're going to explore this and other map projection options in the next section, where we start to look at the map Viewport. This will really set the stage for the incredible variety of geo-display options we have when working with spatial data.

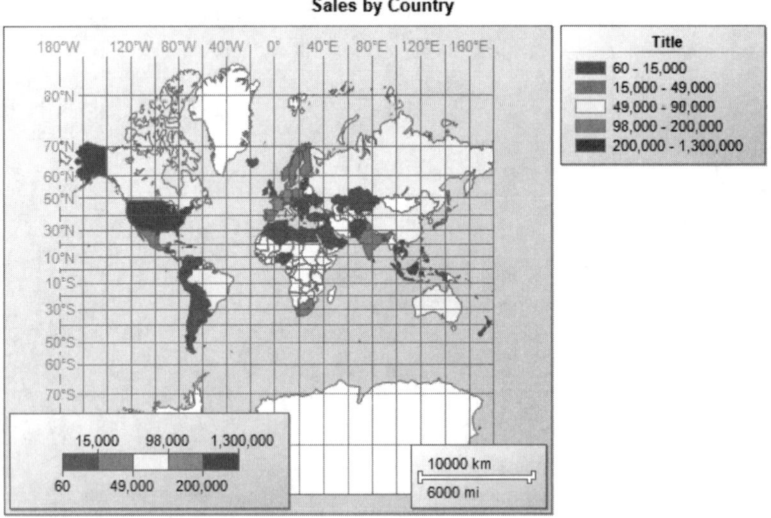

Figure 3-41 *Report Builder: rendering the world map*

Modifying the Map Geography Viewport

This section will enhance the map display with a few simple adjustments of distance scale to show easy-to-interpret labeling of the analytical values that are displayed on the world map. We will also look at the types of "projection" that significantly affect the way a two-dimensional map looks when portraying geo-areas (polygons) that actually come from a three-dimensional spherical globe.

Figure 3-42 starts our world map design process, in this case without using the Report Builder Map Wizard.

1. Right-click the map itself, in the central design pane (Step A).
2. Click the Show Meridians pop-up menu choice (Step B) to uncheck the Meridian display.
3. Right-click the map again, and click the Show Parallels pop-up menu choice again (Step C) to uncheck the Parallels display.
4. Right-click the Color Scale (Step D), and select the Color Scale Properties pop-up menu choice (Step E) to display the Map Color Scale Properties dialog box.
5. In the Map Color Scale Properties dialog box | Number pane, select the Currency choice in the Category list pane (Step F), and click the Use 1000 Separator (,) check box (Step G).

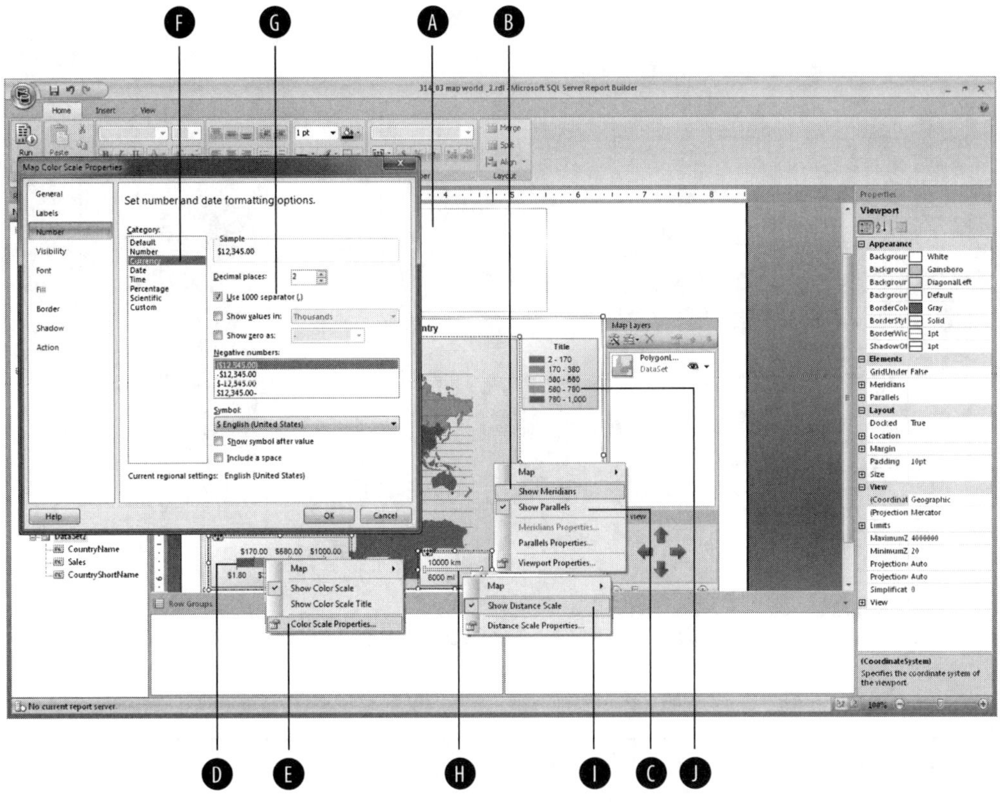

Figure 3-42 *Report Builder: configuring the map meridians, parallels, distance scale, and color scale*

6. Right-click the Distance Scale on the map (Step H), and click the Show Distance Scale pop-up menu choice (Step I) to uncheck the Distance Scale display.
7. Right-click the legend on the map (Step J), and click the Delete Legend pop-up menu choice to remove the legend from the map display.

Figure 3-42 is a pretty standard map display configuration change (which we've done before) with the addition of labeling the Color Scale, but the Meridians and Parallels choices hint at more significant map design considerations of real-world displays on a spherical globe. We'll look at these considerations with Figure 3-43, where we adjust the Projection.

1. Right-click the map itself, in the central design pane (Step A).
2. Click the Viewport Properties pop-up menu choice (Step B) to display the Map Viewport Properties dialog box.

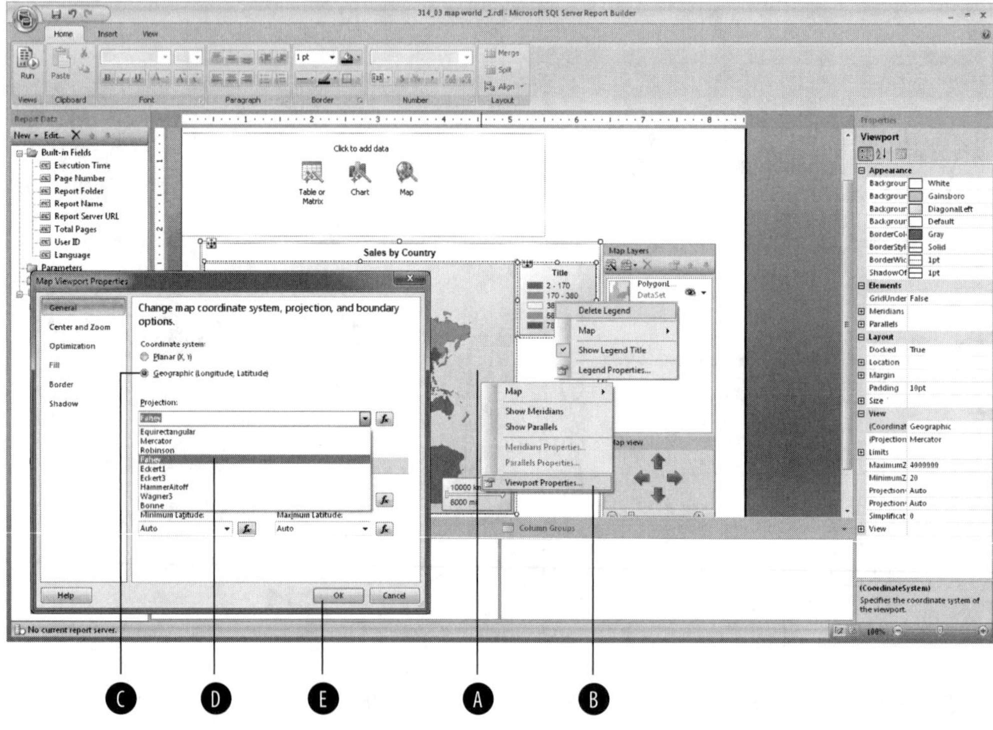

Figure 3-43 *Report Builder: configuring the Map Viewport Projection display*

3. In the Map Viewport Properties dialog box | General pane, choose the Geographic (Longitude, Latitude) option button for the Coordinate System (Step C).
4. Select the "Fahey" choice in the Projection drop-down menu (Step D).
5. Click OK (Step E) to save changes.

In Figure 3-44 you see the rendered result of our world map, with a color scale that makes sense in that it clearly indicates the currency sales levels—against a map that clearly shows the relative distribution of sales levels by country. Not surprisingly, there are no sales occurring in some of the poorest countries, and the highest sales are being registered in the United States and the United Kingdom, which are known to be larger consumers of goods.

BI TIP

As a general rule, it makes sense to have only one legend or scale on a map report; that helps the user interpret the analytical data value ranges. Typically this is a legend, or a distance scale, or a color scale.

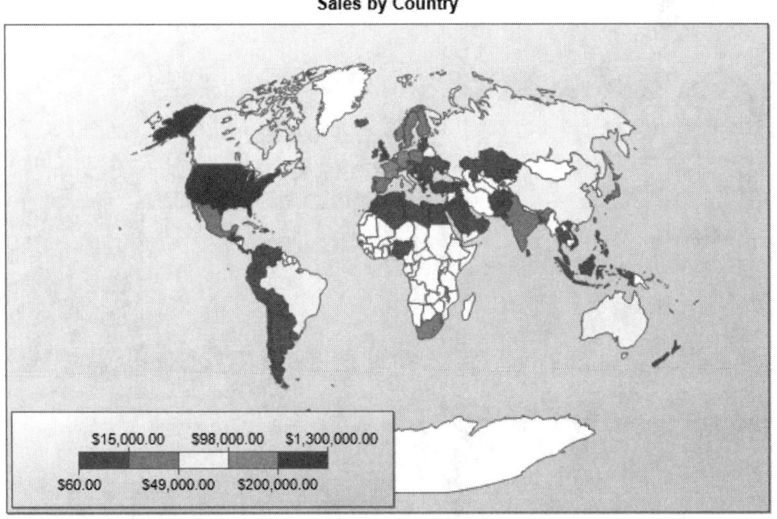

Figure 3-44 *Report Builder: rendering the world map*

Before we leave this section, we'll explore the Viewport Zoom and Projection options that can change the map in Figure 3-44. This way you can actually look at the different projection methods that have been used for many years to depict maps of the Earth, for purposes ranging from flat informational displays to realistic curved, globe-like representations of geo-visualizations. Figure 3-45 shows the steps we take to start the Projection exploration process.

1. Right-click the Color Scale (Step A) and uncheck the Show Color Scale (Step B) to simplify the map display.
2. Right-click the map itself, in the central design pane (Step C), to display the Viewport pop-up menu, and select Show Meridians (Step D) and Show Parallels (Step E) to enhance the map Projection visualizations.
3. On the same Viewport pop-up menu, select the Viewport Properties menu choice (Step F) to display the Map Viewport Properties dialog box.
4. In the Map Viewport Properties dialog box | Center And Zoom pane (Step G), change the Zoom Level (%) to 50 (Step H) to produce smaller Map Projection Examples.
5. Select the Equirectangular choice in the Projection drop-down menu (Step I).
6. Click OK (Step J) to save changes, and click Run to render each Projection example show in Table 3-2.

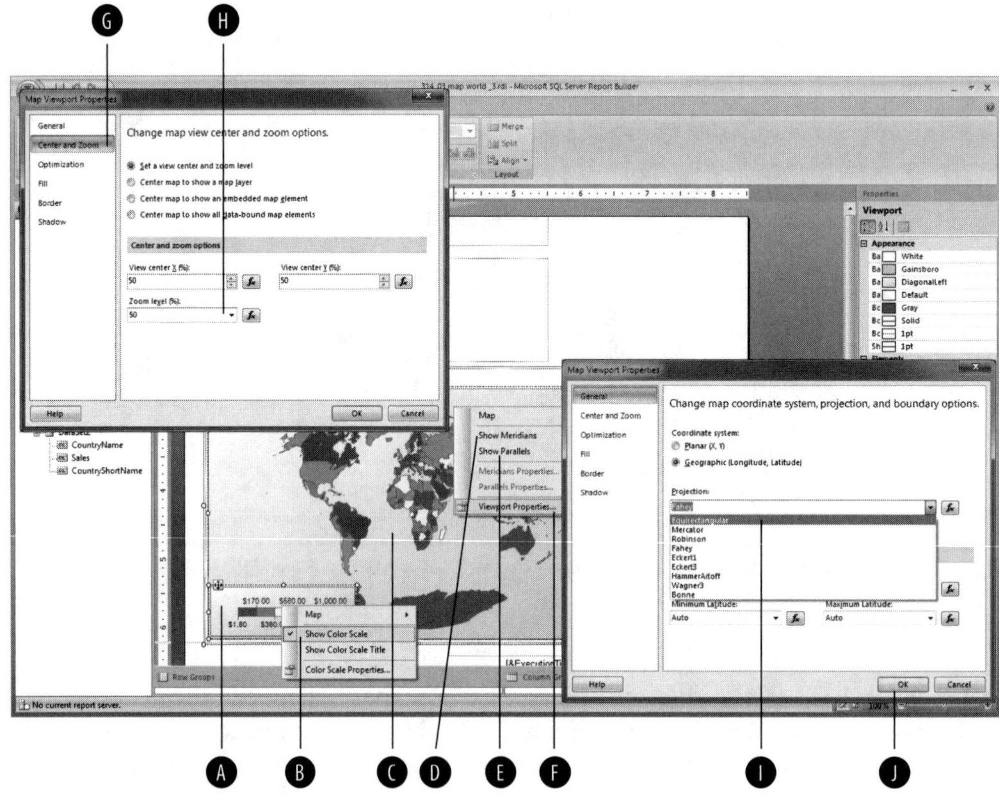

Figure 3-45 *Report Builder: changing the viewport zoom and projection*

Note the following key of map projection terminology, which can be used in the discussion of projection methods in Table 3-2:

- Meridan = VERTICAL = Longitude
- Parallel = HORIZONTAL = Latitude

As we look at Figure 3-45, it would be interesting to add a chart analytic to the map display—if we can do so in a manner that adds to the user's understanding and does not detract from the simplicity of the analytical values on a spatial display. We'll explore this in the next section.

Map Example	Map Projection	Description
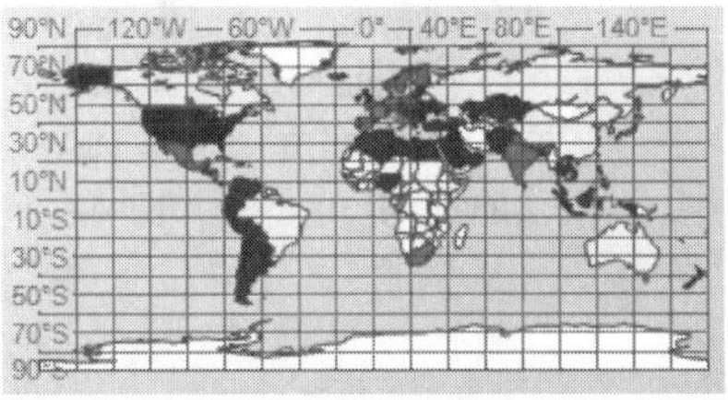	Equirectangular	A projection that displays longitude and latitude presented as rectangular coordinates.
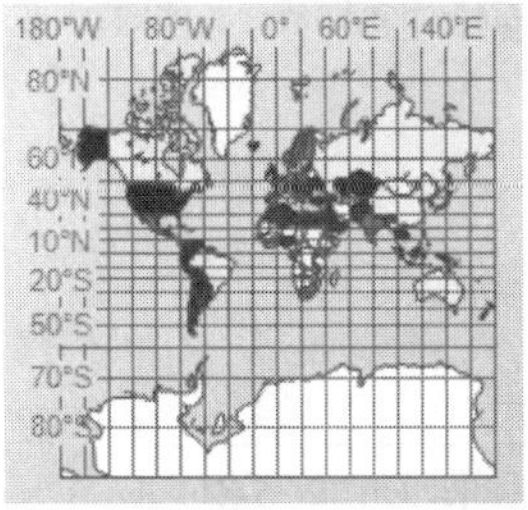	Mercator	A projection that displays less distortion around the equator.
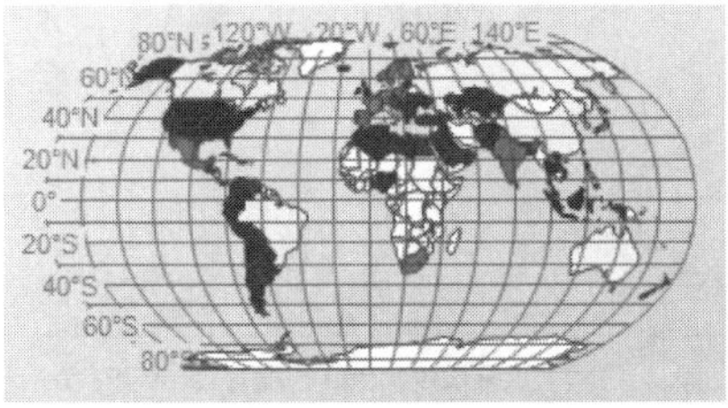	Robinson	A projection that displays less distortion of large areas from the equator to the poles.
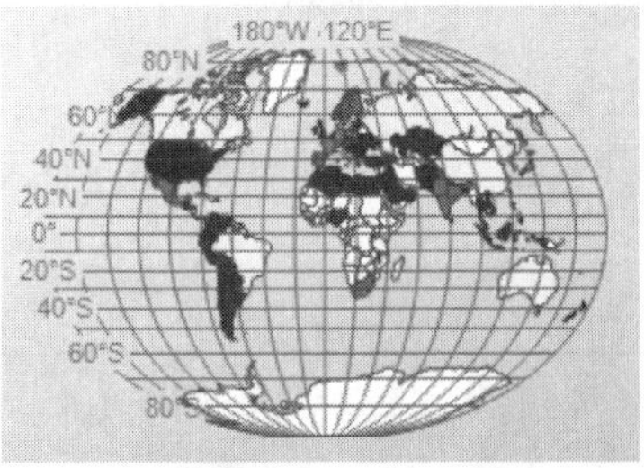	Fahey	A projection that displays less distortion of large areas from the equator to the poles, but more spherical than Robinson.
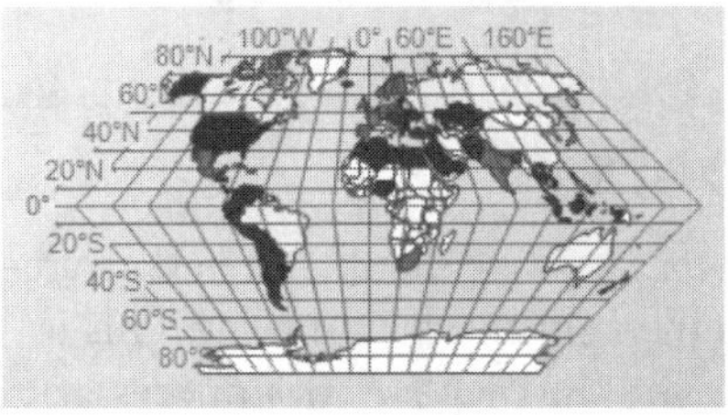	Eckert1	A projection that displays equally spaced parallels = horizontal latitude, and straight lines for meridians = vertical longitude.

Table 3-2 *Map Projection Examples (Continued)*

Map Example	Map Projection	Description
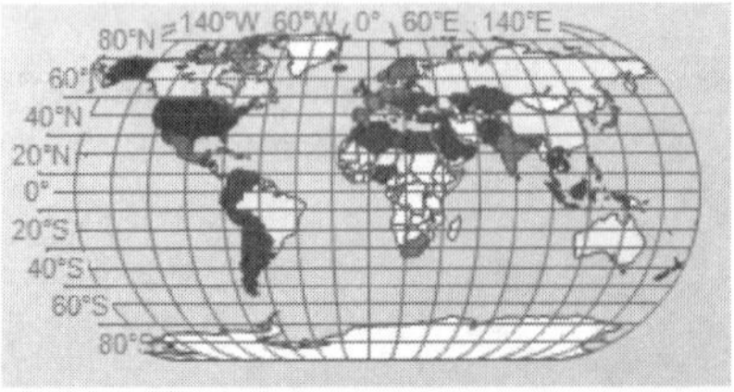	Eckert3	A projection that displays equally spaced parallels = horizontal latitude, and curved lines for meridians = vertical longitude.
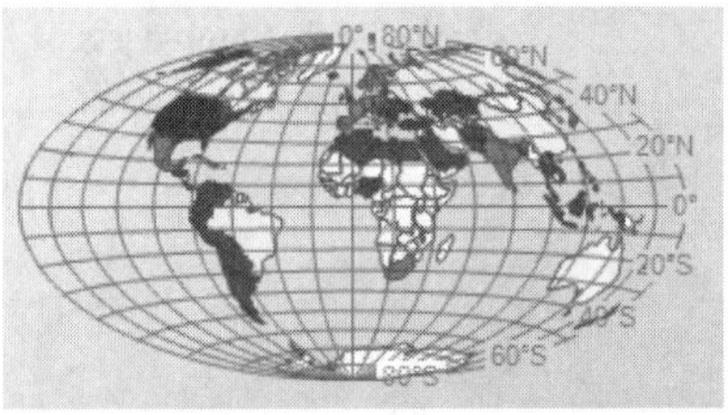	HammerAitoff	A projection known as polar maps.
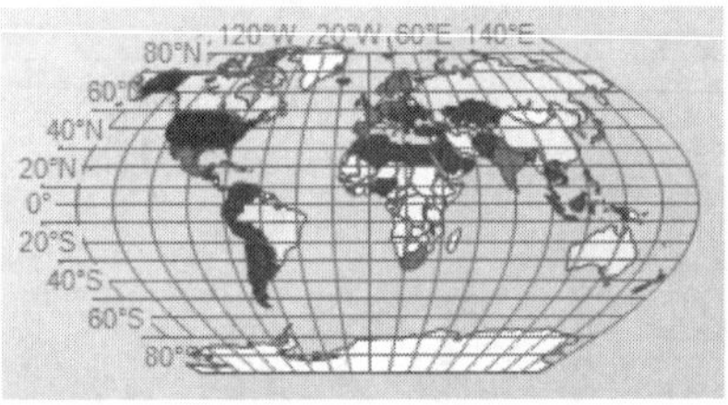	Wagner3	A projection that is common for world maps.
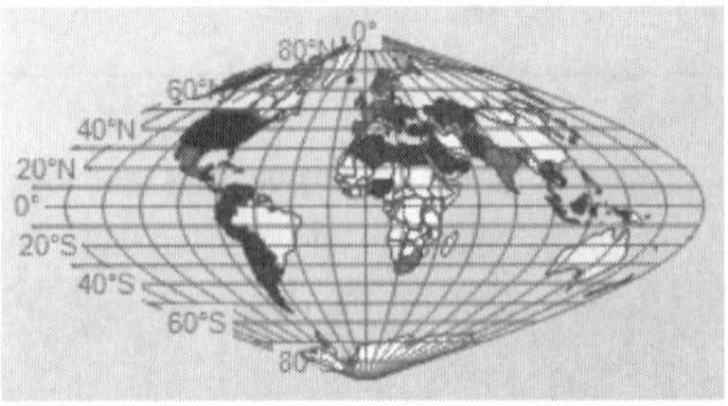	Bonne	A projection that is sometimes used in atlases.

Table 3-2 *Map Projection Examples*

Adding Charts to the Map Report

This section is one of the most important in the chapter, since we'll enhance and arrange the map elements, and create chart elements that complement the map display. This is easier than it sounds, since it becomes a matter of keeping the map free of unnecessary clutter, and creating charts that show the map data in slightly different but valuable ways that are easy to interpret when viewed next to the map in the overall report.

And although one might wonder why charts are handled here in a chapter about maps—it actually makes sense to combine the two presentation devices so that each provides its own unique view of the same data story where the "anchor object" for the report is the map and the charts amplify the map information.

Figure 3-46 shows the starting point for our final map design process, with the addition of a chart to the map report that we're building the Report Builder design interface.

1. Right-click the DataSource1 item in the report designer left-pane tree of report elements (Step A), and choose Add Dataset from the pop-up menu (Step B).
2. In the Dataset Properties dialog box | Query pane, type **Top_5_Countries** for the Name (Step C, no spaces allowed in the name), and choose DataSource1 in the Data Source drop-down menu (Step D).

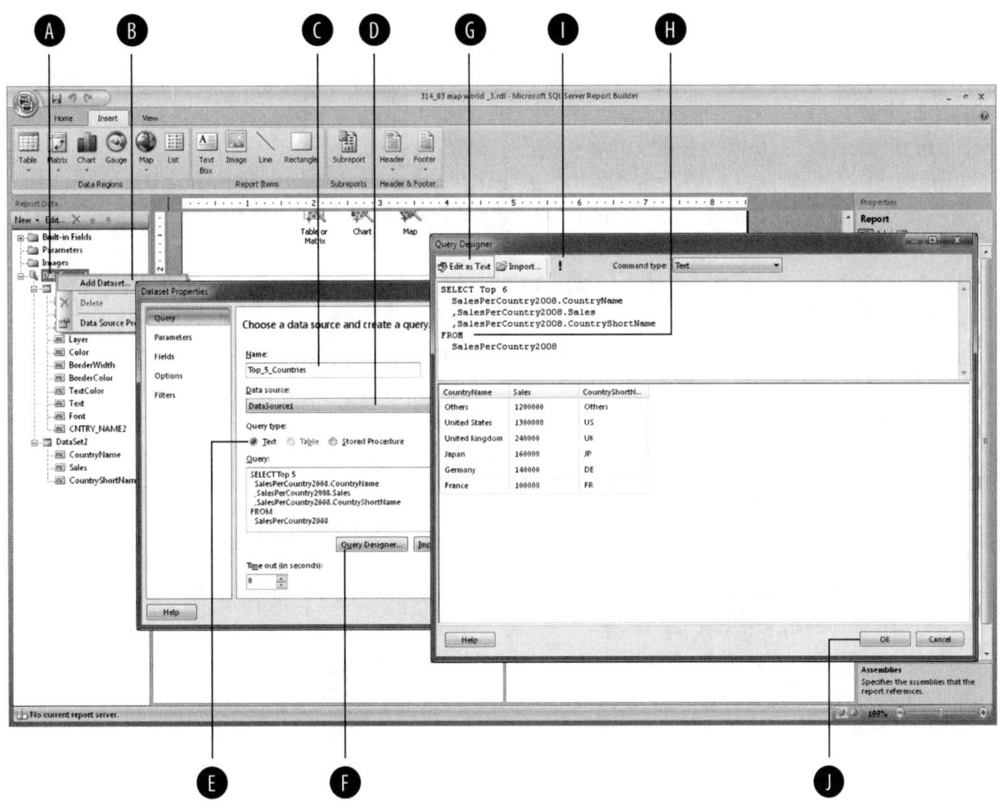

Figure 3-46 *Report Builder: adding a dataset for a Top 5 Pie chart*

3. In the Dataset Properties dialog box | Query pane, choose Text for the Query Type (Step E), and click Query Designer (Step F) to display the Query Designer dialog box.
4. In the Query Designer dialog box, click Edit As Text at the top menu (Step G), and enter the following SQL clause (Step H):

```
SELECT Top 6
  SalesPerCountry2008.CountryName
  ,SalesPerCountry2008.Sales
  ,SalesPerCountry2008.CountryShortName
FROM
  SalesPerCountry2008
```

5. In the Query Designer dialog box, click the ! icon (Step I) to test-run this chart data query.
6. Click OK (Step J) to save the query.

Note in the Figure 3-46 query we are using the old tried-and-true method of manually typing (or copy and paste) SQL for our dataset, since we're creating something more than a simple Select statement. We are retrieving the Top 6 Countries to effectively get the Top 5, because one of the Country data returns is "Others" as we see in the query test.

Figure 3-47 continues our process of creating datasets, in this case for Total Sales by Year—to support a chart for complementary analysis in the map report.

1. Right-click the DataSource1 item in the report designer left-pane tree of report elements (Step A), and choose Add Dataset from the pop-up menu (Step B).
2. In the Dataset Properties dialog box | Query pane, type **Sales_by_Year** for the Name (Step C, no spaces allowed in the name), and choose DataSource1 in the Data Source drop-down menu (Step D).
3. In the Dataset Properties dialog box | Query pane, choose Text for the Query Type (Step E), and click Query Designer (Step F) to display the Query Designer dialog box.
4. In the Query Designer dialog box, click the + button on the TotalSalesPerYear node in the Database View tree (Step G) to expand and display the data elements of the TotalSalesPerYear table.
5. In the Query Designer dialog box, click the check box on the TotalSalesPerYear node in the Database View (Step H) to select all the Spatial Data elements for the Selected Fields right-side pane.
6. In the Query Designer dialog box, click the ! icon (Step I) to test-run this chart data query.
7. Click OK (Step J) to save the query.

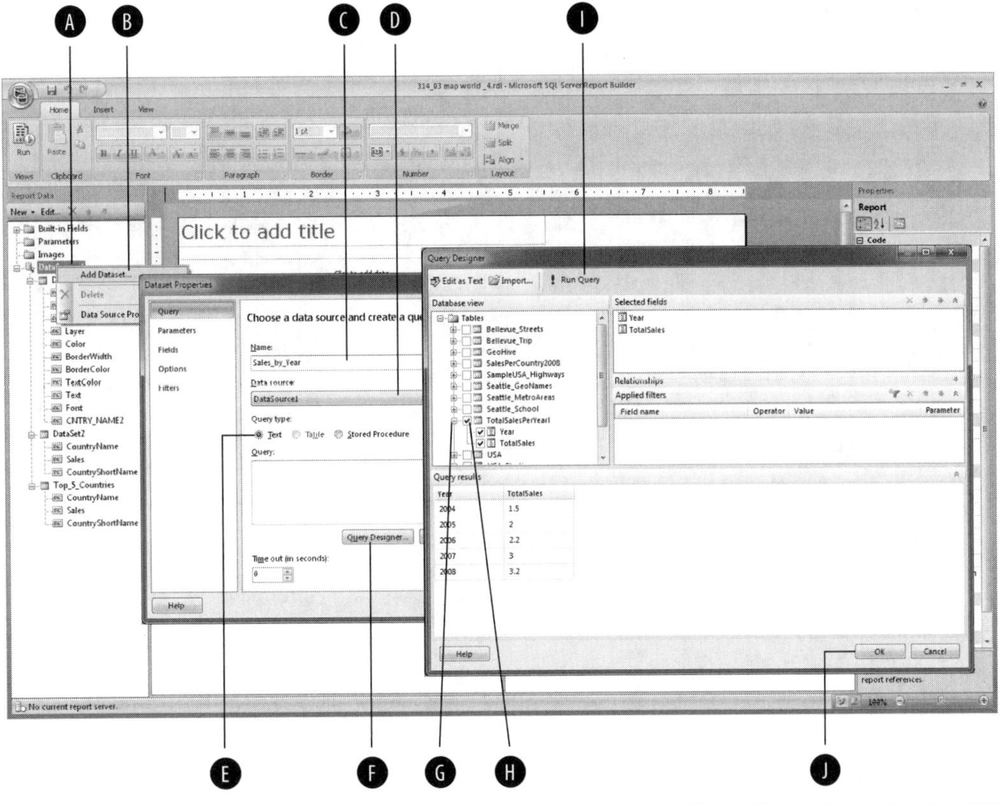

Figure 3-47 *Report Builder: adding a dataset for a Total Sales column chart*

So far this is pretty normal material, and we really haven't done anything new except use the Query Designer in a manual way to create a chart dataset with a Top N clause. In Figure 3-48 we put the query to use in creating a complementary chart for the map.

1. Click the Insert menu tab, on the Report Builder top ribbon menu (Step A).
2. Choose the Chart Wizard icon on the pop-up menu (Step B).
3. In the New Chart dialog box | Choose A Dataset pane, select the "Choose an existing dataset in this report" option button (Step C), select the Sales_by_Year dataset in the list pane (Step D), and click Next to continue.
4. In the New Chart dialog box | Choose A Chart Type pane, choose the Column chart type in the list pane (Step E), and click Next (Step F) to continue.

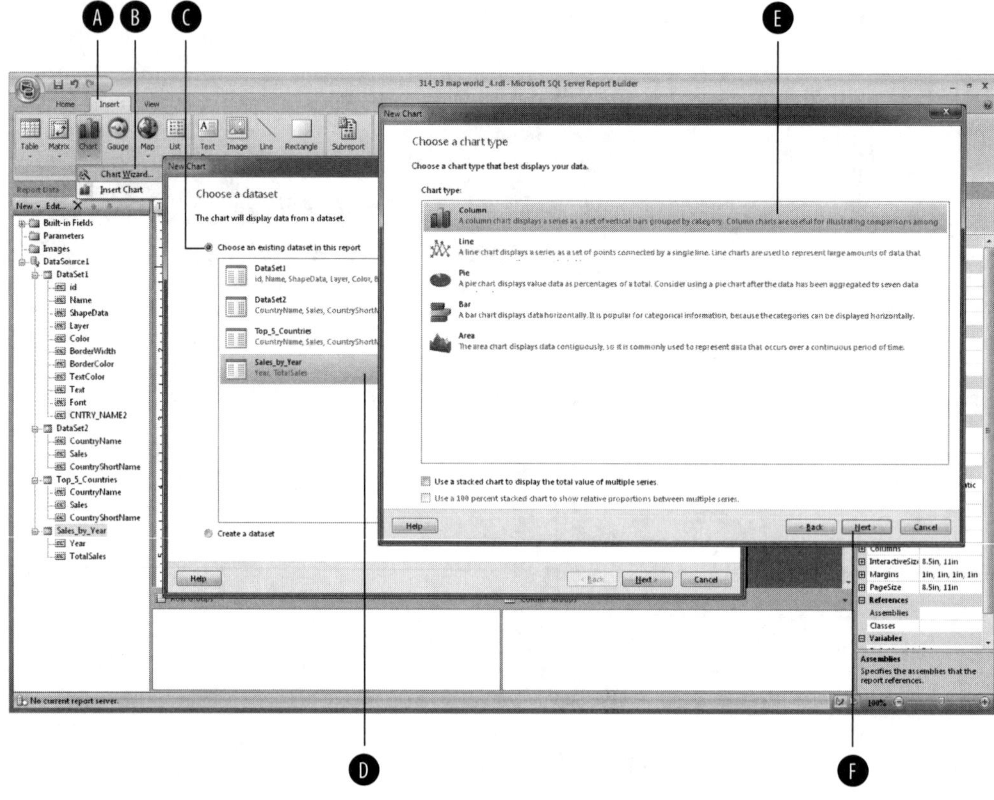

Figure 3-48 *Report Builder: creating the Column chart*

Note in Figure 3-48 we are using a Column chart type because it's the most straightforward way to represent a simple time series of data—in this case Sales by Year. The choice of chart type can be changed later if we wish, by simply right-clicking the chart once it's in the map design display and choosing Change Chart Type.

In Figure 3-49 we continue the process of configuring our simple Column chart in our Chart Wizard step-by-step dialog boxes.

1. In the New Chart dialog box | Arrange Chart Fields pane, drag the Year choice from the Available Fields list pane (Step A) to the Categories list pane (Step B).
2. In the New Chart dialog box | Arrange Chart Fields pane, drag the TotalSales choice from the Available Fields list pane (Step C) to the Values list pane (Step D), which automatically changes to Sum(TotalSales) when dropped into the Values pane.

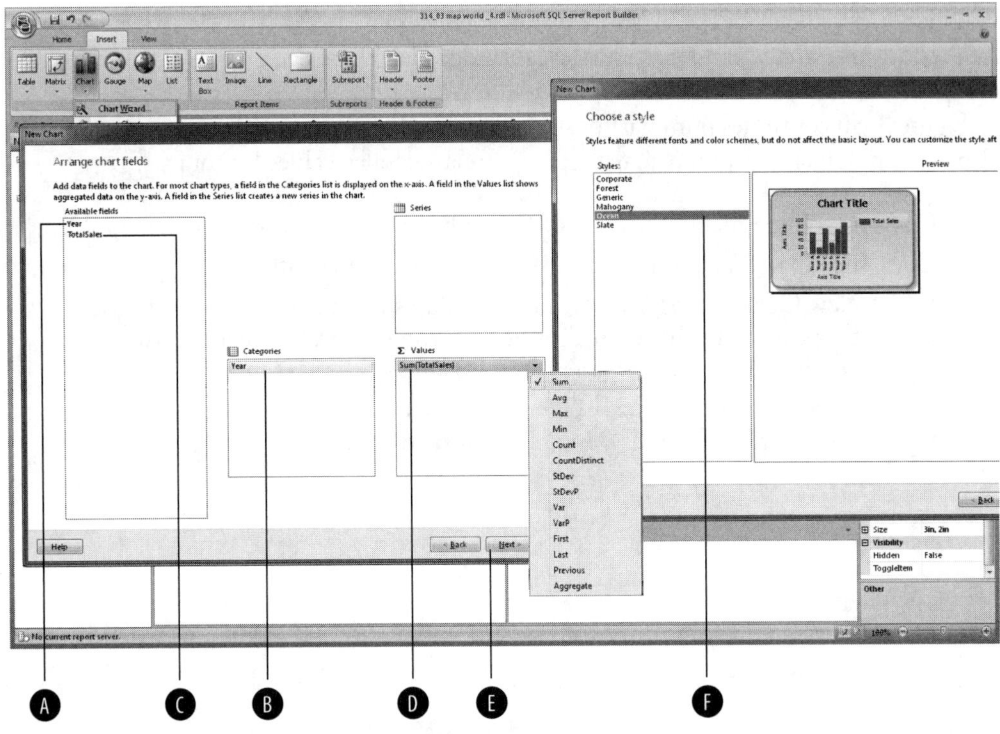

Figure 3-49 *Report Builder: choosing the Column chart data elements and style*

3. Click Next (Step E) to continue.
4. In the New Chart dialog box | Choose A Style pane, select the Ocean style for the chart (Step F), and click Finish to save the chart configuration.

Figure 3-49 shows off a simple but effective user interface for designing the chart. The Categories pane is meant to hold the group by field for the chart, which in this case is Year, and the Values pane is meant to hold the numeric data field to be aggregated in the chart. This is why the Chart Wizard changes TotalSales to Sum(TotalSales) for us automatically. We can click the drop-down arrow for the resulting Sum(TotalSales) Value field, to change the aggregation method for the numeric data as shown in Figure 3-49.

BI TIP

It's usually best to design a simple single-series chart that will be added to a map display. This is because we'll already have a lot of visual interpretation for the end user with the map, and an added chart should provide just one more simple means of seeing the data distribution that corresponds to the map geo-regions.

The Series pane is meant to hold an additional series for a multiseries chart—which might be appropriate for a stacked chart, for example, where each series is a horizontal component (series) of the stacked-series columns.

Figure 3-50 continues our chart design process, where we choose a Pie chart that will also be complementary to our map display of relative sales values by country.

1. Click the Home menu tab, on the Report Builder top ribbon menu (Step A).
2. Click the Chart Wizard icon on the main design pane (Step B).
3. In the New Chart dialog box | Choose A Dataset pane, select the "Choose an existing dataset in this report" option button (Step C), select the Top_5_Countries dataset in the list pane (Step D), and click Next to continue.
4. In the New Chart dialog box | Choose A Chart Type pane, choose the Pie chart type in the list pane (Step E), and click Next to continue.

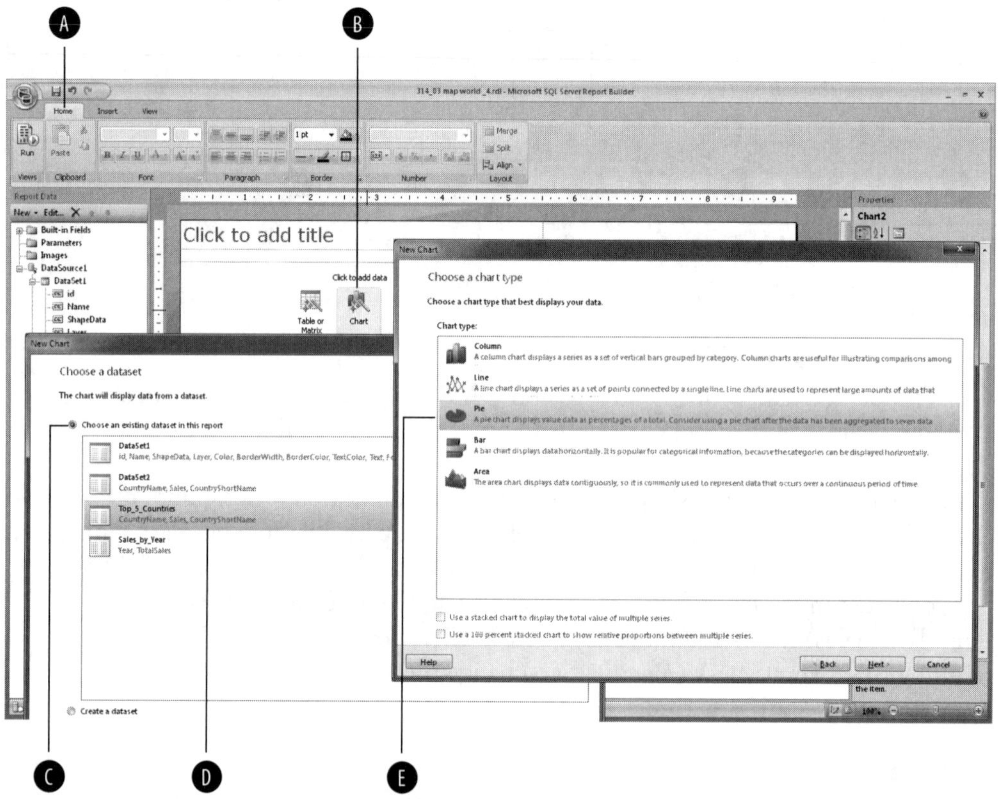

Figure 3-50 *Report Builder: creating the Pie chart*

Note in Figure 3-50 we are using a Pie chart type because it's the most straightforward way to represent the relative size of aggregate values of data—in this case Sales by Country. However, this chart will provide a focused perspective of that aggregate data, by showing only the Top 5 Countries—which consumers of the map report should be able to correlate to the geo-display. It's a nice way to add actual numeric labels to important data, without cluttering the map display with numeric labels that would be hard to discern across the many countries of the world map. The choice of chart type can be changed later if we wish, by simply right-clicking the chart once it's in the map design display and choosing Change Chart Type.

In Figure 3-51 we continue the process of configuring our simple Pie chart in our Chart Wizard step-by-step dialog boxes.

1. In the New Chart dialog box | Arrange Chart Fields pane, drag the CountryShortName choice from the Available Fields list pane (Step A) to the Categories list pane (Step B).

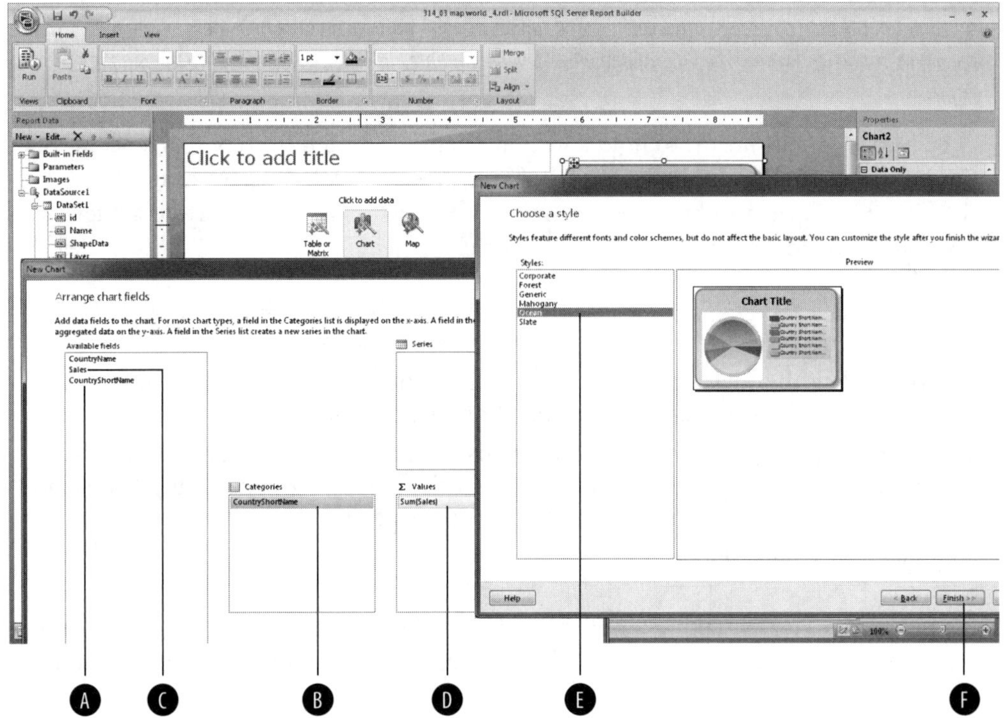

Figure 3-51 *Report Builder: choosing the Pie chart data elements and style*

2. In the New Chart dialog box | Arrange Chart Fields pane, drag the Sales choice from the Available Fields list pane (Step C) to the Values list pane (Step D), which automatically changes to Sum(Sales) when dropped into the Values pane.
3. In the New Chart dialog box | Choose A Style pane, select the Ocean style for the chart (Step E), and click Finish (Step F) to save the chart configuration.

Figure 3-51 shows off the same effective user interface for designing the chart. The Categories pane is meant to hold the group by field for the chart, which in this case is Country (or CountryName), and the Values pane is meant to hold the numeric data field to be aggregated in the chart. The Chart Wizard changes Sales to Sum(Sales) for us automatically. We can click the drop-down arrow for the resulting Sum(Sales) Value field, to change the aggregation method for the numeric data as shown in Figure 3-51.

BI TIP

It's usually best to use a time series to show a chart of aggregated data by year, for example, that will complement a map display of aggregated data by country, for example—or to use a shortened list of aggregated data by country that will complement the map display of aggregated data by country. This way, the consumer of the map can see relative color-coded ranges of aggregates across the geo-areas of the map—but see actual numerically labeled values of a few top-level aggregates in a chart that is next to the map in the report.

The Series pane is meant to hold additional series for a multiseries chart, where each series is a horizontal component (series) of stacked-series columns, for example.

In Figure 3-52 we do a bit of re-arranging of the charts on the report, to achieve a pleasing relative positioning of map and chart elements.

1. Right-click the Distance Scale (Step A) and uncheck the Show Distance Scale menu item (Step B) to remove it from the map display.
2. Right-click the Legend (Step C) and choose the Legend Properties menu item (Step D) to display the Map Legend Properties dialog box.
3. In the Map Legend Properties dialog box | General pane, click the option button at the four o'clock position (lower right) of the Position graphic (Step E), in the Change Legend Layout And Position Options pane.
4. Click OK (Step F) to save changes.

In Figure 3-52 we are taking familiar steps to configure the Distance Scale and Legend elements of the map display—and we take the further step of positioning the legend using

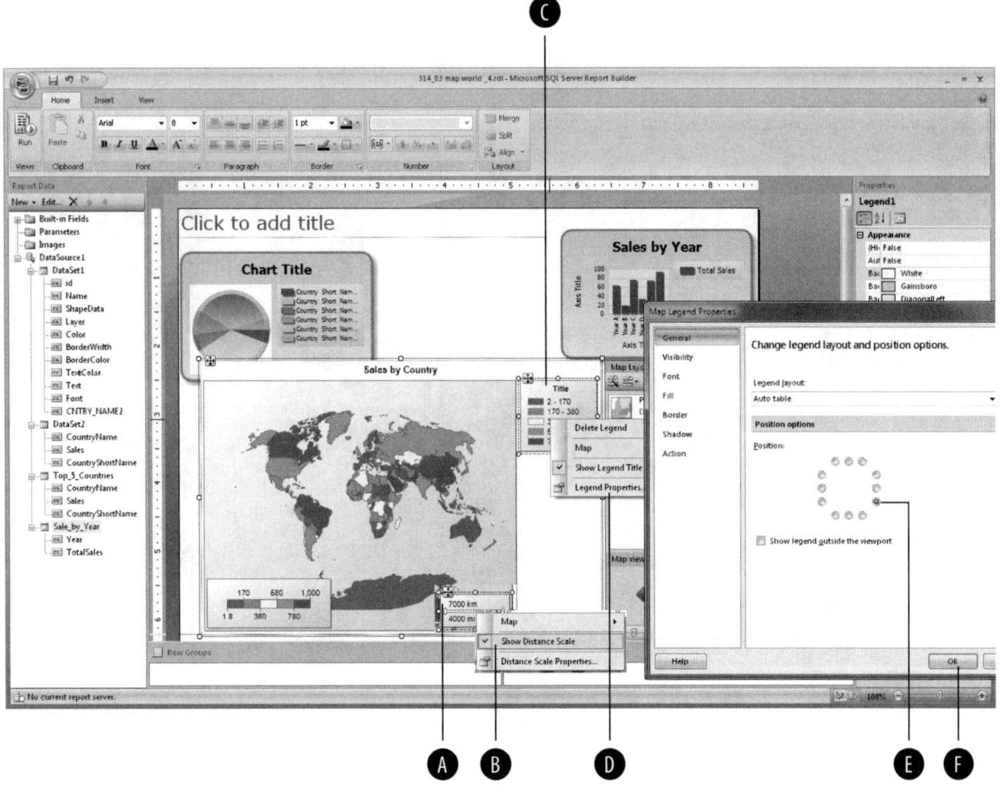

Figure 3-52 *Report Builder: arranging the charts and map display elements*

a nice positioning icon in the Map Legend Properties dialog box. Figure 3-53 shows how we take a final couple of steps to improve the simple chart display and positioning.

1. Right-click the Column chart (Step A), and click the Delete Legend menu item (Step B) to remove the legend from the chart.
2. Click the vertical-axis label on the Column chart, and change the text to read **Billions** (Step C).
3. Click the title to select it in the Column chart (Step D), and change the title to read **Sales by Year**, and do the same for the Pie chart (Step E), changing the title to read **Top 5 Countries**.
4. Click the chart to select the entire Column chart within the report (Step F), and drag and drop it so that it's positioned just to the right of the map.
5. Perform the same drag-and-drop positioning of the Pie chart (Step G) so that it's positioned just to the right of the map and beneath the Column chart.

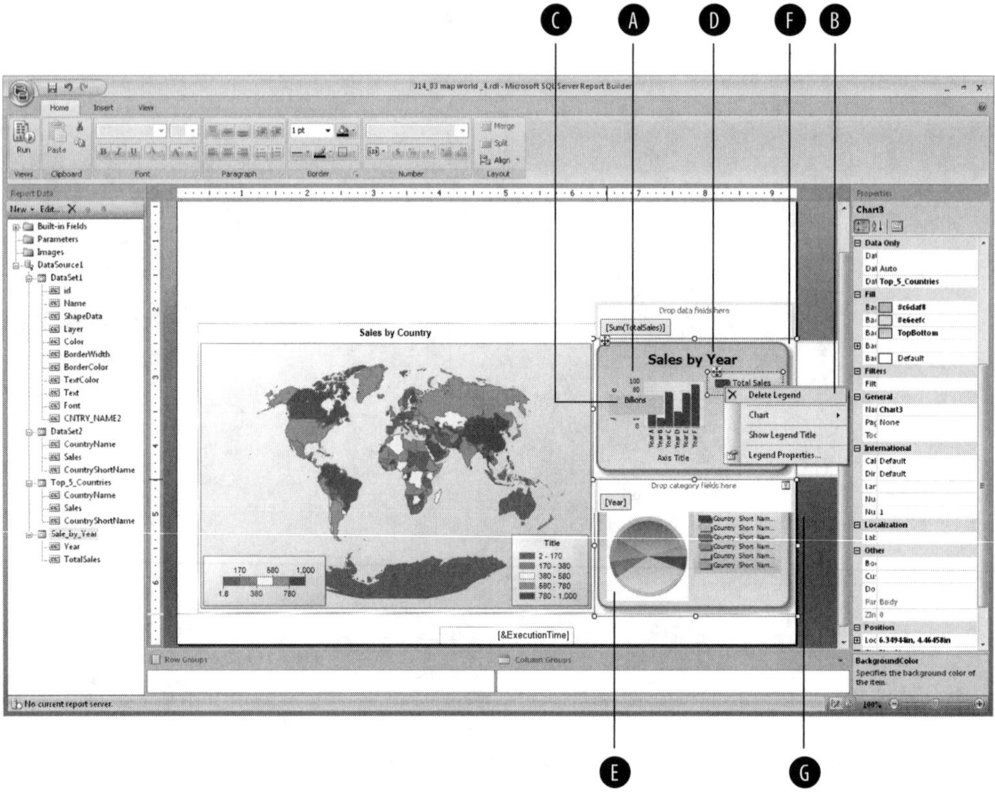

Figure 3-53 *Report Builder: configuring the chart display*

In Figure 3-54 you see the final result: an attractive map with two charts that really add value to the overall map report in the following manner:

- The map, titled "Sales by Country," shows an easy-to-understand country-by-country range of Sales aggregate values (Sum(Sales)), where red represents the worst-performing and green represents the best-performing countries.
- The map has a distance scale with values showing the five aggregate ranges of the map colors, from 60 to 1,300,000 and with thousands separators.
- The Column chart, titled "Sales by Year," shows a simple year-by-year aggregate of Sales values (Sum(Sales), which are actual aggregate values, not ranges of values), where the years provide a complementary but different type of information that allows the report consumer to easily compare country results to year results.

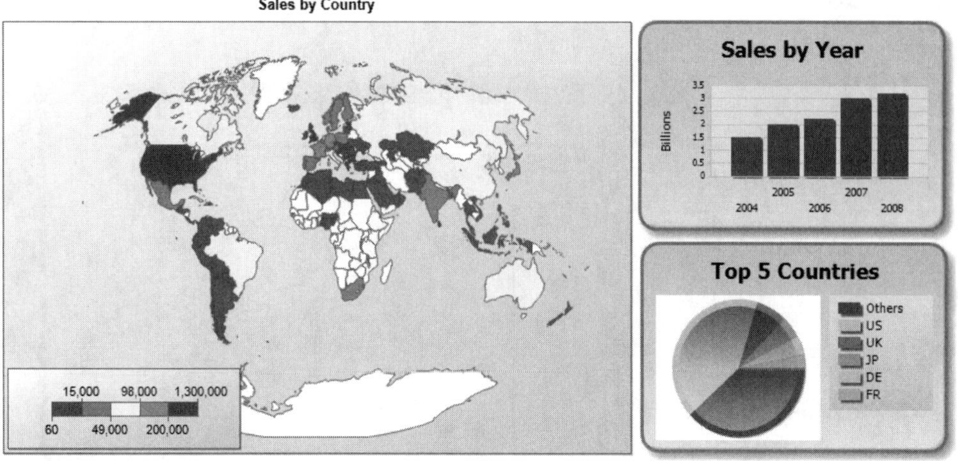

Figure 3-54 *Report Builder: rendering the map and chart report*

- The Pie chart, titled "Top 5 Countries," displays a simple country-by-country aggregate of Sales values (Sum(Sales), which are actual values, not ranges of values), where the country names are the short abbreviated form for faster reader interpretation.
- The charts are positioned to the right of the map, and sized so that the top of the Column chart is horizontally aligned with the top of the map, and the top of the Pie chart is horizontally aligned with the bottom of the map.

In reality the design of the map and chart elements shown in Figure 3-54 is a matter of personal taste, but it does help to keep the overall information display simple enough for users to understand without having to ask the report designer for help in interpreting the data. This is perhaps the strongest point in favor of map displays—that people are usually quick to understand data presented in a geo-display that reflects the world in which they live.

Let's take a final jump into the map design process, by adding a matrix to the top of our working map report. This will show the detail data, with the ability to cross-tab Sales by Population—which should produce an interesting result. Figure 3-55 shows how we start the process of adding a matrix.

1. Click the Insert tab in the ribbon menu at the top of the design screen (Step A), select the Matrix icon (Step B), and select the Matrix Wizard menu choice in the pop-up menu (Step C) to display the New Table Or Matrix dialog box.

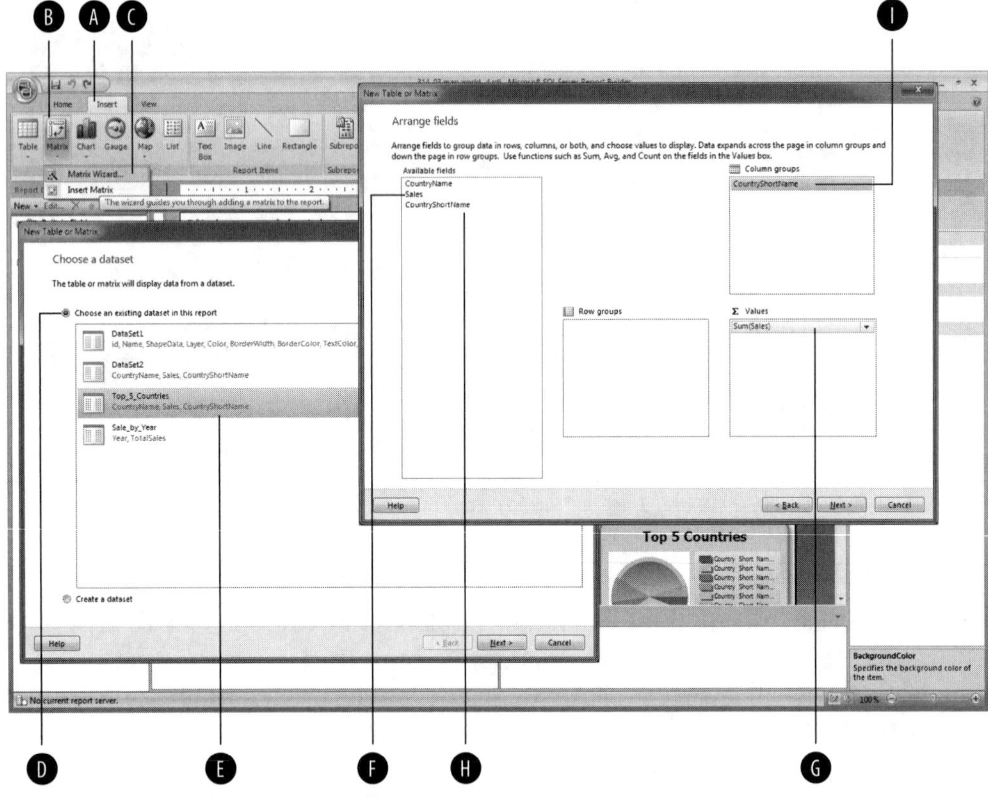

Figure 3-55 *Report Builder: adding a matrix display, dataset, and fields*

2. In the New Table Or Matrix dialog box | Choose A Dataset pane, click the "Choose an existing dataset in this report" option button (Step D), and select the Top_5_Countries choice (Step E); then click Next to continue.
3. In the New Table Or Matrix dialog box | Arrange Fields pane, drag the Sales field from the Available Fields pane (Step F) to the Values pane (Step G).
4. In the New Table Or Matrix dialog box | Arrange Fields pane, drag the CountryShortName field from the Available Fields pane (Step H) to the Column Groups pane (Step I); then click Next to continue.

The steps in Figure 3-55 are familiar from our work with charts, and for the matrix we are simply choosing a cell field and a column header of Country. In Figure 3-56 we finish the Matrix Wizard steps.

1. In the New Table Or Matrix dialog box | Choose The Legend pane, simply click Next (Step A) to accept the defaults for the Matrix layout.
2. In the New Table Or Matrix dialog box | Choose A Style pane, select the Ocean choice in the Styles list pane (Step B), and click Finish (Step C) to save the Matrix configuration.

Figure 3-56 shows the relatively easy step of choosing the style for our matrix. Although this "fourth object" in our map report might seem a bit much, a matrix can add immediate clarity if it occupies a minimal space on the report design. In this case, it almost functions as a legend for the map!

In Figure 3-57 you see the rendered map report, made up of four objects.

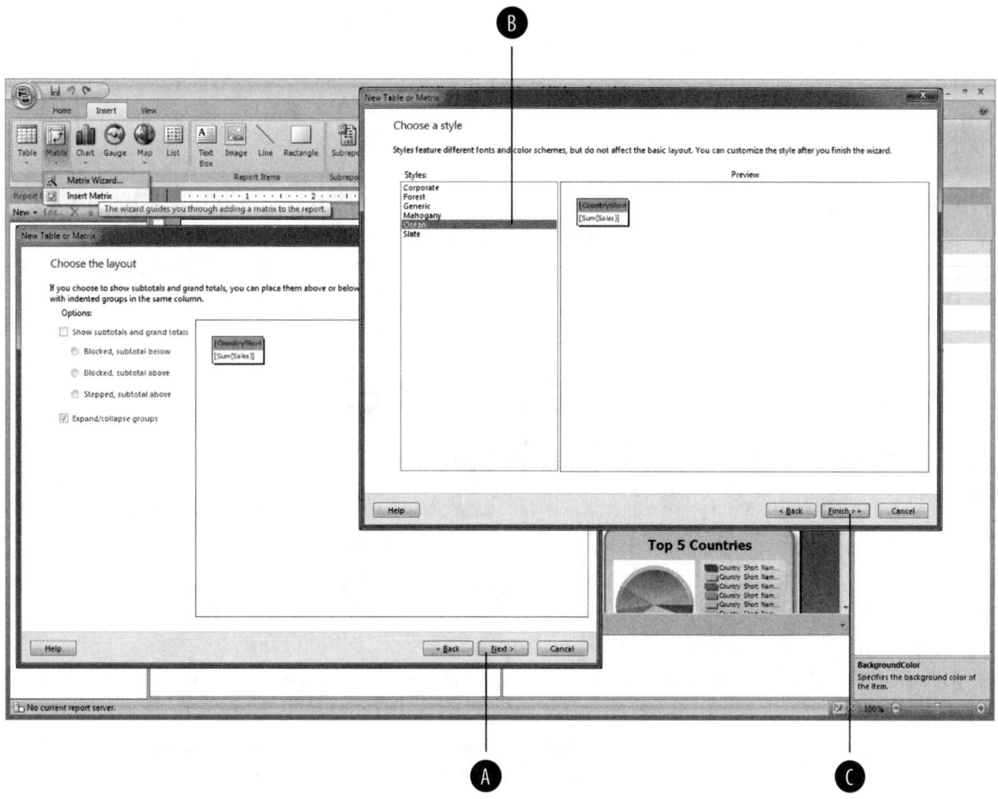

Figure 3-56 *Report Builder: adding a matrix display, layout, and style*

DE	FR	JP	Others	UK	US
140000	100000	160000	1200000	240000	1300000

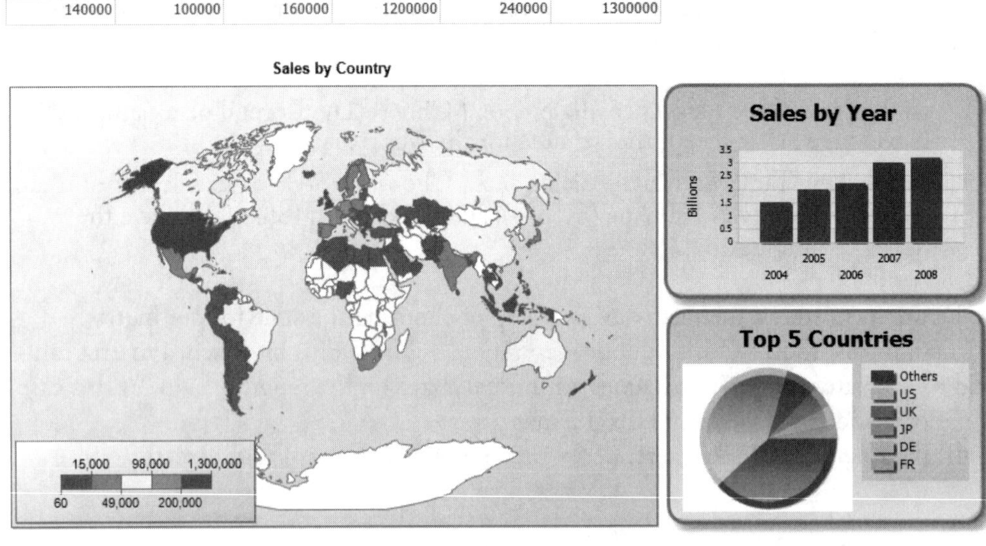

Figure 3-57 *Report Builder: rendered map with simple matrix and charts*

The overall map report presentation tells a coherent story, with the map occupying the central space—surrounded by a matrix-legend, and two charts that portray a graphical view of the sales data, grouped by year and "top 5 countries." In the next and final section we'll add a couple of "nice to have" items to the map report.

Adding a Tooltip and Custom Point with Action to the Map Report

ToolTips are actually very important, since they allow us to add detail to maps on a polygon-by-polygon basis (in this case country-by-country)—where the map would normally be too busy-looking with all data points showing. Report consumers expect this kind of interaction with any report display today, and as you'll see, the Report Builder dialog boxes make it easy to accomplish.

Figure 3-58 shows how we start the task of adding ToolTips to our world map.

1. Click the map itself, in the central design pane (Step A). Click the map again to cause the Map Layers pop-up menu to display.

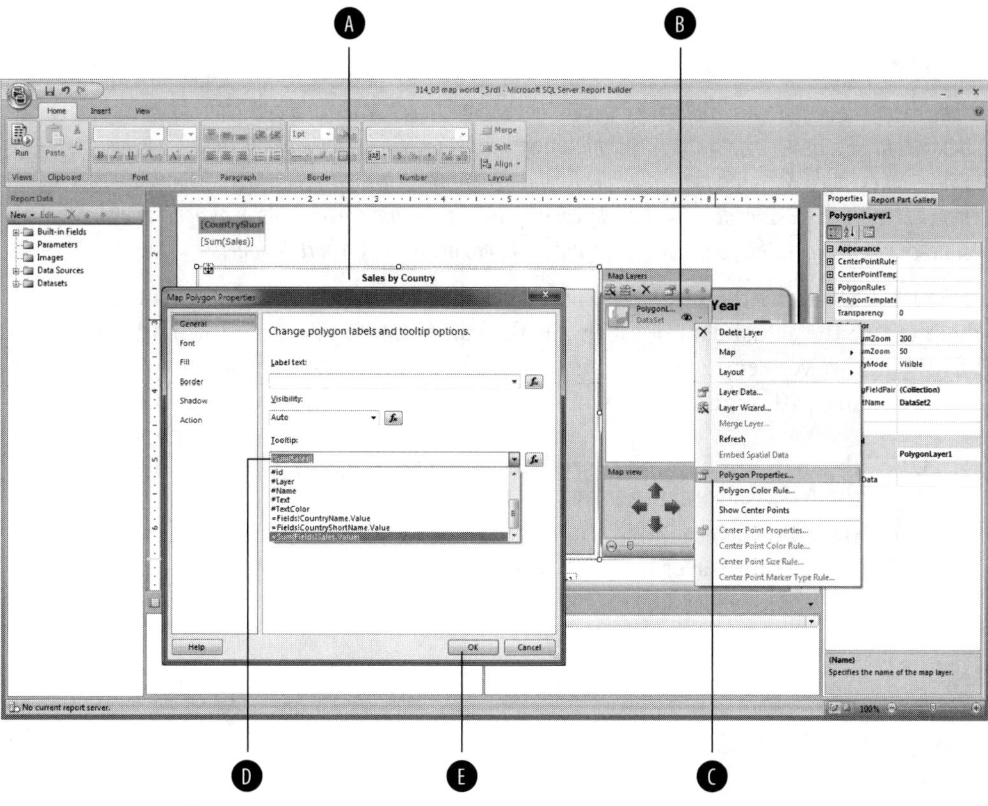

Figure 3-58 *Report Builder: adding a ToolTip*

2. Click the PolygonLayer1 choice in the Map Layers pop-up menu (Step B), and choose Polygon Properties in the Polygon pop-up menu (Step C).
3. In the Map Polygon Properties dialog box | General pane, choose the "=Sum(Fields!Sales.Value)" in the ToolTip drop-down menu (Step D).
4. Click OK (Step E) to save this configuration.

In Figure 3-58, it helps to understand that maps are made up of polygons—thus the dialog box guides us to apply a ToolTip formula to the polygons that make up the world map. The Report Builder already understands that our world map is made up of countries (country polygons)—and automatically provides a drop-down choice for the SUM of sales per country (per polygon).

BI TIP

The geographic design tools available in the past have been difficult to use and generally required a map designer to be a "geo-jockey" with a deep understanding of map display technology. This is no longer true—where, for example, Microsoft Report Builder is typical of the modern map design tools that make it easy to match SUMING formulas of data like sales by country, with maps that are made up of recognizable country-state-county displays. This puts map design into the hands of everyday report designers!

Figure 3-59 shows the result of hovering the mouse over a country on our world map, where we see the actual data point that is the summed sales amount for that country.

Now that we've seen how easy it is to add ToolTips to the map, let's explore Custom Points, starting with Figure 3-60, where we bring up the map layer menus.

1. Click the map itself, in the central design pane (Step A). Click the map again to cause the Map Layers pop-up menu to display.
2. Click the Add Layer icon at the top of the Map Layers pop-up menu (Step B), and choose Point Layer in the Add Layer pop-up menu (Step C).

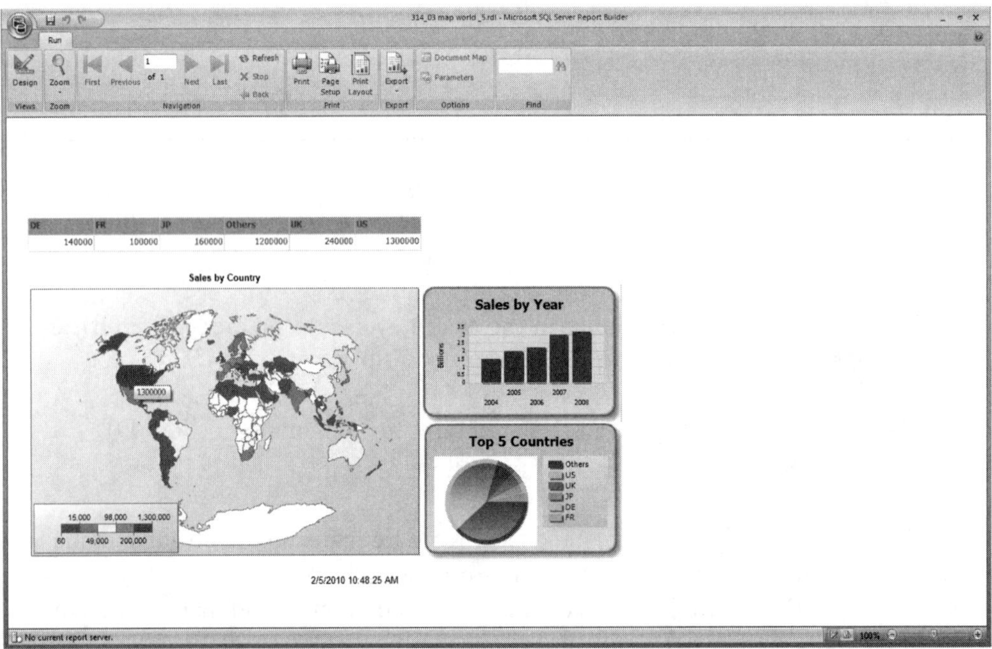

Figure 3-59 *Report Builder: rendered map with ToolTip*

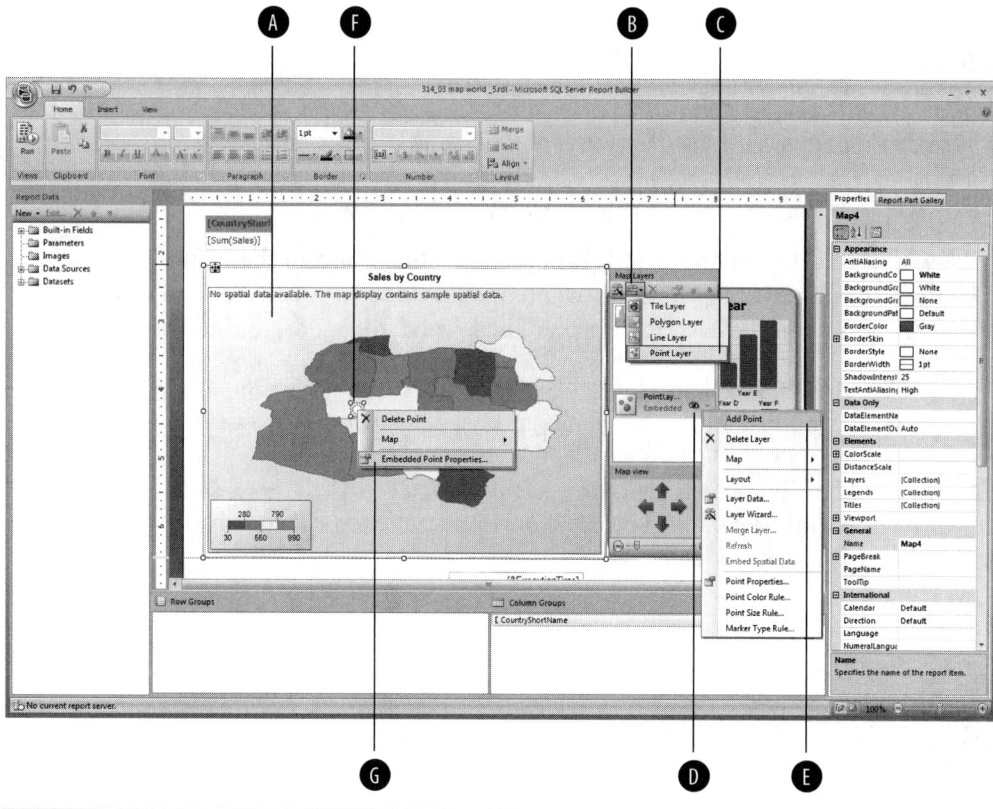

Figure 3-60 *Report Builder: adding a custom point—Point layer*

3. Right-click the new Point Layer choice in the Map Layers pop-up menu (Step D), and choose Add Point in the Polygon Layer pop-up menu (Step E).
4. Move the cross-hair mouse pointer to the location desired, on the map itself (Step F), and click to place the new Point on the map.
5. Right-click the new Point on the map, and choose Embedded Point Properties on the Point pop-up menu (Step G) to display the Embedded Point Properties dialog boxes for the next section!

In Figure 3-60 you find that it's easy to add an approximate location to the map. And although we could add the point with exact longitude-latitude coordinates, it's really quite useful to simply drag and drop the approximate location of our Home Office (for example), since it does not have to be exact in its location. This is a quick and simple means of annotating a map.

BI TIP

Although it's generally a good idea to use exact data in any report presentation, there are many instances where it's good enough to simply annotate the report display with an added piece of visual information that conveys some meaning that does not depend on exact data. The report designer must exercise good judgment in deciding when to use exact data, and where a simple annotation adds value.

Now that you've seen how easy it is to add a custom point to the map, let's explore PushPins, starting with Figure 3-61, where we continue with Embedded Properties pop-up menus from the custom point. We'll also add an Action to the custom point!

1. In the Map Embedded Point Properties dialog box | General pane, check the "Override point options for this layer" check box (Step A) to display additional menu tab options in the dialog box.
2. In the Map Embedded Point Properties dialog box | Marker pane, choose PushPin in the Marker Type drop-down menu (Step B), and change the Marker Size to 14pt (Step C).

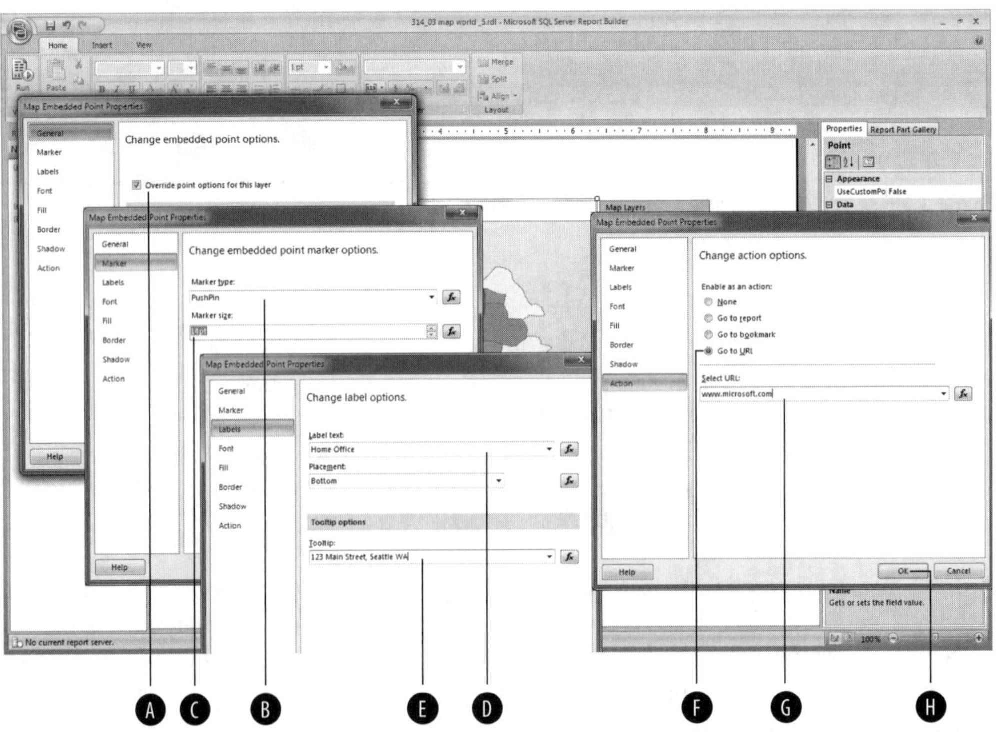

Figure 3-61 *Report Builder: adding a custom point—Embedded Point Properties*

3. In the Map Embedded Point Properties dialog box | Labels pane, in the Label Text box, type **Home Office** (Step D); in the ToolTip text box, type **123 Main Street, Seattle WA** (Step E).
4. In the Map Embedded Point Properties dialog box | Action pane, select the Go To URL option button (Step F); and in the Select URL text box, type **www.microsoft.com** (Step G).
5. Click OK (Step H) to save the configuration.

In Figure 3-61 you see an incredible number of steps that are available in a single set of dialog boxes dealing with our custom point. Not only are we easily able to add/change the PushPin to display over our Customer Point "Home Office," we are able to connect a useful action to the custom point that allows an end user to click it and navigate to the Home page of our Home Office.

BI TIP

Actions are an important part of interactive report design. An action can be as simple as the URL web navigation in our example, or as sophisticated as providing a parameter value to a separate report that can then display in its own window—which can also be described as a subreport scenario where a map can be the main report and a detail report can be the subreport.

Figure 3-62 shows the finished report, with an overlay of the URL Home page that displays in a separate window when an end user clicks on the map's custom point.

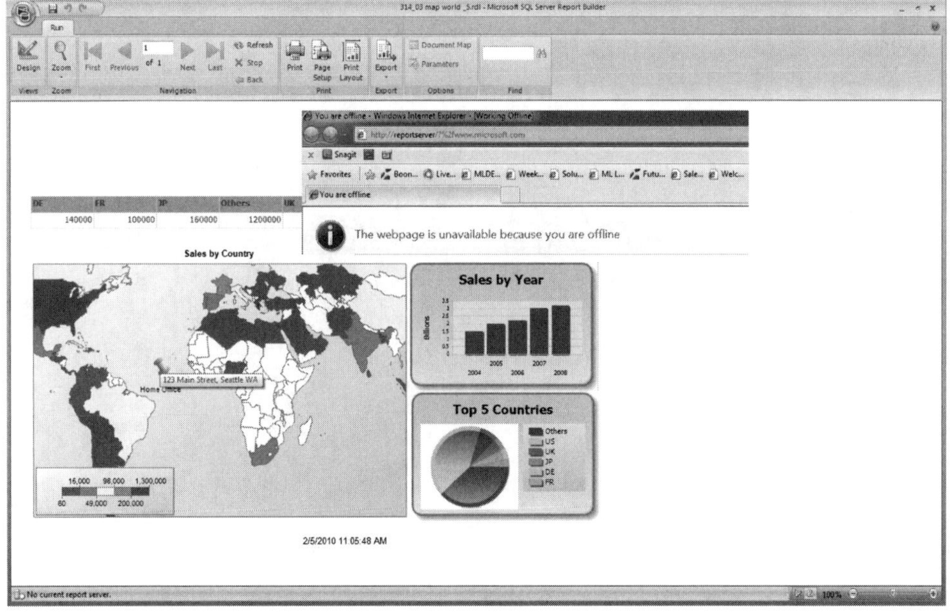

Figure 3-62 *Report Builder: adding a custom point—Embedded Point Properties*

This is an example of several report objects working together in a map display, with an active interface that is configured to display additional information when clicked.

Wrap-Up

It's interesting to note, in summary, that the original mission of business intelligence is fulfilled in our production of displays and graphics with SQL Server 2008 Report Builder—that is, to provide analytical displays of data that immediately connect to the real world in which users live, and to the business processes that users are tasked with controlling for the overall mission of an organization. The Report Builder helps report designers accomplish this mission with the ability to include map geo-displays in reports—without having to be terrifically knowledgeable about the underlying mapping technology.

As this chapter showed, we need a source of spatial data to construct a base map display, to which we can add analytical data that has a matching field to correspond with the spatial data subregions such as countries. The rest is simply a matter of enhancing, labeling, and positioning the map elements—and then adding complementary charts if desired. The result is a professional-quality map-chart report that is connected to real data and can be rendered as needed to show real-time analytical business information.

Chapter 4

Data Visualization Delivery

In This Chapter

- Consuming Visualizations
- SQL Server Report Manager Overview
- Adding a Reporting Services Report to a SharePoint Page
- Microsoft Office SharePoint Server 2007: Reporting Services Integrated Mode
- Creating Dashboard Pages
- PerformancePoint Server 2007
- Putting It All Together: Using Charts and Gauges in Information Delivery
- Best Practices and Special Tips for Intelligent Business Information Delivery
- Wrap-Up

We have been examining the different ways to visualize data and information in this book. I have been examining Charts and Gauges, and my colleagues have been explaining the workings for maps, geographic displays, and data mining. The goal of this chapter is to explore several of the many ways these visual display items can be presented to an audience, and to discuss a variety of considerations to make as you construct information displays for your audience. Microsoft has a rich product portfolio with many integration possibilities, but we will focus on SQL Server Reporting Services (SSRS), Microsoft Office SharePoint Server (MOSS), and PerformancePoint Server (PPS). These are the main platforms for presenting reports, dashboard pages, and collaboration sites—all necessary ingredients for great business intelligence.

We have investigated the many different chart types, the best chart types for the data relationship being displayed, and new ways to create small multiples, like Sparkline reports. We have looked into how gauges are created, the various gauge types that are available, and the use of gauges to display Key Performance Indicators (KPIs) and other key business metrics. We have seen how map and geographic displays can be particularly valuable for communicating spatial information. All of these display types can be used to create a rich, contextual display of key information that can be easily absorbed by the report audience. The way to present this information is to serve it up by one or all of these Microsoft servers (SSRS, MOSS, and PPS) through a client web browser. Using the web browser as the client application gives maximum flexibility in the ability to share this information to a geographically dispersed audience. And the server components give tremendous flexibility to create specific, personalized, and portable displays.

In this chapter, we will cover the following topics:

- Using SQL Server 2008 R2 Reporting Services (SSRS)—Report Manager and Report Server in both native mode and integrated mode
- Using Microsoft Office SharePoint Server (MOSS) 2007 to display reports, report libraries, and dashboard pages
- The integration of PerformancePoint Server with MOSS and Reporting Services, using SSRS Reports in PerformancePoint dashboards, and publishing and using dashboard items as SharePoint web parts
- The future integration of these products

BEST REFERENCES

This chapter is about integration, so we feel compelled to include references for several components. For a variety of perspectives on business intelligence, visit the following sites:

- *Perceptual Edge (Steven Few)   www.PerceptualEdge.com*
- *Intelligent Enterprise Magazine   www.IntelligentEnterprise.com*
- *Dashboad Insight   www.DashboardInsight.com*
- *The B-Eye Network   www.b-eye-network.com*
- *Information Management Review Magazine   http://www.information-management.com/*
- *The DashboardSpy   www.enterprise-dashboard.com/*
- *SharePoint Server Developer Center   msdn.microsoft.com/en-us/office/aa905503.aspx*
- *PerformancePoint Server Developer Center   msdn.microsoft.com/en-us/office/bb660518.aspx*
- *Reporting Services Developer InfoCenter   msdn.microsoft.com/en-us/library/ms159162.aspx*

There are some great blogs available on all the preceding topics; here is a sampling of my favorites:

- *Sean Boon's blog   blogs.msdn.com/seanboon/*
- *Nick Barckley BI-Lingual   feeds.feedburner.com/NickBarclay*
- *SQL Server Developer Center (Blog Heaven)   msdn.microsoft.com/en-us/sqlserver/bb671054.aspx*
- *Teo Lachev's Weblog   prologika.com/CS/blogs/blog/default.aspx*

Consuming Visualizations

In this chapter, we turn our attention to how to deliver these data visualizations to stakeholders and audiences. We are going to include more conceptual content in this chapter, as well as a larger dose of Basic Intelligence (BI) Tips. Here is a special tip from my colleague Ekaterina Shcherbakova:

BI TIP

Always keep in mind the audience the reports are going to be used by. Understand what the final result should be like and show the reports as you develop them because your interpretation of your business requirements, regardless of how well it's written, may not be what the user had in mind. Always prototype—the end users may not be able to visualize the final product as easily as the developer can; therefore, pictures / wireframes help them to understand what the UI may look like. Don't try to guess what the result should look like—ask for the end-user feedback! Start off the design by asking questions—What does the user need? What do you foresee the end result to look like? Who are the users? Do not focus on technology in the beginning, focus on the needs.

This tip underscores an often-overlooked requirement of great information delivery, and that is a deep understanding of the user experience and information needs. To create the best design will rely on your interpretation of delivering exactly what the user needs, understanding that the most important needs will be unarticulated. How intuitive is the interface? Will users know where to click to drill down into detailed information? Delivering beyond expectations is what delights users and makes our job fun.

There are many ways to deliver reports, and each method has its own options, benefits, and challenges. The goal of this chapter is to describe the variety of delivery methods and best practices available using Microsoft products, in particular: SQL Server 2008 R2 Reporting Services, Microsoft Office SharePoint Server 2007, and PerformancePoint Server 2007. Depending on the application architecture at your location, more than one of these options may be available to you. Each delivery method has its own set of pros and cons, which is affected by the objectives your reporting strategy is trying to achieve. Each organization has a unique information culture based upon its technology, processes, people, and leadership strategy. Finding the best way to deliver information requires consideration of each of these factors. The same information can be delivered in multiple ways and that may be appropriate. The context in which the information is received can have a powerful impact on the capability of taking action based on the knowledge transferred. If quality information is received immediately before a critical decision, it will help inform that decision and may affect the alternatives and choices made.

Take into account how the information will be delivered—large CRT monitor, mobile phone, netbook, laptop? All of the above? Determine information urgency and importance, and whether it warrants mobile broadcast via RSS feed or email subscription (Alert).

The first consideration is to determine if the information should be delivered individually, as a traditional report; or integrated with other information web parts in a dashboard. Some information is best delivered as a traditional, self-contained report. When the information needs to be presented holistically, needs to be portable (printed or forwarded), or needs special permissions and protection, then a traditional report may be the best method of presentation.

Dashboards are one-page displays of information web parts. In current BI lingo, if those web parts display information from more than one data source, it is called a *mash-up*. The Microsoft Business Intelligence platform supports mash-up dashboards or dashboards sourced from a singular, controlled data source, like a data warehouse or individual line of business application database. Dashboard design warrants a consideration of the priority of the information and its importance in the decision-making processes at work in the organization. This information will help to drive a good dashboard design by helping to determine where on the dashboard to place the information.

Just like physical property, screen real estate also has variable desirability—location, location, location! Figure 4-1 shows the major divisions of the screen based on how our eyes scan information. We have combined these zones with examples of information web parts that are most appropriate for that screen location.

- Our eyes are naturally drawn to the upper left-hand corner of the display as the starting place for a scan that moves left to right and up to down.
- Try to size components to fit onto a standard screen without scrolling (1024 × 768 for example). If it must be oversized, scrolling up and down seems to be more acceptable. If you end up having to scroll both horizontally and vertically, you should rethink your design and perhaps remove components.

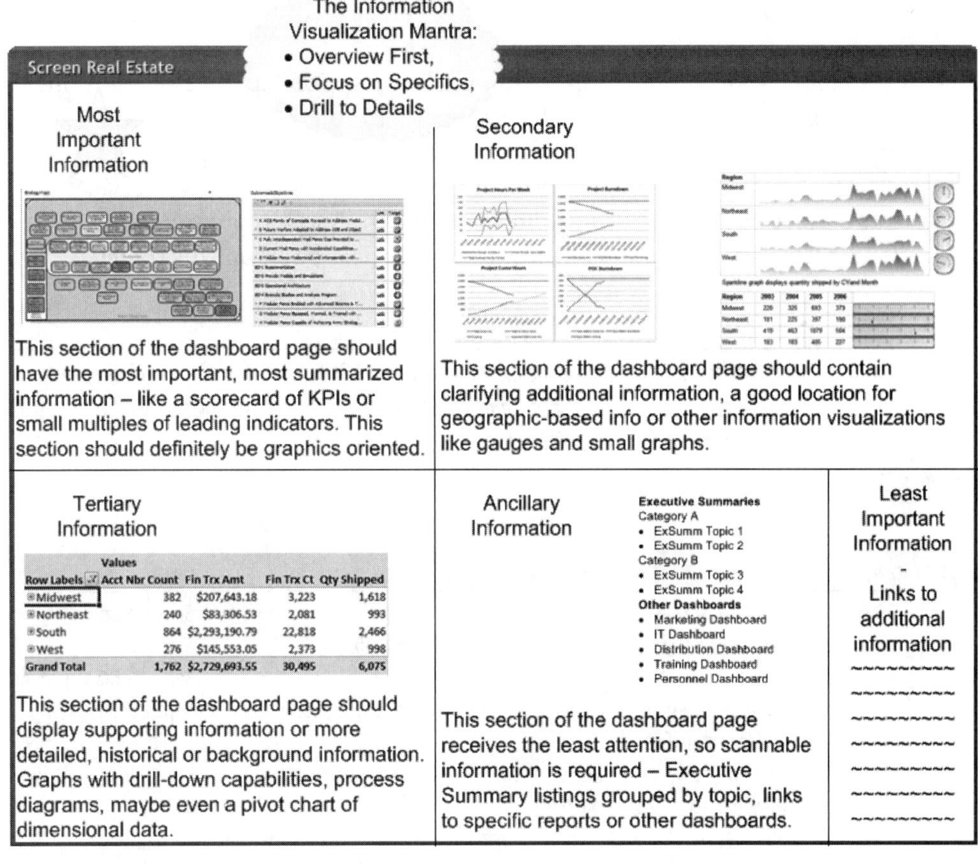

Figure 4-1 *Display screen real estate*

- Design the dashboard to contain the most important information in the upper-left quadrant. This information should be highly summarized and visually appealing. Business or Balanced Scorecards of KPI information and linked strategy maps are good content for this section.
- Secondary and supporting information should be in the top-right quadrant of the display. Graphical images, maps, charts, Sparkline reports, gauges, and small tables all work for this section. These parts should support and answer questions that may arise from the initial information presented in the top-left quadrant.
- Tertiary information, like pivot tables of dimensional data, are best positioned in the lower-left quadrant.
- Finally, ancillary information, links to additional resources, links to related content, and scanable content are best situated in the lower-right corner. Do not put important, "must see" information down here unless there is a corporate standard for that position.

We will examine some of these information delivery options, and we will examine the configuration of these solutions to deliver reports to your report audience.

SharePoint 2010 will integrate the environment even further, providing PerformancePoint Services, Visio Services, Excel Services, and Shared Services in a much more functional way. It is beyond the scope to examine SharePoint 2010 / Office 2010 in more depth here—but watch for our next book on this topic!

BI TIP

Here is a quick rule of thumb for determining the best configuration of SQL Server Reporting Services native mode versus integrated mode. If you need to display reports outside of the SharePoint environment, then install in native mode. This will give you the most flexibility for delivery to other web pages, Outlook, or a custom viewer application.

Environment	Pro	Con
SQL Server 2008 Reporting Services: native mode	Web browser client Easy to navigate, good security model, security trimming Report Builder Good management of reporting environment, including Subscriptions and Execution Snapshots Easy-to-deploy reports and data sources to multiple environments (development, test, production) Still can integrate to SharePoint—Using Page Viewer web part with URL Parameters renders reports as cleanly and easily as utilizing SharePoint integrated mode	Single-purpose application Separate management Separate security schema

Environment	Pro	Con
SQL Server 2008 Reporting Services: integrated mode SharePoint 2007	Web browser client SharePoint integration and available features Report Builder available from within SharePoint SharePoint Alert capability Uses SharePoint security Able to mash up information on dashboards Can display RS reports alone or combined with other, related information	Cannot use deploy for new reports KPI list only Limitations in ability to filter all web parts with page filter reports Must upload reports and data sources instead of publish
SQL Server 2008 Reporting Services: integrated mode SharePoint 2007: with PerformancePoint Server 2007	Can display a variety of related content—KPIs in scorecards, Visio Strategy Maps, RS Reports, PerformancePoint Reports, etc. Able to mash up information on dashboards Robust KPI definitions and data source access Dashboard filters	Kerberos double-hop challenges Multiple configuration points (Reporting Services, SharePoint, PerformancePoint)

We will work our way from the simplest to the more complex integration environments, starting with the stand-alone solution of using SQL Server Report Manager in native mode.

SQL Server Report Manager Overview

The most likely option available for displaying reports created with SQL Server Reporting Services (SSRS) Report Designer or Report Builder will be the SSRS Report Manager in native mode (meaning not integrated with SharePoint). Report Manager is a stand-alone, browser-based application that has a myriad of useful features beyond the display of reports. Report Manager has a flexible, role-based security model, supporting ease of access as well as providing a mechanism for well-controlled content. Report Manager has all the features needed for managing an enterprise-wide report delivery system. In addition to storing and displaying reports, Report Manager supports point-in-time report creation using snapshot execution. Multiple versions of a report can be stored and compared. Subscriptions allow the report audience to set up predetermined schedules of report execution and delivery to an e-mail box or file share. The user interface for Report Manager makes it easy to organize all the items needed to present reports and support ad hoc report creation. Data Sources can be shared and controlled, and it is very easy to generate a report data model for Report Builder use. Report Builder launches from the Report Manager interface; it is a button on the toolbar.

Figure 4-2 shows the new Report Manager user interface and its components. The new look has a more muted appearance, putting the focus on the content in Report Manager.

- Across the top right side is the Home menu bar, here you can access Home, My Subscriptions, Site Settings, and Help. Site Settings is where the administrator creates site-wide administrator and user groups, manages schedules, and sets properties for report execution timeout and version history.
- The Banner identifies the folder you are currently located in. The Search Box will match a string of characters in the report metadata (title and description fields).
- The Main menu bar spans the window under the banner and has buttons for New Folder, New Data Source, New Report in Report Builder, Folder Settings, and Upload File, along with a toggle button between Details View and Tile View.
- The main part of the window displays the contents—folders, report items, data source items, report model items. The inset in Figure 4-2 shows the descriptive icons which distinguish the object type.
- The Details view also allows you to move and delete report objects, as well as view other important item details in the Edit view.

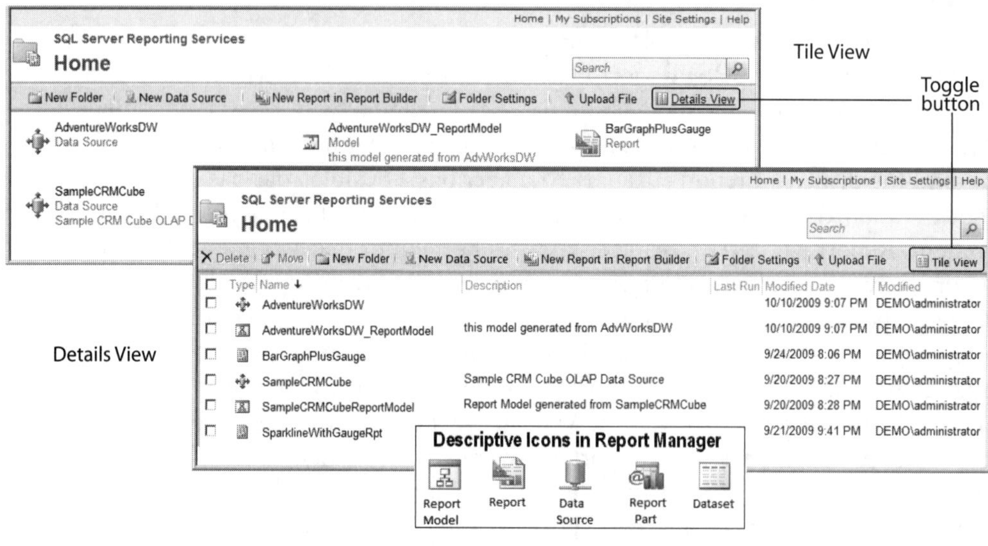

Figure 4-2 *SQL Server Reporting Services: Report Manager user interface summary and Details views*

BI TIP

*Report Manager can manage other file types beside SSRS files. Excel Reports, *.PDF versions of reports, even Word documents can be stored in the Report Manager. This gives the reporting administrator the opportunity to make a unified, integrated report repository for the organization.*

Before launching into the details of Report Manager object types, let's take a moment to discuss how reports and data sources are loaded into Report Manager. For Report Manager in native mode, there are two options: deployment from inside Business Intelligence Design Studio (BIDS); and uploading individual data sources and reports within Report Manager. Using the upload method requires each item to be processed individually.

To upload an item in Report Manager, click the Upload File button, as shown in Figure 4-3. The Upload File dialog box will open. Click Browse and locate the file you wish to upload; if the default name isn't adequate, type in new information. To overwrite an existing item, tick the check box, and then click OK to complete the operation.

BIDS Report Deployment

Let's examine the deployment method where all data sources and reports within a Visual Studio project can be deployed at once. In Business Intelligence Design Studio (BIDS), configure the Project Properties with the Report Server information as shown in Figure 4-4.

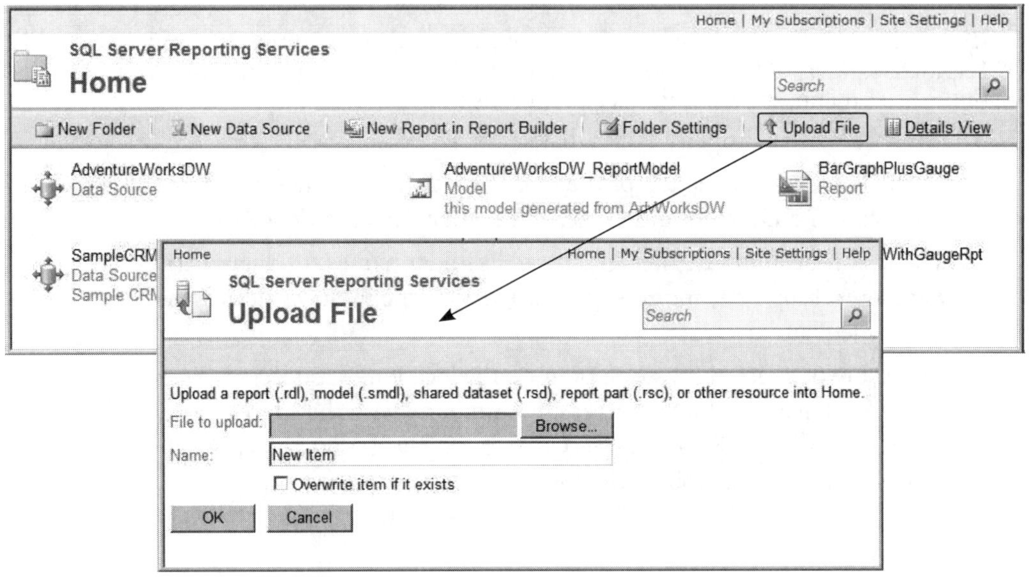

Figure 4-3 *Report Manager Upload File*

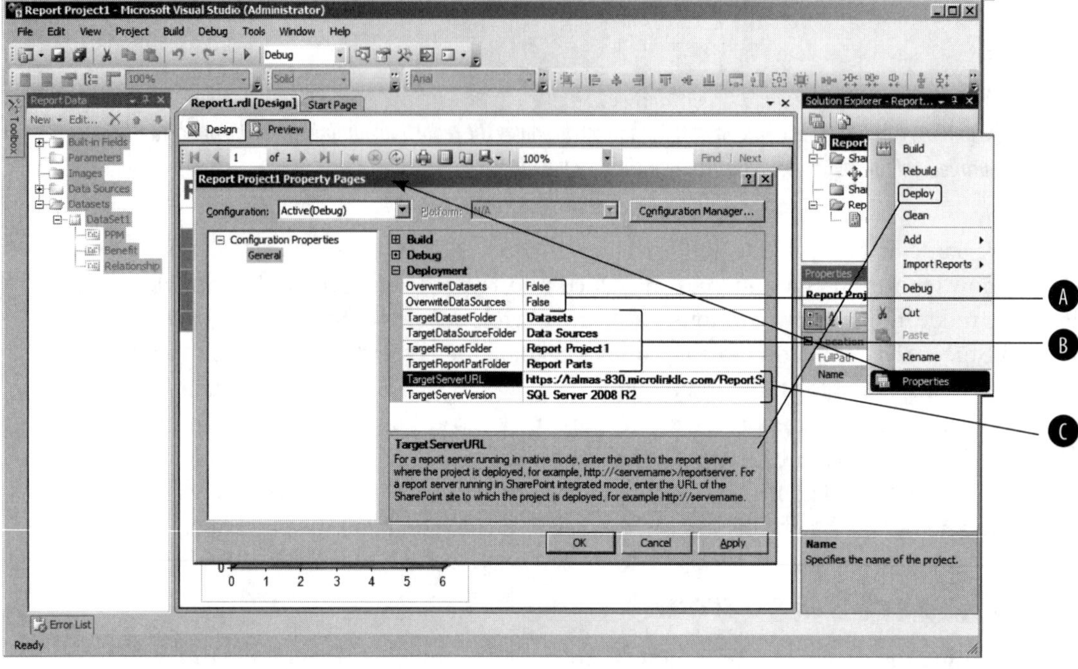

Figure 4-4 *BIDS deployment configuration*

In an open BIDS Report project:

1. Right-click the Project Name at the top of the tree display in the Solution Explorer pane of BIDS, as shown in Figure 4-4. Alternatively, you could navigate the Project menu, selecting Project Properties there.
2. The Report Project Property Pages dialog box will display.
   A. In the Deployment section of the Configuration Properties, the default value for Overwrite Datasets and Overwrite Data Sources is False.
   B. The next four items are the default target folder names for datasets (new), data sources, reports, and report parts (new). Type in new values if the defaults aren't adequate.
   C. The last two items are most important—the location of the Report Server to deploy to. Fill in the Target Server URL property with the address of your organization's SQL Reporting Services Server. The Target Server Version supplies choices in a drop-down box.

Once the Report Server is configured, it is time to deploy your report items (reports, report parts, datasets, and data sources). To deploy report items, right-click the Project Name at the top of the Solution Explorer pane of BIDS, and choose Deploy from the context menu. An output window will open at the bottom of the BIDS design surface and show the progress of the deployment. If there are any failures, the Error List will pop up and display error details. When the deployment process is complete, you will see that final line in the Output window—Deploy: X succeeded, X failed, X skipped. This is the only message of deployment completion. You should now be able to see your newly deployed report items in the Report Manager interface.

Choose the best method, deployment or upload, for your situation, depending upon your development/production environments and security setup.

Report Manager Object Types

Let's take a moment and explore the different item types in Report Manager and their context menus. Understanding the various object types, their purpose and functionality will allow you to exploit the usage of this tool. The Report Manager interface has appropriate context menus for each item type. Figure 4-5 shows all the different item type context menus. Starting in the first column:

- Report Models predefine data relationships and data sources, and make the ad hoc report creation experience much simpler. The Report Model context menu has choices for Move, Delete, Manage Dependent Items, Load In Report Builder, Security, Manage, and Download.
- Reports are the main information delivery vehicle. Report Manager doesn't distinguish between *.rdl files created by Report Designer or created by Report Builder. The Report context menu has Move, Delete, Edit In Report Builder, Subscribe, Create Linked Report, View Report History, Security, Manage, and Download choices. Notice you can subscribe to a report without having to open it!
- Folders are used to organize items. You can mix content types within a folder. The Folder context menu has Move, Delete, Security, and Manage choices. Security can be applied at the folder level, making it easy to secure a group of reports for a particular staff level or department.
- Data Sources are the fundamental building blocks of reports, and specify the data connection string to a server and data source. The Data Source context menu has Move, Delete, View Dependent Items, Generate Report Model, Security, and Manage choices. The View Dependent Items pane shows a listing of report models and reports that use the data source in their definition. This is especially useful to assess what impact a change to a data source may have.

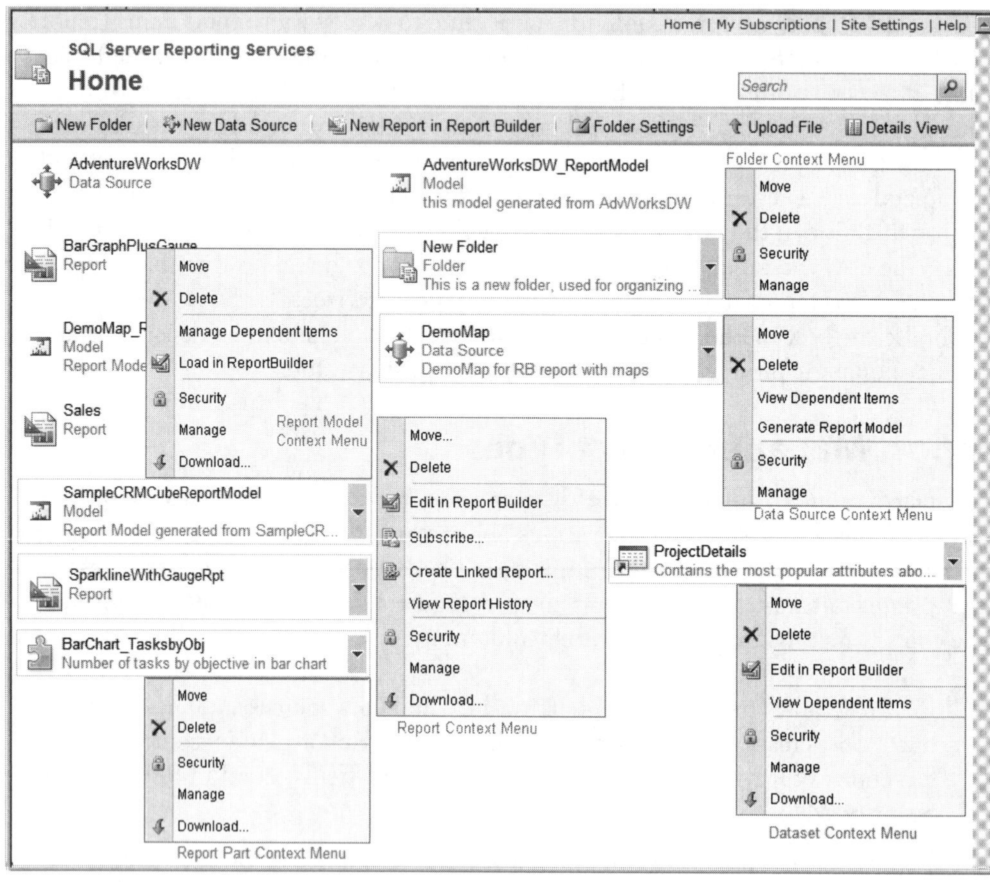

Figure 4-5 *Report Manager context menus for Reporting Services object types*

- Datasets are a new reporting services object type introduced with SQL 2008 R2. They are reusable query or stored procedure result sets. Making datasets available as reusable objects improves information consistency and allows for easy creation of alternate reports and visualizations. The Dataset context menu has Move, Delete, Edit In Report Builder, View Dependent Items, Security, Manage, and Download choices.
- Report Parts is another new feature with this release of SQL Server 2008 R2. Report Parts are reusable, formatted report components, like tables, matrices, charts, or gauges. The Report Parts context menu includes Move, Delete, Security, Manage, and Download. Notice there is no way to edit the report part outside of Report Builder.

Let's examine the properties for Data Sources and Reports, since they are the most important object types.

Data Source Properties

Data sources are the initial building blocks for a report, because it will not render without a data source. If you created a data source for your report when it was created, it can be uploaded or deployed to Report Manager. A data source can use any of the native drivers for SQL Server database, Analysis Services database, ODBC or OLE DB data connection, Oracle database, XML document, SAP Netweaver BI, or Hyperion Essbase source, or a custom data connection. As shown in Figure 4-6, data source metadata has four display panes: Properties, Subscriptions, Dependent Items, and Security. The Properties pane contains the following information:

- A name is required.
- A description is optional, but I would encourage the habit of typing one in; I suggest using the environment and database or application name (example: Production Data Warehouse, Development Timekeeping App). This will help other report developers reuse existing data sources instead of creating multiple objects for the same source.
- The data source type identifies the type of data that will be available.
- A connection string must be in the correct format for the connection type selected.
- There are check boxes for Hide In Tile View and Enable This Data Source.
- There are several security options:
  - Credentials supplied by the user running the report.
  - Credentials stored securely in the report server (i.e., service account) can either be used as Windows credentials or impersonate the authenticated user after a connection has been made.
  - Windows integrated security is available.
  - The last choice is Credentials Are Not Required.
- Press the Test Connection button to ensure your settings work correctly.
- There is one button at the bottom of this display: Apply (save changes). To cancel changes, simply navigate away from this page without clicking Apply.
- There are several operations available on this page, shown as buttons above the main data display: Delete, Move (move this data source to a different location within Report Server), and Generate Model (Report Builder Report Model).

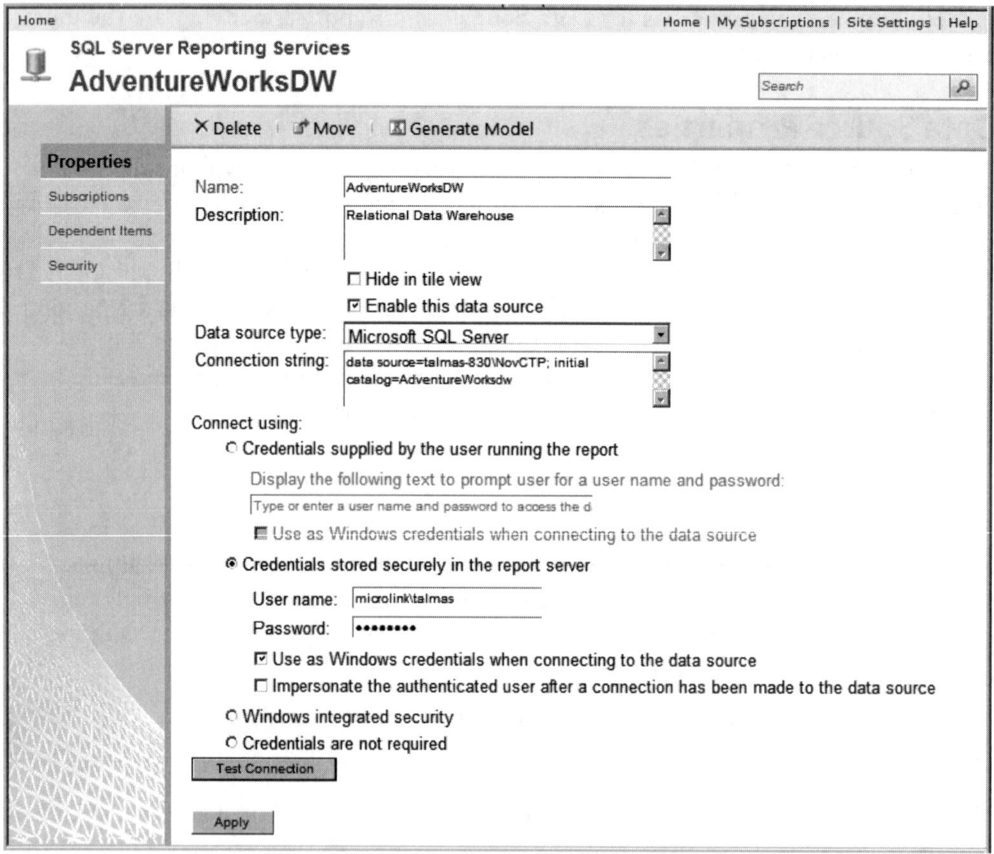

Figure 4-6 *Report Manager data source properties*

Report Manager Data Sources are the main connection between the enterprise data resources and report delivery. They can be designed to provide consistent, enterprise-wide access to the organization's important line of business and reporting data.

BI TIP

Use Data Source metadata as members of the metadata repository that provides valuable information to users, stakeholders, and audiences about the quality, lineage, and trustworthiness of the shared data sources. Use the Name and Description fields to capture correct, relevant keywords that have search value.

Report Properties

Reports are the main Reporting Services objects that can be displayed. Let's cover some of the more important properties available. You may have entered values for some of these properties during report construction, if not, you can edit them through Report Manager. To view and manage report properties, right-click the report item in Report Manager, and select Manage from the context menu, as shown in Figure 4-7. The initial Properties pane displays the report metadata and the report name and description. Several operations can be accomplished from this location by using the buttons in the toolbar: Delete, Move, Create Linked Report, Download, and Replace.

There are a variety of report properties, but we want to highlight several that will impact how your report item is displayed. Figure 4-8 displays the Processing Options and Snapshot Options Properties panes.

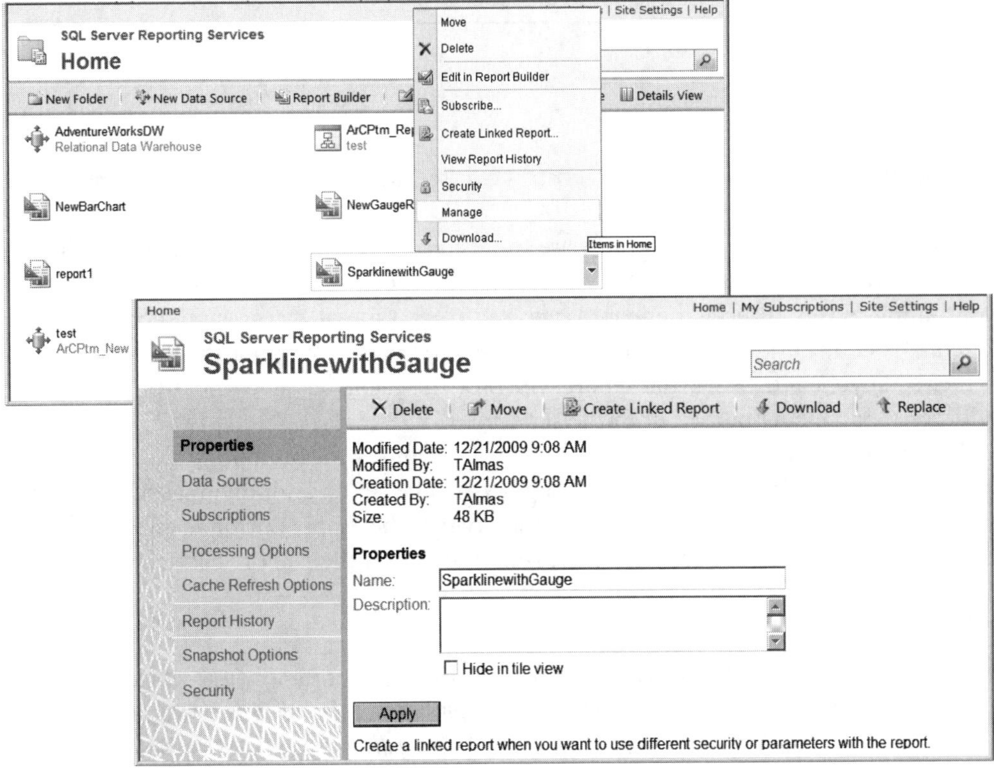

Figure 4-7 *Report Manager, Report Item properties*

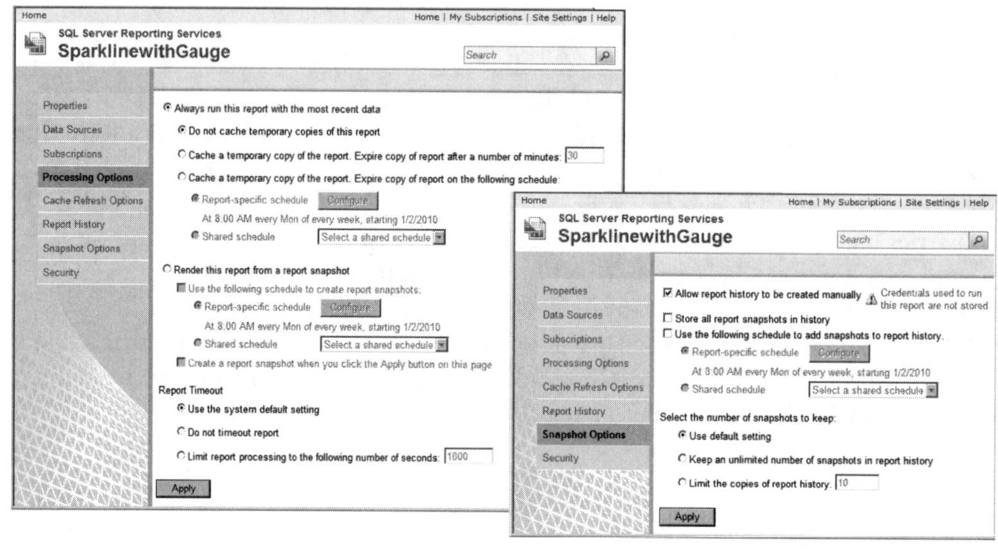

Figure 4-8 *A variety of report properties*

Processing Options is where the settings controlling the report processing are set, as shown in Figure 4-8.

Caching The first set of options are for caching a temporary copy of the report. You may want to cache a copy of the report if the report is large, complex, or time-consuming to run; if the audience is large; and if the time of access is predictable. Caching a copy of the report will store the rendered report temporarily on the report server, so anyone retrieving that report will view the cached copy without putting an additional processing burden onto the server.

Render from Snapshot The second set of options is for presenting the report based on an execution snapshot. The snapshot can be set on an individual schedule, set on a shared schedule, or created immediately (when the Apply button is clicked). Using an execution snapshot reduces the processing burden on the Report Server.

BI TIP

Remember when setting up snapshots that the data source must have the credentials needed to run the report stored securely on the Report Server. Also, if the report has parameters, default parameter values must be set. That is because snapshots require unattended execution, *meaning that the report must be able to render without user interaction (such as gathering parameter values or user credentials). This is the perfect example of the utility of using a service account for report execution.*

Report Timeout This set of options controls how long the report is allowed to process before timing out and returning an error. The value set for the Report Timeout will apply regardless of configured execution method.

Snapshot Options is where the detailed settings for an execution snapshot are stored. Execution snapshots can be used to preserve point-in-time actual values in reports, and they can be stored (and later archived) to provide an audit trail. The second group of options allows you to control the number of snapshots to keep.

BI TIP

By setting up execution snapshots and configuring the Processing Options to use those snapshots, the processing burden on the Report Server and Database Server(s) can be controlled and managed. Consider doing this for any report that is voluminous and/or regularly produced, as it will improve report delivery consistency and significantly reduce wait time.

Report Manager Security

Report and information security are increasingly important, and Report Manager makes it easy to secure your report items as much as necessary, at each level of granularity—from the site, individual folder, and detailed item level, using a role-based security model. This makes implementing security in Report Manager easy to accomplish if an information security schema using Activity Directory Security Groups has already been established. The functional roles provided by Report Manager make it easy to segregate duties among administrators, report authors, ad hoc report creators, and browsers who only view reports. Figure 4-9 shows the Security pane and the New Role Assignment pane for adding a user to Report Manager.

To make a new Role Assignment for the entire site, click the Site Settings menu link. To create a new role assignment for a particular folder, navigate to that folder and click the Security pane. One or multiple roles can be assigned to an individual or group account. The button Revert To Parent Security only appears on items that have customized their security schema.

Report Manager Security allows the organization to provide as broad or restricted access to report items as is necessary. Folder structures can be used to organize and secure content to specific groups with defined roles.

BI TIP

If you create a service account to use for report execution, it must have at least a Browser role assignment for the site.

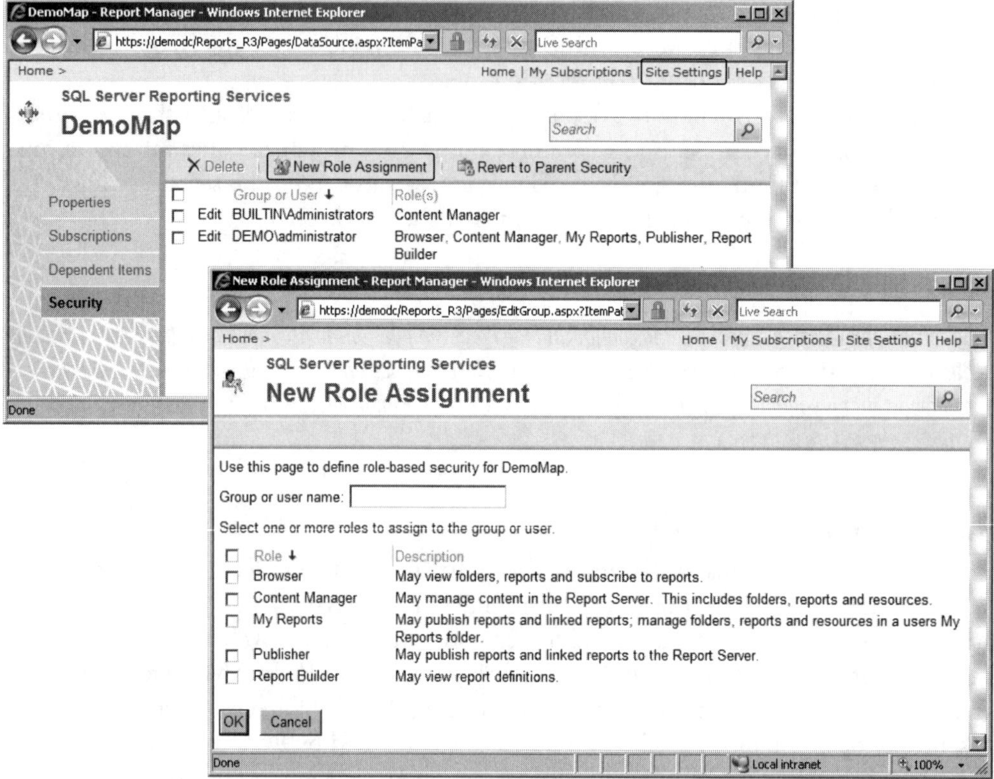

Figure 4-9 *Report Manager role-based security*

Report Subscriptions

Another very useful feature of Report Manager is Subscriptions. A user can subscribe to a report and have it delivered on a preset schedule automatically. Figure 4-10 shows the various options and screens associated with a report subscription.

1. On the Report Delivery Options pane, the report can be delivered via E-Mail or File Share.
   A. If the choice is E-Mail, specify the e-mail address of the recipient, a subject line, a priority, comments, and whether the report or a link is included.
   B. If Windows File Share is preferred, set a filename, path, format, and overwrite options.

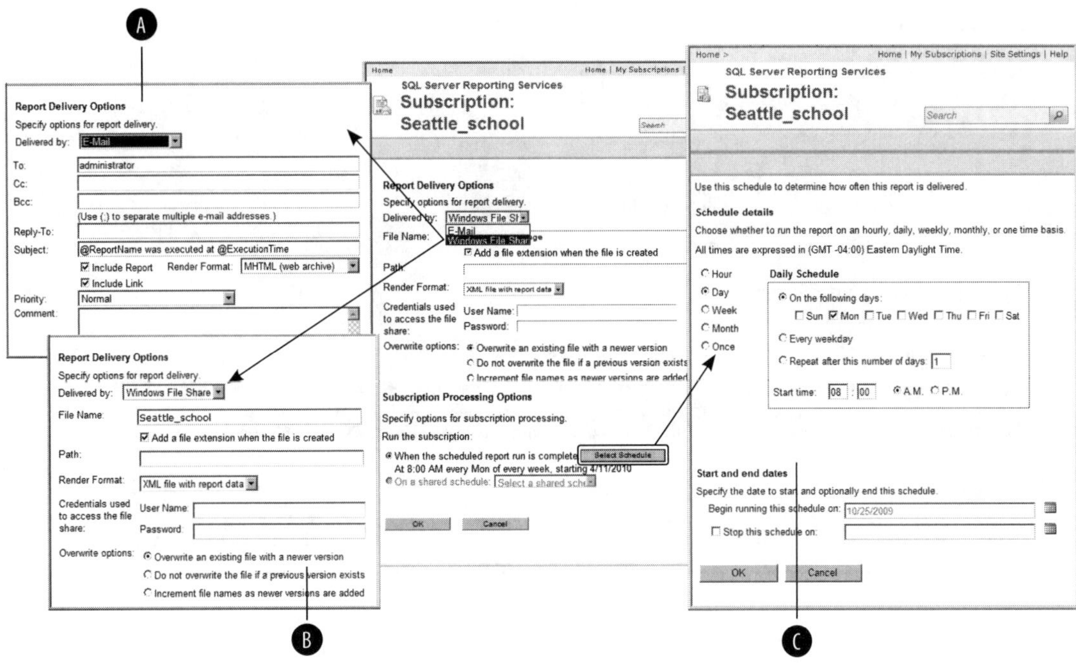

Figure 4-10 *Report Manager Subscriptions*

2. Under the Subscription Processing Options, set up a schedule for this item, or choose a shared schedule to be used for processing the report. Administrators can set up shared schedules that take advantage of server off-peak times for report processing.

   C. Schedule configuration provides plenty of flexibility, having start and stop dates, frequency options (hour, day, week, month, once), and even report processing start times.

3. The last item to configure is Report Parameters Values. If the report has parameters, a value must be chosen or it cannot process. Using a default setting makes the report more consistent.

Using subscriptions for routine report delivery has many benefits: it reduces the administrator's workload by ensuring timely information delivery, it cuts down on unexpected report server processing loads by using schedules to confine report execution to known times, and it provides more consistent report results by processing on the user's requested schedule. Do not overlook the utility of having the report delivered to the stakeholder's e-mail inbox (Figure 4-11). Users have come to expect that if there is anything important going on, they will be notified through their e-mail experience. Leveraging e-mail subscriptions for important reports can provide an easy way to increase awareness, communication, and satisfaction with information services.

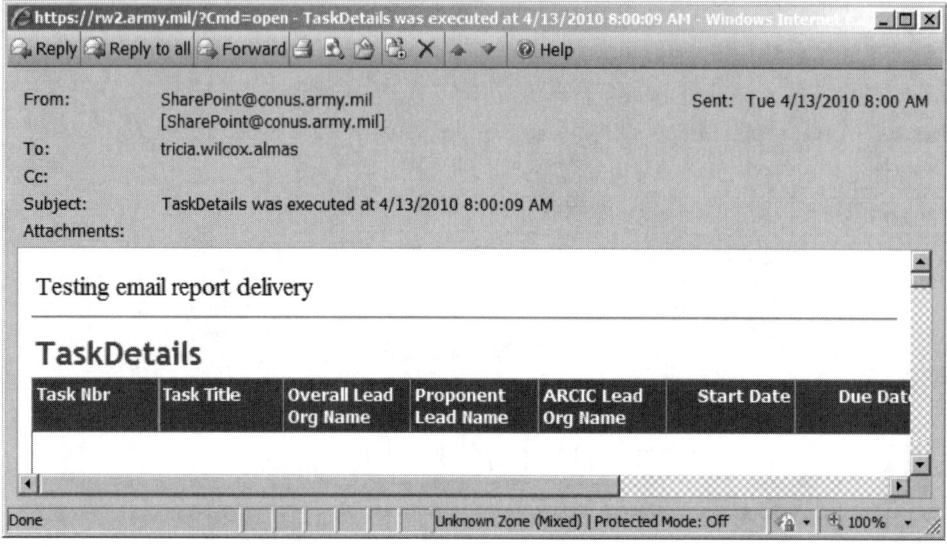

Figure 4-11 *Report rendered in Outlook*

Rendering Reports in Report Manager

Report Manager runs and displays reports natively, meaning if you click a report item, it will process the report on demand and display it in a Report Manager pane. Figure 4-12 shows a map-based report in a Report Manager pane.

A. This report has parameters, and the selection mechanism for parameters is shown in the bar above the display controls.

B. The display controls allow navigation through the report by paging or jumping to a specific page.

C. The zoom control allows you to increase or decrease the size of the display, independently from the zoom control on the browser.

D. The Find text box allows searching of report content.

E. The floppy disk icon displays the export options: XML, CSV, Atom Data Feed, Acrobat, MHTML (web archive), Excel, TIFF (image), or Word.

F. The recycle icon refreshes the report display.

G. The printer icon brings up the Print dialog box.

H. The last icon sets up an RSS data feed.

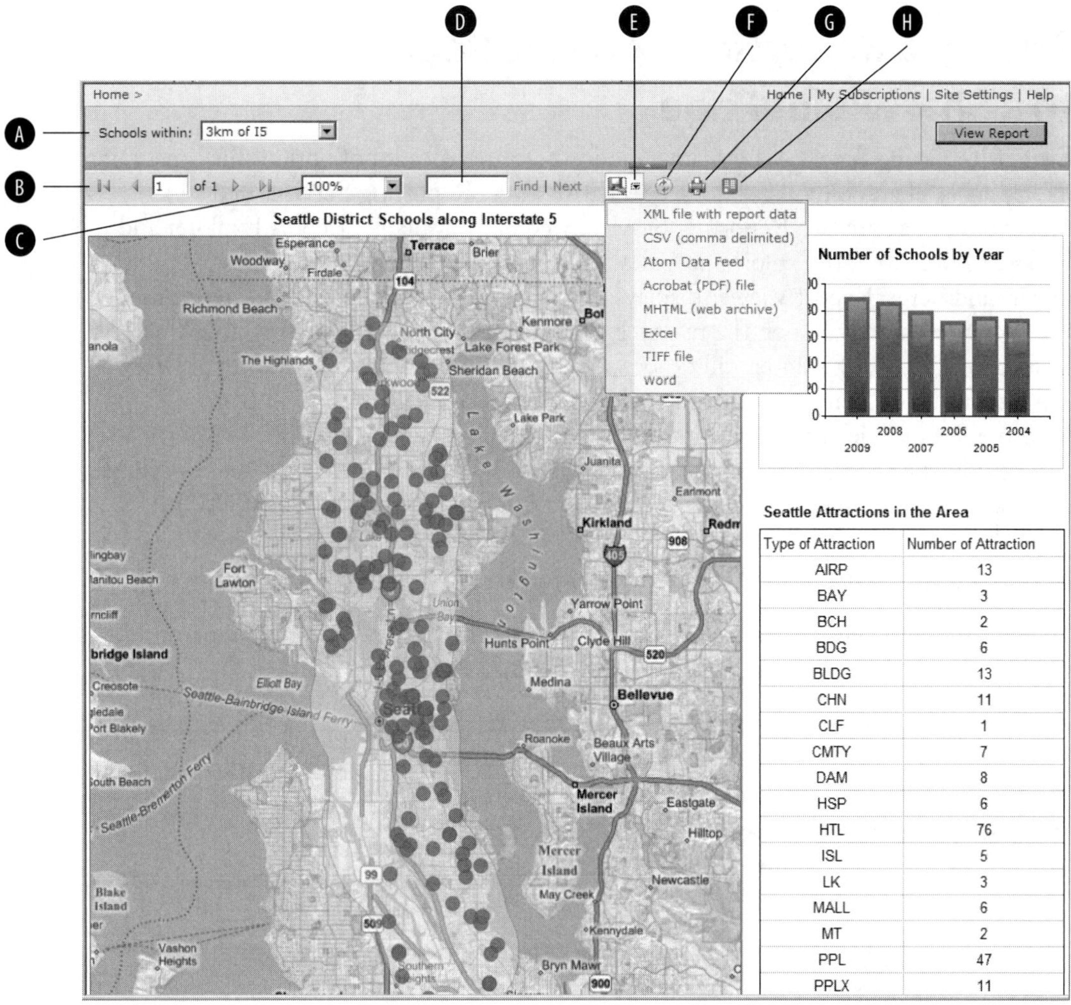

Figure 4-12 *Report Manager report display*

Displaying reports using Report Manager is an easy way to get report content into the audience's hands in a secure manner. Because the report displays as a web page, the only client application required for viewing reports is a web browser. Even if Report Manager is configured to run in native mode, reports can still be delivered into SharePoint pages by using the Reporting Services web parts, and connecting back to the Report Server. We will tackle that topic next.

Adding a Reporting Services Report to a SharePoint Page

Even if Reporting Services is in native mode, there are still a lot of options for consuming the report in SharePoint pages. To access native mode Reporting Services items in SharePoint, there are two Reporting Services web parts available: Report Explorer and Report Viewer. Report Explorer provides the Report Manager–type of view that displays folders and items; Report Viewer displays one report. These two web parts can be used together or separately. When the two web parts are configured to work together through connections, Report Explorer will expose a particular folder structure and Report Viewer will display the chosen report. If you want to embed a particular report in a SharePoint page, use Report Viewer and link it to the specific report item to display.

The following scenario assumes that the Reporting Services web parts (rswebparts.cab) have already been installed into your SharePoint Global Assembly Cache (GAC).

Linked Report Explorer and Report Viewer Web Parts

To add the Reporting Services web parts to a SharePoint dashboard page, open the page in edit mode, as shown in Figure 4-13.

1. Click the Add A Web Part button in the frame at the top of the web part zone.

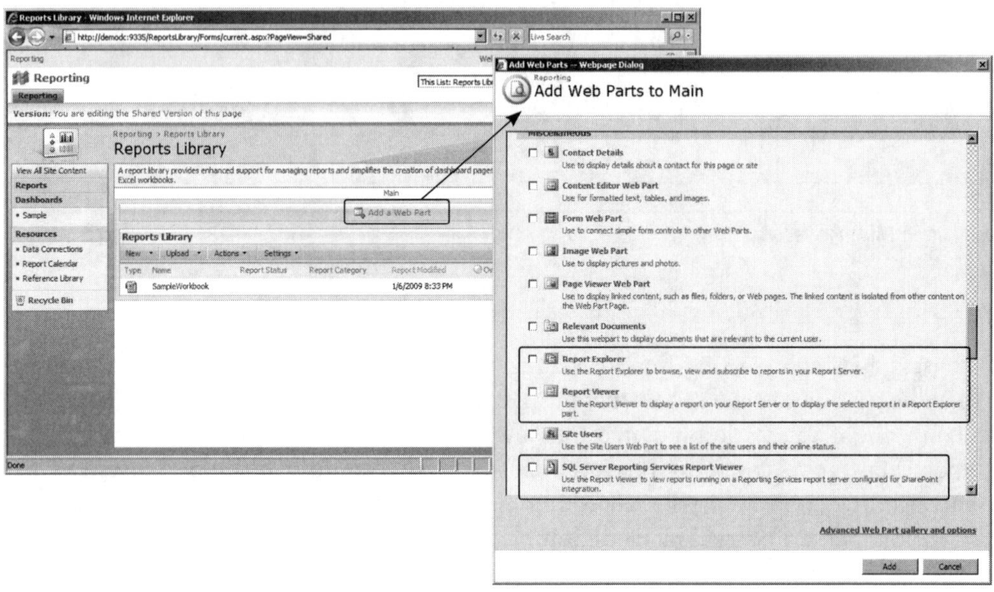

Figure 4-13 *Add Reporting Services web parts to SharePoint page*

2. The Add Web Parts dialog box will appear, listing all available web parts for this site collection. They are grouped in categories. The Report Explorer, Report Viewer, and SQL Server Reporting Services Report Viewer web parts are found under the Miscellaneous category. Use Report Explorer and Report Viewer for Reporting Services native mode reports. Use SQL Server Reporting Services Report Viewer for reports stored in SharePoint integrated mode.
3. Since this is the native mode example, tick the check boxes next to Report Explorer and Report Viewer, and click the Add button at the bottom of the dialog box.
4. The new web parts will display below the existing Report Library web part on the page.

Once the web parts are on the page, configure their connection to the Report Server (Figure 4-14).

1. Click the Edit drop-down for the Report Explorer web part, and click Modify Shared Web Part from the menu (Step A).
2. The configuration pane along the right side of the page will display. In the Report Manager URL, type in or paste the URL for your Report Manager (Step B).

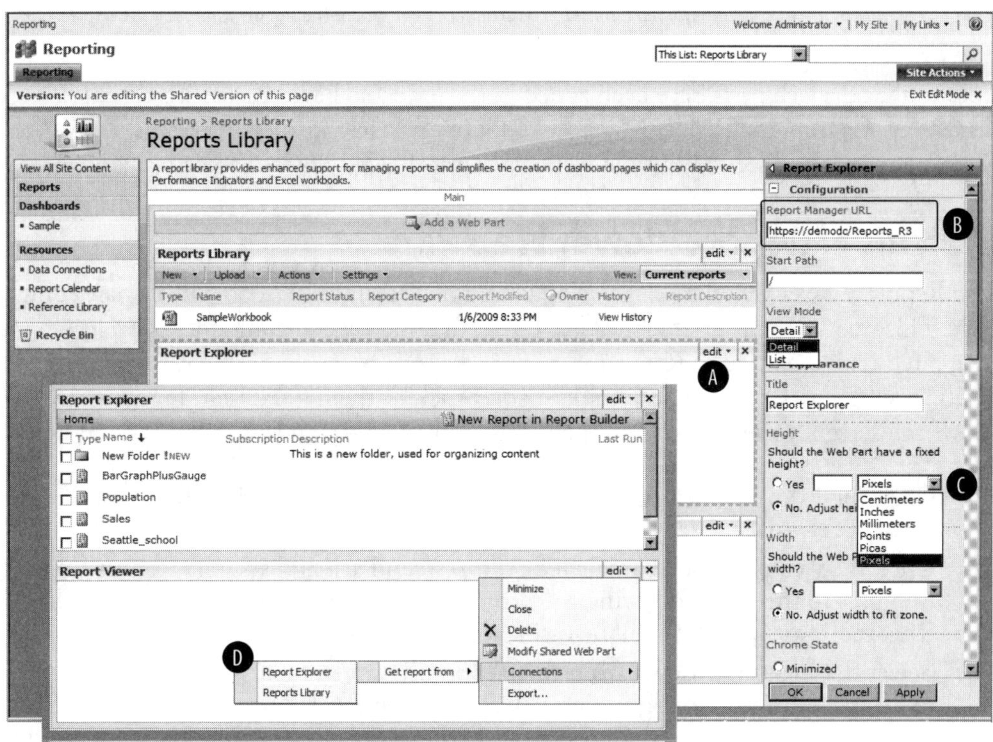

Figure 4-14 *Configure Reporting Services web parts in SharePoint*

3. The Start Path text box allows you to display any segment of a folder structure. This example starts at the root folder.
4. View mode determines whether it is Detail or List view.
5. There are controls for specifically setting the web part height and width, if desired. We find it particularly useful to set the Report Viewer Height setting to be at least 4 to 5 inches, to reduce the need for scrolling (Step C).
6. When the properties are set as desired, click the OK button at the bottom of the pane.
7. The Report Explorer web part will now display the folder structure identified in the Start Path.
8. Click the Edit drop-down from the Report Viewer web part.
9. This time, choose Connections from the menu, then Report Explorer (Step D). This will establish the link between the two web parts, and when a report is selected in Report Explorer, it will render in the Report Viewer web part.

BI TIP

Notice that in the menu bar for the Report Explorer web part, there is a button for New Report in Report Builder. Even though Reporting Services is not in SharePoint integrated mode, Report Explorer provides the connection to launch Report Builder, removing the need for report authors to navigate to the Report Manager site in order to launch Report Builder.

Now that the web parts have been added to the page and have been configured to display reports from the Report Manager, test it out by clicking a report name listed in Report Explorer and see it display in Report Viewer. The results are shown in Figure 4-15!

Individual Report Viewer Web Part

The Report Viewer web part can also be used alone to embed a report in a SharePoint page. This may be appropriate for a dashboard that has several components on it, integrated with a particular Reporting Services report. If your report consists of multiple subreports, you can access and display each of them separately. Figure 4-16 shows the screen for setting up an embedded report in a dashboard page.

1. Click the Edit Page selection in the Site Actions menu found at the upper-right corner of the page (Step A).
2. Click the web part zone bar labeled Add A Web Part, and add the Report Viewer web part to the page, following the procedure previously described (Step B). The Report Viewer web part will be displayed in that zone.
3. Select the Edit drop-down from the Report Viewer web part (Step C), and in the Report Viewer Configuration pane, configure the connection to the specific report you want to embed. In the Report Manager URL text box, paste or type in the URL for your Report Manager.

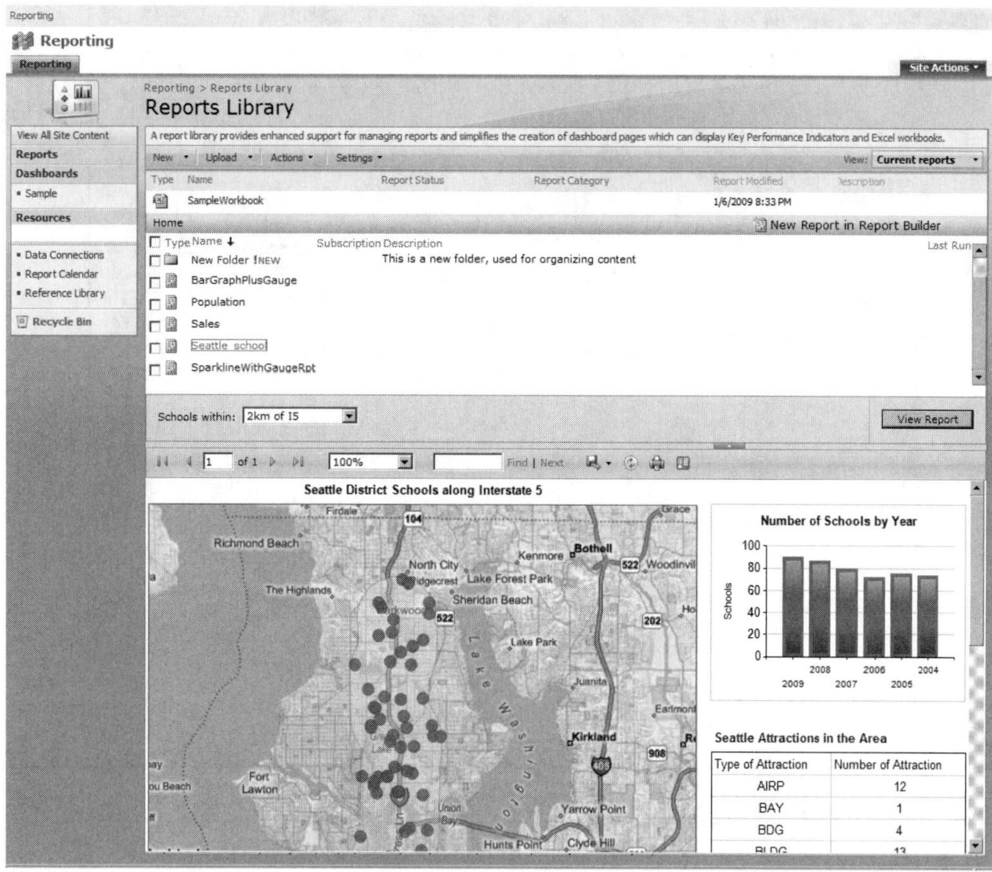

Figure 4-15 *Report Viewer web part displaying the selected report*

4. In the Report Path text box, type in the report name, including the folder path (Step D).
5. If you want to adjust the size of the web part, specify the size under the Appearance section (Step E).
6. Click the OK button at the bottom of the pane (Step F).

As you can see, SQL Server Reporting Services in native mode gives you many options for displaying reports, natively through the Report Manager interface, or embedded in SharePoint using the Report Explorer and Report Viewer web parts. There is another option when integrating Reporting Services and SharePoint, and that is SharePoint integrated mode, which we will cover next.

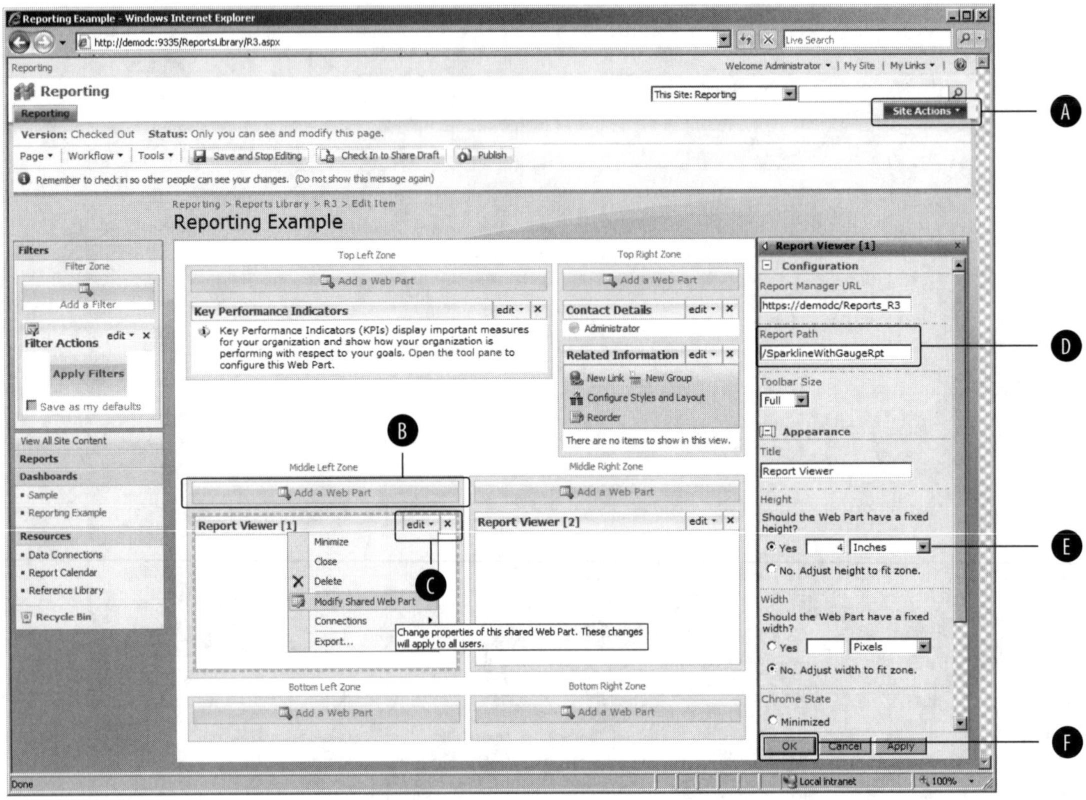

Figure 4-16 *Embedded report in a SharePoint dashboard page*

Microsoft Office SharePoint Server 2007: Reporting Services Integrated Mode

The implementation of installing Reporting Services in SharePoint integrated mode is begun when Reporting Services is initially configured after installation. It is beyond the scope of this chapter to provide that instruction, but suffice it to say that the New Configuration Wizard has been drastically improved over the previous several versions. We assume that the SQL Server Reporting Services configuration and the SharePoint Central Administration Reporting Services Integration has been completed. The most obvious way to expose the SharePoint–Reporting Services integration is to create a SharePoint Site (or Site Collection) based on the Report Center Site Template. Doing so creates a SharePoint Site with the Report Server object types predefined as content types, and a Reports Library document library that has report server content types included.

Reporting Services in SharePoint integrated mode behaves a little differently than in native mode, and the filename extensions for Data Sources vary as well. When you create a new data source file in SharePoint, it is tagged as an *.rsds (report sharepoint data source) file; if you create a data source in Report Manager or BIDS, it is an *.rds. Even though you can set the content type to be a data source on an *.rds file, it just doesn't behave the same as an *.rsds file in SharePoint integrated mode.

BI TIP

Do not import or upload your data source files into the SharePoint Reports Library; re-create them to ensure they are of the proper format and will work in SharePoint integrated mode.

The main functionality of Report Manager in native mode is mimicked in the SharePoint Reports Library. Report and data source files are stored and organized by folders. Security is applied using the SharePoint security model. See the following table for a comparison of default security role equivalencies. Keep in mind that to achieve more granular control over the security features accessed in SharePoint, the system administrator can create new SharePoint roles that have more specific permissions.

Security Feature	Report Manager Roles	SharePoint Roles
Read-only access	Browser	Site Visitor or Reader
Upload content, manage content	Content Manager	Site Member or Contributor
View/edit report definitions	Report Builder	Site Member or Contributor
Publish reports and linked reports to the Report Server	Publisher	Site Member or Contributor
Personalized reports only	My Reports	My Site

The Reports Library in the Report Center is most likely the library that is being synchronized with the Report Server Database, but that can be changed through configuration settings in SharePoint Central Administration, and you can add a Reports Library to any site no matter what site template was used to create that site. The SharePoint library that stores your report server items should have Report Server content types enabled. Figure 4-17 shows a view of the SharePoint Reports Library and the different file content type icons that you will encounter.

SharePoint Reporting Services file types include

- Excel Reports (*.xlsx) that can be used through Excel Services
- Dashboard Pages (*.aspx) that contain web parts
- Report Files (*.rdl) created by either Report Designer (BIDS) or Report Builder 3.0
- Report SharePoint Data Source (*.rsds) to be used with Report Designer and Report Builder

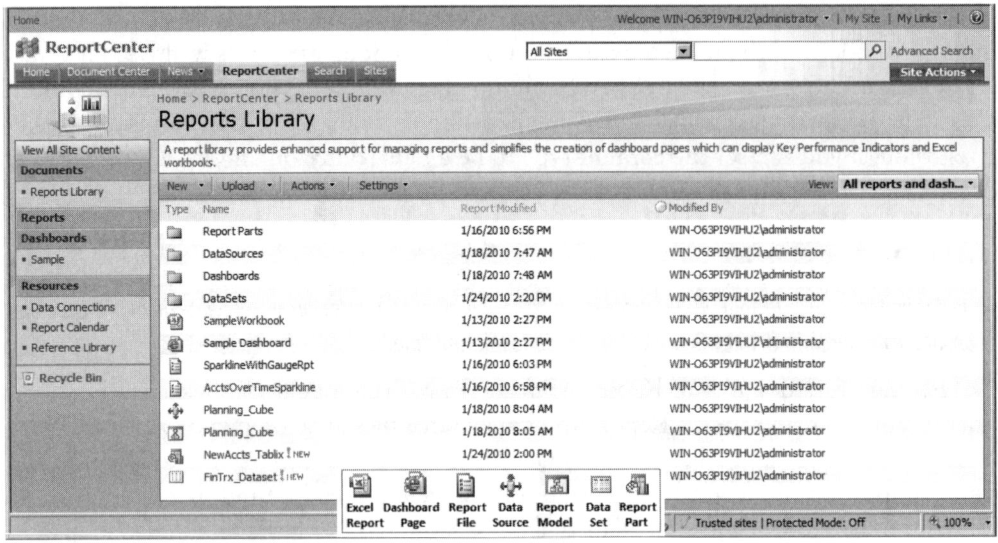

Figure 4-17 *SharePoint Reports Library home and icons*

- Report Model (*.smdl) to be used by Report Builder
- Report DataSet (*.rds) to be used by Report Builder
- Report Part (*.rsc) to be used by Report Builder

Maximize your information delivery flexibility by taking advantage of the new Report Part and DataSet report objects. Small, modular, reusable parts make it easy to build dashboard pages customized for a particular perspective or functional area. This, combined with the fact that Report Builder can now use data sources as well as report models, makes visualization creation swift and easy.

BI TIP

Use folders to organize content and apply access permissions. This will also streamline report deployment and management of like objects. Utilize the available rich metadata, like description fields, to make it easy to find objects for a certain topic or category. Don't forget that you can add custom columns to the Reports Library to collect organization-specific information and make search results more accurate.

So now that we have looked at all of the possible containers for report files, let's talk about how to use them as web parts. As discussed in a previous section, you can display an individual report in a web part, and you can have multiple web parts on a dashboard page. So plan out what you need and create all the parts before starting to construct the dashboard page.

Creating Dashboard Pages

Dashboard pages in SharePoint divide the page up into *zones* in order to provide designers a way to control web part placement and spacing. Let's look at a generic SharePoint dashboard page and discuss the different elements you will find. Figure 4-18 shows a generic SharePoint page with the zones and navigation elements identified.

- At the top of the page is the SharePoint page header, which cannot be modified without SharePoint Designer. It contains the site name, tabs for any subsites, the account name of the person logged in, a link to My Site (if enabled), My Links, a link to Help, the standard Search functionality, and the Site Actions menu.
- Immediately below that is the Site page header, which contains the site navigation breadcrumbs and the Site Page Name.

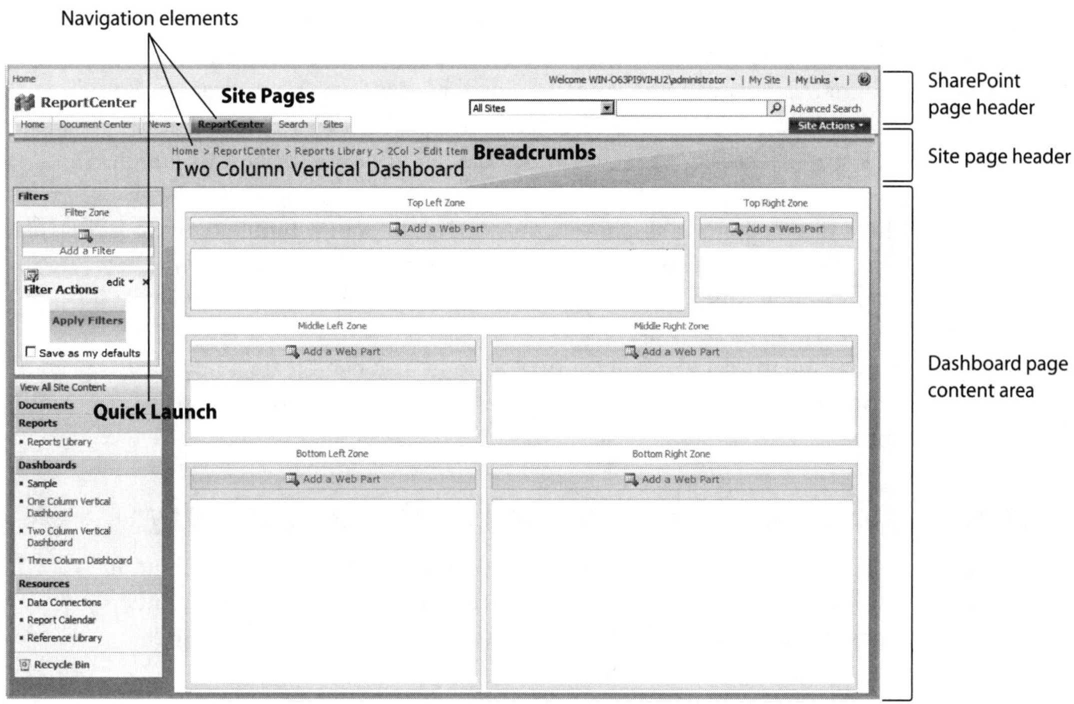

Figure 4-18 *SharePoint dashboard page areas*

- Along the left column is the default area for navigation, and where the Quick Launch bar is found. On many dashboard pages, the default Filter Area is also found at the top of the left column above the Quick Launch bar.
- The main content holding area of the page may contain one or more zones, depending upon the page template being used. If there is more than one zone, the horizontal rows are generally referred to as the Top or Header zone, the Middle zone, and the Bottom or Footer zone. Vertical columns are generally referred to as Left, Left Middle, Middle, Right Middle, or Right.
- Page zones may organize their web parts horizontally or vertically, depending on how the page template designer sets the properties. The default is vertical.

Zones are defined in the page layout templates and are usually specified as a percentage of the page width and/or height. As you will see, zones do not need to be symmetrical, but they do have some specific behaviors to be aware of. Web parts have size controls for height and width and may be set to specific measurements (centimeters, inches, millimeters, points, picas, or pixels) or set to adjust to fit zone for automatic sizing based on the content and the zone size. For pages where there are multiple vertical zones, like the two-column vertical zone in the example, the zones will stay aligned no matter how different the individual content web part sizes are. For example, if you put a web part in the middle-left zone that is 4 inches wide, and a web part in the bottom left zone that is 2 ½ inches wide, that left zone will be at least 4 inches wide consistently.

If you cannot find an acceptable page layout, you can create a new template with SharePoint Designer, but that discussion is beyond the scope of this book. We will examine the standard page layouts available through the Create A New Dashboard and Create A New Web Parts Page options.

To create a new dashboard page, you have two options. You can create a new dashboard page from the new item menu in the Reports Library, or you can create a new Web Part page.

Create a New Dashboard Page in the Reports Library

The SharePoint Reports Library supports the dashboard page content type, making it easy to create a new dashboard. The limitation with this option is that there are only three page templates available. The column count refers to the number of web part zones defined on the page and their orientation.

With this option, here are three choices for page layout:

One-column vertical layout. This layout has two horizontal zones in the header area and one large zone in the body. This layout also has a filter area and the navigation pane along the left side.

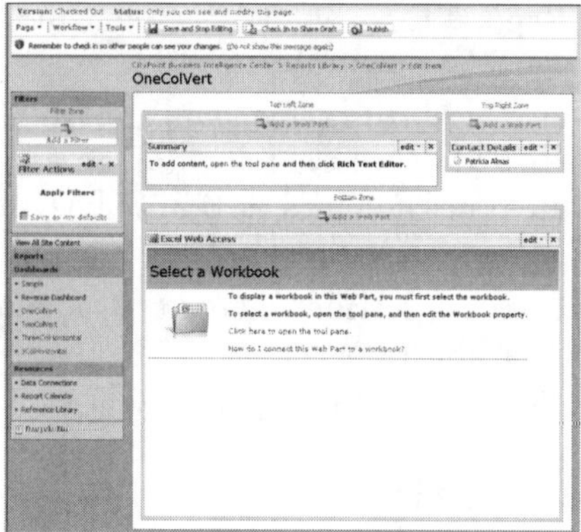

Two-column vertical layout. This layout has two horizontal zones in the header area and four zones arranged in two vertical columns in the body of the page. It also includes a filter area and the navigation pane in the left column.

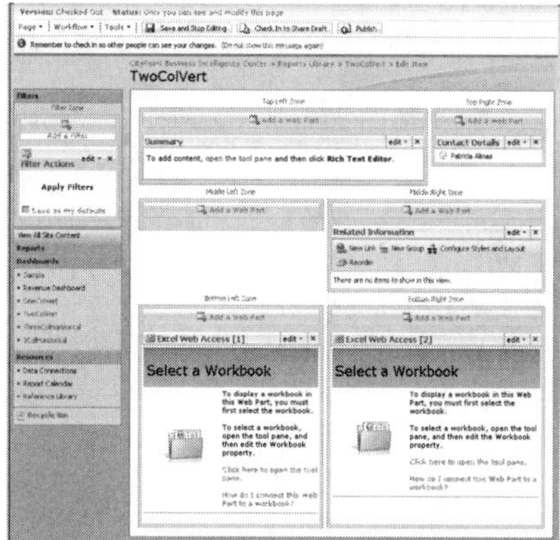

Three-column horizontal layout. This layout has two horizontal zones at the top for header information, a filter zone composed of two columns, three middle zones in the body of the page, and three bottom zones for content. Notice that this page layout does not include the navigation Quick Launch pane on the left side, which gives more area for content web parts but limits navigation to the breadcrumbs and provided links.

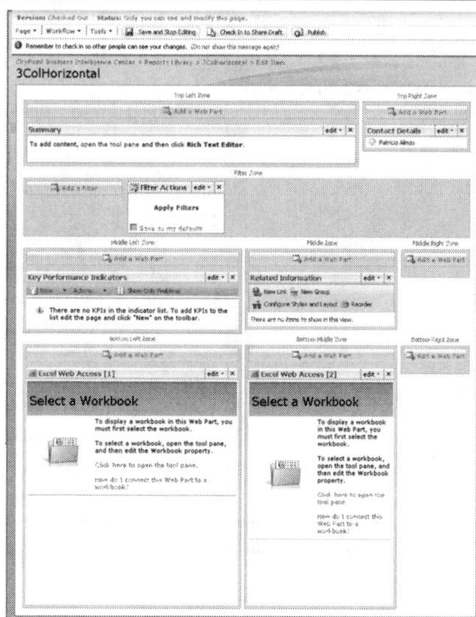

To create a dashboard page in this way, refer to Figure 4-19 and follow this procedure:

1. In the Reports Library, click the New menu button drop-down, and select Dashboard Page from the menu.
2. The New Dashboard screen will appear. Fill in the File Name and Page Title fields—they do not have to be the same. Avoid using spaces in the File Name; spaces are translated into %20 in HTML. To maximize discoverability by the search engine, fill in the description field with rich, keyword-laden text.
3. In the Location section, choose the Document or Report Library and Folder for the new dashboard page.
4. In the Create Link In Current Navigation Bar section, choose whether to display the link for this page in the Quick Launch bar, and if yes, which section the link should appear in.

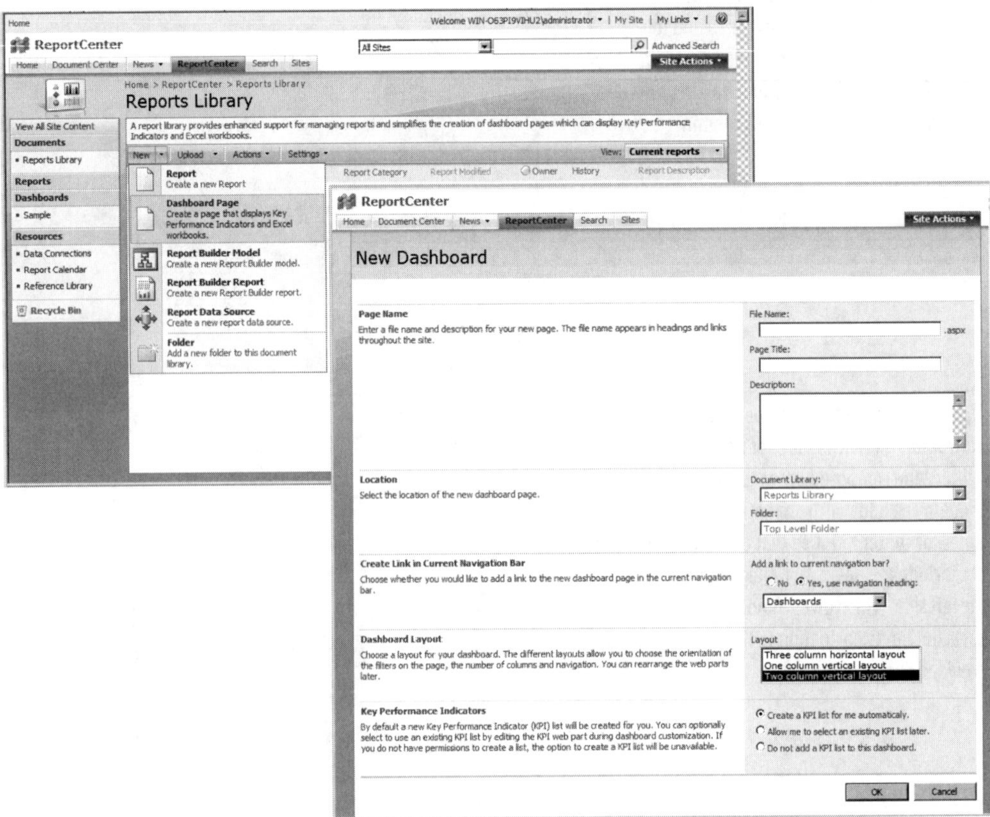

Figure 4-19 *New dashboard page in Reports Library*

5. As described in the preceding table, the Dashboard Layout section presents three choices for your new dashboard page. Choose Three Column Horizontal Layout, One Column Vertical Layout, or Two Column Vertical Layout from the field.
6. The last section, Key Performance Indicators, gives three choices for creating a KPI list to appear on your dashboard: "Create a KPI list for me automatically," "Allow me to select an existing KPI list later," or "Do not add a KPI list to the dashboard." Maximum flexibility is provided by the second choice, allow me to select later.
7. When finished, click the OK button at the bottom of the screen. Click Cancel to finish without saving a new dashboard page.

Your new dashboard page will be found in the library you specified and is now ready for you to edit and add web parts.

Create a New Web Part Page

The second option for creating a new dashboard is to create a new web part page. To increase your web part zone layout options, this second method is to create a new web part page from the View All Items page. There are eight basic zone layout templates, depicted here. None of these layouts includes the left navigation area or the Quick Launch bar. Also, there is less descriptive metadata stored about web part pages—no Page Title or Description fields, and SharePoint will not automatically create a KPI list for your new dashboard. However, the increased layout options make these page templates a little more versatile. Here is a synopsis of the available page layouts for web part pages.

Full Page Vertical. This page layout is one unstructured content area. Multiple web parts will be stacked vertically.

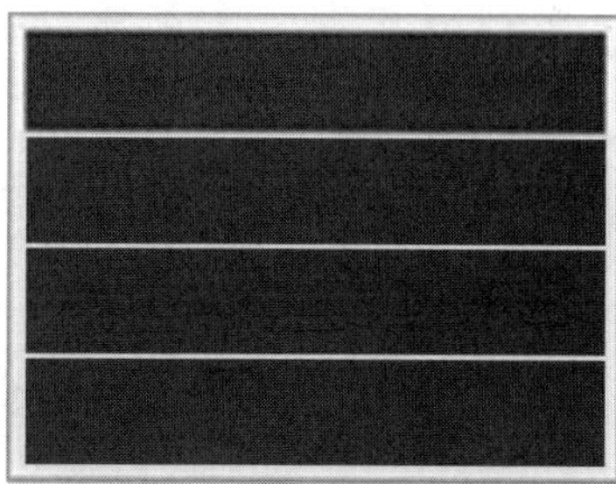

Header Left Column Body. This page layout has a top header zone that spans the page, a left column, and a wide body zone. This layout is particularly useful if you have links in the left column that change the display in the main body.

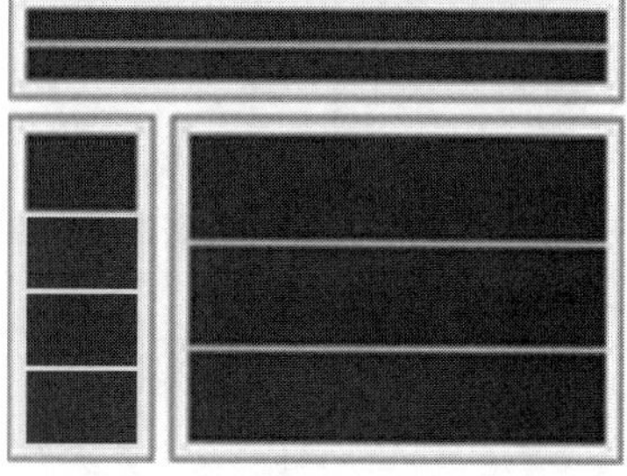

Header Right Column Body. This layout has a top header zone that spans the page, a large body area, and a right column zone. This layout is useful if you want to place links to additional, detailed content in the right column.

Header Footer Three Columns. This layout has header and footer zones that span the page, and three columns in the body area.

Left Column Header Footer Top Row Three Columns. This layout has a left column that spans the page vertically, header and footer zones, a top body zone, and three column body zones.

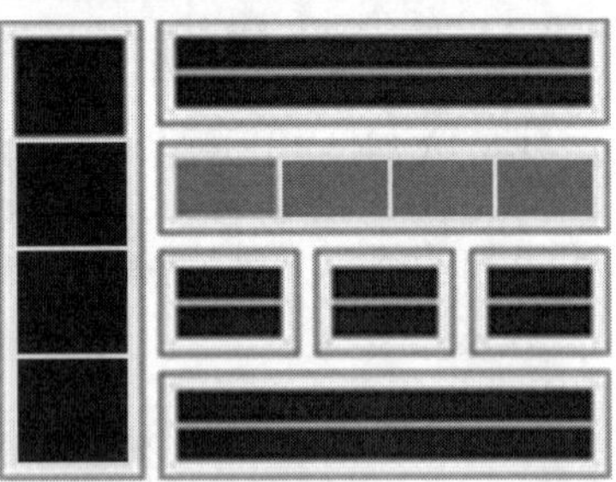

Right Column Header Footer Top Row Three Columns. This layout has a right column that spans the page vertically, header and footer zones, a top body zone, and three column body zones.

Header Footer Four Columns Top Row. This layout has header and footer zones that span the page, left and right column body zones, then a top middle zone and two column body zones in the middle of the page.

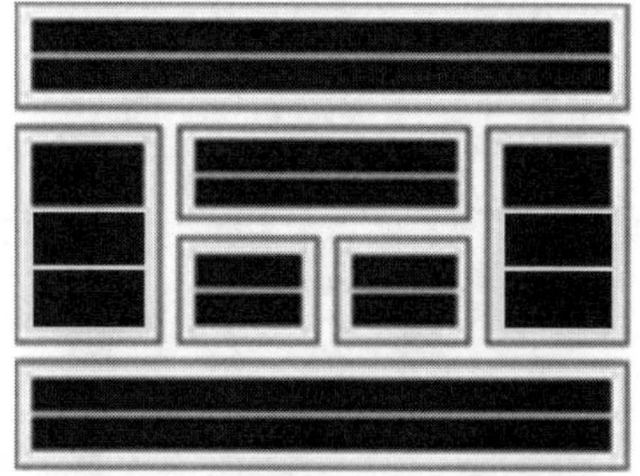

Header Footer Two Columns Four Rows. This layout has header and footer zones that span the page, left and right column body zones, and then four distinct rows in the middle of the page.

To create a new dashboard page in this way, refer to Figure 4-20 and follow this procedure:

1. Click the View All Site Content link that is located at the top of the Quick Launch bar. The All Site Content page will display. Click the Create button directly below the All Site Content page title.
2. The Create page will display, showing all choices for creating new web parts and pages. In the last column to the right, under Web Pages, click the Web Part Page link.
3. The New Web Part Page screen will appear. In the name section, give your new Dashboard a name. This will be the filename for the page, so avoid using spaces in the name, as HTML translates spaces into %20. Notice that there isn't as much metadata associated with web part pages—there are no separate title or description fields to fill in.
4. In the layout section, choose one of the eight layout templates displayed that were described previously. As you click each template name, the thumbnail picture will depict the various zones defined in that template.
5. Choose a location from the drop-down to save your new dashboard page. If you want the dashboard page to reside somewhere not listed, choose Document Library and move the page afterward. Notice that SharePoint does not offer to create a new KPI list associated with this web part page as it did when creating a dashboard page in the Reports Library. You can, however, add a KPI list web part to the page later if you wish.
6. Click the OK button at the bottom of the page when the information is complete, or click Cancel to exit without saving.

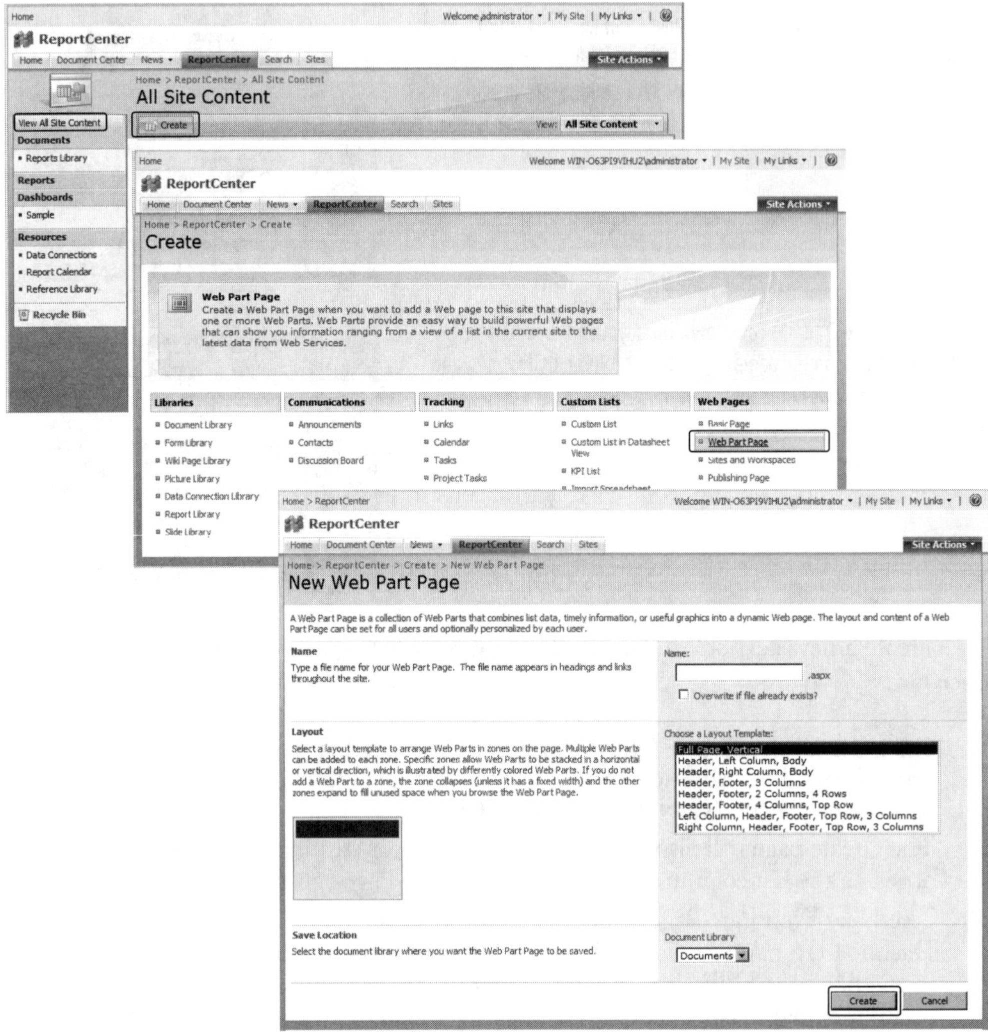

Figure 4-20 *Create a new web part page*

Your new web part page will be found in the library specified, and is now ready for you to edit and add web parts. There is one more topic we should cover before launching into creating some dashboards, and that is page filters.

Page Filters in SharePoint

Page filters are a great feature in SharePoint and allow the page designer to connect various web parts to the same filter so that web part contents can be consistently portrayed. Some filter web parts work in the background and are unseen, like the current user filter. Other filter types allow the user to interact with the dashboard by selecting filter values from a list, or typing in values. The filters can connect with a variety of data sources, including SQL Server Analysis Services data, SharePoint lists, Business Data Catalog lists, or Excel Web Access.

There are three parts to using a filter on a SharePoint page or dashboard:

Add the filter to the web part page. Use the same procedure as you would follow to add any other web part to a page. The dashboard page you create may have a filter zone already defined. If the filter will require user interaction, then consider where on the dashboard page it is located—probably close to the top in either corner.

Configure the filter settings. Each filter web part has its own set of properties that is available to set in the web part tool pane.

Connect the filter to the target web parts. Once the filter is configured, connect it to the various web parts through each web part's Edit menu, then choose Connections, as shown in Figure 4-21.

Here are the options for filter web parts, as shown in Figure 4-22:

1. **Business Data Catalog Filter** If you use the BDC to access line of business data, this filter can contain a list based on those available connections. You can specify both a value column and the description column.
2. **Choice Filter** Choices manually entered by author.

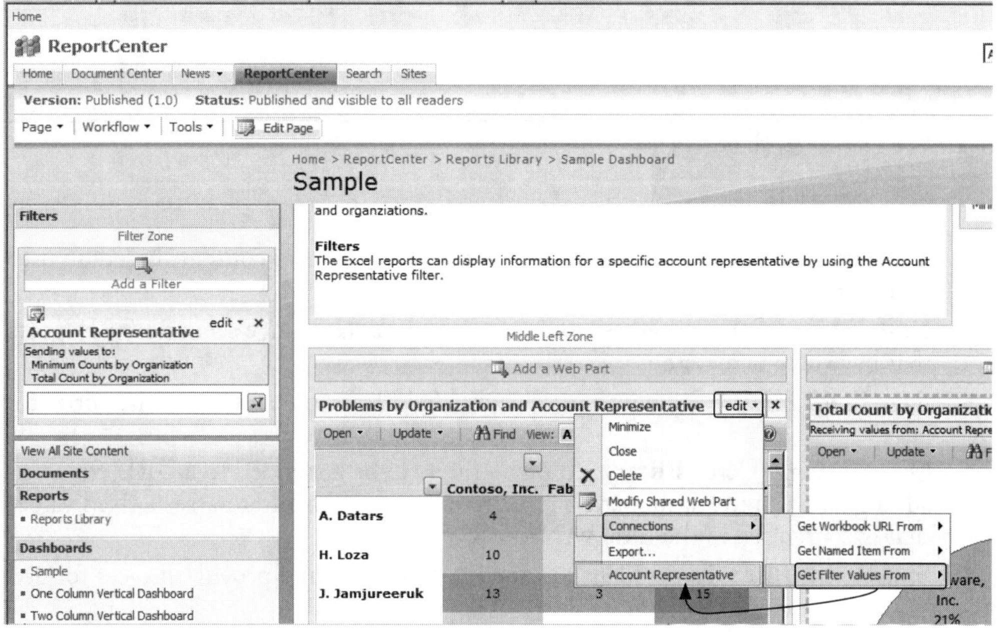

Figure 4-21 *SharePoint filter connection*

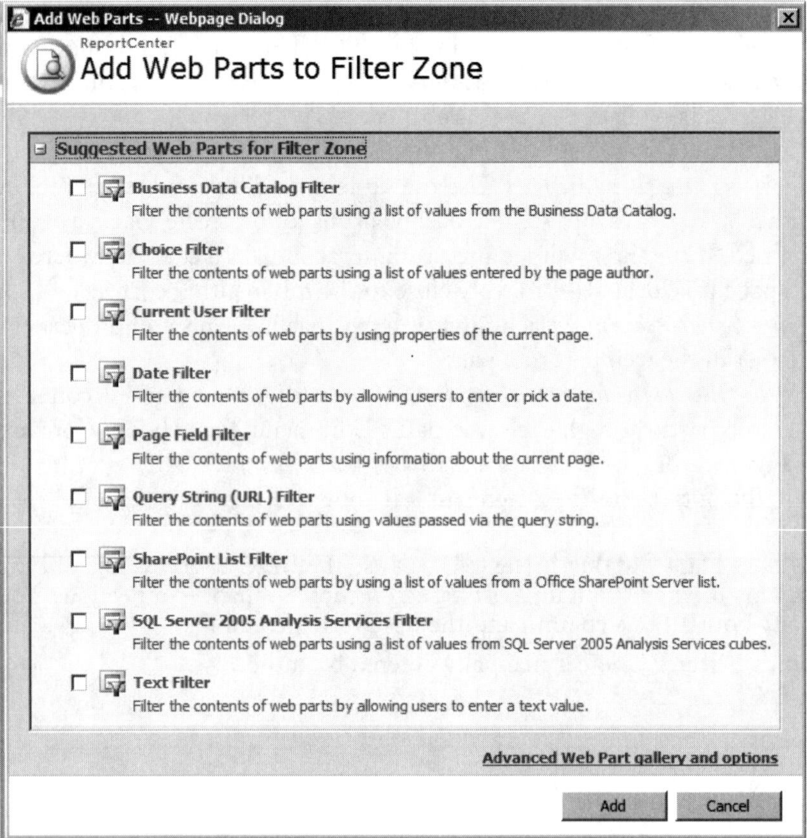

Figure 4-22 *SharePoint filter web part choices*

3. **Current User Filter** Uses the logged-in account to filter contents based on user permissions.
4. **Date Filter** Can be used as a point in time, or a date range scenario for Reports that have date parameters.
5. **Page Field Filter** Provides the value of a field from the list row of the current page.
6. **Query String (URL) Filter** Allows a filters to be appended to a URL, for adding a link to the dashboard on a different page. This filter passes a fixed value that is configured in the filter web part tool pane.
7. **SharePoint List Filter** Identifies the list and column to provide choices for user selection.

8. **SQL Server 2005 Analysis Services Filter** Creates a list filter from an Analysis Services cube dimension.
9. **Text Filter** You can require users to enter text and display based on the value entered. This could be used as an additional security measure.

A wide variety of filter types are available to customize your web pages and dashboards. Each has a specific purpose, and they can be used alone or in combinations to deliver just the right information display. Some filters are not visible to end users but do control the data that is displayed. The current user filter in conjunction with well-designed web parts can present highly customized and secure business intelligence displays. Figure 4-23 shows an example of a connection between a filter web part and a dashboard web part.

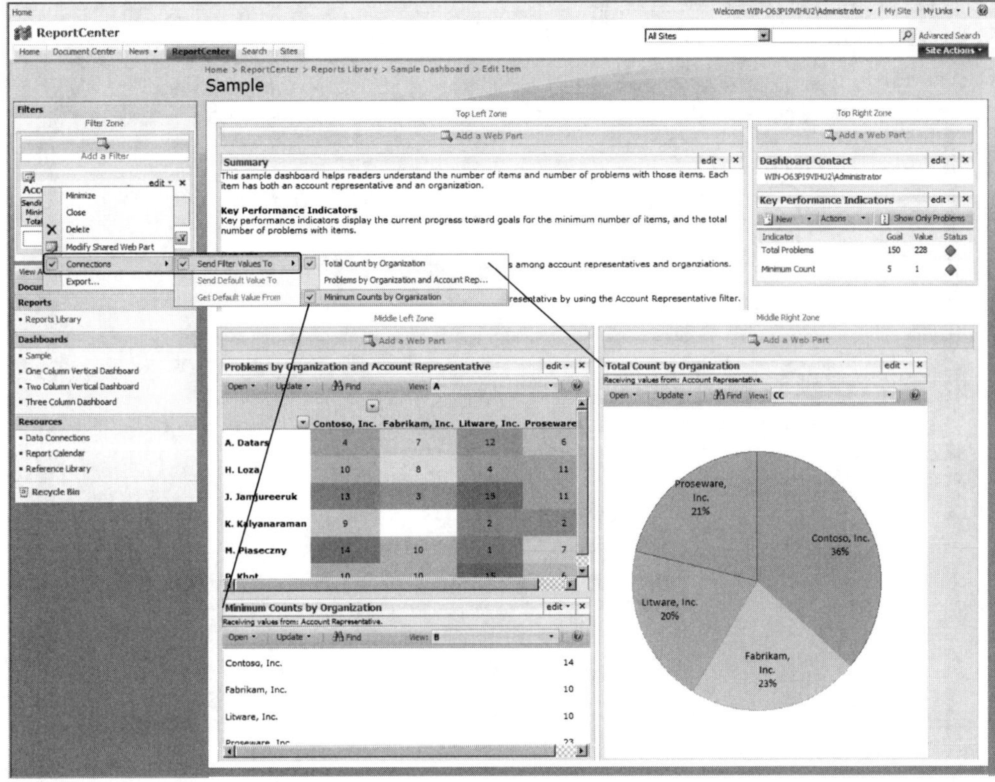

Figure 4-23 *SharePoint filter connections*

PerformancePoint Server 2007

If your company has invested in the Microsoft Business Intelligence Platform, you may have PerformancePoint Server 2007 available to you. This is another great tool for creating visual information displays and can be instrumental to supporting a performance management initiative. PerformancePoint Server provides the database and engine, and Dashboard Designer is the design tool and is a click-once downloaded web application, like Report Builder 3.0. You can launch it from the PerformancePoint Monitoring Central web page, which is generally in the form of "Error! Hyperlink reference not valid." The Monitoring Central page should look something like Figure 4-24. To launch Dashboard Designer, click the Run button adjacent to Download Dashboard Designer.

Figure 4-24 *PerformancePoint Monitoring Central*

BEST REFERENCES

There are great books on configuring and using PerformancePoint. One is Microsoft Office PerformancePoint Server 2007 *by Andersen, Aziza, Fitts, Hoberecht, and Kashani (Wiley, 2008).*

Another is The Rational Guide to Monitoring and Analyzing with Microsoft Office PerformancePoint Server 2007 *by Barclay and Downes (National Press, 2007).*

These works and others provide key insights into how to use PerformancePoint to achieve your performance monitoring objectives using the software tool.

One advantageous feature is the integration between Reporting Services and PerformancePoint. As information delivery professionals, we must leverage every available tool to inform and enlighten. Using PerformancePoint to create dashboards gives the designer options not available through SharePoint alone. The promise of true integration is fulfilled by Microsoft with SharePoint 2010 with PerformancePoint Services. Like Visio Services and Excel Services, PerformancePoint will be part of the code base for SharePoint and provide true interoperability for Business Intelligence information through the collaborative framework provided by SharePoint. For now, we will limit our discussion to what can be achieved with SharePoint 2007 and PerformancePoint Server 2007.

One of my esteemed colleagues, Mr. Steven Dvoranchik, suggested these tips for PerformancePoint.

BI TIP

- *Native drill-through in PerformancePoint Analytic Charts and Grids makes drilling into detailed data very easy. Switch between them to see graphic representations of data.*
- *Have visibility of scorecard KPIs in charts driven by the same metrics. Providing more than one view of the information gives perspective and context.*
- *PerformancePoint filters can work across multiple web parts (reports, KPIs, scorecards, and ProClarity), just as SharePoint filters work on SharePoint web parts.*
- *Mixing bar and line charts renders a cool display but doesn't always render correctly. Test this chart type thoroughly if you intend to use it in a production environment.*
- *When KPIs have metrics using the decreasing is better threshold, sometimes they won't display correctly. Try using the increasing is better threshold, but flip the colors in the indicator where best is red, worst is green. This will usually work and may save a lot of development time.*
- *Calling SSRS reports from PerformancePoint allows the designer to make use of the drill-through action in the SQL Server Analysis Services cube, giving your reports drill-down to details capability!*

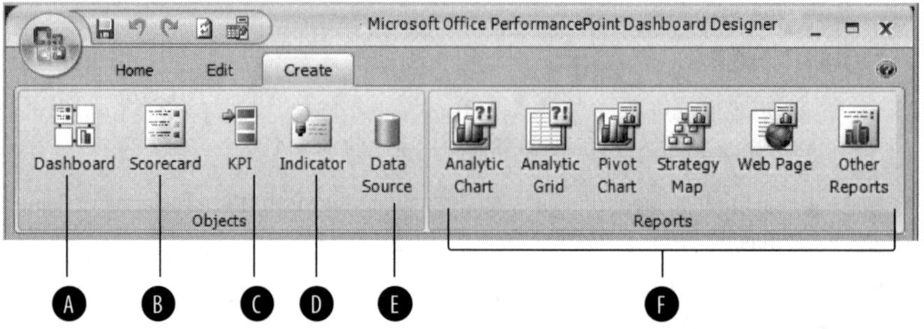

Figure 4-25 *PerformancePoint Dashboard Designer Create toolbar*

A quick review of PerformancePoint object types and their uses is in order, and then we will create some PerformancePoint dashboards and populate them with various items. From the Create menu pictured in Figure 4-25, you can create the following items in Dashboard Designer:

A. Dashboards These are single-page or multipage displays consisting of filters, scorecards. and reports. The reports can be Reporting Services reports or PerformancePoint reports created within Dashboard Designer. PerformancePoint reports created from Analysis Services data sources have the additional capability of supporting dimensional drill-down.

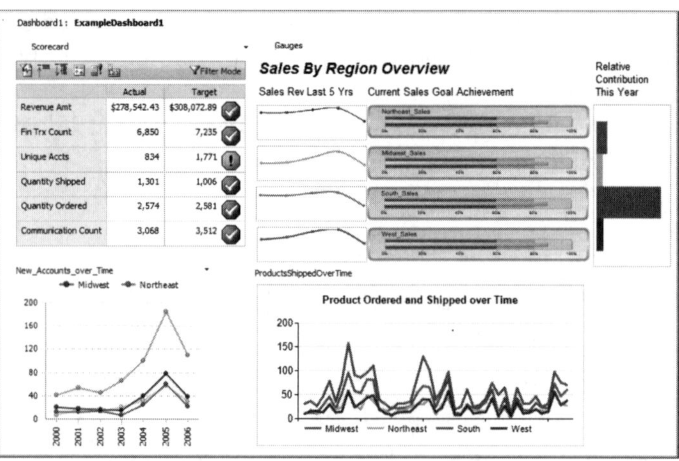

B. Scorecards These are collections of KPIs and indicators that display in a grid. The KPIs are listed in the rows, and the Actual and Target metrics are columns that display values and indicators. Scorecards can display a hierarchy, and they can be filtered by dimensional values or by indicator conditions (for instance, show me only warning indicators).

Test_Scorecard

	Actual	Target
Revenue Amt	$278,542.43	$308,072.89
Fin Trx Count	6,850	7,235
Unique Accts	834	1,771
Quantity Shipped	1,301	1,006
Quantity Ordered	2,574	2,581
Communication Count	3,068	3,512

C. KPI (Key Performance Indicator) KPIs are the feature that ties the data source to the performance measurement. They contain one or more measurement expression(s) that can be actual values or calculated target values. KPIs usually perform a comparison between the actual value and the target value, and they display an indicator that describes what range the value falls into. The most popular type of display is the three-state stoplight with Red = Warning, Amber = Caution, and Green = Favorable conditions.

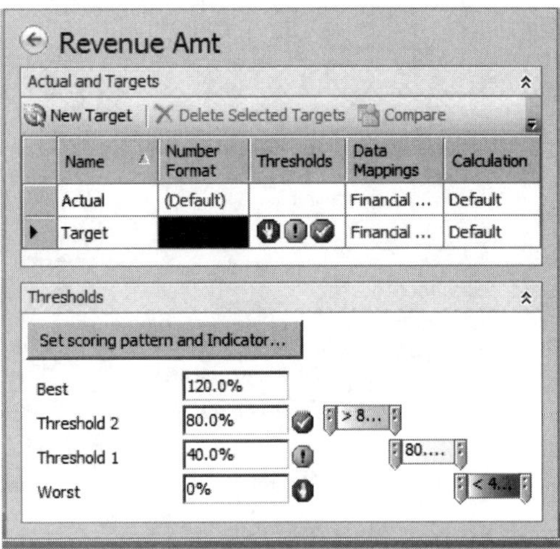

D. Data Sources These are the connections to the available data sources for the solution. PerformancePoint can connect to: Tabular (SharePoint Lists, Excel Services, or Workbook, SQL Server Table/view), Standard Query (ODBC), or Multidimensional (SQL Analysis Services) data sources.

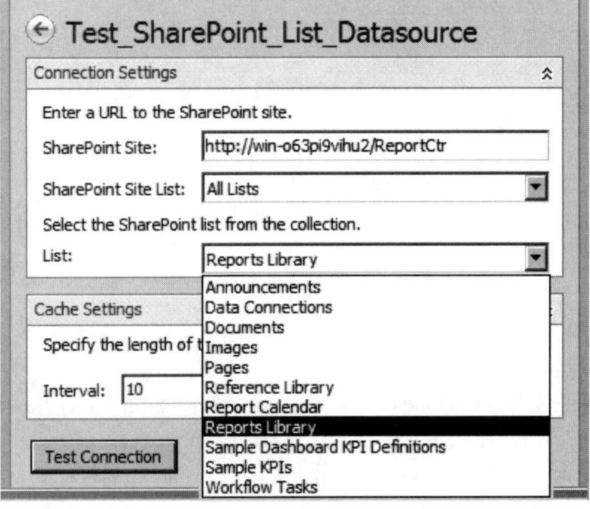

E. Indicators These are the visual elements that convey the rating of a KPI. Common indicators include a variety of Gauges, Stoplights (Red, Amber, Green), Smiley Faces, Clouds, Arrows.

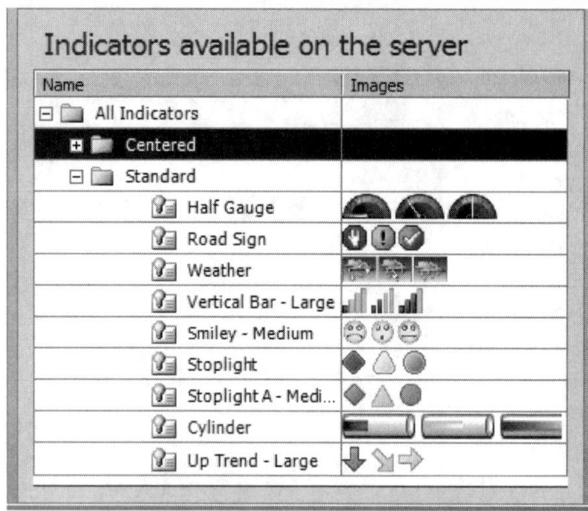

F. Reports There are many types of reports that can be imported or created with PerformancePoint—including Analytic Chart and Grid, Excel Services, SQL Reporting Services, Strategy Maps, and others. See the summary that follows.

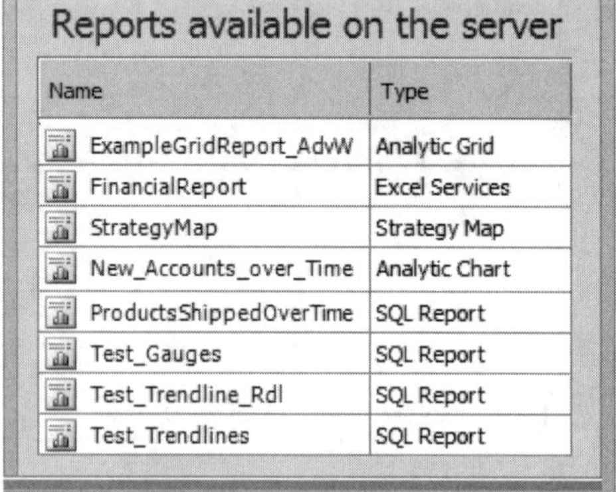

PerformancePoint supports the following report types:

- **Analytic Chart** Uses SQL Server Analysis Services as a data source and OLAP engine. Analytic Charts are limited to chart type (Column, Bar, Line) but support dimensional drill-down and links to reporting services detail reports.
- **Analytic Grid** Is similar to a Pivot Table.
- **Excel Services** Use an Excel Workbook that has been published to the Reports Library.
- **Pivot Chart, Pivot Table (holdovers from SharePoint 2003, they are now deprecated)** This functionality is replaced by SharePoint 2010 Excel Services and PowerPivot. These new features will finally replace the easy-to-use functionality that Pivot Chart and Pivot Table provided, and that Excel 2007 Pivot Table only partially fulfilled.

- **ProClarity Analytics (deprecated)** ProClarity was one of my favorite analysis tools. Some of the functionality will be migrated directly to SharePoint 2010 (Decomposition trees), and some will migrate to PowerPivot (Visual Slicers).
- **Spreadsheet** Uses a regular Excel Spreadsheet as a report.
- **Reporting Services Reports** Can be consumed as Reports in PerformancePoint. The Reporting Services toolbar supports the same functionality, including parameters. See examples later in this chapter.
- **Strategy Map** Links a Visio drawing with KPIs from a scorecard. A whole section on this feature ("PerformancePoint Strategy Maps and Custom Indicators for Diagram Display") appears later this chapter.
- **Trend Analysis Chart (now deprecated)** Better not to use this functionality unless you are willing to convert to a new type when it goes unsupported in SharePoint 2010.
- **Web Page** Uses any web page as content in a report window.

Items that are noted as deprecated will be retired in SharePoint 2010 PerformancePoint Services. There are new features to replace some of the items, and some of the functionality is being absorbed into Office Excel 2010 and PowerPivot. PerformancePoint 2007 is a server-based application; you must create the objects and publish them to the PerformancePoint Server to make them available to SharePoint. Dashboard Designer allows you to save local working files (*.bsx). As a result, it is possible to have development artifacts that are not published on the server. The two most used buttons on the Home menu are Refresh and Publish All!

Creating a New Dashboard

PerformancePoint dashboards come in several page layouts, as they do in SharePoint. PerformancePoint dashboards have zones—very similar to the web part zones in SharePoint dashboard pages. However, there are easier ways to adjust the zones and zone sizes in PerformancePoint.

Figure 4-26 shows the standard dashboard page templates:

- **1 Zone** The dashboard page has one large zone.
- **2 Columns** The dashboard page is divided into two full-length columns.
- **2 Rows** The dashboard page is divided into two full-length rows.
- **3 Columns** The dashboard page is divided into three full-length columns.
- **3 Rows** The dashboard page is divided into three full-length rows.

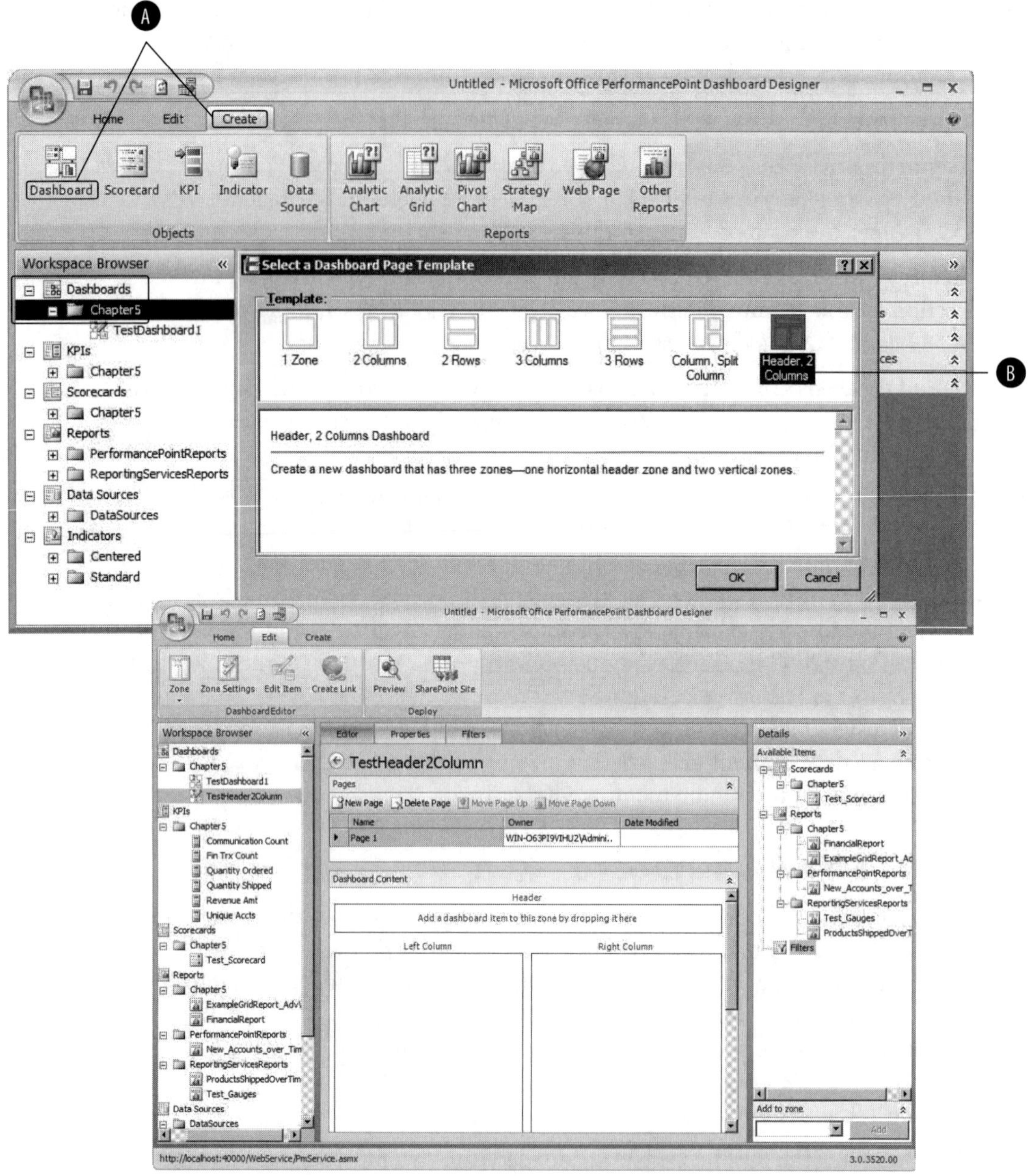

Figure 4-26 *PerformancePoint Dashboard Designer—create new dashboard*

- **1 Full 1 Split Column** The dashboard page has a left, full-length column, and one split column. The proportions of the split column are adjustable. This is a handy layout if you have an item that expands vertically—for example, if you have an analytic grid and the rows are populated by a multilevel dimensional hierarchy that expands downward as you drill down the levels.
- **Header and 2 Columns** The dashboard page has a header full-length row, and two columns below the header row. The header row defaults to 10 percent of the dashboard page size. This is a handy layout if you are going to use visible filters.

In Figure 4-26 the Dashboard Designer is displaying the Create menu and Workspace Browser. To create a new dashboard in Dashboard Designer,

1. Click the Create menu and then choose the Dashboard icon (Step A), or right-click the Dashboard node in the Workspace Browser and select New Dashboard from the context menu.
2. Choose the desired page template from the Select A Dashboard Page Template dialog box (Step B). Highlight your choice and then click the OK button in the lower-right corner.
3. Your new dashboard page will appear in the design surface.

While we are looking at this tool, let me familiarize you with the design surface, represented in Figure 4-27. Much as in the Visual Studio, Business Intelligence Development Studio, or Report Designer, the interface has the Ribbon menu across the top of the page. The Workspace Browser is the explorer panel along the left side of the screen; it displays all the PerformancePoint objects available in your workspace file and on the PerformancePoint Server. The center of the screen is the design surface where the details about the PerformancePoint object are manipulated. The panel along the right side displays the Details or Available Items for the object being worked on. Both the left and right panels are collapsible (by clicking the double angle brackets, << >>) to provide more work area for the center design surface.

So now we have the empty dashboard page, just waiting to be populated by PerformancePoint objects. Rename the dashboard page in the text box at the top of the design surface. You can also add additional pages to your dashboard here by clicking the New Page button (A):

- Add items to the dashboard page by simply dragging the item from the Details/Available Items pane on the right side of the display onto the dashboard page in the design surface (B).

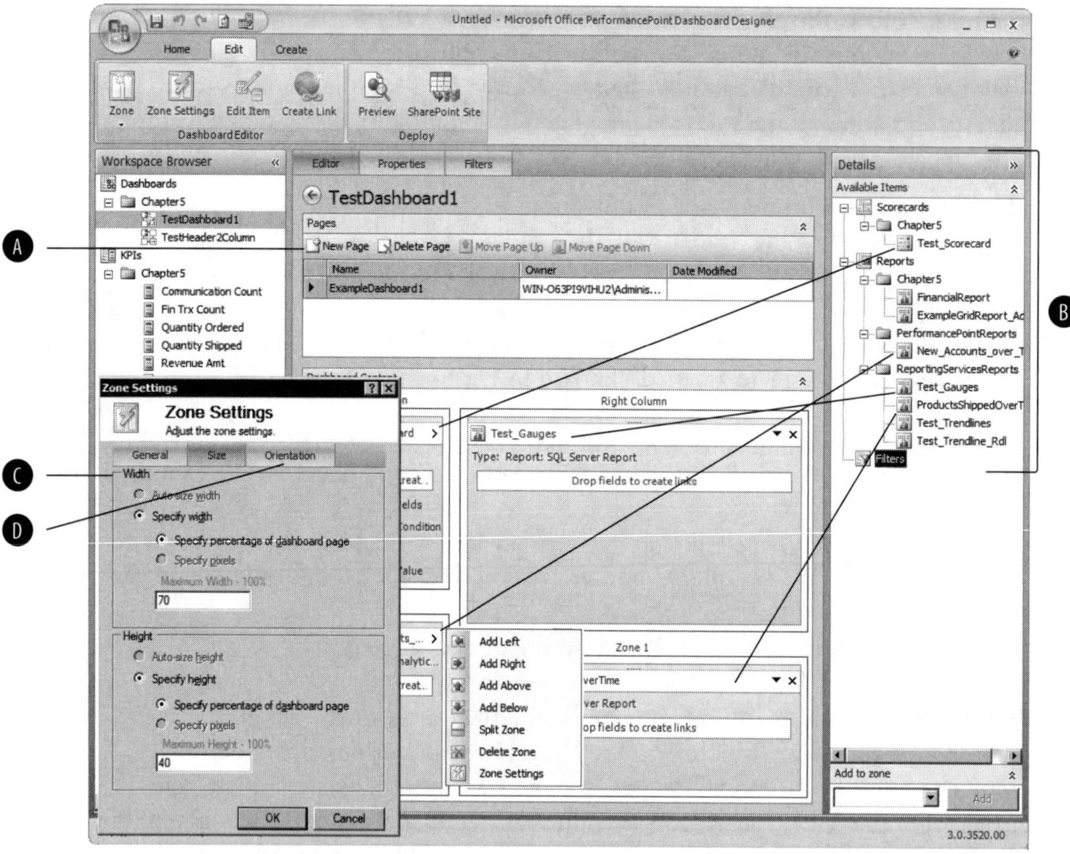

Figure 4-27 *PerformancePoint Dashboard Designer—Design Surface and Zone Settings*

- To adjust, add, or delete a dashboard page zone, right-click the zone border for the context menu, or click one of the Zone menu items that become enabled on the Edit menu ribbon (C). Zone Settings is where you can specify the width and height of a zone, as well as changing the zone area in the General tab or the Orientation.
- The Orientation setting allows you to specify how the PerformancePoint items will be arranged within the zone (D). Available zone orientations are horizontal (side by side), vertical (columnar), or stacked. The stacked orientation is special, in that it allows you to have multiple items in the zone. A drop-down list is presented in the dashboard, and once an item is selected from the list, it is displayed. This can also be used for connecting Parent-Child (Summary-Detailed) items in two different zones.

BI TIP

For the best reference on zone sizing, see the PerformancePoint Services Official Product Team Blog at blogs.msdn.com/performancepoint/archive/2008/01/07/performancepoint-dashboard-sizing-explained.aspx.

One more topic about PerformancePoint dashboards before we move on, and that is filters. Since PerformancePoint web parts do not interact with SharePoint filters, you may need to create a PerformancePoint filter to have the same functionality. Unfortunately, PerformancePoint filters are second-class objects—they are bound by the scope of the dashboard and are not reusable in other dashboards, and you cannot create them dirctly from the Create menu. The good news is that changes in SharePoint 2010!

To create a PerformancePoint dashboard filter, click the Filters tab that appears above the Dashboard Page Title in the design surface, as shown in Figure 4-28. The Select A Dashboard Filter Template dialog box will open. The available filter types are

- **MDX Query** Create a dashboard filter list by using an MDX query on an OLAP data source.
- **Member Selection** Create a dashboard filter that users can interact with to select which members are displayed.
- **Named Sets** Create a dashboard filter list showing Named Sets, which are prebuilt collections of dimension members from an OLAP data source.

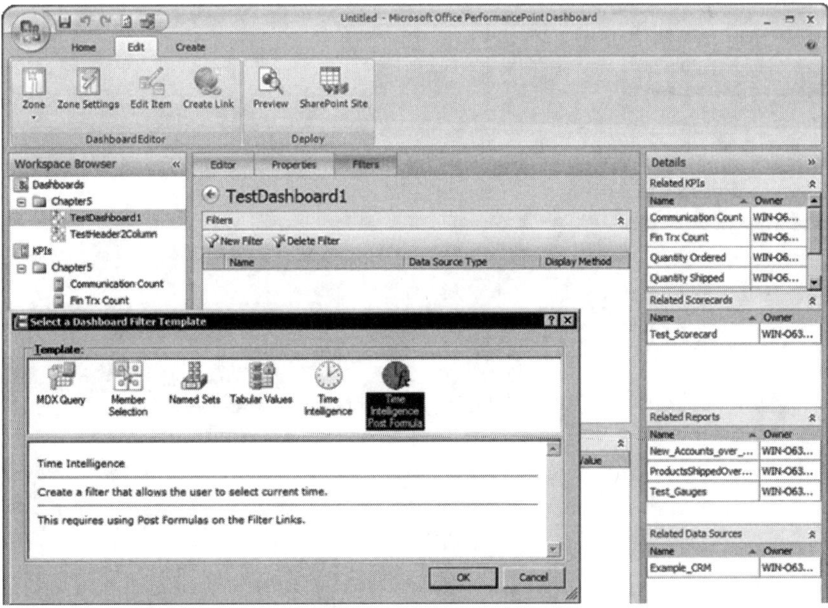

Figure 4-28 *PerformancePoint dashboard filters*

- **Tabular Values** Create a dashboard filter list that is based on values from a database table or view, a SharePoint list, or an Excel Services list.
- **Time Intelligence** Create a dashboard filter enabling users to select specific time elements to display.
- **Time Intelligence Post Formula** Also known as Filter Link Formula. Create a dashboard filter that enables users to select a begin date or other current time period to display. This type of filter uses Simple Time Period Specification (STPS) formulas.

For our example dashboard, we will create a Member Selection Filter, so select Member Selection from the filter template list displayed. The Member Selection filter is a good example to use, because it connects to a data source.

BI TIP

The data source for the filter should match the data source for the item it will be connected to. So when designing your dashboard, take into consideration the subject areas and measurements you want to display, and where those sources of information reside.

Once the OK button is clicked, the PerformancePoint Create a Filter Wizard will appear to collect all the information necessary to create the filter; just fill in the blanks and click the Next button until done! The panels are shown in Figure 4-29 and described here.

- The first panel collects name and description information for the filter.
- The second panel displays available data sources.

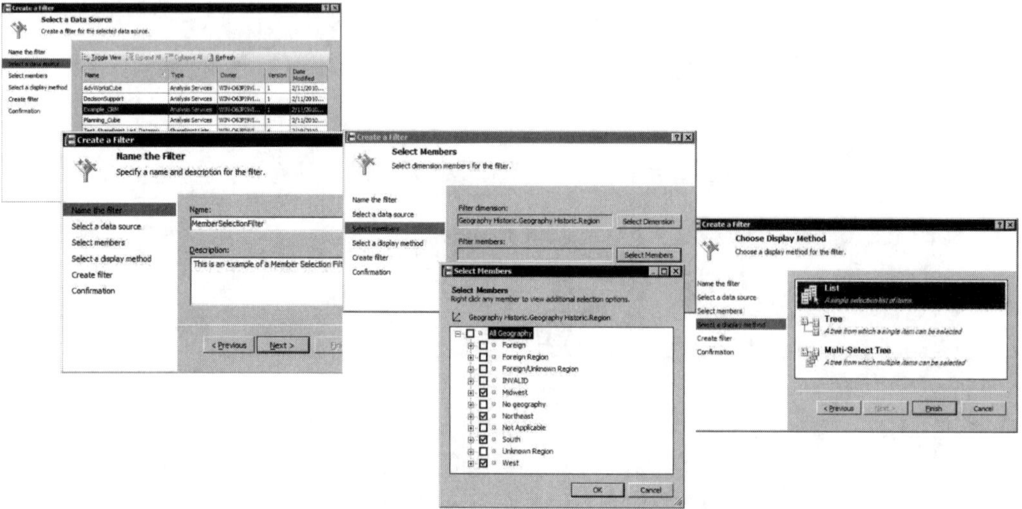

Figure 4-29 *PerformancePoint dashboard filter creation*

- The third panel connects to the data source and allows you to select the dimensions and dimension members to include in the filter.
- The fourth panel of the wizard allows you to select the display method. For the Member Selection filter, there are three choices: List (plain drop-down list), Tree (good if the dimension has hierarchies), and Multi-Select Tree. Select as desired, and then click Next. The final pane of the wizard builds the filter object and displays a confirmation message.

Now that a filter has been created, you connect it to the dashboard items through the Filter Link control, as shown in Figure 4-30. To connect a PerformancePoint dashboard item web part to a filter,

1. Click the drop-down web part menu and select Create Link (Step A).
2. The Filter Link Editor dialog box will appear. In the Link Items tab, click the drop-down box for Filter and select the filter you just created (Step B). In our example it was Member Selection Filter.
3. The Linked dashboard item drop-down should be grayed-out and display the name of the web part you launched the menu from.
4. Click the Link Options tab, and examine the Dashboard item endpoint drop-down (Step C). Recall that our filter was on the regional geography, so select Geography.Geography.Regional from the pick list. That notation stands for the Dimension name (Geography) and the member name (Regional).
5. Under the Source value drop-down, select the Member Unique Name (Step D).

BI TIP

Always use Member Unique Name when linking to an analytic data source, like another dashboard item (scorecard, analytic grid, or chart) or if the filter is based from an OLAP data source.

Previewing and Publishing a PerformancePoint Dashboard

Once your new dashboard has been created, you will want to preview, and then publish the dashboard to a SharePoint Document or Reports Library. Preview allows the designer to see the dashboard rendered in a web page. However, Preview does not display the dashboard using the page template, and some dashboard page functionality may not be available. Previewing a dashboard uses the Monitoring Central Preview site.

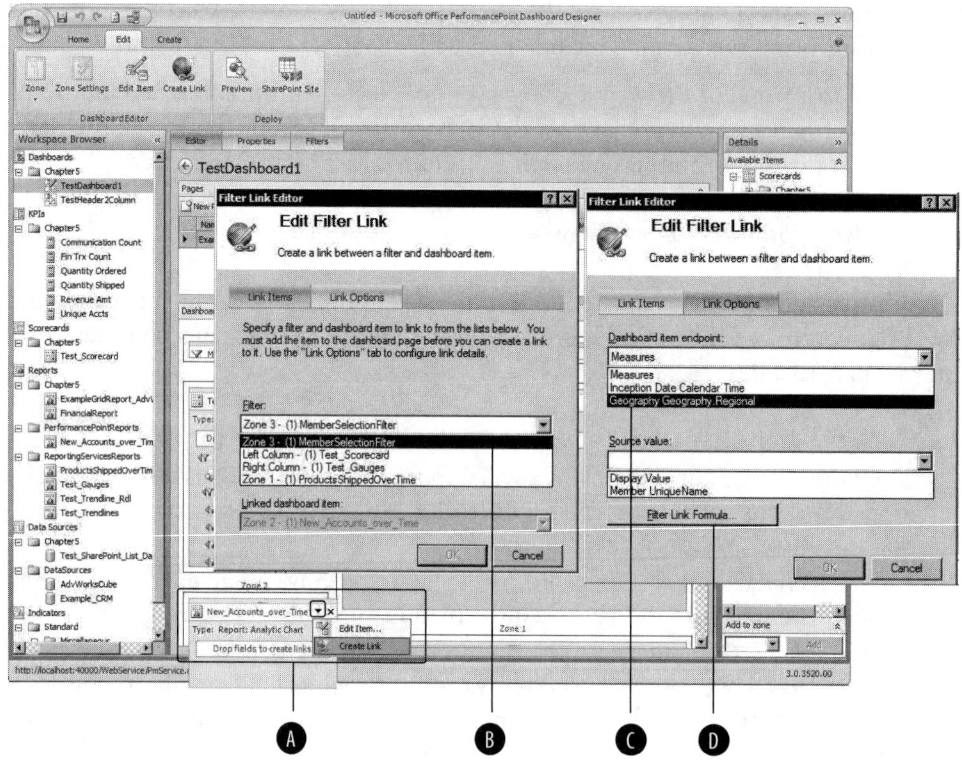

Figure 4-30 *PerformancePoint—connect item to filter*

Publishing actually places a copy of the dashboard into a SharePoint library, making it a saved item. When you publish a dashboard, it saves the container itself, as well as each of the dashboard items. Each of these items then becomes available for use as SharePoint web parts on other web part pages. You can use the dashboard as it is published, or use its components in other web part pages.

To preview a dashboard, select the dashboard in the Workspace Browser, as shown in Figure 4-31, and click the Preview button on the Edit menu. You will be presented with a wizard to collect information and display the dashboard in the preview site.

1. Select the dashboard name from the list on the first panel, Select A Dashboard. Click the Next button in the bottom-right corner.
2. The preview site URL will be prepopulated in the Preview Site Location text box on the Specify A Location panel. Click Finish.
3. The Deploy Dashboard panel will display briefly, and then the Confirmation panel will appear. Click Close. The Dashboard Preview will display in its own browser window, as shown in Figure 4-32.

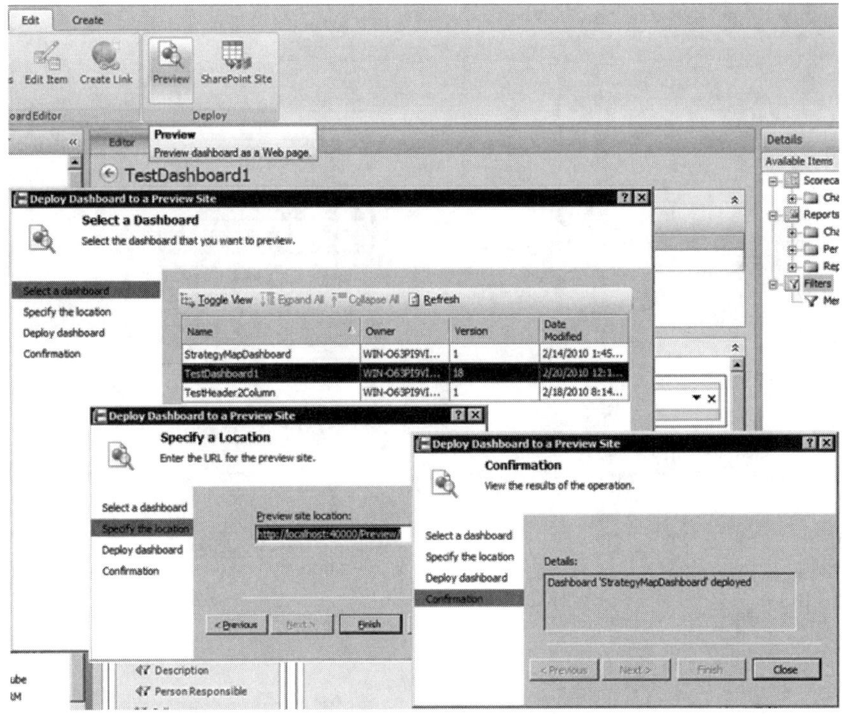

Figure 4-31 *PerformancePoint—preview a dashboard*

Notice that the Preview web page shown in Figure 4-32 is very plain. It is based on the default master page template for the Preview site (http://localhost:40000/Preview) with no embellishments and little navigation—only the breadcrumbs at the very top left of the page. The Dashboard Page Name is displayed under the breadcrumbs. If this had been a multipage dashboard, the page name list would be displayed here. The first web part is the Member Selection Filter, which we had positioned in the header zone of the dashboard page. The purpose of the Preview is to allow the designer to catch any potential errors, to notice spacing and content layout, and test filters. You may need to adjust and re-preview several times to get the dashboard page to display exactly how you would like it. Preview mode is lightweight enough to support that iterative development style.

Dashboard Preview is an important step in the design and development process—do not overlook its utility. Preview allows the designer to see the web parts rendered, make note if sizing and placement adjustments are required, and test data connectivity and chart actions. Once the designer is comfortable with the performance of the chosen dashboard items, it is time to deploy!

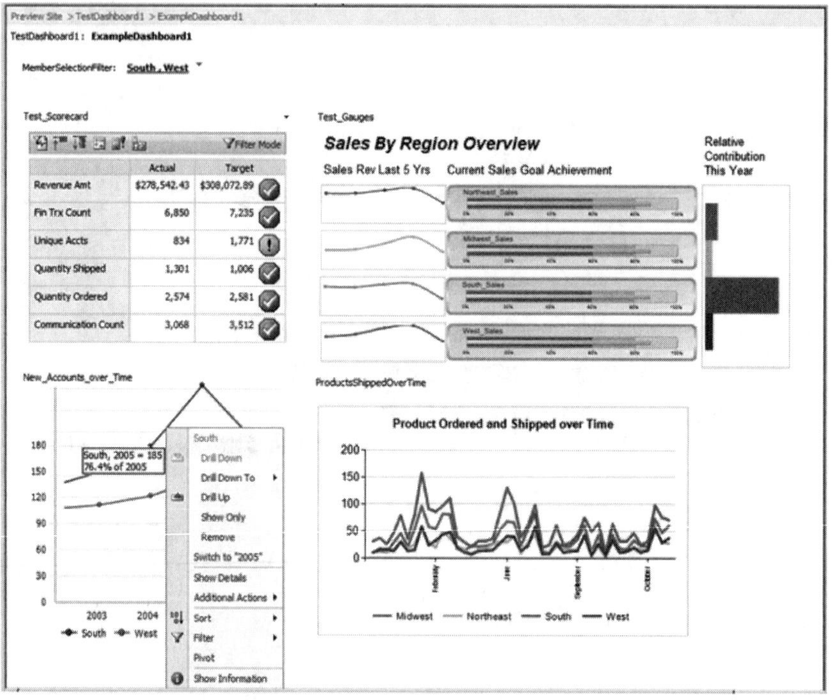

Figure 4-32 *PerformancePoint dashboard preview*

Publishing Dashboards to SharePoint

The next step in presenting the dashboard to the audience is to deploy the dashboard to a SharePoint Library through the publishing process. Publishing a dashboard copies the dashboard (container) and all its components (dashboard items) into a SharePoint Library. To publish a dashboard, follow this procedure, as shown in Figure 4-33:

1. In Dashboard Designer click the Dashboards node in the Workspace Browser. In the Edit Menu, click SharePoint Site in the Deploy section of the menu ribbon.
2. The Deploy A Dashboard To A SharePoint Site Wizard will appear, collecting the information needed to deploy the published dashboard.
3. The first panel, Select A Dashboard, presents a listing of published dashboards. Select from the list and click Next.
4. The second panel, Specify A Location, allows you to enter the URL for the SharePoint Site and select a Document Library. Click Next to proceed.

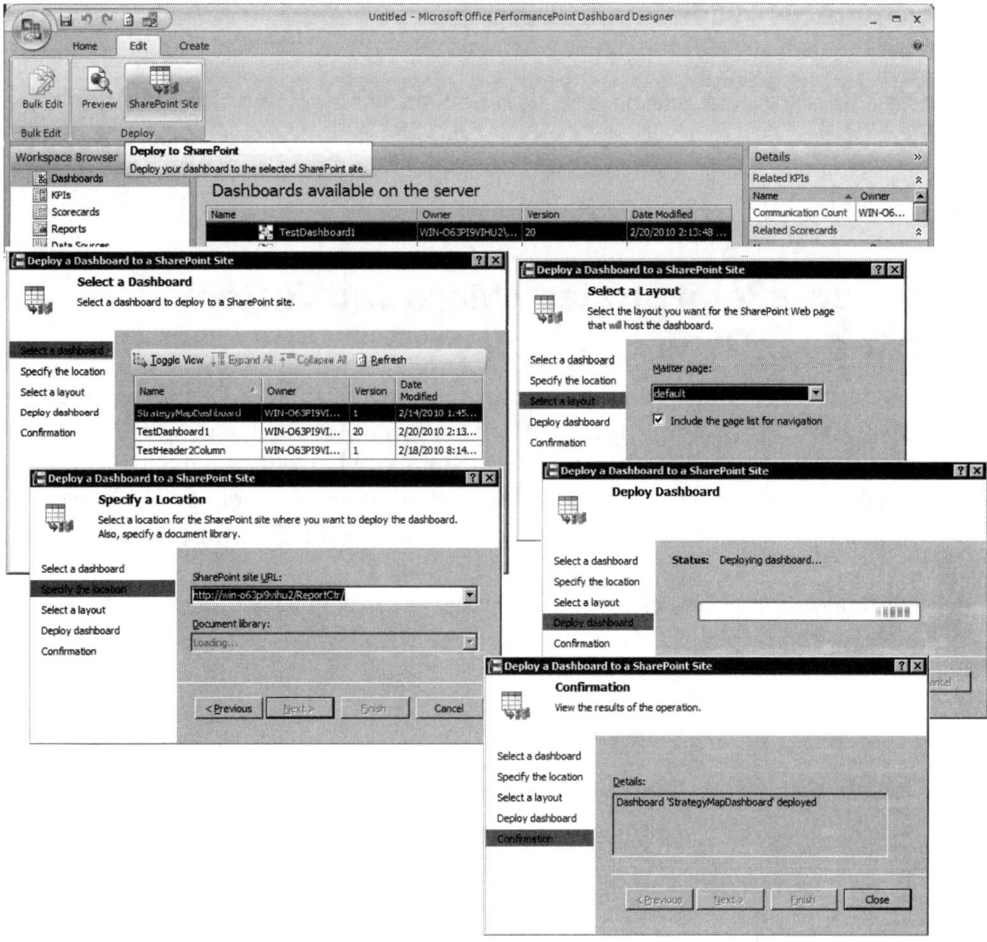

Figure 4-33 *Publish a PerformancePoint dashboard to a SharePoint site*

5. The third panel, Select A Layout, allows the designer to select a master page template from the drop-down list. There is also an option for "Include the page list for navigation." Click Finish.
6. The Deploy Dashboard panel will display progress and end with the confirmation that the selected dashboard has been deployed. A new browser window will open with the dashboard displayed.

The dashboard has now been deployed to the document library selected in the SharePoint site and is available for viewing by the audience.

BI TIP

As a best practice, always communicate to your stakeholders when there is going to be a change to a dashboard they rely on. An explanation of anticipated changes, any increase in data quality or representation, and contact information should be provided. Include before and after screenshots in the communiqué if the page navigation is going to change.

PerformancePoint Strategy Maps and Custom Indicators for Diagram Display

This is a true-to-life example of a lesson learned during creation of PerformancePoint custom indicators. This example is taken from a project that implemented a PerformancePoint Dashboard showing a basic Strategy Map and linked Scorecard for the Leadership dashboard (Figure 4-34). The configuration was very straightforward; all items used indicators that had the default settings. The images used for this example are blurred to disguise the actual data.

During refinement of the design, the decision was made to expand the ratings from Red, Amber, Green stoplights to a custom, five-state display: No Rating, Warning,

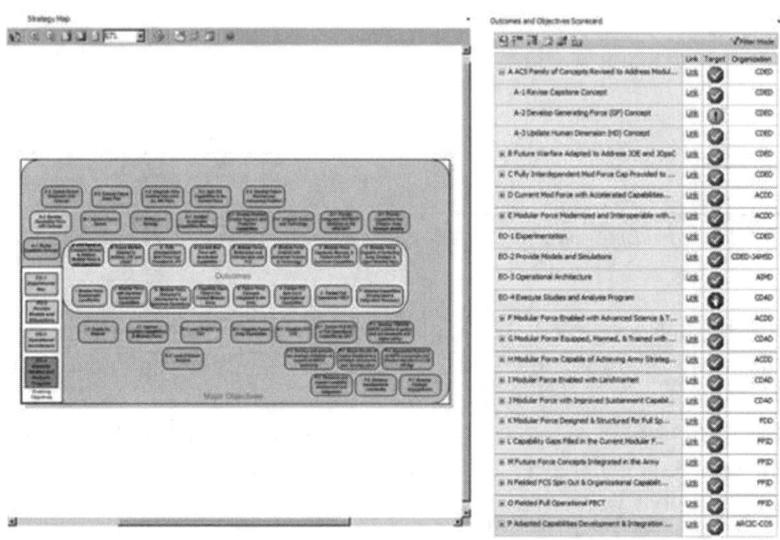

Figure 4-34 *Strategy Map dashboard example*

Caution, Favorable, Completed—adding custom icons for the new levels. Custom indicators were created in PerformancePoint (Figure 4-35). To create a new indicator set,

A. Right-click the Indicators node in the Workspace Browser and select New Indicator from the context menu, or alternatively, click the Indicator icon on the Create menu. The Select An Indicator Template dialog box will appear. For a custom indicator, select Blank Indicator in the explorer pane and click OK.

B. The Create New Indicator dialog box will appear. Fill in the fields and check boxes for Name, Optional Display Folder, and Read Permissions. Click Next.

C. Select the Indicator Type on the next panel. Standard Indicators are used for metrics that have good and bad ratings. Centered Indicators are used for metrics that should be closer to goal. Click Finish to create the Indicator.

Once the Custom Indicator is created, the design surface will display the set and allow configuration of the display name, image, text color, and background color. To select an indicator for a level, click the Edit menu, as shown in Figure 4-36. The choice is to select a standard indicator, or to import a Picture From File. Click the Picture From File selection on the Edit menu. The Windows File Open dialog box will appear, allowing you to select a graphic file to use for your indicator. Repeat this procedure for

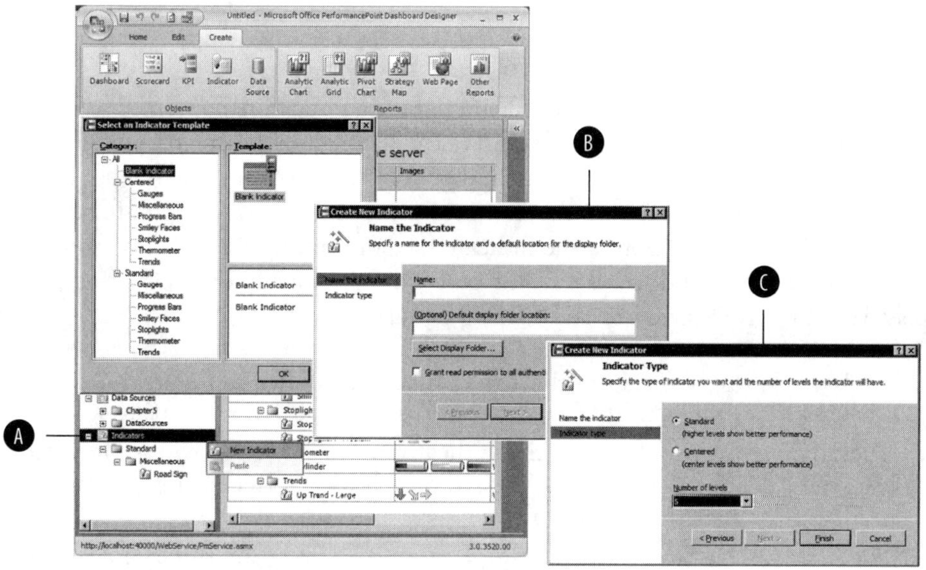

Figure 4-35 *PerformancePoint—create a new indicator*

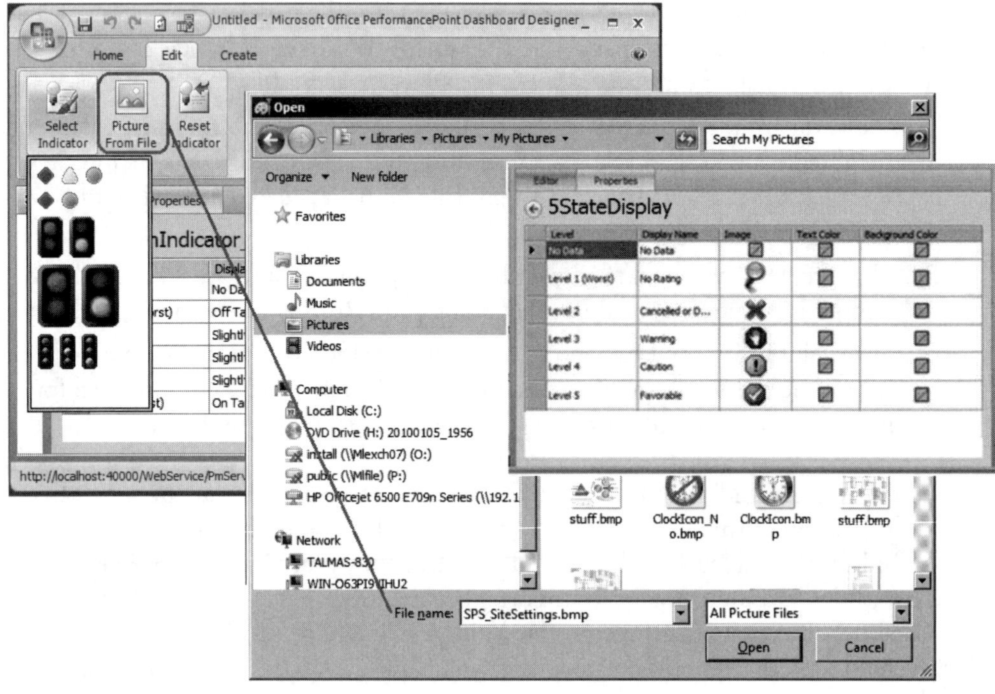

Figure 4-36 *PerformancePoint Custom Indicator settings*

each of the custom indicator levels, until you have the indicators populated as desired. Figure 4-36 shows how our custom five State Indicators look when completed.

Once the custom indicators are created, they can be used by any KPI. Update each of the KPIs on the scorecard with the new indicators and the banding set for the five-state boundaries. The selection of the indicator set and setting the banding values is straightforward. It wasn't obvious that the colors didn't show up on the scoring pattern display. To set the KPI indicator and scoring pattern,

1. Click the Thresholds cell for the Target metric, as shown in Figure 4-37 (A). Clicking there will activate the Thresholds section of the KPI settings.
2. Click the Set Scoring Pattern And Indicator button (B). You will be presented with the Edit Banding Settings Wizard, which will collect the information needed to set these properties for your KPI.
3. The first panel is Select The Scoring Pattern (C). There are three choices for banding method—"Band by normalized value of Actual/Target," "Band by numeric value of Actual," and "Band by stated score." For our KPI, select "Band by numeric value of Actual." Click Next.

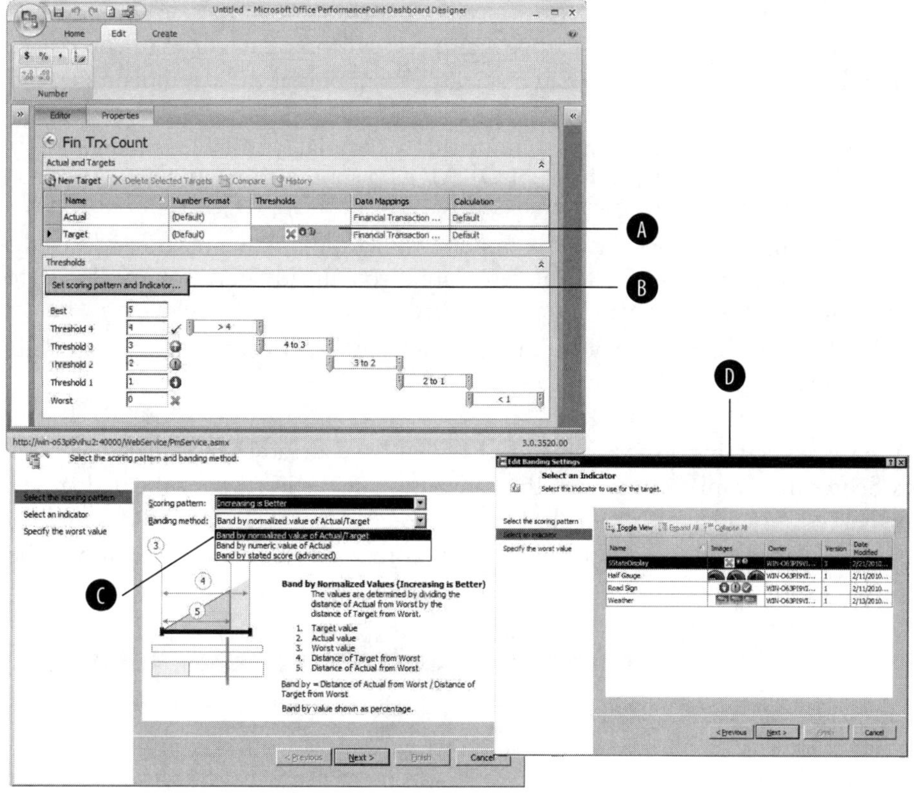

Figure 4-37 *PerformancePoint KPI with Custom Indicator settings*

4. The second pane is Select An Indicator (D). This panel presents all of the indicator types that are in the PerformancePoint Dashboard Designer Browser Workspace. Select the indicator you desire and click Next.
5. If any additional information is needed, like setting the worst value, it is collected on the final panel. Click Finish.
6. You are returned to the main screen, where you can set the threshold values for each banding level.

These KPIs were to display the relative rating of the status of a major objective or outcome. The ratings range from 0 (worst) to 5 (best), with an additional level for "*no rating*", a factor the commander was vitally interested in. This made the scoring pattern easy to set. There is no way to preview a KPI without putting it into a scorecard. So the KPIs were tested by creating a scorecard and using preview to make sure the custom indicator worked.

To create a new PerformancePoint scorecard, click the Scorecard button on the Create Menu in Dashboard Designer, or alternatively, right-click the Scorecards node in the

Workspace Browser and select New Scorecard from the context menu. The Select A Scorecard Template dialog box will appear and present three categories of choices. As shown in Figure 4-38, a scorecard can be created from one of these templates:

1. The first category is Microsoft, and the only template available is the Analysis Services Scorecard. If you have an OLAP data source, this template gives you the most flexibility for using server-based KPIs or creating KPIs from measures.
2. The Standard category has two template choices, Blank Scorecard and Fixed Values Scorecard. Use the Blank template if you already have your KPIs created and just want to pull them into a scorecard.
3. Tabular is the last category and has the Excel 2007, Excel Services, SharePoint List, and SQL Tabular templates.

Since we are creating a scorecard for KPIs that have already been created, choose the Blank Scorecard template, and click the OK button at the bottom of the dialog box. A one-panel wizard will appear to collect the Scorecard Name, Display Folder, and read permissions, and then to create the new blank scorecard when the OK button is clicked.

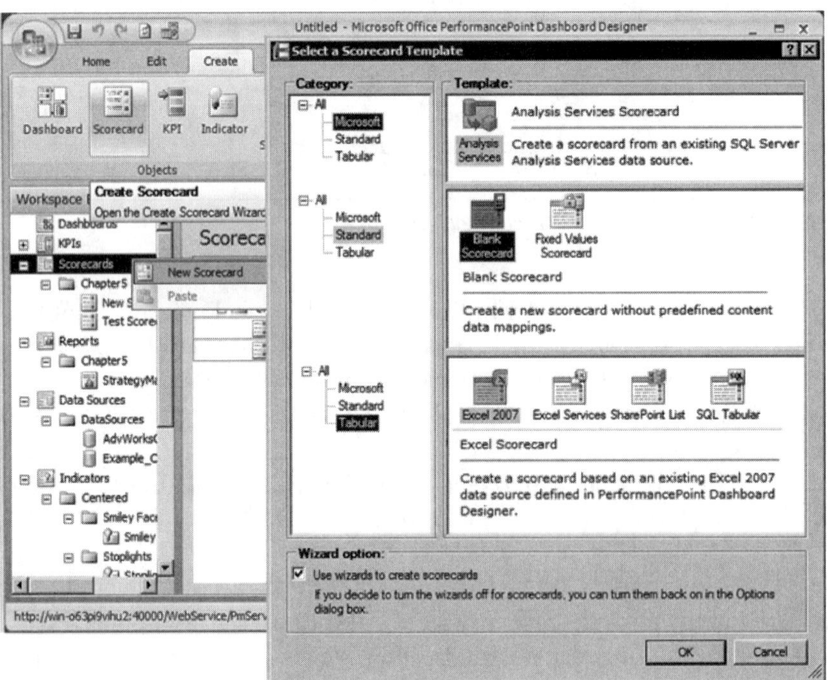

Figure 4-38 *PerformancePoint—create a new scorecard*

Once the new blank scorecard is created, it will be presented on the design surface. Available KPIs are displayed in the Details pane along the right side of Dashboard Designer, as shown in Figure 4-39. Click and drag the selected KPIs onto the rows on the design surface.

Once all the KPIs have been dragged onto the design surface, click the Update button on the Edit menu to refresh the data in the scorecard display. As shown in Figure 4-40, the custom indicators seem to work just fine, displaying appropriately for the values found in the data.

When creating a PerformancePoint Strategy Map, it is unnecessary to have an annotated Visio diagram to start with—you just need the blank shapes on the diagram, because when you link Visio to the scorecard, it will add the KPI names to the shape for you (replacing the existing test). Each shape needs to be connected to its respective KPI from the scorecard (the scorecard controls the list of KPIs displayed as choices).

Create the Visio diagram for your strategy map report. Then in PerformancePoint Dashboard Designer, create a new report, and select Strategy Map from the report types.

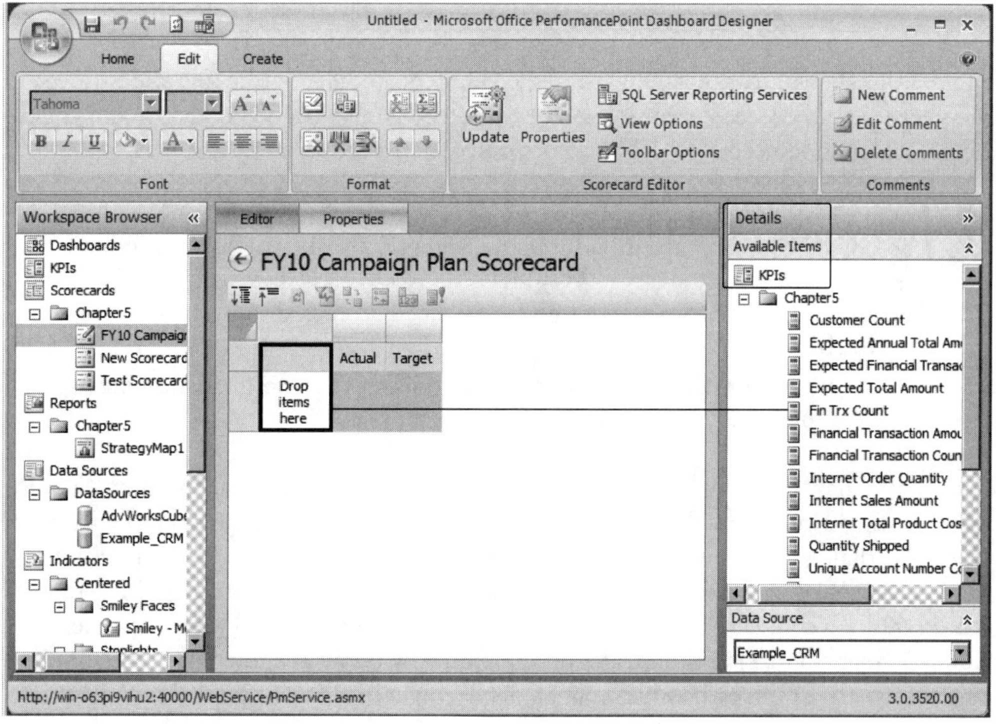

Figure 4-39 *PerformancePoint blank scorecard*

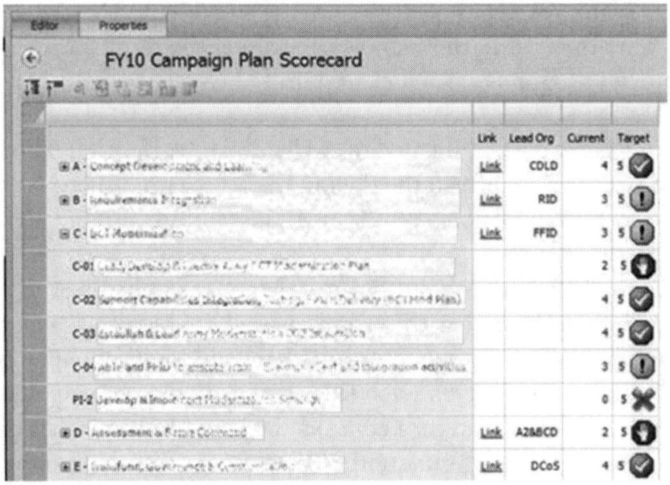

Figure 4-40 *PerformancePoint example scorecard*

Figure 4-41 shows creating a new Strategy Map report. Start by clicking the Strategy Map button on the Create menu. The New Strategy Map wizard will appear and collect all the information needed to create your strategy map report.

1. Name The Report is the first panel for the Create A Strategy Map Report Wizard (A). Give the report a meaningful name, and select a display folder if desired. Tick the check box for Grant Read Permissions and click Next.
2. The second panel allows the designer to select a scorecard to link the strategy map to (B). Click Next.
3. PerformancePoint will create the report and display the Confirmation message when complete (C).

Once the new Strategy Map report is created, click the Edit menu and then click Edit Strategy Map. Click the Open Visio File button and select your Visio file from the Open File dialog box. The diagram from the first sheet will be pulled into the Strategy Map Editor. Remember that the scorecard was selected when the Strategy Map report was created. To connect the shape to the KPI, click each shape, and then click the Connect Shape button in the Strategy Map Editor window as shown in Figure 4-42. The Select A KPI dialog box will appear, displaying a list of available KPIs. Select the appropriate KPI for the shape selected. Ensure the Add KPI Name To The Shape check box is ticked, and click OK. Repeat this process until all shapes are connected.

Charts (Chapter 1)

SQL Server 2008 R2 Reporting Services has an enhanced set of chart features for the display of "grouped data" that makes it easier to see the relative size of data elements, such as in the Pyramid chart shown in the illustration. And there are many chart types, such as the Polar and Pie charts shown, but the real difference is in the ability to combine chart types like the Bar and Trend Line chart, and the Column-embedded-in-Matrix chart.

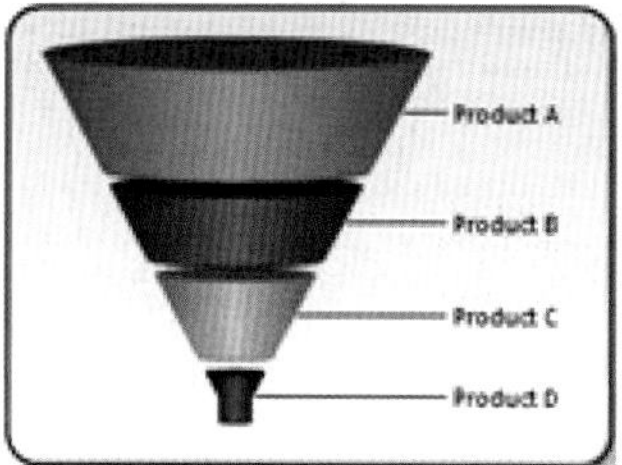

Pyramid chart - For data element size comparison

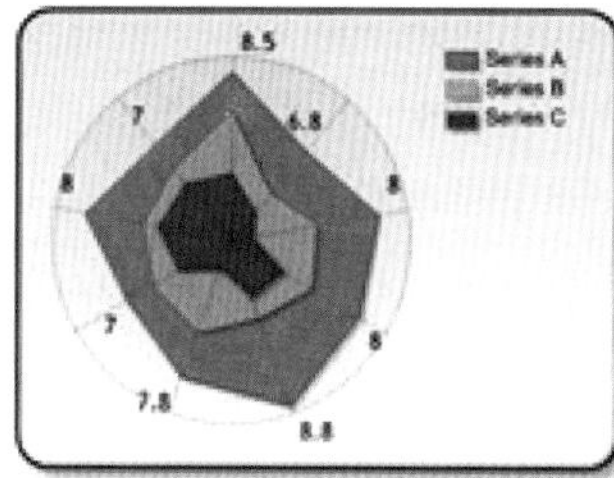

Polar chart - For multiseries range comparison

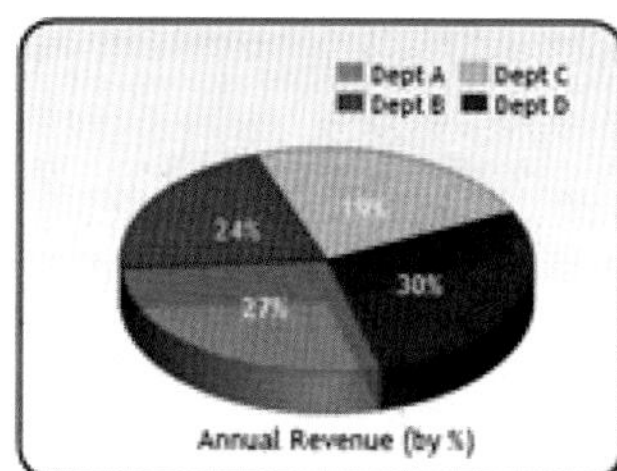

3-D Pie chart with data value labels

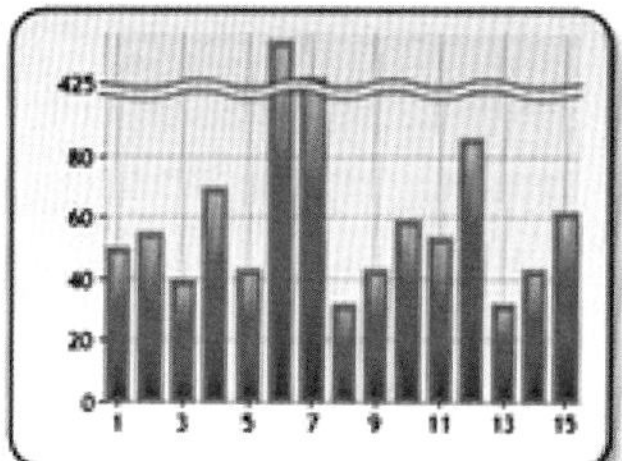

Two charts in one display: Bar chart with trend line

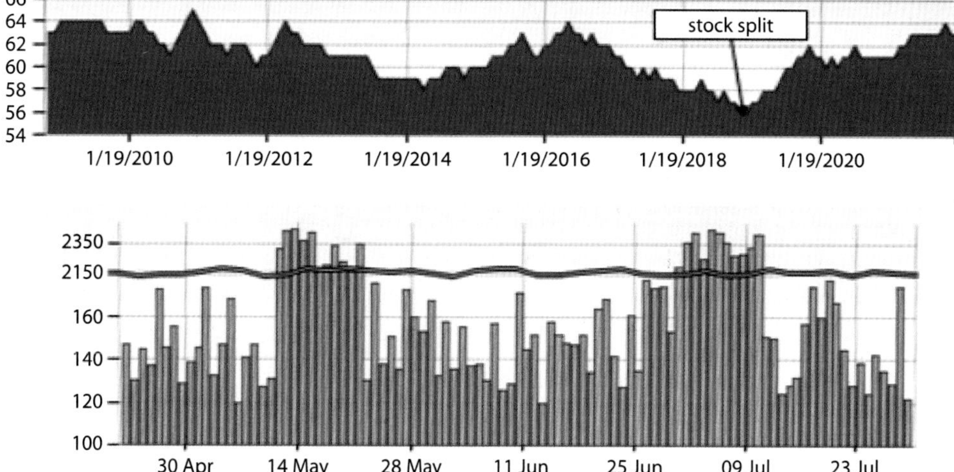

Time Intelligent charts with trend visualization

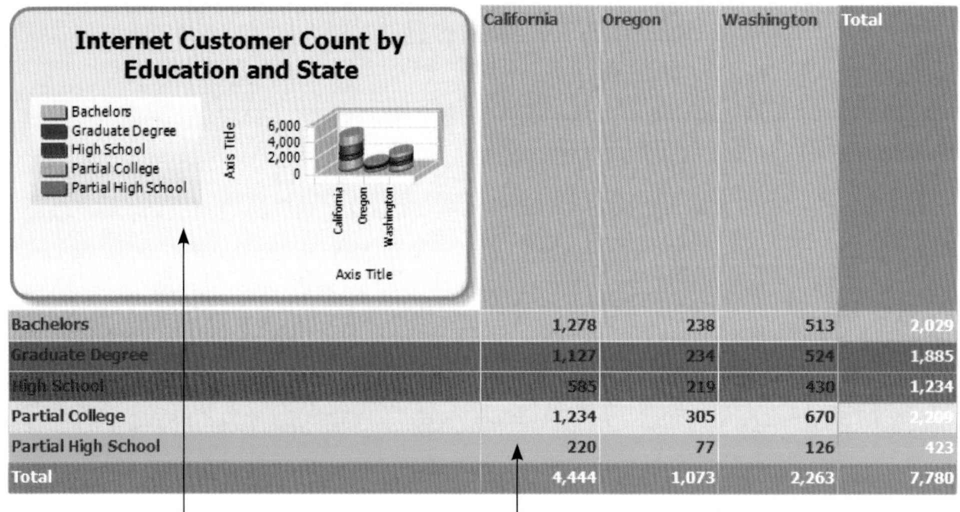

	California	Oregon	Washington	Total
Bachelors	1,278	238	513	2,029
Graduate Degree	1,127	234	524	1,885
High School	585	219	430	1,234
Partial College	1,234	305	670	2,209
Partial High School	220	77	126	423
Total	4,444	1,073	2,263	7,780

Chart embedded in tablix with graphical view of grid data. Column chart shows relative data element sizes, which complements matrix.

Matrix/Tablix with detail grid data. Matrix shows matching color-coded data element values, which complements chart.

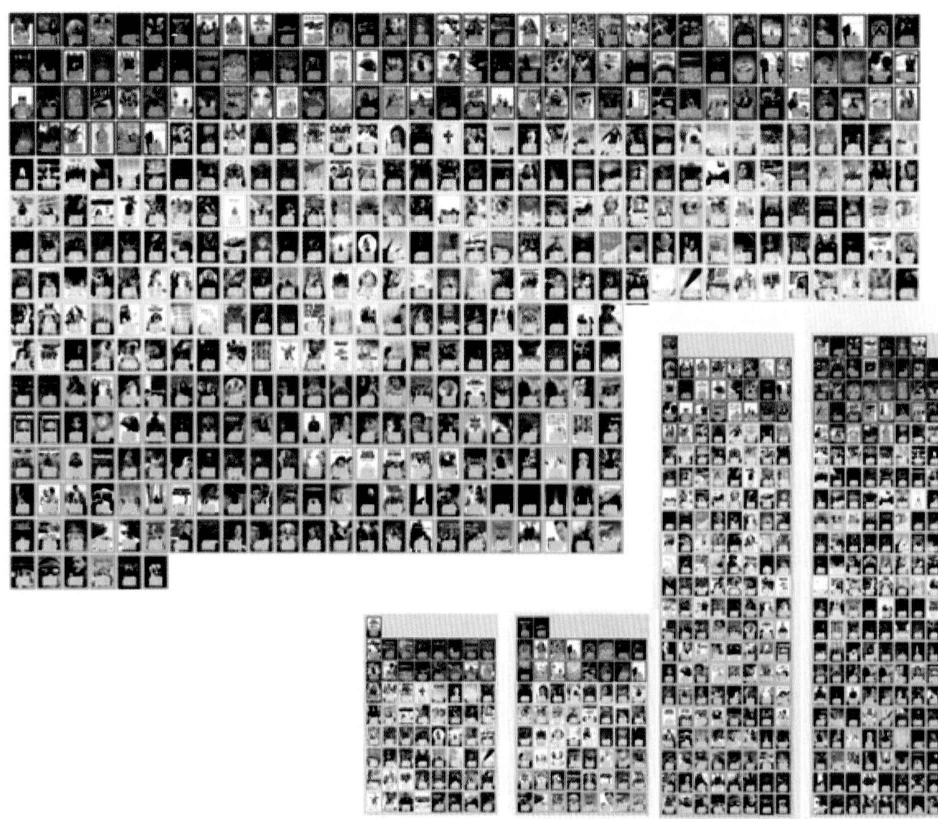

Images in color-coded matrix cells and grouped by category

Sizzling Gauges (Chapter 2)

SQL Server 2008 R2 Reporting Services has a new set of gauge charts for the display of "data with goals" that makes it easier to see the performance of data elements over time, such as in the Radial and Linear gauge charts shown in the illustration. And the gauges can be combined to compare the relative performance of "data groups" as shown in the Horizontal Linear gauge example, and gauges can be combined with other charts such as the Gauges-embedded-in-Matrix chart.

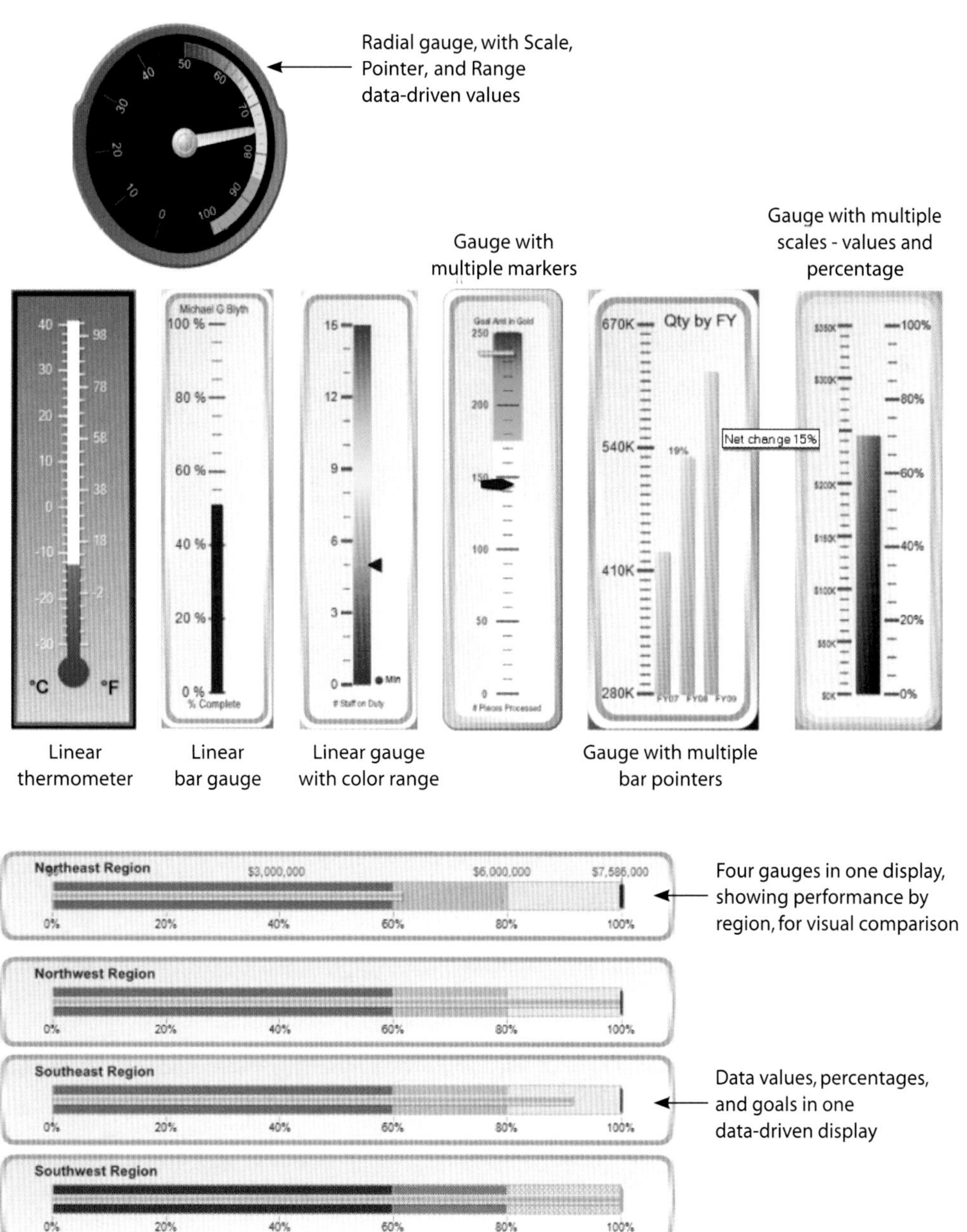

Gauge charts show relative data element sizes, which complements matrix

Multiple gauges showing color-coded data elements embedded in tablix

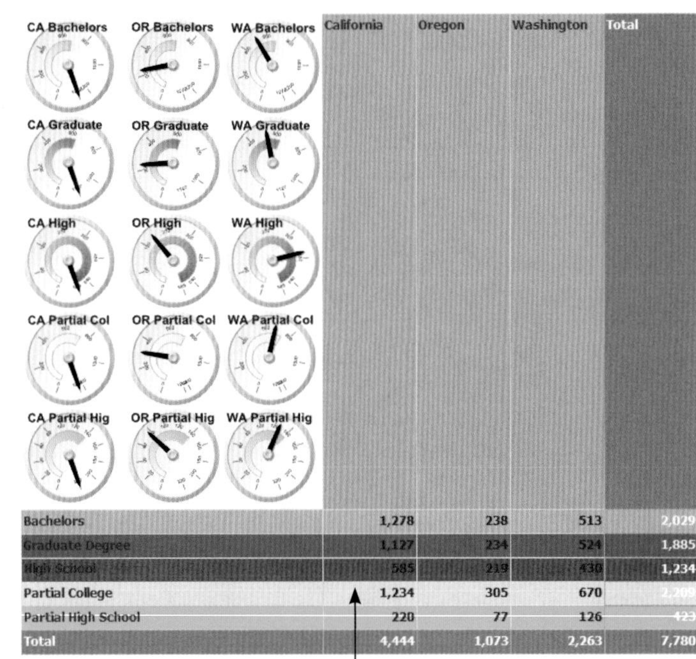

	California	Oregon	Washington	Total
Bachelors	1,278	238	513	2,029
Graduate Degree	1,127	234	524	1,885
High School	585	219	430	1,234
Partial College	1,234	305	670	2,209
Partial High School	220	77	126	423
Total	4,444	1,073	2,263	7,780

Matrix/Tablix with color-coded detail and grid data. Matrix shows matching color-coded data element values, which complements gauges.

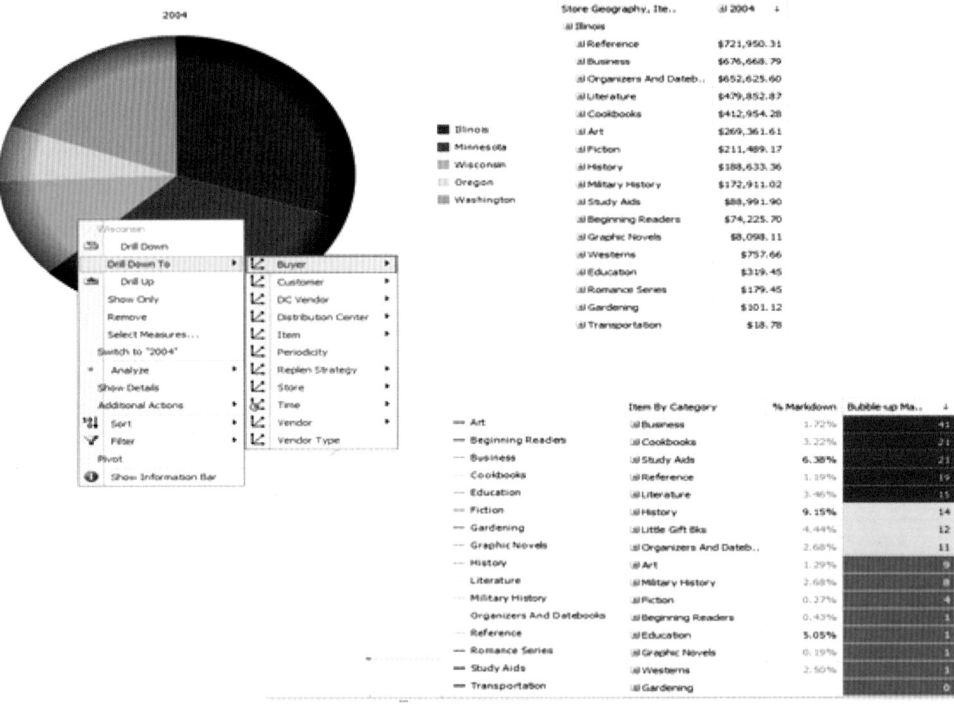

Store Geography, Ite..	2004
Illinois	
Reference	$721,950.31
Business	$676,668.79
Organizers And Dateb..	$652,625.60
Literature	$479,852.87
Cookbooks	$412,954.28
Art	$269,361.61
Fiction	$211,489.17
History	$188,633.36
Military History	$172,911.02
Study Aids	$88,991.90
Beginning Readers	$74,225.70
Graphic Novels	$8,098.11
Westerns	$757.66
Education	$319.45
Romance Series	$179.45
Gardening	$101.12
Transportation	$18.78

Item By Category	% Markdown	Bubble-up Ma..
Business	1.72%	41
Cookbooks	3.22%	21
Study Aids	6.38%	21
Reference	1.19%	19
Literature	3.46%	15
History	9.15%	14
Little Gift Bks	4.44%	12
Organizers And Dateb..	2.68%	11
Art	1.29%	9
Military History	2.68%	8
Fiction	0.27%	4
Beginning Readers	0.43%	1
Education	5.05%	1
Graphic Novels	0.19%	1
Westerns	2.50%	1
Gardening		0

Gauge and chart with drill down

Sparklines (Chapter 1)

SQL Server 2008 R2 Reporting Services has a new kind of chart display known as Sparkline for the display of "data over time" that makes it quick to get an approximate visualization of data elements over time, such as in the Sparkline charts shown in the illustration, where the Sparkline does not show detail data, but rather the visual size of values along an axis. And the Sparklines can be combined with other charts such as the Sparklines-embedded-in-Matrix chart.

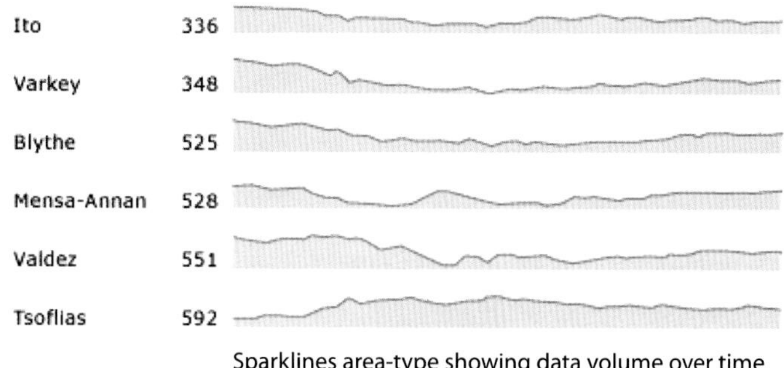

Sparklines area-type showing data volume over time

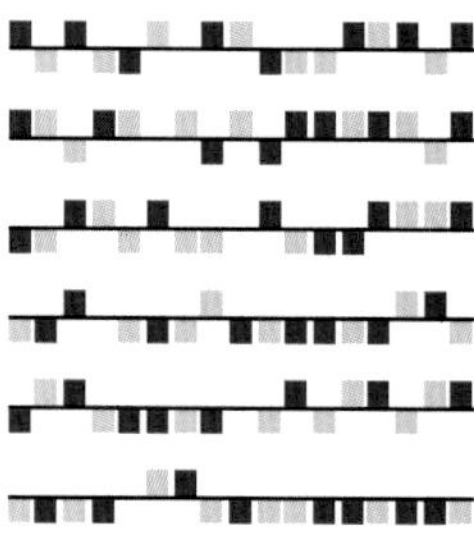

Sparklines column-type showing data values over time

Sparkline showing both Ratio and color-coded Status values, along a timeline

Calendar Quarter	Revenue Value	Expense to Revenue Ratio Value	Expense to Revenue Ratio Goal	Expense to Revenue Ratio Status
Q1 CY 2002	$5,860,884	27.0 %	25.0 %	0
Q1 CY 2003	$6,679,874	35.5 %	25.0 %	-1
Q1 CY 2004	$11,386,315	24.6 %	25.0 %	1
Q2 CY 2002	$6,167,833	28.7 %	25.0 %	0
Q2 CY 2003	$8,357,875	29.4 %	25.0 %	0
Q2 CY 2004	$14,371,807	19.8 %	25.0 %	1
Q3 CY 2001	$4,647,157	32.4 %	25.0 %	-1
Q3 CY 2002	$10,277,073	24.9 %	25.0 %	1
Q3 CY 2003	$13,670,537	20.8 %	25.0 %	1
Q3 CY 2004	$50,841		25.0 %	1
Q4 CY 2001	$6,684,652	23.5 %	25.0 %	1
Q4 CY 2002	$8,368,983	30.1 %	25.0 %	-1
Q4 CY 2003	$13,285,444	21.3 %	25.0 %	1

Matching Matrix/Tablix showing detail data with color-coded Status rows

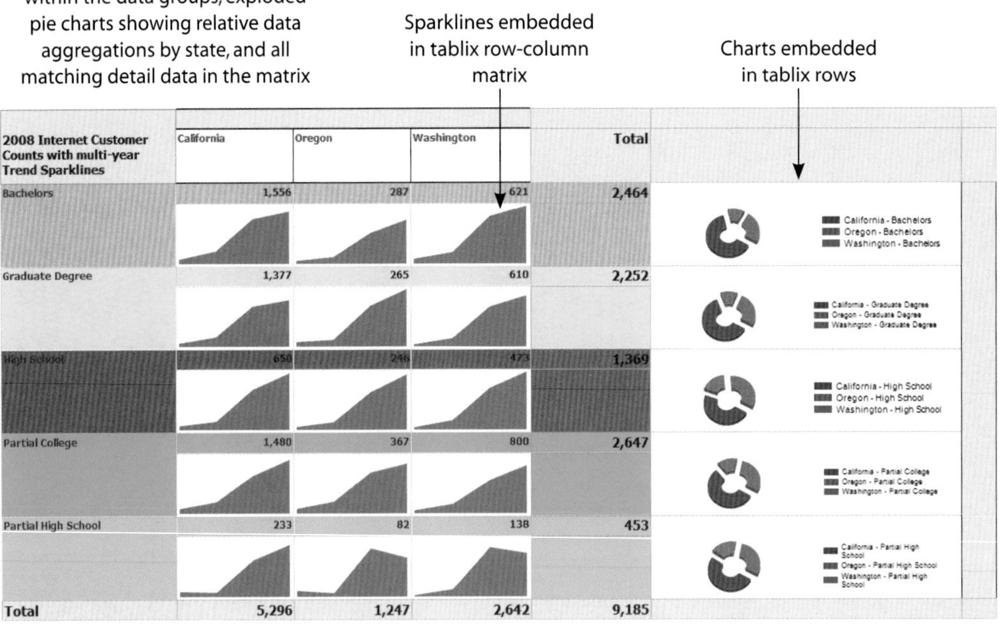

2008 Internet Customer Counts with multi-year Trend Sparklines	California	Oregon	Washington	Total
Bachelors	1,556	287	621	2,464
Graduate Degree	1,377	265	610	2,252
High School	650	246	473	1,369
Partial College	1,480	367	800	2,647
Partial High School	233	82	138	453
Total	5,296	1,247	2,642	9,185

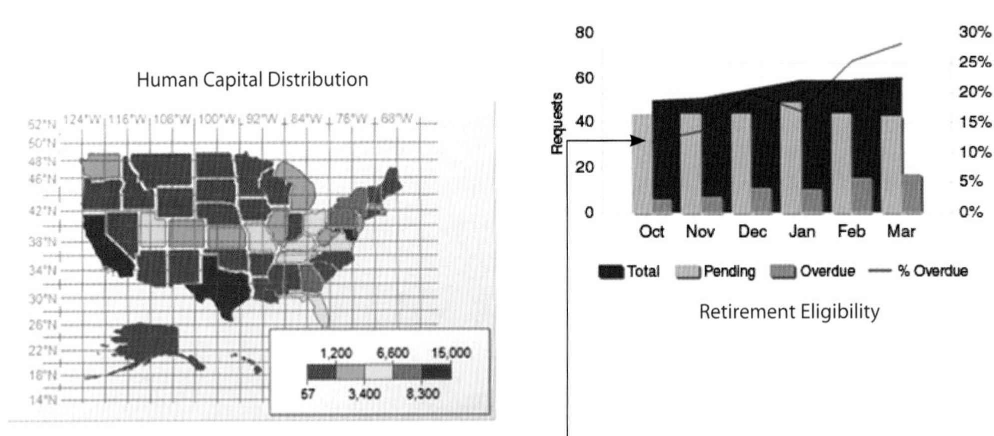

Sparkline complements map display

Maps (Chapter 3)

SQL Server 2008 R2 Reporting Services has a new map display that makes it possible for everyday knowledge workers to create data-driven geographic reports. Analytical data, such as electoral data by state, can be combined with geographic data such as states of the U.S., as shown in the illustration of the 2008 Presidential Election Results. Another example of map layers is shown in the Boundary-Schools-Near-Highway map illustration, which displays a data-driven Boundary of area within two kilometers of a major highway. And the maps can be combined with other charts such as the Map-embedded-in-Matrix.

Color-coded Democratic and Republican states, with relative size bubbles of electoral votes by state

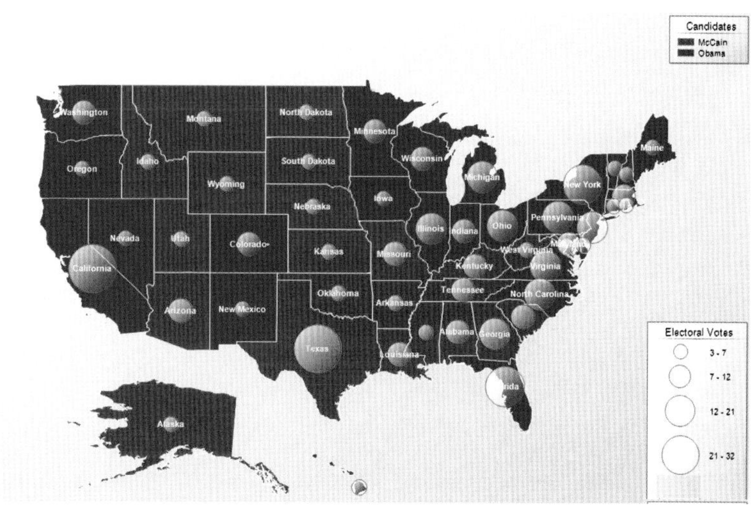

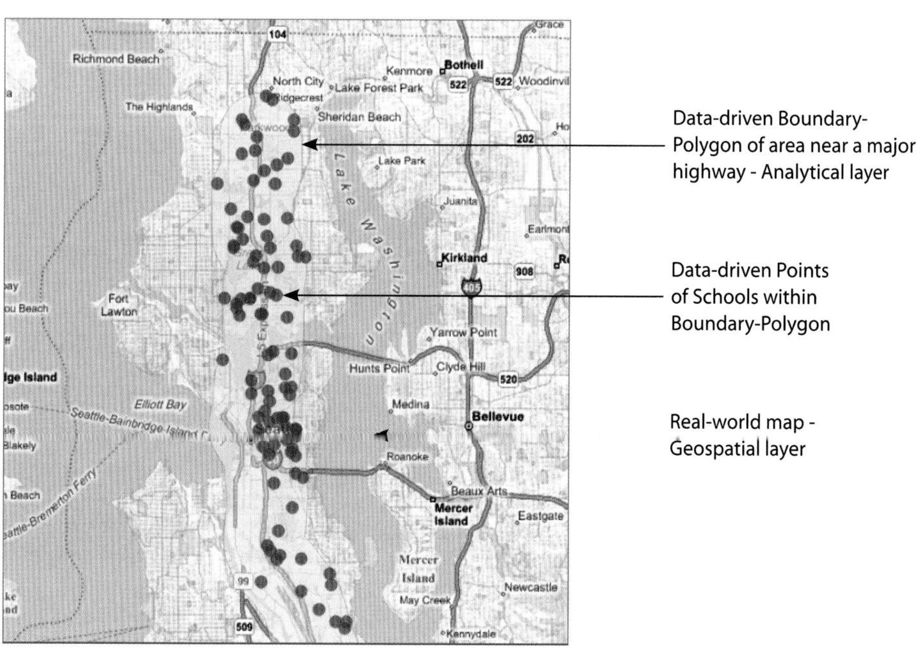

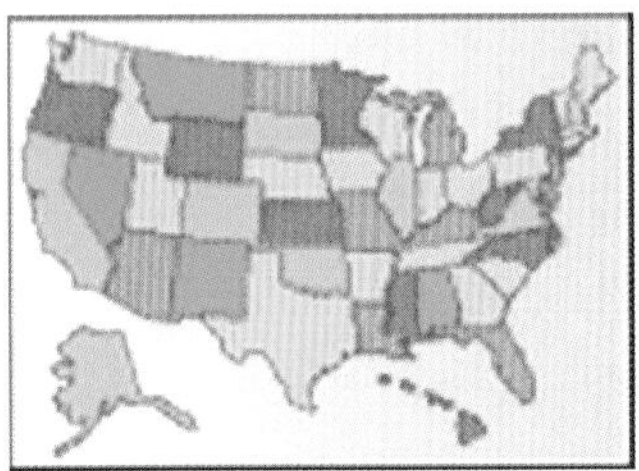

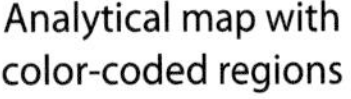

Analytical map with color-coded regions

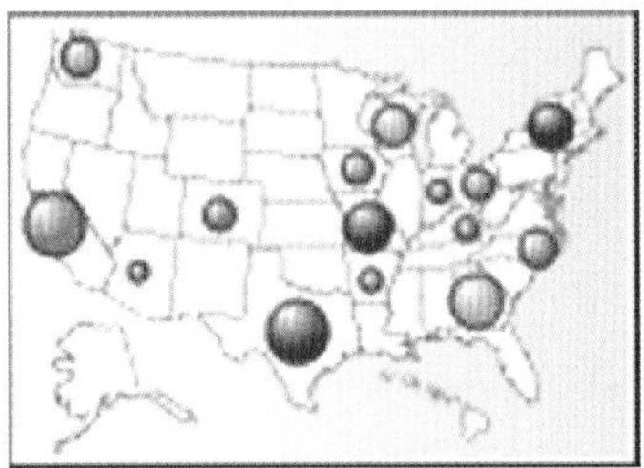

Bubble map with relative-size points

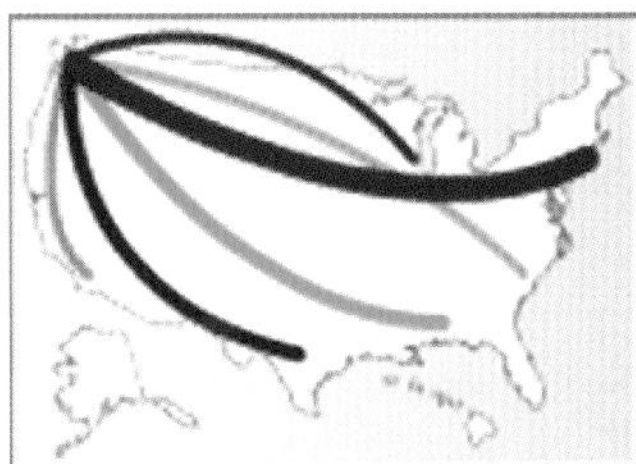

Line map with color-coded routes

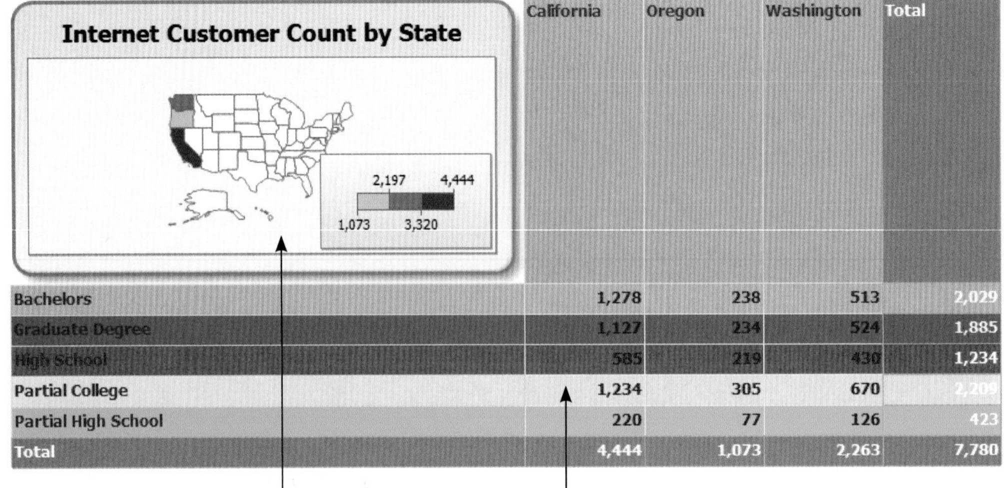

	California	Oregon	Washington	Total
Bachelors	1,278	238	513	2,029
Graduate Degree	1,127	234	524	1,885
High School	585	219	430	1,234
Partial College	1,234	305	670	2,209
Partial High School	220	77	126	423
Total	4,444	1,073	2,263	7,780

Analytical map embedded in tablix. Map shows relative data element sizes, which complements matrix.

Tablix with detail data-grid

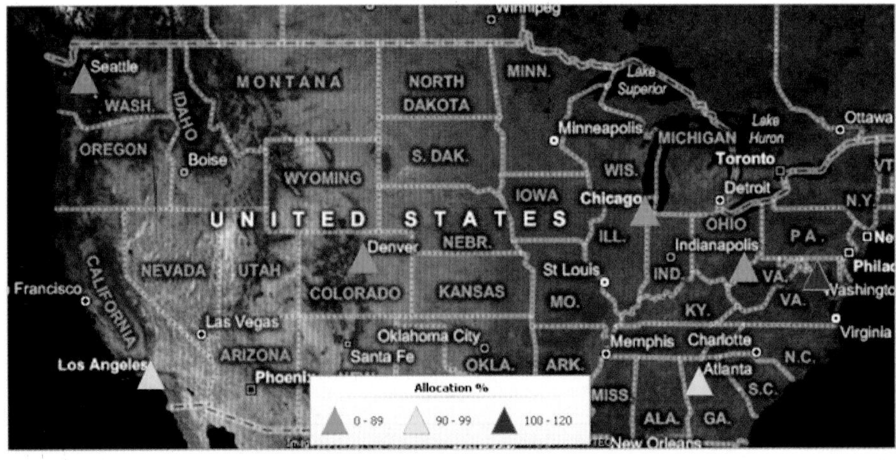

Color-coded status indicators by geo location

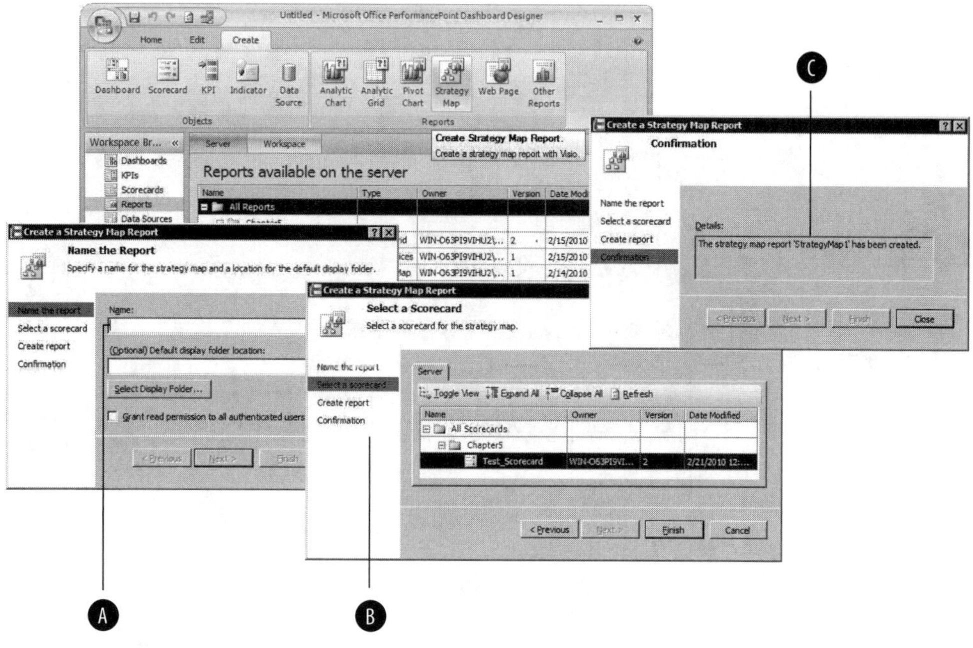

Figure 4-41 *PerformancePoint—create Strategy Map report*

When this process is complete, click Apply in the lower-right corner of the Strategy Map Editor window to save all changes. You will be returned to the Dashboard Designer design surface, with the Strategy Map displayed.

When finished, the colors from the KPI indicators were not displaying on the Strategy Map. When all the obvious culprits for the error were eliminated, I searched the web and found one obscure reference in a Nick Barclay blog post about Custom Indicators and Strategy Maps—the Strategy Maps use the Background Color to light up the shape! The custom indicators created earlier didn't have background colors set. Once the background colors were added to the configuration as shown in Figure 4-43, voilà, the KPI banding and the strategy map have color!

Also, when looking at the KPI banding, the background color shows up on the range indicator! It is easy to create something and not have a full understanding of the utility of every feature, like what those foreground and background color settings were used for. Even the three PerformancePoint books I have don't go into the use of the indicator background color. This tip is shared to spread the understanding. Figure 4-44 shows the final result.

Using the strategy maps feature in PerformancePoint 2007 (and Visio Services/ PerformancePoint Services in 2010) as a way to present interactive visualizations to a dashboard has tremendous potential. Think about using an activity diagram to display

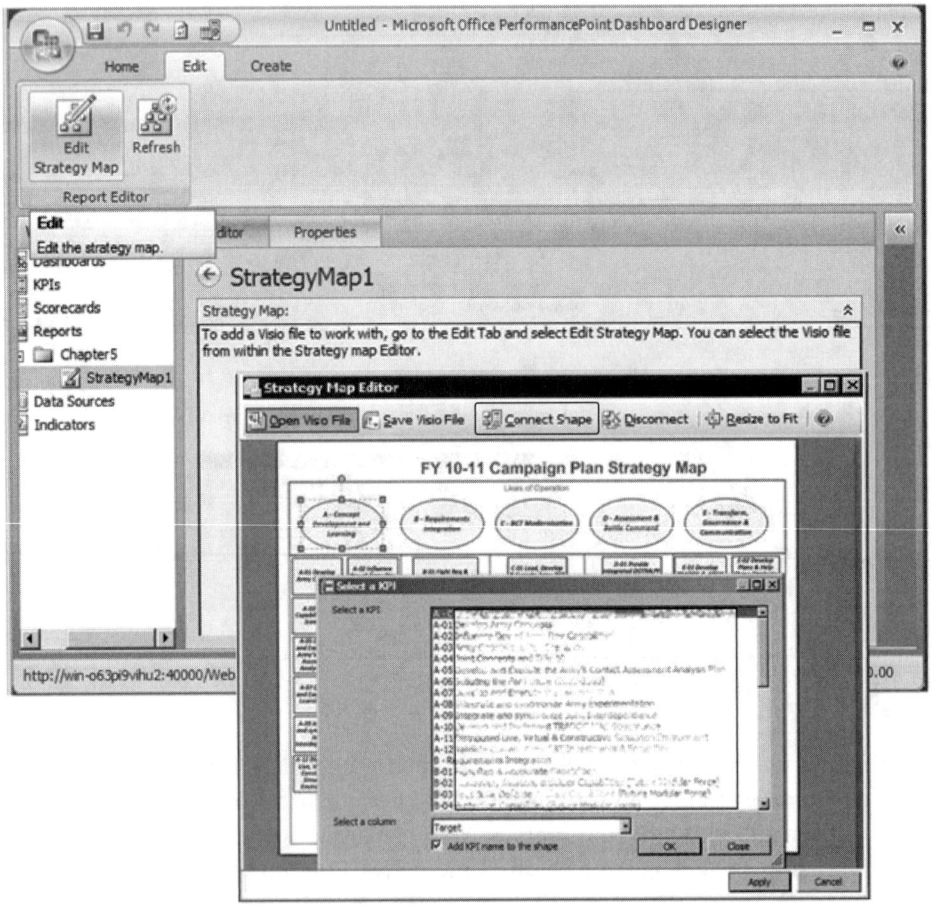

Figure 4-42 *PerformancePoint Visio diagram as a Strategy Map report—connect shape to scorecard KPI*

workflow progress on an operational dashboard. As long as you can figure out how to link the measurement and the diagram shape as part of a visualization, there is no limit on its utility! In PerformancePoint Services 2010, Visio Services will support the shape hyperlink functionality, making it possible to jump to detail pages or detailed reports from clicking a shape on the diagram. This will make the diagrams navigable, opening up a more visual way to traverse the information available.

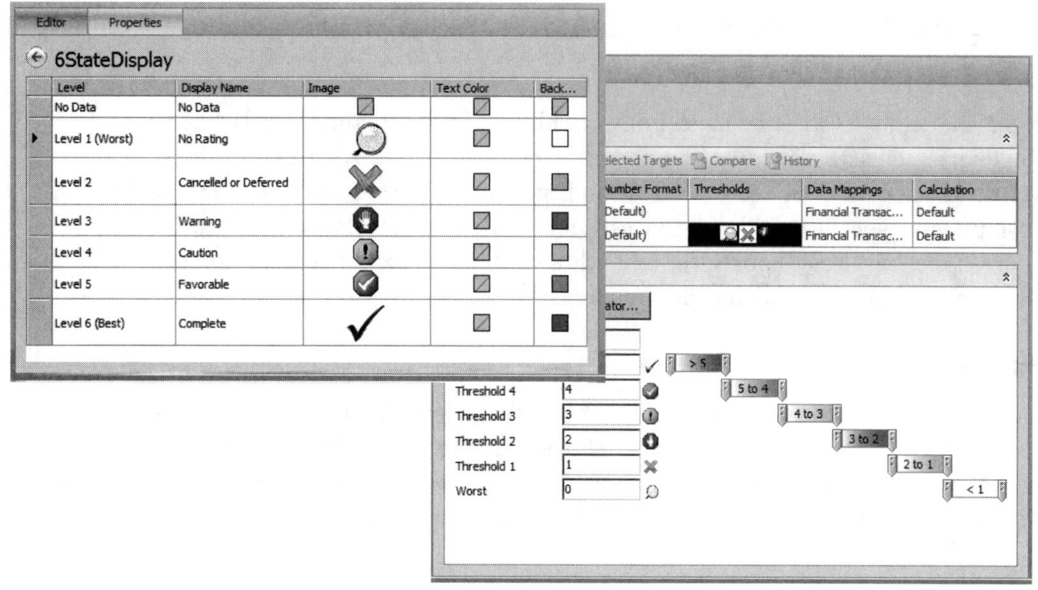

Figure 4-43 *PerformancePoint Custom Indicator with Background Colors set*

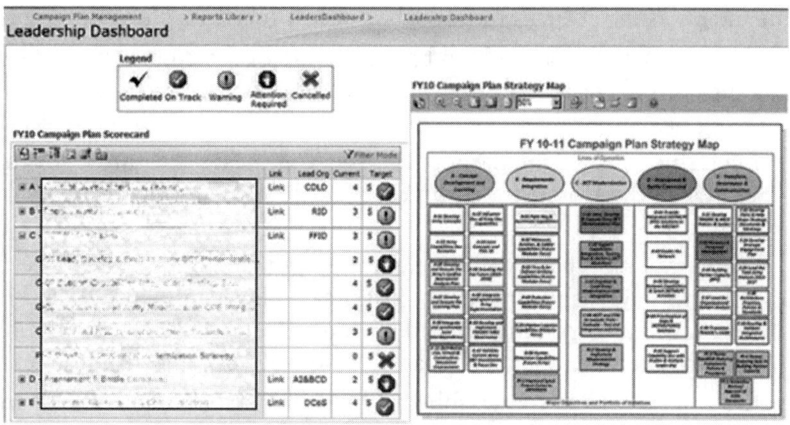

Figure 4-44 *Leadership Dashboard with Strategy Map using Custom Indicators and Colors*

Using PerformancePoint Dashboard Items as SharePoint Web Parts

When you deploy the PerformancePoint dashboard to SharePoint, the dashboard (container) and each individual component is published to the SharePoint site. This gives the dashboard designer a lot of flexibility in adding web parts based on a variety of component types: Reporting Services Reports, PerformancePoint Scorecards and Report, Excel Services Reports, content editor web parts, etc. This means that the dashboard designer should consider how reusable a PerformancePoint item is.

BI TIP

It is generally better to use a complete PerformancePoint dashboard if multiple objects require filtering by the same data source and all components are available through PerformancePoint. It is easy to personalize the entire dashboard using a PerformancePoint filter. If you have multiple web parts (including non-PerformancePoint) from multiple data sources, create a SharePoint dashboard and use the PerformancePoint web parts as components.

Adding a PerformancePoint dashboard component to a SharePoint dashboard page is a two-step process (Figure 4-45). First you select the dashboard that was deployed, and then you select the item from the dashboard to display. To add a component, take the following actions:

1. Put the SharePoint dashboard page in edit mode by clicking on the Site Actions Menu and choosing Edit Page from the context menu, as shown in Figure 4-45.
2. Click the Add A Web Part golden bar at the top of the zone you want the web part to appear in. Select PerformancePoint Dashboard Item from the Add Web Parts dialog box.
3. Once the web part is on the dashboard page, you must configure it for the item you want. Click the Edit drop-down on the Select A Dashboard web part, and choose Modify Shared Web Part.
4. The Web Part Action pane will open on the right side of the page. Click the ellipsis next to the Dashboard text box, indicated by A in Figure 4-46. Find the dashboard you want from the list and click to select, then click the OK button in the lower-right corner. The Dashboard Name will now appear in the text box.
5. Click the ellipsis next to the Dashboard Item text box (B). Select the item you want from the list displayed. The display tree is hierarchical, pages at the top, then items by item type as indented nodes. The item we want is listed under Report Views. Click the item to select it, and then click the OK button at the lower-right corner. The item name will now appear in the text box.

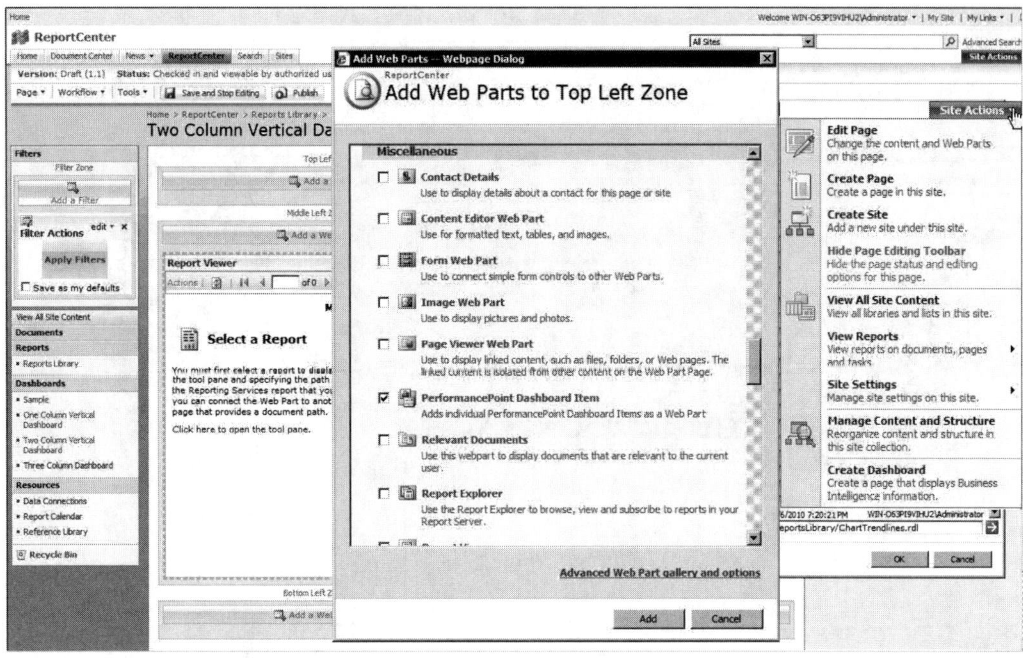

Figure 4-45 *SharePoint Add Web Parts dialog box*

6. Adjust any of the other web part properties, and then click the OK button at the bottom of the Action pane to apply your changes and return to the dashboard page.
7. Your PerformancePoint dashboard item will now be displayed on the page. The page will still be in edit mode. Finish adding web parts, and then click the Publish button to save all changes and publish the dashboard page to the SharePoint Library.

Now that you know how to configure a PerformancePoint web part, let's compare the differences between a Reporting Services Report surfaced using the Report Viewer web part and surfaced used by PerformancePoint and a report generated from a SharePoint Reports Library. The difference between the delivery mechanisms is minimal but can make a difference in usability, depending on how you have constructed the display.

Reports are rendered a little differently, depending on which web part you use on your dashboard. Figure 4-47 shows an example dashboard with a report displayed using the Report Viewer web part and a report from the Reports Library. Notice that the parameters area is located differently. In the Reports Library view, the parameter area is along the side of the display, and the toolbar is still across the top of the report. This takes a little more real estate away from the space used to display the actual report. In either case, showing parameters and toolbars is a display option that can be controlled during report deployment.

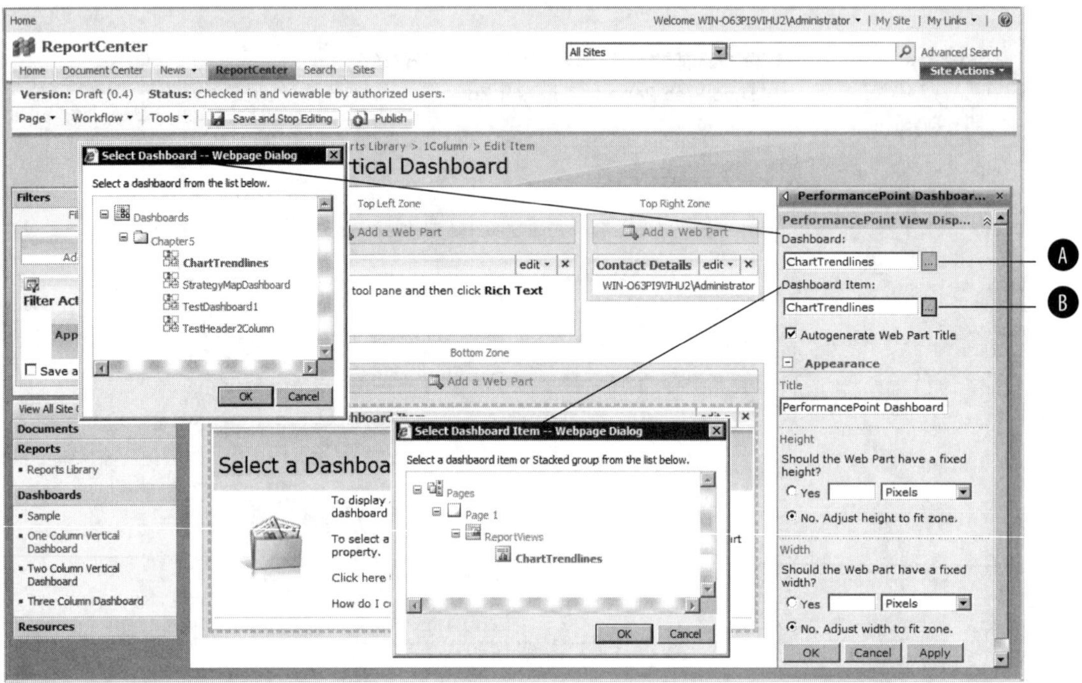

Figure 4-46 *Add a PerformancePoint dashboard web part*

We just wanted you to see the difference so that you could make a better choice about which design fits better in your dashboard design. With the Microsoft Business Intelligence solution, you have many choices for accomplishing the same objective!

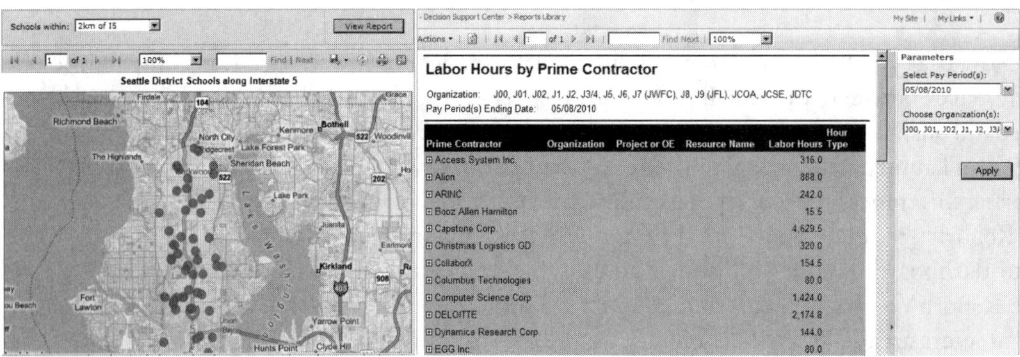

Figure 4-47 *Report through Report Viewer web part vs. Reports Library report display*

Putting It All Together: Using Charts and Gauges in Information Delivery

Now that we have created reporting services objects and some new dashboard pages in SharePoint and PerformancePoint, let's talk about using charts, gauges, maps, and other visual elements in information delivery. It isn't a lie that a picture is worth a thousand words. Because of the human ability to perceive vast amounts of information in a relatively small space, we are challenged to provide relevant, timely, meaningful information that supports decision making and business operations. That means a reporting solution should cover all areas of the organization—from the strategic to the operational. Using a coherent tool set to provide that information is paramount. Your report audience must be able to consume the information, in a manner that is comfortable for them, on a frequency that they choose. These are the reasons we have gone into painstaking detail on some of the more unfamiliar features of SQL Server Reporting Services. So, let's break it down this way:

- Information delivery options: standard reports, personalized reports, and dashboards created to answer specific business questions or allow exploration of available data
- Visualization options: gauges (rates, KPIs), charts (too much variety to list), maps (geographically related information), indicators (KPIs), sparklines (trends). Combine these with matrix and table displays to provide a rich information experience
- Mobile display options: text only or graphic-based (smart phones) options so that information can literally be delivered anywhere
- Information delivery timing: push (subscriptions), on-demand, stored so that the stakeholders receive the information according to their preferences

The world today is connected, linked. Don't try to include too much detail in the top-level report; link to it using Report Actions. Remember the mantra—overview first, focus on specifics, drill down to details. That means start with something graphical. Find out what the most important pieces of information are for the organization, its major divisions and departments, and then present them in a coherent way. Use templates to homogenize the information delivery presentation. If you design a good dashboard template, then folks should be able to understand it no matter which office they are from. For example, they will come to understand and expect that the dashboard's upper-left quadrant always has the department scorecard, and the key issues and reports are in links on the top right. This makes cross-functional communication and support easier and more meaningful. Figure 4-48 shows an example dashboard that demonstrates summary and detailed information.

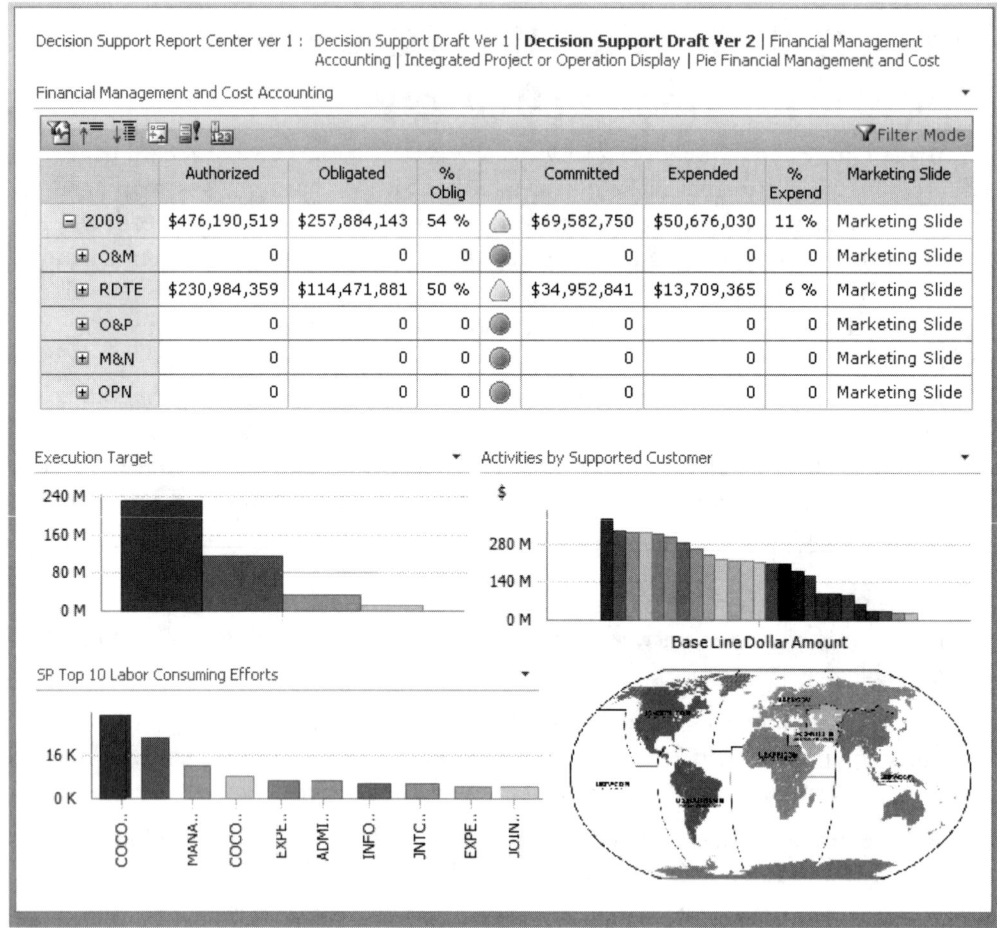

	Authorized	Obligated	% Oblig		Committed	Expended	% Expend	Marketing Slide
⊟ 2009	$476,190,519	$257,884,143	54 %		$69,582,750	$50,676,030	11 %	Marketing Slide
⊞ O&M	0	0	0		0	0	0	Marketing Slide
⊞ RDTE	$230,984,359	$114,471,881	50 %		$34,952,841	$13,709,365	6 %	Marketing Slide
⊞ O&P	0	0	0		0	0	0	Marketing Slide
⊞ M&N	0	0	0		0	0	0	Marketing Slide
⊞ OPN	0	0	0		0	0	0	Marketing Slide

Figure 4-48 *Example dashboard*

If something is important, it should be obvious by looking at it. Make it stand out in some way. Including more context in the visualization will induce better perceptual recognition by the report audience. Remember not everyone sees what you see, so take color-blindness and low vision into consideration when designing reports and dashboards. That means using different symbols as well as different colors to delineate meaning.

If you create a particular analogy to convey a specific piece of information, do not change the visualization of that analogy without thoroughly explaining the change and the new way to read it. We become trained through repetition to derive meaning from presentation. People come to innately recognize certain symbols and colors/positions because of the way they are consistently presented in our culture. For example, you will be hard-pressed to convince the CEO that Red is good and Green is bad. Use those cultural norms to make your report meaning more intuitive.

Creating the report or dashboard is only one facet of the information delivery life cycle. And it, like everything else in our Information Technology (IT) world, does have a life cycle. New information and sources of data will appear and need to be integrated into the environment. They will be updated and analyzed to provide insight into their topic and category. At some point, the data will be overcome by events, become irrelevant, or become false because circumstances have changed. At that point, they will expire and be archived or meet the bit bucket. And the cycle goes on. Make sure that the information provided in reports is timely and relevant. Using a modified date, as of date, report date, or some other indicator of timeliness is a reporting best practice. Figure 4-49 shows a dashboard of data quality metrics that is updated with every

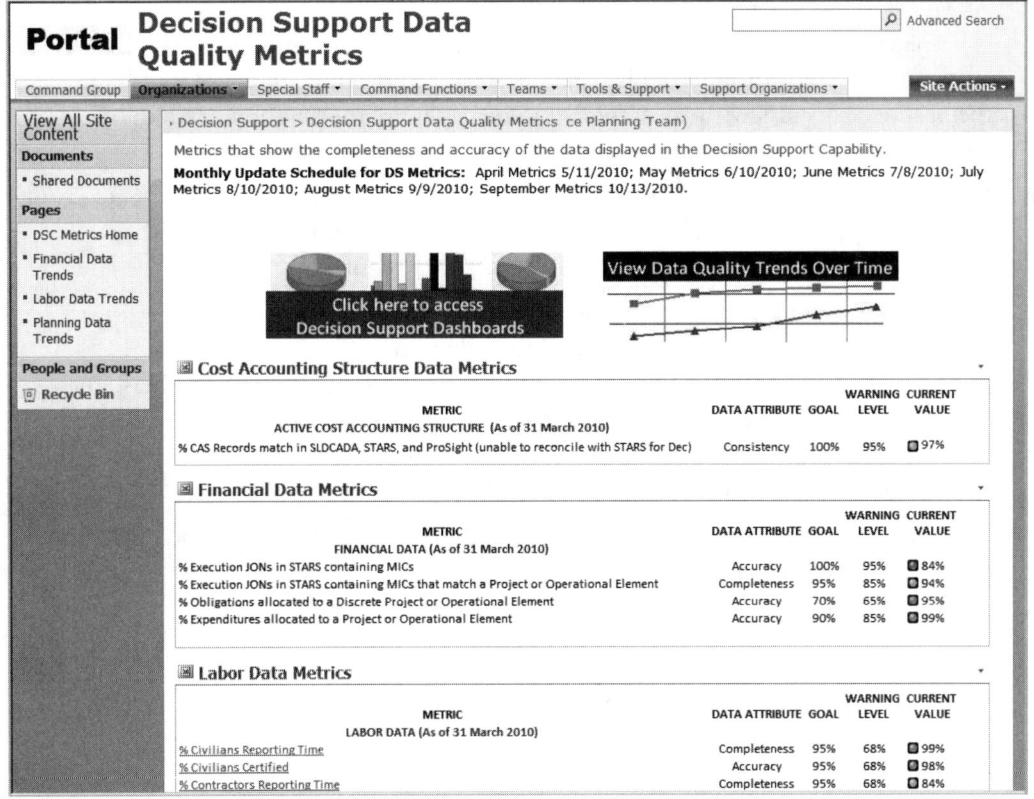

Figure 4-49 *Example dashboard with data quality indicators*

ETL cycle. When users believe the lineage and reliability of their information, they will have more confidence in the reports and displays that are created from it, and your efforts will be a considerable success!

Best Practices and Special Tips for Intelligent Business Information Delivery

As we wrap up this part of the journey, please come to the realization that the hardest part of good business intelligence is not technical. It is understanding the subject matter, being clear on the available means of information distribution, and having a plan that deals with all the intricacies and moving parts that a good solution should have. Take the long-range view and architect a solution that will be extensible, reliable, and dynamic; most of your end users and stakeholders will be pleased. So here are some final points to ponder when working in the information delivery discipline:

- Always start a project by talking to the person who requested the report or information. If you received the requirements secondhand, something may have gotten lost in the translation of business need to technical requirement. Finding the best design starts with accurate requirements and a thorough understanding of your stakeholders' needs.
- Listen to how your stakeholders describe what they are looking for—they may use specific expressions that help you decide what visualization will appeal to them. For example, some folks hate pie charts, others love them.
- Certain industries and professions have standard ways of expressing metrics. Get familiar with these metrics and their baselines; it will allow you to design components that match the experience and expectations of your stakeholders. For example, CPAs are used to using certain ratios in their evaluation of funds. Make sure you have those formulas and use them correctly with your data sources to build KPIs that are meaningful to your report audience.
- Abide by the three-click rule. If your stakeholders cannot navigate to their desired location in three clicks, you will lose their interest.
- We live in an attention deficit environment: if the message is not attention-grabbing, it may not be found over the din of information overload.
- Wise use of push and pull methods to deliver information must figure into your plan for information delivery.

- Always remember that a dashboard must answer questions, not just display a snapshot of current data values. When talking to stakeholders about what they want on their dashboard, always ask what the purpose is, how it will be used, what business questions it will answer.
- Dashboards have the potential to present a lot of rich information in a small space, if properly designed. Location, location, location—the use and placement of information in the four quadrants of a screen is an important gem to remember. The second golden rule is: *"Overview First, Focus on Specifics, Drill to Details."* Thank you to Stephen Few and Edward Tufte for blazing these trails for us.
- Working with a unified data environment makes the designers' job tremendously easier. If you find yourself in an unmanaged environment, try to rationalize your data sources—look for common attributes and dimensions.
- Seek out ways to influence the quality, proper usage, and good understanding of your data environment. Support good metadata by always using contextually rich titles and descriptions. Fill in keywords when available. Make it easy for other designers to understand your work, your data sources, your query logic, and where things are located. Participate in user groups and knowledge management communities.

Wrap-Up

This chapter has been all about data visualization delivery, getting the charts, gauges, and dashboards into the hands of your audience. Using a Microsoft Business Intelligence solution gives you many options for consuming those visualizations. Creating all these cool reports will be worthless unless you can get them into the hands of the users who need them. We started by exploring some dashboard design best practices.

The first report delivery method we reviewed was the SQL Server Reporting Services Report Manager. We looked at the functionality available through Report Manager, the various report item types, and all the properties that report items have. We also walked through deploying Reporting Services reports through the Business Intelligence Development Studio (BIDS), also known as Report Designer. Once those reports are deployed, they can be rendered in Report Manager. Report Manager has many useful features, including execution snapshots, report subscriptions, shared data sources, and folders for organization and permissions control.

Just because you are using SQL Server Reporting Services in native mode doesn't mean you can't display a report in SharePoint. We reviewed the options for using Report Explorer and Report Viewer web parts in SharePoint. You can set up pages to view all available reports in Report Explorer and have them display in a connected Report Viewer web part, or you can configure a solo Report Viewer web part to display a singular report.

Then we explored Reporting Services in SharePoint integrated mode, and the different ways you can interact with reports through this interface. Reporting Services integrated mode has some differences but the basic functionality is the same as with Report Manager; you just don't have the independent Report Manager web site—instead it uses a SharePoint Reports Library.

Then we began to delve into SharePoint features, the various types of SharePoint dashboard pages, where they reside, the different page layouts and zone settings. We discovered how easy it was to create a dashboard page in the SharePoint Reports Library and pull in Reporting Services and other web parts. We also create a new web part page and reviewed all the page layout options for this page type. We also surveyed the many kinds of SharePoint page filters available to help customize and personalize dashboard pages.

PerformancePoint Server 2007 is another tool for presenting information visualizations and consuming Reporting Services reports for display on dashboards. We examined the various PerformancePoint object types, their properties and usage. Reporting Services reports are well supported in PerformancePoint, able to display parameters and the toolbar. We created some PerformancePoint dashboards and looked at previewing and publishing them to SharePoint sites. Once a dashboard has been deployed, its component parts are available to become web parts on SharePoint dashboard pages. Given the limitation of SharePoint filters not interacting with PerformancePoint web parts, we also looked at PerformancePoint filters and their use.

We included a true-life example of using a Visio Strategy Map on a dashboard, and the configuration that goes into getting that to work properly using custom indicators. Finally, we put it all together and examined several examples of using charts, gauges, and maps in dashboards, along with other linked content. We tried to leave you with some advice on Best Practices, and included some special BI Tips from some of my esteemed colleagues. We are in-the-trenches practitioners who work with these tools every day.

Chapter 5

Microsoft and the Cloud

In This Chapter

- So What Is the Cloud?
- Software as a Service
- Platform as a Service: The Windows Azure Platform
- Infrastructure as a Service
- Wrap-Up

Unlike that old Rolling Stones song that asks you to get off of my cloud, the purveyors of the cloud (including Microsoft) want you to get on their cloud. Each vendor that provides "cloud" services has a slightly different approach to providing a solution. We have also seen that different people have a different interpretation as to what the cloud is and how they could potentially use it. We will cover how Microsoft has undergone a significant change in order to make their cloud possible and how SQL Server 2008 R2 (as well as other products) is well positioned to take advantage of this paradigm shift. Steve Ballmer (Microsoft's Chief Executive Officer), speaking at the University of Washington on March 4, 2010, said that Microsoft has added (and looks to continue adding) cloud capabilities to their products as well as providing cloud-based services. Mr. Ballmer also said that Microsoft is "betting the company" on cloud computing. So with Microsoft going "all in" with the cloud, you can bet that there will be some exciting new technologies and innovations coming. But wait, what about some of these offerings that are available today?

To envision some of the cloud capabilities, imagine you had a car and factory service technicians consistently monitored and adjusted your car for you, and they also had the ability to change your engine from a 2 cylinder to a 12 cylinder or from a car into a truck, depending on the need. While it would be a great car, if you take the same paradigm and apply it to enterprise software instead of a car; now you know a small sampling of what the cloud could bring you. Microsoft's Azure services give you this type of a reliable, scalable, and secure functionality in the cloud. One of the premier Azure services is SQL Azure; SQL Azure provides you with the capability to run SQL Server where you can take advantage of all of the power that comes with the database, yet you don't have to do any of the maintenance. Microsoft does the maintenance (backup, monitoring) for you in a secure, zero downtime environment and will even scale the server(s) to fit the changes in your user load automatically!

Microsoft is "all in" with the cloud. What does that mean? Well, this chapter is going to try to describe the cloud and some options you have in order to take advantage of this new and exciting technology. We will describe where Microsoft is with the cloud and how you can take advantage of some of these technologies to help you understand some of the potential of this technology, which includes lower cost, increased efficiencies, and vastly different and new business opportunities (for both the suppliers and the vendors). A lot of people don't realize that Microsoft has been in what has been termed the "cloud" for over 15 years—MSN, Live, and Hotmail are just a few examples—but it makes sense to take a step back and describe what the cloud is.

So What Is the Cloud?

Other than these big fluffy things in the sky that sometimes produce rain, cloud computing has been described in several different contexts. Some people term it a collection of flexible computing resources available on demand. Other people describe it more broadly as services that are available to consumers on the Internet. While it isn't the goal of this chapter to add to this debate, it is a goal to help clarify some of these topics.

In late 2007 Microsoft released a product that helped collect, store, and share health information. This wasn't the first service that Microsoft had that was cloudlike but it is a great example of what is possible with the cloud; this service is called HealthVault. HealthVault is a free service that holds your personal health information (www.healthvault.com). It sets up a personal health record up for you on a Microsoft server and exposes several services for end customers or partners to consume. This record is kept on servers, but it is up to the consumer to decide who can view, use, or add information into your HealthVault account. HealthVault also gives you the capability of connecting devices to your computer to feed data into your HealthVault record: heart rate monitors, blood glucose monitors, oximeters, pedometers, blood pressure, and scales, just to name a few. There are more and different types of hardware coming all of the time. After you use one of these devices, it feeds the data into your personal health record in HealthVault. If you gave access to your physician, then your physician would be able to see records related toward your progress (such as weight). There are even hospitals that have integrated into HealthVault to track progress of their patients. Even though Microsoft doesn't market HealthVault as a cloud service, it behaves just like one. There is a service that is available to the consumer. This service and the data are controlled by the consumer, and the service is both reliable and secure. This service has also spurred several innovations using your personal health records (these are listed under the web applications on the HealthVault web site). Some of these innovations are done by third parties utilizing the service that HealthVault provides. This service is an example of the type of service that is provided and demonstrates some of the potential that cloud services can offer. While this service isn't typically listed as a cloud-based service by Microsoft, it helps demonstrate some of the cloud concepts and how they can be applied and potentially give you a glimpse into some of the innovation that the cloud is bringing.

Microsoft breaks their cloud service offerings into several different products. We will cover some of the components, but it is important to understand that there are several products that Microsoft offers that cover differed categories of services. The marketplace generally breaks the cloud offerings into Software as a Services (SaaS), Platform as a Service (PaaS), and Infrastructure as a Service (IaaS). These categories help describe the services that Microsoft is initially offering to the cloud and where this "all in" move will pay off. The evolution of these services has paid off with Microsoft able to offer a very mature cloud offering. Microsoft's commitment is shown by the company's shift toward the cloud-based services; it has been reported that Microsoft has over 40,000 people (70 percent of the company) working on the cloud today. Microsoft is looking at all of its applications to ensure that they are cloud ready and can meet the current and future needs of a cloud-based computing infrastructure.

Software as a Service

So what is Software as a Service? This is software that is hosted where the functionality of the service is delivered over the Internet. If you are like most business people, you access a computer (either laptop or desktop) each day. On this computer, you have several applications like Microsoft Office or server-based applications like Microsoft Dynamics CRM. In the past these types of applications may have been hosted on a mainframe or similar host-based technology.

These applications then evolved to the personal computer and have made us even more productive. The evolution has continued, and computers have gotten a lot more powerful and more portable (such as the laptop or ultra-portable devices), and some of this capability is making it to our mobile devices (cell phones) every day. Software as a Service endeavors to take these applications from the desktop or server and place them on the Web. In order to use these types of applications, all you need to have installed is a web browser. In traditional information technology systems, you typically have server-based applications and client-based applications. With Microsoft, you can break its SaaS offerings down into client- and server-based applications. A great example of the client-based applications is Microsoft's Office Web Apps. Another example consists of the server-based applications that can be demonstrated in BPOS (Business Productivity Online Standard Suite).

Office Web Applications

This type of software delivers the functionality of the Microsoft Office software suite via a browser. The applications are lightweight copies of their full client versions of Microsoft Office products. The difference is that these applications are hosted in a web browser. Giving users the option to create, modify, and collaborate via these web applications elevates Office to another level. As of the time of the writing of this chapter, the Office Web components are available via:

- An add-in for SharePoint
- Office Live web applications (officelive.com)
- Via Microsoft SkyDrive or Facebook (via www.docs.com)

The only requirement for the Office Web Apps is an Internet browser. You can get most of the full client functionality in a web browser.

You can see in Figure 5-1 that the Office Web Apps look very similar to the full Office client versions. The resulting document format is the same as the full client version as well (so anything that you create in the web application versions works just

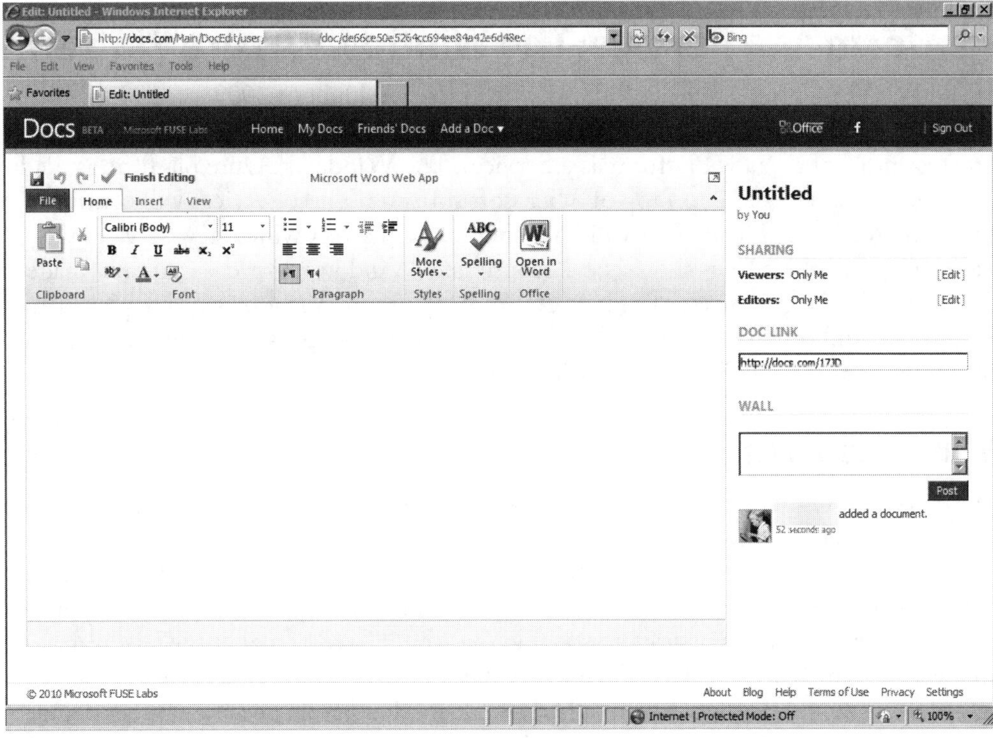

Figure 5-1 *Example of Office Web Apps*

fine in the full client versions). Another nice feature of the web applications is that you do not have to be on Windows; so if you are running another platform, you can take advantage of document sharing.

BPOS (Business Productivity Online Standard Suite)

This suite includes SharePoint Online, Exchange (E-mail) Online, and Office Live Meeting (including Office Communications Server). BPOS is an example of offering packaged products with some of Microsoft's more successful products. Some of the advantages of BPOS are the lower cost (usually done on a per client mode), no on-premise hardware needed, and that you can have your internal IT department focus on internal operations instead of server management and ensuring uptime. Since the servers are maintained in the cloud, you don't have to maintain your own servers (unless you want to commingle cloud services with on-premise equipment).

Platform as a Service: The Windows Azure Platform

Windows Azure hit the market "officially" in the second half of 2009 after a long beta period. It took the market a little time to understand some of the components of this great example of a PaaS (Platform as a Service). The Windows Azure platform is made up of several services built on top of Microsoft software. These services will continue to evolve over time. The market will (and should) help direct which new services will be offered and which ones should be discontinued. Windows Azure is currently made up of the following services: Windows Azure, SQL Azure, Windows Azure platform AppFabric, and codename "Dallas." Each of these services offers different types of technologies that we will go into a little more detail about.

Windows Azure

Windows Azure is an operating system that is sitting in the cloud, but unlike the operating system at your locations, this one can scale up and down, depending on need. Windows Azure also works with your current environment, so that you can take advantage of the scale capabilities when you need them. Imagine if you were an online retailer whose customers bought seasonally. You would have to match the hardware to meet the anticipated peaks in customer volume. You would need to direct resources in order to help this load and hopefully do it before the servers became saturated and turned into a customer satisfaction issue. Now imagine that you could keep some of the capability on your premises and have the capability of dealing with any performance peak that came along. You can use Azure as an integrated part of your solution very easily.

BI TIP

The Azure toolkit has several presentations and is loaded with examples and solutions. This toolkit is more of a package that allows you to learn all about Azure via presentations and demos on how to develop solutions.

You can also migrate your solution over to Azure so that you don't have to maintain the infrastructure yourself (which is very time consuming and expensive).

It is a common misconception that the cloud paradigm has to involve the Internet. There are continuing developments in the area of private clouds. A private cloud is very similar to the cloud except that the cloud components services are managed by the organization within their corporate boundary.

SQL Azure

SQL Azure is a version of SQL Server that is cloud based. This service offers a scalable, reliable, highly available database in the cloud. One of the greatest strengths of SQL Azure is that it looks and behaves similar to a SQL Server instance in your own environment. What is different is that while this service is hosted in the cloud, the database developers don't have to change very much. SQL Azure supports the T-SQL language and can be accessed via the same client access libraries like ADO.Net, ODBC, PHP, and JDBC. In SQL Azure there is even a synchronization model, so that you can keep your on-premises database replicated with SQL Azure using the Microsoft Sync Framework.

BI TIP

You could also use the SQL Server replication features to feed into / out of SQL Azure. You need to pay special attention to the data type, because not all data types are supported in SQL Azure.

You can learn more about the Microsoft Sync Framework from http://msdn.microsoft.com/en-us/sync/default.aspx.

In the following example we will demonstrate how you can set up a SQL Azure database and copy the database from the local instance of SQL Server to an instance of SQL Azure. In order to carry out the following example, you will need to set up an Azure account. If you have an MSDN (Microsoft Developer Network) account, you can utilize that to receive a certain amount of free Azure space and time. If you do not have MSDN, there is currently an option that gives you free space and time on Azure for a trial period (up on www.azure.com).

After you acquire an account, you should then log in to the Windows Azure (or SQL Azure) portal. In the section labeled Existing Windows Azure Platform Users (as shown in Figure 5-2), you can see a link for the portals. Your login is related to your Windows Live ID, which is part of the Azure account provisioning process. In order to do this demo, you should have the sample databases installed on your workstation. The sample databases for SQL Server 2008 R2 are available on http://msftdbprodsamples.codeplex.com. You should install the sample databases named Adventure Works.

BI TIP

On this site there are also example databases for previous editions of SQL Server as well as a sample dedicated to SQL Azure.

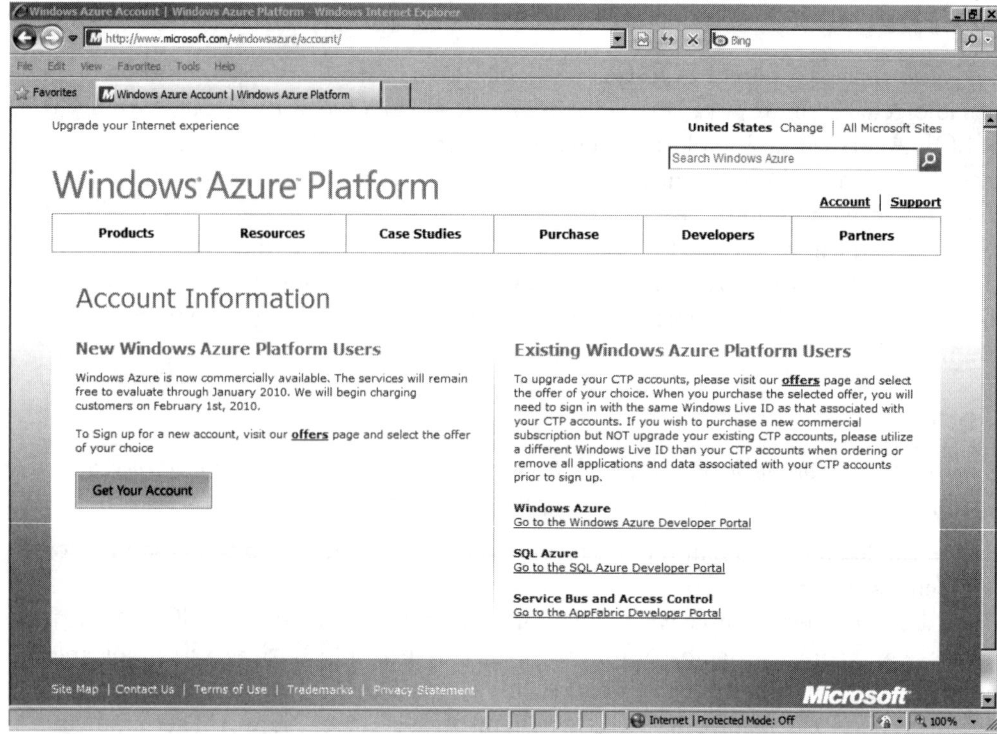

Figure 5-2 *The Windows Azure page on Microsoft.com*

Setting Up a SQL Azure Database

We will be using the sample dedicated for SQL Server 2008 R2, because we will be loading the samples into a SQL Server database and then migrating the database into SQL Azure. After you have the samples installed (either locally, or on a SQL Server that you have access to) you should be ready to go. You will want to go to http://www.azure.com and click the word Account in the top right-hand corner (as depicted in Figure 5-2).

1. Click Go To The SQL Azure Developer Portal (as shown in Figure 5-2) and then log in to the portal with your Windows Live ID.

   After you log in to the portal, you will be presented with a summary of the services that are available to you. In our case we are looking for the SQL Azure portion.

2. Click the SQL Azure section on the left hand side and you are presented with a summary of your SQL Azure setup, as shown in Figure 5-3. Take special note of the Server Name and the Administrator Username (these will be very important later on in this example).

   Next we will create a database container for the database that we are going to move over to SQL Azure.
3. Next scroll down the screen until you see Create Database. Click Create Database and you will be prompted with the dialog similar to Figure 5-4.
4. Put in the database name **AdventureWorksLT**.

The Adventure Works LT database is the lightweight version of the full Adventure Works database.

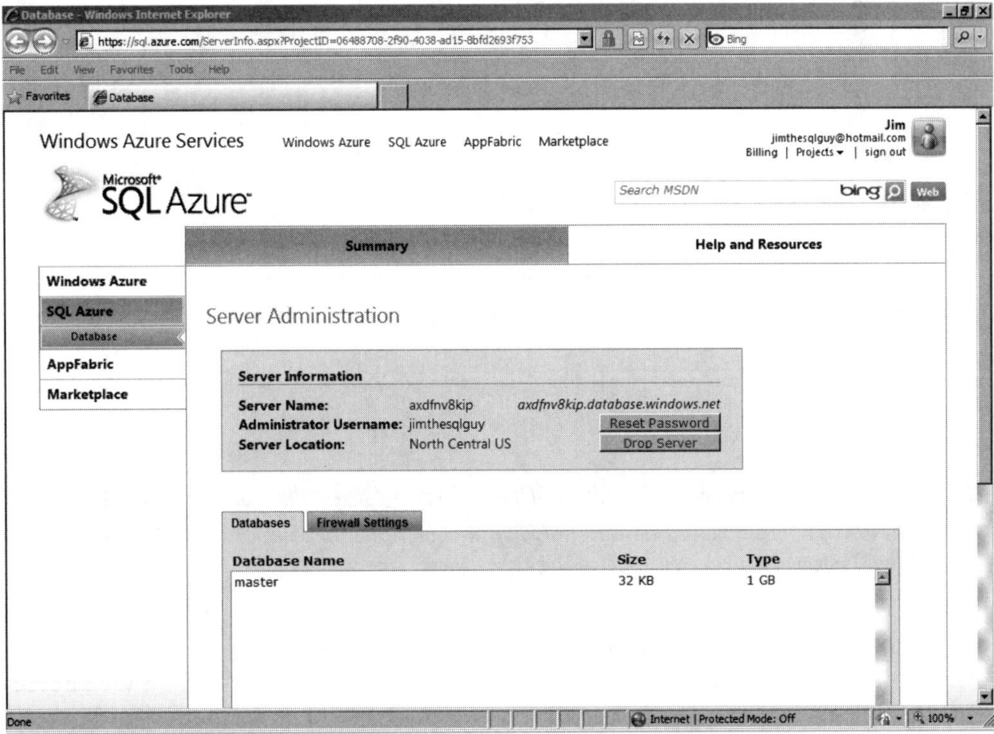

Figure 5-3 *The SQL Azure summary page*

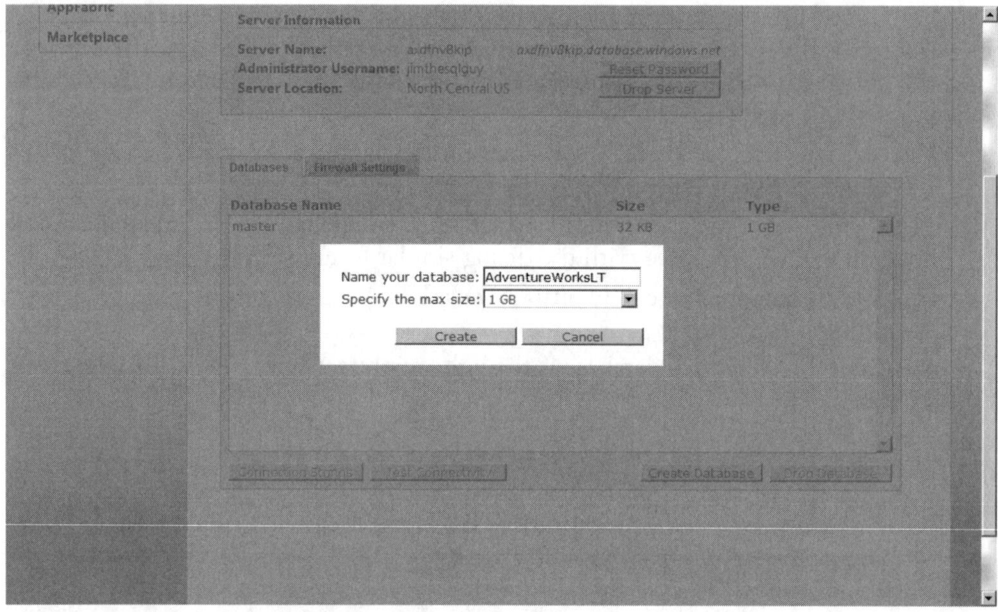

Figure 5-4 *The Create Database dialog*

Allowing Access to the Database

Once we have the database created, we need to allow access to the database. In order to allow access, you will need to specify which IP addresses can communicate with the database. You allow specific ranges of address in the Firewall settings.

1. You will notice that the IP address that you are communicating from appears.

BI TIP

Do not worry if you do not recognize the address (of if the address is different than your workstation's). You will most likely be accessing the Internet via a proxy at some point (if you have a setup like most residential locations, then you will probably have a router). This would be the address of the router.

2. Check the box that says "Allow Microsoft Services access to this server" and be prompted with a dialog as shown in Figure 5-5. You will most likely want to put in a range of addresses that are given access. In our case we allowed from 96.240.0.0 to the highest range that is available, 96.240.255.255. If you want to open up your database to every IP address, you would choose to go from 0.0.0.0 to 255.255.255.255 (though this is not recommended). If you would like to host a database for public consumption, you may want to check out "Project Dallas" later in this chapter.

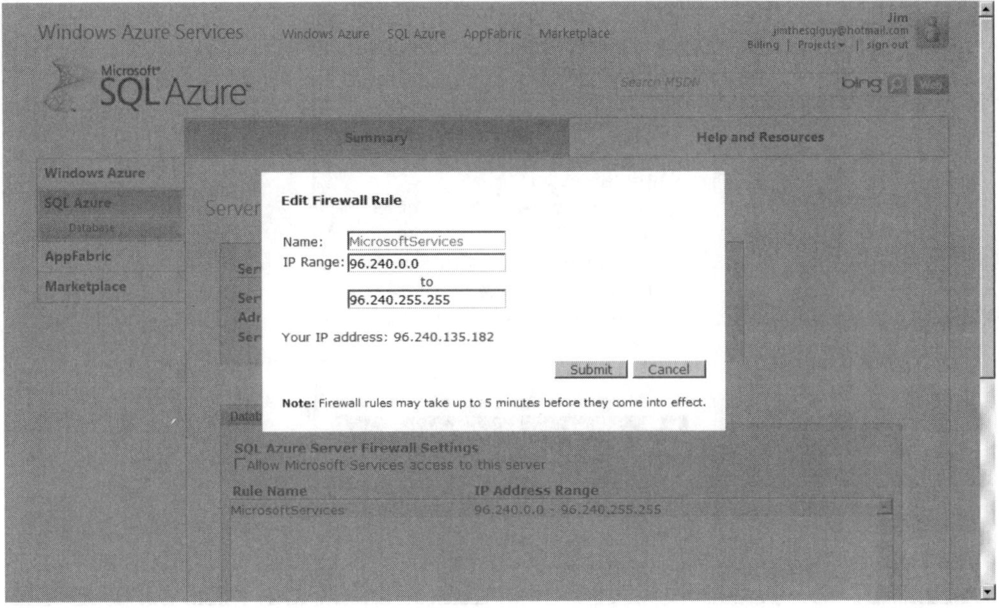

Figure 5-5 *Firewall rules in SQL Azure*

Connecting to the SQL Server Instance

Once you have given access to your IP address, you should be able to connect to that instance of SQL Server as if it were local. To test this, we will connect to this instance with Microsoft SQL Server Management Studio.

1. Launch the SQL Server Management Studio. To do this, open your programs folder and choose Microsoft SQL Server 2008 R2. Under this folder, note the tool called SQL Server Management Studio (as shown in Figure 5-6).
2. Now you should see the sample databases that you have installed on your local SQL Server (or one that you have access to). In this example the samples are installed on a local instance of SQL Server.

   Next we are going to connect the SQL Azure instance to our Object Explorer.
3. Choose the Connect button in the top left-hand corner of the Object Explorer (as shown in Figure 5-7).

Figure 5-6 *Launching the SQL Server Management Studio*

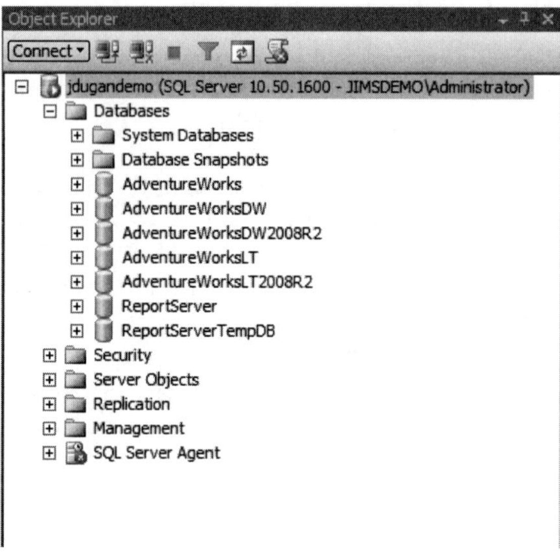

Figure 5-7 *SQL Server Management Studio Object Explorer*

Figure 5-8 *Services from the Object Explorer*

4. You will be asked what type of service you would like to connect to. Choose Database Engine (as shown in Figure 5-8).

   You will then be asked the server name and credentials for logging on.

5. Next input the server to which you are connecting: **<servername>.database .windows.net**.
6. Next choose the authentication type to be SQL Server Authentication and place your user ID and password that you set on the SQL Azure portal. Then click Connect as shown in Figure 5-9.
7. Note that the SQL Server from SQL Azure is registered, as shown in Figure 5-10. Notice that even though this server is located in the cloud, you can manage this database much as you manage a regular SQL Server instance.

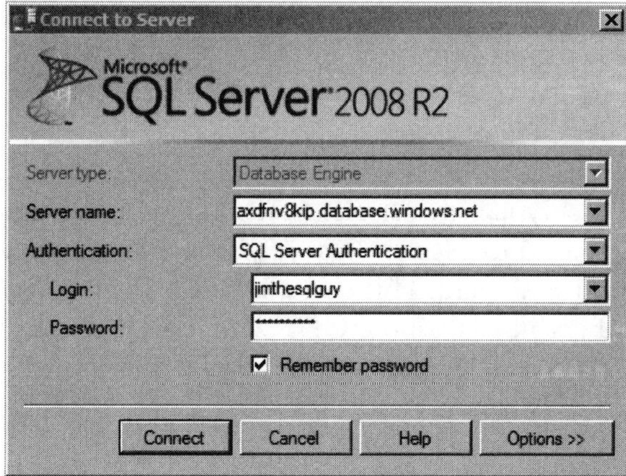

Figure 5-9 *The Connect To Server dialog box*

jdugandemo (SQL Server 10.50.1600 - JIMSDEMO\Administrator)
Databases
System Databases
Database Snapshots
AdventureWorks
AdventureWorksDW
AdventureWorksDW2008R2
AdventureWorksLT
AdventureWorksLT2008R2
ReportServer
ReportServerTempDB
Security
Server Objects
Replication
Management
SQL Server Agent
axdfnv8kip.database.windows.net (SQL Server 10.25.9268 - jimthes
Databases
Security
Management

Figure 5-10 *Object Explorer after your SQL Azure server is registered*

BI TIP

In most applications you need to specify your user name as <username>@<server name>. SQL Server Management Studio allows you to connect to the SQL Azure database with or without the @<servername> in the User ID field.

Loading Data into Azure

Next we are going to copy the data from our local instance of SQL Server up to the SQL Azure instance of the database. There are several ways to load data into your SQL Azure instance (via the Export Data Wizard inside of SQL Server Management Studio, bulk copy, or similar tools). One of the problems with this approach is that not all data types are supported in SQL Server Azure (such as the hierarchy ID, geography, and geographic datatypes). Because almost all of the sample databases contain some kind of unsupported data type, we can't use the default method of moving data into SQL Server, so we will use a tool (from http://sqlazuremw.codeplex.com/) called the SQL Azure Migration Wizard. This tool was written by George Huey and is an invaluable resource for getting data into SQL Azure. This tool even allows you to report on your database to learn which elements won't be able to be ported over to SQL Azure.

Next we are going to install the SQL Azure Migration Wizard tool on our local machine.

1. Launch your Internet browser, go to the address http://sqlazuremw.codeplex.com, and click Download.
2. You will be presented with a license agreement; choose I Agree (as shown in Figure 5-11).

   You can choose either to open the tool or to save it to your local machine. The installation is a compressed file; extract the files to a temporary location to install (running the executable SQLAzureMW).
3. In the section labeled Analyze And Migrate, choose SQL Database as shown in Figure 5-12. This will look at your data and create a report and then migrate the data over for you.

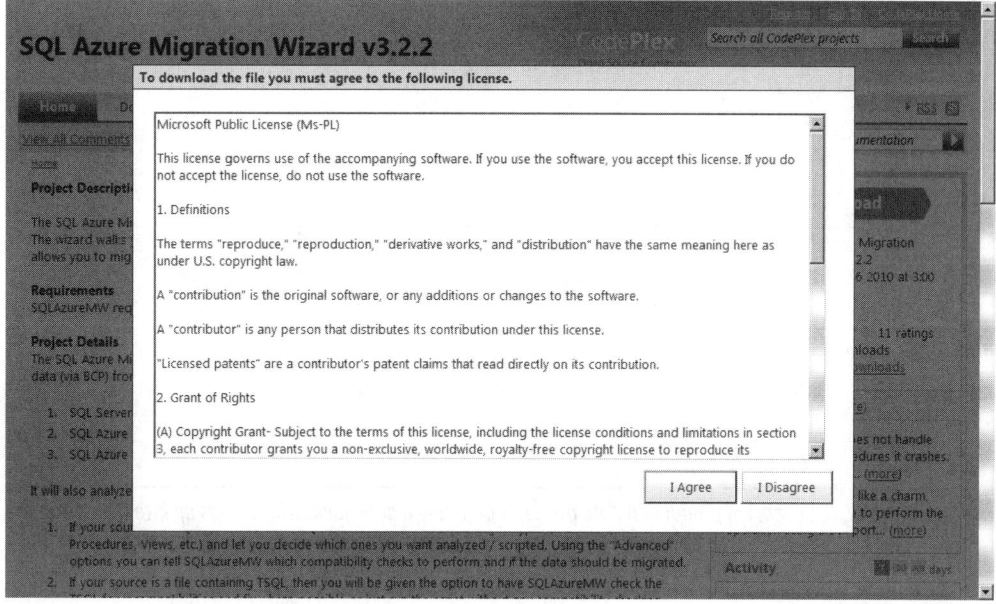

Figure 5-11 *Data migration tool end user license agreement*

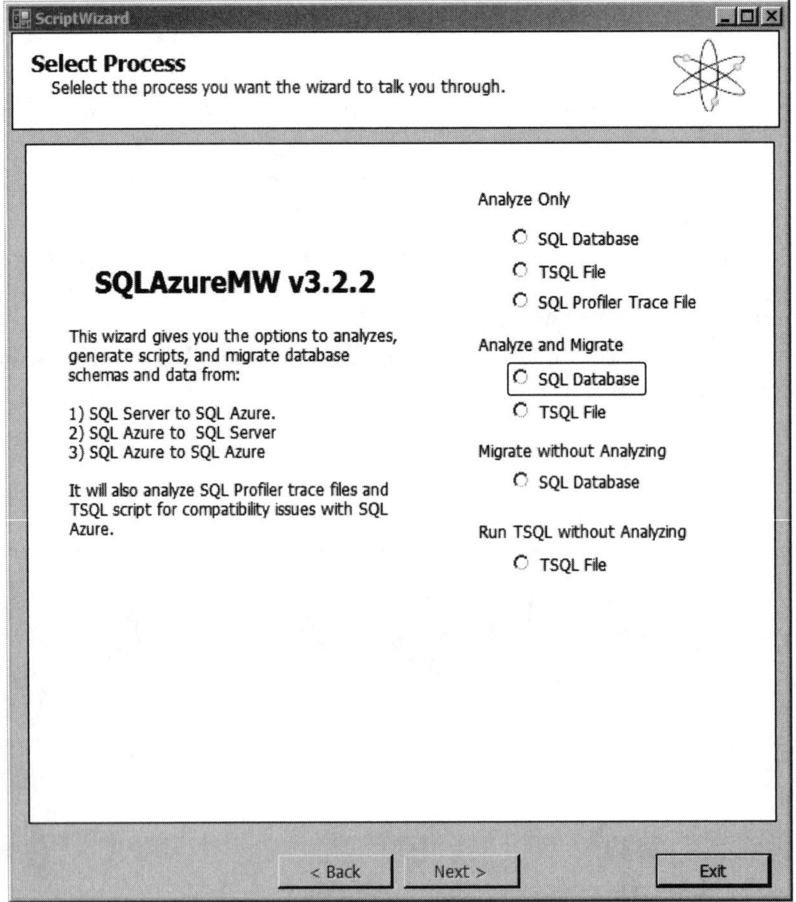

Figure 5-12 *The initial screen for the SQL Azure Migration Wizard*

BI TIP

If you are going to be moving production data over, it is probably a good idea to break this up into two steps. You would first perform an analysis to produce a report, and then later you could come back and migrate without an analysis.

4. You will then be presented with the Select Source dialog. Choose Connect as shown in Figure 5-13 (if the database is on a local instance). If the database is not local to your machine, input the server name and the credentials for the SQL Server and click Connect.

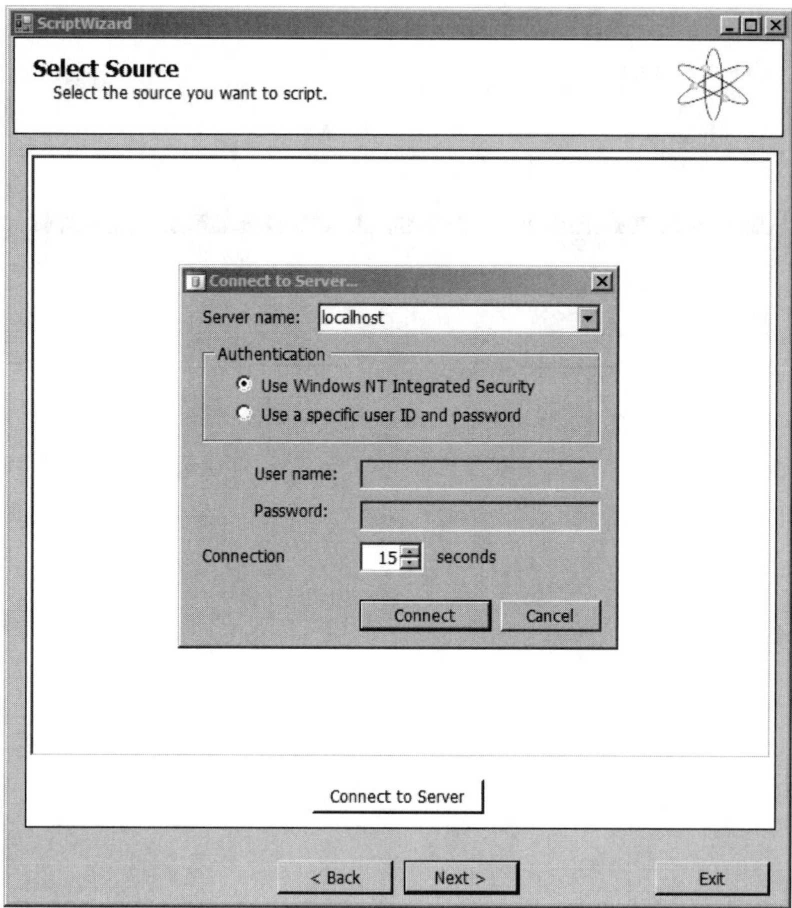

Figure 5-13 *Connect to the local SQL instance (or SQL Azure)*

5. After you log on to the source, you will be presented with the databases that are on the source server. Choose the AdventureWorksLT (the lightweight Adventure Works database) and click Next (as shown in Figure 5-14).
6. You will then be presented with the objects that you would like to move. In this example we will go with the default (which is to transfer all objects). Click Next to continue (as shown in Figure 5-15).

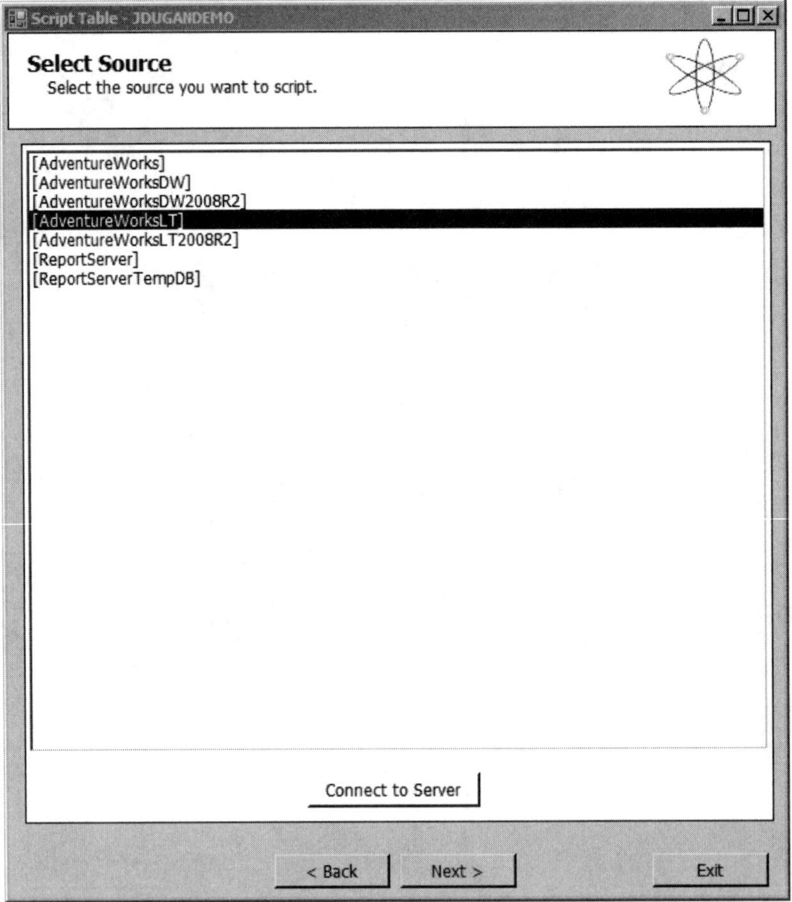

Figure 5-14 *Select your data source.*

7. The next screen is the Script Wizard Summary. This will allow you to view the database, options, and objects that are going to be transferred over to the Azure instance. Click Next to continue (as shown in Figure 5-16).
8. The wizard will now go through the database and produce a report (shown in Figure 5-17), which lists any of the data or objects that won't be transferred over and why. Click Next to continue.

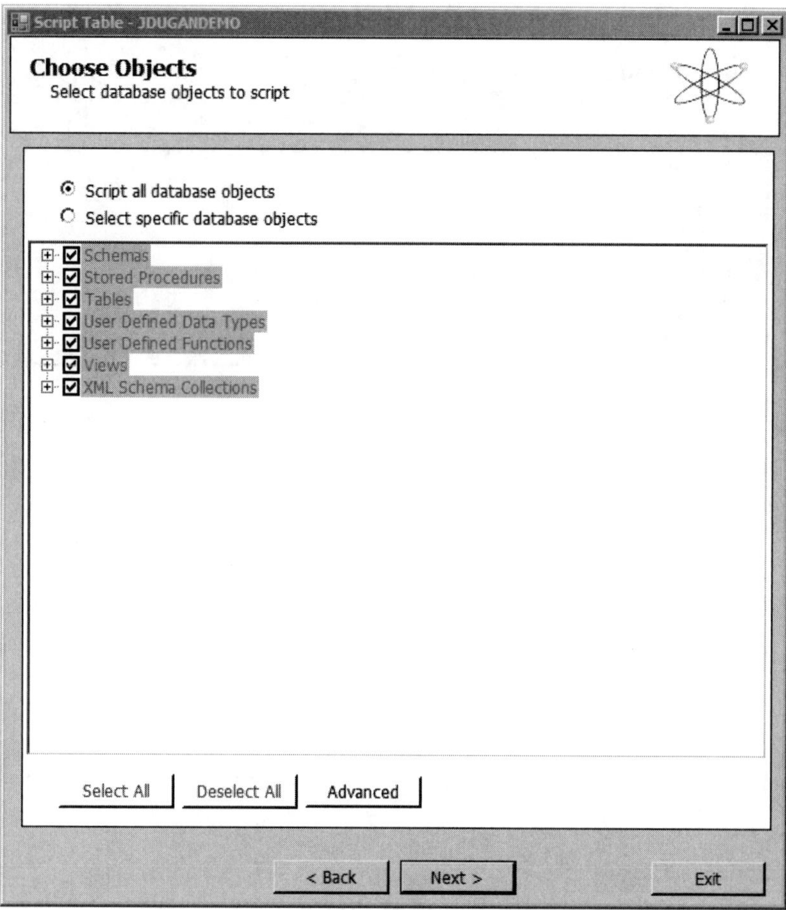

Figure 5-15 *Choose all objects.*

9. Next you will be asked to connect to the SQL Azure server you would like to copy the SQL Azure database over to. Click Connect To Server as shown in Figure 5-18.
10. You will be prompted to enter your server name <servername>.database.windows.net and the username@<servername> in the User Name and Password boxes. Once you enter those values, click Connect (also shown in Figure 5-18).

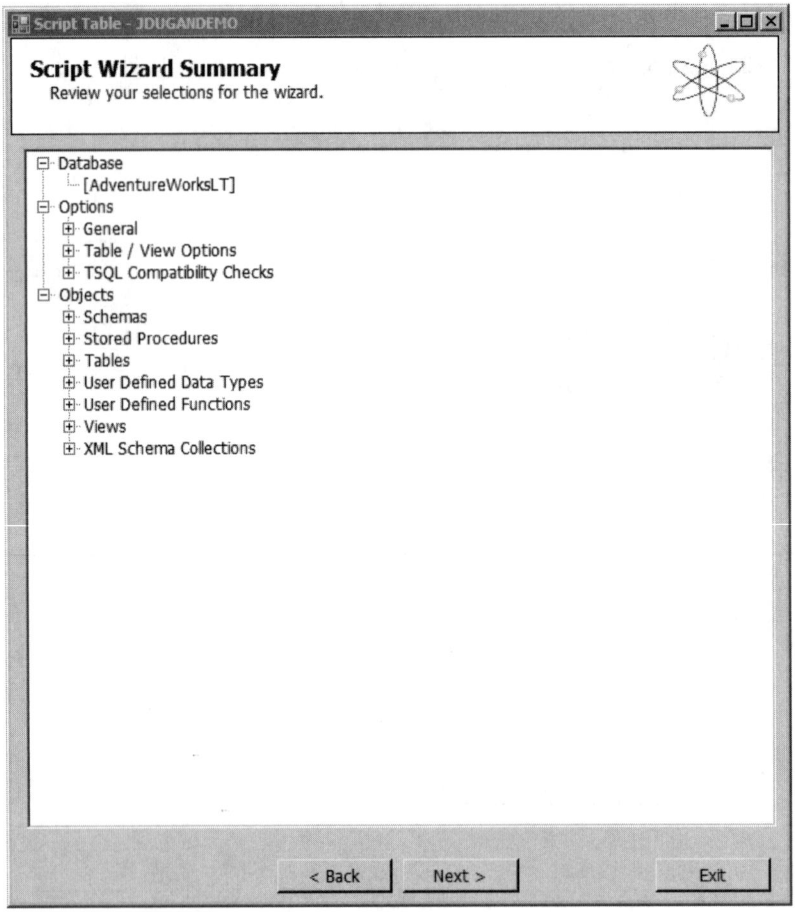

Figure 5-16 *The Script Wizard Summary*

BI TIP

You can also delete an Azure database as well as create a database from this tool as well.

11. You will be asked if you would like to execute the script against the destination server, as shown in Figure 5-19. Choose Yes to begin the processing.

    Because we are just using the lightweight Adventure Works sample, this should transfer relatively quickly (we are only transferring a relatively small database, 3.4MB).

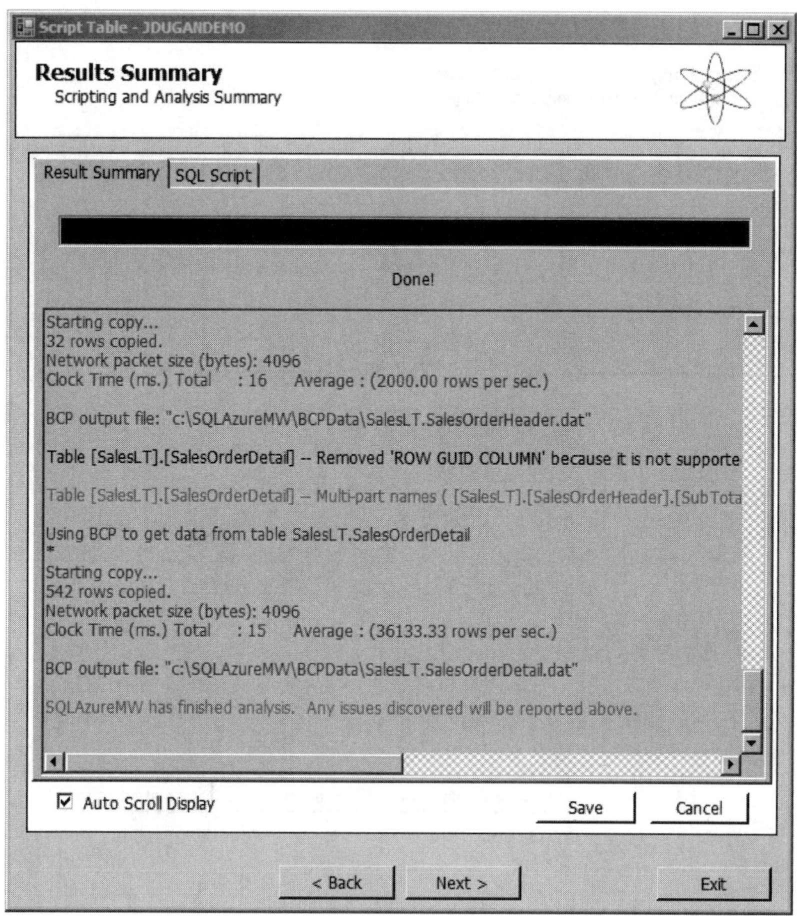

Figure 5-17 *The Results Summary*

12. You should next be presented with the Target Server Response window. If you see an indication of success (as shown in Figure 5-20), click Exit to exit out of the wizard.

    You have now copied the database from a local instance up to an instance of SQL Azure.

BI TIP

You can also use this tool to move data from Azure down to a local SQL Server instance or from one SQL Azure instance to another SQL Server Azure instance.

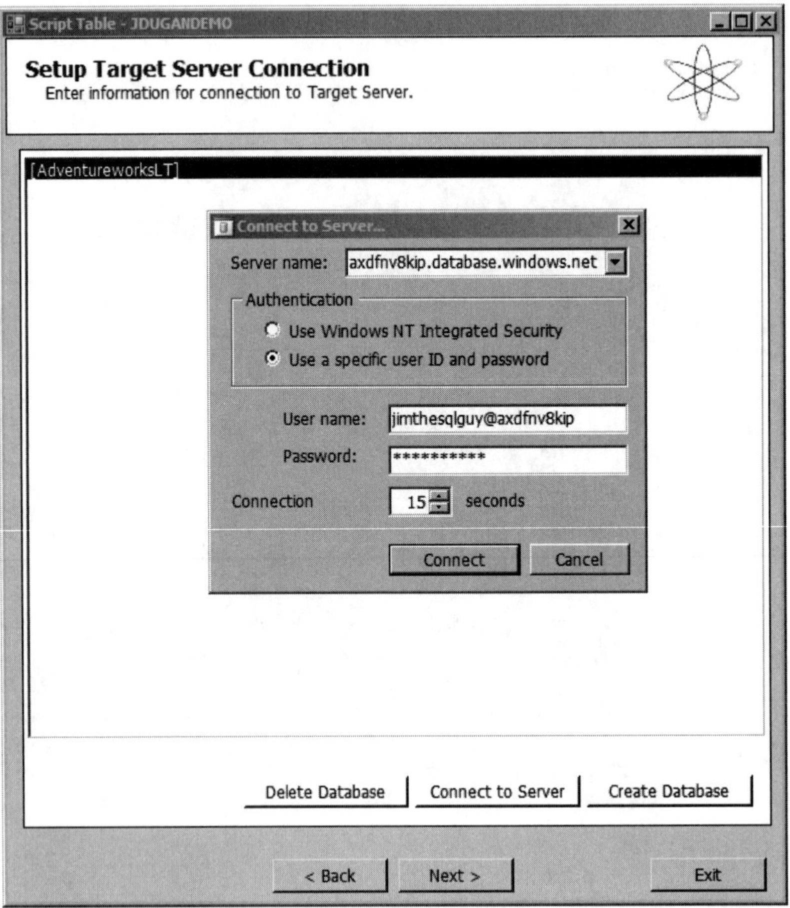

Figure 5-18 *Connecting to the target database*

13. Next go back into your SQL Server Management Studio. Notice that most of the database objects made it over from the local instance to the SQL Server. You can use the SQL Server Management Studio as if the SQL Azure instance were a local instance (as shown in Figure 5-21).

Notice that not all of the objects are the same between an instance of SQL Server 2008 R2 and SQL Azure. There are many differences, but there are even more similarities (this is where some of the power of using SQL Azure shows up). The applications that utilize SQL Server or SQL Azure sometimes don't know, or even care, if the database is in the cloud or if it is local.

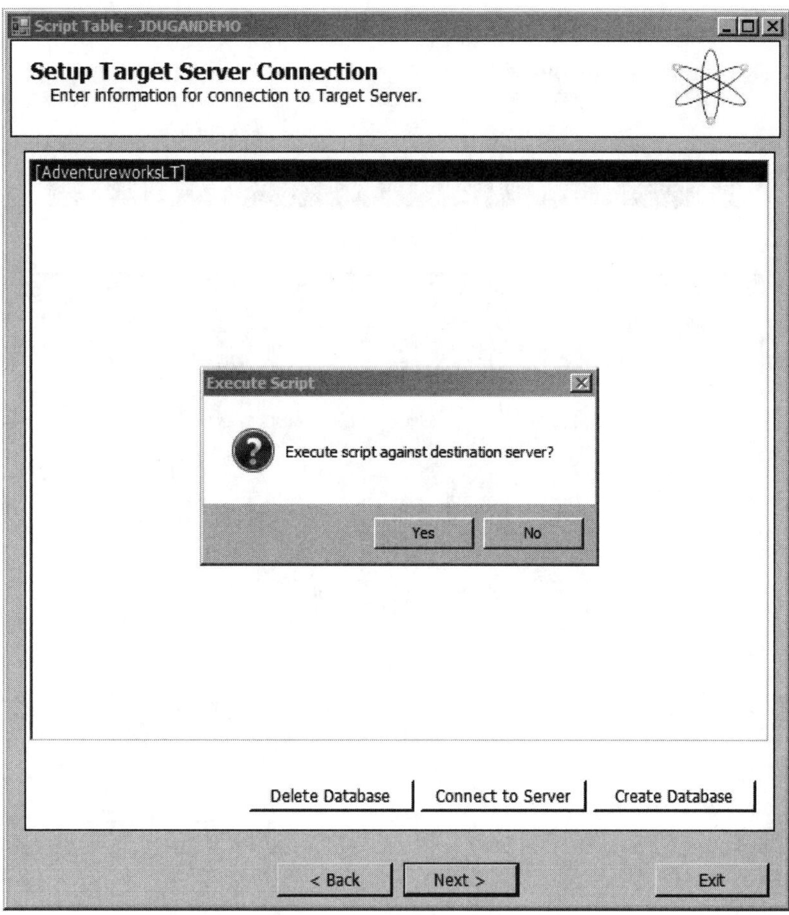

Figure 5-19 *Execute the script against the target database.*

Using Report Builder

In the second example we demonstrate how you can use one such application (Report Builder 3.0). We will create a report with Report Builder 3.0 off of the SQL Azure database instance. We will use the Northwind database that we just transferred over to SQL Azure. Report Builder is available in two different modes, either as a stand-alone tool or launched via SharePoint. The stand-alone version is downloadable in the SQL Server 2008 R2 feature pack (you can find it either from www.officebicentral.com or by searching for "report builder 3.0" from the main web page of Microsoft, www.microsoft.com).

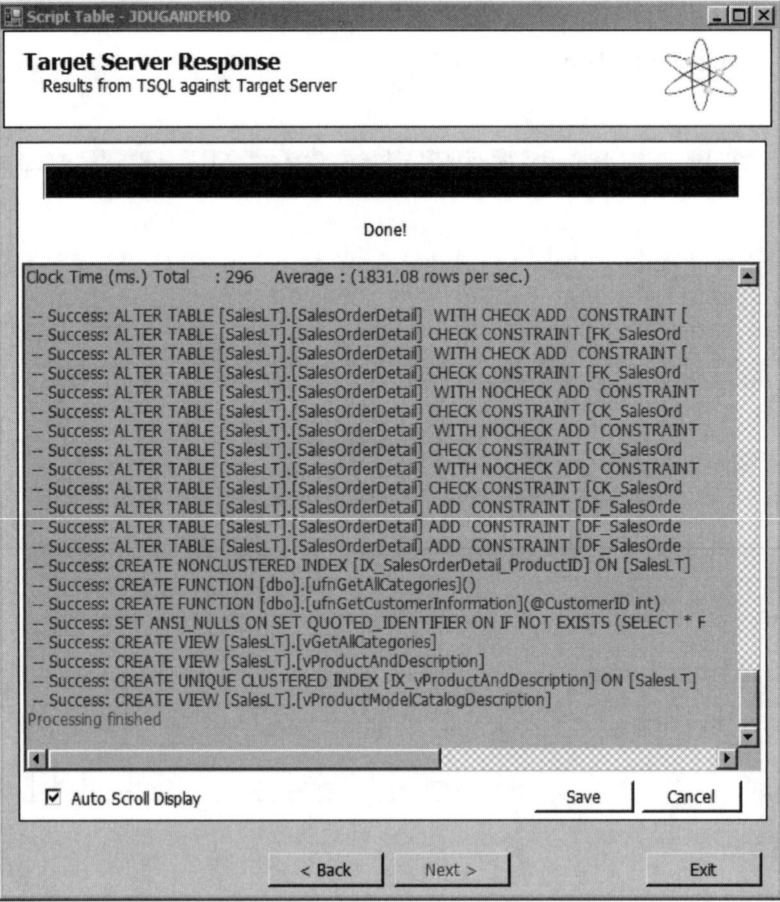

Figure 5-20 *Response from the target database*

Report Builder 3.0 is the ad hoc component of SQL Server 2008 R2 Reporting Services. In order to demonstrate some of the power of the SQL Azure database, we will use Report Builder 3.0 to connect to SQL Azure and create a map chart. Chapter 4 is dedicated to the Reporting Services components, so this example will quickly skim through some of features of Report Builder. Our goal with the next example is to demonstrate how easily SQL Azure can be implemented with existing tools.

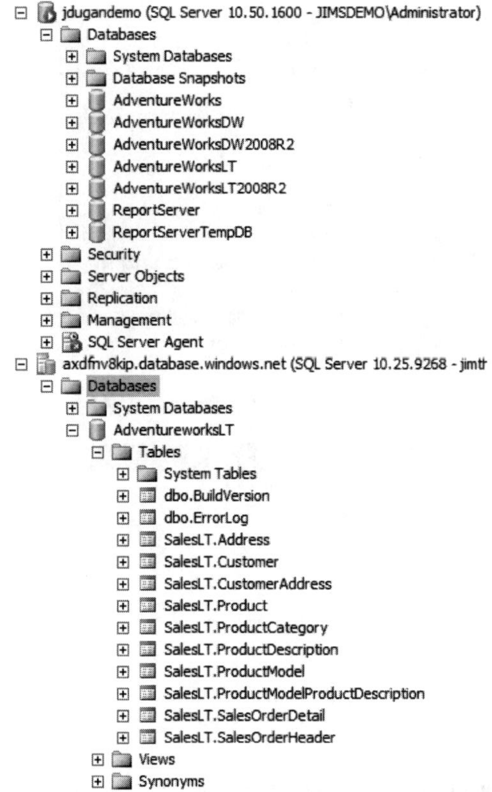

Figure 5-21 *The SQL Azure database in SQL Server Management Studio*

BI TIP

With the initial release of SQL Azure, spatial data types were not available. Geospatial data types are now included with SQL Azure.

1. After you have installed Report Builder 3.0, navigate to your programs folder, choose the folder Microsoft SQL Server 2008 R2 Report Builder 3.0, and choose the executable for Report Builder 3.0 (as shown in Figure 5-22).

BI TIP

You can also launch Report Builder 3.0 from inside SharePoint 2010.

2. Next choose the Map Wizard as shown in Figure 5-23 and choose Next to continue.

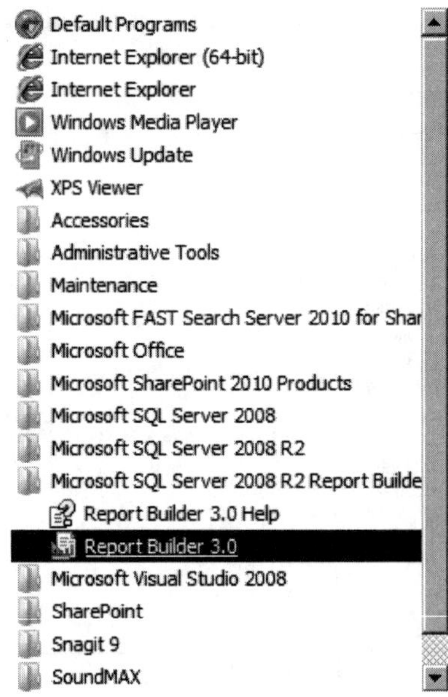

Figure 5-22 *The stand-alone Report Builder 3.0 location*

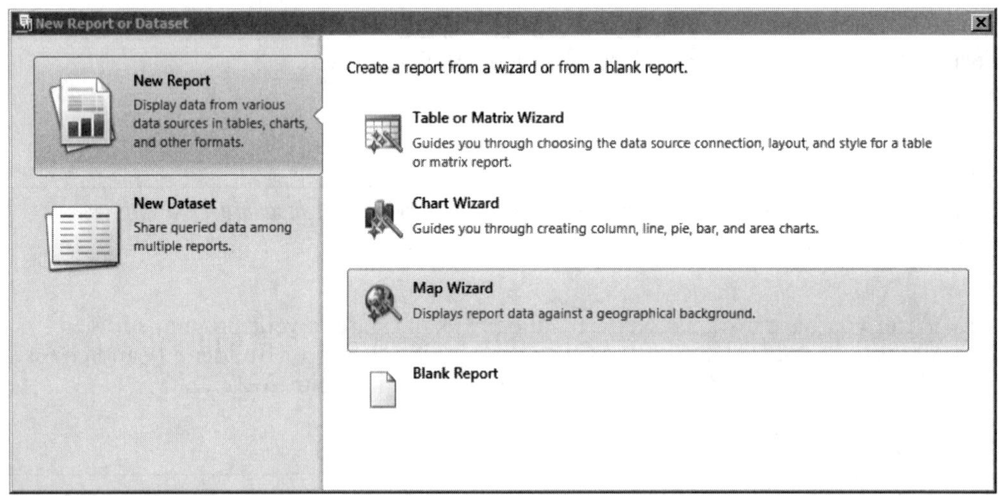

Figure 5-23 *Report Builder 3.0 report design wizard*

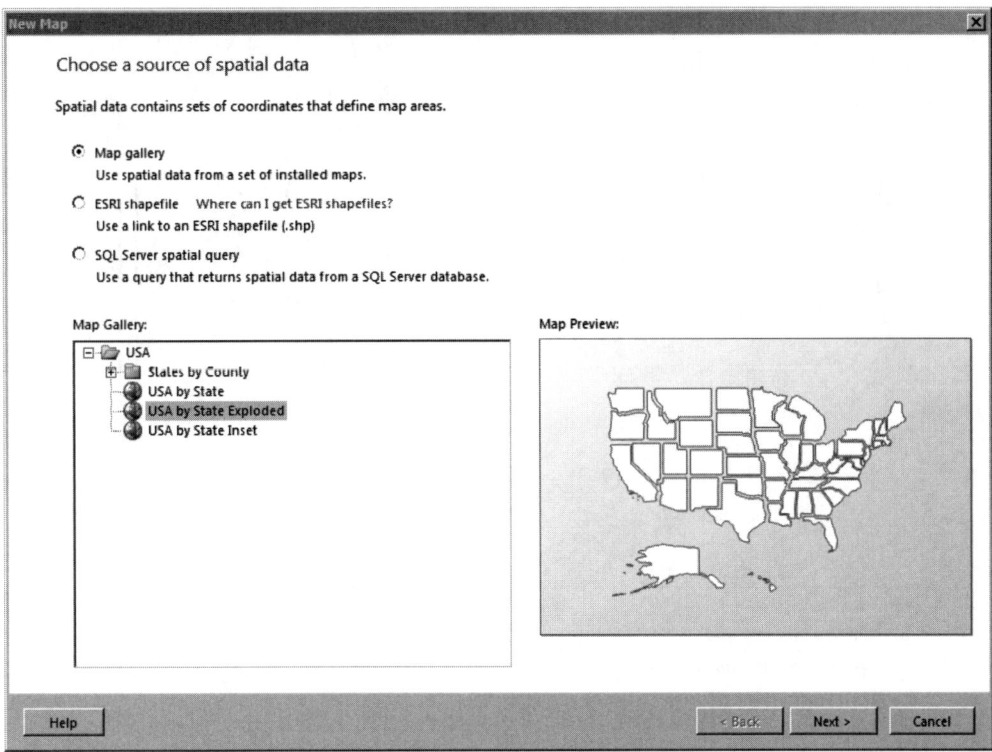

Figure 5-24 *Choose the Map Gallery.*

3. Next you will be taken to the New Map dialog box shown in Figure 5-24. In this screen you can either choose something from the Map Gallery (which offers map backgrounds that are already done for you), import an ESRI shapefile, or run a SQL Server spatial query. In the New Map dialog choose USA By State Exploded and click Next to continue.
4. Because we will be only using a small subset of data, we will need to zoom in (using the slider on the left hand side, which is shown in Figure 5-25). Zoom in on the states of California, Nevada, Arizona, and Utah.
5. Also click the check box labeled Crop Map As Shown Above and click Next to continue (you can also add a Bing Maps layer to the map if you wish).

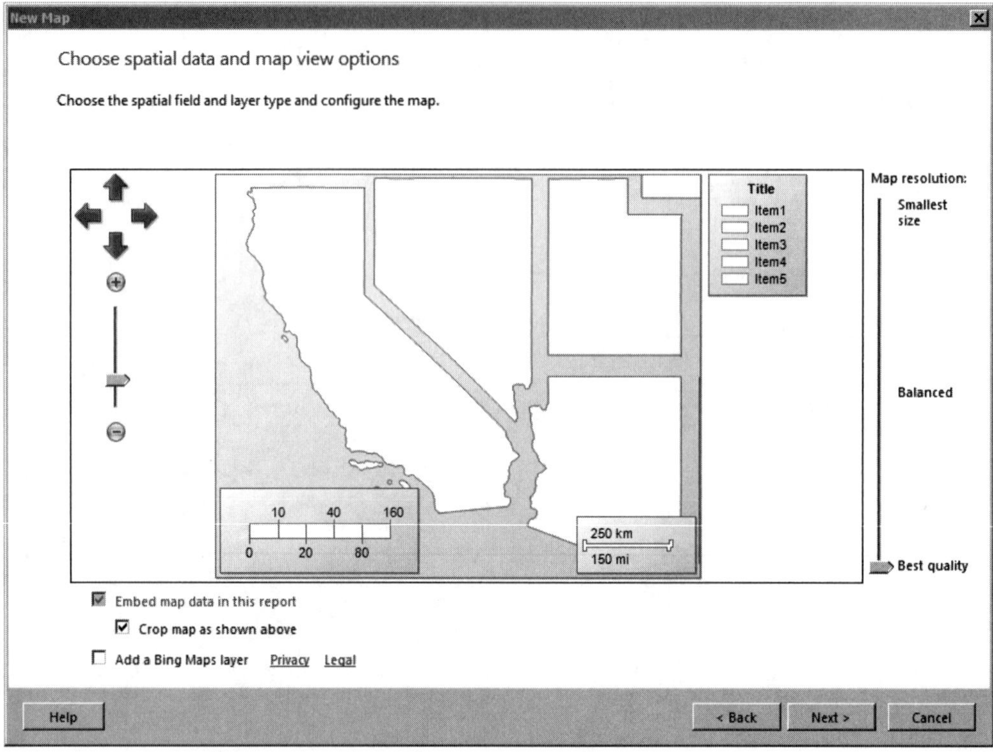

Figure 5-25 *The Map View Options screen*

6. As you see in Figure 5-26, you can choose either a Basic Map (which gives you a simple map), a Color Analytical Map (where you can specify the state colors), or the Bubble Map. In the bubble map you can specify that the size of the bubble is related to a number from your dataset, the color is related to a different data element, and finally the placement of the bubble would be based off of a different data element. Choose Bubble Map and click Next to continue.
7. Since you haven't run a report before (and there are no saved datasets), you should have a screen that is similar to Figure 5-27. Take the default option (which is to create a dataset) and click Next to continue.

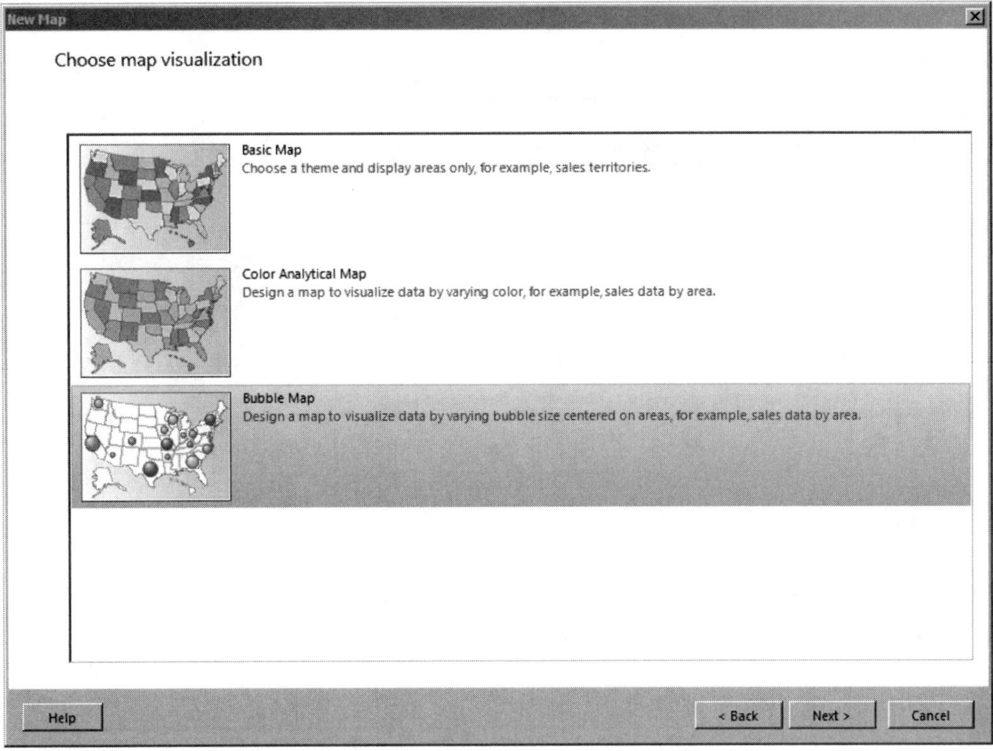

Figure 5-26 *The Choose Map Visualization window*

8. You will next be presented with the Data Source Properties, as shown in Figure 5-28. This is where you specify the connection type (SQL Server, Excel, SQL Azure, etc.) and the connection string. We will use the Build dialog box to build our data source connection string. In the Select Connection Type drop-down list, choose Microsoft SQL Azure. Next click the Build button next to the Connection String box (shown in Figure 5-28).
9. You need to specify the server name (you can obtain this from the SQL Azure developer's portal administration window). The server name should look something like what is depicted in Figure 5-29. The server name is a series of randomly generated letters and numbers followed by .database.windows.net.

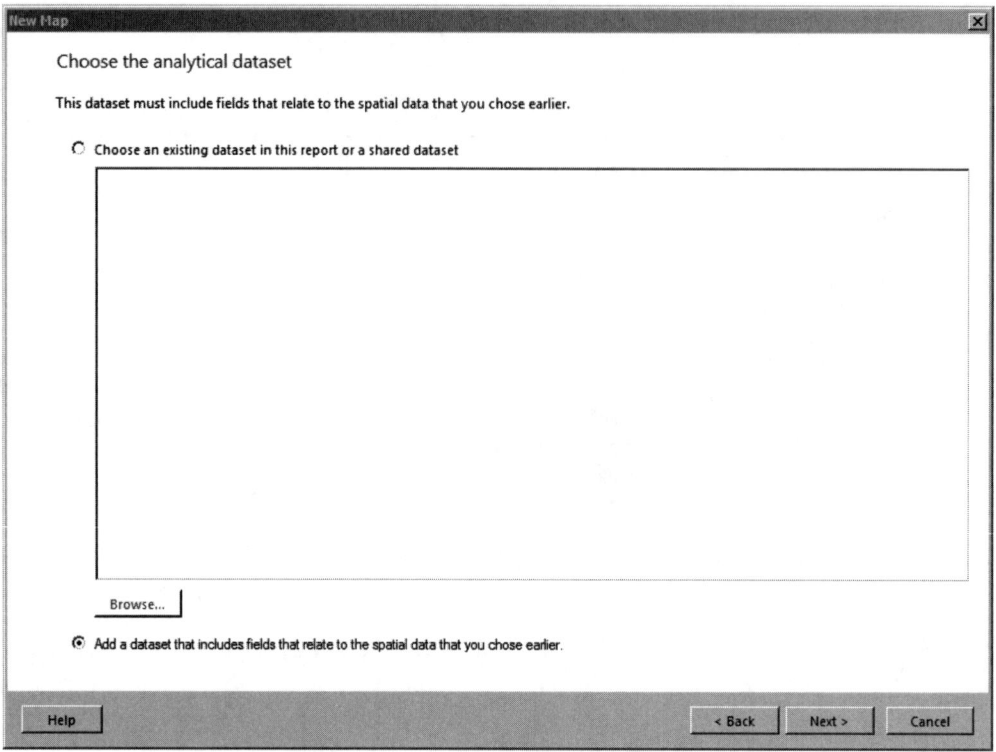

Figure 5-27 *You will need to create a dataset to be used in the report.*

10. Next specify the user name (click Use SQL Server Authentication). You could also find out the user name in the SQL Azure developers' portal. The name should be the user name followed by the @ sign and then the server name; also enter the password (in case you forgot the password, you can reset it in the SQL Azure developers' portal).
11. You will then need to put in the database name, **Adventureworkslt**, in the drop-down list box. Then click OK to continue. Note that in the version of Report Builder 3.0 that we are using, the database name does not populate any of the databases from Azure (you need to type the database in).

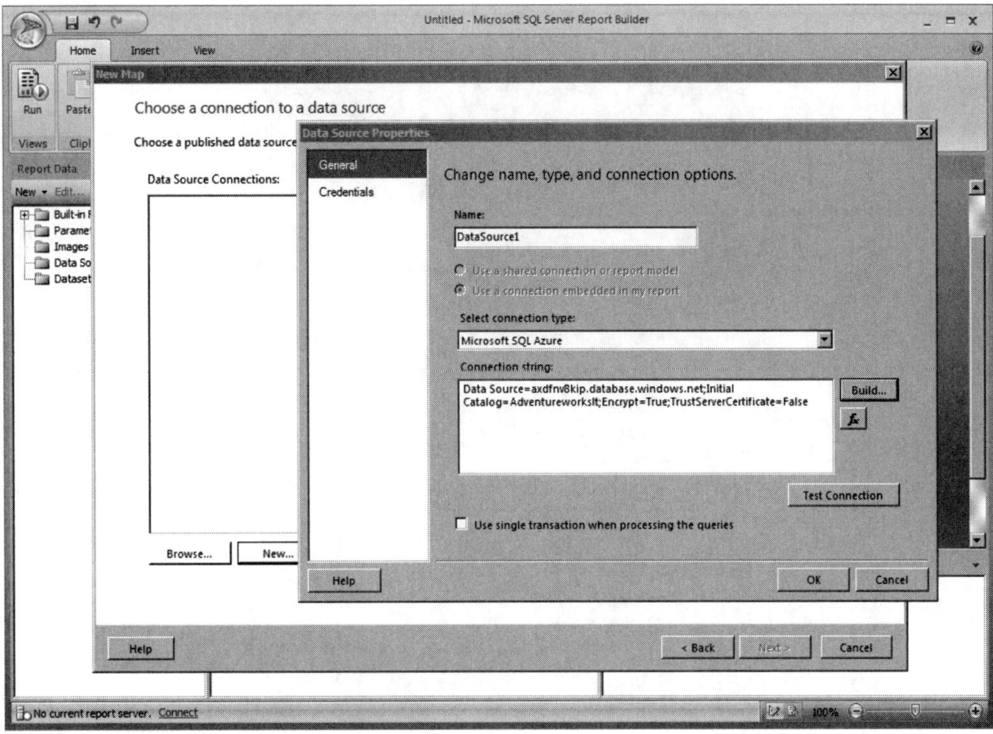

Figure 5-28 *The Data Source Properties window*

12. You should then be placed back in the Data Connections Properties window. Click OK to continue and now the new data source connection should appear in the Choose A Connection To A Data Source window.
13. Choose Next to continue (as shown in Figure 5-30).

    Notice the Query Designer then launches. You can choose as many data elements as you want, but for this example only select 3.
14. You will be presented with the Query Designer window shown in Figure 5-31. Choose from the Address table the column StateProvince and from the SalesOrderHeader table the CustomerID and TotalDue columns.

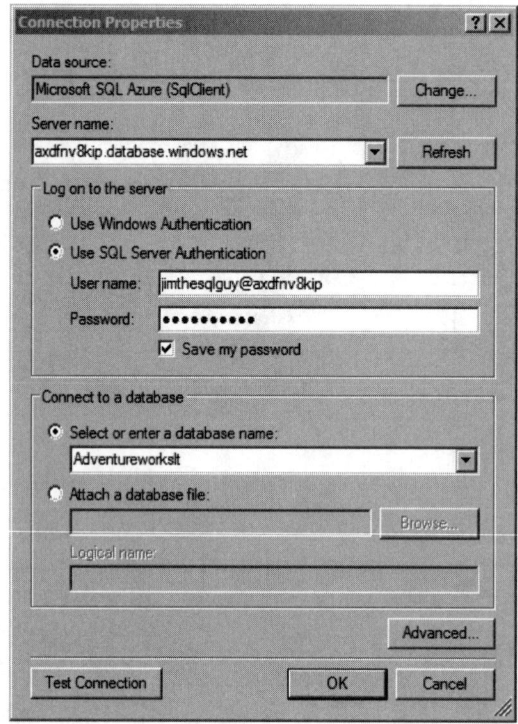

Figure 5-29 *The Connection Properties window*

15. After you choose the columns you want in the report, you will notice that they appear in the Selected Fields window. Choose the TotalDue column and change the Aggregate function to Sum, and in the CustomerID field, change the aggregate to Count. Choose Next to continue.
16. In order to link the data elements that we have chosen in our report to the map, we need to link the state data element in the address to the map state name element. Choose the Statename and in the drop-down list box under Analytical Dataset Fields choose StateProvince. Notice that the Statename in the Spatial Data field matches the StateProvince field. Click Next to continue.

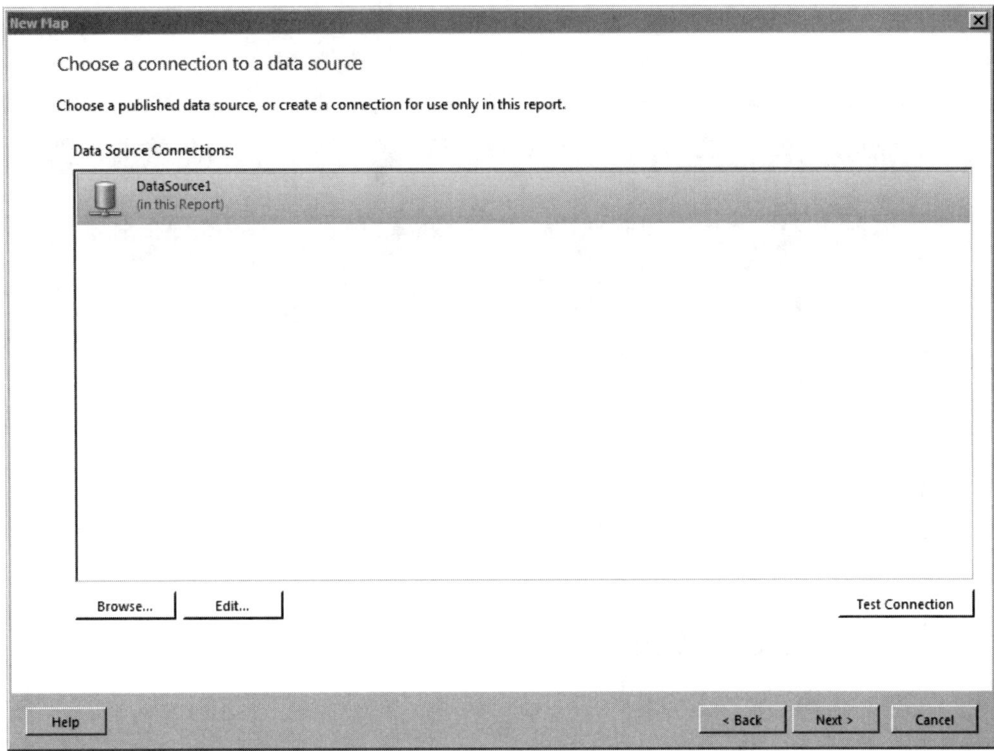

Figure 5-30 *The Choose A Connection window populated with the data source we just connected*

17. You will next have to choose what you want the size of the bubbles to represent, the colors the bubbles to represent, and whether you want to display the data labels or not. In our example we would like the size of the bubble to represent the amount of money that is due and the color would represent the number of customers. We would also like the colors to go from light (fewer) to dark (more) customers. We would also like to have the number of customers displayed on the map.
18. In the New Map Layer window shown in Figure 5-33, choose the Sum of Total Due in the Use Bubble Sizes To Visualize Data drop-down list and then check the box next to Use Polygon Colors To Visualize Data and choose the Sum of Count of Customer_ID from the drop-down list box and change the Color Rule to Light-Dark.

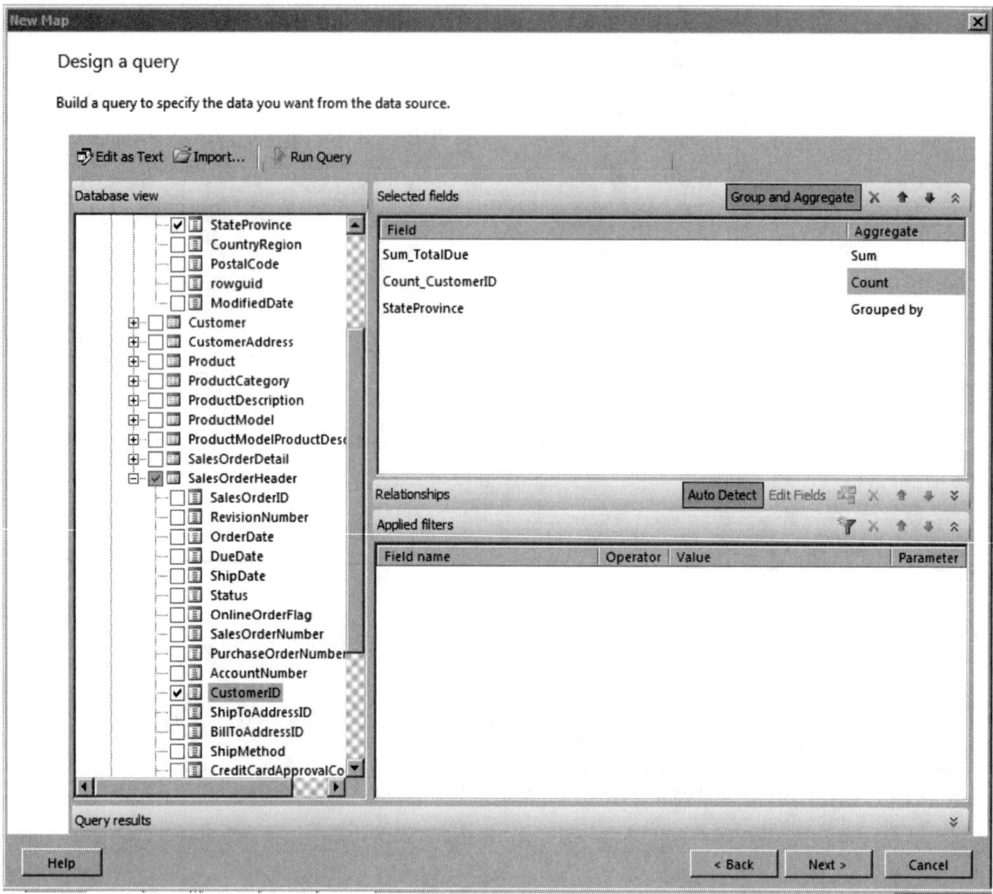

Figure 5-31 *The Query Designer window*

19. Next choose the check box next to the Display Labels field and choose the Sum of the Count of CustomerIDs and choose Finish.

    You will next be placed in the Report Builder design screen. In the design screen you can change anything about the report (as a matter of fact, you can create the map report without going through the wizard).

20. In the design screen choose to run the report (as shown in Figure 5-34).

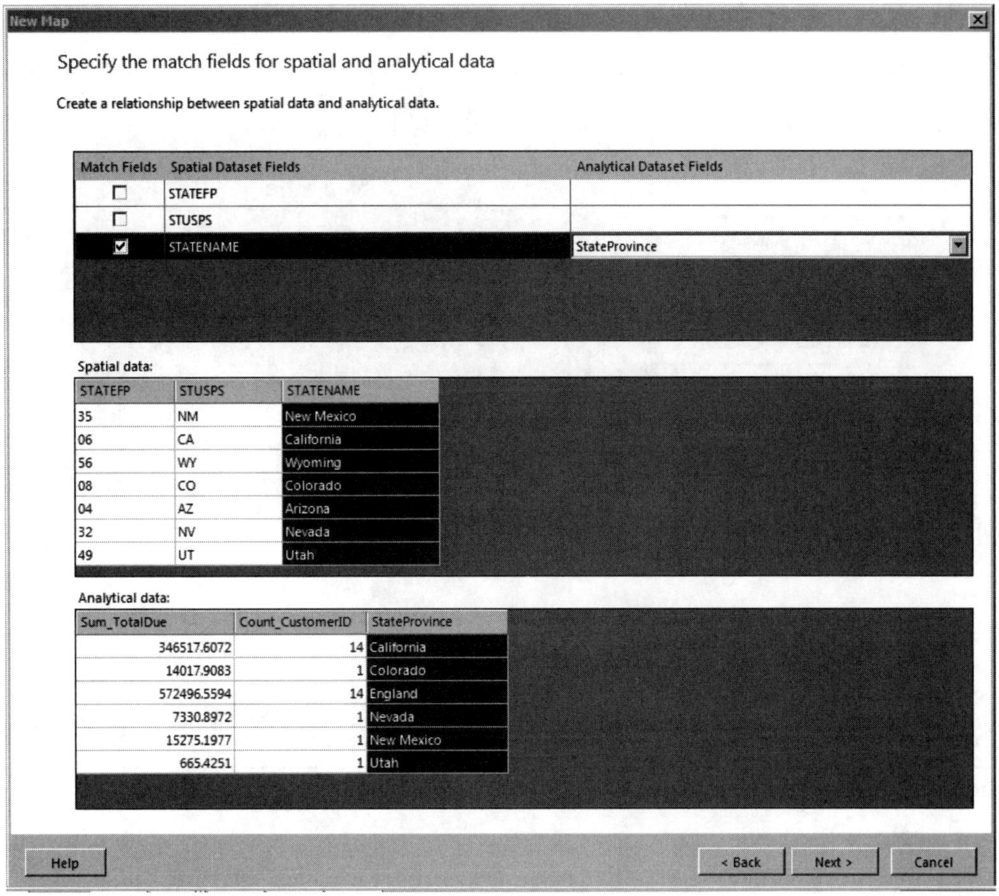

New Map

Specify the match fields for spatial and analytical data

Create a relationship between spatial data and analytical data.

Match Fields	Spatial Dataset Fields	Analytical Dataset Fields
☐	STATEFP	
☐	STUSPS	
☑	STATENAME	StateProvince

Spatial data:

STATEFP	STUSPS	STATENAME
35	NM	New Mexico
06	CA	California
56	WY	Wyoming
08	CO	Colorado
04	AZ	Arizona
32	NV	Nevada
49	UT	Utah

Analytical data:

Sum_TotalDue	Count_CustomerID	StateProvince
346517.6072	14	California
14017.9083	1	Colorado
572496.5594	14	England
7330.8972	1	Nevada
15275.1977	1	New Mexico
665.4251	1	Utah

Help < Back Next > Cancel

Figure 5-32 *The linking screen*

BI TIP

You do not have to go through the wizard each time you would like a report (but it is pretty easy); you could cancel out of the wizard and create the report without the wizard.

You will notice that in Figure 5-35, there are only a few states that are populated with data; this is because we used the smaller AdventureWorksLT sample. You can duplicate this same report with the full Adventure Works dataset if you wish. The data make take a little longer to load up and some of the data elements are a little different, but the principles are the same.

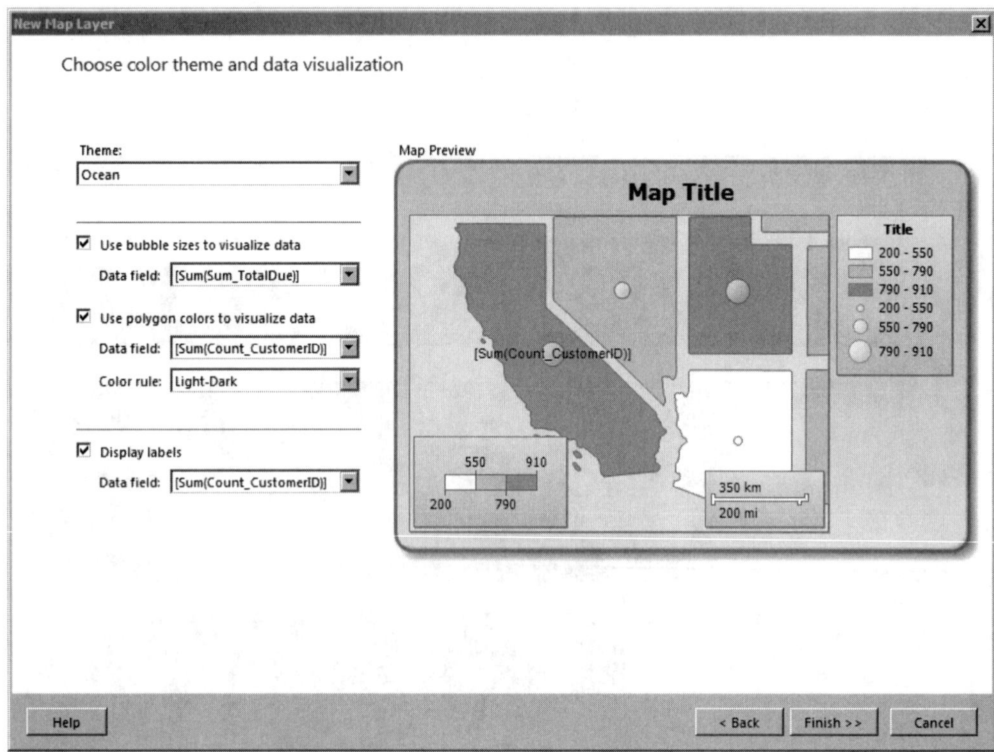

Figure 5-33 *Choosing the theme and visualization*

As hopefully you have seen in this example, working with SQL Azure is relatively easy. It is not hard to get the data into SQL Azure or to use existing tools to get data out of SQL Azure. We should note that this chapter was not meant to provide exhaustive coverage of SQL Azure (We're sure that there will be several entire books dedicated to SQL Azure); rather, it was meant to cover some of the topics surrounding SQL Azure and to demonstrate some of the power of this platform and where SQL Azure fits with in the cloud.

Windows Azure Platform AppFabric

There are two different AppFabric offerings, one that works within your corporate boundaries (Windows Server AppFabric) and provides services to improve the speed, scale, and management of internal applications as well as web-based applications. Some of these services are caching, service, and workflow management. Another AppFabric product is the Windows Azure platform AppFabric. This AppFabric helps connect on-premises applications with cloud-based applications as well as applications running

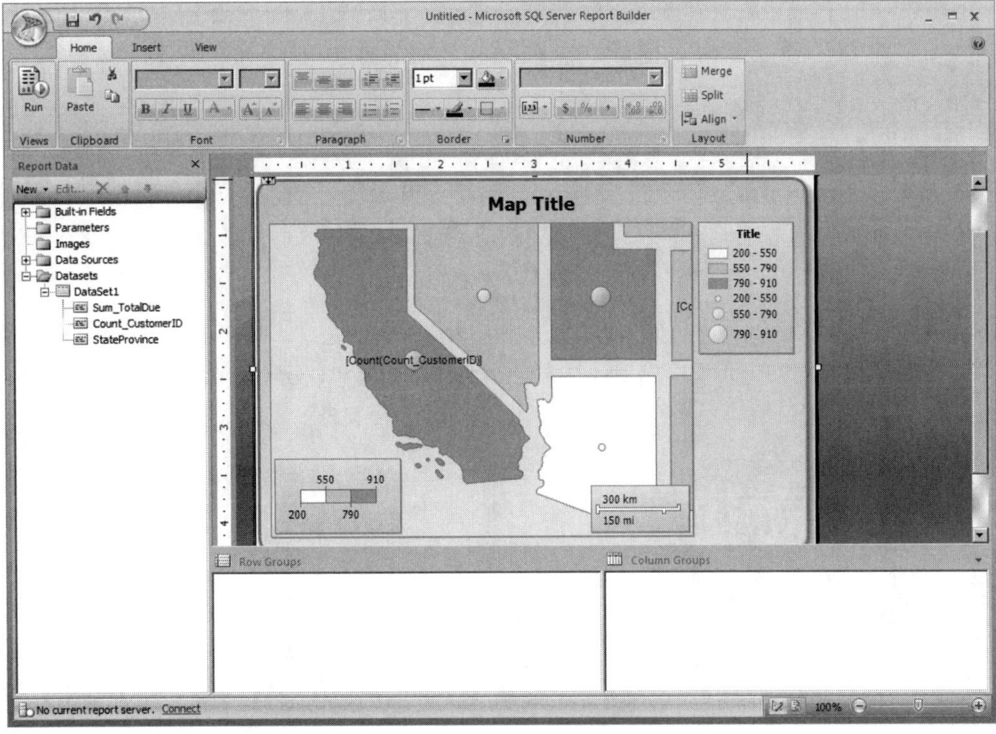

Figure 5-34 *The Report Builder 3.0 design screen*

on other platforms, including PHP, Java, Ruby, and others. These services empower developers with secure communications and coordination between these different platforms. The AppFabric for Azure enables communication between your on-premises applications and the cloud-based services.

Project Dallas

First, Project Dallas is a product currently in beta intended to provide services based on SQL Azure. Second, this service will most likely not have the name "Project Dallas" when it releases, but what is it? Project Dallas is a code name for a new service that allows people to browse and purchase databases online. Project Dallas will also allow you to advertise and house datasets that you own for sale to potential subscribers.

This product is really good for working on data mash-ups. What is a data mash-up? This is where you have different data elements presented together (and in turn these different elements help you gain an understanding of the data or the problem presented). In the example that you just saw, you were given the ability to have different

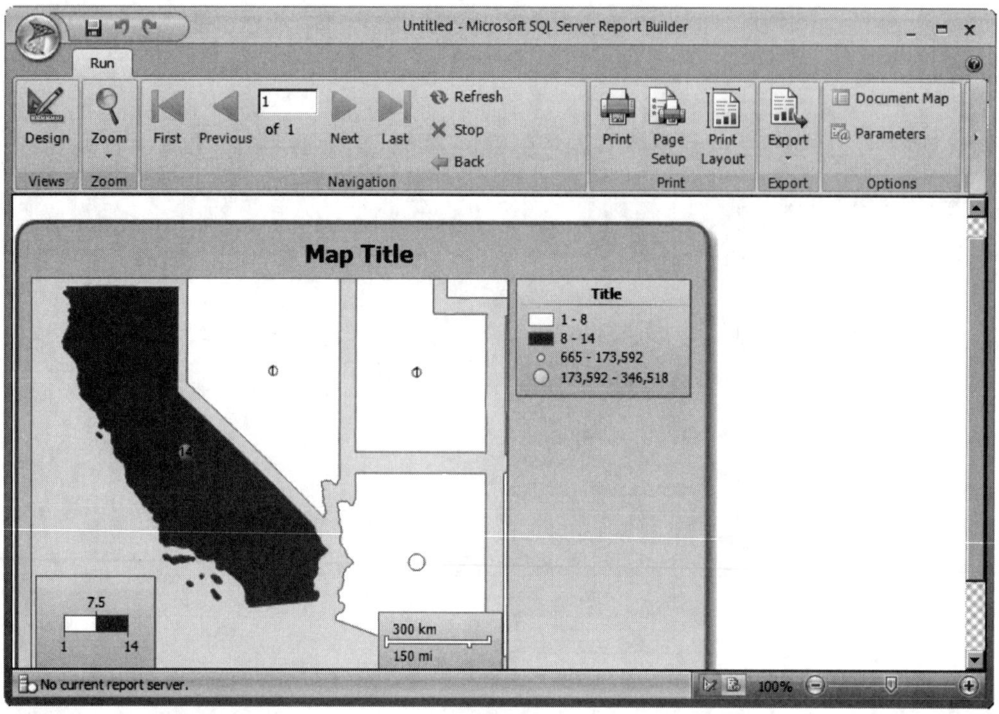

Figure 5-35 *Report Output*

layers of data presented on top of a map image. This is a type of data mash-up, but several others are presented in this book. In Chapter 7, for example, there is a great tool called PowerPivot. PowerPivot gives you the ability to pull in different data sources to be presented inside of Microsoft Excel. In Chapter 4, you learn about the abilities that Reporting Services gives you. With these different datasets that are available from Project Dallas combined with your own data, you can start experimenting with some of the tools that are presented in this book, and so you are well on your way to creating your own data mash-ups. In the initial beta of Project Dallas the datasets are limited, but these will expand over time. One example of using these datasets is provided by OnTerra Systems LLC, a company that specializes in delivering geospatial solutions. This example uses several Microsoft solutions (Microsoft Silverlight, Microsoft Bing Maps, and Project Dallas). This example application was developed with Microsoft Silverlight, which is used to view dynamic web content. The Bing Maps application was used as the geospatial component that gives you the mapping capability, and finally the data comes from Project Dallas. The dataset used is one of the example datasets that was published by a partner (Data.gov) in this case. The data contains the crime data for each state for the years 2006 and 2007. Wouldn't it be great if there were a tool that easily allowed us to combine different datasets and to visualize the data? (Check out Chapter 7 on Microsoft PowerPivot, and yes, you can connect directly from PowerPivot to Project Dallas data feeds.)

This example is based in a web site (http://silverlight.onterrasys.com/crimedemo) and we will demonstrate how you can use the site to view the data. In this case OnTerra used some code to present some Project Dallas data inside of Silverlight (and also used Bing Maps) to demonstrate how crime data can be presented in a very user friendly environment.

1. First launch a web browser and put in the address: **http://silverlight.onterrasys.com/crimedemo** (your screen should be similar to what is shown in Figure 5-36). You will need to have Microsoft Silverlight installed to be able to view this demo. If you do not have Silverlight installed, the page will prompt you to install Silverlight or you can download Silverlight from www.microsoft.com/silverlight.
2. In the Menu page on the web page choose the state of California from the state drop-down list box and choose Violent Crime from the Data drop-down list box. You should see what is depicted in Figure 5-37.

   This example web page pulls in elements from the United States Data.gov site as well as Bing Maps (which also has elements from other mapping solutions). As a developer, you can choose to include additional layers on top of the Bing Map.

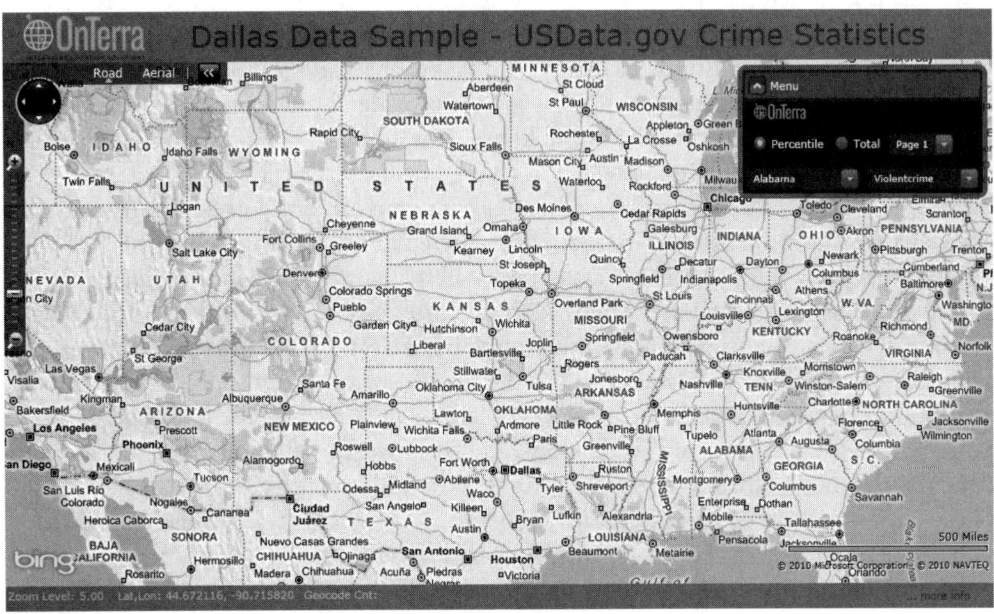

Figure 5-36 *The OnTerra LLC example page*

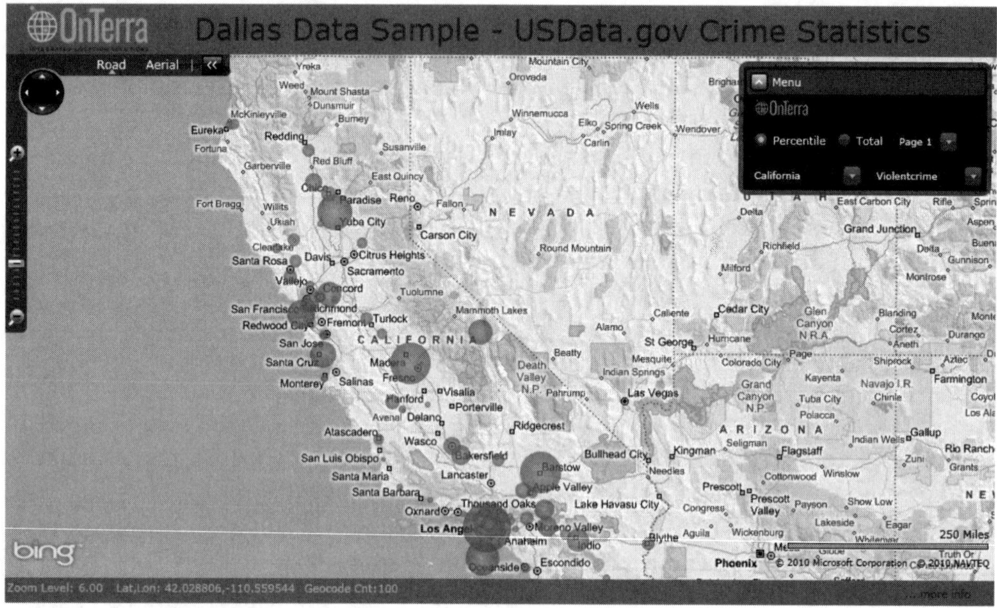

Figure 5-37 *Crime statistics for California*

Dallas is a service that is available in Azure and may be one of many services that sit on top of Azure. In the coming years we believe that there will be additional services. Hopefully Dallas will continue to thrive (and be given a name). Project Dallas should be attractive to the end consumer as well as data providers. It does not cost very much for your database to be consumed or published. It is also easy for a developer to gain access to this data. If you are interested in trying out Project Dallas, launch a web browser and connect to www.sqlazureservices.com. You can browse the databases that are available (since the product is still in beta, there are not a lot of databases listed). I am sure that once this product releases, there will be many more databases available.

The Project Dallas database catalog is shown in Figure 5-38. In order to utilize any of these datasets, you need an account. After you have set up an Azure account, you can subscribe to any of these datasets and use them with several different tools. You could write a web service to pull data from Project Dallas, or you could use a data analysis tool (such as the one depicted in Chapter 7 called PowerPivot). However you use the data, you will hopefully find a repository that is useful for your type of business (such as the ones that were shown in Figures 5-36 and 5-37, where the data elements were populated from Project Dallas and displayed in a web browser.

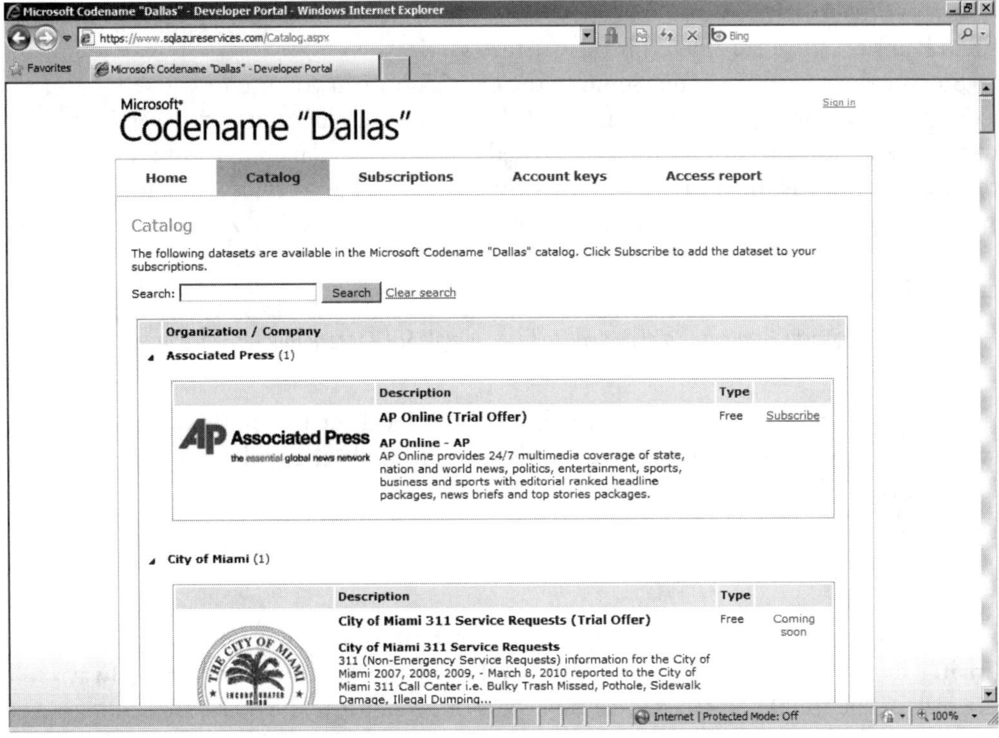

Figure 5-38 *The Project Dallas database catalog*

Infrastructure as a Service

In information technology, the infrastructure components are the routers, switches, and other pieces that make up the physical infrastructure. One of these pieces of physical infrastructure is the desktop PC or laptop that is on the user's desk. Instead of having a physical machine sitting on your desktop, with IaaS, you could have your desktop be virtualized. In this scenario you would be able to connect to your desktop via a browser or a thin client device (such as a terminal). This type of activity would allow you to move from place to place without having to take your desktop or laptop with you. It would also enable some activities that are cumbersome for information technology departments to do today, such as backup/recover of desktops.

There are components of Infrastructure as a Service that are available in BPOS, some in Azure and some in other hosted offerings. We are sure that you will continue to see offerings in Azure that may provide additional infrastructure services, such as hosting virtual machines. Some of the BPOS functions such as hosting Exchange or SharePoint could be considered infrastructure services.

So now that you understand some of the cloud, how can you use it?

As of the writing of this chapter, the SQL Azure data synchronization services were in beta. This meant that they are hosted up on www.sqlazurelabs.com. One of the services there is the SQL Azure Data Sync Service. This service will allow you to synchronize data from your local version of SQL Server to SQL Azure.

BI TIP

SQL Azure Data Synchronization also allows you to keep multiple SQL Azure databases synchronized.

This is a service that keeps data which is in your local version of SQL Server synchronized with SQL Azure data. This is very similar to the replication capability inside of SQL Server.

Wrap-Up

In order for some of these technologies to take off, consumers will have to adjust (mainly by showing trust). As a consumer, you need a service that is reliable (always there all of the time) and secure (from hackers or even just malicious activities). You need to be able to monitor activity, audit transactions, and be notified of suspicious activity. While there are some tools available for monitoring and controlling the services inside of the cloud, we believe that there will be continued development in this area.

Hopefully we have been able to take some of mystery out of the cloud services offerings that are available from Microsoft. We are sure that these services will continue to evolve and some of the services that are currently in development will launch. Steve Ballmer said that 70 percent of Microsoft is working on "the cloud," so you should believe that some very compelling solutions are coming down the line. We are sure that consumers may not like all of the services, but we are sure that there will be quite a few that will change the way that we are working and using data today. We are also sure that the current Azure offerings will continue to be enhanced for some time to come. It is only a matter of time before we will anticipate updated cloud services as we do the next version of Exchange or SQL.

Since Azure has only been out a few months and some of the services that we were demonstrating ("Project Dallas") may change, we will keep www.officebicentral.com updated with the cloud services that are available, and just in case "Project Dallas" does receive a name, we will have a note up there (along with any other errata from this or other chapters in this book).

Chapter 6

Data Mining: Real-World Techniques

In This Chapter

- ► So What Is Data Mining Anyway?
- ► First Steps First: What Is the Data Mining Add-in?
- ► Extended Data Mining Add-In
- ► Wrap-UP

"Information is data endowed with relevance and purpose. Converting data into information thus requires knowledge. And knowledge, by definition, is specialized. In fact, truly knowledgeable people tend toward overspecialization, whatever their field, precisely because there is always so much more to know."

—Peter Drucker, "The Coming of the New Organization," *Harvard Business Review*, January–February 1998

In the past decade there has been an explosion of data, and this shouldn't be a surprise to anyone. What has been surprising is how slow the progress has been in implementing new tools to facilitate better data analysis. The primary goal of this chapter is to show you several techniques that allow you to analyze large sets of data and show you hidden patterns in your data (and hopefully aid you in your decisions). Almost everyone is in some kind of database, probably in several thousand databases (some known and some unknown). If you call or answer the phone, browse the Internet, pay your taxes, take a survey, or buy something, then chances are that data is stored about you in a database somewhere. Databases store all sorts of relational data, blob data (such as binary files), XML data, geographic data, and even more. Since companies are storing more and different types of data, the sizes of databases have increased from megabytes to gigabytes to terabytes and now petabytes (10^{15} or 1,000,000,000,000,000 bytes).

Today, with SQL Server 2008 R2 and Excel 2010, knowledge workers can analyze these incredibly large data repositories with easy-to-understand graphic visualizations like we see in this illlustration:

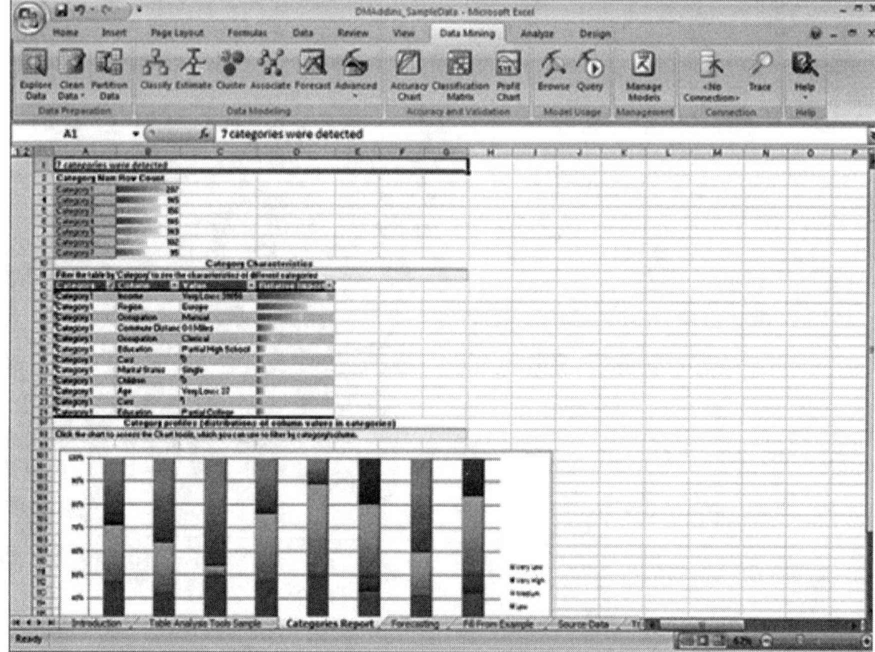

So now, what are people and companies doing with all of this data? Hopefully, companies are finding new and innovative ways to analyze this information to better serve their customers. If companies aren't looking for ways to do things better, faster, or cheaper, then they will quickly find themselves outpaced by their competition. The insight that Peter Drucker has in the quote at the beginning of this chapter from 1998 speaks to the concept of turning data into information and the required specialization. Today, due to several factors, people are required to know as much as the specialist while dealing with an ever-building volume of data. We are very fortunate that the tools that facilitate analysis have become easier. One area, which has seen a lot of specialization, is the field of data mining. A lot of people have been put off by the complex tools and algorithms that they thought this field required. Today, data mining is becoming even easier and is being included in several tools that you may already use.

This chapter demonstrates techniques intended to show how easy data mining can be. Hopefully by the end of this chapter, you will be able to get started using your own data in new and meaningful ways.

So What Is Data Mining Anyway?

Similar to the definition of data warehousing in the late 1990s, the term *data mining* has continued to evolve over time. There are some people who take the statistical definition or the multivariate analysis approach, while others speak to the ability of uncovering hidden patterns in your data. We shouldn't limit data mining to only these definitions; we should continue to expand these definitions to include several additional capabilities. A common misconception is that data mining has to be hard or requires specialized tools. We will go through several data mining techniques using existing tools, such as Microsoft Excel or Microsoft Visio. This chapter is intended as an introduction, so we will start off easy. At some point in their lives, most data processing professionals have had to perform some kind of analysis on a large dataset. (Wouldn't it be great if we could automate this?) It would also be great if we could feed our data into a system and then have it return with something interesting. While data mining isn't quite this simple, with the tools available today it doesn't have to be much harder.

If you are like almost everyone else in the technology industry, you receive a lot of junk mail. You may look at some of this junk mail and wonder how you were picked to receive it, but other times it may look interesting. If you dig deeper into the source of some of this junk mail, you may discover that your receiving it may have been due to your previous buying patterns or a questionnaire that you have filled out. If you were to consider buying something from this junk mail, or actually going ahead and making a purchase, then the companies have successfully targeted you. This is one type of activity that data mining helps facilitate, uncovering higher-potential customers from a larger set of customers (targeting). Another example where data mining can help is with analysis of large volumes of data for specific buying patterns. Imagine that you have a dataset that lists out 30 or so columns of data about purchasers of a product you are selling. Your goal is to uncover something that differentiates buyers from non-buyers; this is another potential fit for data mining.

So Where Can You Use Data Mining?

In short, everywhere! There are very few projects where data mining can't provide some level of assistance. You don't need to worry; you don't have to have any specialized tools or even specialized training or experience in order to use data mining in your project. You can start mining data with a familiar tool from Microsoft called Excel. Excel is part of the Microsoft Office suite of products. If you do not have Microsoft Office, there is an evaluation edition available from the site www.microsoft.com/office. There are times and projects where you will be required to use complex or customized tools to facilitate deeper contextual analysis of your data, but not all of the time. In the following examples we will be using an Excel add-in to help predictive data analysis. You aren't required to have a high level of proficiency with Excel. We have endeavored to make the samples as realistic to real data as possible. With just a few mouse clicks, you can create analysis as depicted in Figure 6-1.

First Steps First: What Is the Data Mining Add-In?

Microsoft Excel is an extremely versatile and powerful tool. There are people who use Excel for its financial worksheet functions, but there are many other people who use Excel for a lot more. I have seen Excel used for personal calendar management, project management, database design, and many other purposes. Although at first glance this may be akin to using a screwdriver where a hammer is needed, Excel is versatile and extensible enough to be used in many different ways. One area where Excel functionality has continued to mature is for use as a business intelligence client. There are several ways of extending functionality inside of Excel (via new features and also via add-ins).

Microsoft's commitment to product innovation shows through with each new version of Microsoft Excel (also evident in all of the other products inside of the Office suite). Another way to augment the capabilities of Excel is via add-ins that can be either developed or downloaded. One such add-in uncovers Excel's often overlooked SQL Server data mining functionality. (We will also explore another Microsoft add-in in Chapter 7, which covers Microsoft PowerPivot.) Hundreds (if not thousands) of Excel add-ins are currently available, with more being developed every day.

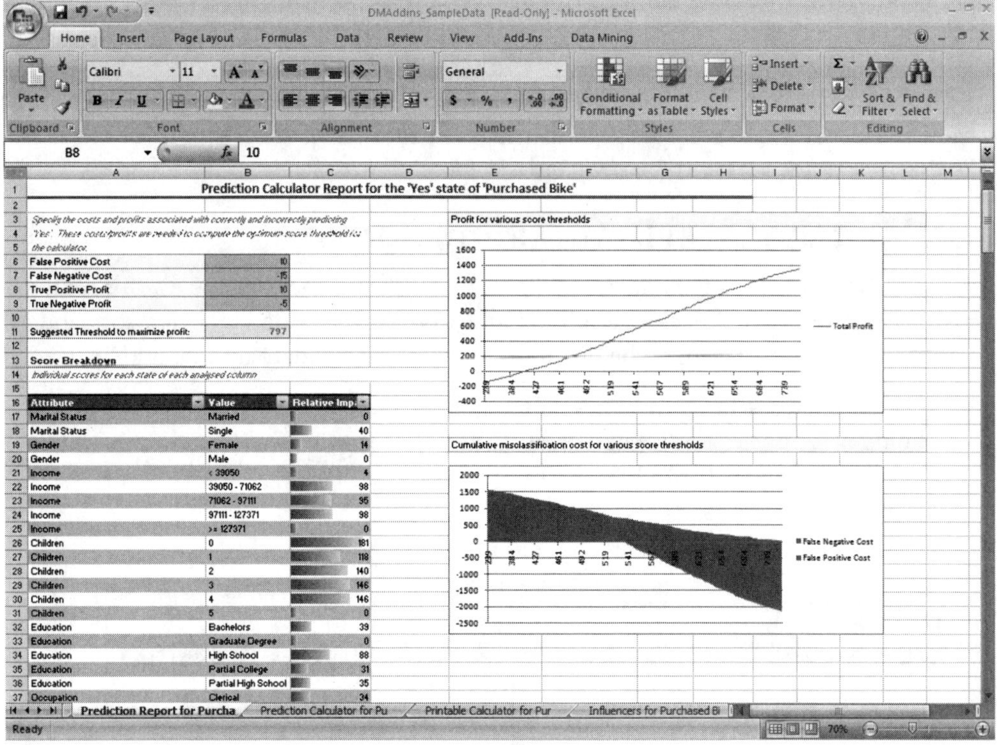

Figure 6-1 *Creating analysis in Microsoft Excel*

BI TIP

In Visual Studio 2010 there is better support for creating add-ins for the Microsoft Office suite, including Microsoft Excel. In the prior versions of Visual Studio, you need VSTO (Visual Studio Tools for Office) to develop add-ins.

Where Is the Excel Data Mining Add-In Available From?

All kinds of add-ins are available from the Microsoft web site dedicated to Excel and other Office products in the Office marketplace. You can go to the Office marketplace at www.microsoft.com/office and search for the data mining add-in. Since the web link for downloading this particular add-in keeps changing, we will put the add-in location up at www.officebicentral.com. You will need to know the version of SQL Server you are running. If you are not running SQL Server, then there is an evaluation edition of SQL Server available from www.microsoft.com/sql.

BI TIP

The Excel 2010 data mining add-in is only available for the 32-bit version of Microsoft Office 2010, which is not a problem, since you can run the 32-bit version of Microsoft Office 2010 with either a 32-bit or a 64-bit version of Windows Server 2008 (or Windows 7) and SQL Server 2008 R2.

Installing the Excel Data Mining Add-In

You can either download the add-in or run it directly from the web site. In this section we will be installing the Excel data mining add-in that is provided by Microsoft, and Figure 6-2 shows how we start the download process for the data mining add-in.

1. Connect to www.microsoft.com and search on the term "data mining add-in." You should also append the version of SQL Server that you would like to use. (Note that this add-in is only available with SQL Server 2005, 2008 and SQL 2008 R2.)

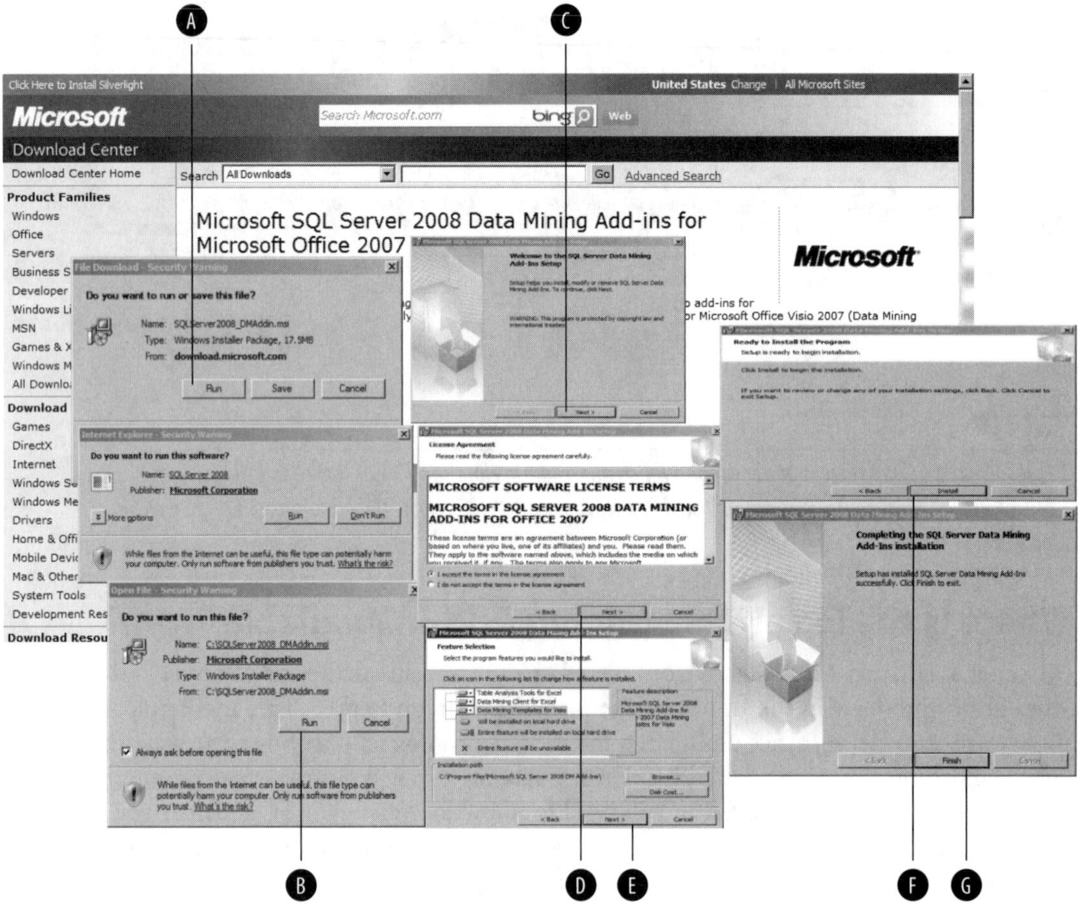

Figure 6-2 *The initial steps for downloading the data mining add-in*

BI TIP

The SQL 2008 data mining add-in works with SQL 2008 R2, and there have been no enhancements to this add-in as of the time of the writing of this book; so the SQL 2008 and SQL 2008 R2 editions of the add-in are identical.

2. Once you have clicked the web page to download the add-in, you should be presented with a window that asks if you want to Run or Save this file. Click on Run (Step A).
3. After you click Run, when you are presented with another window that asks if you want to run the file, choose Run (Step B).

BI TIP

If you do not have Microsoft Excel installed on your machine, you can obtain a 60-day trial version from www .microsoft.com/office/trial.

4. You should now be presented with a Welcome Wizard screen. Choose Next to continue (Step C).
5. The next screen should be the End User License Agreement (or EULA for short). If you do not accept the license agreement, then you can't use the add-in. Choose "I accept" and then click Next to continue the installation (Step D).
6. The next screen that you should see is the feature selection. Choose to have the features installed. If you also have Visio installed on your machine, also choose to install the Visio add-in features as well. Click Next to continue (Step E).
7. The add-in now has enough information to install. Choose Install (Step F).
8. You should now see the final add-in installation screen. Choose Finish to close the installation wizard (Step G).

Now that we have installed the add-in, you should notice additional programs. If you click Start and then All Programs, you will notice the folder called Microsoft SQL 2008 Data Mining Add-ins (Figure 6-3). If you expand this folder, you will see the programs shown in Table 6-1.

Now choose the Server Configuration Utility as shown in Figure 6-3 (or you can just launch Excel, because the configuration tool should be launched unless you have configured the tool before).

Next we will need to configure the add-in for the Analysis Services configuration. Once you launch the Server Configuration Utility, you will be presented with several screens that help guide you through the configuration utility (Figure 6-4). You will need

Feature	Description
Data Mining Visio Template	This program shows up only if you choose to install the Visio tools inside of the add-in. You would launch this to use Visio to view your mining models.
Getting Started	This is a help file that helps you in using the add-in and all of the functionality.
Help and Documentation	This is where you would view the "Books on line" of this add-in.
Sample Excel Data	This is a sample dataset that is used to demonstrate much of the add-in functionality with sample data.
Server Configuration Utility	This allows you to configure the settings necessary for connecting to SQL Server Analysis Services. If you do not choose to use it directly from the menu, the first time that the add-in is loaded inside of Excel, the add-in will prompt you for the required settings.

Table 6-1 *Features That Were Installed with the Data Mining Add-In*

to have Administrative access to a SQL Server Analysis Services server because the Data Mining add-in will require a connection to an Analysis Services engine.

1. The first screen is the Welcome screen (A), where you choose Next to continue.
2. You should now see Step 1 of 4 (B), where you choose the server name where the instance of Analysis Services is installed. Note: you should have Administrative access to this instance, since you will be changing a configuration setting on the Analysis Services instance. Choose Next.
3. In Step 2 of 4 (C), you should notice that you need to have "Allow creation of temporary mining models" turned on inside of Analysis Services (this is why you need to be an Administrator of the instance). Choose Next to continue.

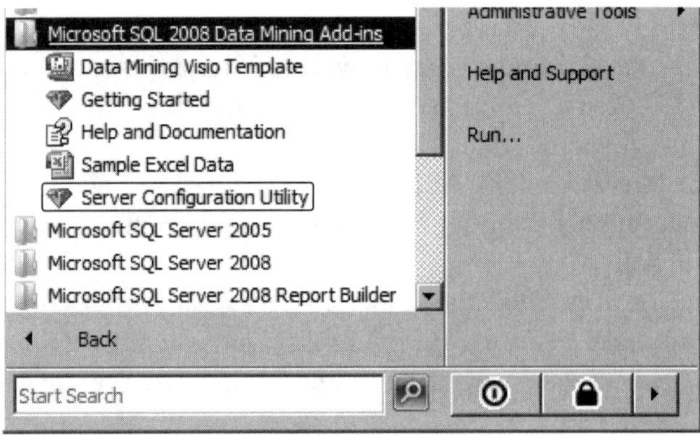

Figure 6-3 *The Server Configuration Utility*

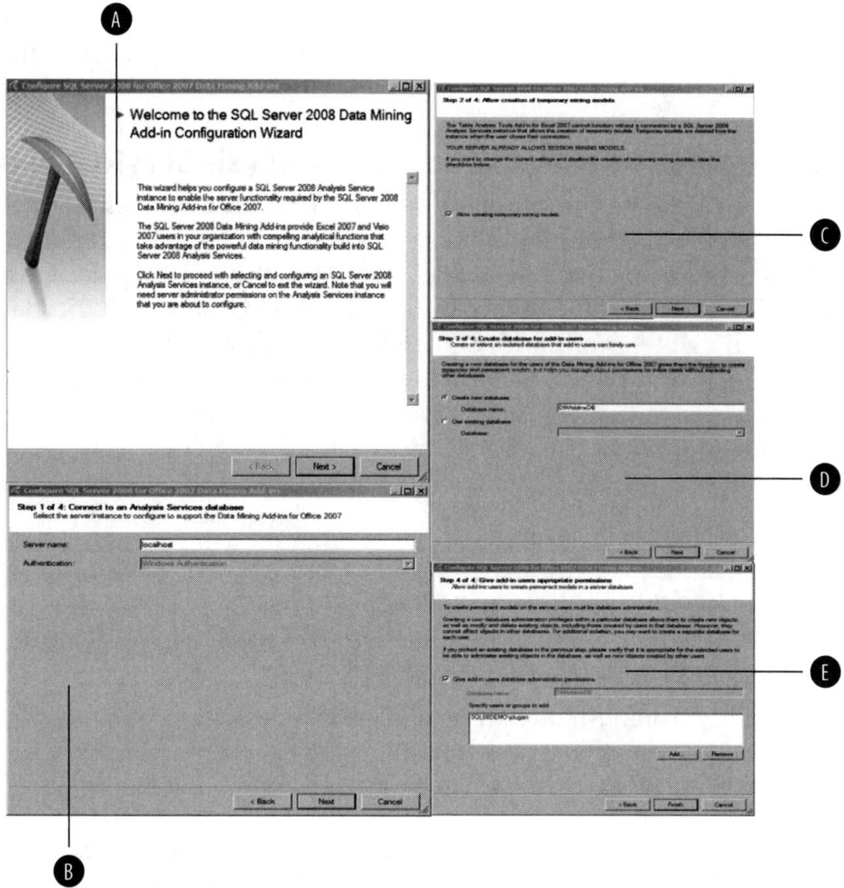

Figure 6-4 *The Server Configuration Wizard*

4. The next window you should see is Step 3 of 4 (D), which allows you to either create a database or connect to an existing database for model creation. If you do not have a database, let the utility create the default database for you (DMAddinsDB). Choose Next to continue.

BI TIP

If you have the sample databases installed on your SQL Server, you can choose to have the data mining add-in point to that database (AdventureWorks or Contoso).

5. You should now see Step 4 of 4 (E). This is the final step of the configuration tool. You should see your user name under users. This screen will try to give the user access to the database that was previously created for your mining models. Choose Finish to continue.

So now you have a new add-in installed inside of Excel. The first time that you run the add-in, you will prompted to configure the add-in to point it to where Analysis Services is installed.

Why Do You Need to Use a SQL Server Analysis Services Server?

The data mining engine is housed inside of Microsoft Analysis Services. Analysis Services is delivered with Microsoft SQL Server (versions 2000, 2005, 2008, and 2008 R2). You need to make sure that you installed the add-in that is appropriate for your version of SQL Server. The 2005 add-in works only with SQL Server 2005, and the 2008 version of the add-in works with SQL 2008 and SQL 2008 R2.

Okay, so now you have the right add-in installed for the correct version of SQL Server. Next you need to configure it. You usually don't have administrative access to the Analysis Services box. If you do have Administrative access, you can follow the wizard to allow the changes necessary to the Analysis Services.

BI TIP

If you want to make the changes yourself (i.e., you are wizard adverse), inside of SQL Management Studio, connect to Analysis Services. Turn on Show Advanced Options, and under DataMining change AllowAdHocOpenRowsetQueries and AllowSessionMiningModels to true.

If you do not have administrative access to the Analysis Services box, you will need to notify the administrators. The wizard will allow you to send an e-mail to your system administrator with the necessary steps. The first step is depicted in Figure 6-5.

1. Choose "Connect to a Microsoft SQL Server 2008 Analysis Services instance to which I have non-administrative access" and click Next to continue.

BI TIP

The wizard also points you to the trial web page (if you don't have SQL installed) or to use an instance that you have administrative authority over. If you are installing on the same box or to a machine that you have administrative authority over, use the second option to install.

2. Now fill out the name and e-mail address of your administrator (and also your name and e-mail) and click Send E-Mail.
3. Now click Close to proceed (as shown in Figure 6-6).

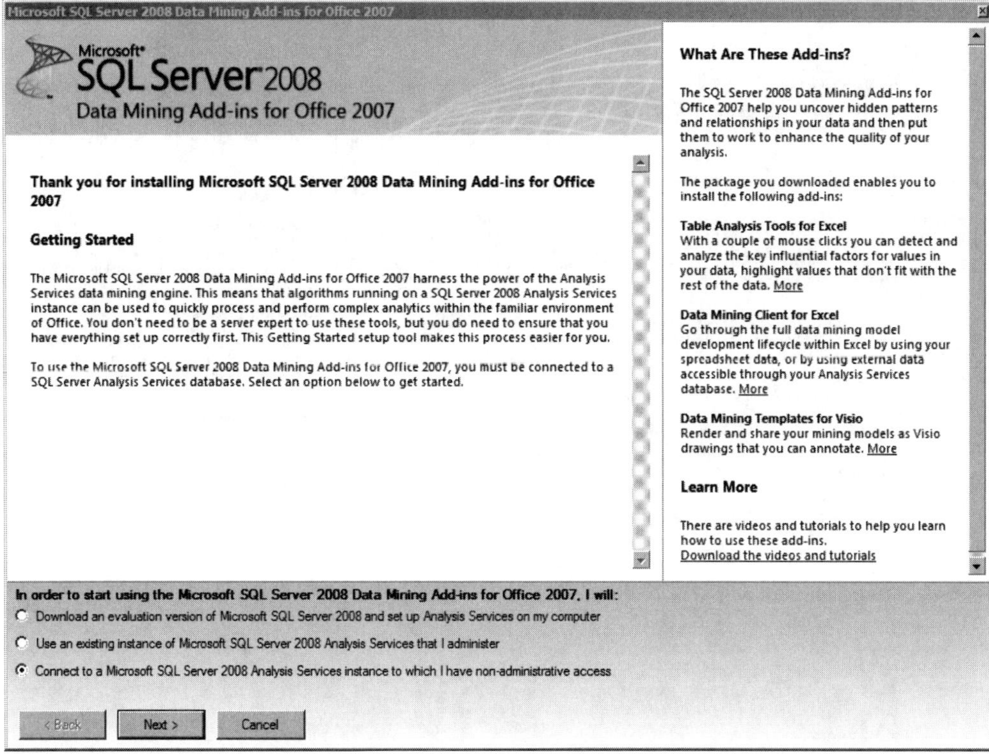

Figure 6-5 *The first step of the Administrative Wizard*

Why Don't I Notice Anything Different?

If you now launch Microsoft Excel, you probably won't notice anything different. This is because in order to use this add-in, the data needs to be formatted as a table inside of Excel. Why is this necessary? The data mining engine (housed inside of SQL Server Analysis Services) expects to deal with data from a relational database and formatted in rows and columns. The Microsoft Excel–formatted table behaves exactly like a relational database record set.

How Do You Format Data as a Table Inside of Excel?

The data mining add-in wants data to be formatted just like a relational database table (rows and columns of data). The only way to ensure that the data is in the right structure is to format the data as a table inside of Excel.

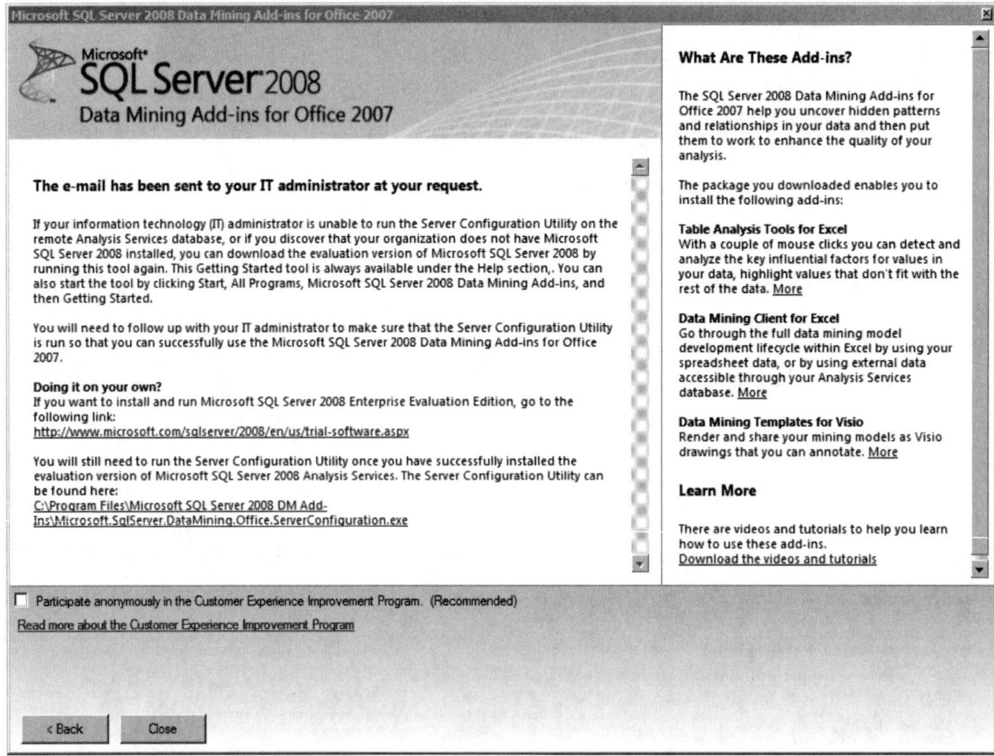

Figure 6-6 *The Administrator mail has been sent.*

There are a couple of ways to format data as a table inside of Excel. On this example spreadsheet I have created a few rows and columns with sample data inside. You would highlight the rows where there is data and press CTRL-T (or choose Insert from the ribbon and then Table). In this case you choose My Table Has Headers and click OK (as shown in Figure 6-7).

1. Highlight the data you would like to make a table and press CTRL-T, or else choose Insert and then Table.
2. Now that you have a created a table, you will notice that when you select the table, the table tools appear at the top of the screen.

You can now use the Excel data mining add-in with any set of data that you want (as long as it is formatted as a table). You should notice two new ribbons installed inside of Excel (as long as you have clicked the table). One of the ribbons is the data mining add-in, and the other is the Analyze ribbon. The Analyze add-in should open

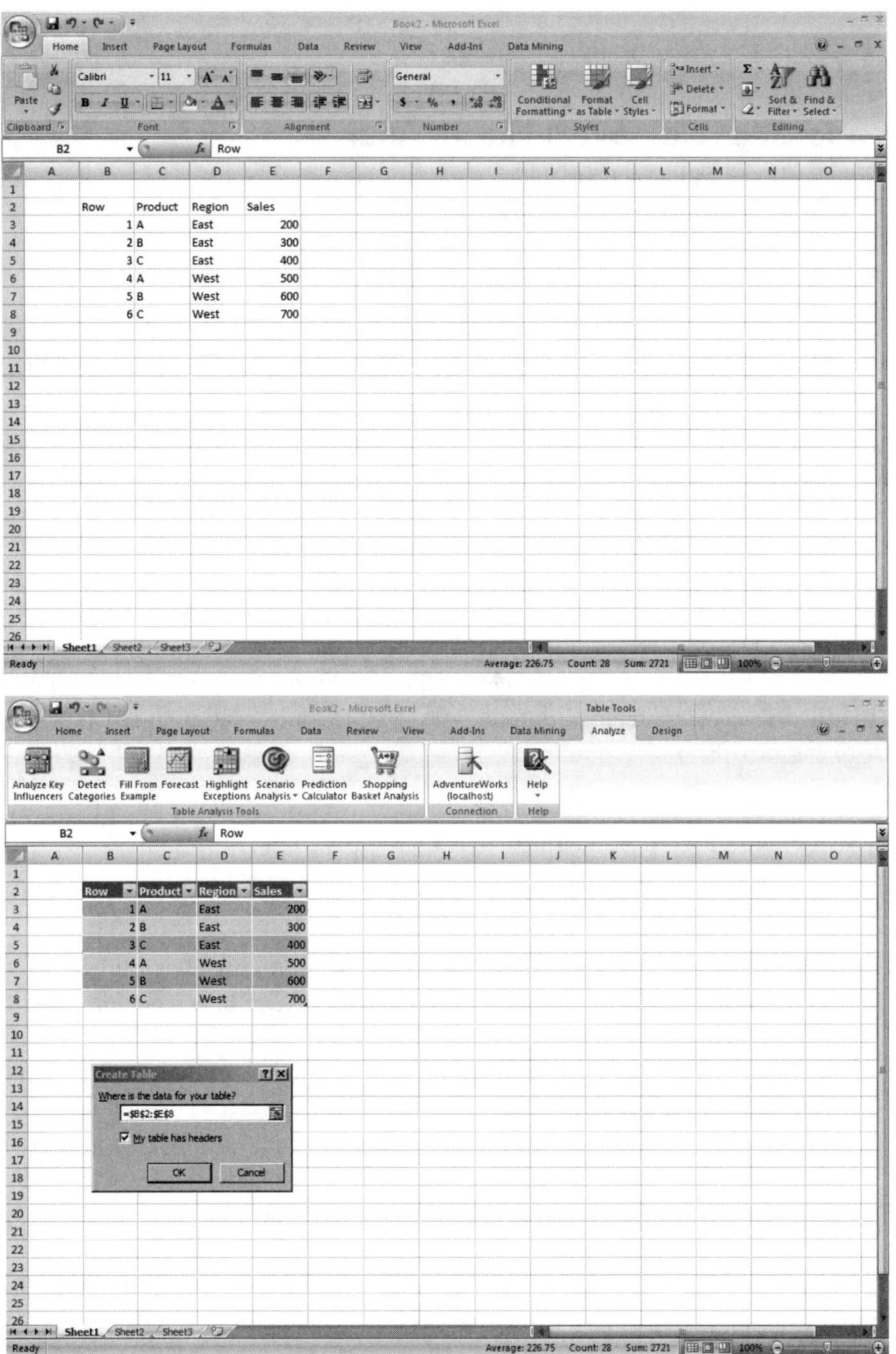

Figure 6-7 *Excel data before and after you make it into a table*

automatically after you create the table. Next we will move on to a scenario where we will use an unformatted text file.

Scenario: Start with a Text File for Analysis

In this scenario we will download a dataset from the web. The dataset contains different characteristics about survivors of the RMS Titanic.

BI TIP

The example spreadsheet that is installed with the add-in is a great example for learning to use the add-in. We want to also show the versatility of this add-in by using it with a text file that was found on the Internet.

The original dataset location is included in the spreadsheet; in this case it is http://biostat.mc.vanderbilt.edu/twiki/bin/view/Main/DataSets?CGISESSID=10713f6d891653ddcbb7ddbdd9cffb79.

This site was kind enough to include the file in .xls (Excel) format, but we won't be using that for this demonstration. Since most samples are in text files, we will start out with the .txt (Text) file. This file is formatted in Quote Comma Delimited (CSV) format. This means that the column values are separated by commas and the text is delimited with double quotes. First save this file somewhere on your machine. (In most browsers all you have to do is right-click the file and choose where to save it.) Then open the file in Excel and change the file type to text. You should then see a window similar to Figure 6-8.

1. Once you have downloaded the add-in, open up the text file. From Microsoft Excel, choose File from the menu and then Open.
2. In the Open dialog box, click Open (Step A).
3. Select Next to continue formatting the text file (Step B).
4. Choose Comma as the delimiter (Step C) and choose Next to continue.
5. Now choose the Finish button to proceed (Step D). You have now imported the text file into Excel.
6. Click the data inside of Excel and choose the entire dataset by pressing CTRL-A (this should choose the entire dataset).
7. Next click CTRL-T to format the data as a table. You should then be prompted with the pop-up window shown in Figure 6-9.
8. Ensure that the check box is selected for My Table Has Headers and click OK.

After you click OK, your Excel worksheet should look like Figure 6-10. If you haven't configured the add-in to point to a database server, you should set the Analysis Services database and server.

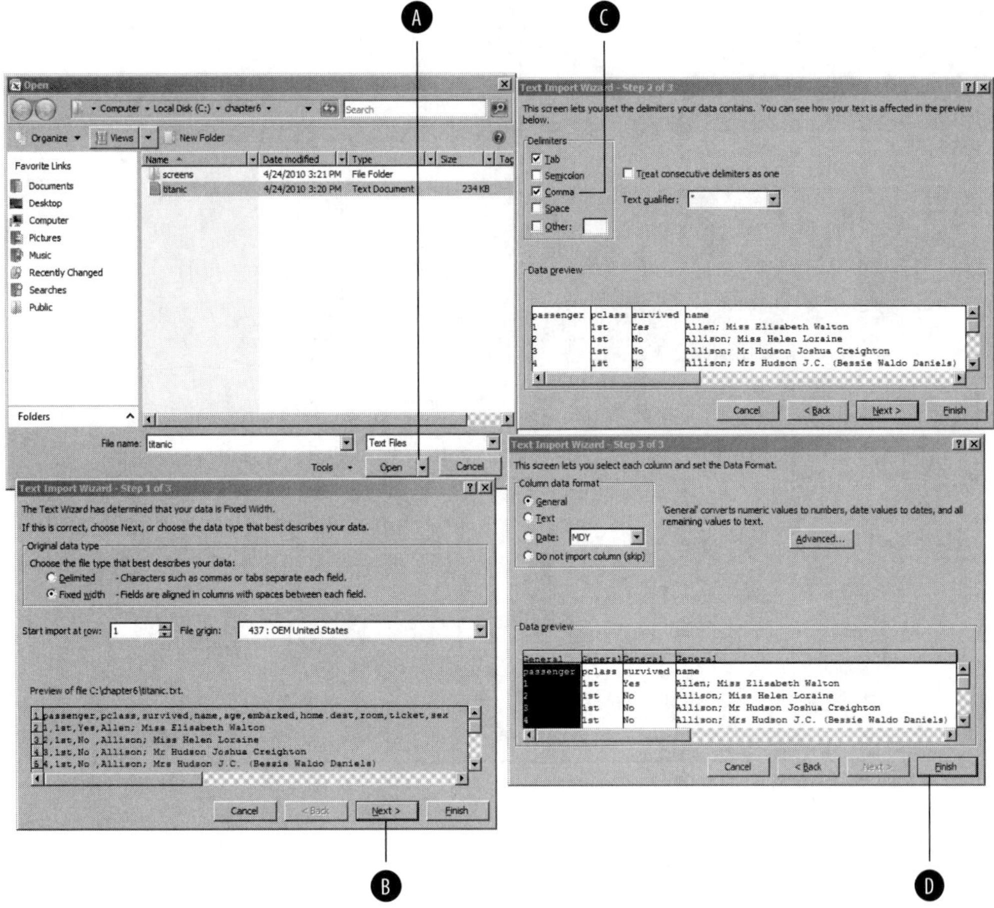

Figure 6-8 *The steps to import a text file*

Figure 6-9 *More steps to import a text file*

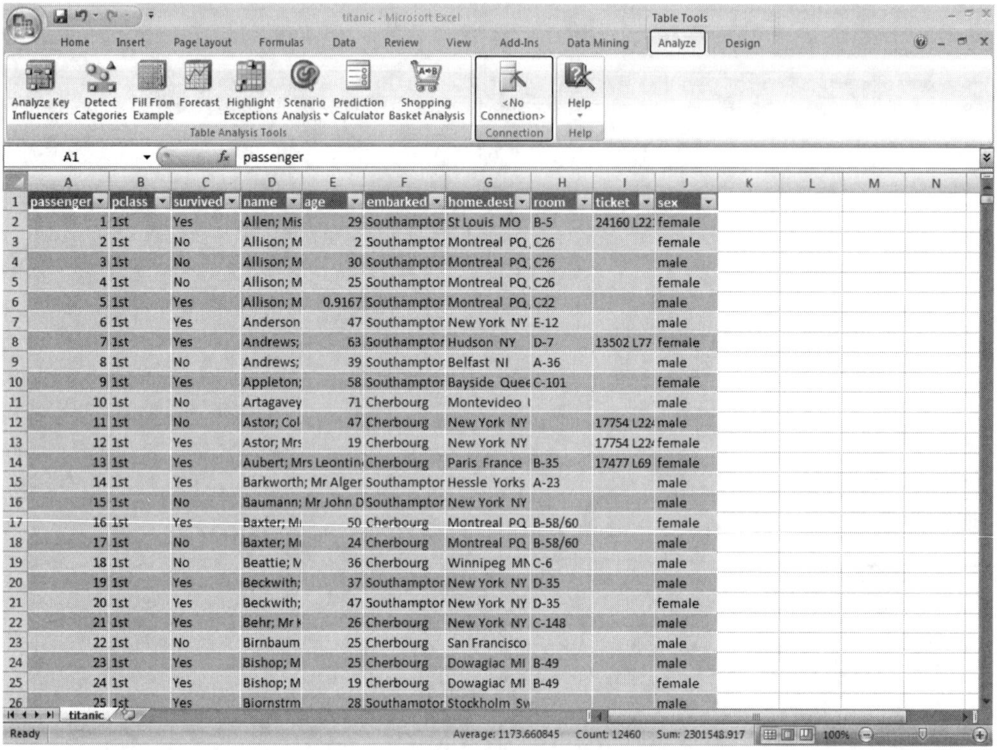

Figure 6-10 *The Analyze tab of the Office data mining add-in*

Once the dataset is formatted as a table, you are ready to start. If you want to skip the previous steps, this sample spreadsheet in Excel 2007/2010 can be downloaded from www.officebicentral.com.

In the next few pages we will go over each option of the add-in. The options in the add-in are shown in Table 6-2.

Add-In: Analyze Key Influencers

Now that we have the data we need, we want to do some analysis on this dataset. To start, choose Analyze Key Influencers from the left side of the ribbon (as shown in Figure 6-11). We would like to analyze the traits of the survivors.

1. Choose Survived in the Column Selection (Step A) and then click Run.
2. Next you will see the "Discrimination based on key influencers" screen (Step B). Choose to add it to the report by choosing Add Report. The discrimination report will show the different options that impact the outcome.

Option	Description
Analyze Key Influencers	Used to see which other columns (or values) impact a given column. This is useful to analyze large datasets where you want to see how something is impacted, such as what factors influence someone who has purchased something.
Detect Categories	Looks at a dataset, showing similarities and the values that make up the categories. This is very useful for targeted mailings or to divide customers into different segments.
Fill From Example	Start filling a few rows in a dataset and this option will fill out the remaining rows by looking for similarities.
Forecast	This will allow you to predict future values based on past performance. The output is a chart with the forecasted values.
Highlight Exceptions	Highlights rows and values where there are data anomalies. This is useful to run against large datasets to see where potentially incorrect data is.
Scenario Analysis	There are two options in this tool: Goal Seek gives you the row(s) that need to be changed in order for a desired value change. What-if allows you to change values and see how the change would impact an outcome.
Prediction Calculator	This option creates a printable spreadsheet with the values that impact a given outcome.
Shopping Basket Analysis	This allows you to analyze sales data to see which products are frequently bought together.

Table 6-2 *The Options That Are Available in the Add-In*

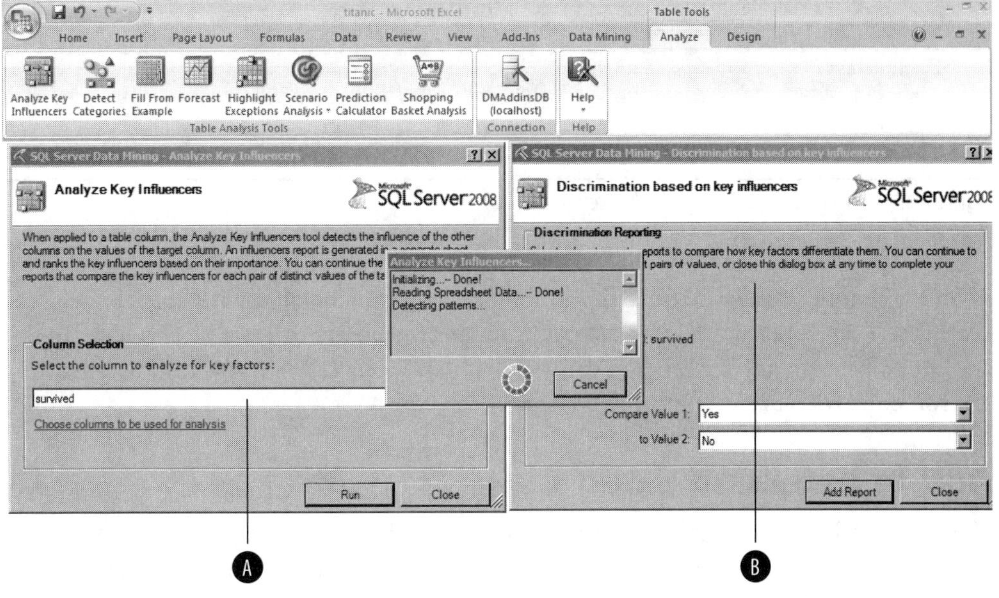

Figure 6-11 *The Analyze Key Influencers process*

	A	B	C	D	E	F	G
3	Key Influencers and their impact over the values of 'survived'						
4	Filter by 'Column' or 'Favors' to see how various columns influence 'survived'						
5	Column	Value	Favors	Relative Impact			
6	sex	female	Yes				
7	pclass	1st	Yes				
8	passenger	< 258	Yes				
9	embarked	Cherbourg	Yes				
10	age	< 18.121504979:	Yes				
11	embarked	Southampton	Yes				
12	passenger	258 - 529	Yes				
13	pclass	2nd	Yes				
14	sex	male	No				
15	pclass	3rd	No				
16	embarked		No				
17	passenger	>= 1043	No				
18	age	Missing	No				
19	passenger	782 - 1043	No				
20							
21							
22							
23	Discrimination between factors leading to 'Yes' and 'No'						
24	Filter by 'Column' to see how different values favor 'Yes' or 'No'						
25	Column	Value	Favors Yes	Favors No			
26	sex	female					
27	sex	male					
28	pclass	3rd					
29	pclass	1st					
30	embarked						
31	passenger	< 258					

titanic | Influencers for survived

Figure 6-12 *The output of Analyze Key Influencers*

You will notice in Figure 6-12 the different values are depicted with bars. The bars under the Favors Yes and Favors No columns specify whether the value of a column appears to be a key influencer. You can see that gender has a big impact on whether or not someone will survive, followed by class.

Add-In Detecting Categories

Now that we have done some analysis on the data, it is time to see if we can break up the data into different categories. In order to do this, you will need to click the Detect Categories tool of the add-in as depicted in Figure 6-13.

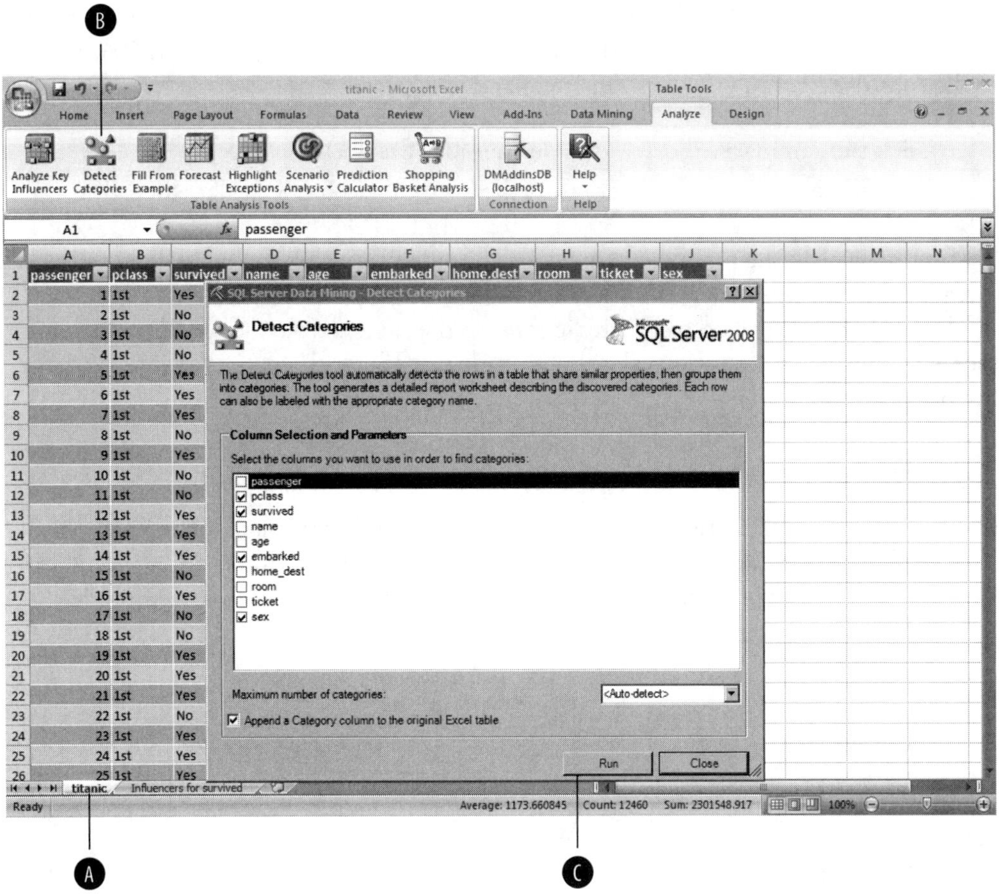

Figure 6-13 *The Detect Categories dialog box*

BI TIP

If these tools do not appear, it is most likely because you have clicked out of the table inside of the worksheet. In order to get the tools to appear again, just click back on the table inside of the Excel worksheet.

1. With the Titanic tab selected (Step A), click Detect Categories from the add-in ribbon (Step B).
2. In the Detect Categories dialog box, click Run (Step C).

The next window will show you the categories and how different data elements have impacted each category (Figure 6-14). If you click the number 2 on the left-hand side of the spreadsheet, you will see a larger expanded category report.

1. Click the summarized categories on the side (Step A).
2. Click the original spreadsheet tab at the bottom left-hand corner (Step B).

If you now click the main data tab (titanic), you will see the original dataset with the category next to each data row (as shown in Figure 6-15).

Next we are going to do some predictions on the same dataset. If you click back on the table, the analyze selections should be available. (If not, then choose Analyze from the ribbon at the top.)

Add-In Prediction Calculator

In order to make a prediction, you need to establish a weighted value for each choice. (You saw this in the analysis of key influencers before in this chapter.) What you didn't have access to before was exactly how much each attribute impacted a given result.

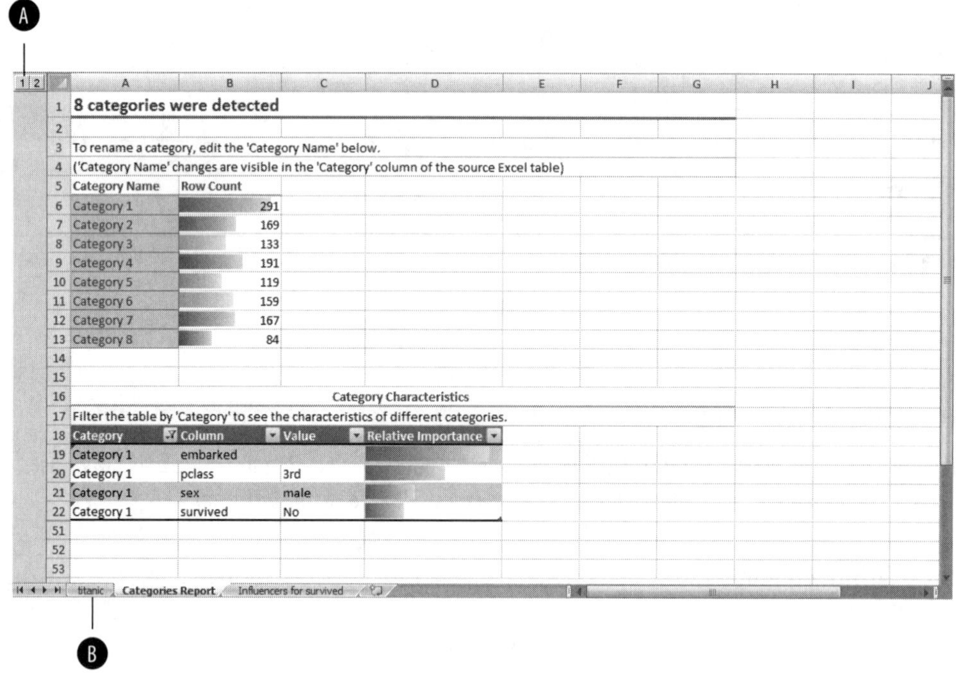

Figure 6-14 *Choose the expanded categories (2) or the summarized categories (1).*

	A	B	C	D	E	F	G	H	I	J	K
1	passenger	pclass	survived	name	age	embarked	home.dest	room	ticket	sex	Category
2	1	1st	Yes	Allen; Mis	29	Southamptor	St Louis MO	B-5	24160 L22	female	Category 6
3	2	1st	No	Allison; M	2	Southamptor	Montreal PQ	C26		female	Category 7
4	3	1st	No	Allison; M	30	Southamptor	Montreal PQ	C26		male	Category 7
5	4	1st	No	Allison; M	25	Southamptor	Montreal PQ	C26		female	Category 7
6	5	1st	Yes	Allison; M	0.9167	Southamptor	Montreal PQ	C22		male	Category 7
7	6	1st	Yes	Anderson	47	Southamptor	New York NY	E-12		male	Category 7
8	7	1st	Yes	Andrews;	63	Southamptor	Hudson NY	D-7	13502 L77	female	Category 6
9	8	1st	No	Andrews;	39	Southamptor	Belfast NI	A-36		male	Category 7
10	9	1st	Yes	Appleton;	58	Southamptor	Bayside Quee	C-101		female	Category 6
11	10	1st	No	Artagavey	71	Cherbourg	Montevideo			male	Category 7
12	11	1st	No	Astor; Col	47	Cherbourg	New York NY		17754 L22	male	Category 7
13	12	1st	Yes	Astor; Mrs	19	Cherbourg	New York NY		17754 L22	female	Category 6
14	13	1st	Yes	Aubert; Mrs Leontin		Cherbourg	Paris France	B-35	17477 L69	female	Category 6
15	14	1st	Yes	Barkworth; Mr Alger		Southamptor	Hessle Yorks	A-23		male	Category 7
16	15	1st	No	Baumann; Mr John D		Southamptor	New York NY			male	Category 7
17	16	1st	Yes	Baxter; Mi	50	Cherbourg	Montreal PQ	B-58/60		female	Category 6
18	17	1st	No	Baxter; Mi	24	Cherbourg	Montreal PQ	B-58/60		male	Category 7
19	18	1st	No	Beattie; M	36	Cherbourg	Winnipeg MN	C-6		male	Category 7
20	19	1st	Yes	Beckwith;	37	Southamptor	New York NY	D-35		male	Category 7
21	20	1st	Yes	Beckwith;	47	Southamptor	New York NY	D-35		female	Category 6
22	21	1st	Yes	Behr; Mr K	26	Cherbourg	New York NY	C-148		male	Category 6
23	22	1st	No	Birnbaum	25	Cherbourg	San Francisco			male	Category 7
24	23	1st	Yes	Bishop; M	25	Cherbourg	Dowagiac MI	B-49		male	Category 6
25	24	1st	Yes	Bishop; M	19	Cherbourg	Dowagiac MI	B-49		female	Category 6
26	25	1st	Yes	Biornstrm	28	Southamptor	Stockholm Sv			male	Category 7

titanic / Categories Report / Influencers for survived

Figure 6-15 *Notice the new category column on the right side of the worksheet.*

Imagine if you had all the attributes with a predicted weight (and you could view these attributes). Now also imagine if you could put these all in one spreadsheet where you could fill out the choices and make the prediction by adding the attribute weights together. So now let's look at the Prediction Calculator tool, shown in Figure 6-16.

1. Choose the Prediction Calculator (Step A).

   You will now choose the columns that you want to predict. You should choose for the target to be survived; the goal here is that you want to try to predict whether a person will survive. The original dataset lists 1 as survive and 0 for those who did not.
2. In the Column Selection choose the target column (in this case survived, Step B).
3. Choose the value in the column that you would like (in this case 1).
4. Now click Run (Step C).

The spreadsheet windows should change, and there should be some processing. Once the processing has finished, you should see something that looks like Figure 6-17.

This spreadsheet tab lists out the data elements and their impacts. This worksheet also has four data elements that you can input: False Positive Cost, False Negative Cost, True Positive Profit, and True Negative Profit. These options help when you are trying to analyze how this prediction will clarify your cost or profit options as shown in Table 6-3.

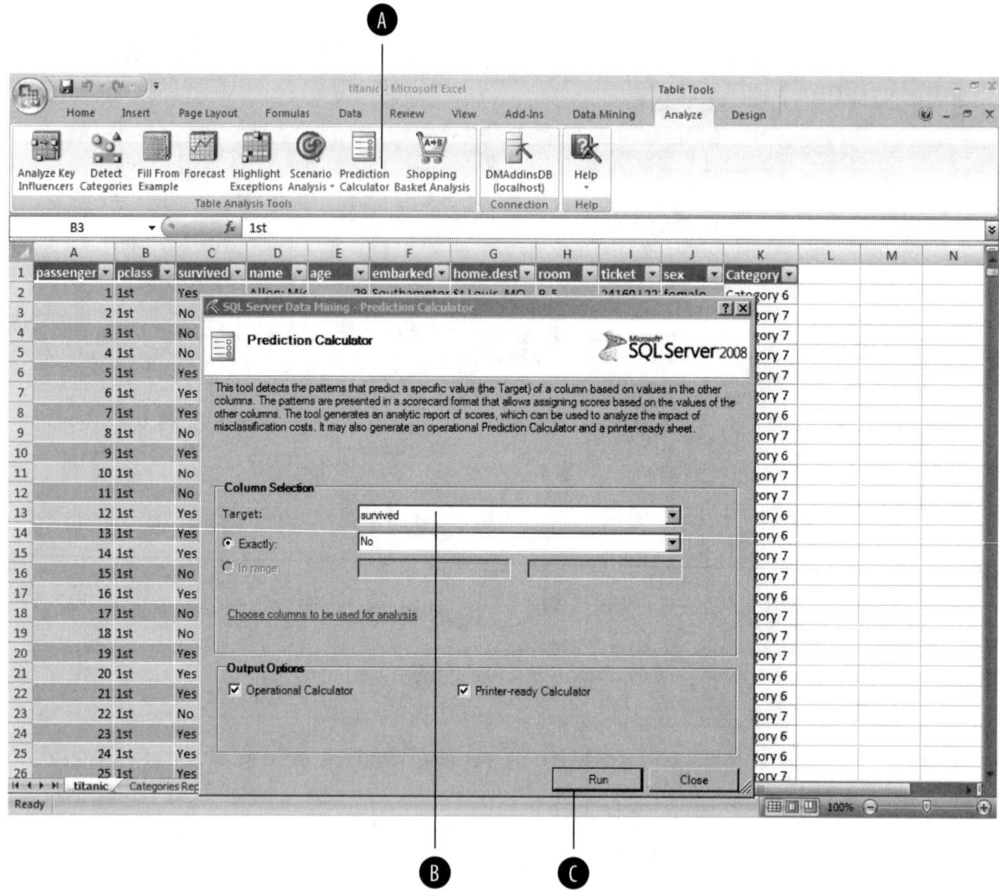

Figure 6-16 *Click the Prediction Calculator process.*

You should notice several different charts that may help you in determining why certain choices were made and the potential impact of these decisions (i.e., how much profit will be gained or lost given a decision).

Next click the Printable Calculator worksheet tab (as in Figure 6-18). In this worksheet, you will see that each column has a data element and a score next to it. This score represents the impacted value of each data element to the desired value (survived in this case).

BI TIP

This table can be printed out, and you will notice that next to each element is a score. If you add up the score next to each of your chosen data elements, you can compare that value to the optimal value that was determined by the data mining engine. Using this method, you're able to compare your chosen values to what the data mining engine would have predicted.

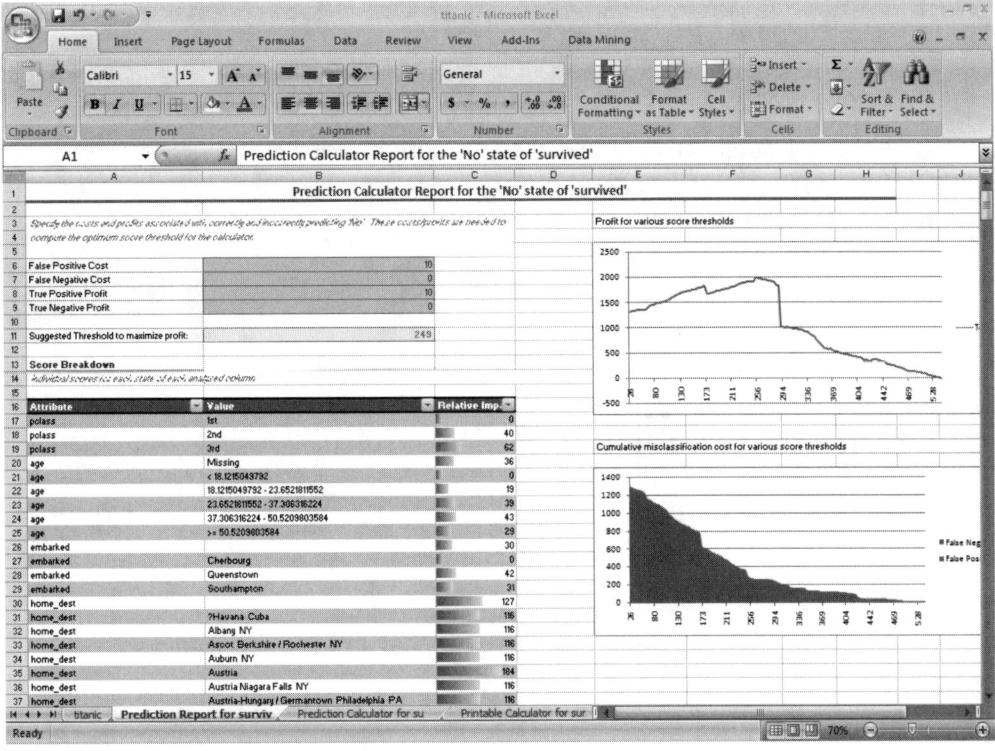

Figure 6-17 *The Prediction Calculator report*

So far in this chapter we have been using real data samples downloaded from the Internet. Now we are going to use the sample that is installed with the data mining add-in. When you install the data mining add-in, a program group is added named SQL Server 2008 Data Mining Add-ins. Under this, launch the Sample Excel Data spreadsheet (as shown in Figure 6-19). This spreadsheet is meant to show off the add-in with sample data. This sample spreadsheet allows you to test out all of the functionality of the add-in.

Element	Description
False Positive Cost	If the model predicted a positive, yet it was wrong, how much does this cost you?
False Negative Cost	If the model predicted a negative, yet it was wrong, how much does this cost you?
True Positive Profit	If the model predicted a positive, and it was right, how much profit will you make from this prediction?
True Negative Profit	If the model predicted a negative and was truly a negative, how much would you have benefited from a correct prediction?

Table 6-3 *The Prediction Calculator Report Returns Options*

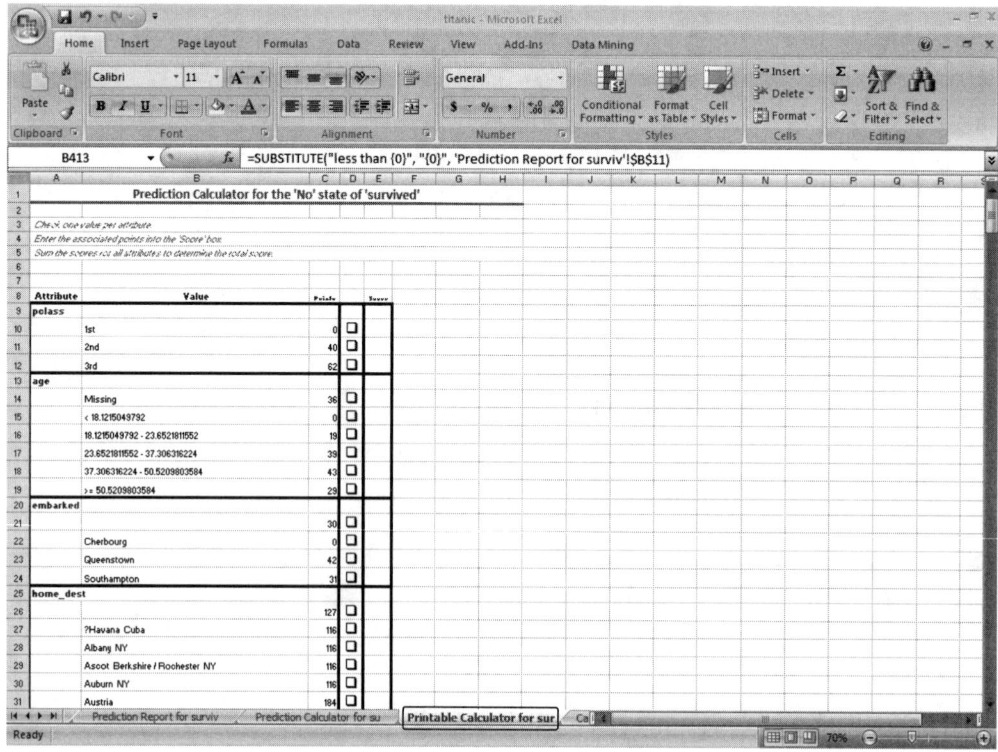

Figure 6-18 *The Prediction Calculator Printable Calculator output*

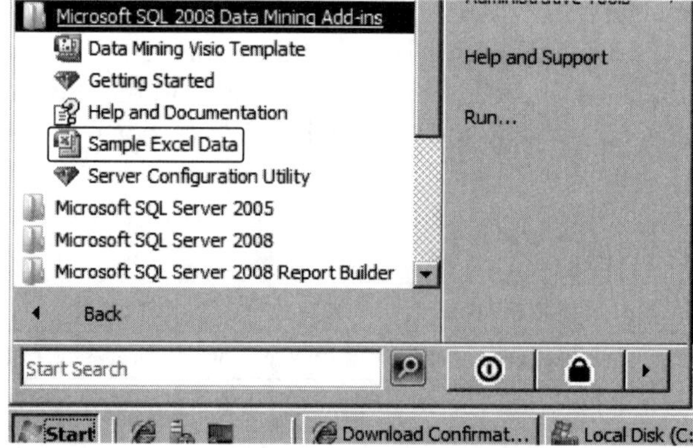

Figure 6-19 *Launch the Sample Excel Data spreadsheet.*

Add-In Fill from Example

Now imagine that you have 500 customers in a spreadsheet and your boss asks you to go through all 500 customers to try to determine if they are good potentials for a purchase. You could spend the day going through all 500 customers line by line (and potentially facing some frustration along the way), or you could just use the Fill From Example tool. In this example you will have the first ten high-valued customer rows filled out, and you will fill out the rest with a few mouse clicks.

1. Select the Sample Excel Data from the program menu (Excel should launch). Once you launch the spreadsheet, you will see several tabs that have different data elements (as in Figure 6-20). Choose the Fill From Example tab.

NOTE

We will be using the sample spreadsheet for the remainder of examples in this chapter.

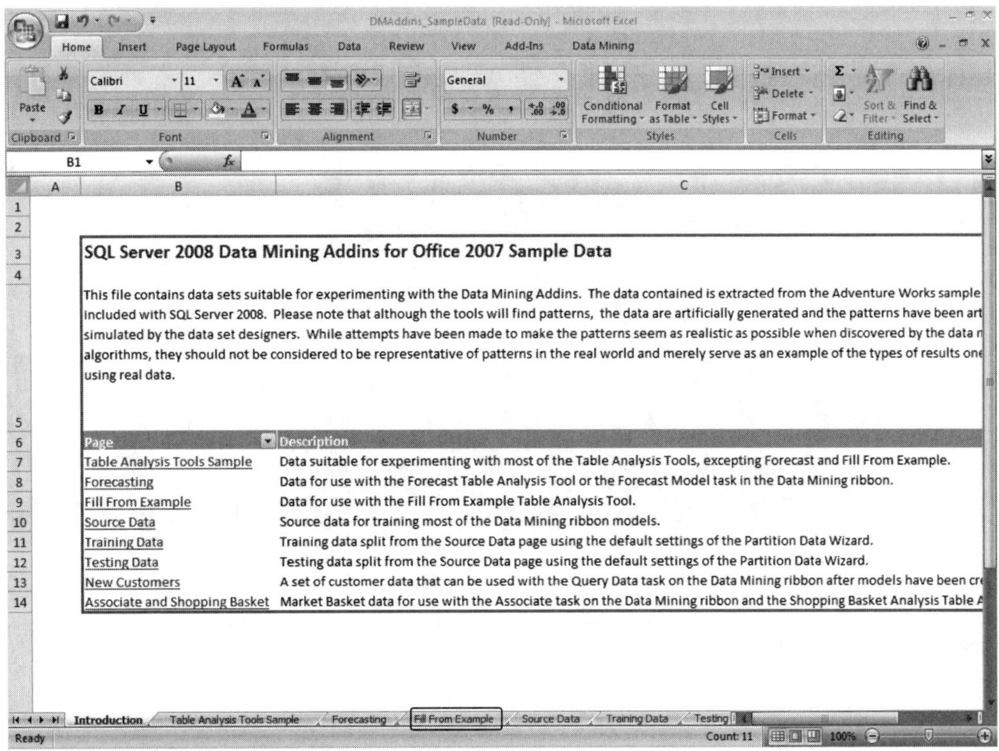

Figure 6-20 *Choose the Fill From Example tab.*

2. In the sample spreadsheet (see Figure 6-21), choose Fill From Example from the ribbon (Step A).
3. Choose High Value Customer from the drop-down list and click Run (Step B).

Once the processing completes, you will be given a spreadsheet of the pattern that was detected by the tool as in Figure 6-22.

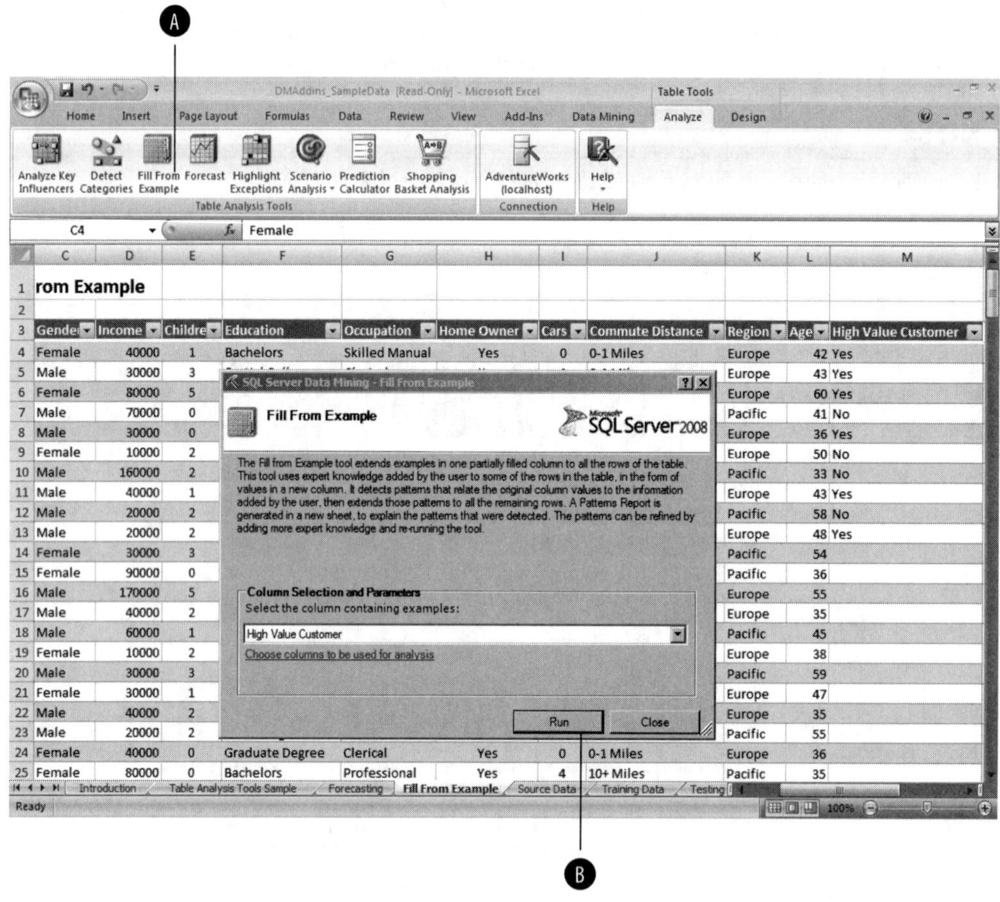

Figure 6-21 *The Fill From Example tool process*

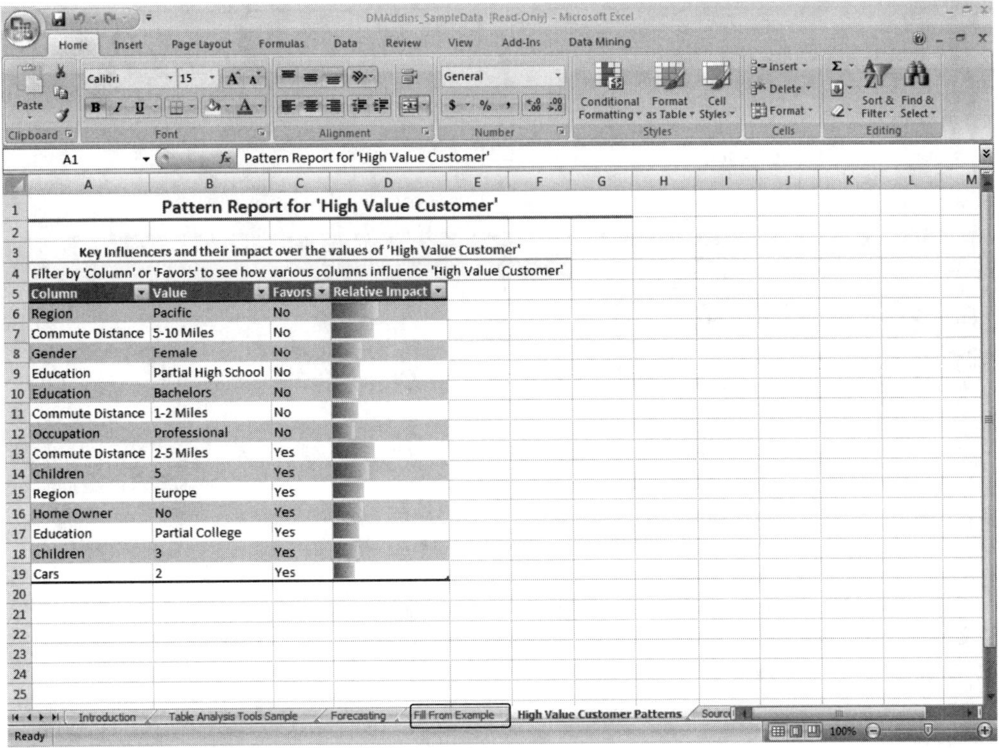

Figure 6-22 *The Pattern report for the higher-valued customers*

The first screen lists out the columns, the values, and the impact on a given value. This visualization is a very powerful tool where you can see which values impact a given outcome. Next we will look at the changes that were made on the original spreadsheet.

If you click the Fill From Example worksheet tab, you will notice that a new column has been added to the dataset. In this case it is called High Value Customer_Extended. This is the value that was filled in based on the sample. You will notice that later rows have been filled in based on the first ten rows (as in Figure 6-23).

From Example

Gende	Income	Childr	Education	Occupation	Home Owne	Cars	Commute Distance	Regio	Ag	High Value Customer	High Value Customer_Extended
Female	40000	1	Bachelors	Skilled Manua	Yes	0	0-1 Miles	Europe	42	Yes	Yes
Male	30000	3	Partial College	Clerical	Yes	1	0-1 Miles	Europe	43	Yes	Yes
Female	80000	5	Partial College	Professional	No	2	2-5 Miles	Europe	60	Yes	Yes
Male	70000	0	Bachelors	Professional	Yes	1	5-10 Miles	Pacific	41	No	No
Male	30000	0	Bachelors	Clerical	No	0	0-1 Miles	Europe	36	Yes	Yes
Female	10000	2	Partial College	Manual	Yes	0	1-2 Miles	Europe	50	No	No
Male	160000	2	High School	Management	Yes	4	0-1 Miles	Pacific	33	No	No
Male	40000	1	Bachelors	Skilled Manua	Yes	0	0-1 Miles	Europe	43	Yes	Yes
Male	20000	2	Partial High Schoo	Clerical	Yes	2	5-10 Miles	Pacific	58	No	No
Male	20000	2	Partial College	Manual	Yes	1	0-1 Miles	Europe	48	Yes	Yes
Female	30000	3	High School	Skilled Manua	No	2	1-2 Miles	Pacific	54		No
Female	90000	0	Bachelors	Professional	No	4	10+ Miles	Pacific	36		No
Male	170000	5	Partial College	Professional	Yes	4	0-1 Miles	Europe	55		Yes
Male	40000	2	Partial College	Clerical	Yes	1	1-2 Miles	Europe	35		Yes
Male	60000	1	Partial College	Skilled Manua	No	1	0-1 Miles	Pacific	45		Yes
Female	10000	2	High School	Manual	Yes	1	0-1 Miles	Europe	38		Yes
Male	30000	3	Partial College	Clerical	No	2	1-2 Miles	Pacific	59		Yes
Female	30000	1	Bachelors	Clerical	Yes	0	0-1 Miles	Europe	47		No
Male	40000	2	Partial College	Clerical	Yes	1	1-2 Miles	Europe	35		Yes
Male	20000	2	Partial High Schoo	Clerical	Yes	2	5-10 Miles	Pacific	55		No
Female	40000	0	Graduate Degree	Clerical	Yes	0	0-1 Miles	Europe	36		No
Female	80000	0	Bachelors	Professional	Yes	4	10+ Miles	Pacific	35		No
Male	40000	2	Partial College	Clerical	Yes	0	1-2 Miles	Europe	35		Yes
Female	80000	5	High School	Management	No	3	5-10 Miles	Europe	56		Yes
Male	40000	2	Partial College	Clerical	No	1	0-1 Miles	Europe	34		Yes
Male	30000	1	Bachelors	Clerical	Yes	0	0-1 Miles	Europe	63		Yes
Male	30000	0	Partial College	Clerical	No	1	0-1 Miles	Europe	29		Yes
Female	100000	0	Bachelors	Professional	No	1	5-10 Miles	Pacific	40		No

Figure 6-23 *Notice the High Value Customer_Extended values.*

The next tool that we will work through will be the Shopping Basket Analysis, using sales receipt data from a fictitious sporting goods company. Our goal here is to see how much data we can gather from sales receipt data.

Add-In Shopping Basket Analysis

This tool will help with one of the more famous data mining tasks, shopping basket analysis. The typical shopping basket scenario could be where you may uncover strange patterns such as the relation between beer, peanut butter, and diapers during the late evening. In this case you are working at a bicycle store. Since you are new, the boss gives you the sales for the past month. Your goal is to decide which items should be placed

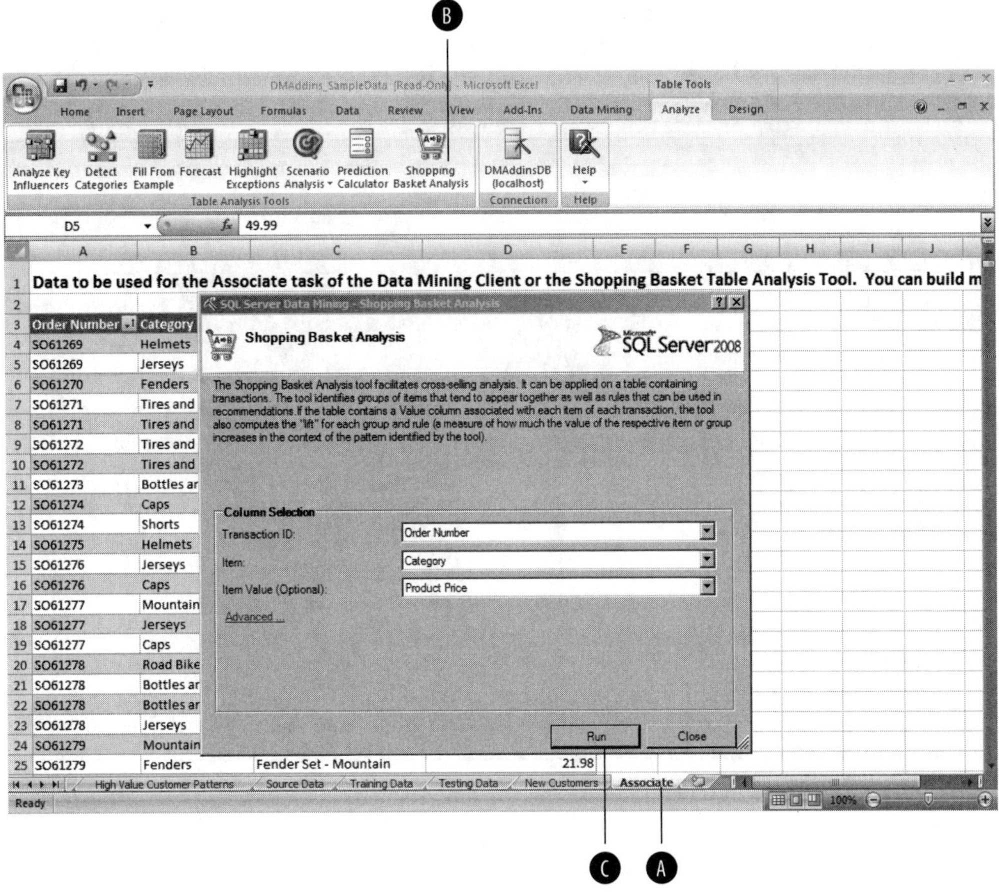

Figure 6-24 *Choose the Associate worksheet tab and then Shopping Basket Analysis from the add-in.*

near each other in the store. As an added bonus, you would also like to determine which items you may want to bundle together. Refer to Figure 6-24 for these steps.

1. Choose the Associate tab inside of Excel (Step A).
2. Choose Shopping Basket Analysis (Step B).
3. You should be presented with a dialog box that has several drop-down list boxes and a Run button. Click Run (Step C).

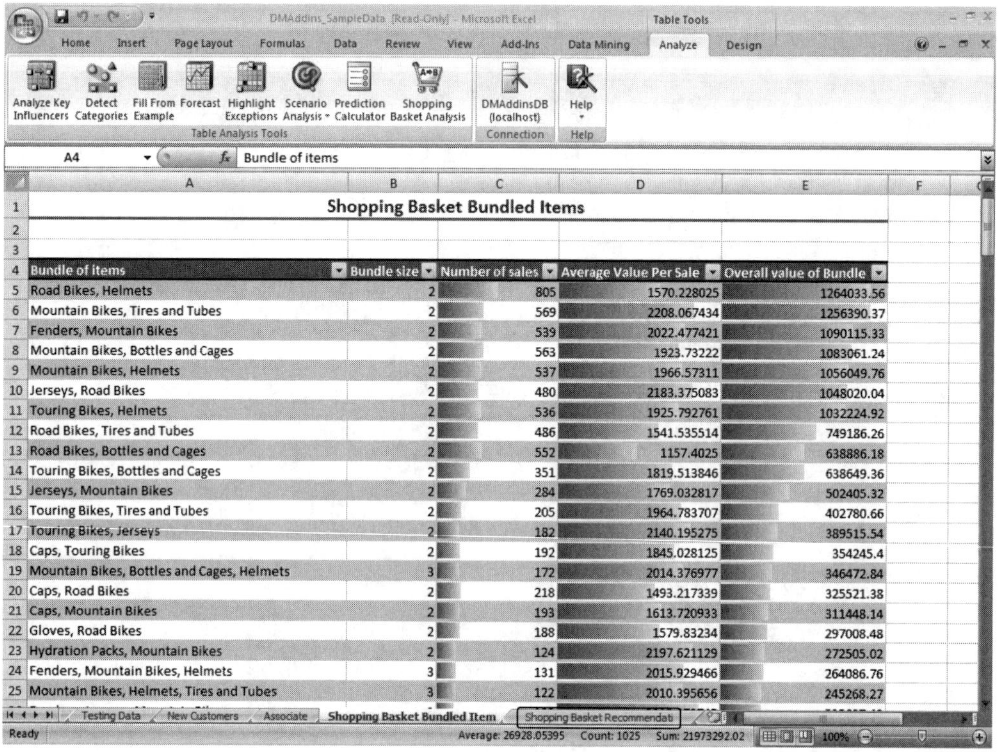

Shopping Basket Bundled Items

Bundle of items	Bundle size	Number of sales	Average Value Per Sale	Overall value of Bundle
Road Bikes, Helmets	2	805	1570.228025	1264033.56
Mountain Bikes, Tires and Tubes	2	569	2208.067434	1256390.37
Fenders, Mountain Bikes	2	539	2022.477421	1090115.33
Mountain Bikes, Bottles and Cages	2	563	1923.73222	1083061.24
Mountain Bikes, Helmets	2	537	1966.57311	1056049.76
Jerseys, Road Bikes	2	480	2183.375083	1048020.04
Touring Bikes, Helmets	2	536	1925.792761	1032224.92
Road Bikes, Tires and Tubes	2	486	1541.535514	749186.26
Road Bikes, Bottles and Cages	2	552	1157.4025	638886.18
Touring Bikes, Bottles and Cages	2	351	1819.513846	638649.36
Jerseys, Mountain Bikes	2	284	1769.032817	502405.32
Touring Bikes, Tires and Tubes	2	205	1964.783707	402780.66
Touring Bikes, Jerseys	2	182	2140.195275	389515.54
Caps, Touring Bikes	2	192	1845.028125	354245.4
Mountain Bikes, Bottles and Cages, Helmets	3	172	2014.376977	346472.84
Caps, Road Bikes	2	218	1493.217339	325521.38
Caps, Mountain Bikes	2	193	1613.720933	311448.14
Gloves, Road Bikes	2	188	1579.83234	297008.48
Hydration Packs, Mountain Bikes	2	124	2197.621129	272505.02
Fenders, Mountain Bikes, Helmets	3	131	2015.929466	264086.76
Mountain Bikes, Helmets, Tires and Tubes	3	122	2010.395656	245268.27

Figure 6-25 *Bundled items output report*

The tool looks at what people have purchased together. This may help us to make a decision about which products should be located in the store together (as shown in Figure 6-25).

The first spreadsheet shows items that were purchased together in the store. Click the Shopping Basket Recommendations tab to see the resulting worksheet, which shows recommendations based on purchases (as shown in Figure 6-26).

These recommendations are based on things that were purchased together. You could come up with this type of analysis, but you would have to go through all of the

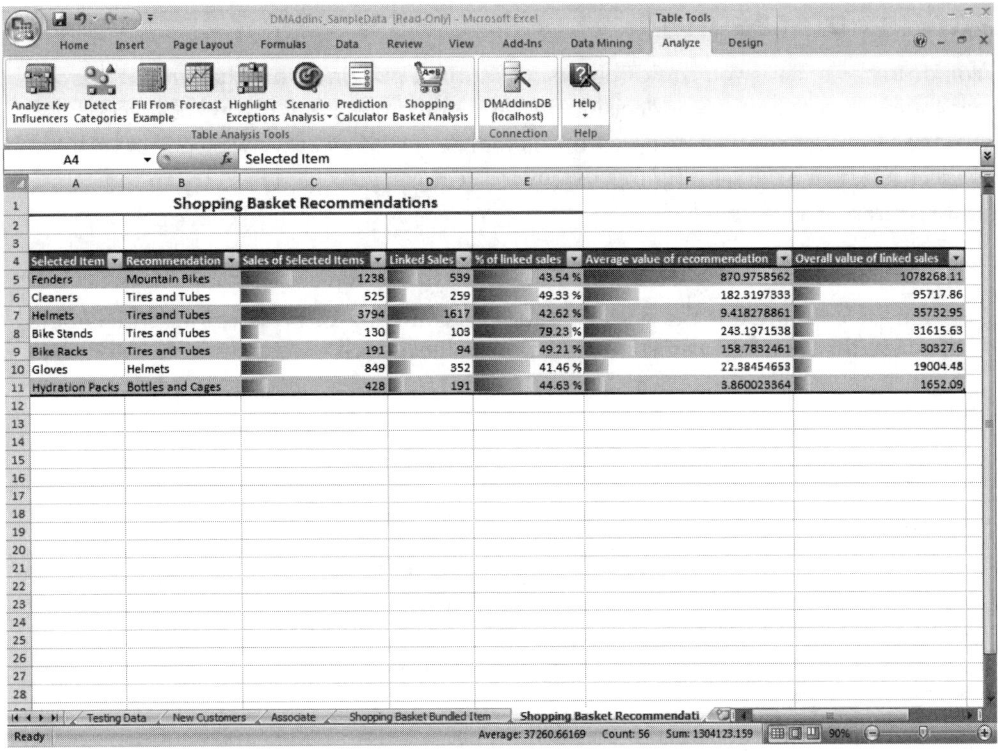

DMAddins_SampleData [Read-Only] - Microsoft Excel
Table Tools
Home Insert Page Layout Formulas Data Review View Add-Ins Data Mining Analyze Design
Analyze Key Influencers
Detect Categories
Fill From Example
Forecast
Highlight Exceptions
Scenario Analysis
Prediction Calculator
Shopping Basket Analysis
DMAddinsDB (localhost)
Help
Table Analysis Tools
Connection
Help
A4
Selected Item
Shopping Basket Recommendations
Selected Item | Recommendation | Sales of Selected Items | Linked Sales | % of linked sales | Average value of recommendation | Overall value of linked sales
Fenders | Mountain Bikes | 1238 | 539 | 43.54 % | 870.9758562 | 1078268.11
Cleaners | Tires and Tubes | 525 | 259 | 49.33 % | 182.3197333 | 95717.86
Helmets | Tires and Tubes | 3794 | 1617 | 42.62 % | 9.418278861 | 35732.95
Bike Stands | Tires and Tubes | 130 | 103 | 79.23 % | 243.1971538 | 31615.63
Bike Racks | Tires and Tubes | 191 | 94 | 49.21 % | 158.7832461 | 30327.6
Gloves | Helmets | 849 | 352 | 41.46 % | 22.38454653 | 19004.48
Hydration Packs | Bottles and Cages | 428 | 191 | 44.63 % | 3.860023364 | 1652.09
Testing Data
New Customers
Associate
Shopping Basket Bundled Item
Shopping Basket Recommendati
Ready
Average: 37260.66169 Count: 56 Sum: 1304123.159
90%

Figure 6-26 *Shopping Basket Recommendations output*

purchased items. In just a few mouse clicks, the Data Mining Wizard went through all of the items that were purchased together and isolated the items that have a higher probability to be purchased together. Now imagine that you were the owner of a bike store; this would be extremely valuable information.

The final tool that we will go through is the Forecast tool. Imagine if you could predict future events from past data trends. Now also imagine if you could do this with only a few clicks of the mouse (that is what we will be doing here).

Add-In Forecasting

Wouldn't it be great if you could forecast the future; imagine what that would do for your lottery, sports betting, or decision-making outcomes. Now if you are successful with the lottery or sports betting with this tool, let us know at www.bicentral.com. In this scenario, you have sales figures for several regions; your goal is to try to forecast the future from past sales trends.

1. Click the Forecasting tab on the bottom of the screen as shown on Figure 6-27. This screen contains the sales data for this company and the regions. You should notice that the data also contains a time value as well.

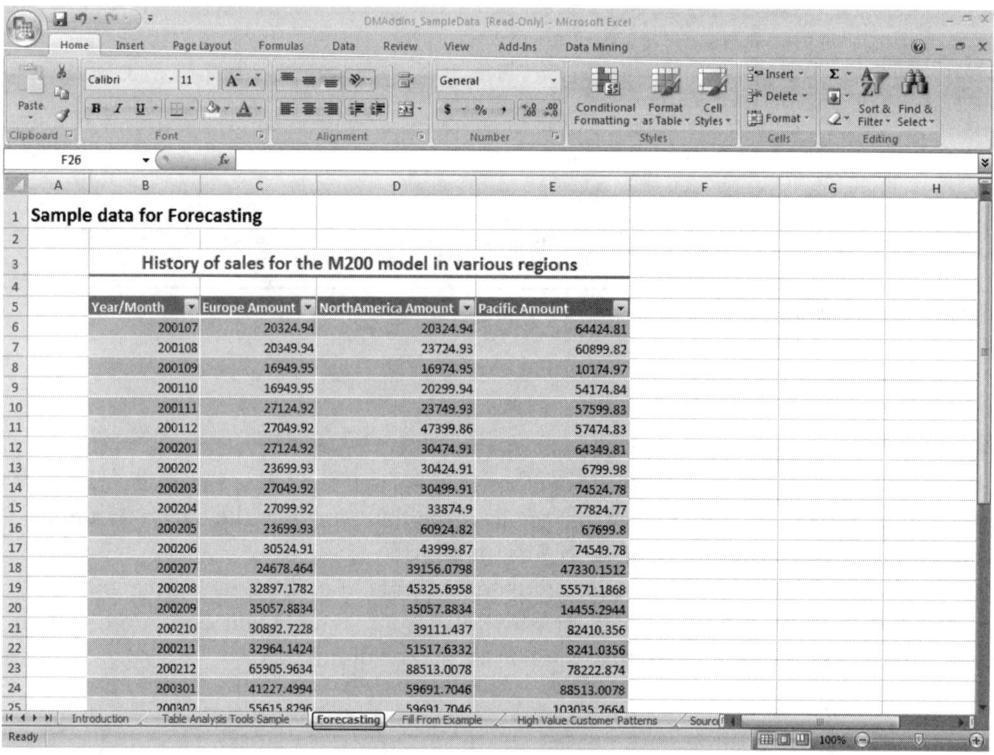

Year/Month	Europe Amount	NorthAmerica Amount	Pacific Amount
200107	20324.94	20324.94	64424.81
200108	20349.94	23724.93	60899.82
200109	16949.95	16974.95	10174.97
200110	16949.95	20299.94	54174.84
200111	27124.92	23749.93	57599.83
200112	27049.92	47399.86	57474.83
200201	27124.92	30474.91	64349.81
200202	23699.93	30424.91	6799.98
200203	27049.92	30499.91	74524.78
200204	27099.92	33874.9	77824.77
200205	23699.93	60924.82	67699.8
200206	30524.91	43999.87	74549.78
200207	24678.464	39156.0798	47330.1512
200208	32897.1782	45325.6958	55571.1868
200209	35057.8834	35057.8834	14455.2944
200210	30892.7228	39111.437	82410.356
200211	32964.1424	51517.6332	8241.0356
200212	65905.9634	88513.0078	78222.874
200301	41227.4994	59691.7046	88513.0078
200302	55615.8296	59691.7046	103035.2664

Figure 6-27 *The Forecasting worksheet*

2. Next, choose the Forecast tool in the Analyze tab (Step A in Figure 6-28).

   You should be presented with the options for different data elements. You will notice there are different selections on this screen. The Number Of Time Units To Forecast defaults to 5, but you can change it to anything that you like. We currently won't be using the Time Stamp field, so leave Periodicity Of Data to Detect Automatically selected.

3. Click Run (Step B).

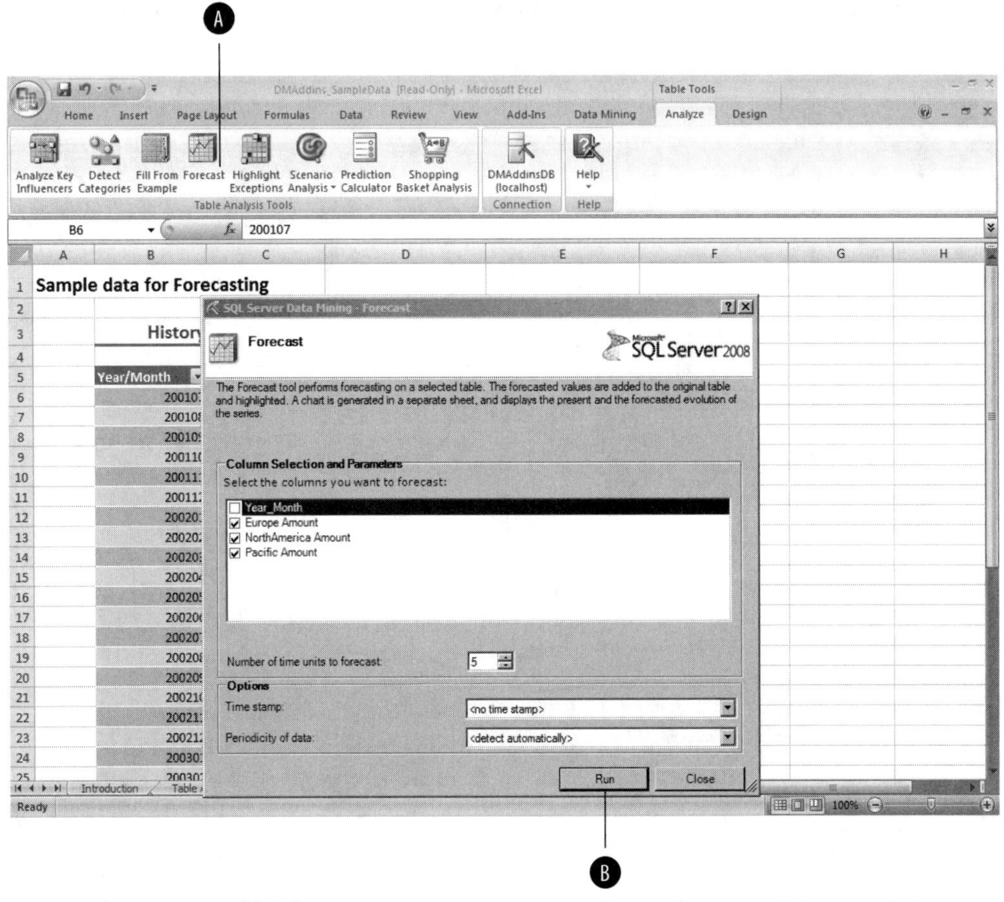

Figure 6-28 *The Forecasting process*

BI TIP

If you choose to use the full Data Mining tab (instead of Analyze), you can set the number of units to forecast as well as additional data items in the viewer. (This is shown later in this chapter.)

The output of the Forecast tool is a chart on a new tab called the Forecasting Report. You should notice that the chart looks very similar to other Excel charts, except that the dashed lines are predicted elements (as shown in Figure 6-29).

So what do the dashed lines mean? Well, the dashed lines are what potentially will happen in the future (based on the past trends). So using this method, you now have a way of potentially predicting the future. So what does the future hold? It is hard to tell,

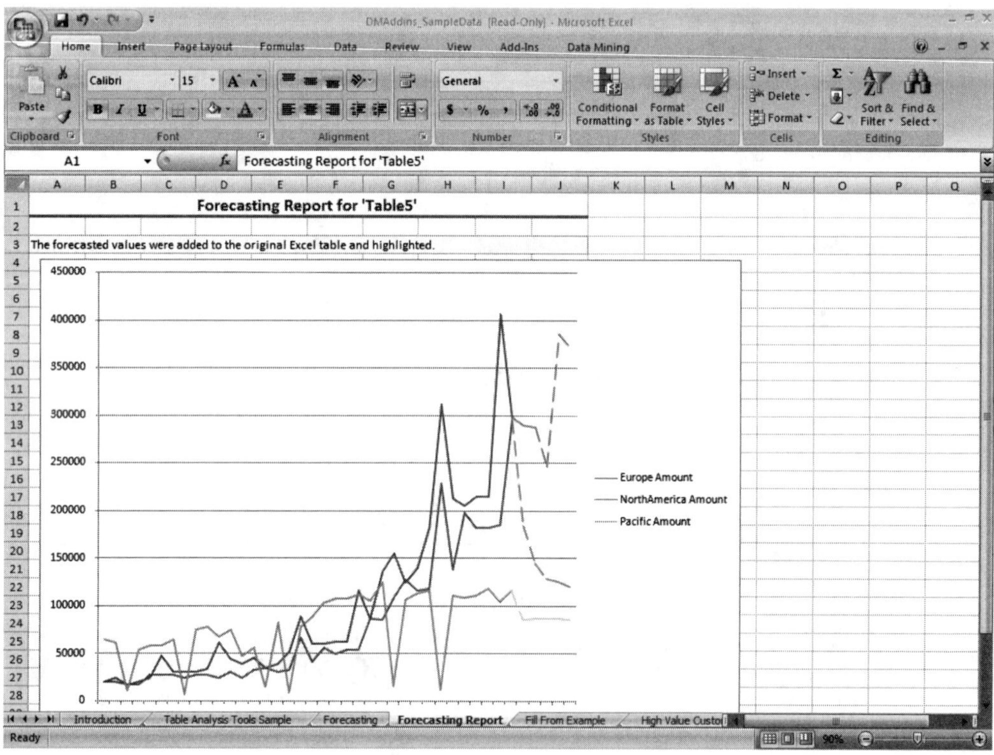

Figure 6-29 *The output of the Forecast tool*

but with the Forecast tool you can at least now know how some of the data elements might behave.

So if you now click the original Forecasting tab, you will see that the add-in updated the original spreadsheet worksheet with the projected values (as shown in Figure 6-30).

In order to use the add-in a different way, we will need to delete the new rows that were created in the last exercise (see Figure 6-31).

1. Highlight the rows that were created by the Forecast tool (Step A).
2. Next click the right mouse button and choose Delete and then Table Rows (Step B). (The dataset should then look just like the original dataset.)

	A	Year/Month	Europe Amount	NorthAmerica Amount	Pacific Amount	F	G	H
25		200302	55615.8296	59691.7046	103035.2664			
26		200303	49379.2494	61897.0526	107133.4628			
27		200304	53499.7672	61785.4456	107289.7126			
28		200305	53522.0886	115329.8556	111209.3378			
29		200306	86597.838	86620.1594	105062.0432			
30		200307	85489.63	135979.41	124579.46			
31		200308	108439.53	154464.33	16139.93			
32		200309	127024.45	124454.46	106169.54			
33		200310	115449.5	138474.4	113029.51			
34		200311	117644.49	182154.21	115374.5			
35		200312	228304.01	311473.65	11524.95			
36		200401	138349.4	212389.08	110734.52			
37		200402	198344.14	205329.11	108539.53			
38		200403	182129.21	214584.07	110859.52			
39		200404	182254.21	214609.07	117619.49			
40		200405	184774.2	405993.24	103849.55			
41		200406	295483.72	297803.71	115249.5			
42			184306.0323	289657.7535	85701.6478			
43			144563.065	287474.2001	85885.22423			
44			127951.9745	246325.1756	85918.73182			
45			125262.3327	385199.6905	85834.37076			
46			119828.9563	371575.1437	85658.65469			
47								
48								
49								
50								

Figure 6-30 *The projected values have been placed in the original worksheet.*

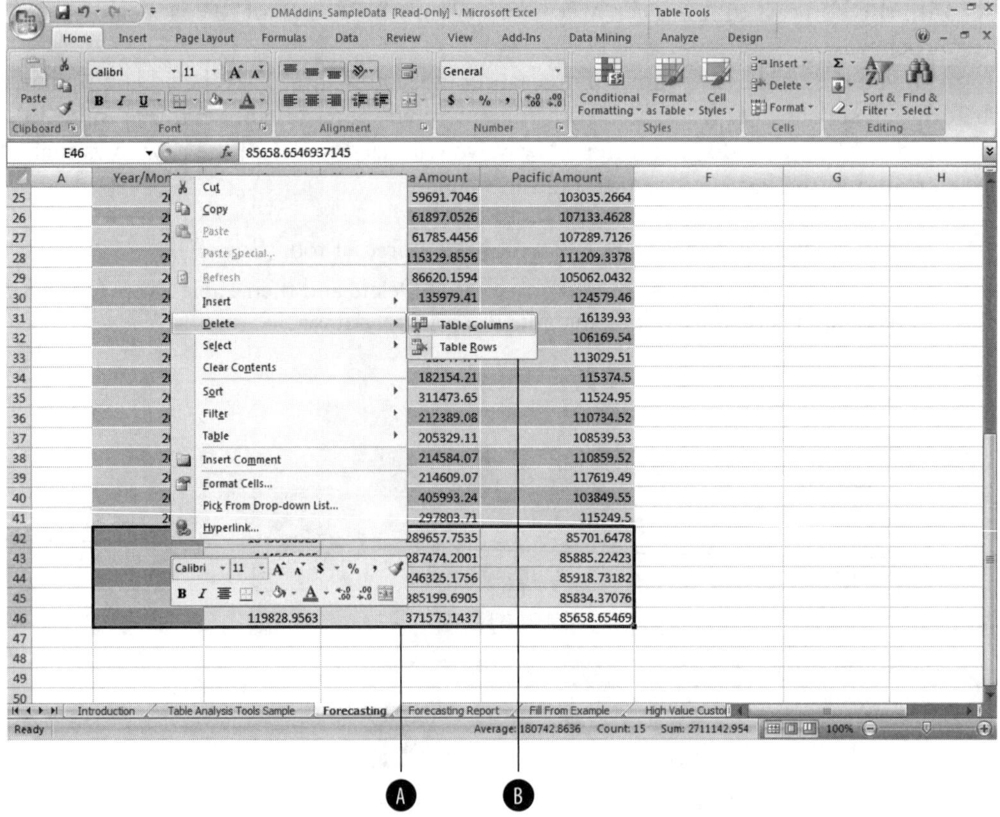

Figure 6-31 *Delete the forecasted rows that were added in this step.*

Extended Data Mining Add-In

Now that we have gone through the Analyze tab, we will go through the Data Mining tab. This tab is designed for more advanced data mining functions. There are also some very useful tools that aren't very complicated. The key difference in these scenarios is that the visualization controls are displayed instead of embedded inside the spreadsheet. You will notice that there is also additional functionality inside of these controls.

Now to see this same example with additional options, choose the Data Mining ribbon from Microsoft Excel. This ribbon should be under Table Tools and slightly to the left (as depicted in Figure 6-31). In order for the data mining add-in to show up, you have to choose a table inside of Excel. When you choose the same table that you used in the preceding example, you should see a new item show up on the ribbon called Data Mining. When you choose this ribbon, you should see the options shown in Figure 6-32.

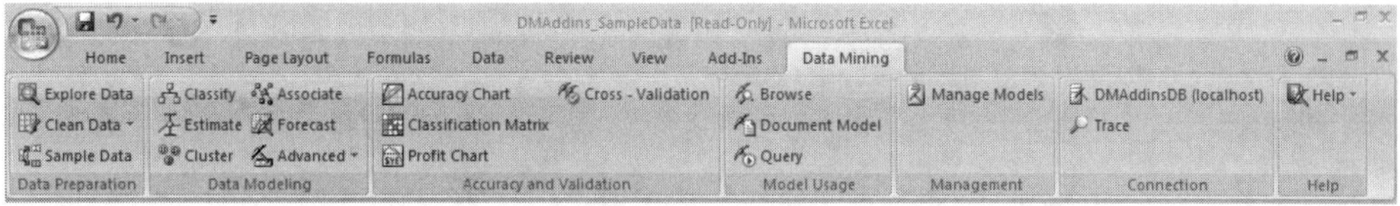

Figure 6-32 *The data mining add-in with additional options*

BI TIP

You can create, browse, document, query, manage, and do a whole lot more with this data mining add-in. One quick start technique that will help you in creating your data mining structure is to start the structure with Excel and set Use Temporary Models. The temporary models will persist after you disconnect from Excel. You only need to change the connection of the model to your relational database.

There are several useful functions that this add-in provides. Our goal in the next step is to duplicate the same visualization that was done by the forecasting add-in with the table tools.

Extended Add-In Forecasting

We are going to go through several of the sections of this add-in, but let's jump forward to the Data Modeling section and choose Forecast (as shown in Figure 6-33).

1. Choose Forecast in the Data Mining tab (Step A).
2. The Getting Started With The Forecast Wizard will pop up (Step B). Click Next to continue.
3. The Select Source Data screen allows you to choose either a spreadsheet range or an alternate data source (Step C). Just click Next.
4. The next screen lists the fields that are available for creation of the model (Step D). In this case they are the input fields. These are the fields that the algorithm will analyze. Click Next to continue.
5. The final screen allows you to name the mining model (stored inside of Analysis Services) with a description (Step E). The Enable Drillthrough check box allows you to pass through the data mining engine into the underlying rows that make up this data. This option would be valuable if you were doing a mailing list based on this data or similar. When you click Finish, you should see what is depicted in Figure 6-34.
6. Click the Show Historic Predictions check box (Step F).
7. Click the Show Deviations check box (Step G).
8. Increase the Prediction Steps to 10 (Step H).

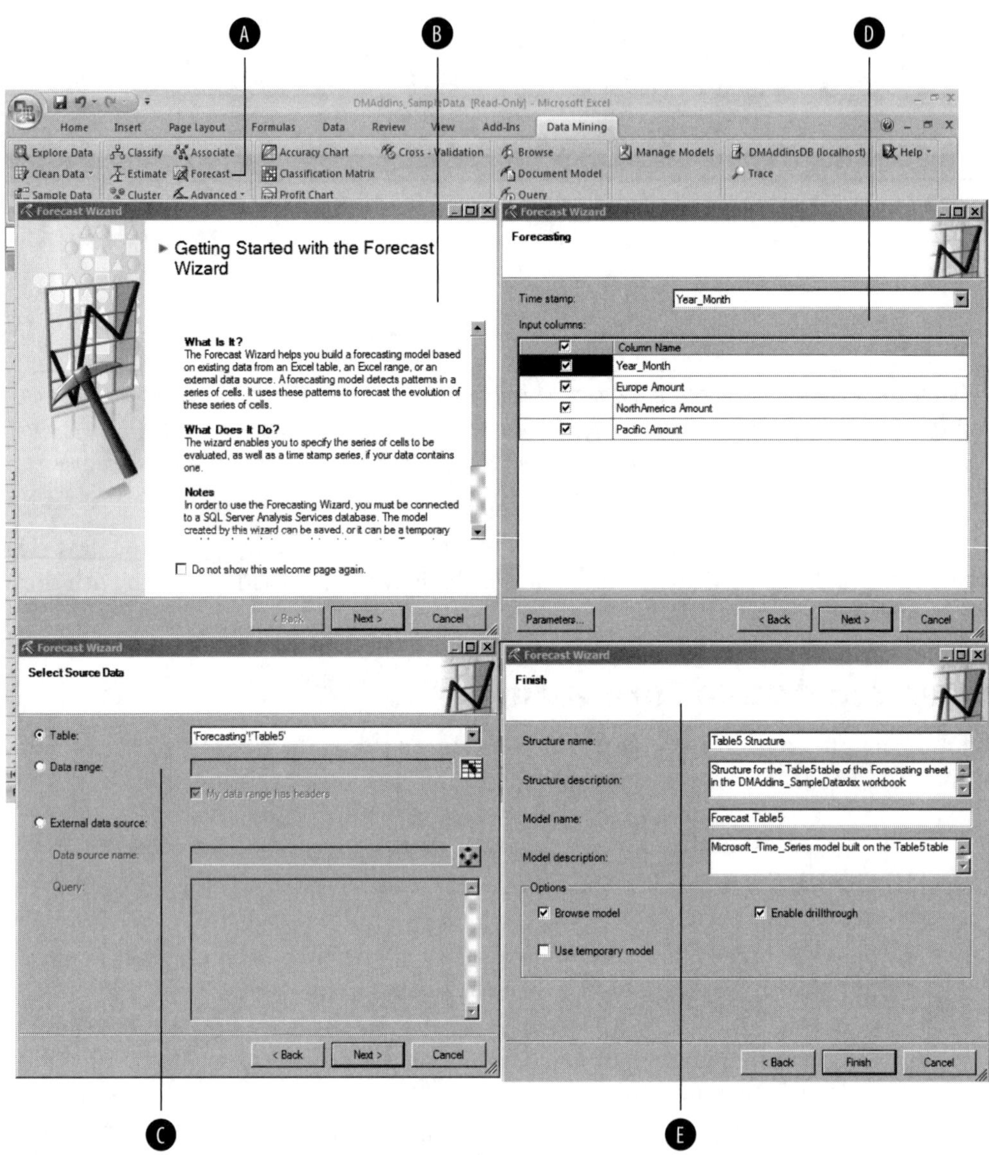

Figure 6-33 *The Forecast tool extended process*

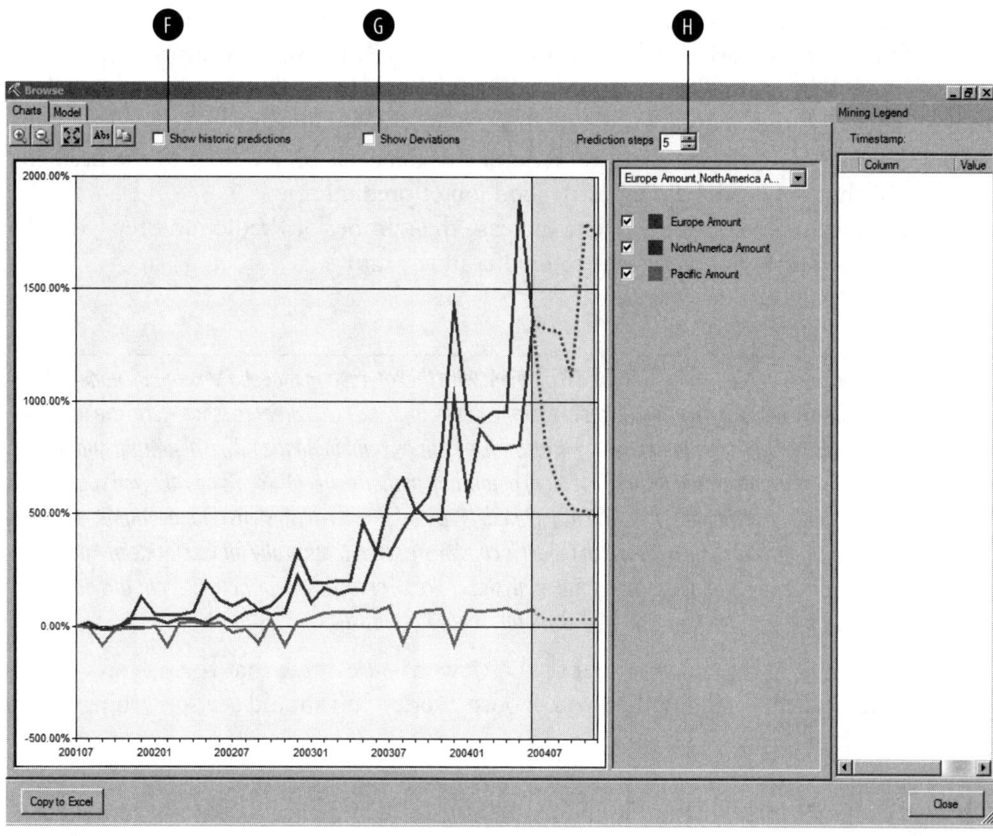

Figure 6-34 *The Forecast output viewer*

You should notice several differences between the Data Mining ribbon tab method and the Analyze tool method. First, the forecast model is now inside of a separate window.

BI TIP

This window contains the data mining viewer controls. These viewer controls are available for you to embed inside of your application if you wish. (More about the viewer controls is available from www.codeplex.com or msdn.microsoft.com.) The web controls are also downloadable as part of the SQL Server 2008 feature pack.

Second, you should also notice that there are more options available inside of the full viewer. The Show Historic Predictions value will tell you the predictions that would have been made at that point in time, so you visually see if the data can be predicted. You can also click the Show Deviations check box, which will show you high/low predicted values. You can see that the trend of this data was pretty close to the predicted model (and that the model did a pretty good job of predicting).

Third, you can also see that you can increase the number of Prediction Steps, which is the amount of time that you want to predict in the future.

BI TIP

In the SQL Server 2008 version, Microsoft fixed a problem with the forecasting model. The original model is based on the ARTxp (Auto Regression Trees with Cross Predict) algorithm, which was great for short-term predictions but was erratic with longer-term predictions. Microsoft fixed this by combining the ARTxp algorithm and the ARIMA (Auto Regressive Integrated Moving Average) algorithm. In this model Microsoft has allowed you to have the best of each model working together. The ARTxp model is used for short-term steps and the ARIMA is used for longer term predictions. The choices for which model is chosen are set automatically for you inside of Analysis Servers. This option can be changed inside of the Analysis Services. For further information about this particular algorithm, see http://msdn.microsoft.com/en-us/library/bb677216.aspx.

Fourth, in the top left-hand corner of the viewer, you can see that there is an additional tab called Model. When you choose Model, you should see something similar to what is depicted in Figure 6-35.

1. Click the Model tab and notice the different visualization (Step A).
2. Click Close (Step B).

This is a different view of the model; in this case it is the decision tree viewer. This gives you a lot more information about which choices were made by the model and why.

Extended Add-In Explore Data

Next we will take a look at the Explore Data tool. This tool does not require any access to SQL Server Analysis Services (so it is self-contained and does not need any outside connection; rather, the tool interacts with the data from the spreadsheet directly). This example uses the Table Analysis Tool worksheet (notice at the bottom of the sample spreadsheet the tab labeled Table Analysis Tools Sample). You will then notice in the Data Mining section of the ribbon at the top of Excel that there are several tools broken down into several different sections. The first section is called Data Preparation;

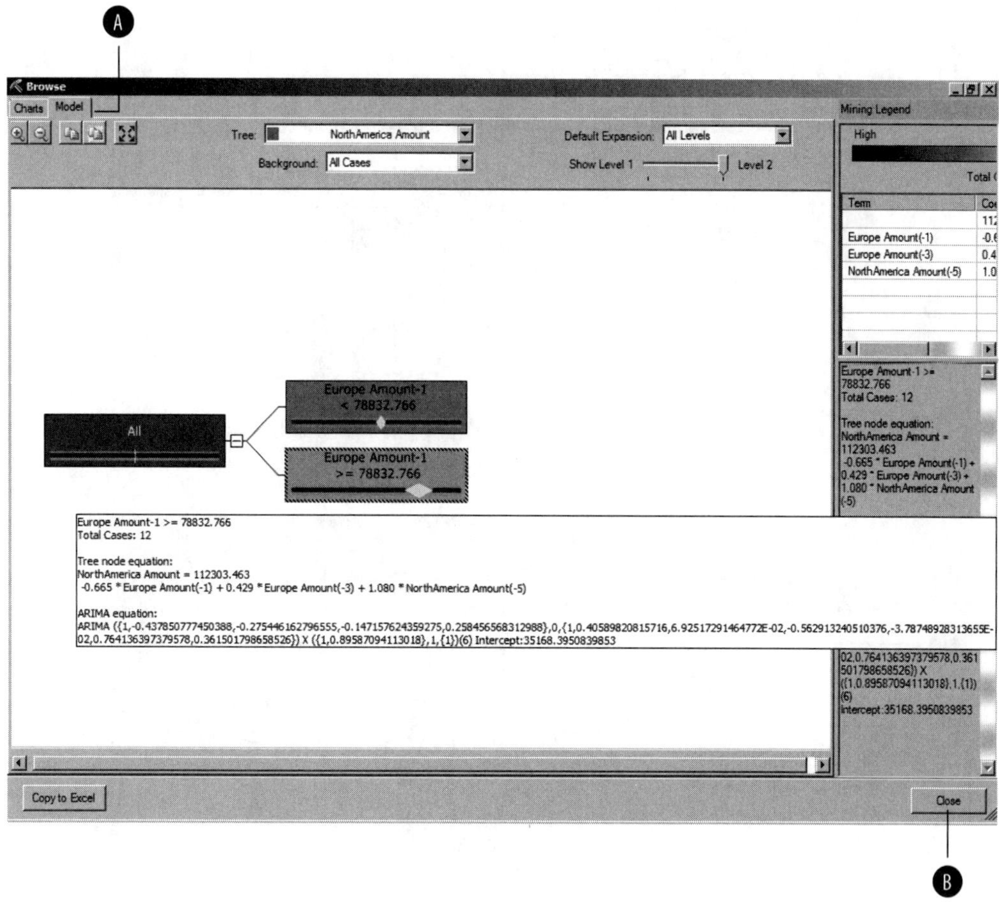

Figure 6-35 *The Model viewer of the Forecast tool*

this section contains tools that are very useful for interacting with your data. In this example we will be choosing the Explore Data tool (as shown in Figure 6-36).

1. Click the Explore Data tool in the Data Mining ribbon (Step A).
2. Click the Table Analysis Tools Sample data tab (Step B).

   After you launch the "Explore Data" tool, you should see the first screen of the Getting Started With The Explore Data Wizard (Step C). Click Next to continue.
3. On the Select Source Data screen, you can either accept or specify a data range (Step D). Click Next to continue.

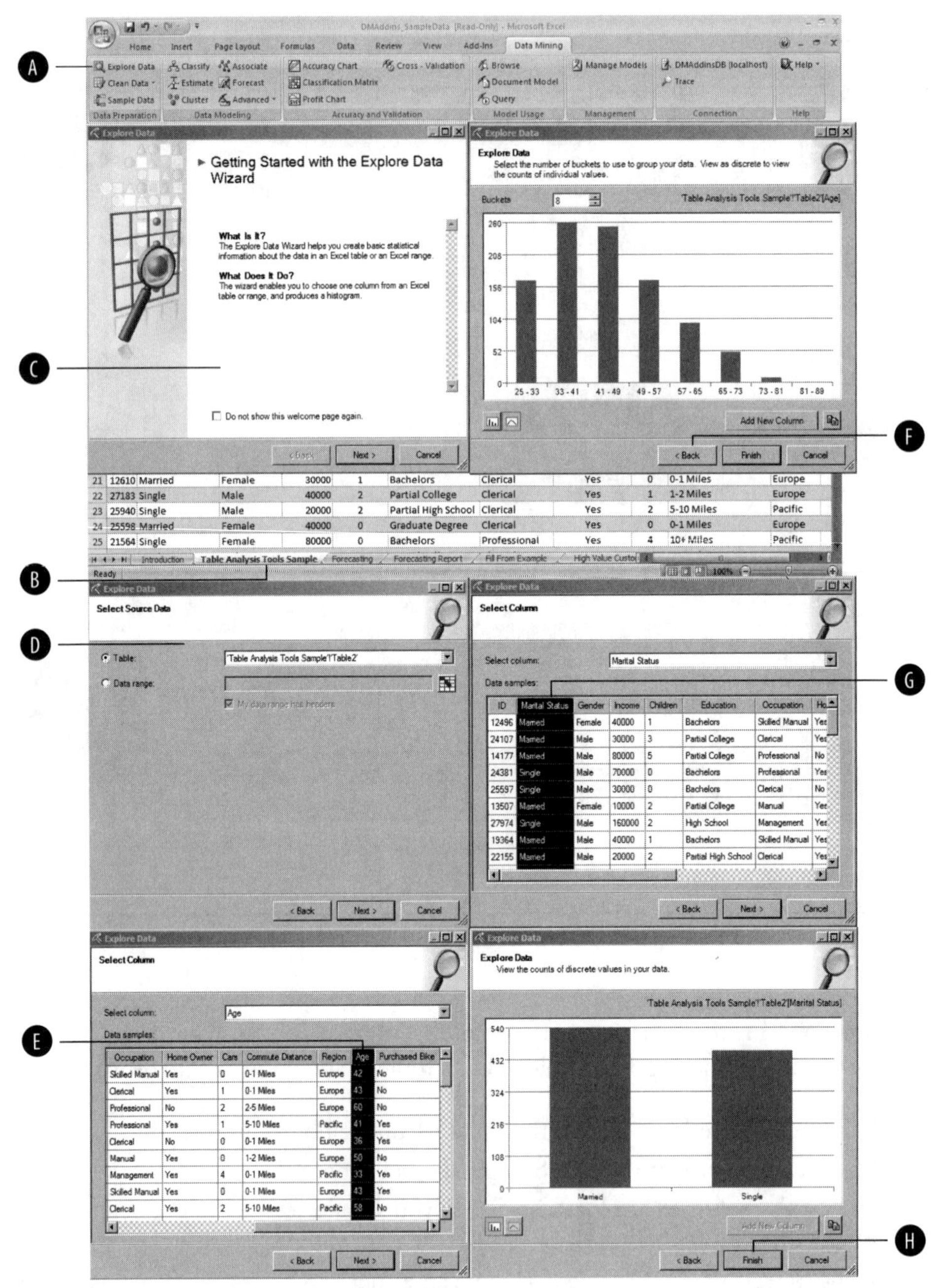

Figure 6-36 *Choose the Table Analysis Tool worksheet and then Explore Data.*

4. Choose the Age column in the Select Column screen (Step E) and then click Next to continue.

   This screen contains the columns that are available from the worksheet. You can choose any of the columns, but in this example choose the Age column. (You can either choose the column from the drop-down list box at the top or click the individual column.) Once you choose Age, you should see the Explore Data screen.
5. On the Explore Data screen, click Back to select a different column (Step F).

   The Explore Data screen shows the data distribution of ages in the dataset. The default is for data to be broken down into eight different buckets, but you can adjust to fit your needs. If you click Back, you should be back at the screen that allows you to choose the columns.
6. Click Marital Status (Step G) and click Next.
7. Click Finish (Step H).

This is the distribution of Married versus Single people in the dataset. This tool will give you a quick overview of the distribution of the data elements.

Extended Add-In Data Preparation

The next tool that we will cover in the Data Preparation section is the Clean Data tool. When you choose this tool, you are presented with two options: Outliers and Re-label. For the next example we are going to pull off a section of the data into a different sheet. You may also notice that you can re-label, sample, or delete from this tool as well. The following steps are shown in Figure 6-37.

1. Click the Clean Data drop-down and select the Outliers (Step A). You should see the Outliers window open up (Step B). Click Next to continue.
2. This next screen allows you choose the default table or specify a data range from an Excel worksheet (Step C). Click Next.

NOTE

You can choose any column, but for this example we will be using Age.

3. Choose the Age column or choose Age from the Select Column drop-down list box (Step D) and choose Next.
4. On the Specify Thresholds window move the Minimum slider up to 31 (or you can type **31** in the text box, Step E).
5. Also on the Specify Thresholds window move the Maximum slider up to 50 (or you can type **50** in the text box, Step F).

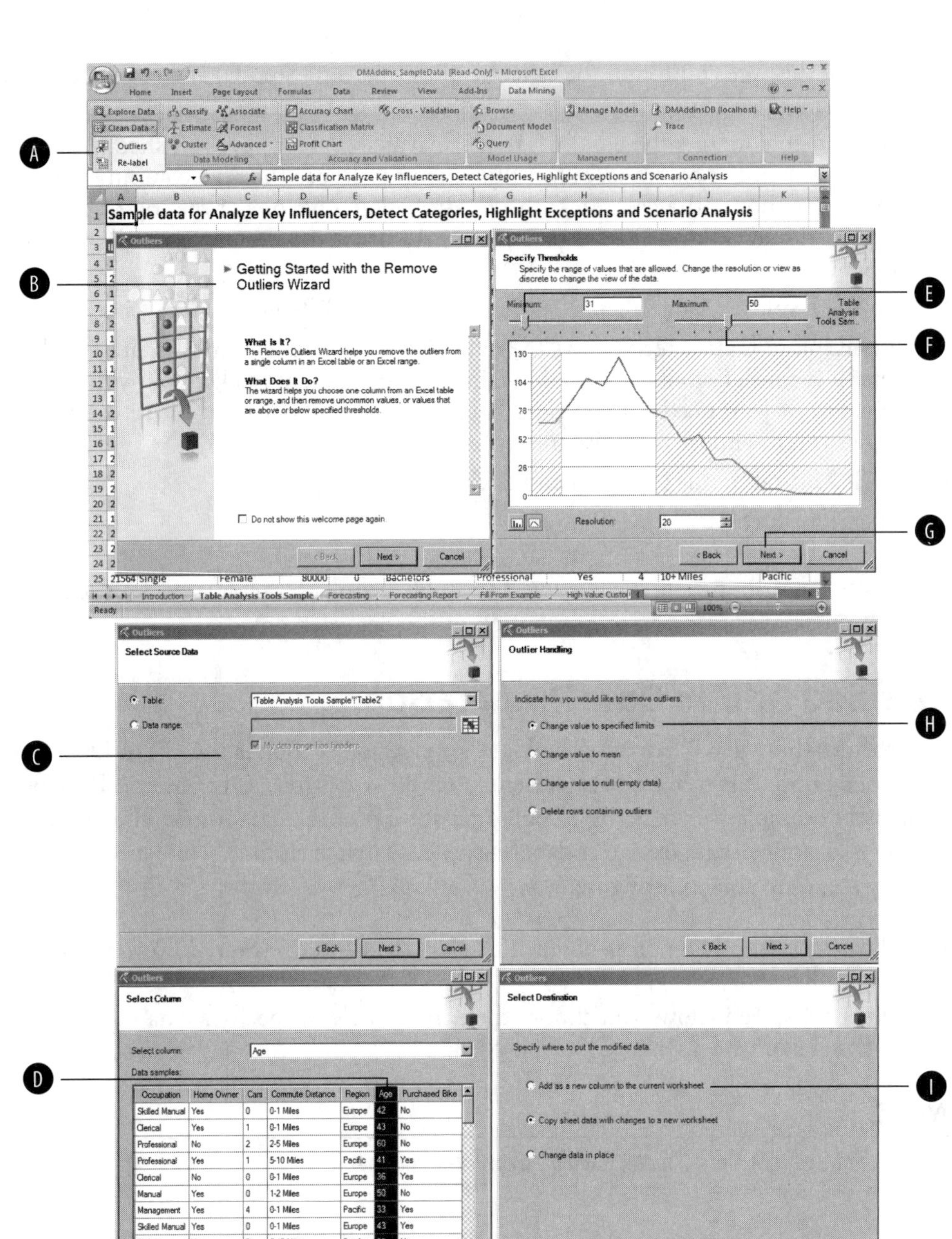

Figure 6-37 *Choose Clean Data and the Outliers tool.*

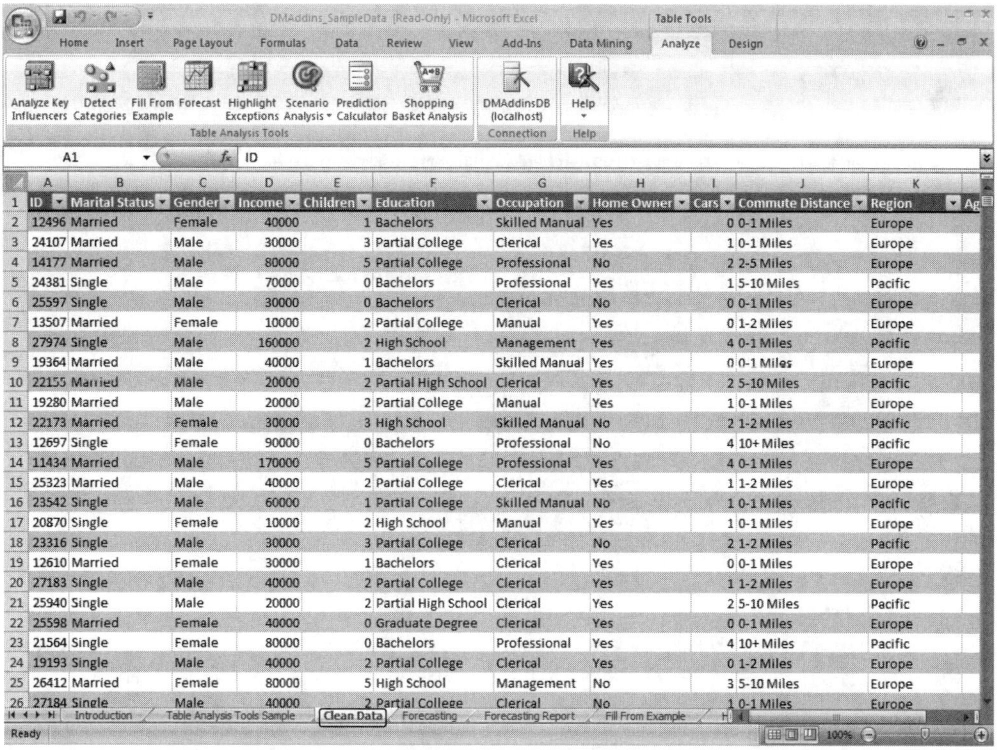

ID	Marital Status	Gender	Income	Children	Education	Occupation	Home Owner	Cars	Commute Distance	Region
12496	Married	Female	40000	1	Bachelors	Skilled Manual	Yes	0	0-1 Miles	Europe
24107	Married	Male	30000	3	Partial College	Clerical	Yes	1	0-1 Miles	Europe
14177	Married	Male	80000	5	Partial College	Professional	No	2	2-5 Miles	Europe
24381	Single	Male	70000	0	Bachelors	Professional	Yes	1	5-10 Miles	Pacific
25597	Single	Male	30000	0	Bachelors	Clerical	No	0	0-1 Miles	Europe
13507	Married	Female	10000	2	Partial College	Manual	Yes	0	1-2 Miles	Europe
27974	Single	Male	160000	2	High School	Management	Yes	4	0-1 Miles	Pacific
19364	Married	Male	40000	1	Bachelors	Skilled Manual	Yes	0	0-1 Miles	Europe
22155	Married	Male	20000	2	Partial High School	Clerical	Yes	2	5-10 Miles	Pacific
19280	Married	Male	20000	2	Partial College	Manual	Yes	1	0-1 Miles	Europe
22173	Married	Female	30000	3	High School	Skilled Manual	No	2	1-2 Miles	Pacific
12697	Single	Female	90000	0	Bachelors	Professional	No	4	10+ Miles	Pacific
11434	Married	Male	170000	5	Partial College	Professional	Yes	4	0-1 Miles	Europe
25323	Married	Male	40000	2	Partial College	Clerical	Yes	1	1-2 Miles	Europe
23542	Single	Male	60000	1	Partial College	Skilled Manual	No	1	0-1 Miles	Pacific
20870	Single	Female	10000	2	High School	Manual	Yes	1	0-1 Miles	Europe
23316	Single	Male	30000	3	Partial College	Clerical	No	2	1-2 Miles	Pacific
12610	Married	Female	30000	1	Bachelors	Clerical	Yes	0	0-1 Miles	Europe
27183	Single	Male	40000	2	Partial College	Clerical	Yes	1	1-2 Miles	Europe
25940	Single	Male	20000	2	Partial High School	Clerical	Yes	2	5-10 Miles	Pacific
25598	Married	Female	40000	0	Graduate Degree	Clerical	Yes	0	0-1 Miles	Europe
21564	Single	Female	80000	0	Bachelors	Professional	Yes	4	10+ Miles	Pacific
19193	Single	Male	40000	2	Partial College	Clerical	Yes	0	1-2 Miles	Europe
26412	Married	Female	80000	5	High School	Management	No	3	5-10 Miles	Europe
27184	Single	Male	40000	2	Partial College	Clerical	No	1	0-1 Miles	Europe

Figure 6-38 *The Clean Data worksheet*

In the example we are looking for ages between 31 and 50. Next we have to choose what to do with these age options. Click Next (Step G).

6. The Outlier Handling window gives you the choice to modify, delete, or leave the dataset as is. Choose the default option (which is Change Value To Specified Limits) and choose Next (Step H).
7. In the Select Destination window the default option is to "Add as a new column to the current worksheet." Choose this option (Step I), then click Finish to continue.

   You should notice a new worksheet called Clean Data as shown in Figure 6-38.

This new worksheet contains data where the age is between 31 and 50. This is a fast way to pull a smaller section of data over to a new worksheet tab.

Extended Add-In Clustering Tool

Previously in this chapter we used the Forecast tool in the Analyze tab. Now we will be using the Cluster tool included with the Data Modeling tools in the Data Mining tab (see Figure 6-39). You will notice that this tool allows you to configure the sampling

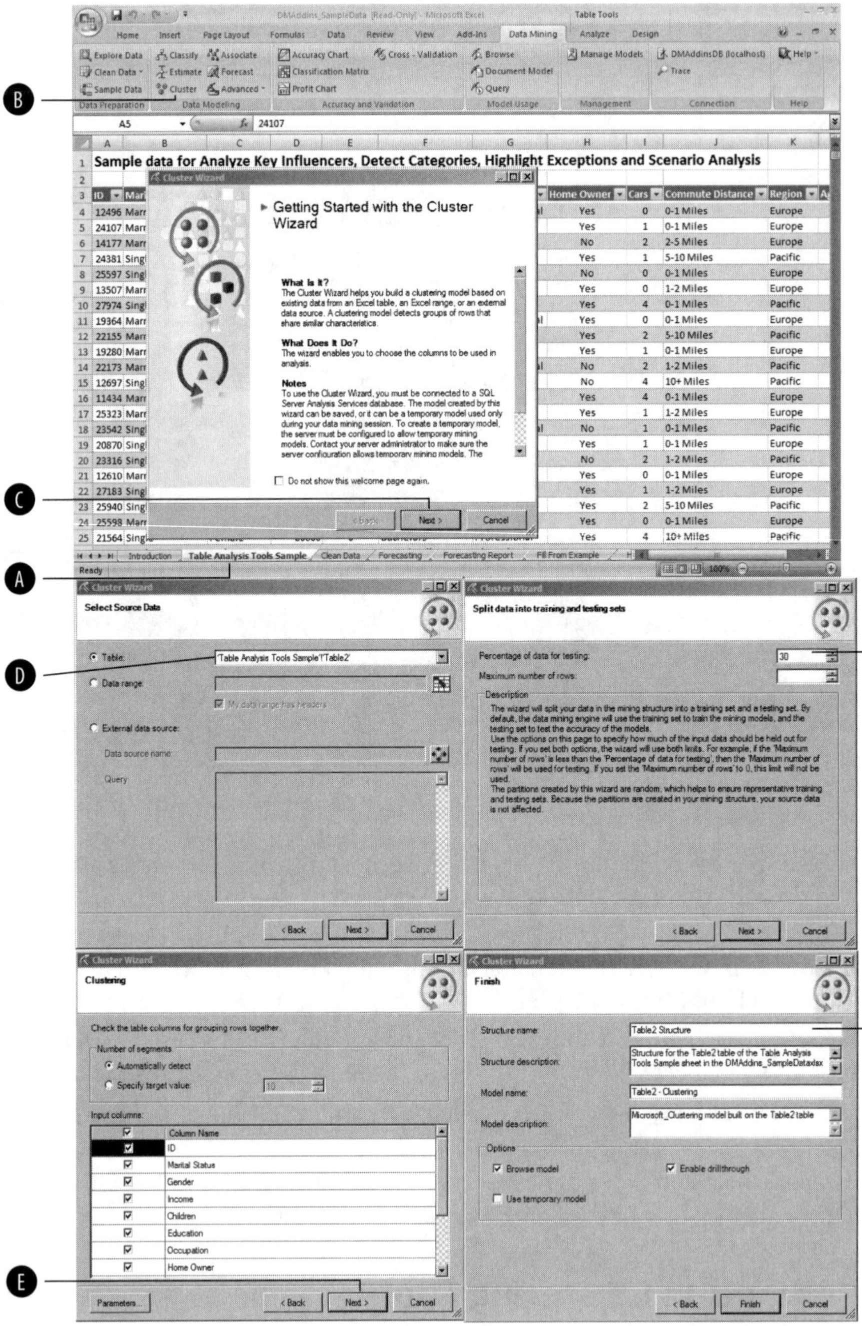

Figure 6-39 *The Cluster Tool process*

set and even allows you to pull data from an external data source. This tool includes additional viewers as well.

1. Click the Table Analysis Tools Sample tab (Step A).
2. Click the Cluster tool inside of the Data Modeling group (on the ribbon, Step B).
3. In the Getting Started window of the Cluster Wizard, choose Next to continue (Step C).
4. Choose the default data source option in the Select Source Data window (Step D) and choose Next to continue.

BI TIP

The options in the Select Source Data window allow you to choose a table, choose a range inside of the Excel spreadsheet, or specify an external data source.

5. Choose Next from the Cluster Wizard Clustering window (Step E).
6. In the Split Data Into Training And Testing Sets window, choose the default option (which is 30%) (Step F) and choose Next to continue.
7. The Finish window allows you to name the model structure and model inside of Analysis Services (Step G). Click Finish to continue.
8. After a few seconds (the time is dependent on computing resources, network capacity, and the like), you should see the cluster viewer depicted in Figure 6-40. Choose the data element that you want to analyze (Step H). Select the Shading Variable as Population (Step I).
9. Also try moving the All Links slider up and down to see the strength of cluster correlations (Step J).

   The darker the line, the stronger the correlation between the clusters and the attribute in the top-right corner of the window. You can change the attribute (such as age or income) to see which clusters complement each other.

The screen shown in Figure 6-40 is the cluster viewer control. Several options allow you to customize or change the view. You should notice that the individual clusters of groups are preliminarily named Cluster *X* (*X* being an auto-incrementing number).

BI TIP

You can edit these cluster names into something more meaningful if you want. All you have to do is right-click the cluster and choose Rename.

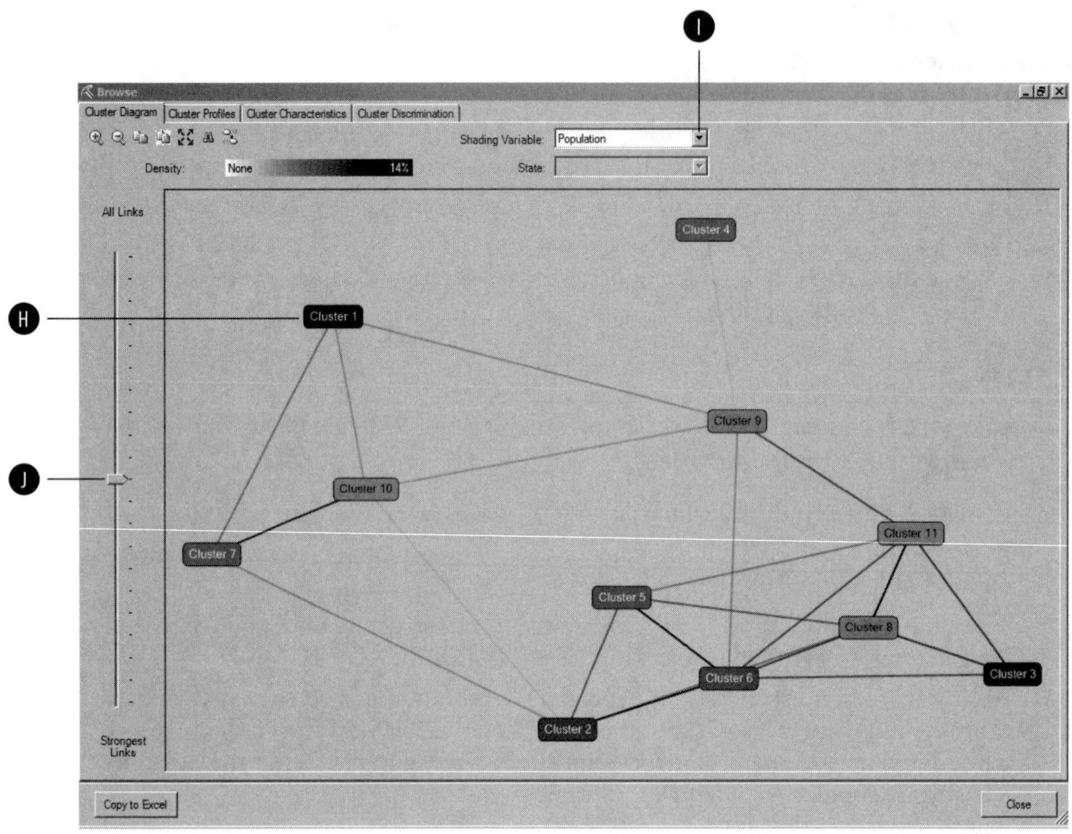

Figure 6-40 *The cluster viewer, where you can move the slider on the left side up and down and change the shading value*

If you move the slider on the left side of the window up and down, you should see the density of the lines between the clusters change.

Next, we will look at the differing cluster characteristics.

1. Click the Cluster Profiles on the top tab (Step A) and you should see something similar to Figure 6-41.

   On this screen you can see in the first column the name of the different data attributes, and in the graphics on the right you can see the different columns where the different clusters are represented. Under the name of the individual cluster, you can see the population. (This is the number of data rows that make up that cluster.)

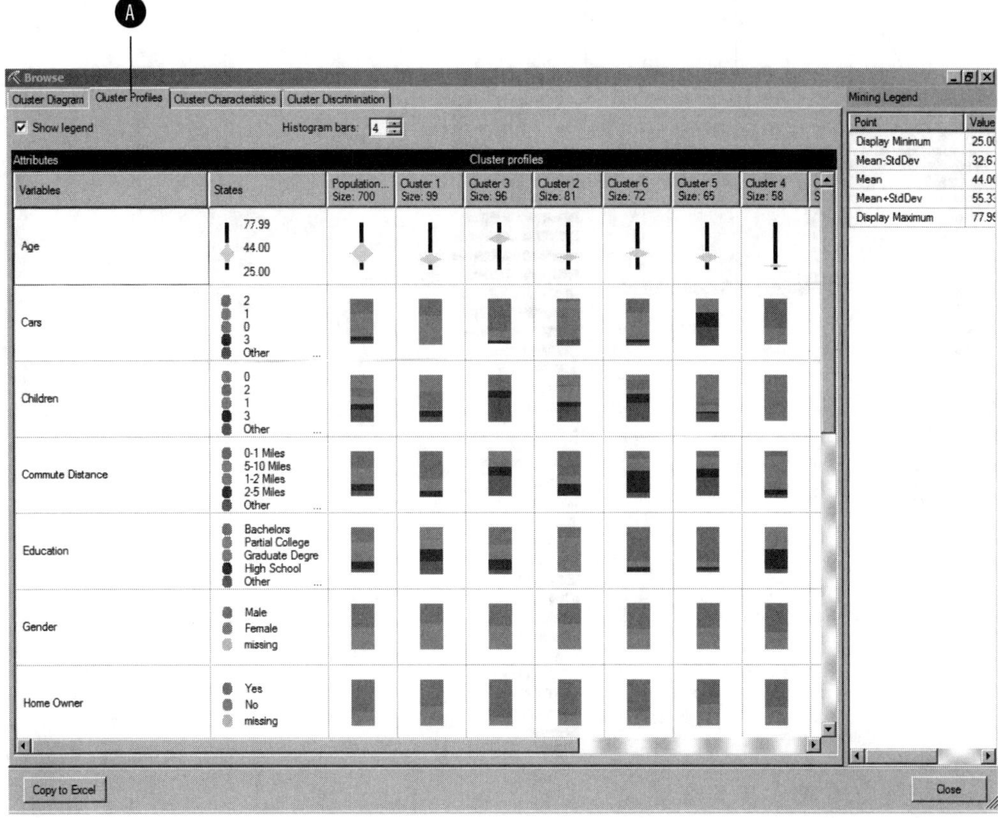

Figure 6-41 *The Cluster Profiles viewer*

2. Now click the tab titled Cluster Characteristics (Step B) to see the screen depicted in Figure 6-42.
3. In the browse window in the Cluster Characteristics tab, choose different clusters with the Cluster text box (Step C).

   The Cluster Characteristics screen shows you the Variables (or the data elements) and the strength or probability that a given value or range appears in that cluster of data. The next view (shown in Figure 6-43) will show how you can compare two different clusters of data.
4. Now click the Cluster Discrimination tab to see what is shown in Figure 6-43 (Step D).

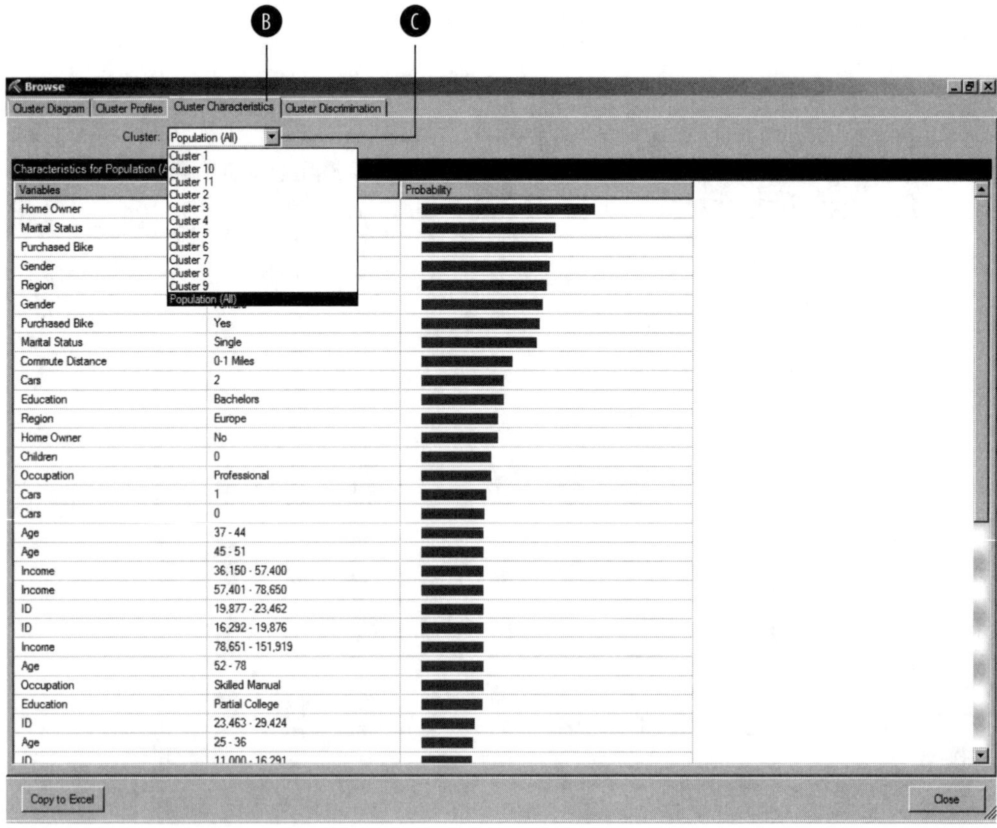

Figure 6-42 *The Cluster Characteristics viewer*

The view in Figure 6-43 shows how you can compare two different clusters. You can choose different clusters from the drop-down list box at the top.

5. Choose different clusters to compare them to each other (Step E).

   The other tools that are in the Data Modeling section allow you to use algorithms or models for different uses, such as Association and Estimation. The next section is Accuracy And Validation. These tools were demonstrated earlier in this chapter, where you went through the Prediction Calculator (the lift charts, cross-validation, and accuracy charts).

Extended Add-In Browsing a Model

The final section that you will walk through is the browsing of a model that was already created for you. You have to install the sample applications on your Analysis Services instance (the SQL Server sample databases are available at

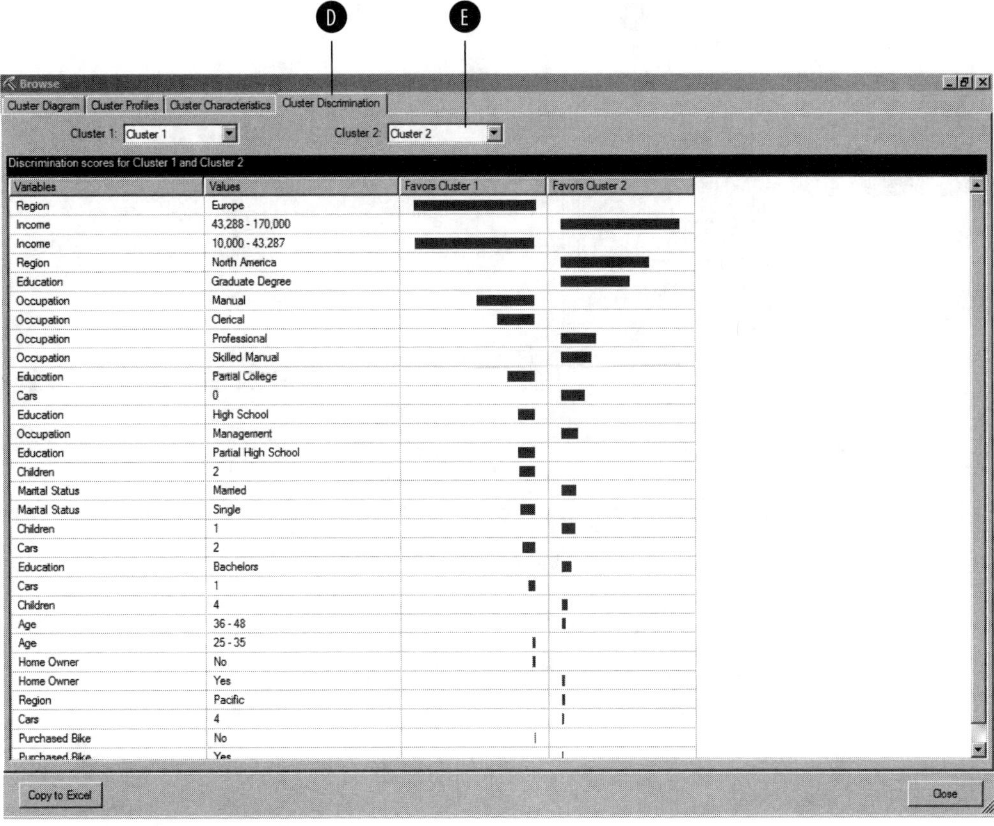

Figure 6-43 *The Cluster Discrimination viewer*

http://msftdbprodsamples.codeplex.com/). Once you have the samples installed for Analysis Services, you need to set the connection inside of the add-in to point to Adventure Works. On the Data tab you should see a group of tools called Connection as shown in Figure 6-44.

1. Click the Connection section of the ribbon (Step A).
2. Click New to create a new connection (Step B).
3. Set the Server Name to the server name where the samples are loaded (Step C).
4. Choose the logon credentials necessary for connecting to the server where the samples are installed (Step D).

   You need to ensure that the connection is set to the server where the samples are located. In this case the samples are located on the same machine on which I am running Excel.

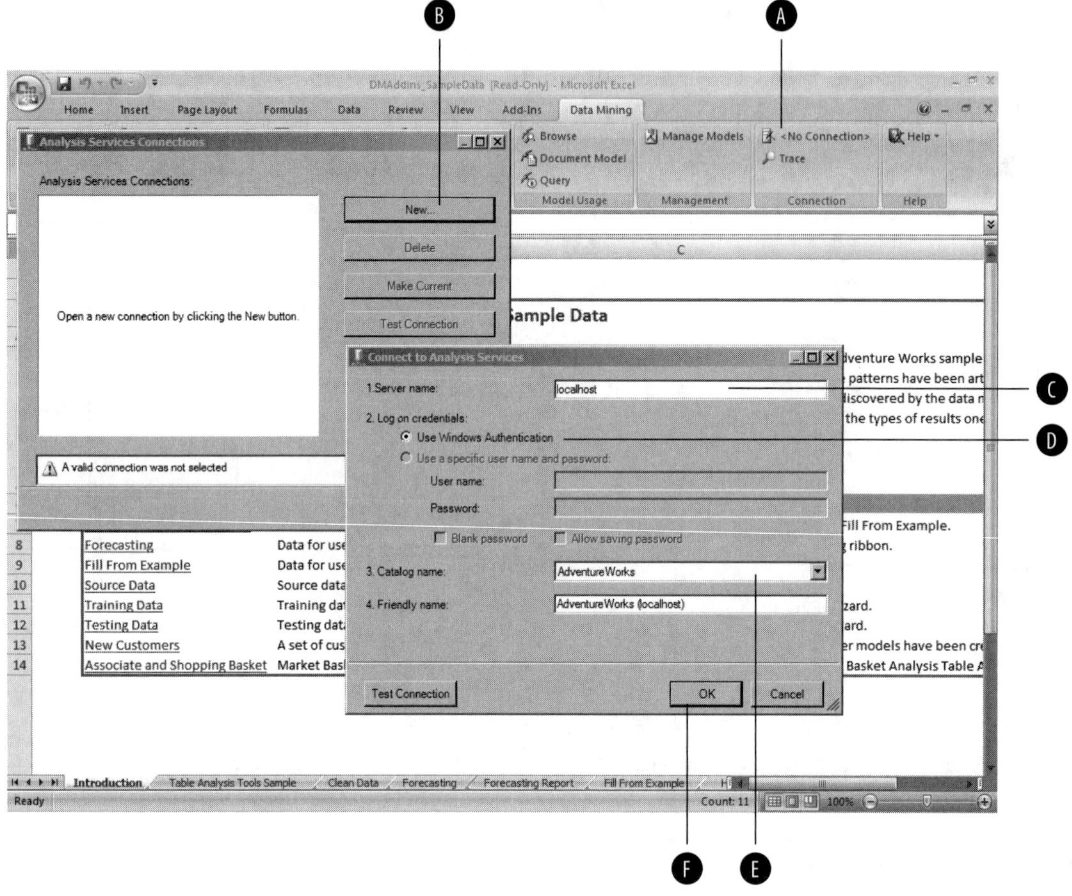

Figure 6-44 *The current connection on the Data Mining ribbon process*

5. Set the catalog name to AdventureWorks (Step E). Also make sure the Friendly Name is set. If AdventureWorks is not listed, then the samples are not installed correctly.
6. Click OK to continue (Step F). You will see a tab that looks like Figure 6-45.
7. You should see AdventureWorks (and the name of your server) in the Connection area (Step G).
8. Select Browse under Model Usage (Step H).
9. In the Browse window under Market Basket, select Association (Step I) and click Next (Step J) to continue.

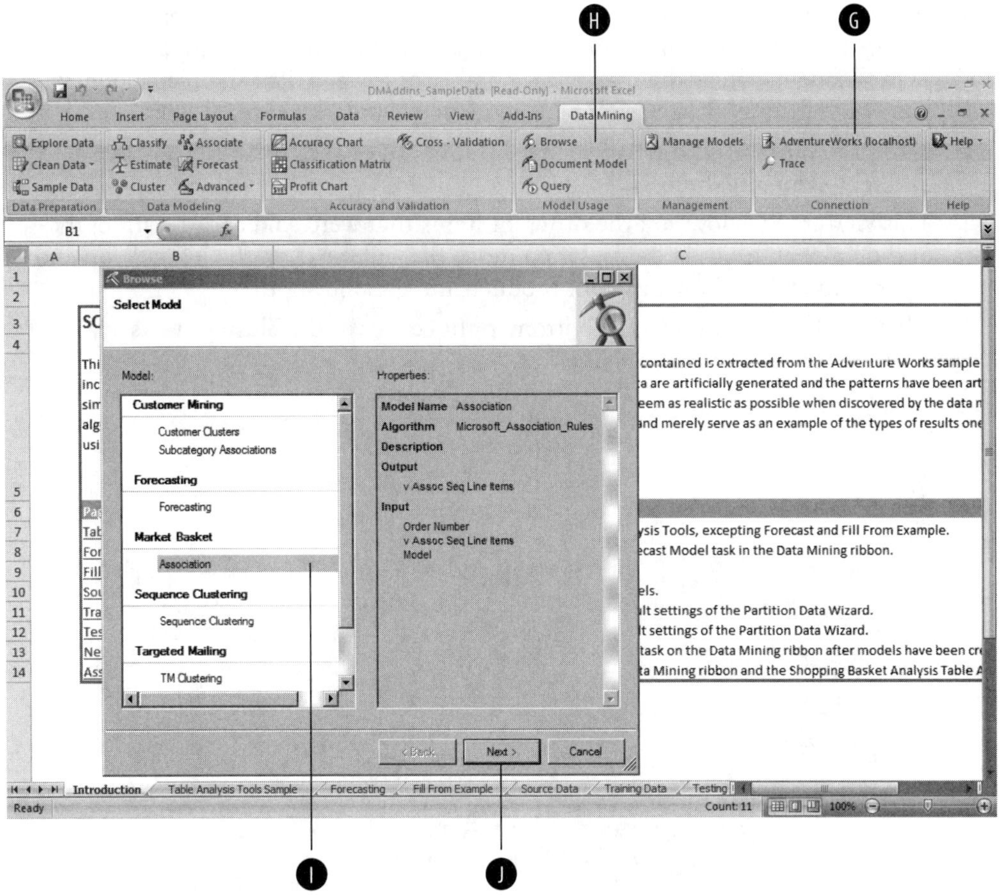

Figure 6-45 *In the Data Mining tab, choose Browse under Model Usage.*

The options on the left side of the Select Model window allow you to browse the models that are on the server, and the window on the right gives you more information about the model, such as the algorithm that was used and the input and output items. Next we will look at a couple of the viewers that we haven't seen yet. (Several are included.)

BI TIP

These viewers are the same viewers that are included with the data mining web controls.

10. After you click Next, your screen should look like Figure 6-46, where you can see the rules that were used and the probability. You can also change parameters in the model (such as the maximum number of rows). Click the Dependency Network tab (Step K) to see the Dependency Network viewer (Figure 6-47).
11. Move the slider up and down to see the strength of the correlations between different elements (Step L).

    This viewer will show you the different items that were sold and the strength of the link between the items. If you move the slider bar on the left side up and down, you will see how different products impact one another.
12. Click the Close button in the bottom-right corner of the cluster browser window (Step M).

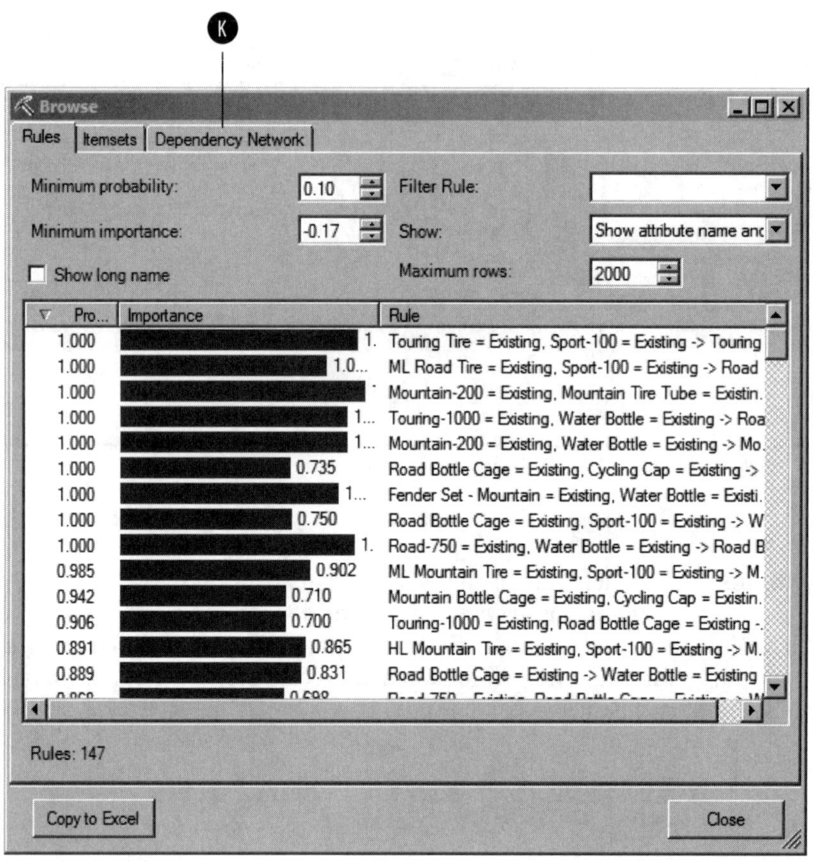

Figure 6-46 *The Rules window*

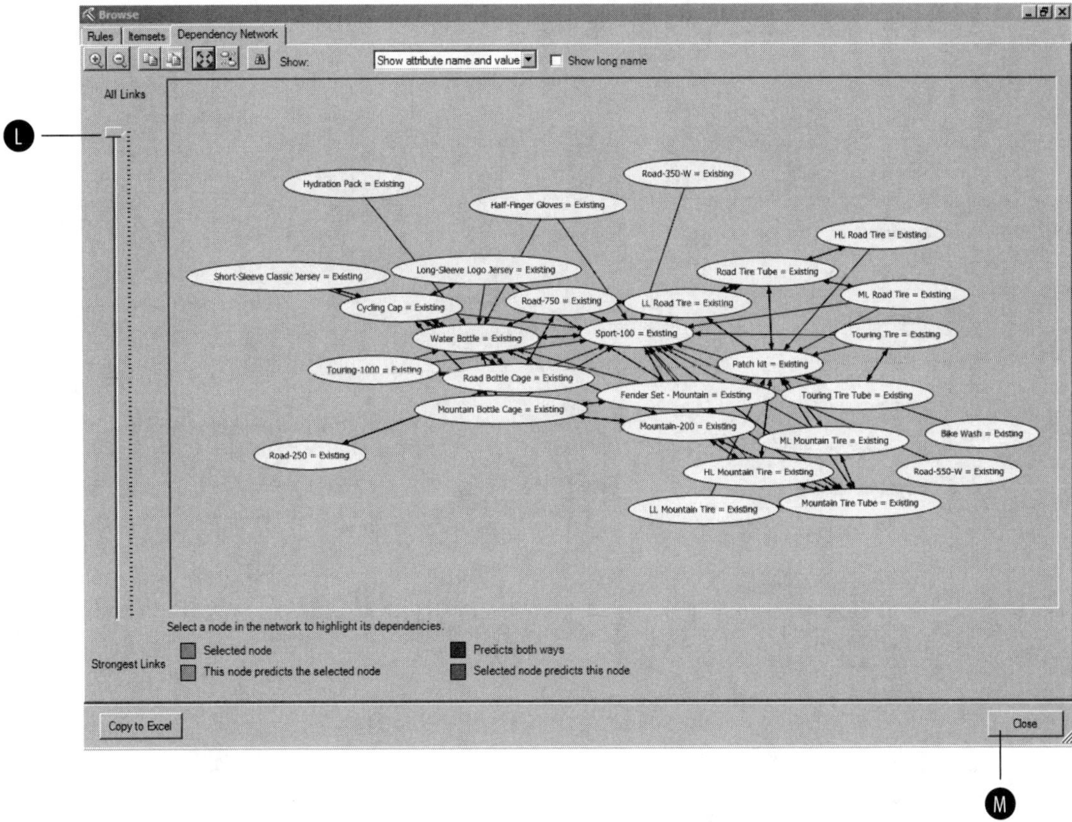

Figure 6-47 *The Dependency Network viewer*

13. Choose Browse Model again to see the screen shown in Figure 6-48. Select the TM Naive Bayes model (Step N) and click Next to continue (Step O).
14. On the Data Mining ribbon select Browse under Model Usage.
15. This time choose TM Naive Bayes and select Next to continue. You should see something similar to what is depicted in Figure 6-49.

    This Dependency Network diagram will show you the impact on different data elements and whether they are a bike buyer. You can move the slider bar on the left side to see which item has the strongest impact on being a bike buyer.
16. Select Close to continue.

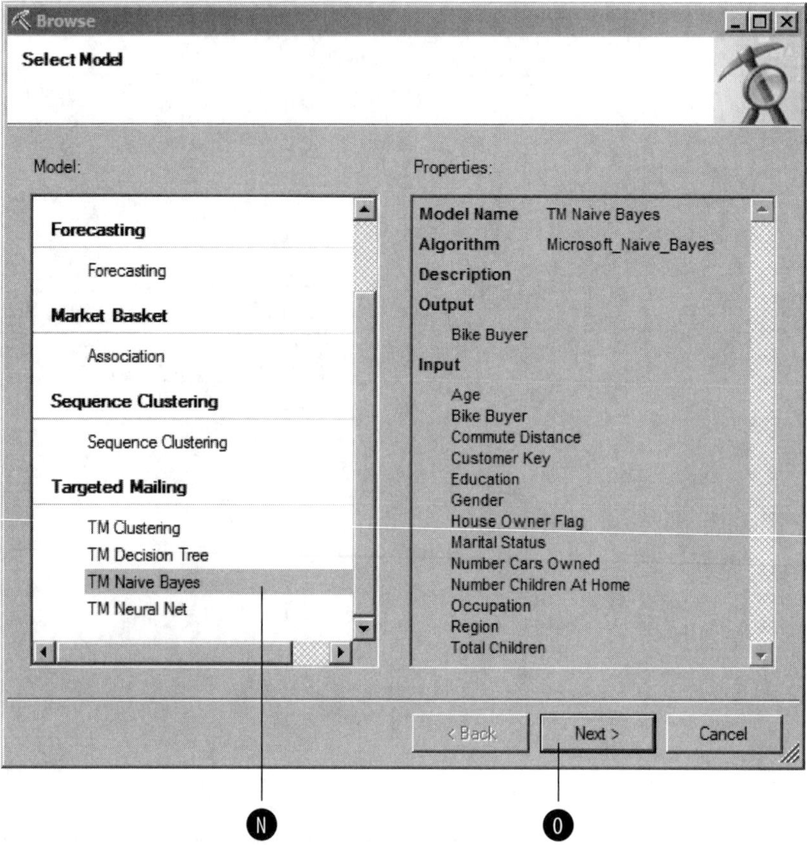

Figure 6-48 *The Select Model screen*

The Visio Add-In Tool

The next tool which we will use is the add-in to Visio. (This was installed as part of the same tool that we have been covering.) The Visio add-in tool is a little different from the tools inside of Excel. The previous tools that we covered were centered on creation and viewing of the mining models, but the Visio tool is used only for viewing models that were previously created. The Visio tool doesn't have the entire complement of models available (as in the Excel add-in), but there are three very interesting ones (dependency, cluster, and decision tree).

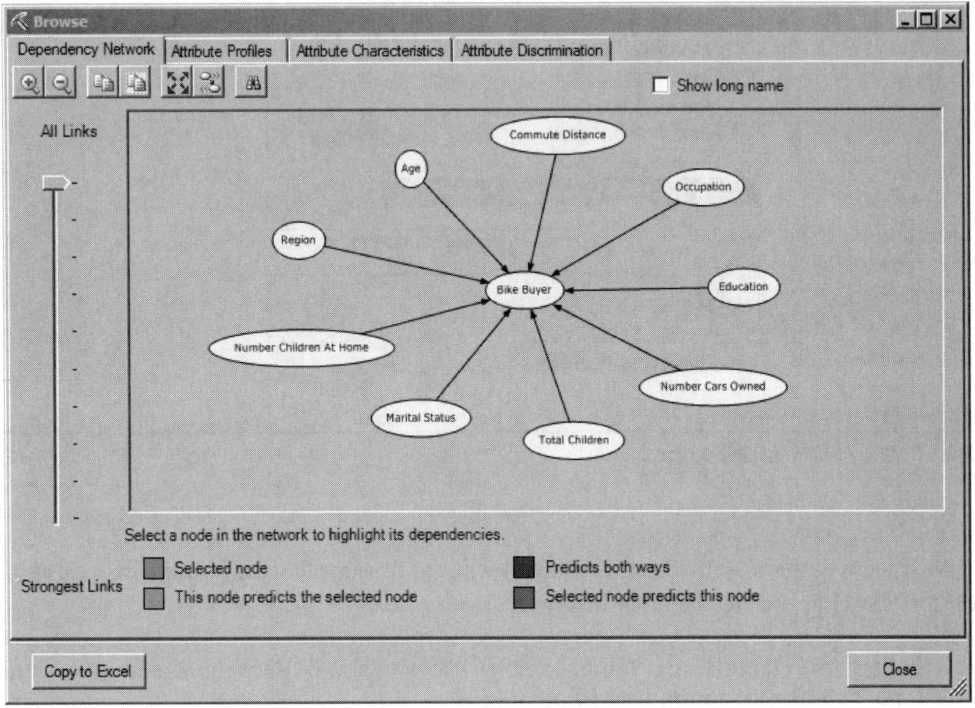

Figure 6-49 *The Dependency Network viewer*

BI TIP

When you install the data mining add-in, you are prompted about whether or not you would like the Visio add-in installed. In order to use the Visio add-in, you should also have Microsoft Visio installed (2007 or 2010 version). An evaluation edition of Visio is available from www.microsoft.com/visio.

In the next section we will launch the Data Mining Visio template.

1. Open the programs folder (choose All Programs) and then the folder Microsoft SQL 2008 Data Mining Add-ins.
2. You should see Data Mining Visio Template. Click this template as shown in Figure 6-50.

BI TIP

If you did not install the add-in with your initial install, you can run the installation again and update the installation to include the Visio add-in.

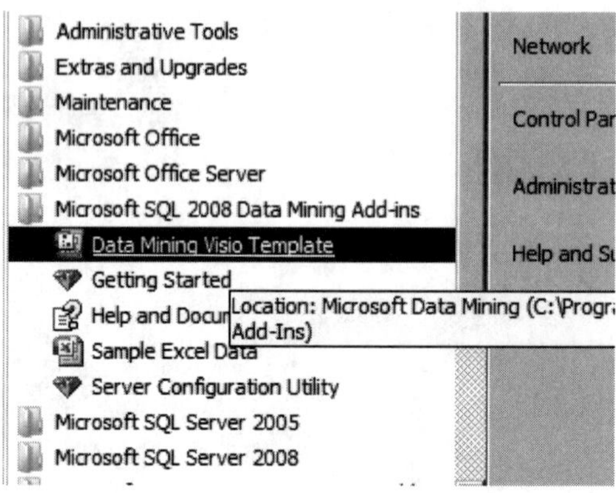

Figure 6-50 *The Data Mining Visio template*

Next we will manage the connections to where our sample data mining structures reside, following the steps shown in Figure 6-51.

1. In the new Data Mining tab inside of Visio, you should see Manage Connections. Choose this menu item (Step A).

   Now that we have a connection to a cube where samples are located, we will use the decision tree viewer.
2. After you click Manage Connections you may see a current connection (Step B). If this is the connection where your data mining structures are located then you should be good. Click Close and proceed to the next sequence of steps.
3. In the Analysis Services Connections window, click New to establish a new connection (Step C).
4. In the Connect To Analysis Services dialog box enter the server (Step D) and database (Step E) where your data mining objects are located and click OK to continue. In this example I have used the AdventureWorks sample database (which is available on www.codeplex.com).
5. Now that you have a connection to the server, either choose to insert a decision tree from the data mining menu or choose Decision Tree from the left panel (Step F).

Next we are going to go into the Decision Tree Wizard shown in Figure 6-52.

1. The first wizard dialog box describes the wizard. Click Next to continue to the connection box (Step A).
2. Verify that the connection is to where the example mining structures are installed (in this case on the localhost in the database AdventureWorks, Step B). Click Next to continue to choose which mining model you want to view.

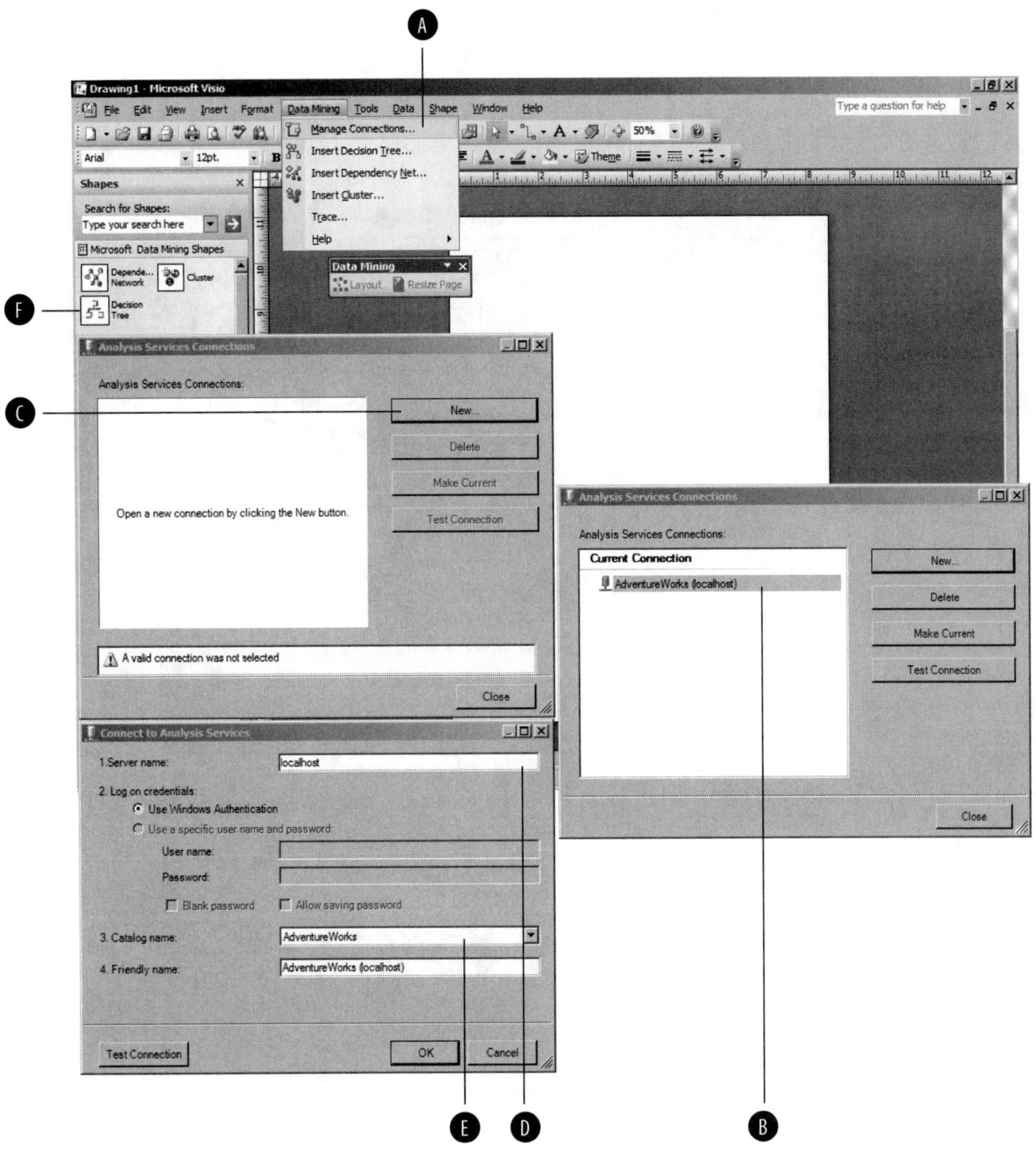

Figure 6-51 *Choose Manage Connections.*

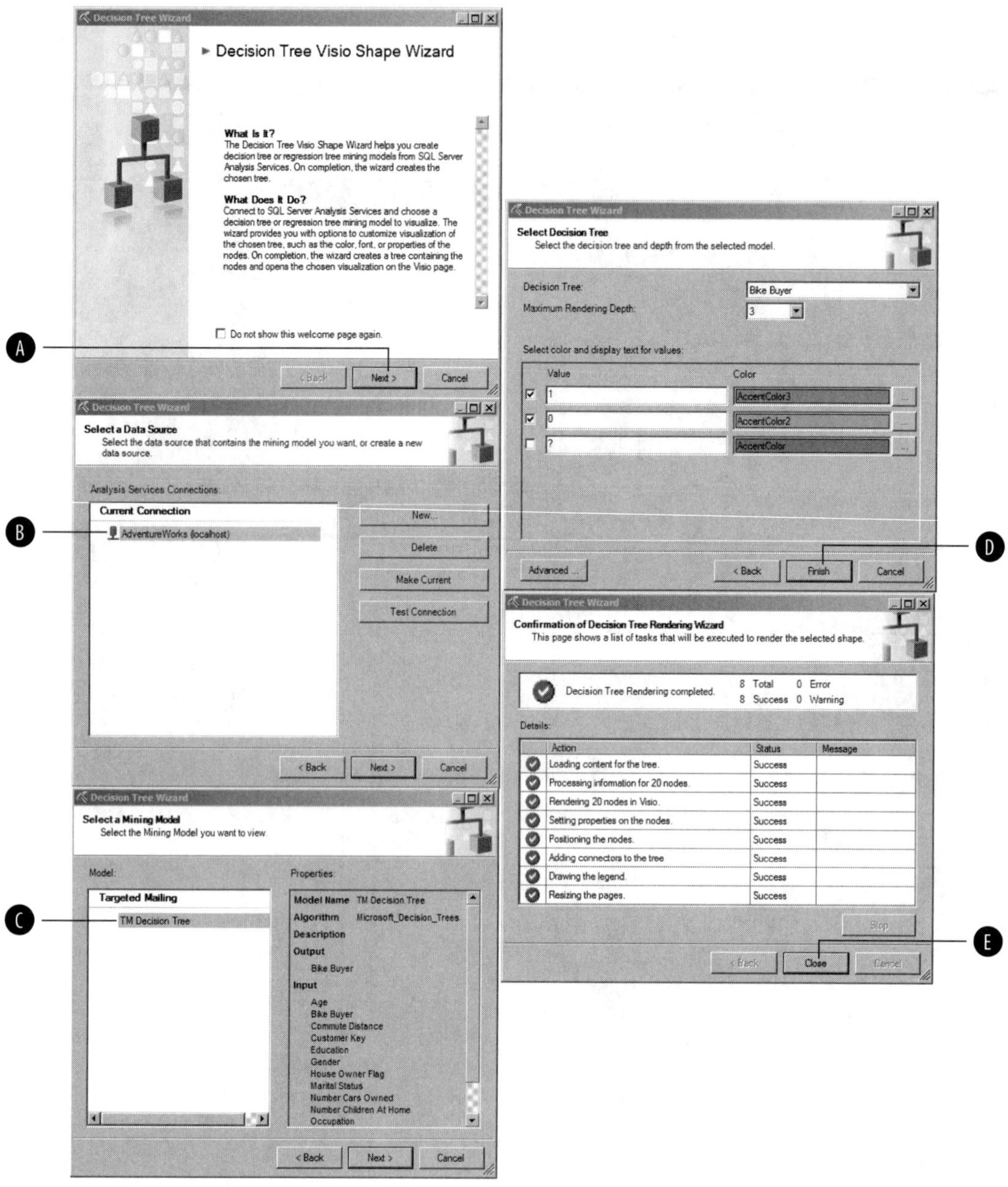

Figure 6-52 *The Decision Tree Wizard process*

3. Choose TM Decision Tree (the default connection if you are using the AdventureWorks sample, Step C). Click Next to continue to the options screen.
4. On the Select Decision Tree screen, next click Finish to begin the rendering (Step D).
5. Once the rendering wizard is finished, choose Close (Step E).

Next we will see the decision tree diagrammed in Visio.

In Figure 6-53 you will see the choices that the decision tree has made and the breakdown for probable bike purchasers.

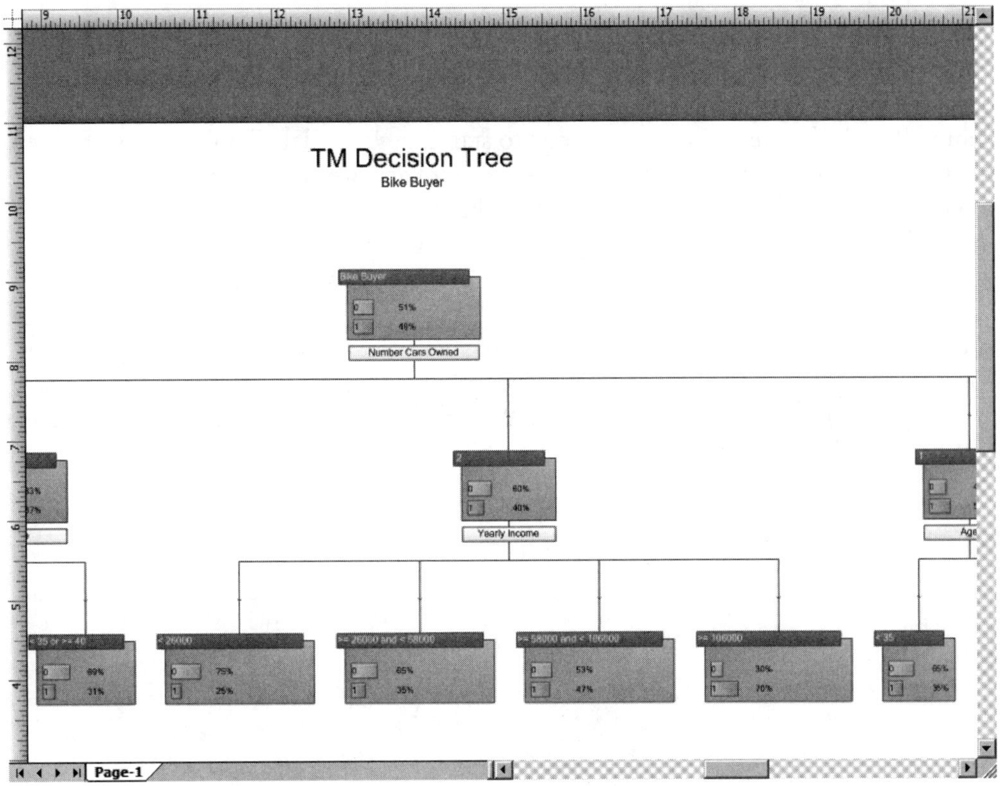

Figure 6-53 *The decision tree output*

BI TIP

You can enhance this output easily by placing a background image. (In this case, you may want to use something from clip art that has to do with bicycles.)

This was only a glimpse into using Visio to view the output of one of the data mining algorithms (MS Decision Tree). You can also use Visio to view the Dependency Network and MS Clustering. You will notice that you can comment and present the data mining model from inside of Visio.

Wrap-Up

This chapter is intended to be an introduction to data mining and this particular data mining tool. Hopefully you have seen that the field of data mining does not have to involve complex tools to produce items that look complex (or have complex models behind them). You were able to use Excel to start analyzing data. You were able to use the tool with data that was designed to use the tool and we also showed how you can modify data to fit the tool. Finally, you were able to see how to use the Visio portion of the add-in to visualize mined data. I am sure that in the future the data mining tools will become easier to understand and potentially even be integrated into some of the tools that we use every day (such as Excel). I am also sure that the field of data mining will continue to grow and evolve. Since this chapter is an introduction to these tools, if you are interested in SQL Server 2008 data mining in greater depth, a great resource is *Data Mining with Microsoft SQL Server 2008* by Jamie MacLennan, ZhaoHui Tang, and Bogdan Crivat (Wiley, 2008).

Chapter 7

Microsoft PowerPivot

In This Chapter

- Why Do We Need This Tool?
- So What Is PowerPivot?
- Installing the PowerPivot Add-in
- Using the PowerPivot Add-in with Sample Data
- Enhancing Charting with PowerPivot
- Extending PowerPivot with DAX
- Wrap-Up

Wouldn't it be great if there were a tool that allowed you to analyze large amounts of information quickly and easily? Wouldn't it be even better if it didn't take up too much space and allowed you to join across multiple sources or tables (without involving a developer or DBA)? And wouldn't it be even better if the tool presented the data in a way that you are already familiar with? This "game-changing" tool is called Microsoft PowerPivot, which is part of SQL Server 2008 R2. With just a few clicks you can create visualizations such as in Figure 7-1.

The dataset that was used to create the PowerPivot in Figure 7-1 was downloaded from the Internet and represents all domestic airline flights for the calendar year 2009 (a total of 6,450,285 flights!). In this chapter we will explore the original source of the data and how we are able to analyze it in ways that were unimaginable before the release of PowerPivot. We will show how to use the PowerPivot client and server to do some interesting visualizations; and this chapter will present the main features of PowerPivot in an overview fashion. Our goal in this chapter is to give you an overview of the tool and demonstrate the creation of compelling visualizations with a lot of data quickly and easily.

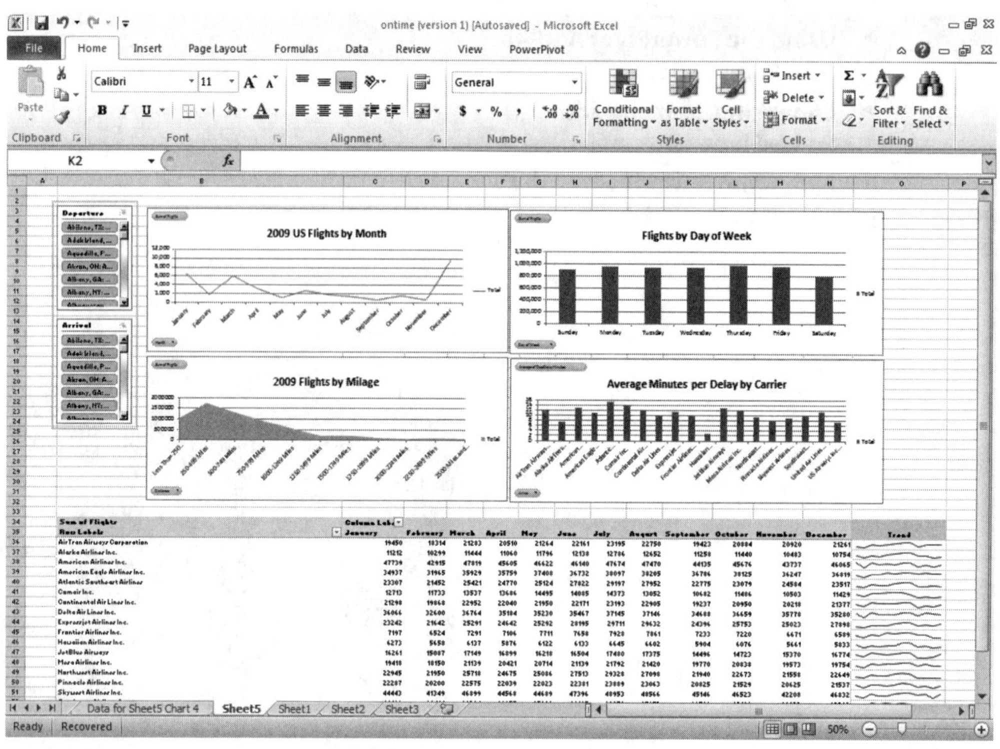

Figure 7-1 *An example of what we will create with PowerPivot*

Why Do We Need This Tool?

A decision is usually based on several different elements; a decision support system endeavors to bring together these different elements (and potentially sources) into something that enables a decision. The more successful decision support systems seamlessly pull together these different sources. One of the problems with creating a decision support system is that it takes a lot of time to integrate most data systems into decision support systems. The second problem concerns the timing of the data; most data takes some time to filter down into a decision support system. The third problem is that if we have the data (and it is semicurrent), we now need some way to view it.

The tool that we are going to explore (PowerPivot) succeeds in dealing with these three problems (and a whole lot more, including self-service analytic capability). As we'll see, the PowerPivot tool augments and extends data warehouse systems, but it is not intended to replace the data warehouse system and tools.

Decision support systems take time to grow and mature; over time they can turn into a data warehouse. The time to mature for a data warehouse is anywhere from months to years to decades and longer. Some of the most successful data warehouses are made up of decision support systems that have worked their way into everyday processes and tools. Wouldn't it be great if there were a tool that allowed you to do some of this work yourself? Imagine how great it would be if there was a tool that allowed you to

- Combine data from different sources easily.
- Work with hundreds of millions of rows of data (on your workstation).
- Visualize data in a tool you already use (Microsoft Excel).

BI TIP

The PowerPivot tool is an Excel 2010 add-in and ships with SQL Server 2008 R2. The Excel PowerPivot add-in does not require a connection to a SQL Server 2008 R2 Analysis Services server, but the server (SharePoint) deployment does.

We won't cover the entire history, but Microsoft has been good at introducing technologies to the marketplace that have been "game changers." From Windows in the 1980s to low-cost databases in the early 1990s, when Microsoft entered the business intelligence marketplace in 1998 with the release of OLAP Services with SQL Server 7.0, the primary goal was to establish BI for the masses. We have been the beneficiaries because we have seen easier-to-use tools and more business intelligence solutions and projects entering the market every day.

With SQL Server 2008 R2, Microsoft introduced PowerPivot. PowerPivot is a new and exciting technology that will enable you to analyze enormous amounts of data both quickly and easily on your laptop. One of the driving factors of PowerPivot is the need by users to create their own solutions. The goal of this chapter is to introduce you to this technology and hopefully demonstrate some techniques that will have you developing your own PowerPivot solutions quickly.

So What Is PowerPivot?

PowerPivot is an exciting new set of technologies that ships with SQL Server 2008 R2 and allows you to do things with data that have been impossible before. PowerPivot has two different components: a server component and a client component. The server component is housed inside of Microsoft SharePoint 2010, and the client is housed inside of Microsoft Excel 2010. This tool is a departure from the standard business intelligence tool in that it places the power with the user. This can be termed self-service business intelligence. Our goal is to introduce this tool (with a real-world example) and to demonstrate how you can use data to make decisions (without involving your IT department).

A Couple of New Things in Excel 2010 (PivotTables, Slicers, and Sparklines)

Because PowerPivot is a tool that is exposed inside of Excel it makes sense to start there. There are a lot of exciting new features inside of Excel 2010; we are going to go over a couple of the most important ones. These features are available without PowerPivot, but since we are going to use these inside of our examples, we wanted to describe them at the beginning of this chapter.

BI TIP

Because PowerPivot is an Excel 2010 add-in, it makes sense to understand how to use the other Excel 2010 business intelligence tools that do not require PowerPivot but can be used in conjunction with PowerPivot for everyday analysis and reporting.

PivotTables in Excel 2010

PivotTables inside of the Excel client have changed over time. A PivotTable allows you to choose different data elements in an easy-to-use summarized form. Historically, PivotTables gave you a very interactive way to deal with relational data. One of the drawbacks was that you had to pull the entire dataset down in order to view the summarized data. This changed when Analysis Services allowed you to connect to a cube. As with all technologies, things evolve, and we now have a very powerful tool that will allow us to view summarized data without having to pull all of the data into the spreadsheet or have someone stand up a cube for us to connect to. That tool is called PowerPivot, which has been described as PivotTables on steroids.

In Figure 7-2 we see the view of a PivotTable inside of Microsoft Excel 2010. There are a few items to note on this spreadsheet worksheet: on the left-hand side is the PivotTable; this is where the summarized numbers are displayed. In the middle of the figure is the PivotTable chart; this chart (and the PivotTable) are both controlled by the third item, on the right-hand side of the page, the PivotTable field list. This field list contains items that are available to display or summarize on the report (we will go over the field list in more detail later in this chapter).

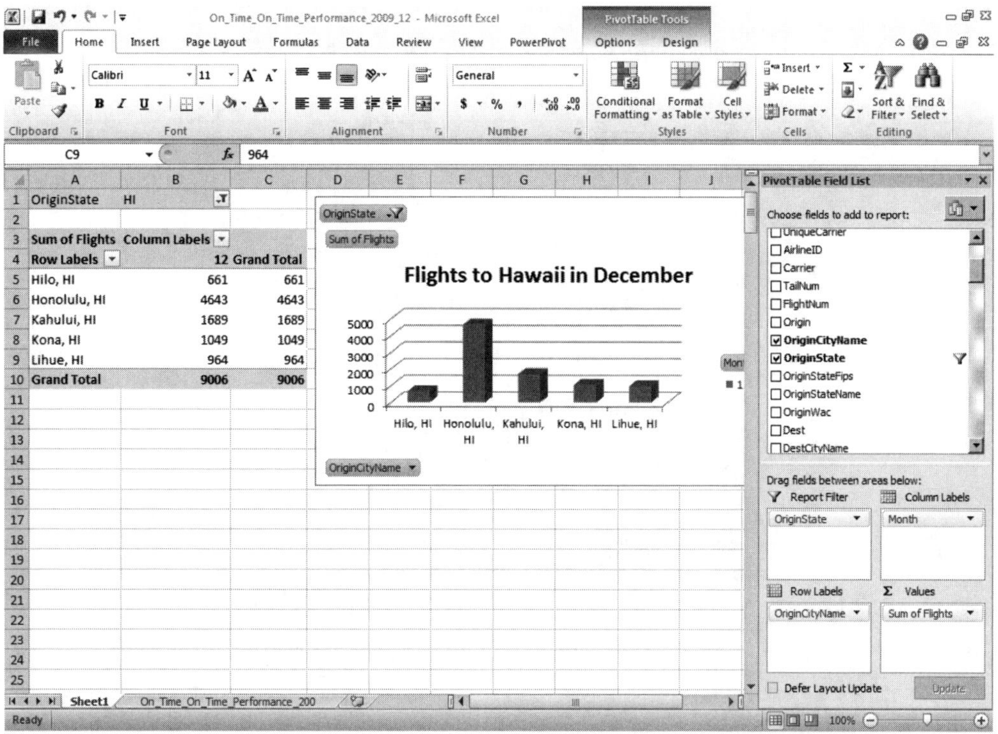

Figure 7-2 *A PivotTable inside of Excel*

Slicers in Excel 2010

Slicers allow you to change the visualization in a simple and easy way. In Figure 7-3 you will see a chart where the data can be controlled by selecting options, which are called slicers. The slicers change the chart or grid on the same sheet. A slicer can control one chart or grid or be configured to modify any number of charts or grids on a page.

What is the difference between a slicer and a report filter?

Both of these items filter out data from the PivotTable. The key difference is that the slicer is meant to be more interactive. You can also use a slicer to control one chart or many charts and tables. You will see how to implement a slicer inside of your data later in this chapter.

BI TIP

A slicer in Excel 2010 acts like a truly interactive report filter—but it can be used to select and de-select the data being displayed, on the fly, while viewing and working with data in Excel 2010.

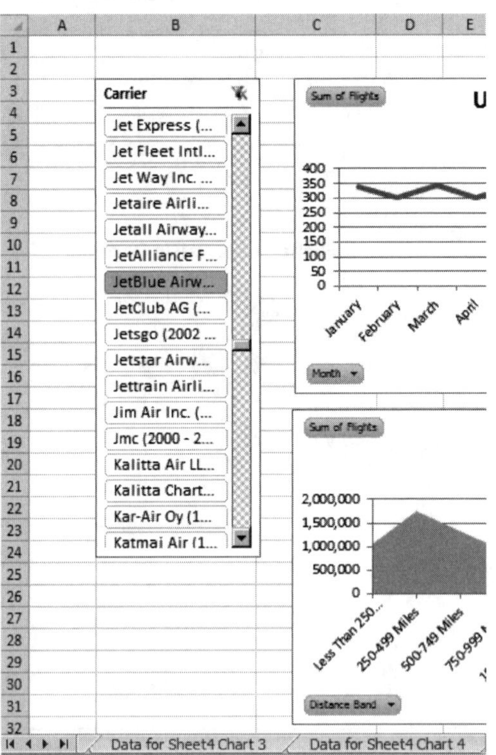

Figure 7-3 *An example of a slicer*

Sparklines in Excel 2010

Sparklines are trend graphs that are inside of a cell. In order for the trend line to work, you need to have a series of data points (in Figure 7-4 the data series is months). The sparklines are valuable for visualizing trends over time in a very small space. Sparklines are not specific to PowerPivot, but are one of the new features inside of Excel 2010. Later in this chapter you will create a sparkline inside of a spreadsheet.

So Why Can't We Just Do This in Excel?

So no solution is useful unless there is a problem (or even better, multiple problems). You can do some truly incredible things with Excel (and it gets even better with each new version). While Excel can do some wonderful things, Excel does have some limitations that we are going to address, namely:

1. Excel 2010 is limited to one million rows of data.
2. Excel is not a replacement for a database, meaning that some large data volume interactions are cumbersome.
3. If you store a lot of data in Excel, the size of the spreadsheet will be huge.
4. It is hard to join differing datasets together into one view.

BI TIP

How do you tell which version of Office you are running? Inside of Excel choose the File menu item and then choose Help. You will notice that there is a section called About Microsoft Excel and the version number. Next to the version number it will say either 32-bit or 64-bit.

Sum of Flights	Column Labels												
Row Labels	January	February	March	April	May	June	July	August	September	October	November	December	Trend
Less Than 250 Miles	86309	78607	88627	85737	87590	90392	94762	92385	85598	88461	83350	85582	
250-499 Miles	144640	132243	149637	146060	149523	151884	156998	153867	141258	146355	139529	141661	
500-749 Miles	109176	99888	113150	109731	111845	114551	118857	116535	104079	109041	103544	106660	
750-999 Miles	75848	69756	81006	76997	77782	77596	80398	79165	69860	73843	71019	74527	
1000-1249 Miles	46510	43334	50200	47976	45182	44605	46300	45478	40313	42226	43607	47344	
1250-1499 Miles	18139	17048	19839	18335	18619	19258	20262	19949	17735	18352	17633	18879	
1500-1749 Miles	19329	18135	21036	19872	20187	20780	21821	21171	18273	19087	18536	19918	
1750-1999 Miles	10011	9057	10403	10066	11040	11471	11975	11641	10134	10508	10035	10564	
2000-2249 Miles	6600	5979	6876	6676	7122	7733	8188	7893	6647	6732	6281	6663	
2250-2499 Miles	8955	8177	9430	9139	10244	11135	11751	11597	9707	9852	9258	9873	
2500 Miles and Greater	6822	6186	7218	7204	7698	8189	8822	8620	7248	7342	6748	7598	

Figure 7-4 *A sample sparkline*

So How Is PowerPivot Different?

As we described in the preceding chapter, the PowerPivot client is an Excel add-in. The PowerPivot add-in actually launches a separate tool within Excel 2010 on a client machine. For the client, the Excel integration is seamless (as you will see in the example that we are creating). There is also a server-based component to PowerPivot (which we will cover later in the chapter). The PowerPivot add-in allows you to work with huge amounts of data outside of Excel and still deliver the output (charts and grids) of the data inside of the Excel client. PowerPivot allows you to easily accomplish the following tasks:

- Join multiple data elements together.
- Interact with data (via PivotTables and slicers).
- Share analytic views and data with others.

BI TIP

Unlike the data mining add-in, the PowerPivot add-in comes in both 32- and 64-bit versions. The 64-bit version facilitates better use of memory on the client machine—and it should be noted that new desktop and laptop computers are 64-bit machines. Welcome to the future!

Installing the PowerPivot Add-in

You can download the PowerPivot add-in from the Microsoft web page (www.microsoft.com/office) or from www.officebicentral.com. The steps for installing the PowerPivot add-in are relatively easily, as you can see in Figure 7-5. You need to match the add-in with the version of Microsoft Office that you have installed (32-bit or 64-bit).

1. Download the add-in or run it from the installation location. After you click Download, you will be asked if you would like to run the add-in; choose Yes. You will be presented with a Welcome screen. Click Next to continue (Step A).
2. You will next be presented with the license agreement. Choose "I accept the terms in the license agreement" (Step B) and select Next (Step C) to continue.
3. You will next be presented with registration information. Click Next to continue (Step D).
4. You will then be presented with a processing screen. Wait until the processing screen finishes and when you are finally presented with a completion screen, click Finish (Step E).

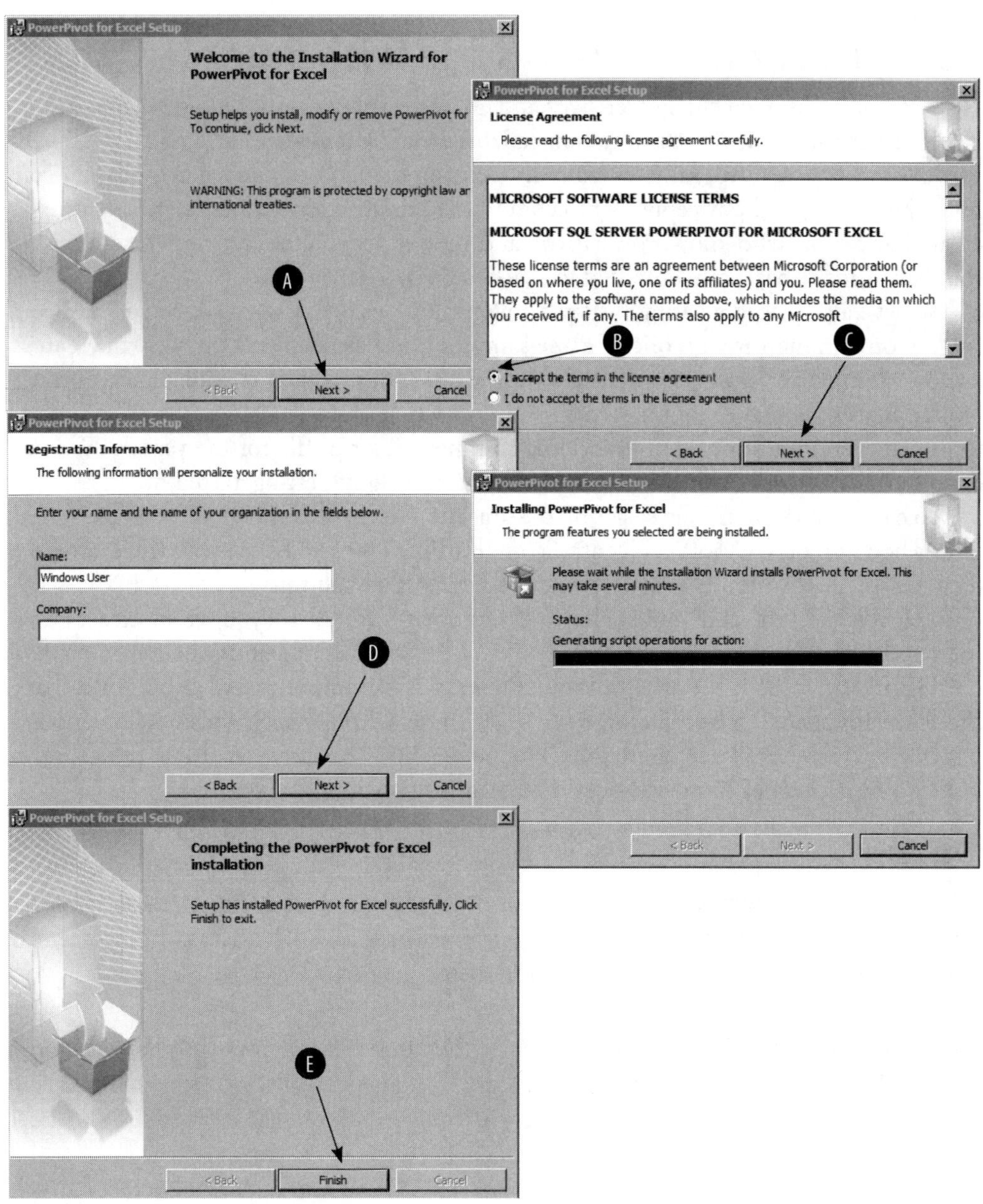

Figure 7-5 *The PowerPivot installation screens*

Using the PowerPivot Add-in with Sample Data

Now you have installed the PowerPivot add-in, you may not notice a big change in Excel (other than now there is a ribbon called PowerPivot as seen in Figure 7-6). There are all sorts of PowerPivot samples from different Internet locations such as Codeplex.com, powerpivot.com, and powerpivot-info.com (just to name a few). These samples were created by people who know PowerPivot, and they allow you to learn from examples that have already been implemented in real-world data environments.

We have also placed a listing of PowerPivot examples up on www.officebicentral.com. Instead of working through one of these samples that has been created, we will create our own sample and interact with real-world data. This real data is available from the United States Federal Aviation Administration (FAA). This data contains all of the flight data for domestic and international commercial air traffic for the year 2009. This data is available for download from www.transtats.bts.gov/gettingstarted.htm.

We have also made things easier by posting the Excel spreadsheet and text files used in this book up on www.officebicentral.com. Furthermore, we have made the example data file smaller by eliminating several unnecessary data columns.

After you have the add-in installed and you open Excel 2010, you will notice a new item in the ribbon called PowerPivot. We will be using this add-in in the next steps to create different visualizations with PowerPivot. It is also important to understand that the PowerPivot add-in launches in a separate window from Excel. This window looks just like Excel, but it is a separate tool. The PowerPivot tool creates a PivotTable/chart in the original Excel 2010 worksheet that is already open on the client.

BI TIP

Microsoft Office applications all use the common theme of ribbon menus. *These are top-level menus that form strips of control buttons across the top of the user interface, with a standard "ribbon" grouping of common tasks that save and open files and work with the data on the screen.*

1. First choose the PowerPivot ribbon and then under Launch choose PowerPivot Window (as shown in Figure 7-6).

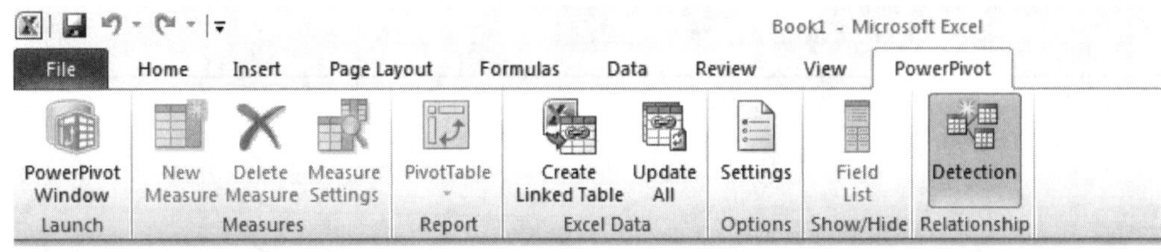

Figure 7-6 *The PowerPivot add-in*

2. You will notice that PowerPivot is not launched inside of Excel; it actually launches in a separate tool, shown in Figure 7-7.
3. The first thing that we need to do is obtain data to work with. You will notice the Get External Data group. You can get data from a database (the different types are listed in Table 7-1), but here you should choose From Text.

Loading the Text Files

Next we are going to choose the data from a text file that we will work with. When downloaded from the original data sources (the FAA web site), the text file sample is just over 250 megabytes. We are going to load all 12 months into a PowerPivot worksheet. The size of the resulting spreadsheet will be under 250MB, achieving over a twelve-fold compression (yes, PowerPivot has incredible compression as well). The amount of compression will depend on several factors, including data type, size, and sparseness of the data.

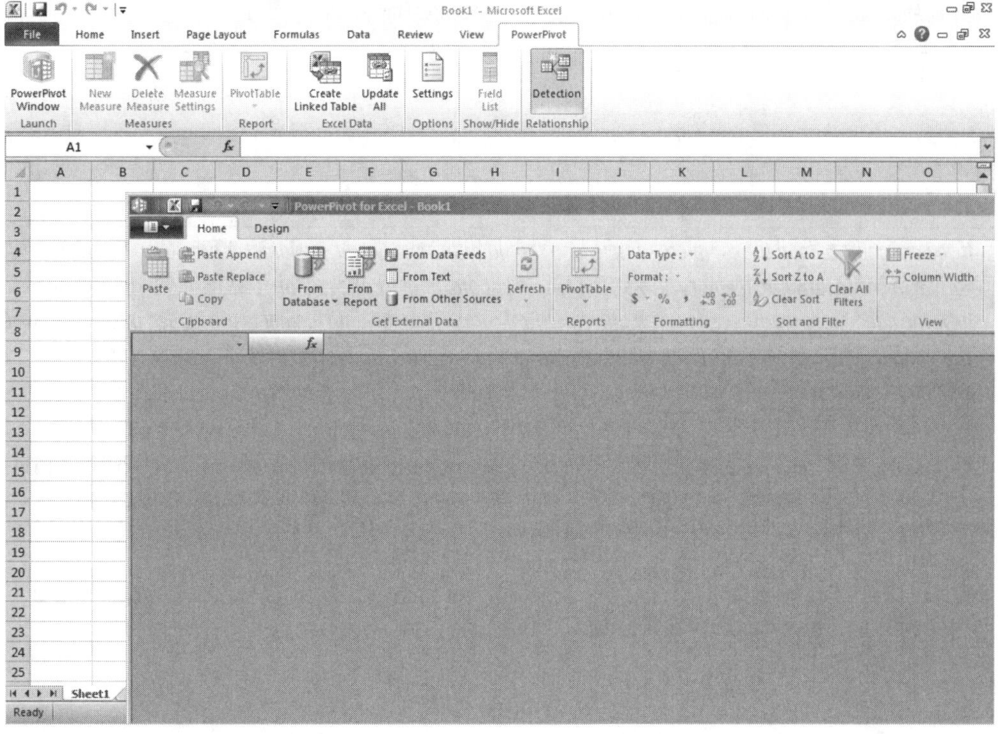

Figure 7-7 *The PowerPivot add-in launches*

Data Type	Version
Microsoft Access	2003, 2007, 2010
SQL Server	2005, 2008, 2008 R2, Microsoft SQL Azure
Oracle	9*i*, 10*g*, 11*g*
Teradata	V2R6, V12
Informix	
IBM DB2	8.1
Sybase	
OLE/DB Provider or ODBC	
Text files	
Microsoft Excel	97, 2003, 2007, 2010
PowerPivot (other workbooks)	Microsoft SQL Server 2008 R2
SQL Server Analysis Services cube	2005, 2008, and 2008 R2
Data feeds (also used to pull in data from Reporting Services reports, Atom service docs, and single data feeds)	Atom 1.0 format, any DB exposed via the ADO.Net Data Services Framework

Table 7-1 *PowerPivot Supported Data Sources*

BI TIP

If you are going to load the complete sample, you should be using a 64-bit version of Office 2010. The 32-bit version of Office runs into memory errors after loading approximately one million rows with this dataset (we have included the spreadsheet on www.officebicentral.com). Once the data elements are loaded into PowerPivot, you shouldn't have any trouble loading the created spreadsheet in 32-bit form (a lot of memory is used when loading the data into PowerPivot format).

1. After you choose From Text, you will be presented with the Connect To Flat File dialog box. Input or browse to where the sample flat file is located and choose the "Use first row as column headers" option. (Your screen should look similar to Figure 7-8.) Next click Finish to launch a processing window.
2. It should take a few minutes to load the text file. Once it is finished, you should see a window similar to Figure 7-9. Click Close.

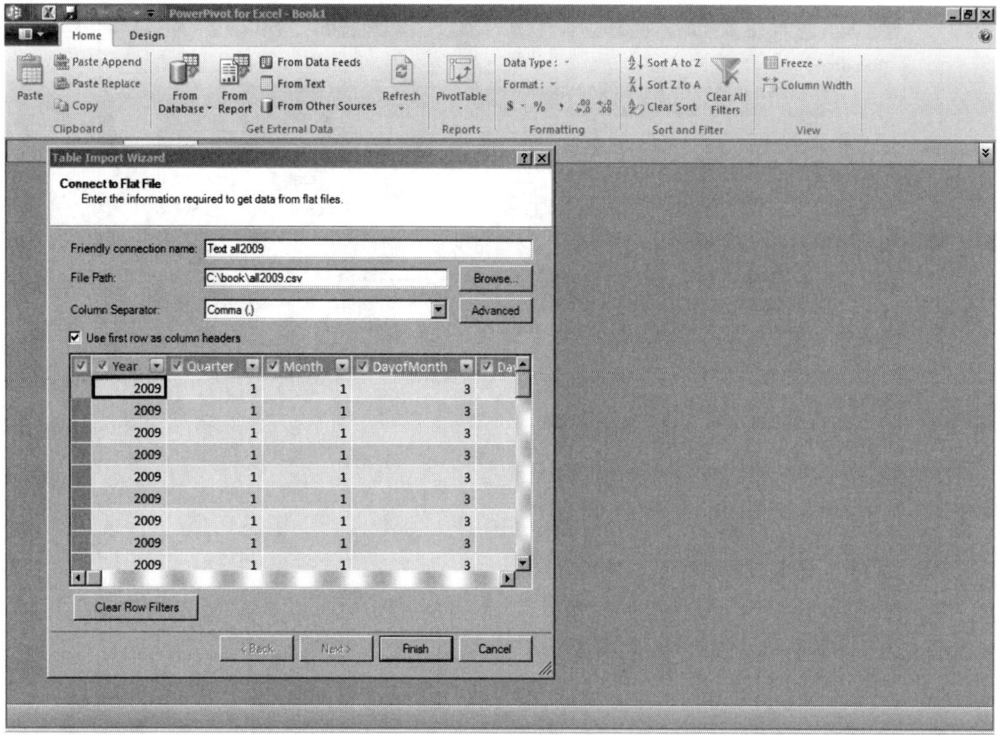

Figure 7-8 *The Connect To Flat File dialog box*

3. Now you have loaded the text file into the PowerPivot tool, next you should follow the same process that you used to load the all2009 flight sample to load additional text files (Arrival, Departure, Cancellation, Distance, Months, Day_of_week, and state text files).

   Once you have all of the files loaded, your screen should look similar to Figure 7-10.

BI TIP

These text files are also available on the FAA site and www.officebicentral.com.

Joining the Tables

Next we are going to create a join between these tables. A *join* allows the two tables to interact and be viewed as one table. For example in Figure 7-10 the Day of Week is listed as 1–7, but what we want is the day listed out (such as Sunday or Monday).

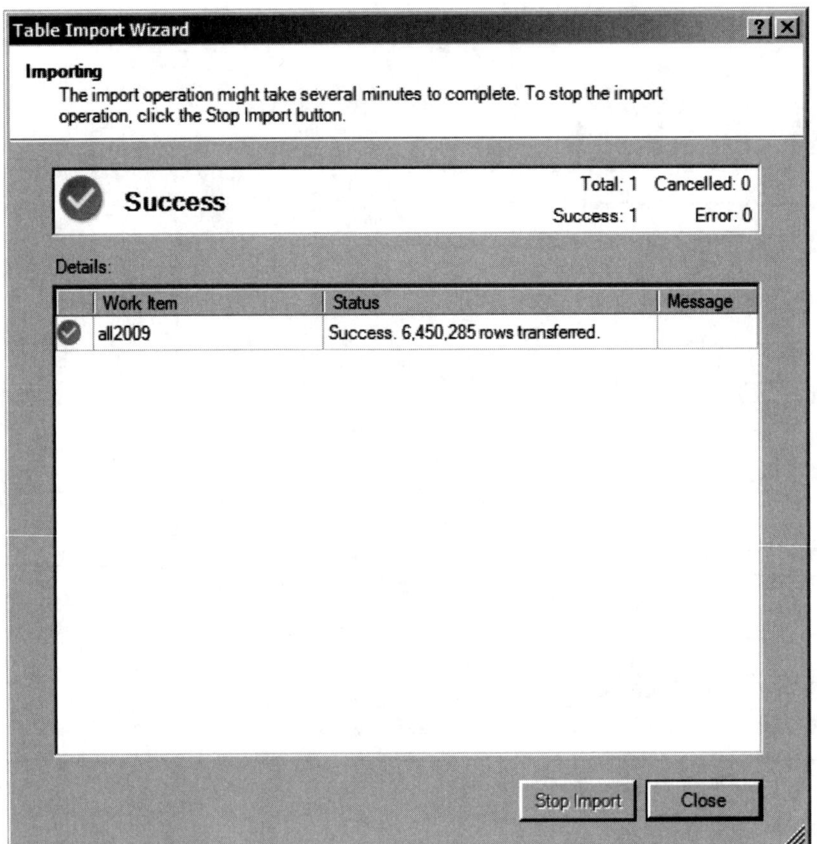

Figure 7-9 *The Table Import Wizard processing window*

The Day_of_week table contains a code (1–7) and a description field that lists the days (Sunday etc.). We need to create a join between these tables.

1. Choose the Design ribbon from the PowerPivot tool (Figure 7-11).
2. Choose Create Relationship from the ribbon.
3. You should now be presented with the Manage Relationships screen. Choose Create (also notice the Manage Relationships button, which is where you would manage relationships that were already created).

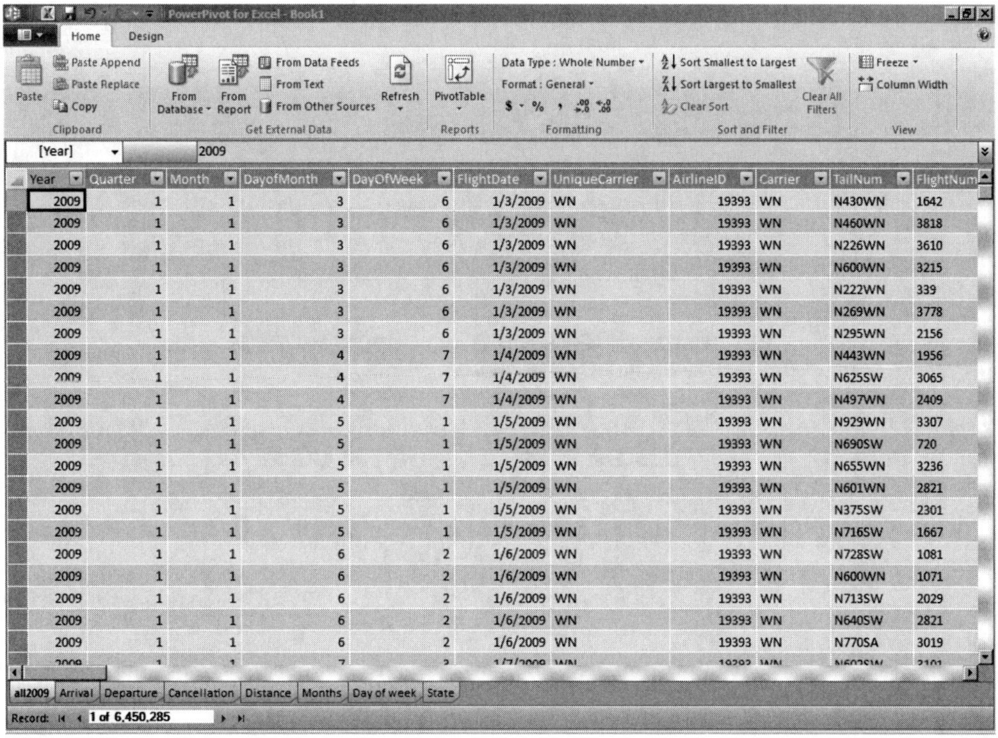

Figure 7-10 *The PowerPivot tool with all sample files loaded*

4. In the Create Relationship dialog box (Figure 7-12), choose the all2009 table in the Table drop-down list box and Dest as the Column, choose Arrival as the Related Lookup Table and Code as the Related Lookup Column, and click Create (we are going to do this several times).
5. Next do the same thing with the Distance, Cancellation, Month, Day_of_Week, OriginState, and DestinationState tables. The columns are listed in Figure 7-13 and also in Table 7-2.

Now that the tables relate to one another, it is time for us to add these back to Excel. Next we will place a PivotChart and table back to Excel from the PowerPivot client. This time when we add the items back to Excel, they will be in summarized form, in a PivotTable or a PivotChart. Remember that Excel has a one million row limit. But before we do that, let's briefly examine what we can do inside of the PowerPivot client.

Home
Design
Add
Delete
Hide and Unhide
Calculation Options
Existing Connections
Create Relationship
Manage Relationships
Table Properties
Undo
Redo
Columns
Calculations
Connections
Relationships
Properties
Edit
Manage Relationships
Create
Edit
Delete
Table
Related Lookup Table
Create Relationship
Create a lookup relationship between two tables
Select the tables and columns you want to use to create the relationship.
Table:
Column:
Related Lookup Table:
Related Lookup Column:
Create
Cancel
all2009
Arrival
Departure
Cancellation
Distance
Months
Day of week
State
Record: 1 of 6,450,285

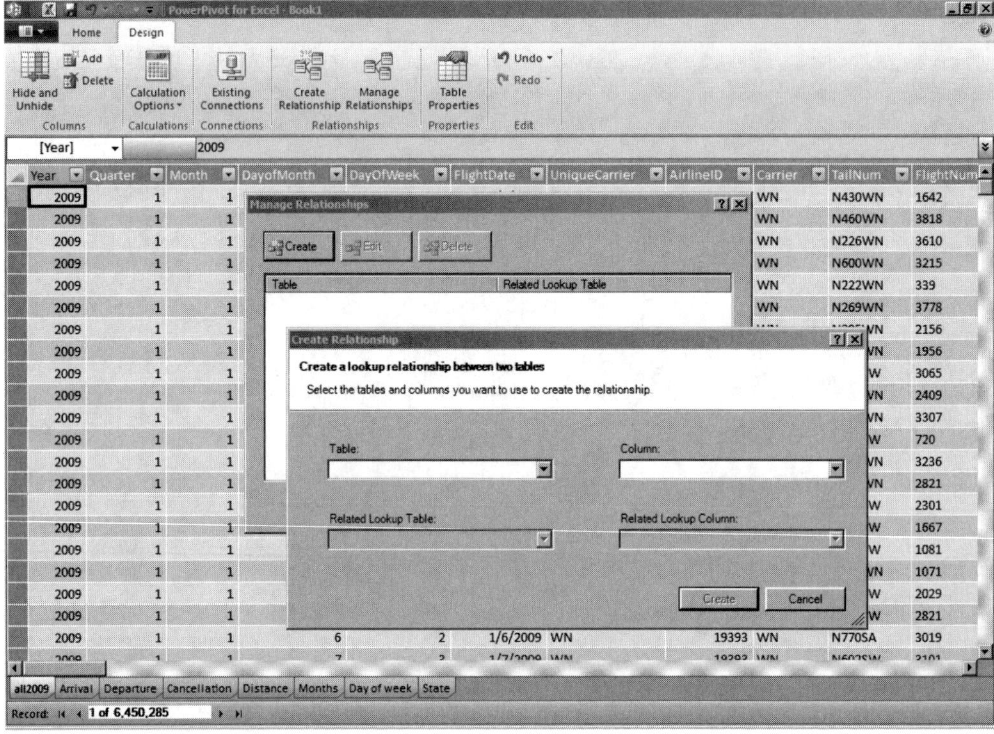

Figure 7-11 *The Design ribbon*

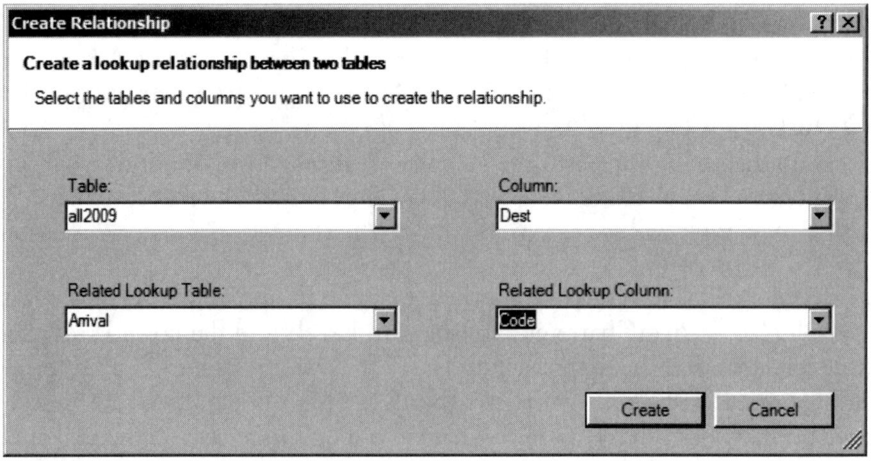

Create Relationship
Create a lookup relationship between two tables
Select the tables and columns you want to use to create the relationship.
Table:
all2009
Column:
Dest
Related Lookup Table:
Arrival
Related Lookup Column:
Code
Create
Cancel

Figure 7-12 *The Create Relationship window*

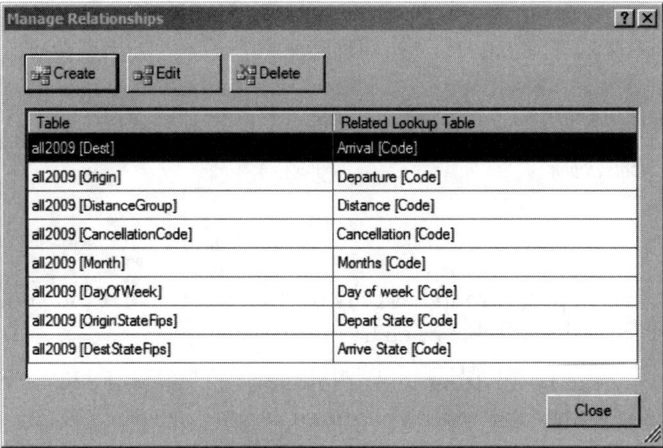

Figure 7-13 *The fully populated Manage Relationships window*

The PowerPivot Home Ribbon

The first ribbon is the Home ribbon (as shown in Figure 7-14); this is the default or first ribbon that pops up. This contains tools gathered into six separate groupings that describe what each tool does.

- **Clipboard** The clipboard grouping allows you to copy, paste, and append rows of data in the PowerPivot worksheet.
- **Get External Data** The Get External Data group allows you to populate data into your worksheet, and the Refresh tool allows you to refresh the current worksheet or all of the worksheets.

Text File	Column	Related Lookup Table	Related Lookup Column
all2009	Dest	Arrival	Code
all2009	Origin	Departure	Code
all2009	DistanceGroup	Distance	Code
all2009	CancellationCode	Cancellation	Code
all2009	Month	Months	Code
all2009	DayOfWeek	Day of week	Code
all2009	OriginStateFips	Depart State	Code
all2009	DestStateFips	Arrive State	Code

Table 7-2 *Table and Column Relations*

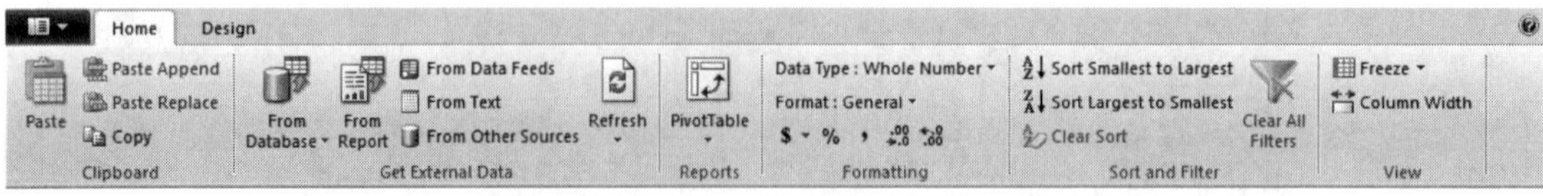

Figure 7-14 *The PowerPivot Home ribbon*

- **Reports** The Reports group has only one tool, the PivotTable tool; this is the tool that places a PivotTable or chart into Excel.
- **Formatting** The Formatting tools allow you to change the data type of a column or the default formatting of the column.
- **Sort And Filter** The Sort And Filter group allows you to filter out the dataset or to sort by the largest number to smallest or smallest to largest (you should try using this tool on the all2009 data and notice how fast you can sort data of all 6,450,285 rows). This is because PowerPivot loads this data in an in-memory store (which is also very compressed). You can work with datasets that are hundreds of millions of rows of data on a 32-bit client machine or even more on a 64-bit machine.
- **View** These tools allow you to freeze and unfreeze a column (which is where the column will not be able to be updated). You can also set the column width via this tool as well.

NOTE

You can get to a majority of these tools by right-clicking the column / table.

The Design Ribbon

The other ribbon in the PowerPivot client is the Design ribbon (see Figure 7-15). This ribbon contains tools which will aid in adding things to your PowerPivot worksheet.

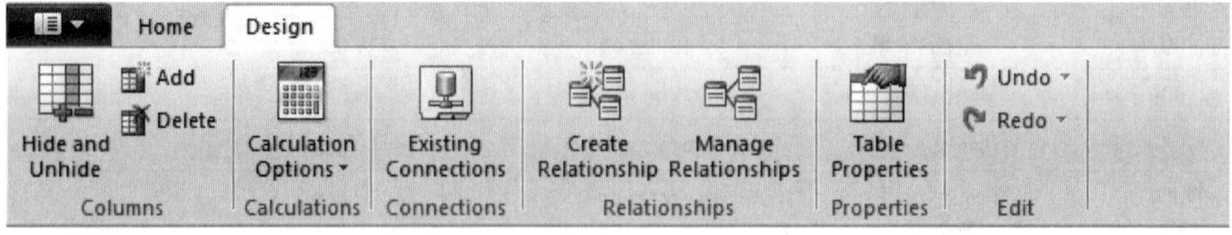

Figure 7-15 *The Design ribbon*

This ribbon is broken down into six different sections: Columns, Calculations, Connections, Relationships, Properties, and Edit.

- **Columns** These tools allow you to hide and unhide data in the worksheet. You may want to keep a column on the worksheet that isn't exposed to Excel via the PivotTable/chart data. You will be able to view the data in the PowerPivot worksheet, but not inside of Excel. There is also the ability to add and delete columns from this set of tools as well.
- **Calculations** There are two different modes you can set for calculations: manual and automatic. If you have any formulas that use changed data, they will not be automatically updated if you choose manual calculation.
- **Connections** This tool will allow you to view any connections to data sources that are part of this PowerPivot worksheet. You can browse, open, edit, refresh, and delete the sources from this ribbon selection.
- **Relationships** These tools are where you create and manage relationships between tables (similar to database joins).
- **Properties** These are used if you wanted to go back to the original source (in our example we will be pulling in the data from a text file). You can filter out rows or columns that you want to use inside of PowerPivot.
- **Edit** Just link inside of Excel; you can undo changes that you have made (you can also redo changes if you decide to undo too many changes).

So now that we have gone over what is in the PowerPivot client ribbons, we will actually take the data that we have used and place a PivotTable / PivotChart into Excel. We will be doing this from the PowerPivot client with only a couple of mouse clicks.

1. Click the Home ribbon, choose the PivotTable tool, and choose Chart and Table (Vertical) as shown in Figure 7-16.

   This will open a dialog box inside of Excel that will ask us if we want to place this inside of Excel.
2. You now have the choice to either create a New Worksheet or use an Existing Worksheet. For this example, choose a New Worksheet as in Figure 7-17 and click OK.

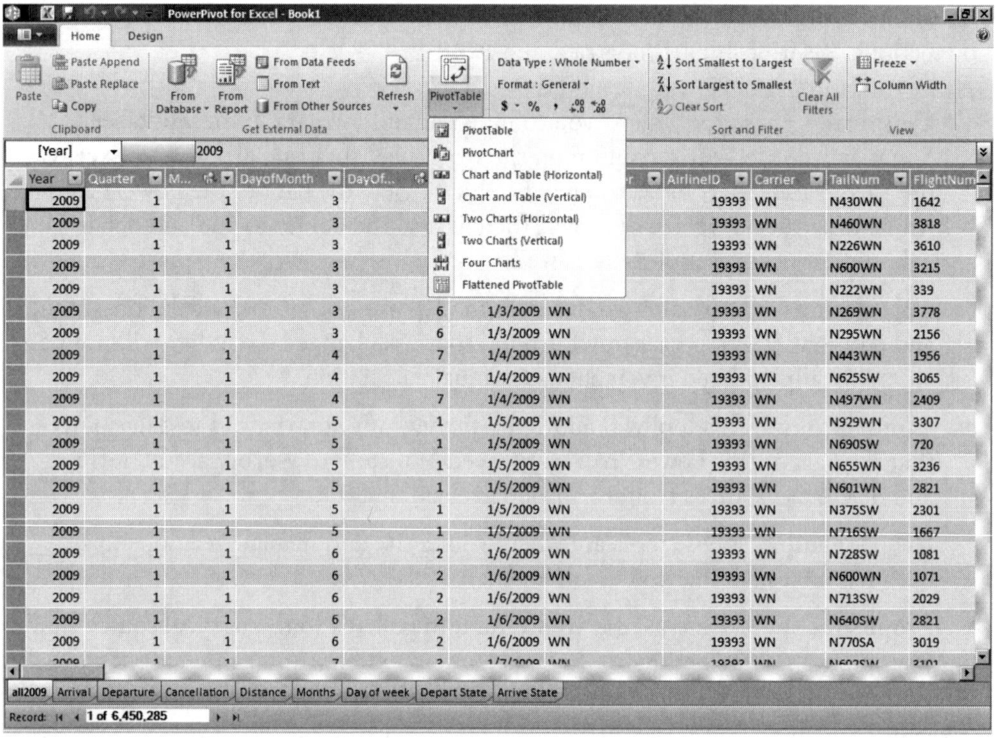

Figure 7-16 *To insert a PivotTable from the Client into Excel*

You should notice several items on your Excel worksheet as shown in Figure 7-18. Namely that there is now a PowerPivot field list on the right, a chart on the upper portion of the screen, and a PivotTable on the bottom. We will mainly be working with the PowerPivot field list on the right-hand side.

3. Scroll down the data items in the PowerPivot field list and place a check mark next to Flights, as shown in Figure 7-19. This will place Flights into the Values field.

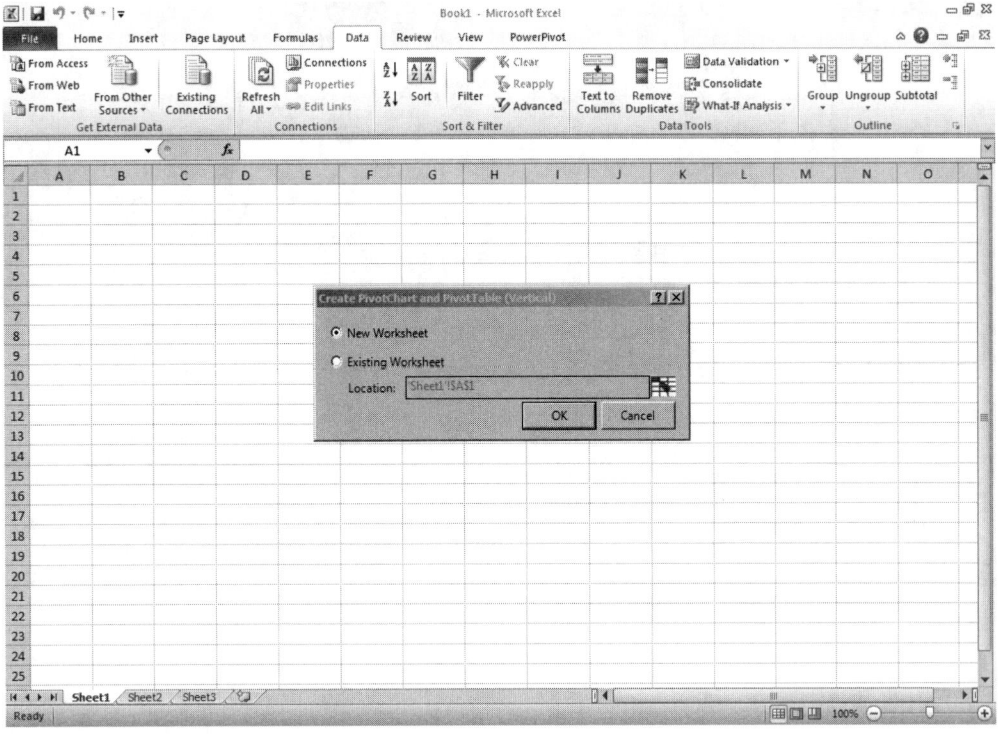

Figure 7-17 *The Create PivotChart and PivotTable location*

You can either place a check mark next to an element that you would like to use or drag the item down to one of the windows below (slicers, filter, labels, or values). The default behavior is to sum (or aggregate) the flights count. You can also choose other aggregate functions, including Sum, Count, Min, Max, and Average. Next we will add the Month to the row label.

4. Next scroll down to Month and either check the check box under Months | Month or drag the Month down to the Row Labels window at the bottom. You should notice something similar to Figure 7-20.

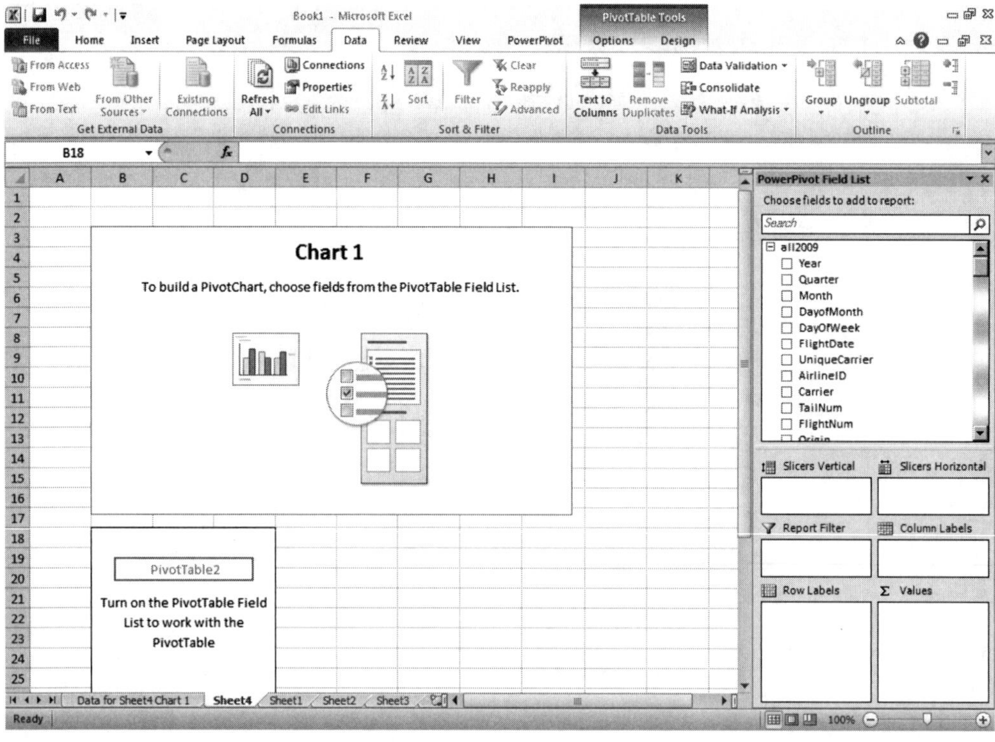

Figure 7-18 *The Excel worksheet after inserting from the PowerPivot client*

Adding a Slicer

Now that we have a worksheet that has data in both the PivotChart and PivotTable, let us see how we can add a slicer. The slicer allows us to filter out the data in an easy-to-use window inserted next to the PivotChart or PivotTable.

1. You have can either choose the Options window under the PivotTable Tools (or PivotChart Tools) and Insert Slicer (as shown in Figure 7-21) or you can drag the item that you would like to use down to the Slicers Vertical or Slicers Horizontal boxes (at the bottom of the PowerPivot field list). For this example we will be using the Day of Week as our Vertical Slicer. You can either choose Day of Week from the drop-down list box that is displayed after you click Insert Slicer, or drag Day of Week from the PowerPivot field list down to Slicers Vertical to see the view shown in Figure 7-22.

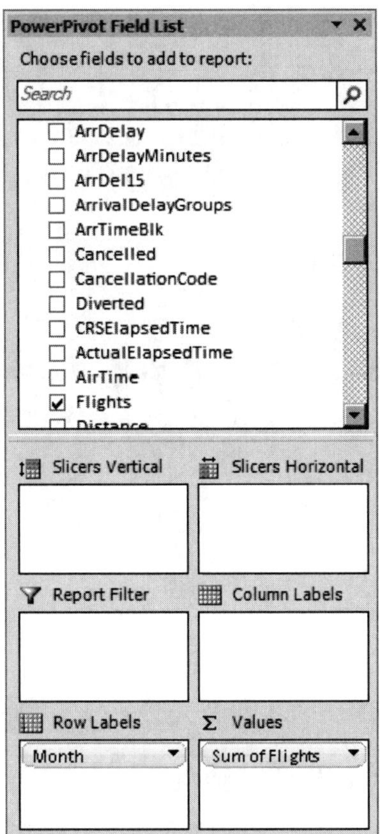

Figure 7-19 *The PowerPivot field list*

2. After you insert the slicer, you can control the slicer in a couple of different ways. If you click any day of the week, you will notice that the data displayed will change to only what is chosen in the slicer. You can hold down the CTRL key and click different days or the SHIFT key while you click to choose between two days. You will notice that this will only show for either the PivotTable or PivotChart, but in this case we want to have this slicer linked to both the PivotTable and the PivotChart. We will do that next.

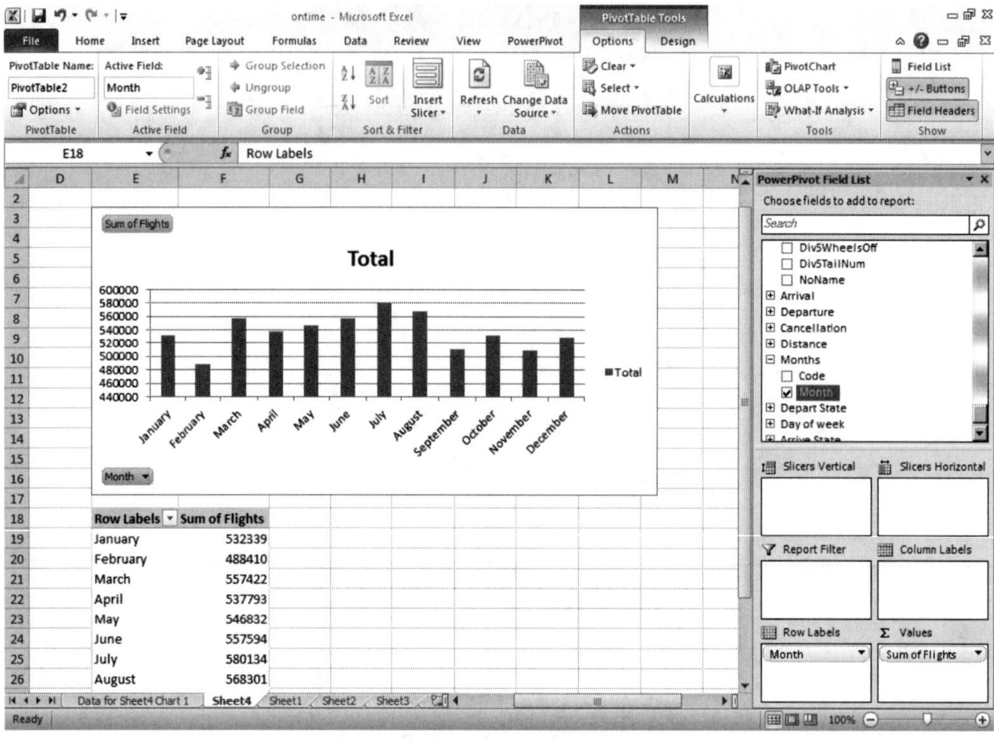

Figure 7-20 *Drag the Flights to Values and Month to Row Labels*

3. Next click the slicer. Notice that the Slicer Tools entry shows up in the ribbon. Choose Options and then PivotTable Connections (as shown in Figure 7-23).
4. You should see a screen similar to Figure 7-24. Click the check marks next to both PivotTable1 and PivotTable2 (so that the slicer will control both the chart and the grid).

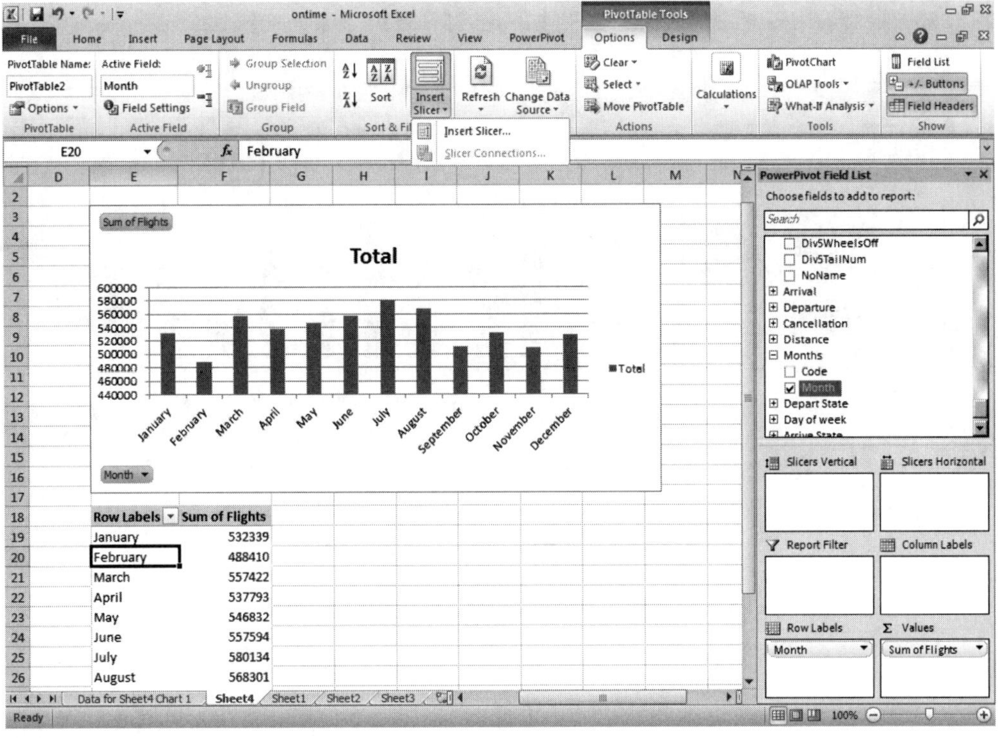

Figure 7-21 *The Insert Slicer process*

5. Next we are going to put a slicer above the chart. Inside of the PivotTable field list, scroll down to Cancellation. Click Cancellation and drag it over to Slicers Horizontal, as shown in Figure 7-25 (alternatively, you could choose the PivotTable Tools options from the ribbon and select Cancellation from the drop-down list box). You should also ensure that the second slicer (Cancellation) is linked to both the chart and the grid (using the process described in Steps 3 and 4).

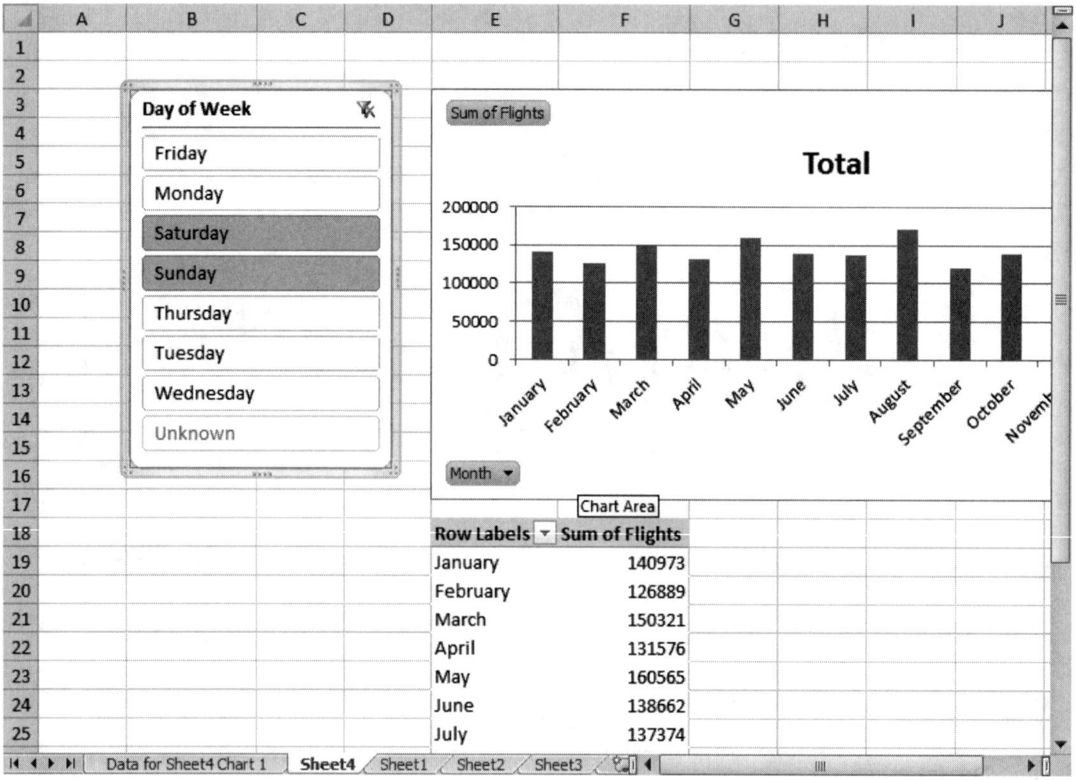

Day of Week

Friday
Monday
Saturday
Sunday
Thursday
Tuesday
Wednesday
Unknown

Sum of Flights

Total

200000
150000
100000
50000
0

January February March April May June July August September October Novemb

Month

Chart Area

Row Labels	Sum of Flights
January	140973
February	126889
March	150321
April	131576
May	160565
June	138662
July	137374

Data for Sheet4 Chart 1 | Sheet4 | Sheet1 | Sheet2 | Sheet3

Figure 7-22 *The view after the slicer has been inserted*

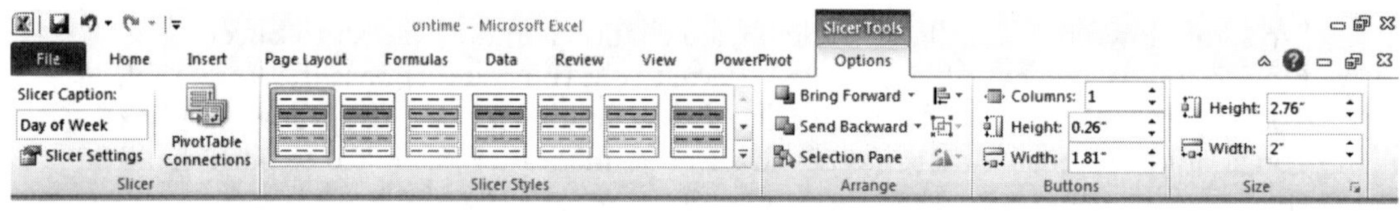

Figure 7-23 *The Slicer Tools ribbon*

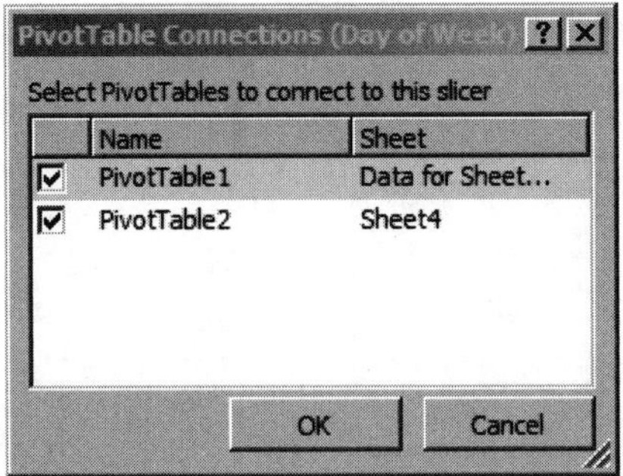

Figure 7-24 *The PivotTable Connections dialog box*

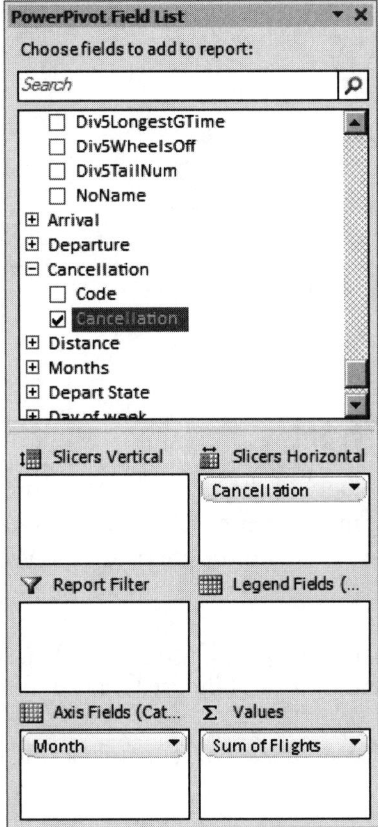

Figure 7-25 *How to put a slicer above the chart*

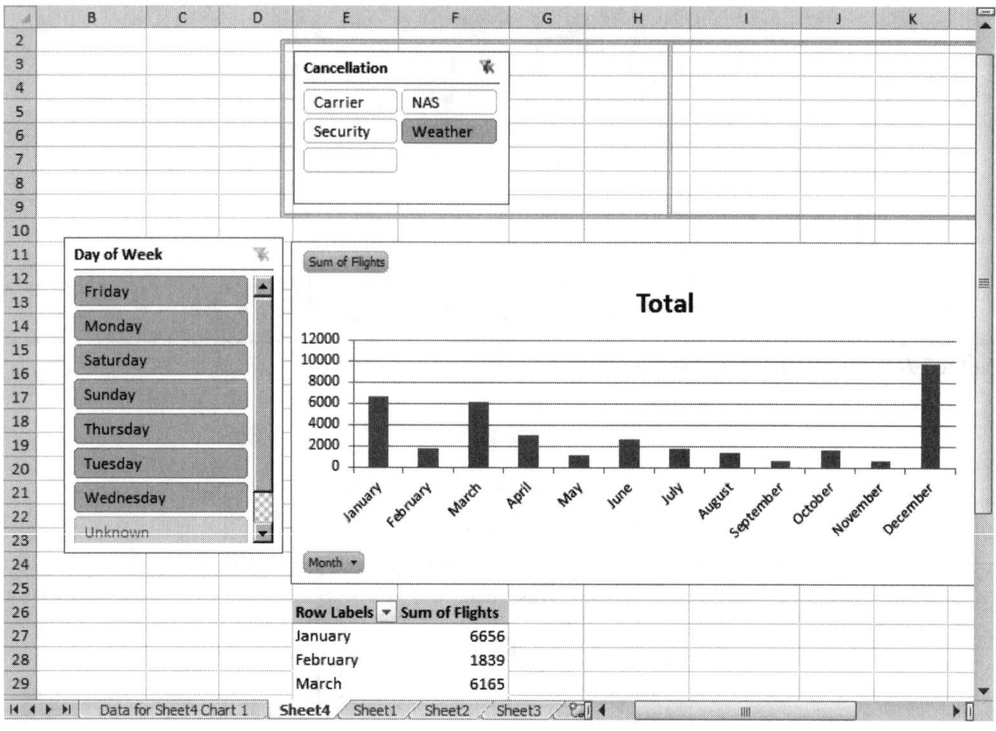

Figure 7-26 *The chart with two different slicers*

Customizing the Chart

Now that you have a decent-looking chart (similar to Figure 7-26) with multiple slicers, you may now like to make some cosmetic changes to the chart. There are hundreds of customizations that you could make on the chart or grid. We are going to explore just one of these customizations.

1. On the PivotChart click the right mouse button. You will be presented with something similar to Figure 7-27. Choose Change Chart Type from the menu to launch a window.
2. Now choose the Line type for the chart and click OK to continue (Figure 7-28).

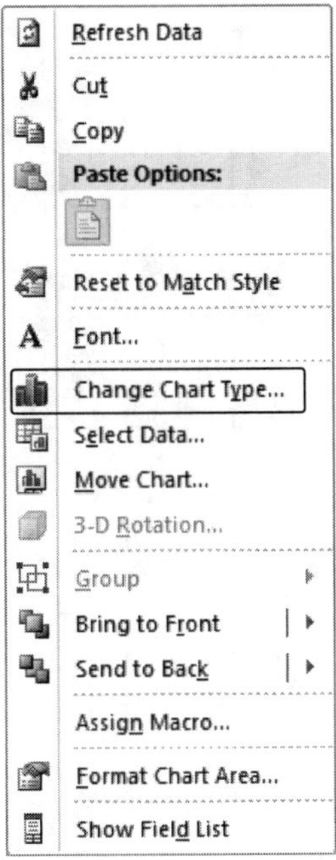

Figure 7-27 *The PivotChart options menu*

BI NOTE

You should be able to choose any type of chart from the list except the XY Scatter, Bubble, or Stock chart types with PowerPivot.

Shown in Figure 7-29 are some different chart types that can easily be chosen (there are many more, but this just gives you a general idea of some of the chart types).

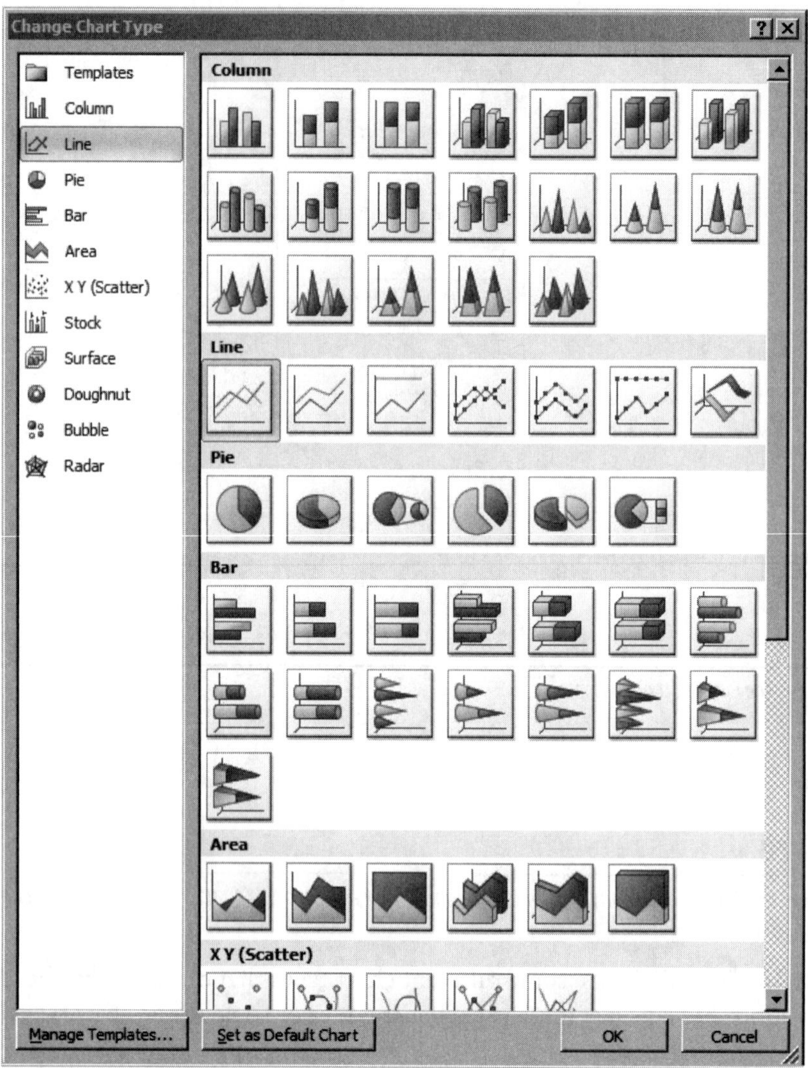

Figure 7-28 *The different chart types*

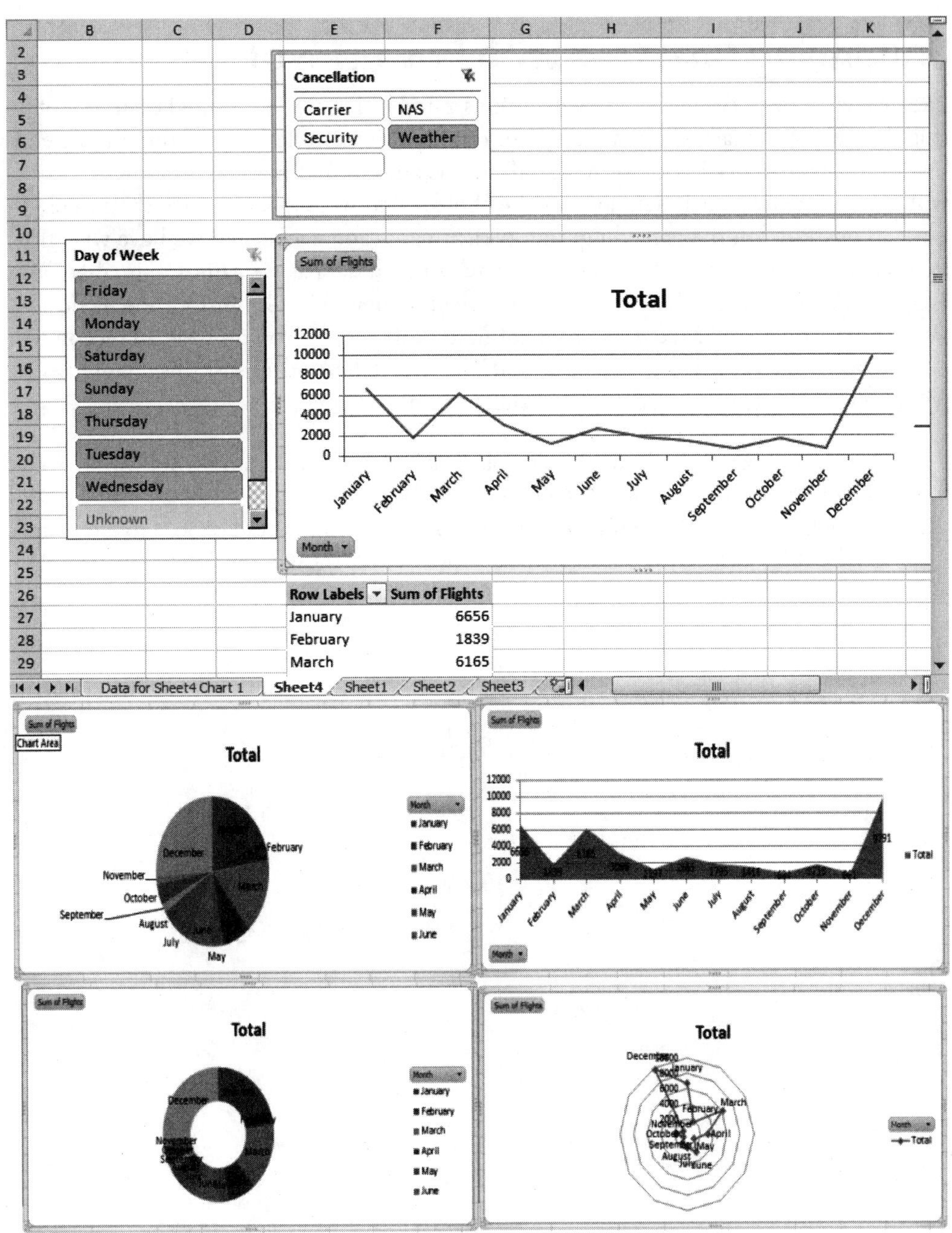

Figure 7-29 *Demonstration with different chart types*

Enhancing Charting with PowerPivot

Next we will create the chart that we demonstrated in Figure 7-1 at the beginning of this chapter. This chart will consist of four charts, a PivotTable (which contains a trend line), and finally two slicers. Since we will not be adding that much new content, we will not go into too much detail about the choices that were made (unless they were not demonstrated in the preceding example). An additional goal that we have with this example is that we would like to demonstrate as much data as we can in a small amount of space. We also have iMac users who also need to view this. Currently, there is no PowerPivot add-in for Macintosh users of Microsoft Office. You do have an option to allow those users via Microsoft SharePoint, so in the later portions of this chapter we will cover adding this PowerPivot worksheet to SharePoint.

1. Start by choosing the PowerPivot ribbon and then Four Charts from the PivotTable drop-down list as shown in Figure 7-30.
2. You will then be presented with a dialog box where you should choose to create this in a New Worksheet. Click OK to view the four charts as shown in Figure 7-31.

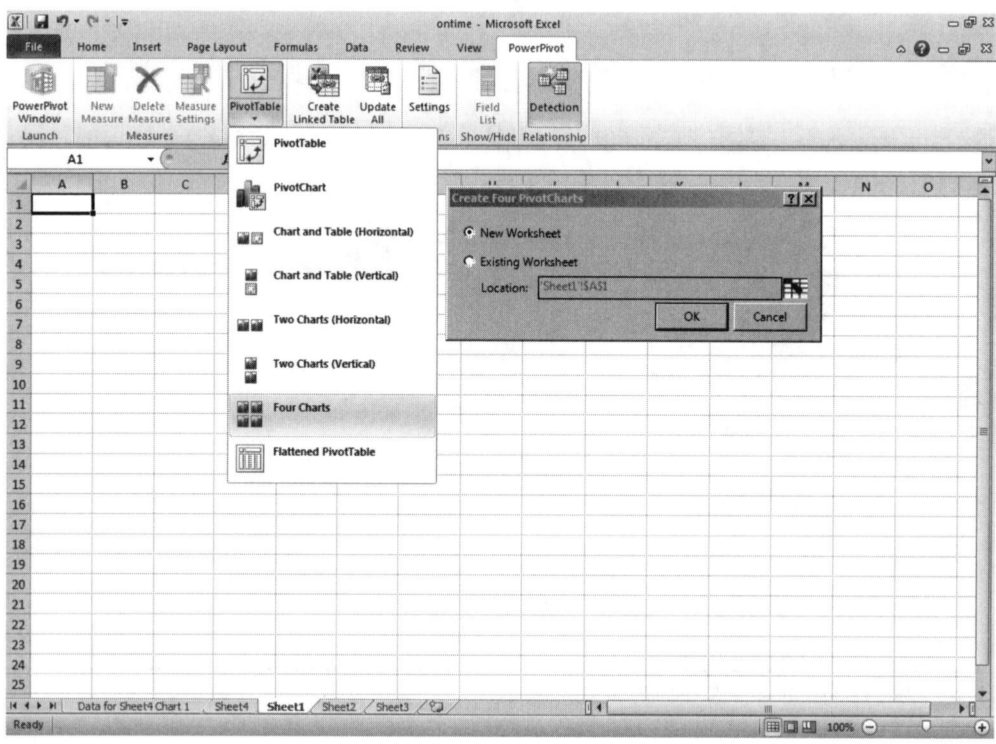

Figure 7-30 *Adding four charts to a table*

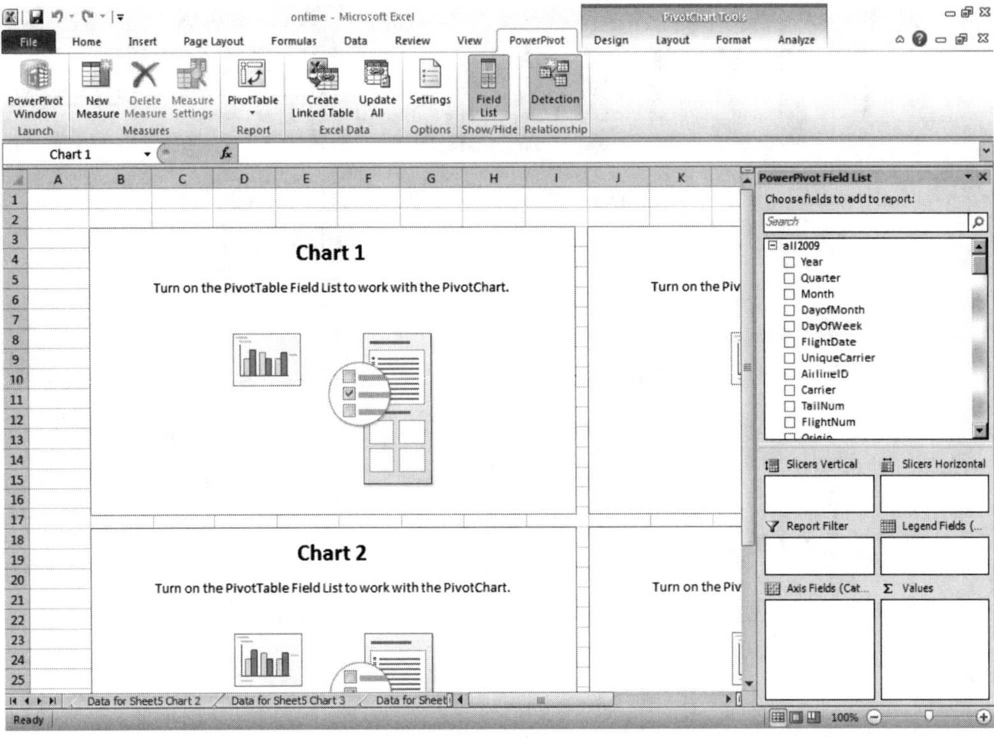

Figure 7-31 *Four charts on a new worksheet*

These four charts are just like the charts in the previous example. In order to choose what is on each chart, click in the chart box. The first three charts are much like the previous example; for the fourth chart you will be changing several things.

3. In Chart 1 create a "Flights by Month" line chart (which is similar to the previous example, except that you will choose month instead of day of week). You should have Flights in the Values box and Month in the Axis Fields box. You should also change this chart type to be a line type chart.
4. In Chart 2 create a "Flights by Mileage" area chart; this is similar to chart 1 except that you should choose Flights by Mileage in the Axis Fields box. You should also set the chart type to be an area chart.
5. In Chart 3, which is almost exactly like the previous example, use Flights in Values and Day Of Week in the Axis Fields box. The chart type should be bar.

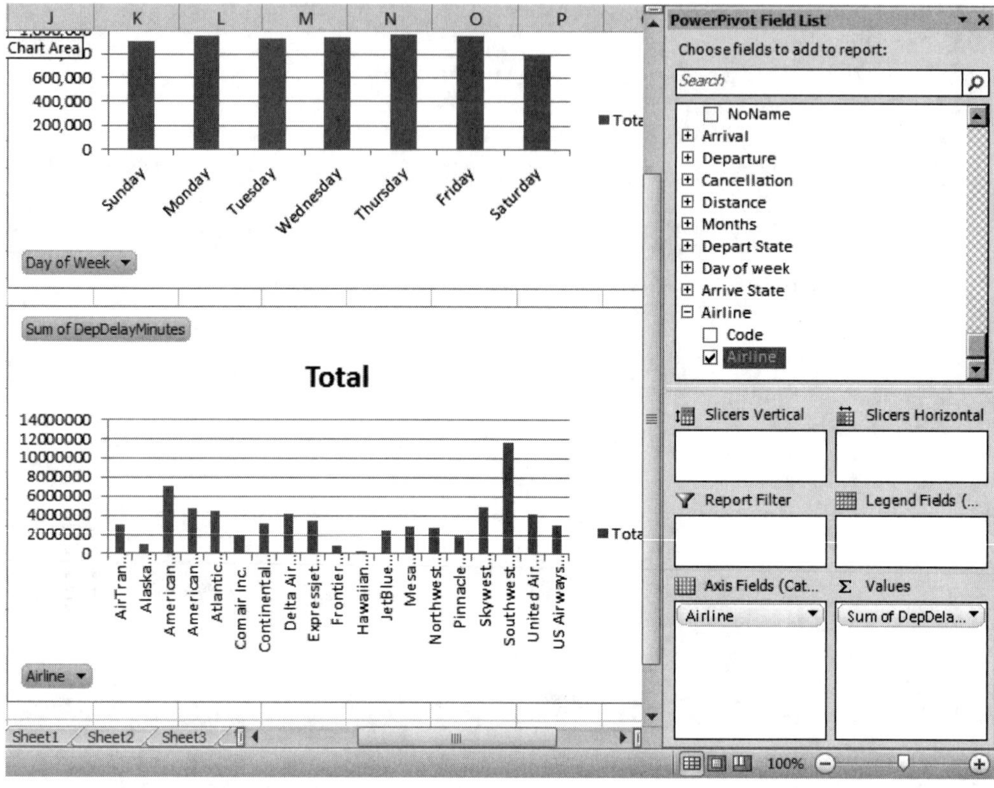

Figure 7-32 *Pivot field list for Chart 4*

In Chart 4 there are some slight modifications, which we will cover in the next steps.

6. With Chart 4 put Airline in the Axis Fields box, as in Figure 7-32.
7. Put the Sum of DepDelayMinutes in the Values field.

   If you just want to have a chart that lists the total amount of delays per airline, then you can skip the next step. We want to know the average minutes per delay by carrier.
8. We would like the change the DepDelayMinutes so that it doesn't sum all of the numbers (which is the default option). Click the Sum of DepDelayMinutes and you will be presented with a list box as shown in Figure 7-33. In the list box choose Summarize By and then choose Average (the other aggregate functions are Sum, Count, Min, and Max).
9. You can also click the title of a chart and type in what the chart is demonstrating (as also shown in Figure 7-33). This makes it easier for the consumer of the report to understand what she is seeing in the chart.

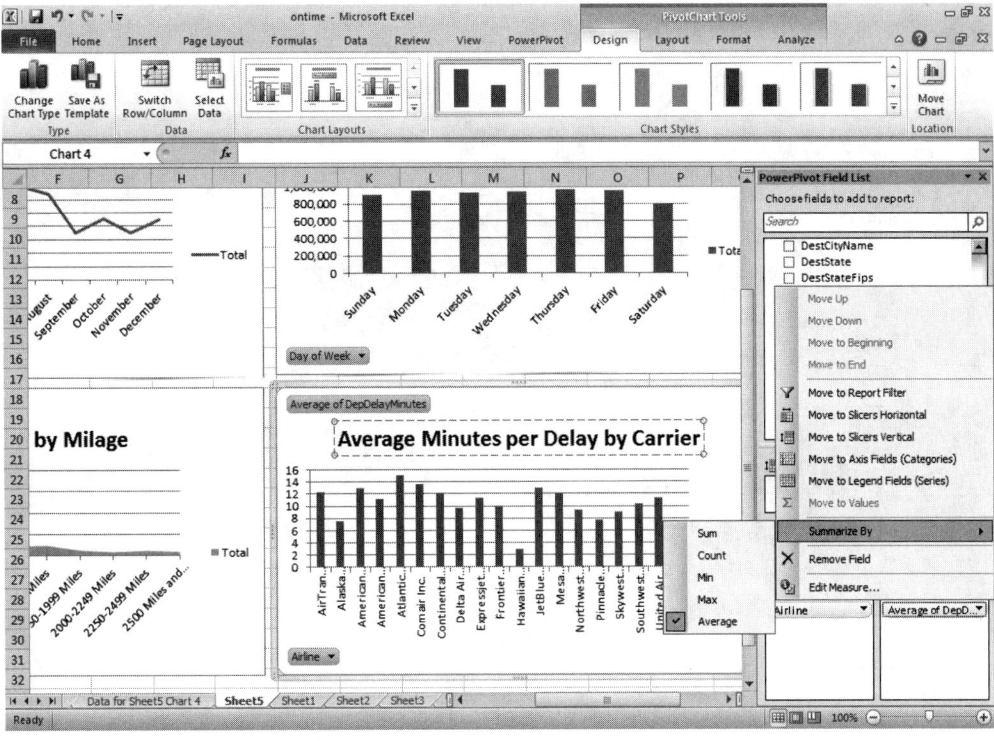

Figure 7-33 *How to change the Aggregate function*

10. Now that you have the charts looking pretty good, try adding a new PivotTable to the bottom of this chart. Click into a cell below the charts (following Figure 7-34, place the chart in cell B:34).
11. From the PowerPivot ribbon choose PivotTable and then PivotTable from the drop-down list. You should then be presented with a choice as to where to place the PivotTable. Choose to place it in the Existing Worksheet (as also shown in Figure 7-34).

Changing PivotTable Options

In the next set of steps we will change options in the PivotTable.

1. For this PivotTable click next to Flights or drag Flights down to the Values box, place Airline in the Row Labels box and Month in the Column Labels box (shown in Figure 7-35).

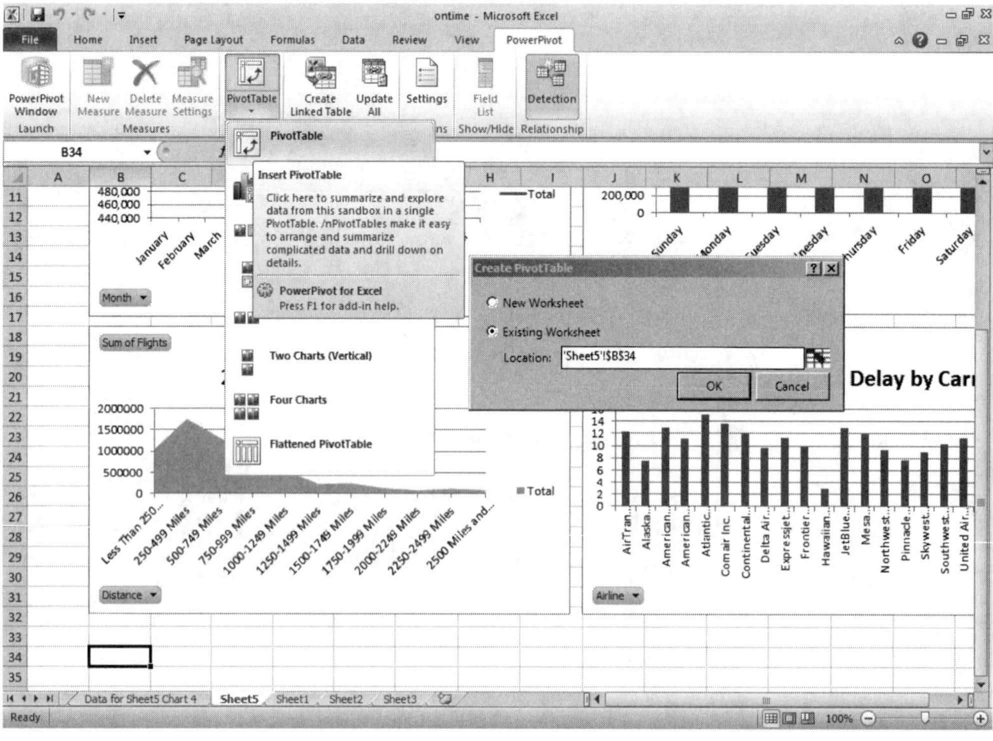

Figure 7-34 *Adding a PivotTable to the worksheet*

This will create the default PivotTable in the worksheet, but we would like to change an option in this PivotTable; we would like to hide the Grand Total column.

2. Right-click the PivotTable and choose PivotTable Options from the drop-down list box. This will present you with the PivotTable Options screen (also shown in Figure 7-35). Click the Totals & Filters tab, uncheck the box that says Show Grand Totals For Rows, and then click OK to continue (also shown in Figure 7-35). You could also choose Design under the PivotTable Tools on the ribbon and then under Grand Totals and choose for Columns only.

   Now that we have the PivotTable like we want it, we should add a sparkline (a trendline) to where the rows grand totals were located. In order to do this, we will use the Insert ribbon in Excel.

3. Click the Insert ribbon to see which other items you can insert into the worksheet. Choose in the Sparklines section to add a line (as shown in Figure 7-36).

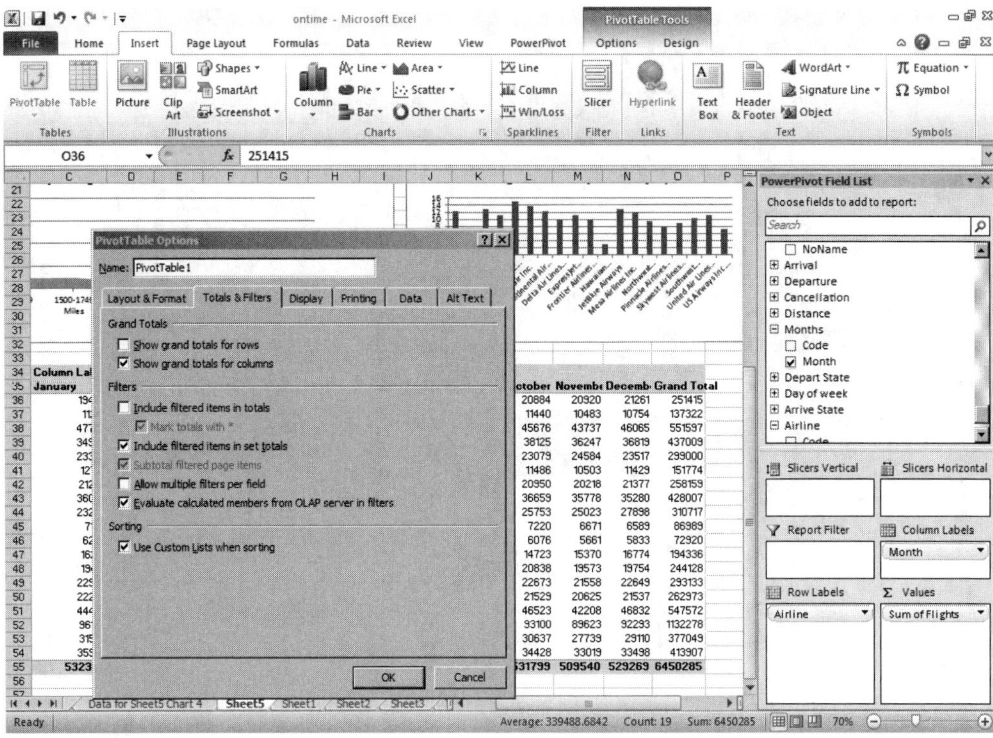

Figure 7-35 *Changing the options in the PivotTable*

4. You will next be presented with a box (as depicted in Figure 7-37). Choose the Data Range to be the inside of the PivotTable that you just put down (in the example case, from column C to column N and row 36 to row 54—C36:N54). You can either insert this into the box or use your mouse to highlight those rows.
5. Next you need to choose where you would like the sparkline to be located. We would like this to be in column O and go from rows 36 to row 54 ($O$36:$O$54). You can also use your mouse to highlight the location where you want the sparkline to be located.

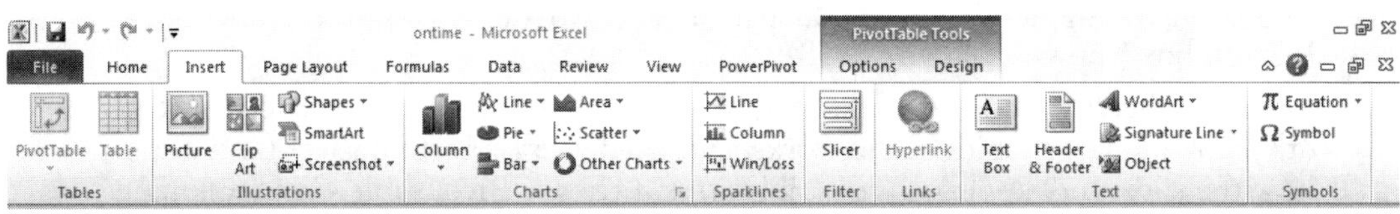

Figure 7-36 *The Excel Insert ribbon*

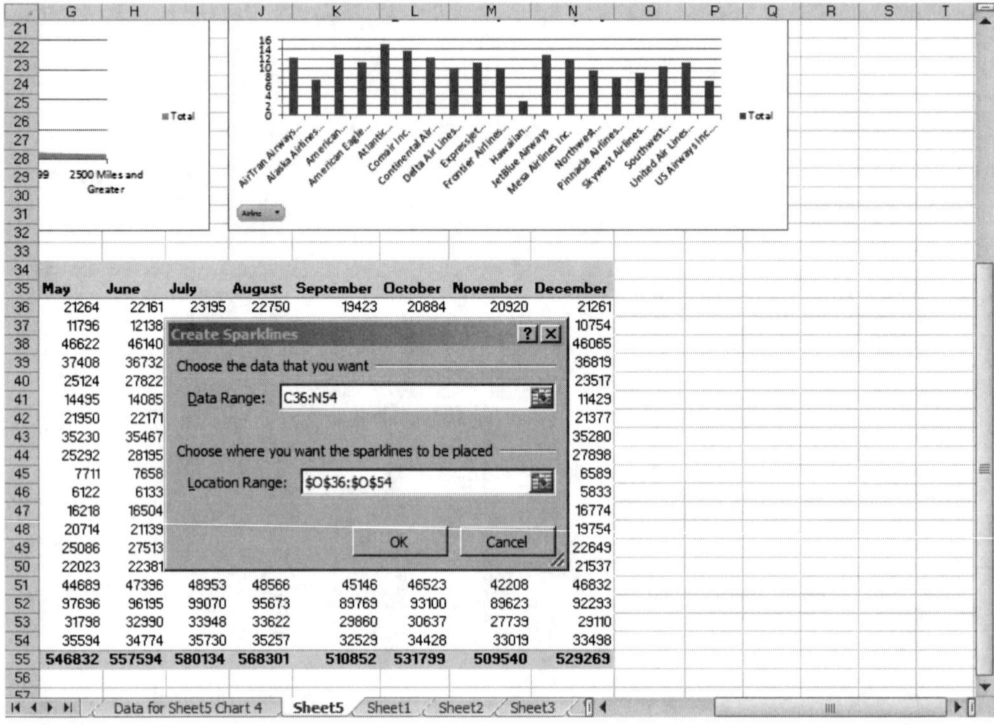

Figure 7-37 *The Create Sparklines range selection*

Placing Slicers

Now that we have a PivotTable looking the way we want, next we would like to place a couple of slicers on the sheet. We want these slicers to change all of the charts that we have created if a certain departure or arrival destination is changed (we want to be able to pick different airports to see how all of the flights and carriers did across the whole year). To do this, we will need to add slicers.

1. There are two ways of adding a slicer: via the menu that you have used previously, or by dragging the items into the PowerPivot field list, which is the way we will be demonstrating here. Drag the Departure and Arrival fields into the Slicers Vertical box (shown in Figure 7-38).
2. Once the slicers are on the worksheet, next you need to connect the slicers to the other PivotChart / tables in the worksheet. Click the Departure slicer (and notice how the slicer tool appears in the ribbon) and choose PivotTable Connections (as shown in Figure 7-38). Place a check mark next to each PivotTable in the box (this will link the slicer to all other PivotTables).

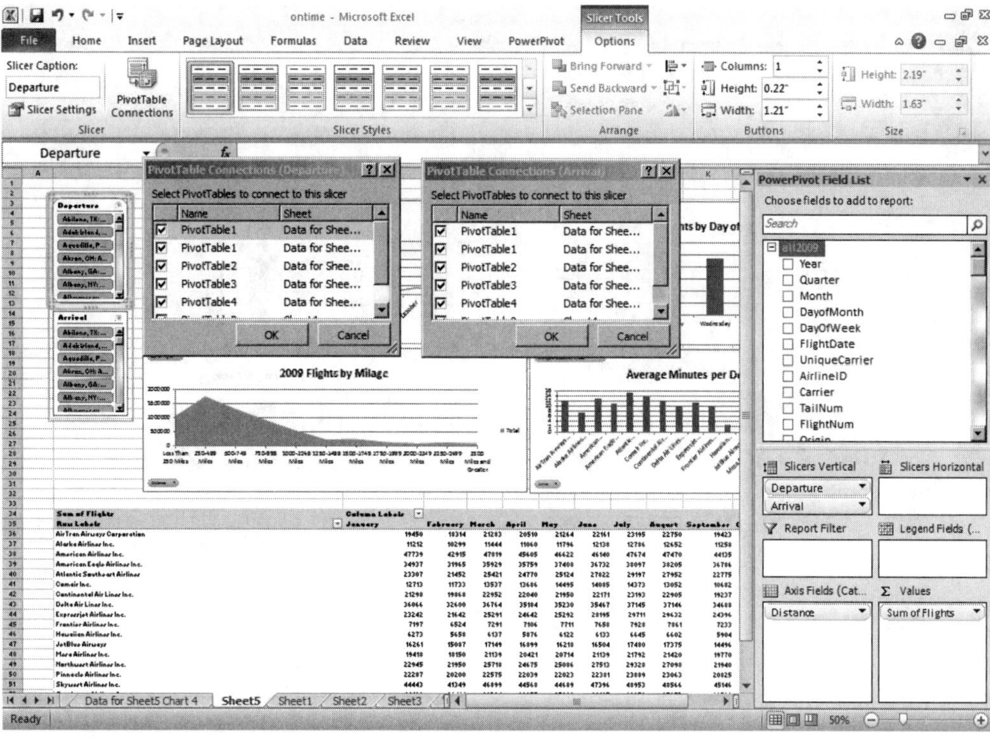

Figure 7-38 *Adding slicers to the worksheet*

3. You will need to do the same thing with the Arrival slicer; in the Slicer Tools choose PivotTable Connections and place a check mark next to every PivotTable in the list.

Now you should have a screen that looks similar to Figure 7-39. This visualization is just another small sample of what you can do with PowerPivot. Several books are dedicated just to PowerPivot and the power that this tool gives the end users. If you are interested in learning more about PowerPivot, you should check out some of these wonderful books that are available on PowerPivot and/or visit www.powerpivot.com or www.powerpivot-info.com (these are great resources for further information). We also have additional resources updated information up on www.officebicentral.com.

Sharing PowerPivot

Next we will be moving into the server component of PowerPivot (which is based in Microsoft's Office SharePoint Server). SharePoint is an integrated suite of capabilities that PowerPivot resides in. We won't spend very much time going through SharePoint,

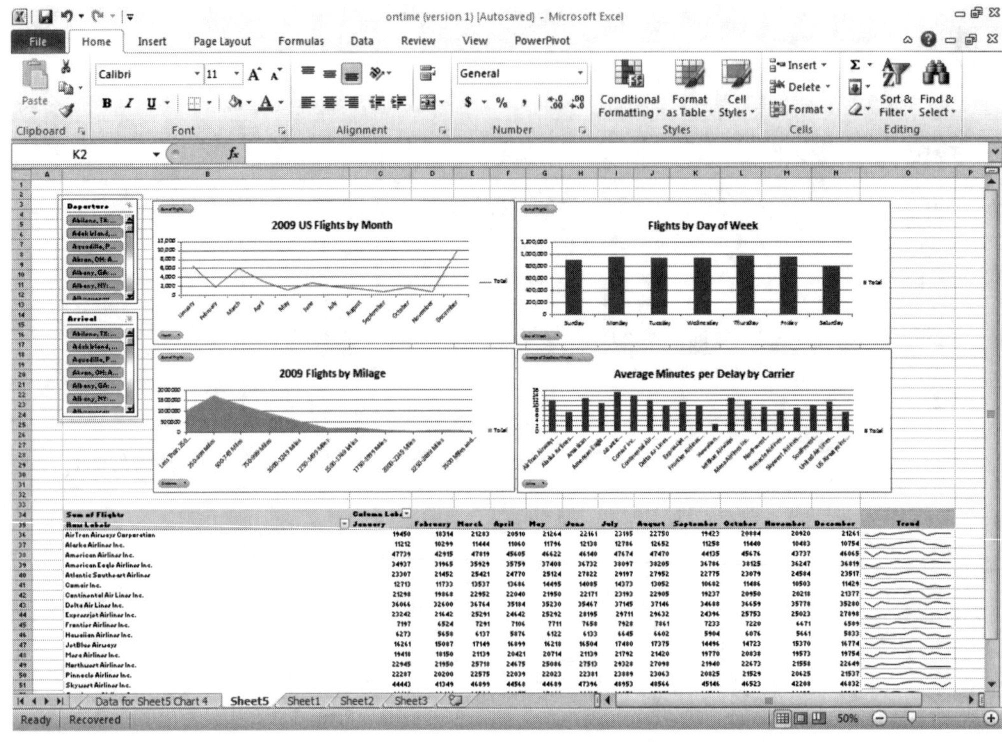

Figure 7-39 *The completed example*

but it is important to note that you will require SharePoint Enterprise and SQL Server 2008 R2 Enterprise and above in order to install the PowerPivot components. You should also note that you need to install the Analysis Services components with your installation of SQL Server 2008 R2 in order to have PowerPivot options. We won't go through the further requirements to install PowerPivot in SharePoint, but there are great examples up on www.powerpivot-info.com and also references on www .officebicentral.com.

Once you have a SharePoint implementation installed, you will be able to share your visualizations with other people (as shown in the next few steps).

1. First click the File button in the upper left-hand corner (shown in Figure 7-40).
2. In the column choose Save & Send. This will give you several additional choices; choose Save To SharePoint (shown in Figure 7-40).
3. If you have already saved worksheets to a SharePoint site, they will show up in this window, or you can browse for additional locations.

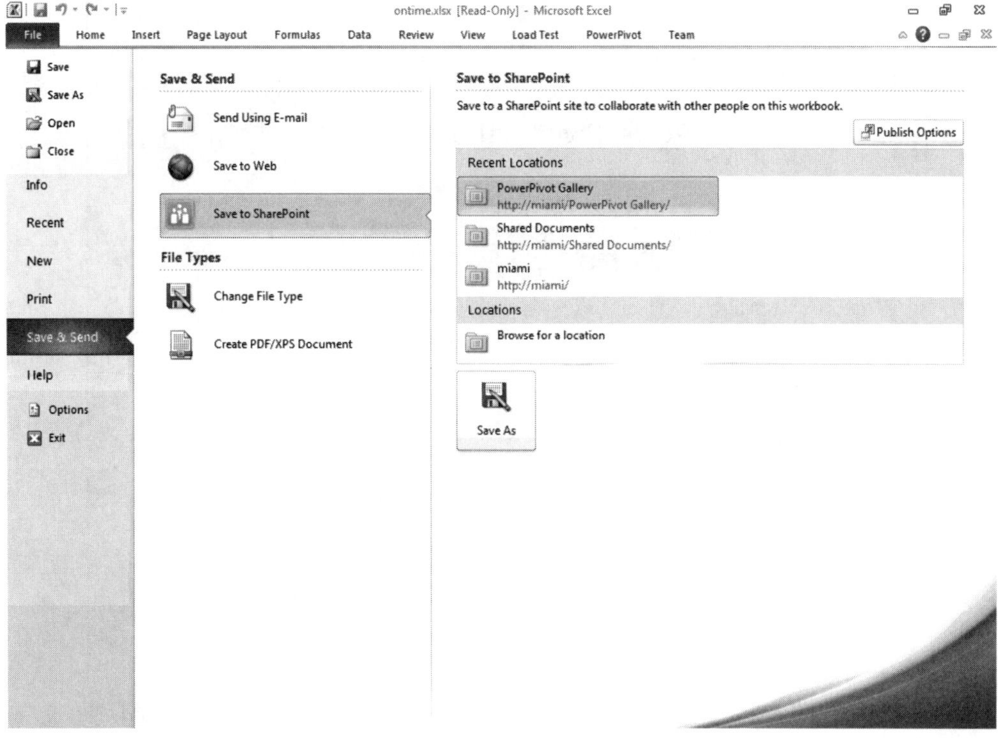

Figure 7-40 *Saving your worksheet to a SharePoint site*

4. You will next be presented with a Save As dialog box (shown in Figure 7-41). Choose the filename and the gallery you would like to save the worksheet to (in this example we are saving it to the PowerPivot Gallery). Click Save to continue.
5. After you click Save, SharePoint will ask the type of content you are saving. Choose PowerPivot Gallery Document from the drop-down list box and click OK to continue (depicted in Figure 7-42).

   By default after you save the worksheet up to SharePoint, it will open the worksheet. This is a nice way to view the visualization that you just created as other users would see it using a browser. This is shown in Figure 7-43. You will notice that this should look almost exactly as it does inside of the full Excel client (except that there is no ribbon and it is in a browser).

   You will notice if you scroll down the page that the trend lines are there and the slicers also change the data on the charts.
6. Click the PowerPivot Gallery (as shown in Figure 7-44).

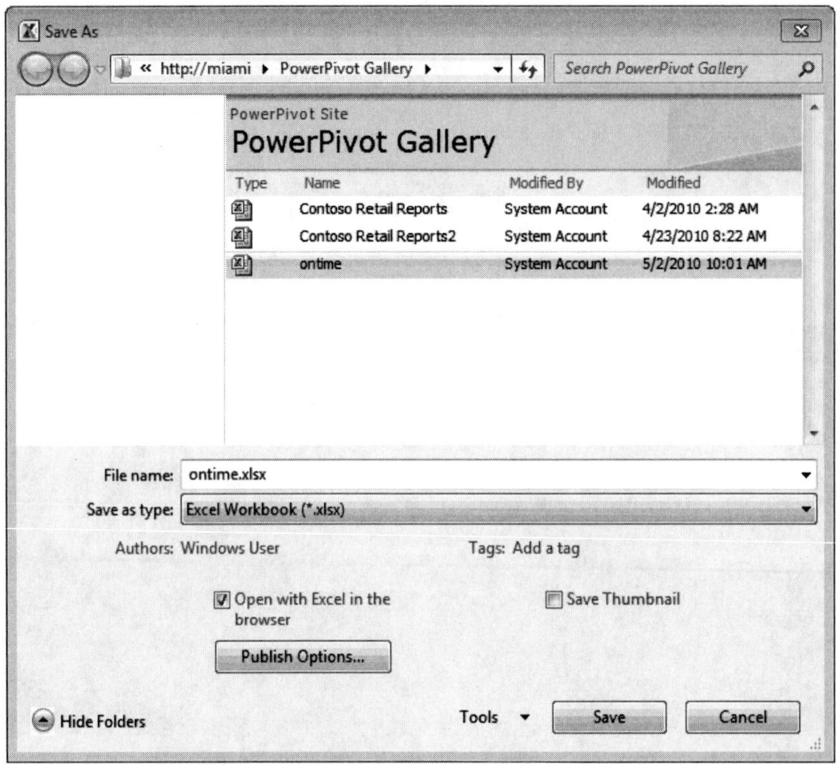

Figure 7-41 *The PowerPivot Gallery save options*

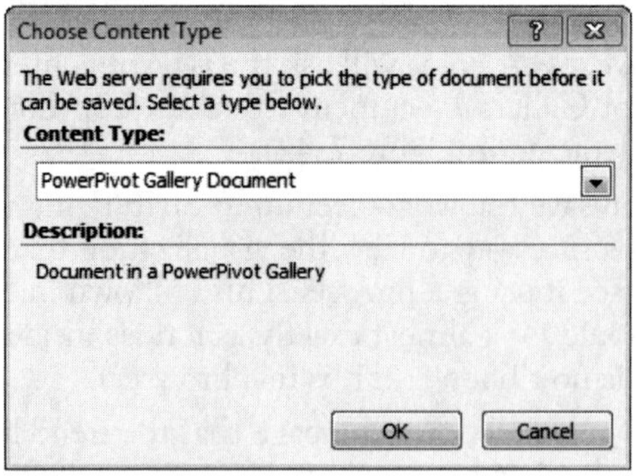

Choose Content Type
The Web server requires you to pick the type of document before it can be saved. Select a type below.
Content Type:
PowerPivot Gallery Document
Description:
Document in a PowerPivot Gallery
OK Cancel

Figure 7-42 *Choosing the content type in SharePoint*

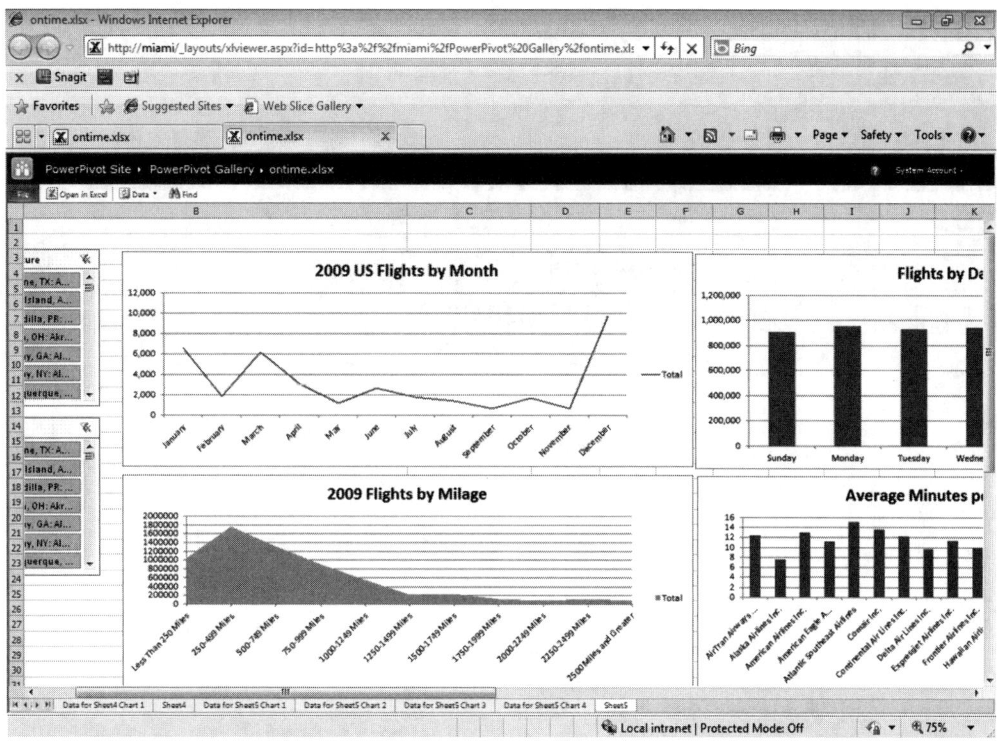

Figure 7-43 *The example PowerPivot worksheet in SharePoint*

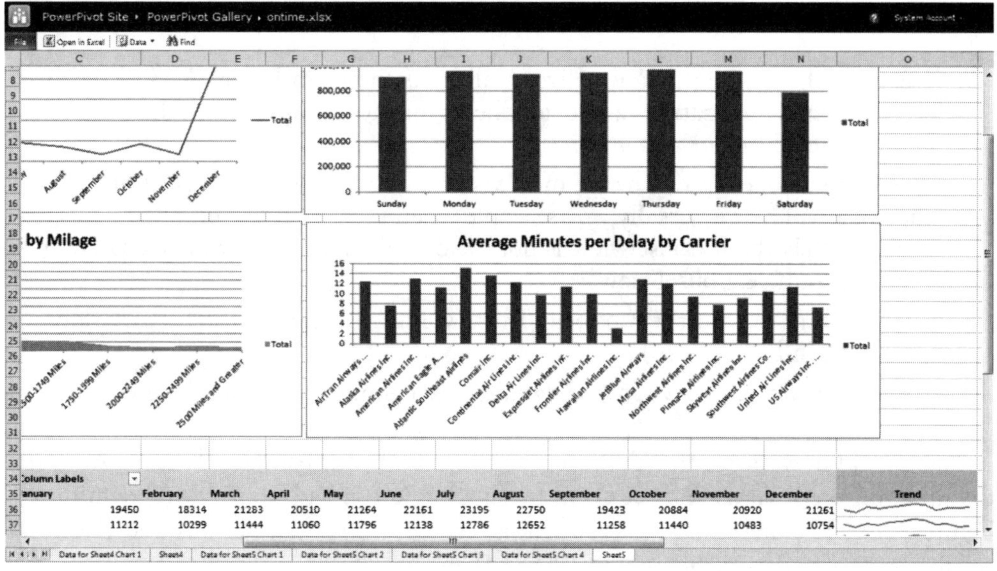

Figure 7-44 *Moving around the worksheet*

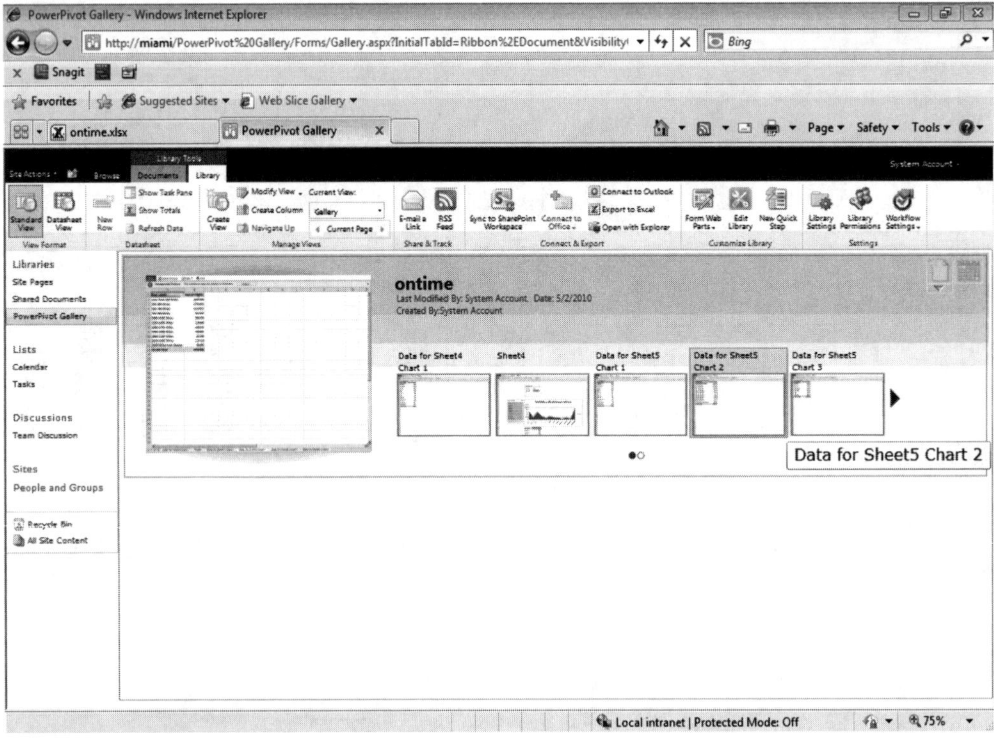

Figure 7-45 *The PowerPivot Gallery*

7. Next you should see the PowerPivot Gallery as shown in Figure 7-45. You should see all of the visualizations and chart sheets for the example. Click the different charts to see different visualizations.

   The Carousel view is one of the most visually compelling views inside of the Gallery. This view really wows people when they see it the first time, but unfortunately the Carousel view is not the default view, so we will be changing the view to the Carousel view.

8. In the library tools at the top select Library. This will display the Library ribbon (as shown in Figure 7-46).
9. Under the Current View drop-down list box, choose the Carousel view.

You should now notice the Carousel view inside of your browser. This allows you to pull in different views and see them by clicking left or right buttons (shown in Figure 7-47). The one thing that you will notice with this example was that Excel publishes all of the worksheets to the SharePoint site.

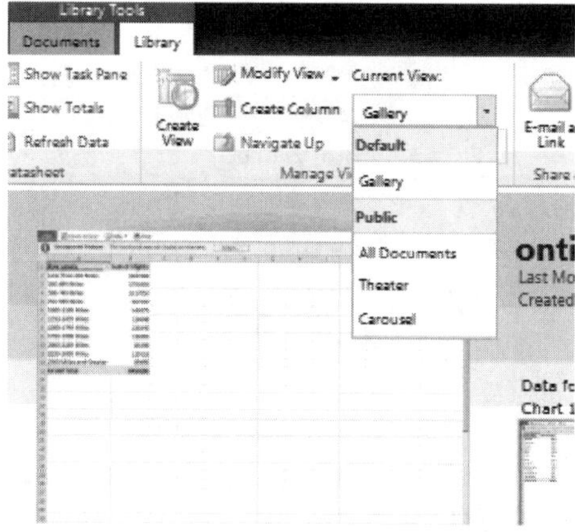

Figure 7-46 *How to get to the Carousel view*

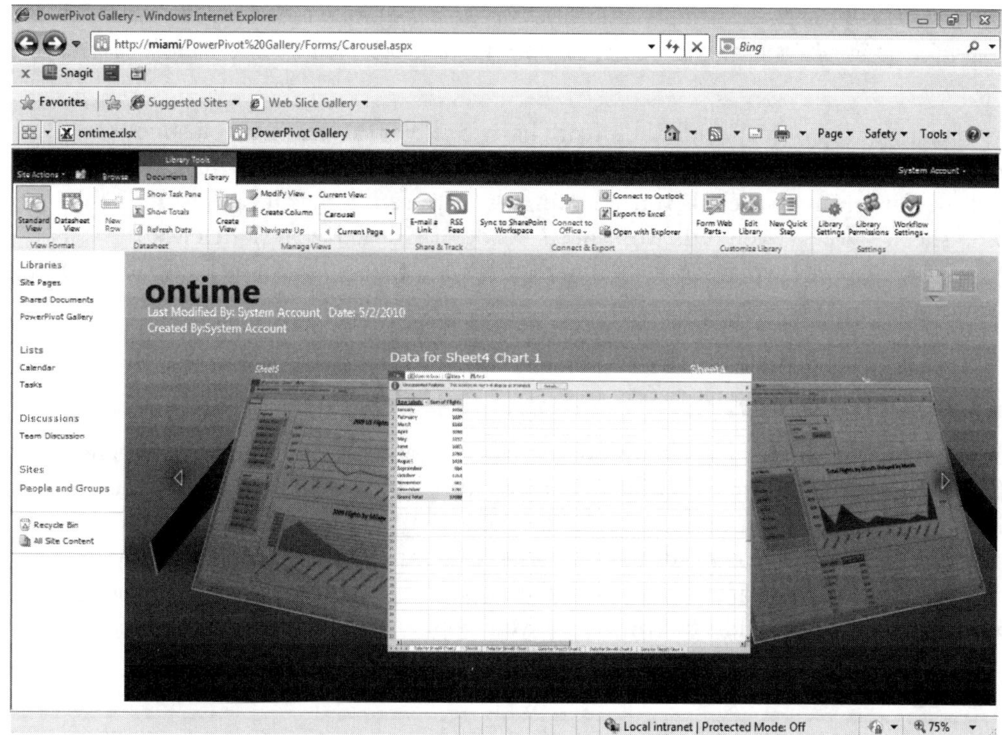

Figure 7-47 *The Carousel view*

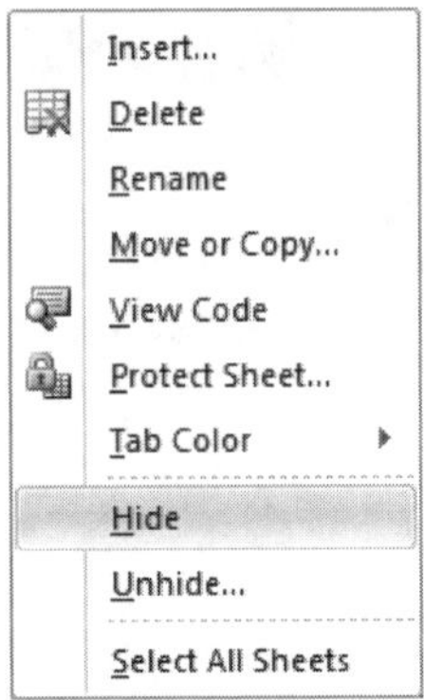

Figure 7-48 *The worksheet options inside of Excel*

BI TIP

To make only the items you want to publish to SharePoint, you would choose the Save And Send menu choice and then Save To SharePoint. This will list a dialog box where you can choose the items under the publishing options section.

If you want to only include the PivotCharts or PivotTables, then you should only publish those. If you publish all or use the default save method, you will also publish out the data sheets as well. If you are going to only use Excel, you can just hide the worksheets. How do you hide worksheets inside of Excel? If you right-click the Worksheet tab, you will be presented with the menu that is shown in Figure 7-48. You would want to hide any sheets before you save to SharePoint.

Extending PowerPivot with DAX

It is amazing what we can do with PowerPivot without having to make any changes. Sometimes the problem is that the data isn't exactly the way we need it. You can go back to the original source to make these changes, but sometimes that isn't possible or practical. Sometimes you need to modify the data or perhaps even combine multiple fields to achieve your intended visualization. In order to do that, you need some way of interacting with the fields. In PowerPivot you would use DAX.

BI TIP

DAX is meant to be user friendly, but it is extremely powerful. There is a lot more information about DAX on the web page www.powerpivot-info.com.

What Is DAX?

While the name DAX was very popular with *Star Trek*, this DAX is a data expression language used inside of PowerPivot. DAX (the term stands for Data Analysis Expressions) is exposed via PowerPivot. DAX is based on of the familiar Excel functions that hard-core Excel users are used to. There are a couple of differences between DAX and Excel functions:

- In DAX you deal with the complete table or column of data, and in Excel you typically deal with individual cells.
- DAX can return a table of values.
- The DAX Date functions return a datetime; Excel date functions return an integer.

In DAX you can use the filter function to limit the items from a table or a column. In several other functions you can apply the filter directly (one such example is the Calculate function).

Where Would We Use DAX?

DAX is used primarily in two places within PowerPivot: measures and calculated columns. It is important to understand where to use Excel functions and where to use PowerPivot functions. Excel functions are used in Excel worksheets, and DAX is used inside of PowerPivot (or inside of the PowerPivot-created table or chart). We will go through a demonstration of creating a calculated measure and a calculated column inside of PowerPivot.

Example of Creating a Calculated Column

In this example we will be using the same ontime.xlsx file that we either created or downloaded earlier. In this flight data example we have various elements of United States domestic flight data. We have two columns that we will be using in these data elements, distance and airtime, to determine the average speed per minute, then we multiply times 60 to get the average miles per hour. The distance is the air miles that the flight has flown and the airtime is the time in minutes that the flight took. Our calculation is simple: distance divided by airtime and then multiplied by 60 to get the average miles per hour the flight has flown.

BI TIP

If you would like to get the average kilometers per hour, you would first multiply the mileage by 1.609344 (that would give the distance in kilometers).

1. Open the PowerPivot window (if you open the spreadsheet you will see the PowerPivot ribbon—choose PowerPivot in the Launch Section). Choose the Add Column (which is a column on the far right of the worksheet). When you select the column, the entire column will be highlighted as in Figure 7-49.
2. Above the column but below the ribbon you should notice the function line (this is where you input functions). In this case insert the following DAX script:

   =IF(ISBLANK(all2009[ActualElapsedTime]),0
   (all2009[Distance]/all2009[ActualElapsedTime])*60)

   If we pick apart this function, the first statement is an IF statement. We need to check and see if we are going to cause a divide by zero error, so we will test to see if in the table all2009 in the column ActualElapsedTime is blank; if it is blank we return a zero. If ActualElapsedTime is not zero, we then divide the column Distance by the column ActualElapsedTime and then multiply by 60.

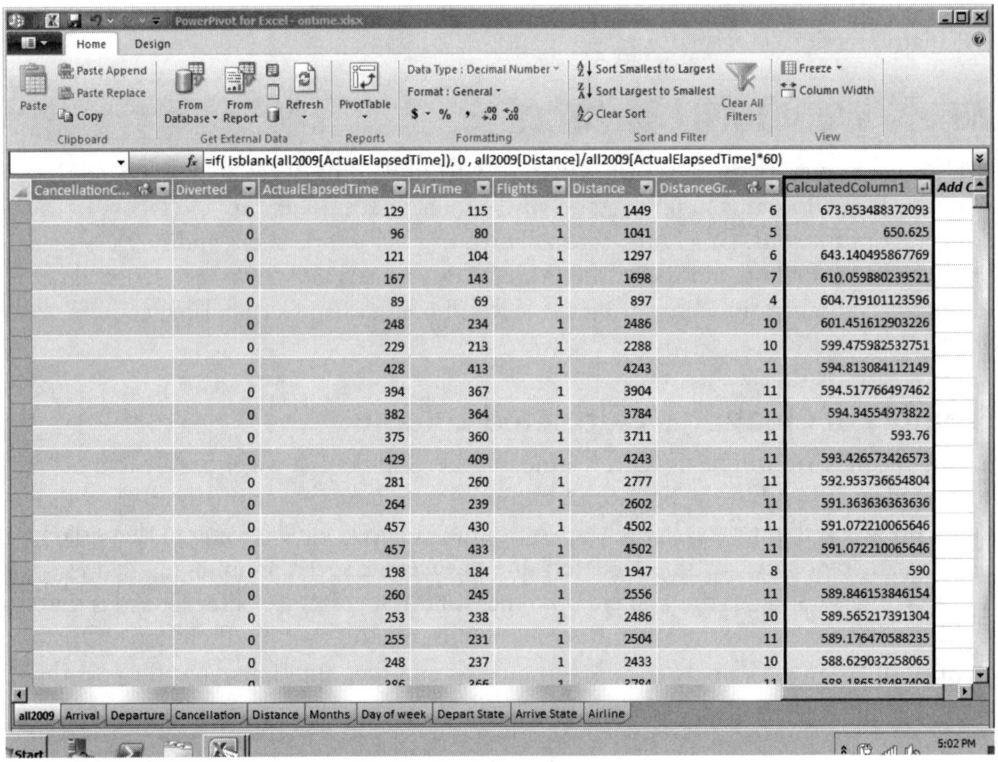

Figure 7-49 *Creating a calculated column*

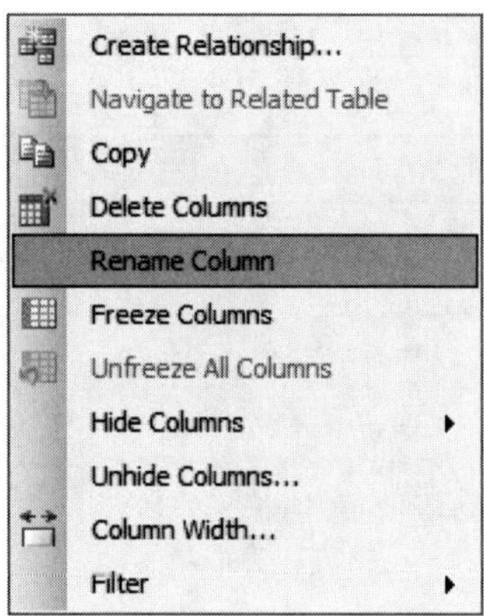

Figure 7-50 *How to rename a column in the PowerPivot worksheet*

3. The default name for the column will be CalculatedColumn1, but we would like to change the name to something more meaningful. Right-click the column and you will be presented with a list as depicted in Figure 7-50. Choose Rename Column and set the name to something like **Average Flight MPH**.
4. Now we will format the new column so that it only displays whole numbers. There are two ways that you can do this. One way is to use the DAX function Round(the_number, the_number_of_digits). The second way is to choose the Home ribbon from the PowerPivot tool and then under the Format drop-down list in the Formatting section choose Whole Number, as in Figure 7-51.

   Now if you make changes to the PowerPivot worksheet while you have active charts, you do not have to restart your spreadsheet. You will receive a notification at the top of the PowerPivot field list that you need to refresh, as in Figure 7-52.
5. If you click the Excel worksheet that has the example PivotTables and charts in it, you will notice on the top of the PowerPivot field list a notification that there were modifications to the PowerPivot data. Choose Refresh to continue. You will notice that there is a new column named Average Flight MPH.

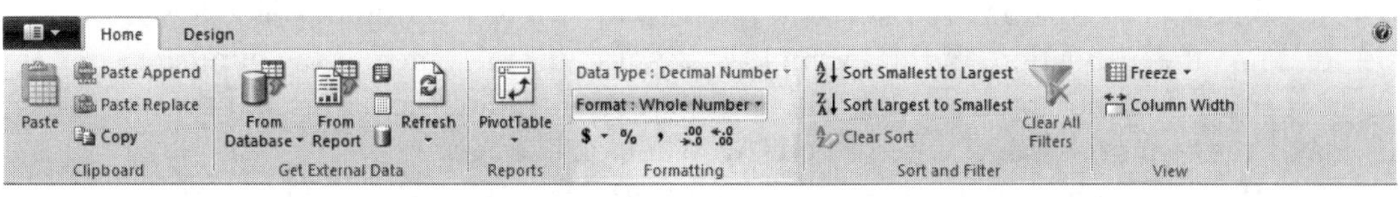

Figure 7-51 *Formatting columns in the PowerPoint*

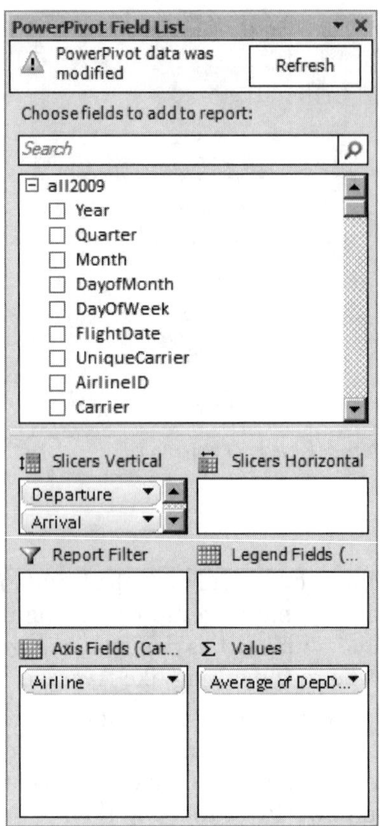

Figure 7-52 *A PowerPivot field list that needs to be updated*

Example of Creating a Calculated Measure

In the preceding example we created a new column that we could use in a PivotTable or chart. In this example we will be creating a calculated measure. The main difference between the calculated column and the calculated measure is when each of the calculations takes place. In the calculated column, it is done on the worksheet and as data is inserted. In the calculated measure, the calculation is done when you use the measure. The reason for this is that in the calculated measure we will be filtering the data down before doing the calculation. In this example we want to try to figure out the number of flights per day. In order to do this, we will need to first sum all of the flights and then divide by the count of distinct dates. The DAX will look like this:

```
=ROUND(SUM(all2009[Flights]) / COUNTROWS(DISTINCT(all2009
[FlightDate])),0)
```

So let's pick apart this function from the inside out. The DISTINCT() function will return just distinct dates for the table all2009 and the column FlightDate. We next use the COUNTROWS() function to return the number of rows that are a distinct date. Next we divide by a SUM() function of all of the dates, and finally we round the number so that we don't have any decimal places. The number that should be returned is the flights per day. If you place a row or a column label, you should see the number of flights broken out by those labels (such as the number of flights by carrier per day).

1. In the Excel worksheet, choose the PivotTable on the lower portion of the charts (this is the one that has the sparklines). When you click the table, you will notice that in the PowerPivot window you can see New Measure in the Measures section. Click New Measure as shown in Figure 7-53.
2. You should notice the Measure Settings dialog box open. Set the Measure Name to Flights per Day as shown in Figure 7-53.

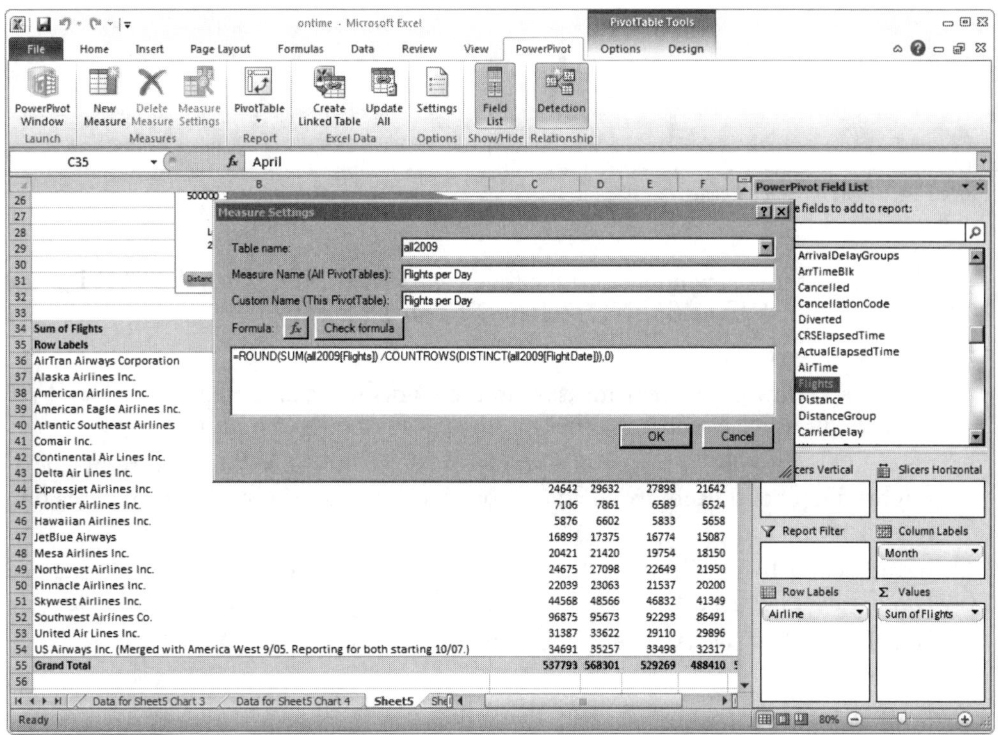

Figure 7-53 *How to create a calculated measure*

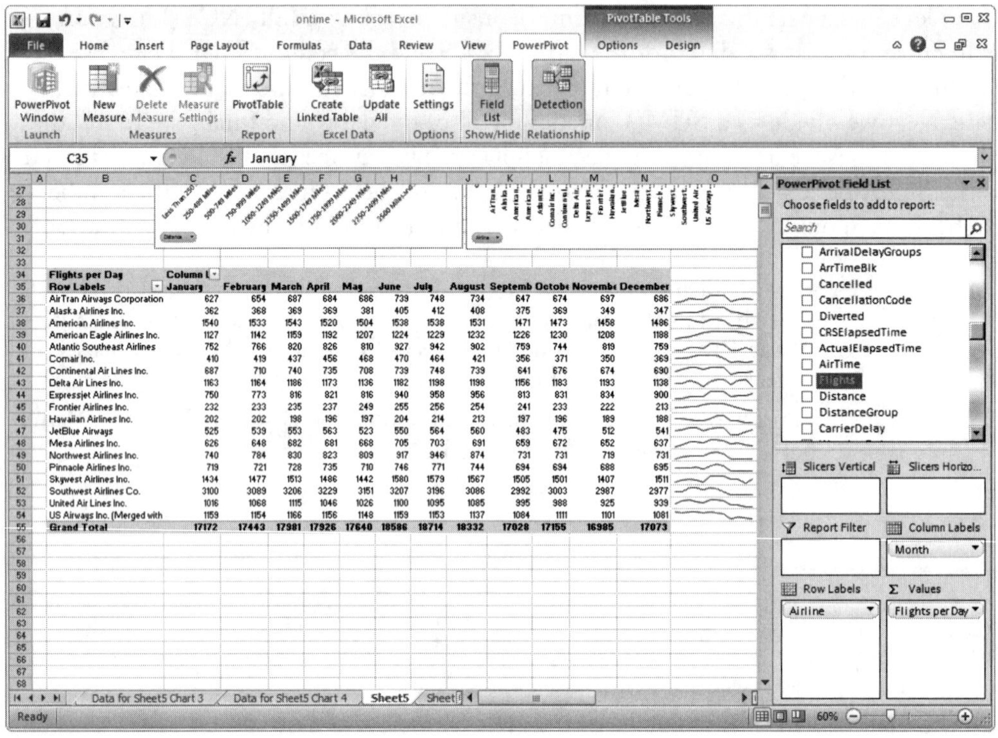

Figure 7-54 *Using the new calculated measure*

Next in the formula window type the following: **=ROUND(SUM(all2009[Flights]) / COUNTROWS(DISTINCT(all2009[FlightDate])),0)**

3. Click OK to continue.

   You should now have a new measure in the worksheet called Flights per Day. We can use this as we would any other number, as Figure 7-54 indicates.

4. You can now use the measure that you just created. In the Values field right-click Flights and choose Remove Field (or you can just drag Flights to a blank area on the worksheet).

5. In the field list you will notice the measure that you just created called Flights per Day. Either click next to this entry or drag the entry down to the Values field.

6. You should also have Airline in the Row Labels box.

Now you have used the new measure that you just created in a PivotTable. You can use regular and calculated measure in the same way inside of PowerPivot.

In this section of the chapter we have only touched on what is possible with extending PowerPivot with DAX.

BI TIP

There are about 135 DAX functions, and if you are interested in more information, there is a listing up on http://powerpivot-info.com/post/16-powerpivot-dax-function-list-with-samples (or you can also find this link on www.officebicentral.com).

Wrap-Up

If you were wondering how PowerPivot works, the PowerPivot add-in installs something called VertiPaq (which is similar to a local instance of SQL Analysis Services). VertiPaq is an in-memory engine that PowerPivot communicates with via AMO / ADOMD.NET (common multidimensional data connections). VertiPaq is also what SharePoint uses for PowerPivot communication. Since VertiPaq has external providers, we believe that you will see additional solutions that extend the functionality of PowerPivot in the near future.

This chapter was meant as an introduction to these abilities that PowerPivot gives you. We are hopeful that you have learned a little bit about how you can utilize this tool to create some compelling solutions using Excel and PowerPivot. We have created a portion of the web site www.officebicentral.com, which lists some additional sites that contain blog entries, additional samples, and further information about this great tool.

Chapter 8

SQL Server 2008 R2 Analytic Design Techniques

In This Chapter

- Report Builder Elements: An Overview of Matrix, Chart, and Map Objects with SQL Server Reporting Services
- Creating an OLAP Data Source for Our Model Report
- Creating a Matrix for Our Model Report
- Creating a Chart for Our Model Report
- Creating a Map for Our Model Report
- Creating a Gauge for Our Model Report
- Creating a Parameter Dataset for Our Model Report
- Creating a Parameter for Our Model Report
- Adding the Parameter to the Dataset for Our Model Report
- Model Report First Draft and Changes
- Naming Conventions
- Modifying the Display Elements for the Model Report
- Modifying the Data Display for the Model Report
- Report Element Display and Position Changes to the Model Report
- Wrap-Up

We start this chapter with an immediate example, a model report with tablix, map, and chart report objects that tell the data story of "customer counts"—each in its own unique way, and yet in a complementary manner. This model report, if we've done our work correctly, should show the status of a business process at a glance.

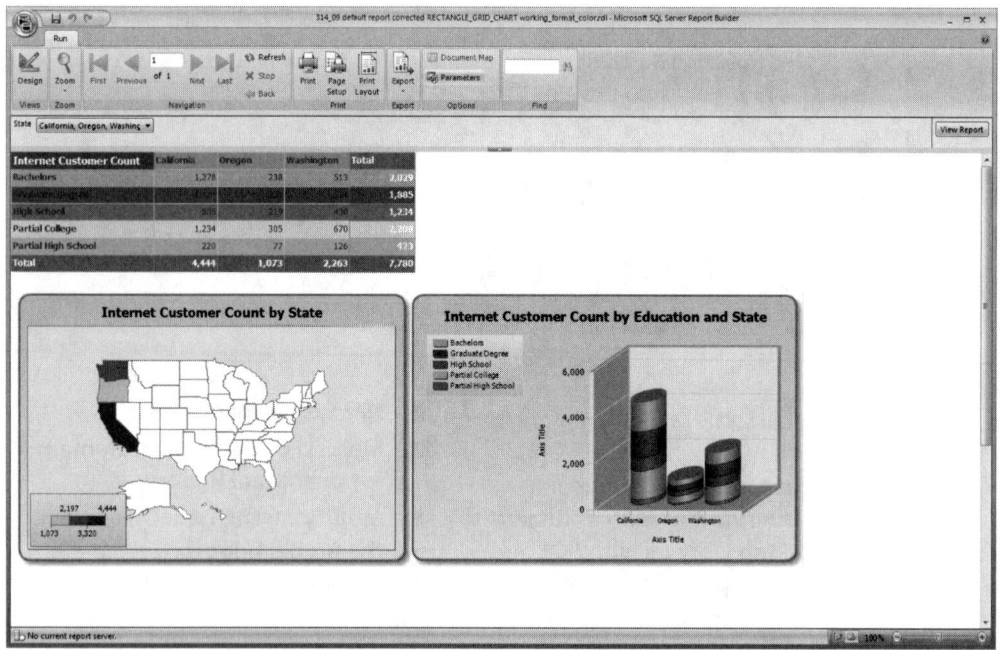

As you'll see in this chapter, there is a good deal of work that goes into making such a report, and the core lesson you'll learn is "pay attention to the details." It is rarely sufficient to stop with a default report presentation; rather, the report designer should take the extra steps to portray a graphical presentation of a data story that understands the business audience that will be consuming the report. In summary, the report should be something the report designer can be proud of, that reflects the look and feel and the mission of the organization.

Report Builder Elements: An Overview of Matrix, Chart, and Map Objects with SQL Server Reporting Services

SQL Server Reporting Services has leveraged the Visual Studio integrated design environment (IDE) to deliver its Report Designer to end users since the introduction of Reporting Services with SQL Server 2000. SQL Server 2005 saw the introduction of the Report Builder as a companion report design interface, delivered in its own "click once" module that can be downloaded from SQL Server to any Windows client machine.

The Report Builder tool is a web solution in that client machines can download it over a LAN/WAN connection, but it is a .NET client application (once it's installed on the client PC) with the robust feature set of an advanced report-writing tool. With SQL Server 2008, and more so with 2008 R2, the Report Builder design experience has really matured and is today the tool of choice for everyday report-writing people. For information purposes, Report Builder version 3.0 is the version that comes with SQL Server 2008 R2.

Reporting Services is part of the three major business intelligence tools that are delivered with SQL Server; the other two being Integration Services and Analysis Services. These three SQL business intelligence services (or tools) can work independently for reports, data extraction, and OLAP analysis respectively—or in an integrated fashion where Integration Services is used to "extract, transform, and load" data from multiple data sources of different formats; where Analysis Services accepts the automatic updating of data from Integration Services into an OLAP cube data structure; and where Reporting Services queries and displays the Analysis Services data in a report presentation.

BI TIP

The Report Builder is the most commonly used Microsoft report-writing tool, with its easy-to-understand Office-like ribbon menu user interface; whereas the Report Designer is the most sophisticated Microsoft reporting tool with its Visual Studio integrated design environment (IDE).

With SQL Server 2008 R2, which releases to market in 2010 as a "business intelligence refresh" improvement for the SQL Server 2008 platform, Microsoft has significantly enhanced the Report Builder to make use of the market-leading Dundas Chart, Map, and Gauge technology—which Microsoft has natively "baked" into the SQL Server reporting tool set (SQL Server itself comes with all these features and requires no third-party licensing nor installation). This chapter will take a step-by-step approach to building a model report using these components. In reality, what constitutes a good model report (or best practices report) is a subjective judgment call that involves both the data story and the report consumer personality. However, we will clearly show the common steps (and a few missteps) that are involved in creating a usable report.

Our model report will incorporate a matrix, a chart, and a map—with a parameter that filters the data for all three elements. We'll take a brief look at placing a gauge on the report—and then provide some comments about where gauges work in reporting. So, to get started, note the blank report design screen we have when starting the SQL Server Report Builder as shown in Figure 8-1.

A. **Report Data pane** This is an expandable tree view of all data elements and report objects in the report being created or edited.

B. **Ribbon menu** This is the Office tab-menu for top-level editing functions, and for inserting new report objects. The common actions available in this top menu are also available by right-clicking report objects in the main report design pane—as with all Microsoft Office applications.

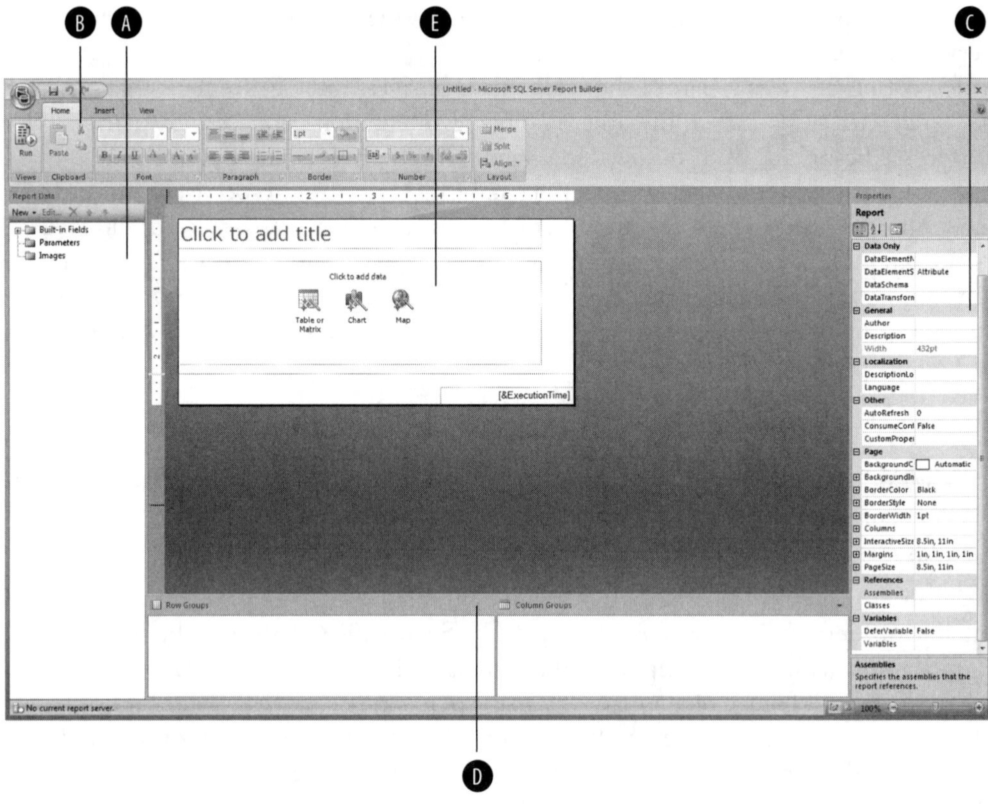

Figure 8-1 *SQL Server 2008 R2 Report Builder: a .NET Windows application*

C. **Properties pane** This is an expandable tree view of all report elements, although it dynamically changes to display configurable properties for the report element currently selected/highlighted in the main report design pane. The common properties available in the right-side pane are also available by right-clicking report objects in the main report design pane (which is the properties configuration methodology used in this chapter).

D. **Row Groups and Column Groups** This is an interactive field display of data elements in a matrix object in the main report design pane, although the matrix data elements are presented in a more useful manner through the right-click pop-up menus and dialog boxes available directly on the matrix object in the main report design pane (which is the matrix configuration methodology used in this chapter).

E. **Main Report Design pane** This is the central drag-and-drop report design area, where report objects are arranged, and where report objects support right-click pop-up menus and dialog box user interfaces.

The wizard approach to creating new report objects is a dominant theme in Report Builder, and it's strongly recommended by the Microsoft product team because it walks the user through the data selection and report object configuration/visualization process to produce report elements that convey information to the consumer of the report (in the context of business intelligence, where we strive to create data visualizations that place information in a display that provides some analytical value).

So let's get started with the Report Builder, version 3.0—and create a data source for our model report as shown in Figure 8-2.

Creating an OLAP Data Source for Our Model Report

This section takes an interesting journey, using a multidimensional online-analytical-processing (OLAP) cube for the report data source. This is different from using an everyday relational database for the data source, since an OLAP cube contains better organized data that has been drawn from a relational data source, and the OLAP cube has its own internal relationships that support data analysis in a more intuitive way.

Since it is becoming more common today to see OLAP cubes that are created by data professionals in support of report designers, we're choosing to show off the Report Builder capabilities using an Adventure Works cube as a data source, that can be freely

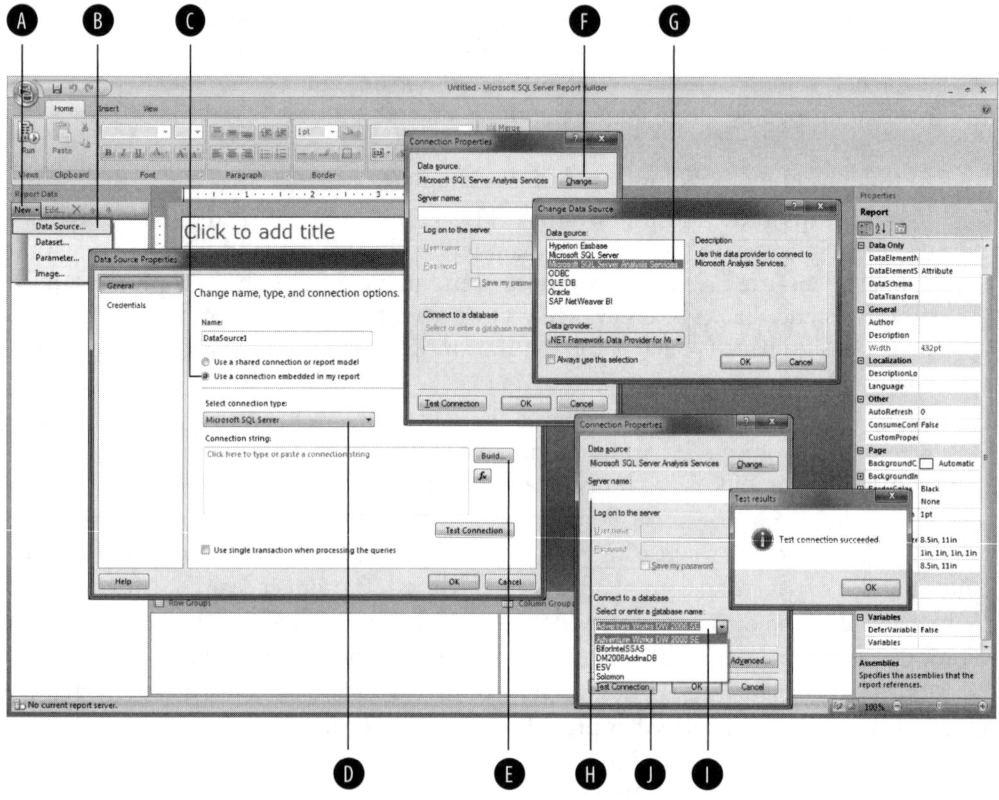

Figure 8-2 *Report Builder: creating a new data source for an Analysis Services cube*

downloaded from Microsoft websites. Figure 8-2 starts this process of choosing an OLAP cube for a data source.

1. Click the New drop-down in the upper-left corner of the Report Designer screen (Step A).
2. Choose Data Source (Step B) to create a new data source.
3. In the Data Source Properties dialog box | General tab, choose the option button "Use a connection embedded in my report" (Step C), in the Select Connection Type drop-down select Microsoft SQL Server (Step D), and click Build (Step E).
4. In the Connection Properties dialog box, click Change (Step F) to display the Change Data Source dialog box.
5. In the Change Data Source dialog box, choose Microsoft SQL Server Analysis Services in the list box (Step G), and then click OK.

6. In the Connection Properties dialog box, in the Server Name text box type a . (a period) (Step H) to designate a local server (or type the name of your desired SQL Server), and click in the "Select or enter a database name" drop-down list to choose "AdventureWorks DW 2008 SE" (Step I).
7. In the Connection Properties dialog box, click Test Connection (Step J) to display the Test Connection Succeeded pop-up message box, and click OK.

In Figure 8-2 we are creating a data source to a SQL Server OLAP cube. This is significant because a cube data source provides a uniquely organized structure that makes it easy to use for analysis and reporting—once you become familiar with the concept of dimensions and measures. In this case we're using a Microsoft-provided cube: Adventure Works DW 2008 SE, which is a well-organized hierarchical cube (data warehouse design–star schema) for SQL Server 2008 Standard Edition.

BI TIP

OLAP cubes, also known as multidimensional data sources, are a best-practices source of data for report designers because the data relationships are organized in a manner that makes them easy to choose when creating a report with Microsoft's Report Builder.

What Is an OLAP Cube?

When people need to group and total data in a flexible manner, online analytical processing (OLAP) can provide an intuitive way to look at the rows of information and use the OLAP measures and dimensions in reports such as our working model report. Since we want to look at sales amounts grouped by state and education, it makes sense that the OLAP dimensions of state and education provide a way to do this.

Frankly, the dimensions of a well-designed OLAP cube provide groups of data that have already been analyzed by the cube designer—to make it easy to summarize numeric data that might be associated with the dimensions. In our working report we summarize the number of customers by state and education level. It's worth knowing that the power of OLAP cubes extends beyond just analysis and actually provides a way to look at large amounts of data. Cubes are capable of providing split-second access to millions of rows of data because the cube pregroups the data, making it ready for end-user analysis and reporting!

BI TIP

OLAP cubes are an increasingly common part of business intelligence, where we require fast totaling and subtotaling of data according to different groupings of data that we choose in an ad hoc manner. OLAP cubes require a special database server, known as SQL Server Analysis Services, that is designed to host OLAP cubed data.

Continuing with the Data Source and Datasets

The data source in Figure 8-2 is an embedded data source because we're creating it on-the-fly for our working model report—and thus it will be part of our model report and not available to other reports. Shared data sources are actually a better way to work with report design in an organization, because knowledgeable database administrators (or just people who know the data source) can take some time to create good data sources, from either relational or multidimensional (cubes) data, and place the resulting data sources in a SharePoint repository for all report designers to use.

For now, we'll just work with a data source that draws from a pre-existing cube, and go with a default methodology of leaving the data source embedded in the report. Looking again at Figure 8-2, we've really taken the easy road to creating a data source, by choosing Microsoft SQL Server Analysis Services in the Data Source drop-down menu, simply entering a period for the Server name, and then choosing Adventure Works DW 2008 SE for the cube data source.

BI TIP

It's a real time-saver to simply type a period (.) when entering a SQL Server machine name for a report data source. The period tells Report Builder to look for a local instance of SQL Server and connect to it—which is also made easier if one's network login ID and password will work to gain read access to the local SQL Server (as opposed to having to enter a SQL Server–specific ID and password).

In Figure 8-3 we continue the configuration of the OLAP cube data source for our working model report—by using the wizard dialog boxes to create a dataset from the data source. This dataset stage is an important step, since we're choosing a measure for our report. The measure is the numerical part of the report, and although we can certainly choose multiple measures to include in a report, we're going to use just one measure for our working model—and then add dimensions that will effectively provide a "group by" on either rows or columns (once we get to the task of actually designing the report), for summing the measure we've chosen. As we see in Figure 8-3, the measures and dimensions depend on our having chosen a data source cube from SQL Server Analysis Services.

1. Select the DataSource1 node in the left-hand pane (Step A), and right-click to choose Add Dataset from the pop-up menu (Step B).
2. In the Dataset Properties dialog box | Query tab, in the Data Source drop-down choose DataSource1 (Step C).
3. Click Query Designer (Step D) to display the Query Designer dialog box.
4. In the Query Designer dialog box, click the + Measures (Step E) and the + Internet Customers nodes (Step F) to expand the Adventure Works left-pane tree.

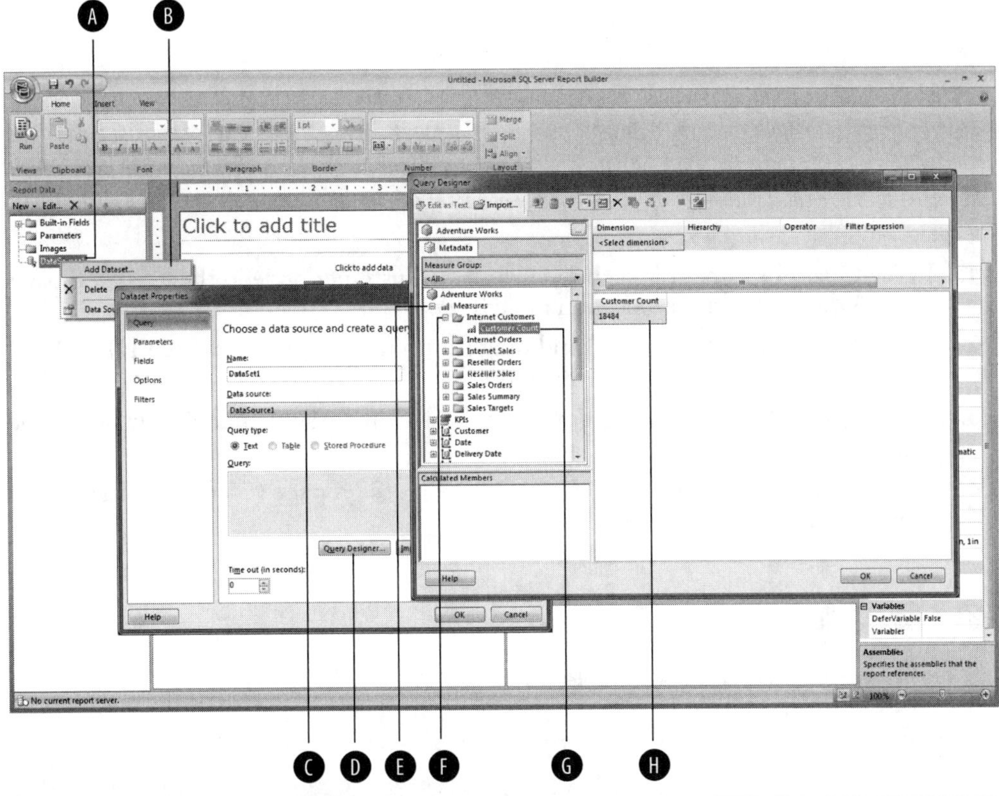

Figure 8-3 *Report Builder: creating a new dataset from cube measures and dimensions*

5. In the Query Designer dialog box, select Customer Count (Step G) and drag it into the main design pane (Step H) as the numeric element to be displayed in our report.

Now that we have our measure as the numeric aspect of the report, we can choose the dimensions as shown in Figure 8-4. Since we are only at the dataset stage of working with our cube data, we simply drag the desired measures into columns that make up a dataset. In a later stage we will design the working report by choosing which measures are appropriate for rows and which measures are appropriate for columns.

Note that in Figure 8-4 we are accomplishing two tasks: choosing measures and choosing a filter to retrieve only a subset of the available data source data. This will make our working report reasonable to render because we're using the filter to ensure that less data is retrieved from the SQL Server Analysis Services cube—which is then subsequently available to the actual report design, as we'll see in later steps.

BI TIP

The job of creating a report that renders in a fast manner (a few seconds) is part dataset configuration and report parameter configuration. The dataset should use a filter to retrieve only the subset of original server data that will be useful to the report, and the parameter should encourage parameter choices that result in a useful report—such as a chart with an appropriate number of bars or columns that can easily be viewed on the report.

1. In the Query Designer dialog box, click the + Customer node in the left-hand pane (Step A), and click the + Location node (Step B).
2. Select State-Province (Step C) and drag it into the design pane (Step D) as the first column to be displayed in the query.
3. In the Query Designer dialog box, click the + Demographic node in the left-hand pane (Step E).
4. Select Education (Step F) and drag it into the design pane (Step G) as the second column to be displayed in the query.

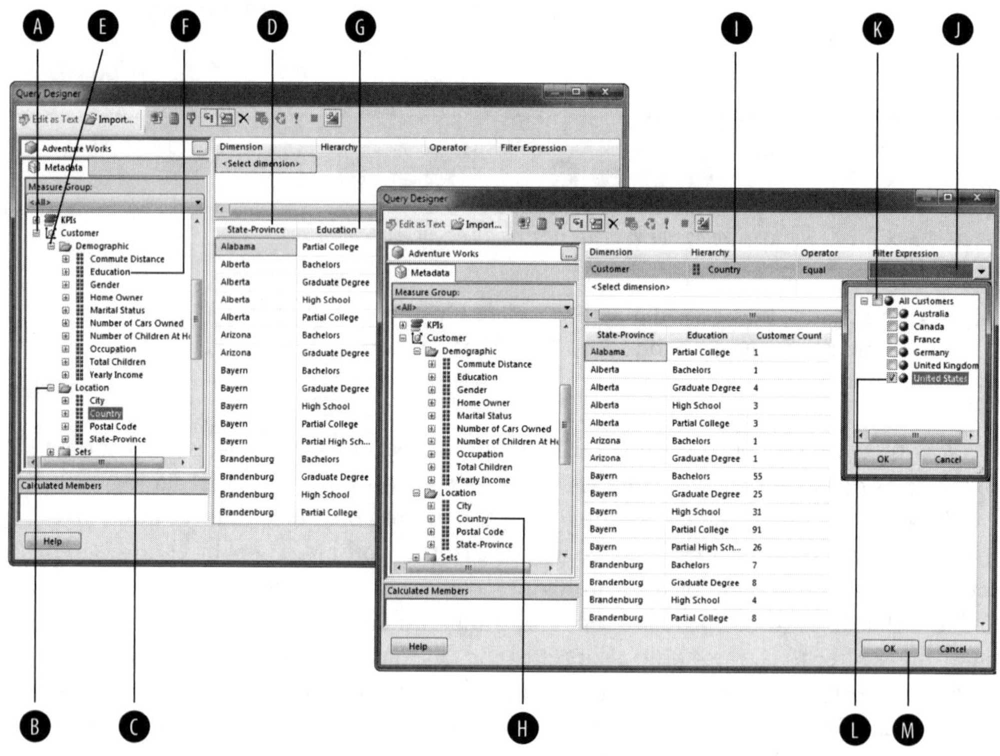

Figure 8-4 *Report Builder: choosing measures and dimensions for the dataset*

5. From the Location node, select Country (Step H) and drag it into the <Select Dimension> cell above the query design pane (Step I), to create a filter that will limit the data return set.
6. Click in the Filter Expression cell above the query design pane (Step J), and click the drop-down to open the Filter Elements list.
7. Click the All Customers check box (Step K) to unselect all choices, and check the United States check box (Step L) to select only United States State-Province elements for the data return set that will be available to the report.
8. Click OK (Step M) to save the query.

In Figure 8-4 we are making the determination that our report will deal only with a single country, and then allow the user to choose states with the country. For our working model we're using a dataset filter to limit the data actually retrieved from the SQL Server cube—in this case, to that of the United States. We could alternatively create reports for other countries, or even create a two-level parameter that forces the user to choose a country, and then states-provinces with the country.

We'll see how to make these choices in later steps when configuring the parameter for our working report. For now, however, we'll proceed in the next section with the task of creating a matrix object for our working report—which will provide some immediate feedback on the visualization of the data source, and the dataset, in an actual rendered report.

Creating a Matrix for Our Model Report

In this section we'll take on the task of creating a matrix object in our model report. A matrix is basically a cross-tab mini-spreadsheet that is flexible enough to allow us to place any desired data elements on the rows or columns. While it often makes sense to create a multipage report of grouped rows, we're going to create a single-page report with multiple distinct objects such as the matrix. The goal is to end up with a report presentation that accurately shows a single data story at a glance, with minimal interpretation required from the report consumer that is viewing the report.

One of the neat aspects about the Microsoft Report Builder design experience is that it separates the data source design process from the report design process. In our working example, we are in good shape knowing that the data source–dataset(s) have all the data elements we'll need for multiple report elements, and now we can focus on placing the right data on the rows and columns of a tablix report object!

Figure 8-5 shows how we start the process of creating the matrix report object.

1. Click the Table Or Matrix icon in the report main design panel (Step A) to start a new matrix element for the report.

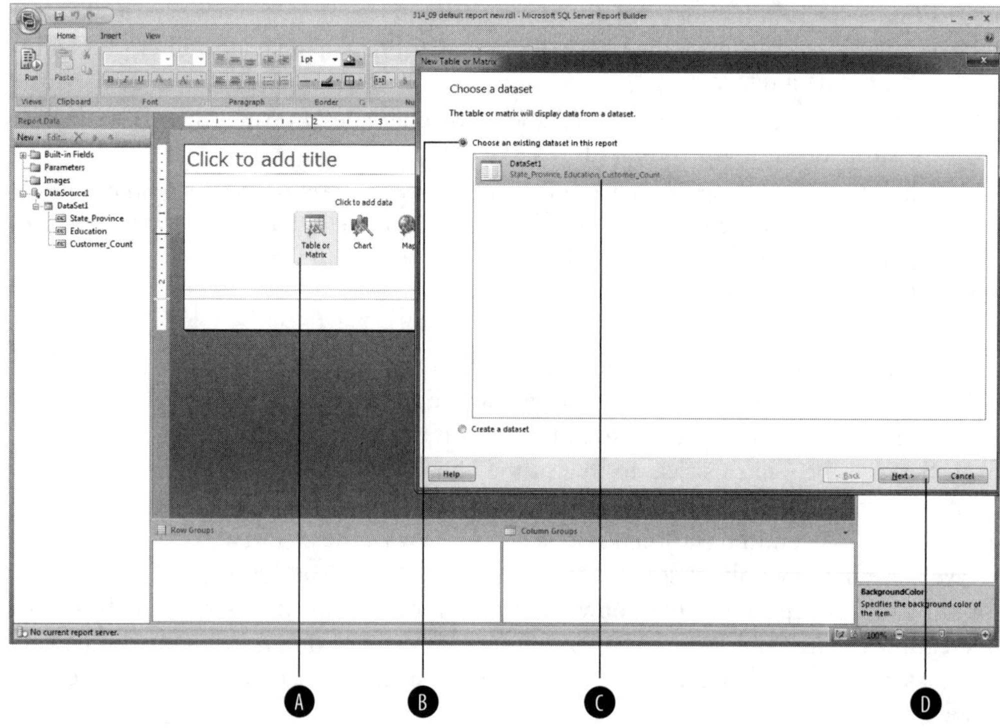

Figure 8-5 *Report Builder: creating a new matrix*

2. In the New Table Or Matrix dialog box, select the "Choose an existing dataset in this report" option button (Step B), and select DataSet1 in the list of datasets (Step C).
3. Click Next (Step D) to continue.

Figure 8-5 shows how we start the wizard dialog box process of creating a matrix by clicking the matrix icon in the center of our blank report design pane. We're using the data source that draws on the OLAP cube data, which is particularly well suited for a matrix object where we have cells displaying the "measure" numeric data element that we earlier designed into the data source configuration. The final matrix will have the on-screen capability to automatically sum/re-sum the cell-by-cell numeric display, as the report user expands or contracts the hierarchical row or column dimensions. This is similar to the PivotTable construct that is familiar to Excel users—which is often connected to OLAP cube data as well for the same dynamic row-column behavior.

BI TIP

A matrix in a report works much like an Excel PivotTable. It is basically a dynamic cross-tab report that sums rows and columns. However, the matrix rows and columns are preset in the design of the matrix and cannot be changed by the report consumer (which makes the matrix simpler than a PivotTable for most users).

Figure 8-6 continues the process of choosing data elements for the matrix, where we drag a measure and dimensions into the matrix design panes.

1. In the New Table Or Matrix dialog box, in the Available Fields list box, select State_Province (Step A) and drag it to the Row Groups list box (Step B).
2. In the New Table Or Matrix dialog box, in the Available Fields list box, select Education (Step C) and drag it to the Column Groups list box (Step D).
3. In the New Table Or Matrix dialog box, in the Available Fields list box, select Customer_Count (Step E) and drag it to the Values list box (Step F, note that it automatically changes to "Sum(Customer_Count)" to provide a sum-by-group element for the new report).

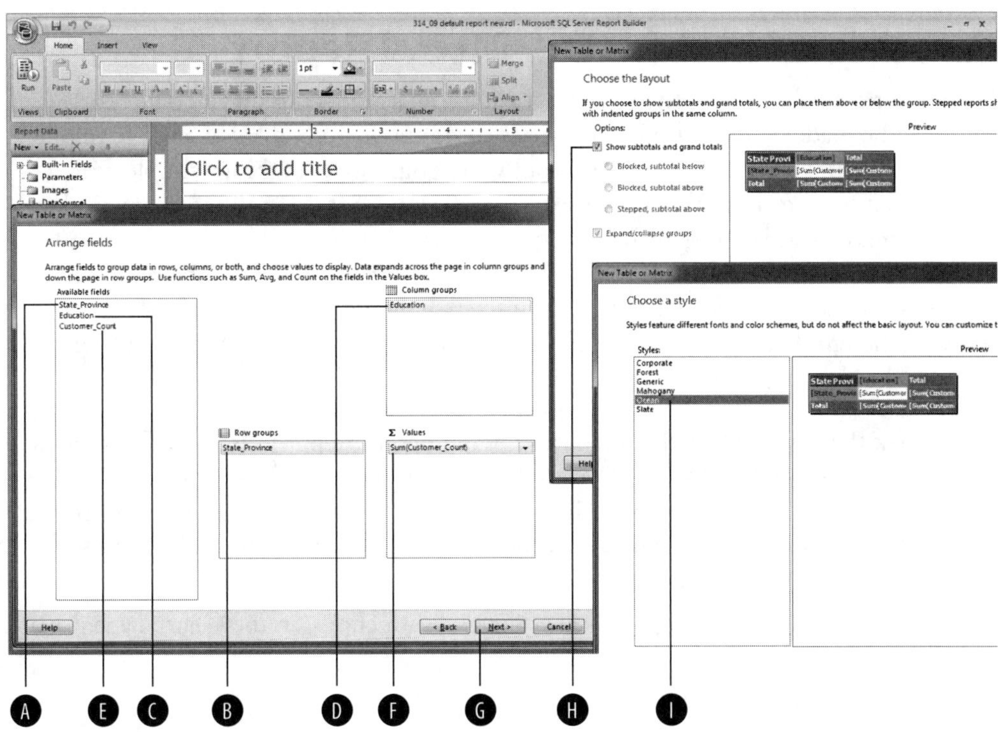

Figure 8-6 *Report Builder: new matrix data element and display choices*

4. Click Next (Step G) to continue.
5. In the New Table Or Matrix dialog box, check the Show Subtotals And Grand Totals check box (Step H) to provide a full matrix cross-tab display for the new report.
6. In the New Table Or Matrix dialog box, select Ocean (Step I) for the style of the matrix.
7. Click OK to save the matrix configuration.

Notice in Figure 8-6 that when we drag Customer_Count into the Values pane, it automatically changes to "Sum(Customer_Count)," which supports the automatic summing of the numeric measure, by whichever row and column dimensions are placed on the matrix. For the model report, we're placing State_Province into the Row Groups pane, and Education into the Column Groups pane. As you'll see later in the design process, these can be changed or swapped at any time in the report design process.

The next section starts the process of adding a chart to our model report. As you'll see, there are many choices for chart types—which is an improved part of Microsoft Reporting Services with the new 2008 R2 release in 2010.

Creating a Chart for Our Model Report

In this section we'll take on the task of creating a chart object in our model report. A chart can be made up of multiple data series to simultaneously display more than one numeric measure at a time on a chart—but we're going to keep things simple with a single series for the chart. We'll then spend some time coordinating the chart display with the matrix display so that they complement each other.

The goal is to make it easy for the report consumer to look at both the matrix and the chart on one page, and understand intuitively how they relate to each other and show a coherent data story together. Figure 8-7 shows how we start the process of creating the chart report object.

1. Click the Insert tab in the top-level ribbon menu (Step A), click the Chart icon (Step B), and choose Chart Wizard in the pop-up menu (Step C).
2. In the New Chart dialog box, click the "Choose an existing dataset in this report" option button (Step D), and select the DataSet1 choice in the list box (Step E).
3. Click Next (Step F) to continue.
4. In the New Chart dialog box, select the Column choice in the Chart Type list box (Step G).
5. Click Next (Step H) to continue.

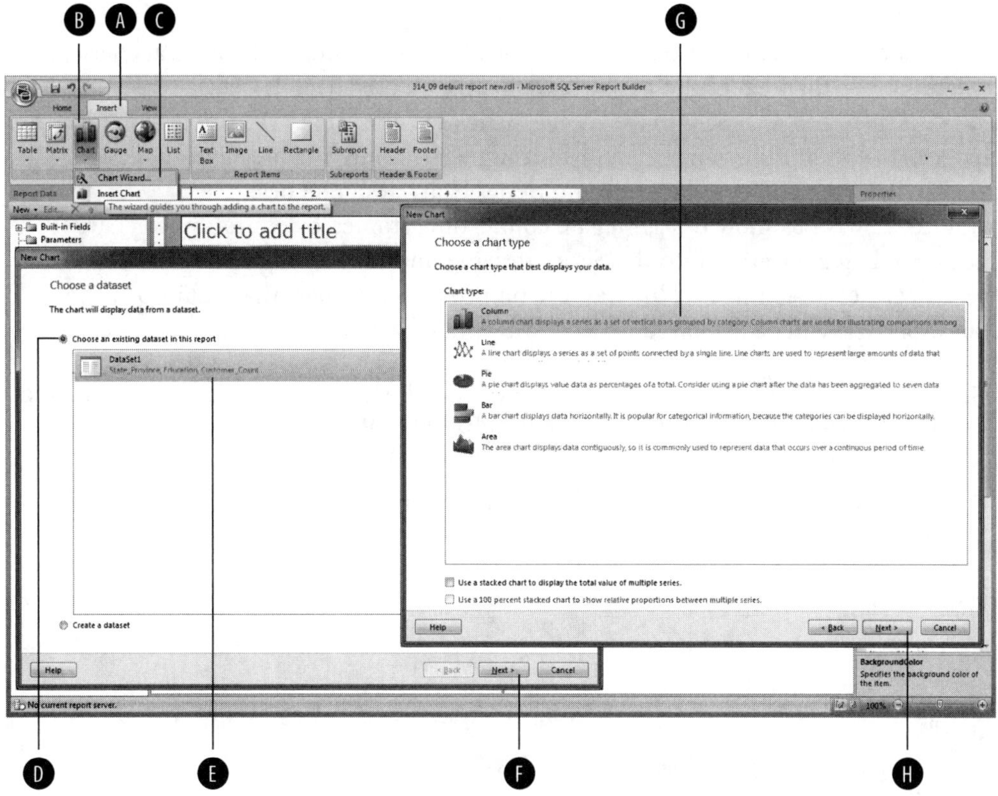

Figure 8-7 *Report Builder: creating a new chart*

Figure 8-7 shows how we are again dependent on the data source–dataset that we designed previously for our model report. The dataset can be changed at any time, but it certainly helps to put some thought into its configuration from the beginning. In fact it's even better to work with a database administrator or someone who really knows the data, to design a dataset that can be used by many different report designers. Such reusable datasets can be stored in a SharePoint Data Connection Library (DCL) for retrieval by report authors who are members of the SharePoint environment.

BI TIP

A Data Connection Library (DCL) in SharePoint is an important way to improve report writing and report rendering productivity. This is because report designers can retrieve a prebuilt data connection that has been validated by data-knowledgeable experts, and report consumers can run reports with properly maintained data connections from the DCL that largely eliminate data connection errors (and the tech support associated with data connection errors).

For now, however, we'll proceed with the report-specific data connection and dataset that are already available for our model report. Figure 8-8 shows the critical chart design options that determine the series displayed in the chart. It makes sense that we drag Customer_Count into the Values pane (and the Chart Wizard automatically changes it to "Sum(Customer_Count)" for us)—but it might a bit more challenging to decide what goes into the Category and Series chart design panes.

Since we wish to show the aggregate counts of customer, by education level, we choose to drag Education into the Series design pane and to drag State_Province into the Categories design pane. This way, the number of customers that fall into each education type will be displayed on a state-by-state basis.

1. In the New Chart dialog box, in the Available Fields list box, select State_Province (Step A) and drag it into the Categories list box (Step B).
2. Select Education (Step C) and drag it into the Series list box (Step D).
3. Select Customer_Count (Step E) and drag it into the Values list box (Step F).

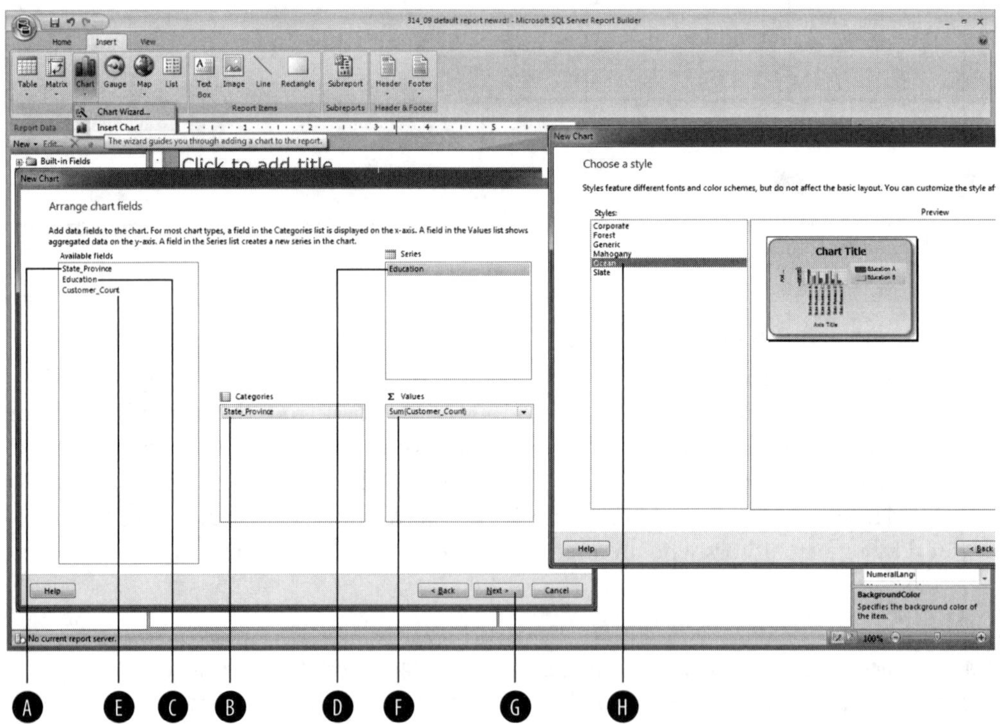

Figure 8-8 *Report Builder: new chart options*

4. Click Next (Step G) to continue.
5. In the New Chart dialog box, in the Styles list box, select the Ocean choice (Step H).

The next section starts the process of adding a map to our model report. This is a new capability with Microsoft Reporting Services in the new 2008 R2 release. As you'll see, it's an amazing leap forward to be able to provide geospatial visualization in our model report—and the new Report Builder use of advanced chart and map technology makes it reasonable for everyday report designers to accomplish.

Creating a Map for Our Model Report

In this section we'll take on the task of creating a map object in our model report. A map can be made up of many layers to simultaneously display more than one plane of information at a time on a map—but we're going to keep things simple with a U.S. map layer and a color-coded "customer count" analytic layer. We'll then spend some time coordinating the map display with the chart and matrix displays so that they complement each other.

The goal is to make it easy for the report consumer to look at the matrix, map, and chart on one page, and see at a glance that they each tell a version of the same data story. Figure 8-9 shows how we start the process of creating the map report object.

1. Click the Insert tab in the top-level ribbon menu (Step A), click the Map icon (Step B), and choose Map Wizard in the pop-up menu (Step C).
2. In the New Map dialog box, click the Map Gallery option button (Step D).
3. In the New Map dialog box, in the Map Gallery list box, click the + for the USA node (Step E), and select the USA By State Inset choice in the list box (Step F).
4. Click Next (Step G) to continue.
5. In the New Map dialog box, click Next (Step H) to accept the default options for the Spatial data and map view options.

Figure 8-9 shows how we are can choose from one of the built-in map layers that are delivered with Report Builder 3.0. This is really good because, frankly, much of our geo-reporting involves the United States—which can be state-by-state or down to the county level.

BI TIP

The best way to get started with map reports is to use the included map layers that pop up in the first step of the Map Wizard in Report Builder. That way, you can become familiar with the concept of a map layer—and add analytic layers for data visualization on top of the map layer.

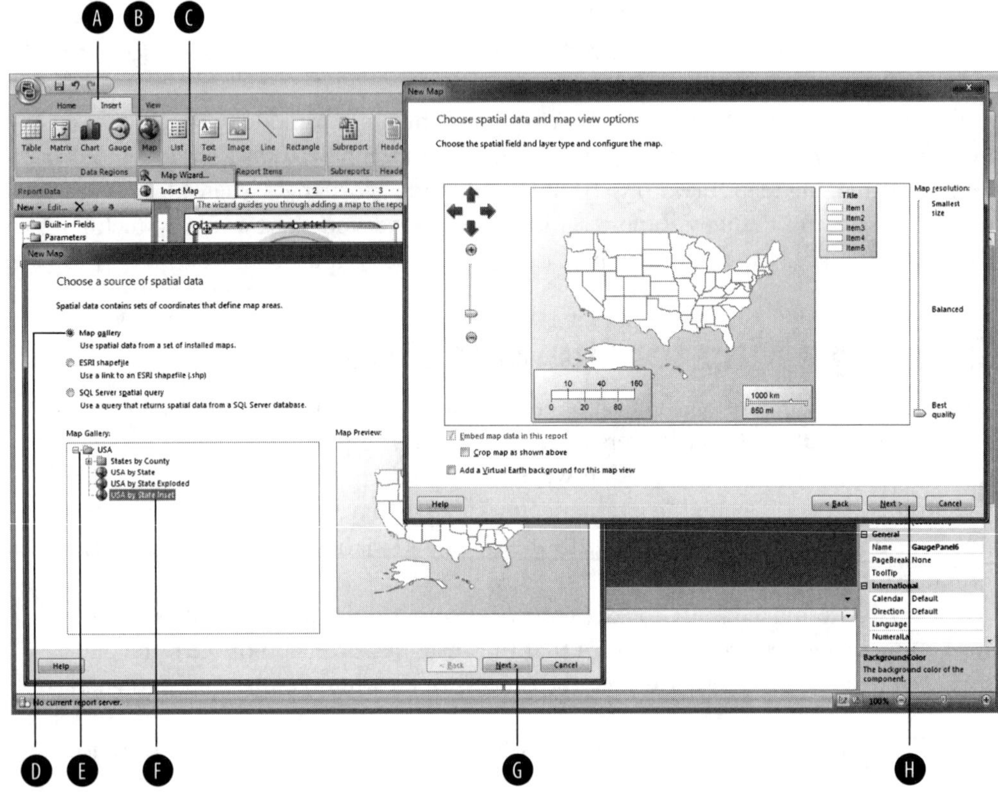

Figure 8-9 *Report Builder: creating a new map*

Figure 8-10 takes us to the next step of adding an analytic layer to our map object—which is really where the magic happens in showing data on a state-by-state basis.

1. In the New Map dialog box, select the Color Analytical Map choice (Step A), and click Next to continue.
2. In the New Map dialog box, click the "Choose an existing dataset in this report" option button (Step B), select the DataSet1 choice in the list box (Step C), and click Next to continue.
3. In the New Map dialog box, click the STATENAME check box (Step D), as the Spatial Dataset Field to match to the Analytical Field.
4. In the New Map dialog box, click the drop-down cell that is next to the checked Spatial Dataset Field, and select the State_Province choice (Step E) to match it to the Spatial State Field.

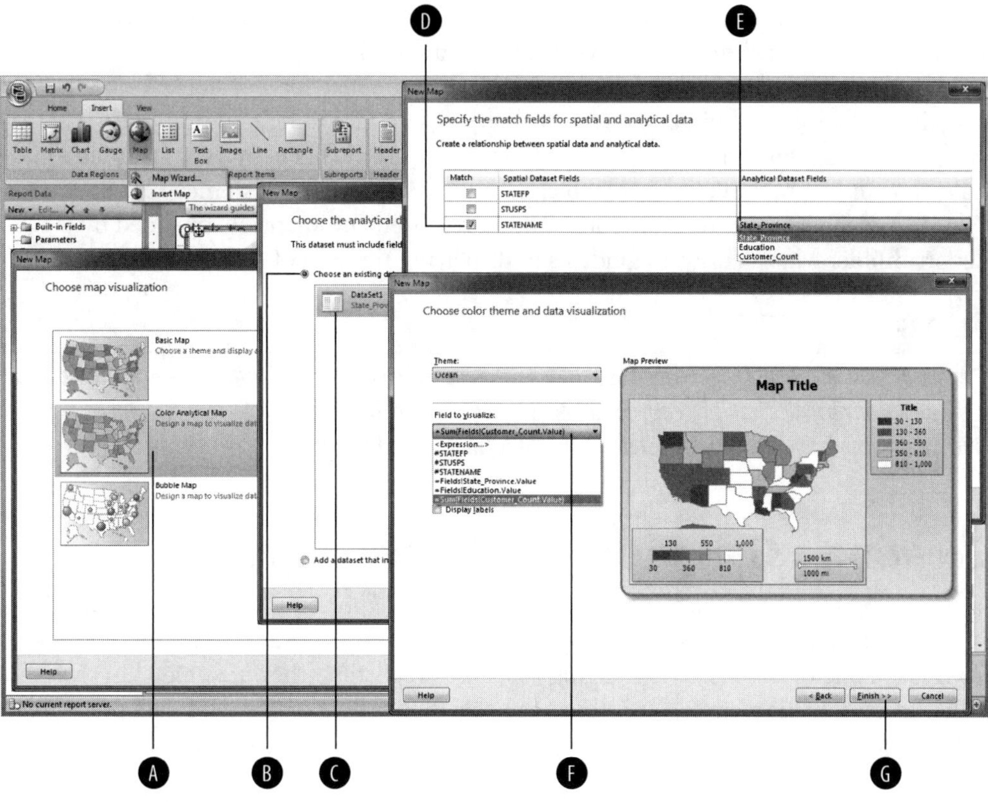

Figure 8-10 *Report Builder: new map options and spatial-analytical matching*

5. In the New Map dialog box, click the drop-down for Field To Visualize and choose "Sum(Fields!Customer_Count.Value)" (Step F).
6. Click Finish (Step G) to save the map configuration.

In Figure 8-10 we first choose to create a color analytical map, which is the most commonly used Report Builder map construct. Although we could instead choose to design a bubble map at this point, it makes more sense to create an analytical map with color-coded analytic values that fill out the state-by-state areas (also known as polygons). We can always add a Bubble effect if we wish—although it would probably be too much to display on our working model report, where we're already going to have a matrix, map, and chart.

Figure 8-10 uses the same dataset as the matrix and chart, which makes sense because we want to show a geographic visualization of the same data story in all three report objects. And as you'll see, all three objects have unique ways of portraying the data story with their different data visualization methods.

The other significant step in Figure 8-10 involves the matching of fields for spatial and analytical data. Report Builder uses a nice dual-list interface to help us intuitively match the geographical state entity with the analytical state entity. Then, in the subsequent dialog box in Figure 8-10, we're able to choose the "Sum(Fields!Customer_Count.Value)"—which is an aggregation formula that has been automatically provided by the Report Builder Map Wizard to guide us in displaying the sum of customers by state.

BI TIP

A map display can be easily understood as a reporting "group by" method of visualizing data—where we group the sum of an analytical value by each geographic area on the map. Then we add color-coding to make it easy to see which geographic areas (such as states) have the highest or lowest counts!

Creating a Gauge for Our Model Report

In this section we'll take on the task of creating a gauge object in our model report. A gauge can be in a radial format (like a gas gauge) or a linear format (like a thermometer). Gauges are one of the more challenging aspects of reporting; they are unique in their ability to portray progress toward a goal, but they don't show a variety of data points like a chart does.

BI TIP

A gauge is excellent for showing progress toward a goal in either a radial gas gauge display or a linear thermometer display—for a singular data point. Multiple data points can be displayed by using multiple gauges, such as a linear gauge for each row of a matrix report—where each gauge might be used to display a row total against the backdrop of the overall matrix total, for example.

We're going to try a gauge on our model report and see how it fits. Figure 8-11 shows how we start the process of adding a gauge in Report Builder.

1. Click the Insert tab in the top-level ribbon menu (Step A), and click the Gauge icon (Step B).
2. Select the Radial tab, and select the top-left Radial Gauge type (Step C).
3. Click OK (Step D) to continue.
4. Select the Gauge on the main report design pane (Step E), and right-click to display the pop-up menu.
5. Choose Gauge on the pop-up menu (Step F), and then choose Gauge Properties on the secondary pop-up menu (Step G).

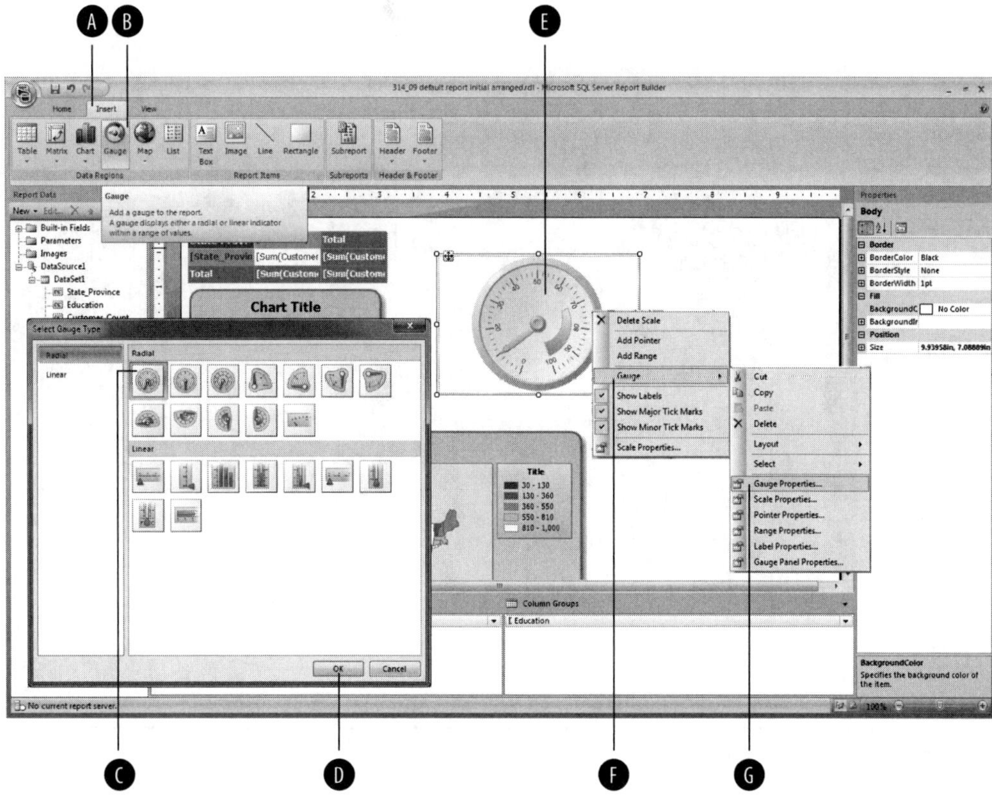

Figure 8-11 *Report Builder: creating a new gauge and properties*

In Figure 8-11 we are using the Gauge Wizard, which walks us through a series of dialog boxes to configure a gauge—and we're simply choosing a default type of Radial gauge to see how it fits on the report. We then click the gauge to right-click to get to the Gauge Properties for configuration of the data to display in the gauge.

However, we can already see in Figure 8-12 that the gauge does not really fit on our model report! This is not necessarily because it might not display data in a helpful way—rather it's because we can immediately see that four objects is making our model report look too cluttered. We already have a matrix, a map, and a chart on the report display (and remember, we're aiming for a single-page model report display)—and the gauge as a fourth major report object just takes up too much space on the report page. Hence we show how to delete the gauge in Figure 8-12, and go back to the job of arranging the other three objects in a way that makes sense.

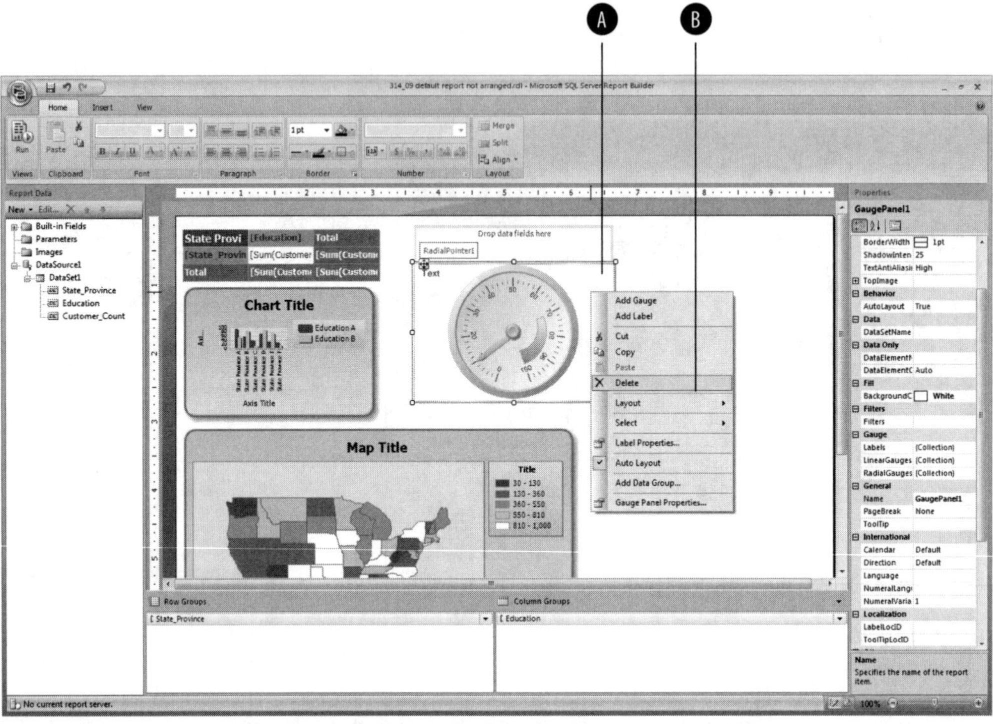

Figure 8-12 *Report Builder: deleting gauge*

BI TIP

It's important to keep a report simple enough for report consumers to understand at a glance. Too many objects on the report can really distract from the task of easily conveying meaning to people who read the report—and since Report Builder has so many options for report objects (such as matrix, map, chart, gauge), we find that we have to carefully choose the appropriate objects to visualize the data.

1. Select the Gauge on the main report design pane (Step A), and right-click to display the pop-up menu.
2. Choose Delete on the pop-up menu (Step B) to remove the Gauge from the report.

In the next section we'll jump to a new aspect of reporting—that of parameterization. This is important because we can connect the parameter to all objects on the report so that they work together in a coherent manner to display the data story.

Creating a Parameter Dataset for Our Model Report

In this section we'll take on the task of creating a parameter object for our model report. A parameter typically has its own dataset that provides a list of unique values (we don't want duplicates in a parameter list) for the end user to choose in filtering the report. Basically, the parameter allows the end user to narrow the dataset being returned in the report.

BI TIP

A parameter when correctly designed is an ad hoc interface for users. It allows them to dynamically choose the data to be displayed in the report—and gives the user a feeling of control over the data being displayed.

We'll also see that the parameter configuration affects the look and feel of our model report, since the main objects look different when they display more data (for example, the matrix will have more rows or columns if a broader dataset is provided to it via parameterization). Figure 8-13 shows how we create the dataset for our parameter.

1. Select the DataSource1 node in the left-hand pane (Step A), and right-click to choose Add Dataset from the pop-up menu (Step B).
2. In the Dataset Properties dialog box | Query tab, in the Data Source drop-down choose DataSource1 (Step C).
3. Click Query Designer (Step D) to display the Query Designer dialog box.
4. In the Query Designer dialog box, click the + Measures (Step E) and the + Internet Customers (Step F) nodes to expand the Adventure Works left-pane tree.
5. In the Query Designer dialog box, select Customer Count (Step G) and drag it into the main design pane (Step H) as the numeric element to be displayed in our report.
6. In the Query Designer dialog box, click the + Customer node in the left-hand pane (Step I), and click the + Location node (Step J).
7. Select State-Province (Step K) and drag it into the design pane (Step L) as the first column to be displayed in the query.
8. Select Country (Step M) and drag it into the <Select Dimension> cell above the query design pane (Step N), to create a filter that will limit the data return set.
9. Click in the Filter Expression cell above the query design pane (Step O), and click the drop-down to open the Filter Elements list.
10. Click the All Customers check box to unselect all choices (Step P), and check the United States check box (Step Q) to select only United States State-Province elements for the data return set that will be available to the report.
11. Click OK to save the query.

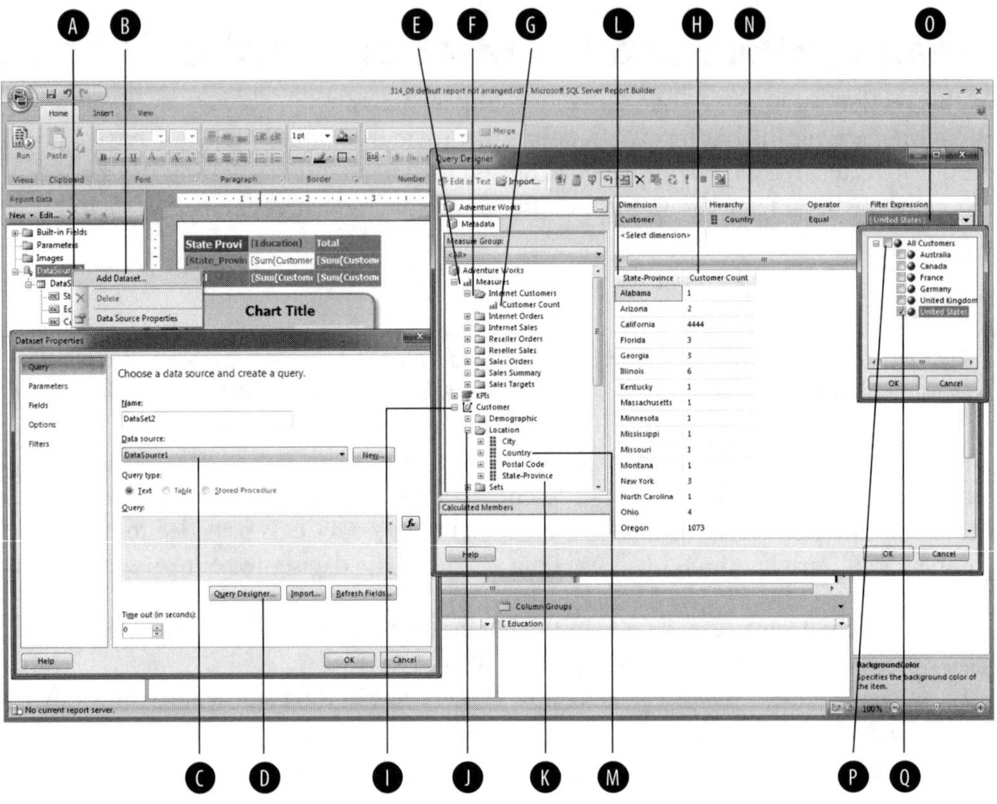

Figure 8-13 *Report Builder: creating a parameter dataset*

There are quite a few steps in Figure 8-13; where we are choosing the same Data Source as used elsewhere in the report, but creating a different Data Set for the parameter values. Note that we had to choose a measure for the dataset, even though the parameter is only going to display the text data choices of U.S. states. This is because a dataset from an OLAP cube must by definition include a numeric measure—so we simply choose Customer_Count even though we really only want the unique list of states.

The list of state-provinces is narrowed to states of the United States by including a filter in the dataset. This has the dual benefit of returning data faster, since only the U.S. states will be returned from the server data source, and of guiding our model report to be a report for U.S. states only. As you'll see in subsequent sections, this will affect the look and feel of our model report as we strive to produce a single-screen display that shows one or more states of customer counts.

In the next section we'll continue with the configuration of our parameter, based on the dataset we now have for the parameter.

Creating a Parameter for Our Model Report

Now that we have a dataset that returns state values, we need to create a parameter that displays the dataset values to the end user, before running the report—as shown in Figure 8-14.

1. Select the Parameter node in the left-hand pane (Step A), and right-click to choose Add Parameter from the pop-up menu (Step B).
2. In the Report Parameter Properties dialog box | General tab, in the Name drop-down choose ReportParameter1 (Step C); in the Prompt drop-down choose ReportParameter1 (Step D); in the Data Type drop-down choose Text (Step E); check the Allow Multiple Values check box (Step F); and under Select Parameter Visibility choose the Visible option button (Step G).

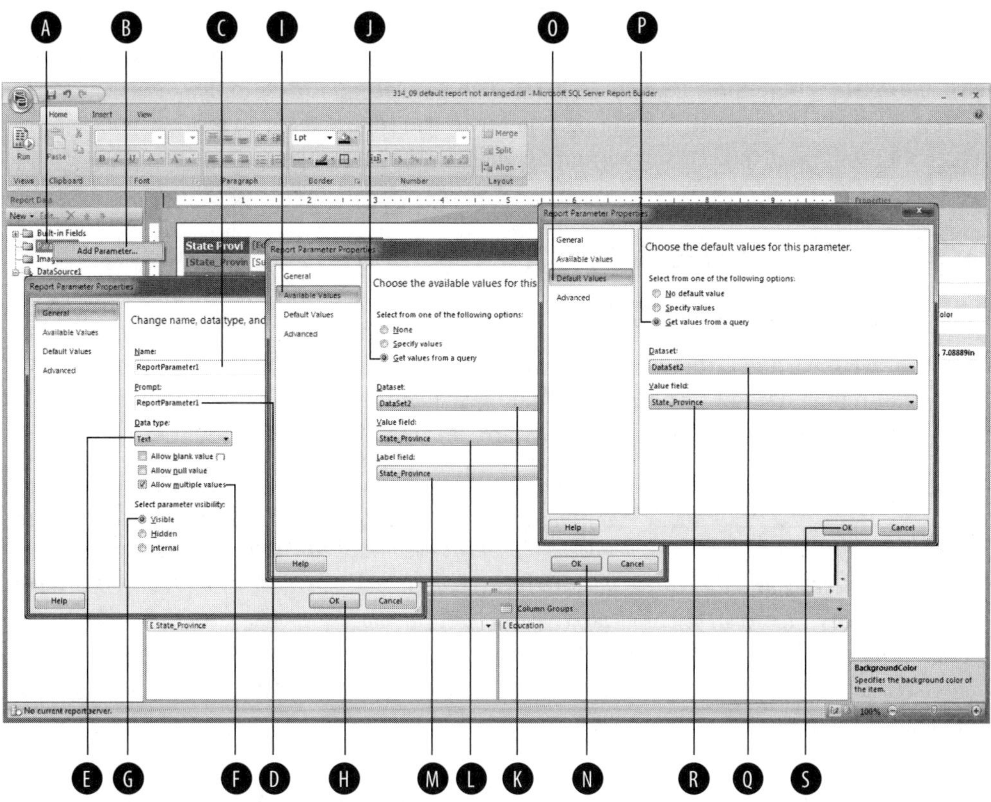

Figure 8-14 *Report Builder: creating a parameter*

3. Click OK (Step H) to continue.
4. In the Report Parameter Properties dialog box | Available Values tab (Step I), under "Select from one of the following options" choose the Get Values From A Query option button (Step J); in the Dataset drop-down choose DataSet2 (Step K); in the Value Field drop-down choose State_Province (Step L), and in the Label Field drop-down choose State_Province (Step M).
5. Click OK (Step N) to continue.
6. In the Report Parameter Properties dialog box | Default Values tab (Step O), under "Select from one of the following options" choose the Get Values From A Query option button (Step P); in the Dataset drop-down choose DataSet2 (Step Q), and in the Value Field drop-down choose State_Province (Step R).
7. Click OK (Step S) to save the parameter configuration.

It's important to realize how many configuration options are available in Report Builder for parameters. As you see in Figure 8-14, the parameter has both Values (where we selected the Value Field) and a Label (where we selected the Label Field). As you'll see later, the configuration of default values from a query affects the quality of presentation to the end user, who wants to be able to easily choose State parameter values and end up with a good-looking report that could be used in a meeting, for example.

In the next section we'll add the parameter to the report itself to guide the choice of values that will be displayed in the matrix, map, and chart objects.

Adding the Parameter to the Dataset for Our Model Report

Now that we have a parameter with its own dataset, we can embed the parameter into the overall report dataset to narrow the data visualization for all report objects. This involves first making the report dataset aware of the parameter as shown in Figure 8-15.

BI TIP

The importance of a properly designed parameter cannot be overemphasized. It literally makes the report usable, by presenting the end user with parameter choices that make sense—and then feeding the user-chosen parameter values to the report objects for good visualization of the broader report dataset. If users like the parameterization of the report, they will like the report that is rendered with data that is guided by the same parameter values. If the parameter is designed to return a reasonable subset of data values, the report itself can render more quickly—which in and of itself is a large part of user acceptance.

1. Select the DataSource1 node in the left-hand pane (Step A), and expand it to display the datasets.

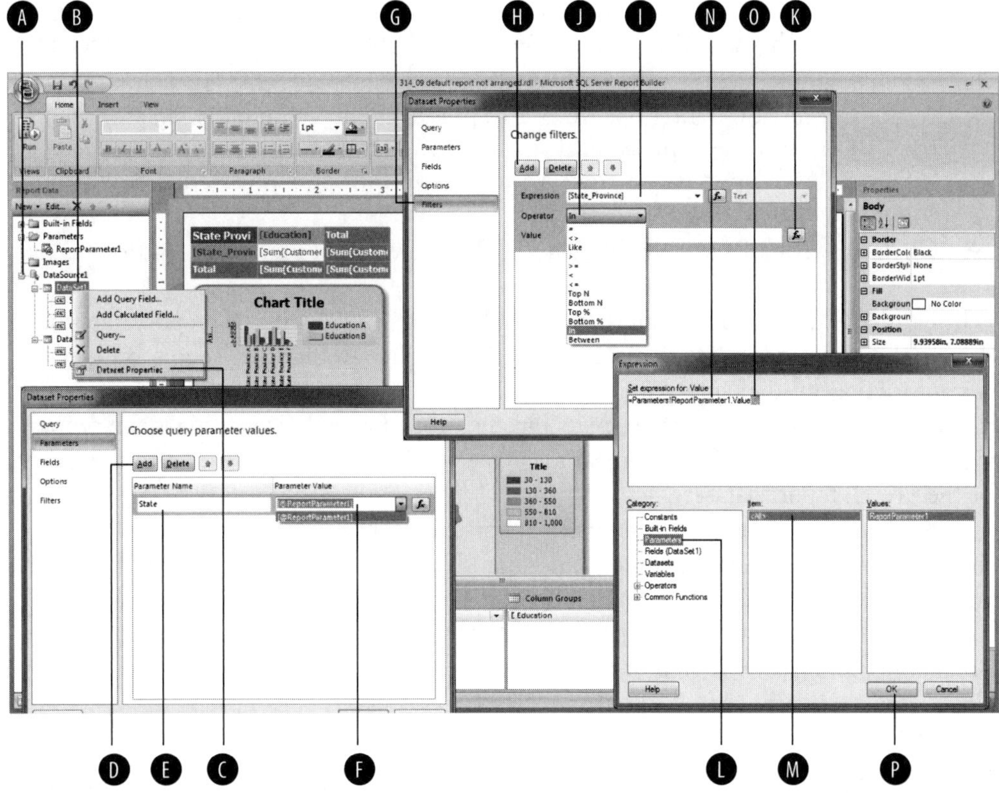

Figure 8-15 *Report Builder: adding parameter and filter to the dataset*

2. Select the DataSet1 node (Step B), right-click to display the pop-up menu, and choose Dataset Properties on the pop-up menu (Step C) to display the Dataset Properties dialog box.
3. In the Dataset Properties dialog box | Parameters tab, click Add to add a parameter (Step D); in the Parameter Name text box type **State** (Step E), and in the Parameter Value drop-down choose @ReportParameter1 (Step F).
4. Click Next to continue.
5. In the Dataset Properties dialog box | Filters tab (Step G), click Add to add a filter (Step H); in the Expression drop-down choose "[State_Province]" (Step I); in the Operator drop-down choose In (Step J) to support multiple parameter values to filter the report dataset.
6. In the Dataset Properties dialog box | Filters tab, for the Value field, click the *fx* button (Step K) to display the Expression dialog box.

7. In the Expression dialog box, in the Category list box click Parameters (Step L); in the Item list box choose <All> (Step M); in the Values list box select ReportParameter1 and drag it into the upper Set Expression For Value pane (Step N).
8. In the Expression dialog box, in the Expression For Value pane, delete the "(0)" part of the expression if it is showing (Step O)—thus leaving "=Parameters!ReportParameter1.Value" as the correct expression that will support multiple values.
9. Click OK (Step P) to save the Dataset Parameter and Filter configuration.

In Figure 8-15 we're doing some more sophisticated work with the report dataset. Note in the Dataset Properties dialog box | Parameters tab that the Report Builder Wizard (dialog-by-dialog box step-by-step approach) automatically portrays the Parameter Value as [@ReportParameter] in the drop-down choices. This is the proper configuration (using the @ nomenclature) for embedding the parameter into the query for the overall report dataset.

In the Dataset Properties dialog box | Filters tab, it makes sense we choose "[State_Province]" in the drop-down choices for which Dataset field to actually filter with the parameter. Then we choose In for the Operator (which is admittedly a bit of SQL magic) to allow multiple choices for State_Province. This simply means the end user can choose more than one state for the report.

BI TIP

Most parameters need to support multiple choices, meaning the end user can choose more than one parameter value at a time to render the report. In SQL terminology this is known as using the In operator, which supports multiple choices in the WHERE *clause that will filter the dataset to be returned from the data server.*

In Figure 8-15 we also corrected an anomaly with the embedding of the parameter into the report dataset—by removing the "(0)" from the end of the Filter Expression that was automatically created by the Dataset Properties dialog box | Filters. The "(0)" would limit the parameter values to a single value, which is not correct, so we simply eliminated the problem with a quick side trip into the expression for the filter.

Now that we have a parameter with its own dataset, and the parameter is embedded into the report dataset—we'll see how it affects the look and feel of our main report objects as they display the returned dataset in the next section. Note that because we embedded the parameter into the dataset used by all the report objects, the parameter values chosen by the end user will affect the matrix, map, and chart objects—which all display data from Dataset1.

Model Report First Draft and Changes

Figure 8-16 shows the newly rendered report—and it easy to see that the matrix takes over the screen and pushes the map and chart off the immediate display. This is something we really need to fix on our model report, because even though it's technically showing an accurate set of data, it is not easily viewed by the end user.

1. On the Home tab on the top ribbon menu, click the Run icon (Step A) to render the report.
2. If the report displays "Parameter . . . missing a value," then in the Run Viewing pane, click the upper-left Parameter drop-down, and select the "(Select All)" check box (Step B) to choose all States.
3. In the Run Viewing pane, click the upper-right View Report button (Step C) to render the report.

In Figure 8-16 we see an immediate problem: the default values of all states produce a matrix that overwhelms the display. In Figure 8-17 we take the step of altering the

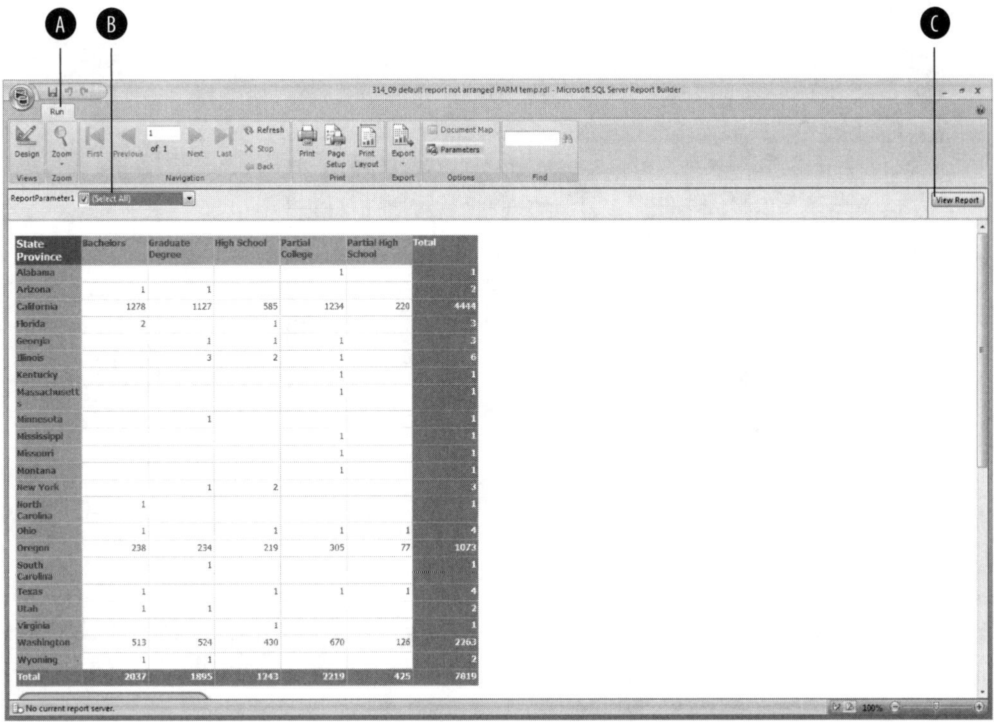

State Province	Bachelors	Graduate Degree	High School	Partial College	Partial High School	Total
Alabama				1		1
Arizona	1	1				2
California	1278	1127	585	1234	220	4444
Florida	2		1			3
Georgia		1	1	1		3
Illinois		3	2	1		6
Kentucky				1		1
Massachusetts				1		1
Minnesota		1				1
Mississippi				1		1
Missouri				1		1
Montana				1		1
New York		1	2			3
North Carolina	1					1
Ohio	1		1	1	1	4
Oregon	238	234	219	305	77	1073
South Carolina		1				1
Texas	1		1	1	1	4
Utah	1	1				2
Virginia			1			1
Washington	513	524	430	670	126	2263
Wyoming	1	1				2
Total	2037	1895	1243	2219	425	7819

Figure 8-16 *Report Builder: report rendered with default parameter values ALL*

default values that make up the parameter configuration, with the goal of achieving a better default display for our single-page model report.

1. On the left-side Report Data pane, click the + to expand the Parameters node (Step A), and select ReportParameter1 (Step B).
2. Right-click the ReportParameter1 node, and choose Parameter Properties on the pop-up menu (Step C).
3. In the Report Parameter Properties dialog box, click Default Values on the left pane (Step D).
4. Select the No Default Value option button (Step E) to remove the automatic parameter value selection for the report.
5. Click OK (Step F) to save the configuration.

With the default values removed for the report parameter, in Figure 8-18 we can now see the matrix, chart, and map on the same report screen when we choose four states.

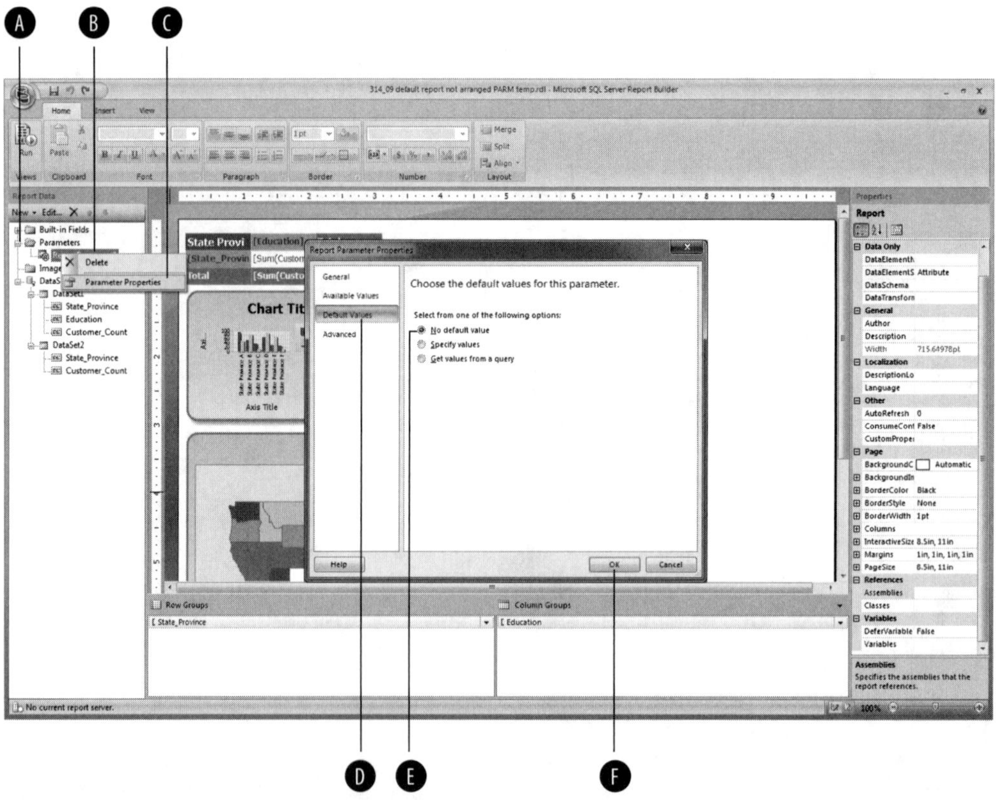

Figure 8-17 *Report Builder: removing default parameter values*

BI TIP

Default values for parameters are an important part of the experience of running a report. The end user is encouraged to choose parameter values, based on the default values showing (or no default values)—which in turn affects the aesthetics of the rendered report, as it might be designed to better display fewer parameter-driven data values. In any case, the parameter default values should be configured to best complement the final report layout when it's run with real data from the data server.

1. On the Home tab on the top ribbon menu, click the Run icon (Step A) to render the report.
2. In the Run Viewing pane, click the upper-left Parameter drop-down, and select Alabama, Arizona, California, and Florida (Step B).
3. In the Run Viewing pane, click the upper-right View Report button (Step C) to render the report.

Figure 8-18 shows the rendered report with default values removed, such that we are now displaying only four states in the result dataset for matrix, chart, and map.

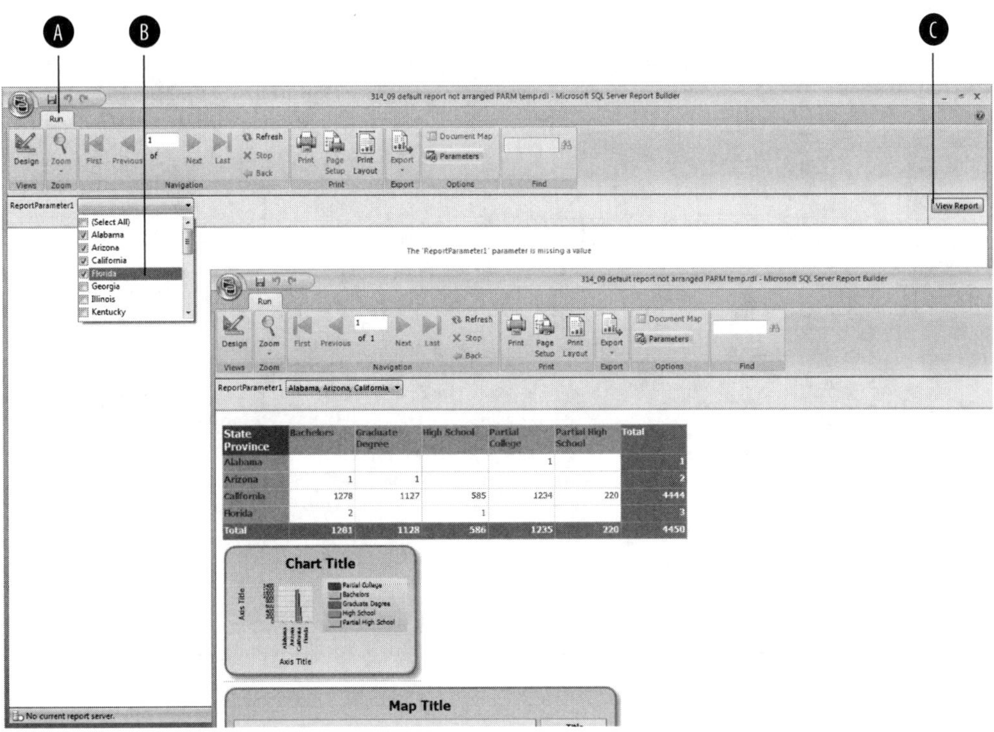

Figure 8-18 *Report Builder: rendered report with no default values*

However, we now see another problem: the three report objects are stacked vertically in a manner that is not appealing given the one-page report format. Figure 8-19 shows how we address this issue with the built-in Report Builder drag-and-drop capabilities.

1. On the main report design pane, select the chart and drag it to the right (Step A), making room for the map to fit to the left of the chart.
2. Select the map and drag it up (Step B), placing it to the left of the chart. As you move either the chart or the map, a horizontal alignment blue-line will appear to help position the two report elements in an exact horizontal alignment.

In Figure 8-19 we have highlighted an interesting aspect of good report design: the horizontal and vertical alignment of report objects. In this case it seems to make sense that the matrix is at the top, while the map and chart occupy the lower space, in a horizontally aligned manner. This drag-and-drop capability is sometimes termed "snap-in-grid" because the report design screen actively helps to guide mouse movements to align and position report objects in a grid or in alignment with nearby report objects.

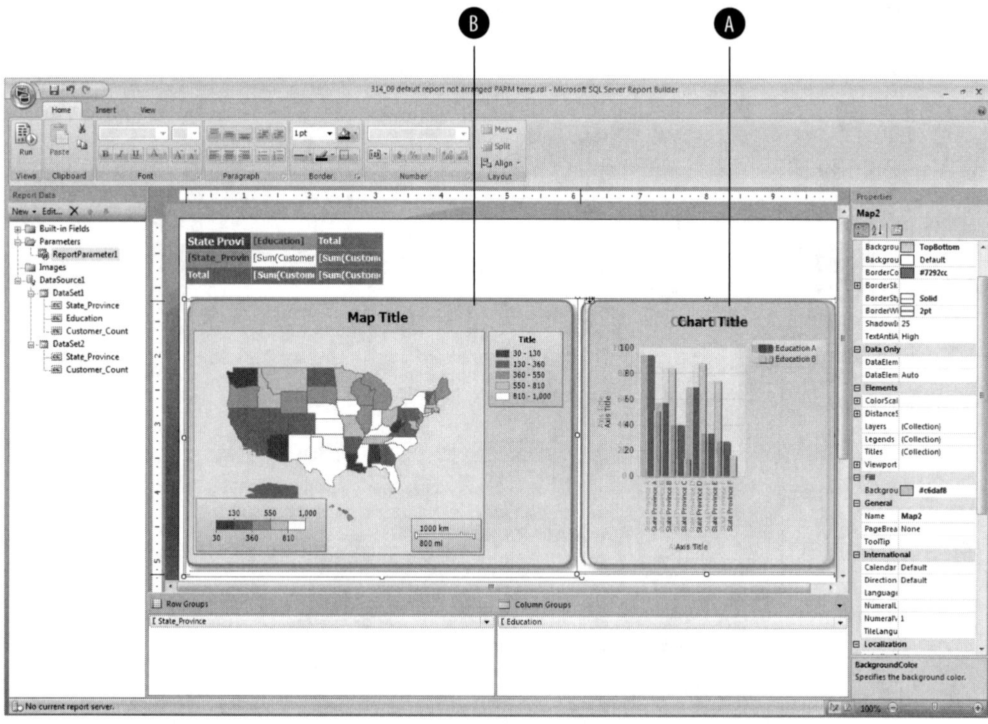

Figure 8-19 *Report Builder: moving map and chart*

BI TIP

Alignment of report objects is critical for a well-designed report. People are remarkably quick to spot misaligned columns and rows, for example—which can be so distracting that a report consumer is paying attention to "something that bothers their eye" instead of analyzing the report data story. It is good practice and part of professional report design to horizontally and vertically align all the objects on a report display, from top to bottom and left to right—which complements the way readers consume report information.

1. On the Home tab on the top ribbon menu, click the Run icon (Step A) to render the report.
2. In the Run Viewing pane, click the upper-left Parameter drop-down, and select Alabama, Arizona, California, and Florida (Step B).
3. In the Run Viewing pane, click the upper-right View Report button to render the report (Step C).

Figure 8-20 shows an improved report, with a matrix, a map, and a chart that are beginning to look like they belong together. We'll see in the following sections, however,

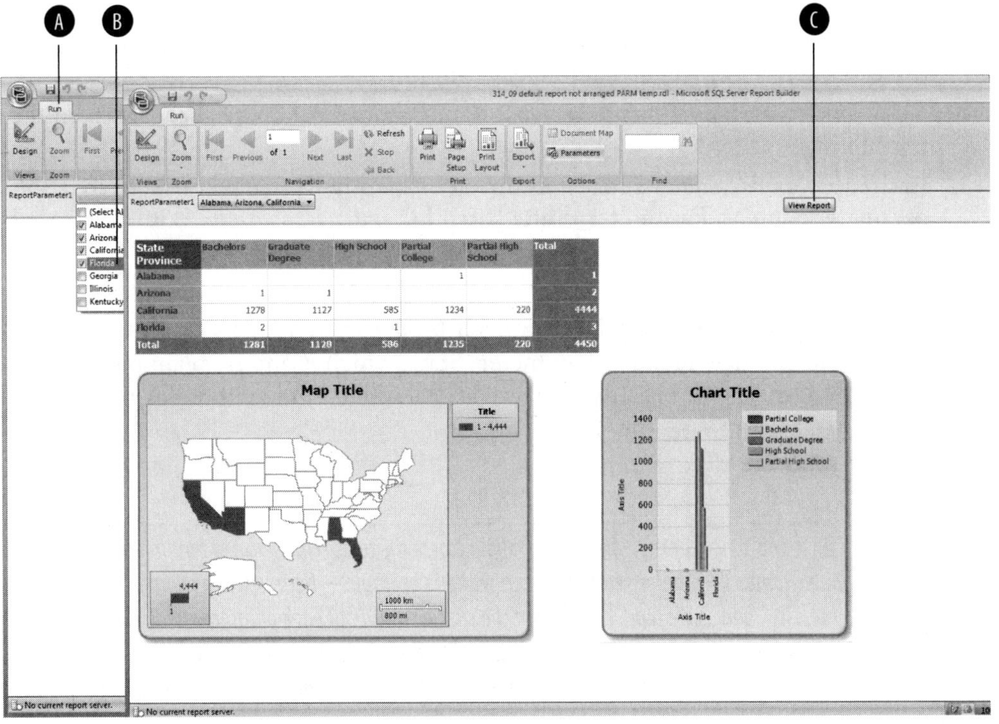

Figure 8-20 *Report Builder: rendered report with arranged map and chart*

that there are quite a few more steps to improving both the layout and the end-user rendering experience for our model report.

Naming Conventions

This section deals with a part of report design that is too often overlooked: that of proper naming conventions when constructing data repositories, data sources, datasets, and so forth. In fact, we really should have followed this "best practices" methodology of naming conventions when first creating the report elements—since so often we have to hurry development-to-production and deploy the report in support of a real-world business process that can't wait!

BI TIP

Commonsense naming of report data and display elements should be accomplished as soon as possible in the process of report design. This avoids the introduction of embarrassing report names such as the infamous "test report" nomenclature that designers will temporarily put into a draft and forget to remove when rushing to production!

Figure 8-21 shows how we start the process of naming/renaming the elements of our model report, beginning with the parameter.

1. On the left-side Report Data pane, click the + to expand the Parameters node (Step A), and select ReportParameter1 (Step B).
2. Right-click the ReportParameter1 node, and choose Parameter Properties on the pop-up menu (Step C).
3. In the Report Parameter Properties dialog box, in the Name text box, change the parameter name to **Parameter_State** (Step D).
4. Click OK (Step E) to save the Parameter configuration.

In Figure 8-21 we're accessing the Parameter properties to rename the parameter. Note that we chose a new name of Parameter_State, which is a fairly plain piece of terminology. However, it does show us that it's a parameter and it shows us that it's likely a parameter with State values.

BI TIP

A good convention for naming report elements is to follow a general-to-specific sense of terminology. Thus a parameter might be named Parameter_State as in our working example—because then all parameters will appear together in a list, and as we read left-to-right the specific nature of each parameter will be evident (where in our working example we see the parameter is for State values). The underscore is a convenient word separator that is commonly used in naming conventions and satisfies the frequent requirement that the report element name must not contain spaces.

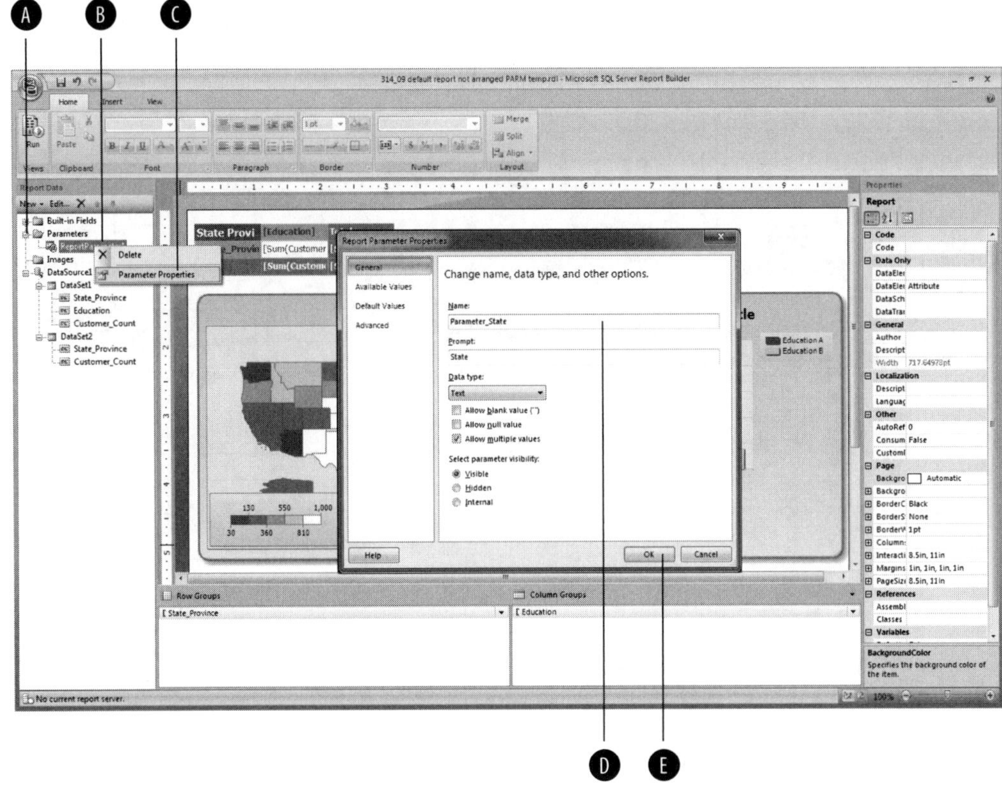

Figure 8-21 *Report Builder: renaming report parameter design labels*

In Figure 8-22 we continue with our naming convention exercise by accessing the report data element properties.

1. On the left-side Report Data pane, right-click the DataSource1 node (Step A); choose Data Source Properties on the pop-up menu (Step B) to display the Data Source Properties dialog box.
2. In the Data Source Properties dialog box | General tab, in the Name text box change the Data Source name to **Cube_AdventureWorks** (Step C).
3. Click OK to save the Data Source configuration.
4. On the left-side Report Data pane, click the + to expand the DataSource node, and select DataSet1 (Step D).
5. Right-click the DataSet1 node, and choose Dataset Properties on the pop-up menu (Step E).

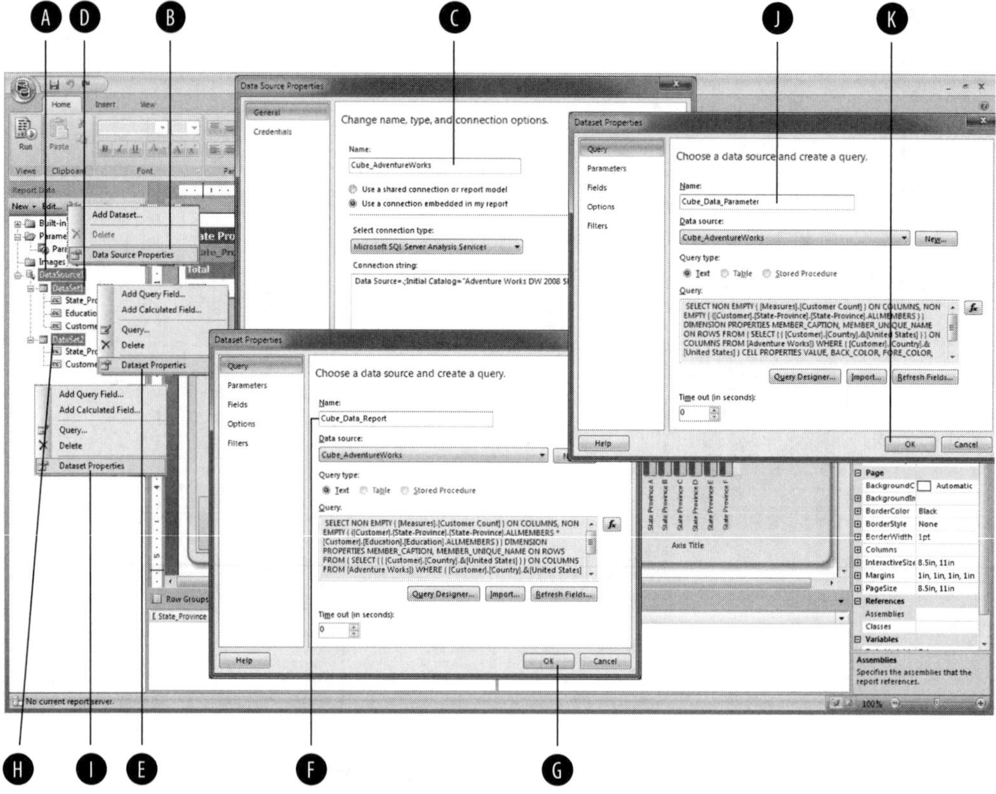

Figure 8-22 *Report Builder: renaming data source and set labels*

6. In the Dataset Properties dialog box | Query tab, in the Name text box change the Dataset name to **Cube_Data_Report** (Step F).
7. Click OK (Step G) to save the Dataset configuration.
8. On the left-side Report Data pane, select DataSet2 (Step H).
9. Right-click the DataSet2 node, and choose Dataset Properties on the pop-up menu (Step I).
10. In the Data Properties dialog box | Query tab, in the Name text box change the Dataset name to **Cube_Data_Parameter** (Step J).
11. Click OK (Step K) to save the Dataset configuration.

In Figure 8-22 we're covering a lot of ground—dealing with both the data source for the entire report (hence the new name of Cube_AdventureWorks) and the datasets that provide queries for parameter and report object values in the report. Since all data elements in our working model report are derived from a SQL Server Analysis Services OLAP cube, we decided to follow a naming convention that starts with the term "cube."

With Cube_Data_Parameter and Cube_Data_Report datasets as our new names, we are ready to proceed with running the report again—however, Figure 8-23 displays a surprise error message that gives us an opportunity to explore report debugging.

1. On the top-left side Report Builder menu Office button (Step A), open a saved version of the report.
2. If an error message pops up with the message "Failed to open report . . . DataSet1 is not valid . . . ," click OK (Step B) to continue.

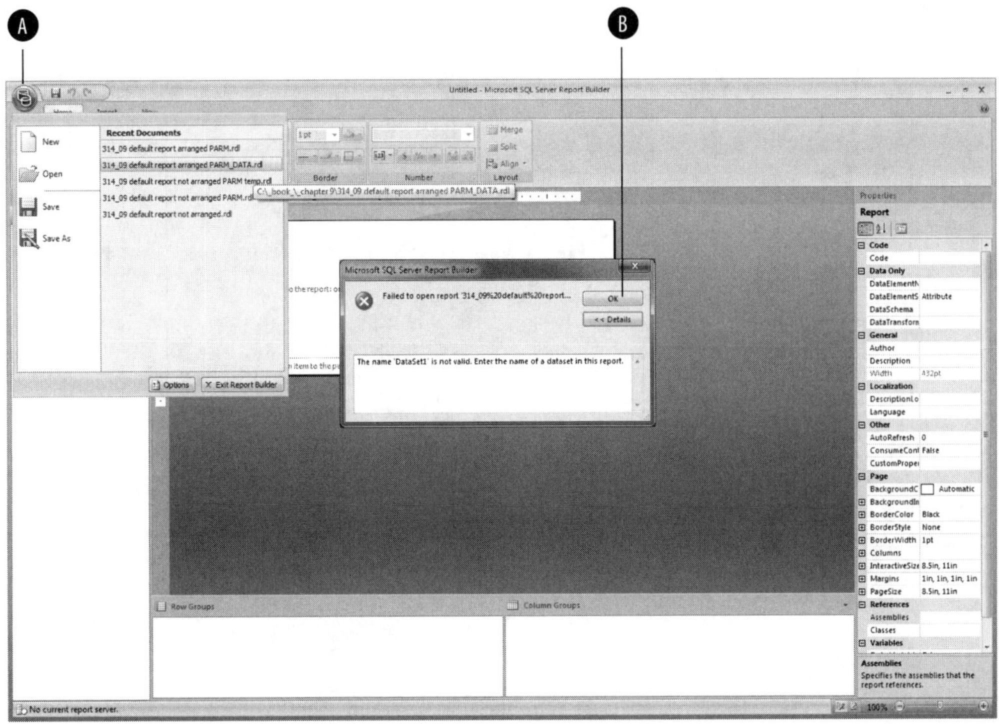

Figure 8-23 *Report Builder: Data Element Errors—Unable to Open Report*

In Figure 8-23 we're trying to run our report with a renamed parameter, data source, and datasets. However, we find there is an error message that prevents the report from running. In this case we see a reference in the error message to "the name DataSet1 is not valid . . . ." It's actually a straightforward data error that we'll fix starting with the steps in Figure 8-24.

BI TIP

By far the most common report error messages are data error messages. And although they stop the report from running (which seems catastrophic in a sense), they are often the easiest to debug. Simply remember to "follow the data" from server, to data connection, to data source, to dataset. Somewhere along the line a configuration error, or an incorrect or outdated ID or password, is disrupting the flow of data.

1. Using Notepad, open the problematic report (Step A).
2. Click the Notepad top-menu Edit choice (Step B), and select Replace.

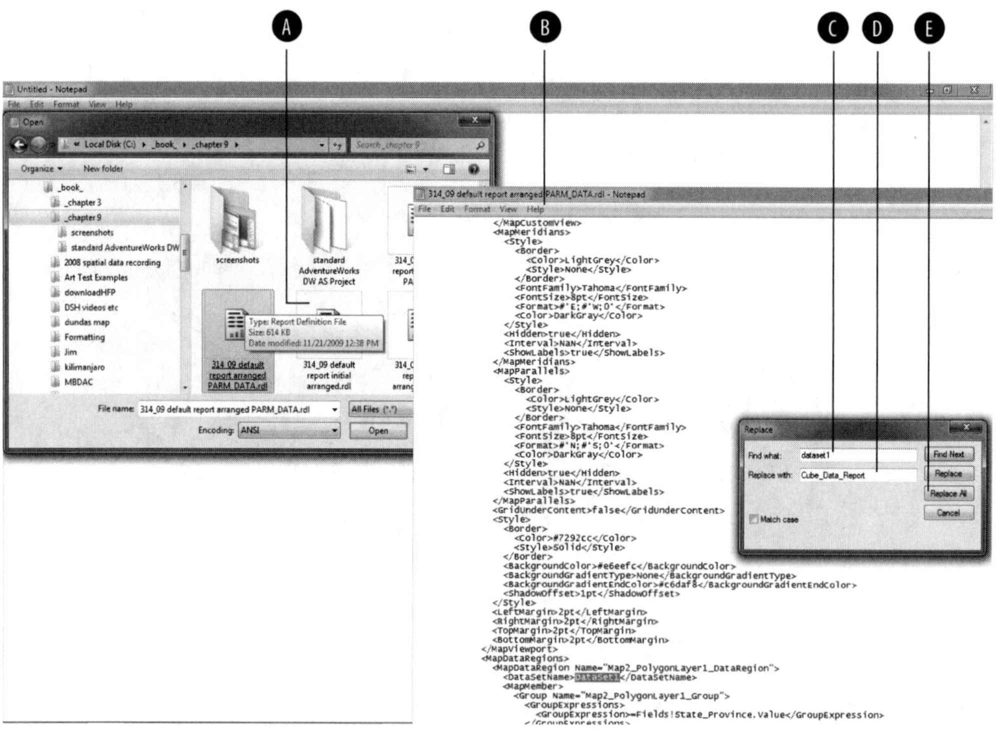

Figure 8-24 *Report Builder: using Notepad to fix Open Report Error*

3. In the Notepad Replace dialog box, in the Find What text box enter **dataset1** (Step C) and in the Replace With text box enter **Cube_Data_Report** (Step D), and click Replace All (Step E).
4. Save the changes and exit Notepad.

In Figure 8-24 we use the Notepad application to open the report .RDL file—because one of the remarkable things about Microsoft report files is that they are simply .XML files that can be edited with something as simple as Notepad. While it's not recommended to do this, we can use the approach in a pinch to fix an internal error with a Report Builder report. In this case, the report simply will not open/reopen with the Report Builder to fix the errors.

So, it is normally recommended that we use the application that created the report object, to correct the report object; we have to resort to Notepad because in this case Report Builder will not open the incorrect report at all. This is an example of outside-the-box thinking that can be applied to an open format such as the .RDL files of Microsoft Reporting Services.

For now we'll replace the text "dataset1" with the new name of "Cube_Data_Report" and save the resulting file without making any other changes. Figure 8-25 shows what happens next when we again try to run the report.

1. Using Report Builder, open the problematic report; click Run (Step A) to render the report.
2. If an error message pops up with the message "Failed to preview report . . . the report parameter . . . refers to a dataset which does not exist . . . ," or " . . . the query parameter . . . refers to a non-existing report parameter . . . ," or " . . . the filter . . . refers to a non-existing report parameter . . . "—click OK (Step B) to continue.

As we attempt to again run our model report, we notice that we are in fact able to open the report with Report Builder. Thus we can now fix the remaining errors that we inadvertently introduced with our naming convention section earlier in the chapter. Figure 8-26 shows how we methodically track down the errors for Parameter, Query, and Parameter and fix them with the Report Builder application by simply accessing the appropriate Properties dialog boxes.

1. On the left-side Report Data pane, expand the Parameters node (Step A); select the Parameter_State node (Step B); and choose Parameter Properties on the pop-up menu (Step C) to display the Report Parameter Properties dialog box.
2. In the Report Parameter Properties dialog box | Available Values tab (Step D), in the Dataset drop-down change the Dataset to Cube_Data_Parameter (Step E), which is the correct dataset for the parameter.
3. Click OK to save the Parameter configuration.

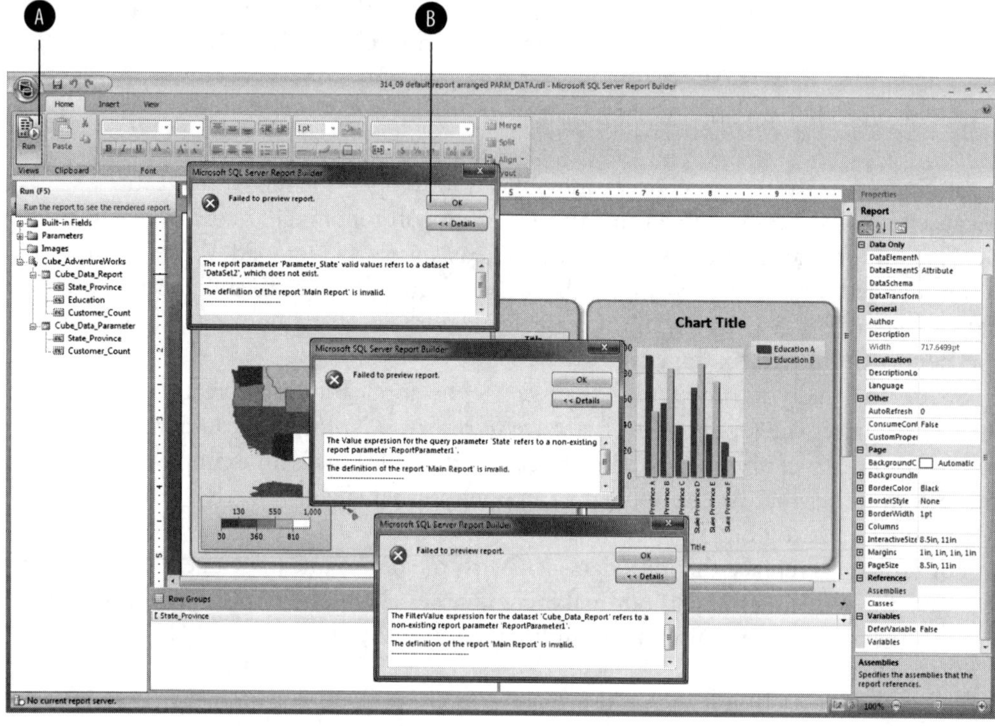

Figure 8-25 *Report Builder: Data Element Errors—Unable to Render Report*

4. On the left-side Report Data pane, click the + to expand the DataSource node, and select Cube_Data_Report (Step F).
5. Right-click the Cube_Data_Report node, and choose Dataset Properties on the pop-up menu (Step G).
6. In the Dataset Properties dialog box | Parameters tab (Step H), in the Parameter Value drop-down change the selection to [@Parameter_State] (Step I), which is the correct parameter for the dataset.
7. In the Dataset Properties dialog box, Filters tab (Step J), in the Value drop-down change the selection to [@Parameter_State] (Step K), which is the correct filter for the dataset.
8. Click OK (Step L) to save the Dataset configuration.

With the report being in a corrected state with regard to naming conventions, and now running successfully, we can again turn to the look and feel of our model report. This is actually an important point—the report really is not done until we've accomplished all we

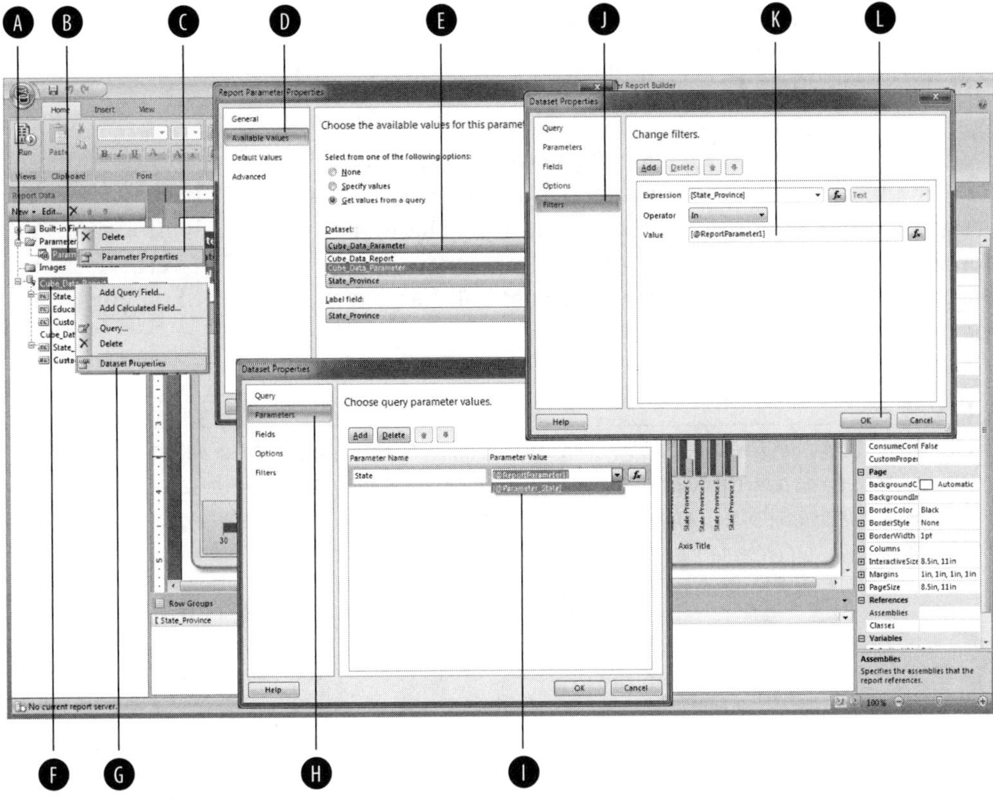

Figure 8-26 *Report Builder: fixing Data Element Errors*

can (in a reasonable time frame, such as hours) to make it presentable to end users. We continue this pursuit of model appearance in the next section.

Modifying the Display Elements for the Model Report

Realizing our goal for the model report is to present a data story on one page, and to have the report elements work together to tell the data story—we see that the chart can be improved to support our Customer Count by State and Education story. In Figure 8-27 we continue this process of report improvement by changing the chart type.

1. Select the chart on the main report design pane (Step A), and right-click the pop-up menu to choose Change Chart Type (Step B).

2. In the Select Chart Type dialog box | Bar tab (Step C), select the first Bar icon (Step D) to choose a horizontal bar chart.
3. Click OK (Step E) to save the chart configuration.

Figure 8-27 shows off the new chart type choices that are available with Report Builder 3.0, where Microsoft introduced the Dundas chart types to enhance the report design process. In this case we're choosing a Bar chart type, with a straightforward horizontal arrangement. The goal here is to arrange the states along the vertical axis of the chart—which follows the vertical column of states on the left side of the matrix at the top of the report.

BI TIP

The concept of horizontal and vertical alignment can be continued in the arrangement of data across various elements of a report. It helps knowledge workers who are visually interpreting the report, to see the arrangement of groups ("States" in our model report) follow the same top-down or left-to-right paradigm throughout the report presentation.

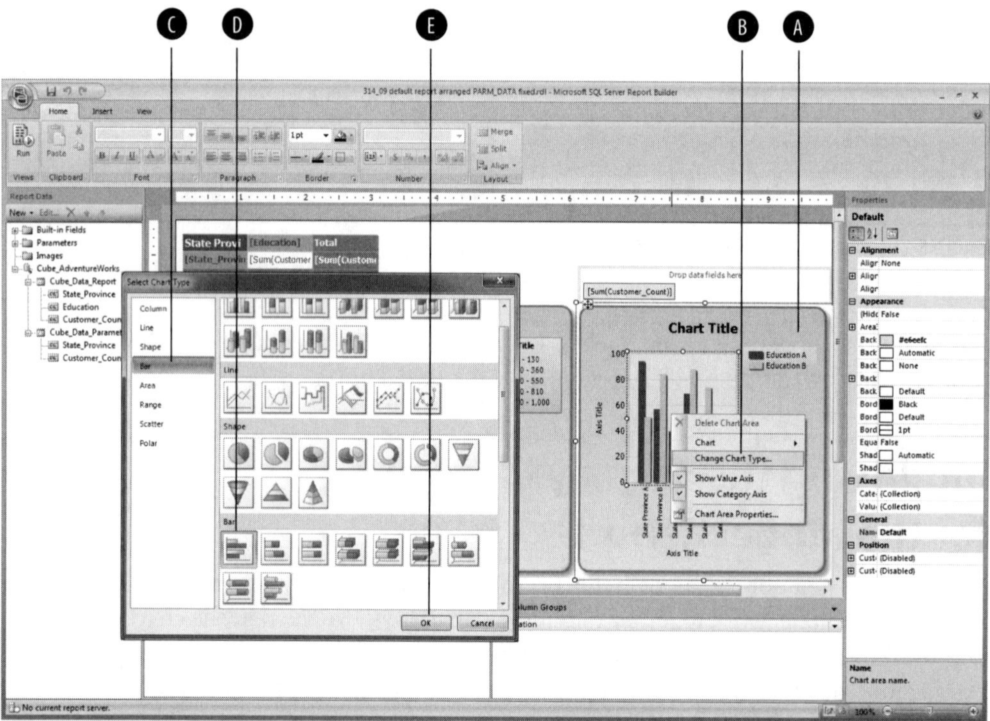

Figure 8-27 *Report Builder: chart type change*

In Figure 8-28 you see the result of our model report with the rearranged chart.

1. On the Home tab on the top ribbon menu, click the Run icon (Step A) to render the report.
2. In the Run Viewing pane, click the upper-left Parameter drop-down, and select Alabama, Arizona, California, and Florida (Step B).
3. In the Run Viewing pane, click the upper-right View Report button (Step C) to render the report.

Figure 8-28 is certainly looking better, but now we can see a new problem. The parameter values of states, which can be from 1 to 50, depending on what the user chooses when running the report, create a matrix that can run too tall vertically and push the map and chart off the immediate screen. While we could say the end user should simply scroll to see the entire report, there is a better way to enhance this part of the report experience, as we see with the steps in Figure 8-29, where we modify the matrix.

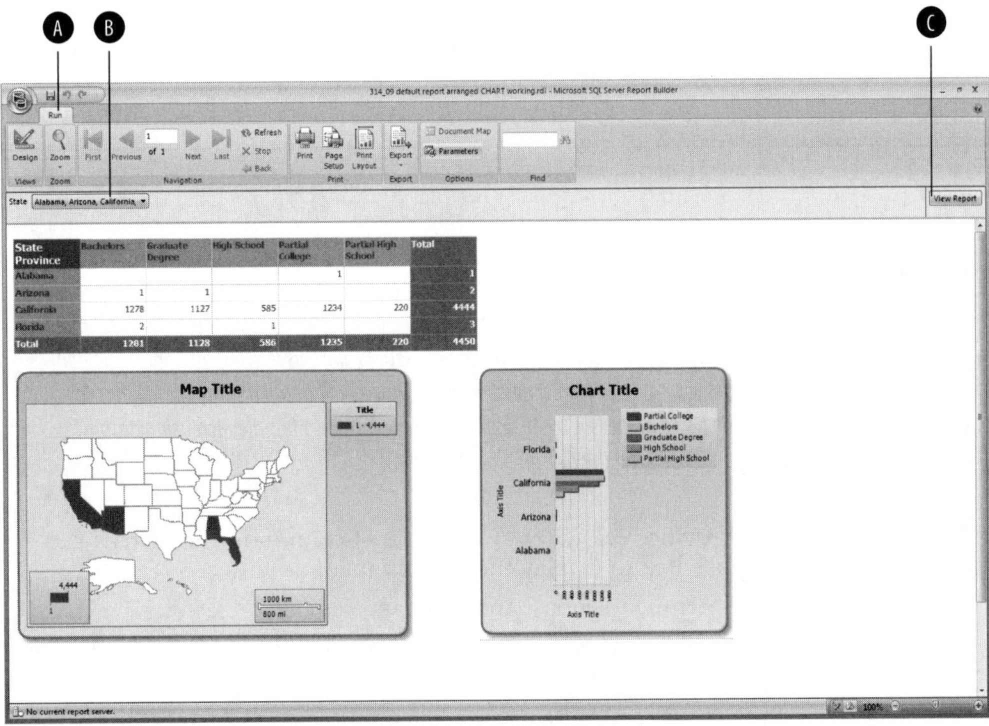

Figure 8-28 *Report Builder: working report rendered with revised chart*

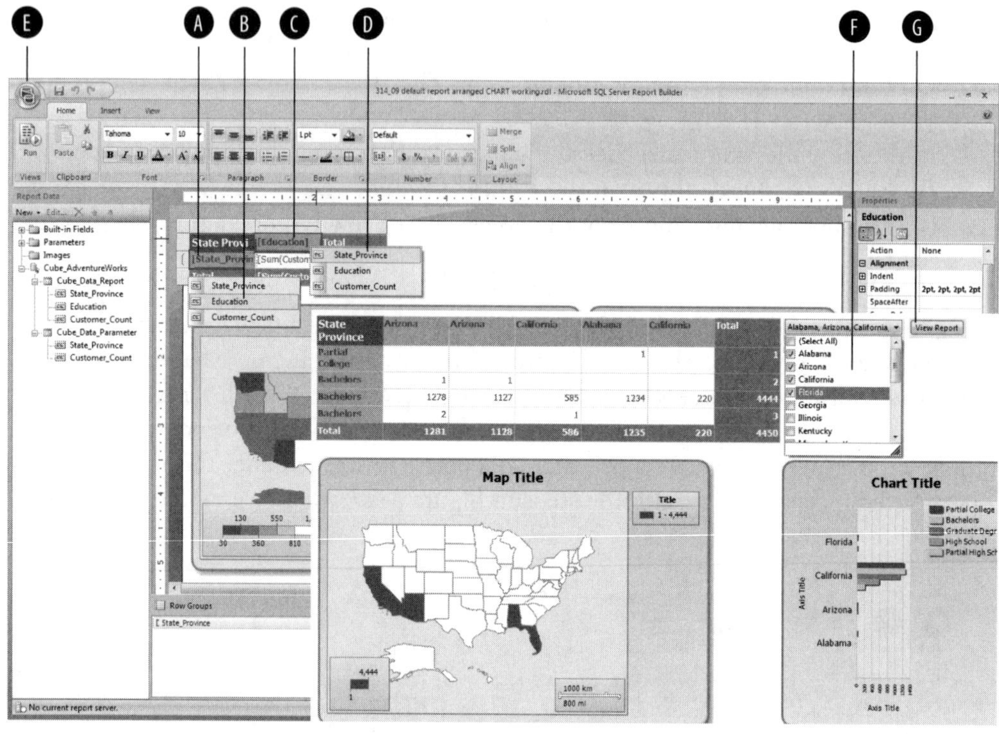

Figure 8-29 *Report Builder: working report rendered with revised grid*

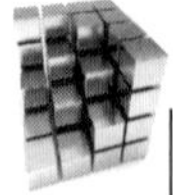

BI TIP

The interaction of parameter values and report rendering involves a balancing act that attempts to produce a good-looking report, no matter what parameter values are chosen. While this is often an impossible goal because so many data values can be chosen that they overwhelm the report detail display (at least as far as the end user is concerned), we can try to address it by designing the report to best handle increasing data by growing horizontally or vertically—depending on the overall report design.

1. Select the State_Province cell (Step A, or the first column in the matrix; the data cell), and right-click to display the pop-up menu.
2. Select Education (Step B) to choose the row data element.
3. Select the Education cell (Step C, or the second column in the matrix; the data cell), and right-click to display the pop-up menu.
4. Select State_Province (Step D) to choose the column data element.
5. On the Home tab on the top ribbon menu, click the Run icon (Step E) to render the report and view the revised matrix.

6. In the Run Viewing pane, click the upper-left Parameter drop-down, and select Alabama, Arizona, California, and Florida (Step F).
7. In the Run Viewing pane, click the upper-right View Report button (Step G) to render the report.

Figure 8-29 shows off the nice features of the Report Builder graphical user interface, where we are able to select columns and rows and change the entire makeup of the matrix. In this case we're placing State to render as column headers—which can then run horizontally to the right as far as they need to.

And in Figure 8-30 we take the next step in this new paradigm of displaying States horizontally, by changing the chart to reflect the same behavior.

1. Select the chart on the main report design pane (Step A), and right-click the pop-up menu to choose Change Chart Type (Step B).
2. In the Select Chart Type dialog box | Column tab (Step C), select the second Column icon on the second row (Step D) to choose a vertical (column) 3-D stacked chart.

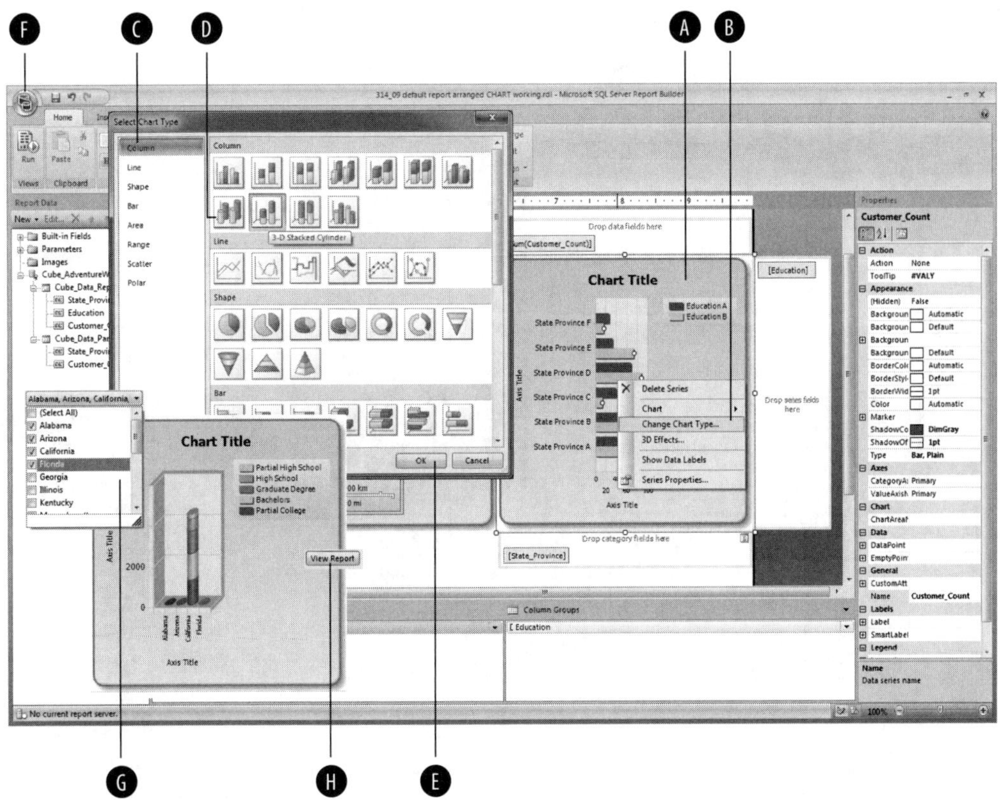

Figure 8-30 *Report Builder: working report with revised grid and chart*

3. Click OK (Step E) to save the chart configuration.
4. On the Home tab on the top ribbon menu, click the Run icon (Step F) to render the report and view the revised matrix.
5. In the Run Viewing pane, click the upper-left Parameter drop-down, and select Alabama, Arizona, California, and Florida (Step G).
6. In the Run Viewing pane, click the upper-right View Report button (Step H) to render the report.

Figure 8-30 shows that we can change the chart to display States along the horizontal X axis—and we can also choose a "stacked" column effect that shows the makeup of Customer Counts by Education, with a vertical column for each State chosen by the user in the Parameter values. This complements the matrix which shows the detail numbers for the combinations of States and Education, and does so with a consistent vertical arrangement of Education types.

Figure 8-31 continues our quest for consistency, by showing how we change the Education legend to the left side of the chart—which is similar to the Education breakout showing on the left side of the matrix! These seemingly small steps can make a big difference in the overall presentation of a data story to end users.

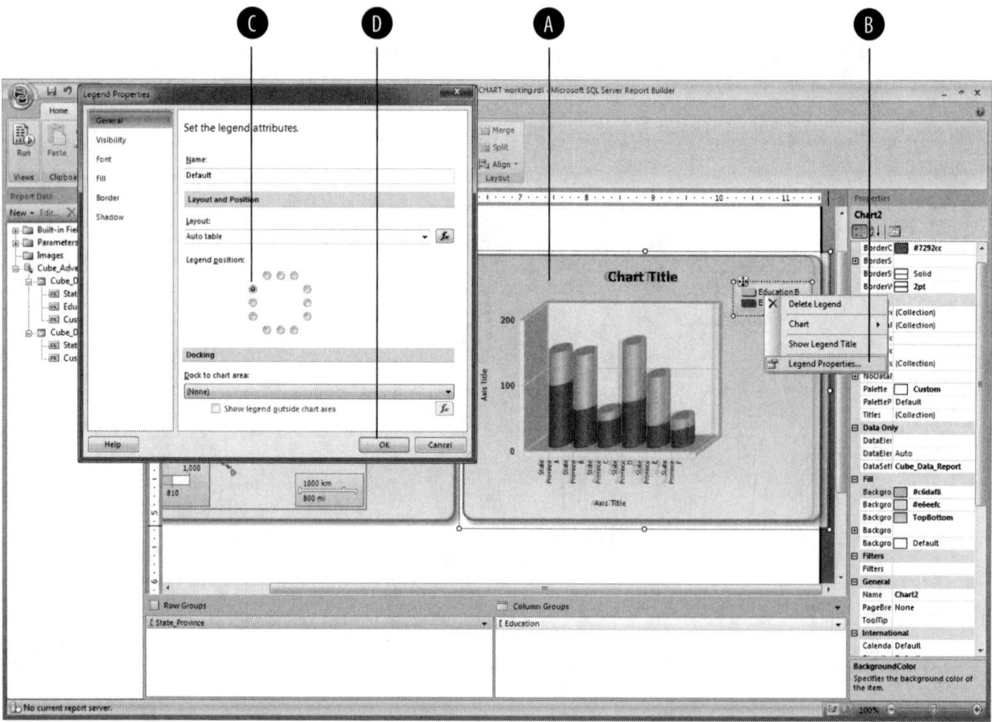

Figure 8-31 *Report Builder: working report—revising chart again*

BI TIP

As a good design for report presentation is achieved through the steps outlined in this section, the process can be continued with other reports. The result can be a consistent look and feel to the reports that is so consistent that end users actually know the reports come from the same business organization. The benefit is that knowledge workers can more readily interpret the various reports because they become faster at interpreting the consistently formatted reports!

1. Select the chart on the main report design pane (Step A), and then click again on the legend inside the chart design pane, and right-click the pop-up menu to choose Legend Properties (Step B).
2. In the Legend Properties dialog box | General tab, in the Legend Position pane, click the upper-left (10 o'clock position) on the graphical position display (Step C) to move the legend to the upper-left inside the Chart pane.
3. Click OK (Step D) to save the legend configuration.

The results of Figure 8-31 are shown as we render the model report again in Figure 8-32. It's clearly becoming a better report, with the matrix showing the detail cell-by-cell data for Customer Counts by State and Education, the map showing the relative summation of customer counts by State (without Education information), and the chart showing the relative makeup of Education types by State.

1. On the Home tab on the top ribbon menu, click the Run icon (Step A) to render the report and view the revised matrix.
2. In the Run Viewing pane, click the upper-left Parameter drop-down, and select Alabama, Arizona, California, and Florida (Step B).
3. In the Run Viewing pane, click the upper-right View Report button (Step C) to render the report.

Figure 8-32 shows a new problem, however. The matrix is now showing redundant Education rows and redundant State columns—it's clearly out of whack! The fix is pretty straightforward, as we see in Figure 8-33, where we rebuild the matrix.

1. Select the matrix element in the main report design pane (Step A), and press the DELETE key to remove it from the report—so that it can be re-created.
2. Click the top ribbon menu Insert tab (Step B), click the Matrix icon (Step C), and select the Matrix Wizard on the pop-up menu (Step D).
3. In the New Table Or Matrix dialog box, choose a dataset, select "Choose an existing dataset in this report" (Step E), and select Cube_Data_Report in the Dataset list box (Step F).

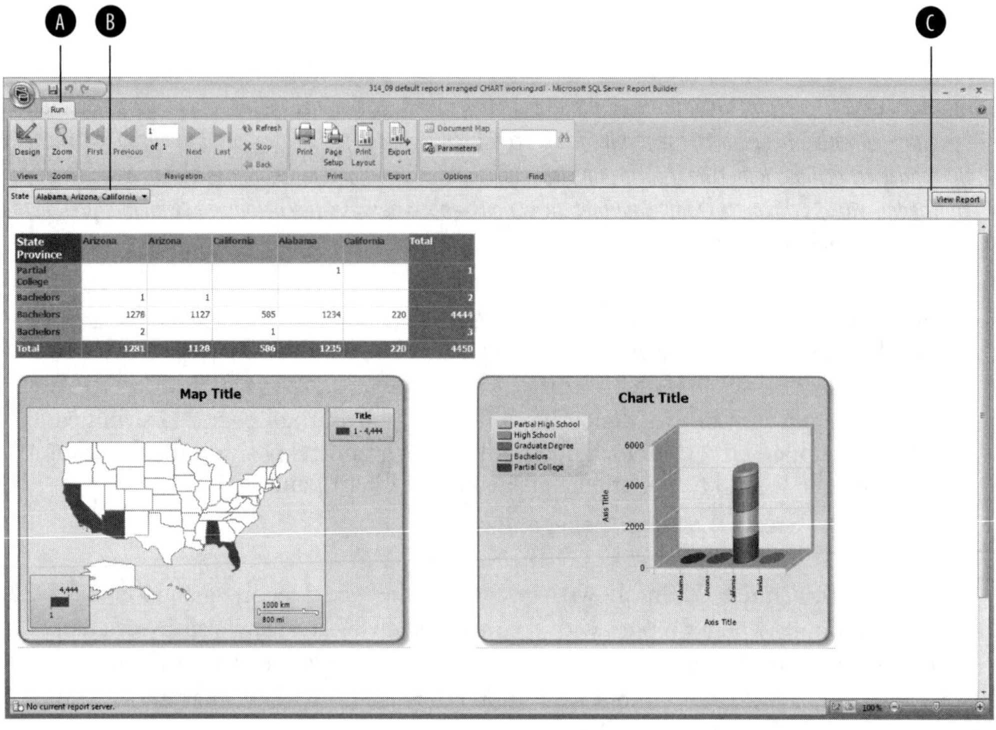

Figure 8-32 *Report Builder: working report—revised chart again rendered*

4. In the New Table Or Matrix dialog box, in the Available Fields list box, select State_Province (Step G) and drag it to the Column Groups list box (Step H).
5. In the New Table Or Matrix dialog box, in the Available Fields list box, select Education (Step I) and drag it to the Row Groups list box (Step J).
6. In the New Table Or Matrix dialog box, in the Available Fields list box, select Customer_Count (Step K) and drag it to the Values list box (Step L). Note that it automatically changes to "Sum(Customer_Count)" to provide a sum-by-group element for the new report.
7. Click Next (Step M) to continue.
8. In the New Table Or Matrix dialog box, check the Show Subtotals And Grand Totals check box to provide a full matrix cross-tab display for the new report.
9. Click Next to continue.
10. In the New Table Or Matrix dialog box, select Ocean for the style of the matrix.
11. Click OK to save the matrix configuration.

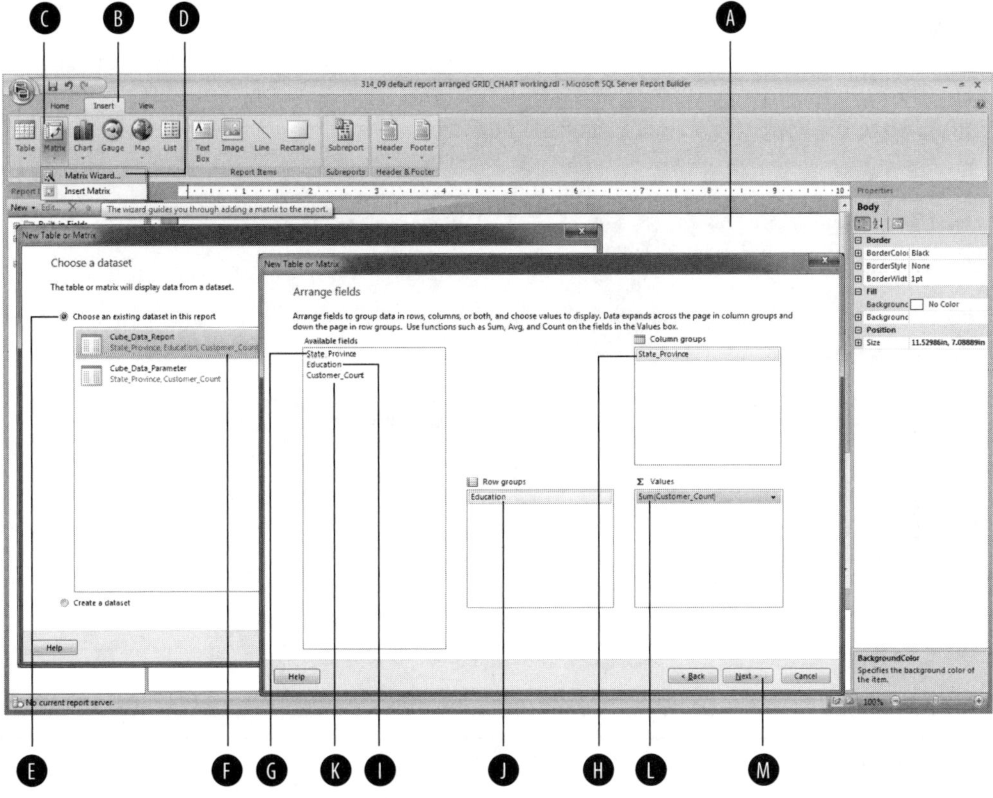

Figure 8-33 *Report Builder: working report—rebuilding the matrix*

In Figure 8-33 we use the solution of re-creating the matrix, because we knew the data presentation problem was not due to a data problem—because the map and chart were displaying correctly using the same dataset. Figure 8-34 shows the newly corrected model report.

1. On the Home tab on the top ribbon menu, click the Run icon (Step A) to render the report and view the revised matrix.
2. In the Run Viewing pane, click the upper-left Parameter drop-down, and select Alabama, Arizona, California, and Florida (Step B).
3. In the Run Viewing pane, click the upper-right View Report button (Step C) to render the report.

Figure 8-34 shows a report that is looking good—but yes, there is still another issue. The chart data is not showing in sorted order with regard to the Education legend. We'll continue our process of improving such details with the data in the next section.

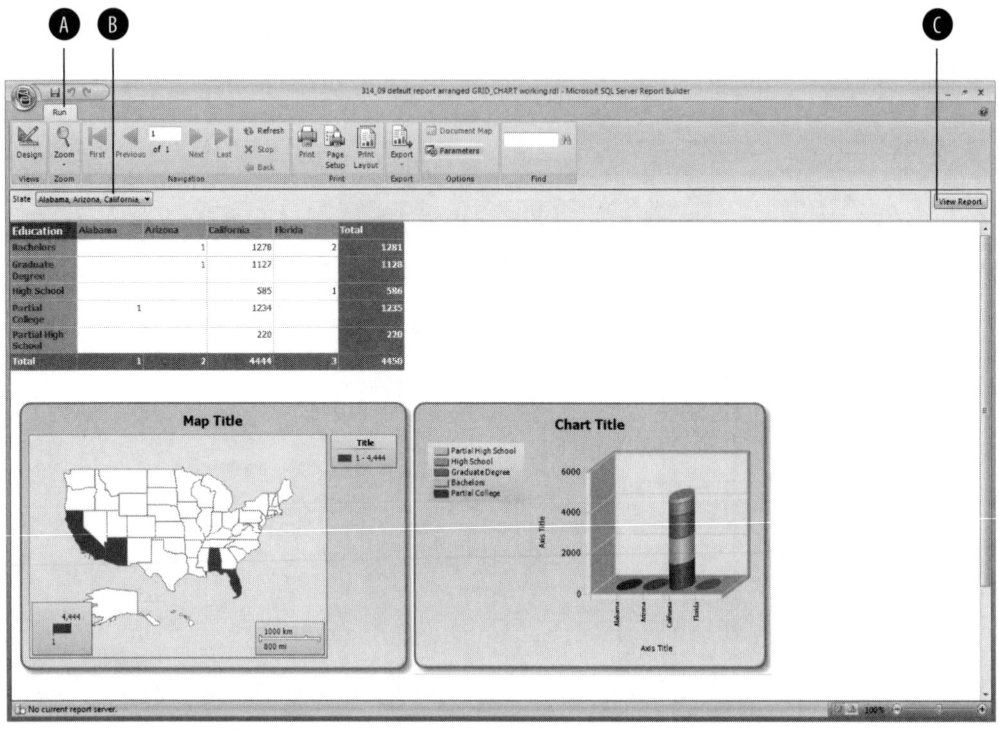

Figure 8-34 *Report Builder: working report—corrected matrix*

Modifying the Data Display for the Model Report

Our working model report is pretty far along, but fixing the smaller data details is like fixing misspellings in a document—it's necessary to achieve a professional result that can be confidently deployed into production use. After all, if knowledge workers are going to use our reports to run the business, we should do everything we can to produce a top-quality, accurate report that is totally consistent in its presentation of a data story.

Figure 8-35 shows how we jump back into the chart configuration to adjust the legend data display.

1. In the main report design pane, select the chart (Step A) to display the Chart Properties in the right-hand Properties pane.
2. Expand the Group node (Step B); click in the SortExpression node and click the ellipses (. . . , Step C) to display the Series Group Properties dialog box.

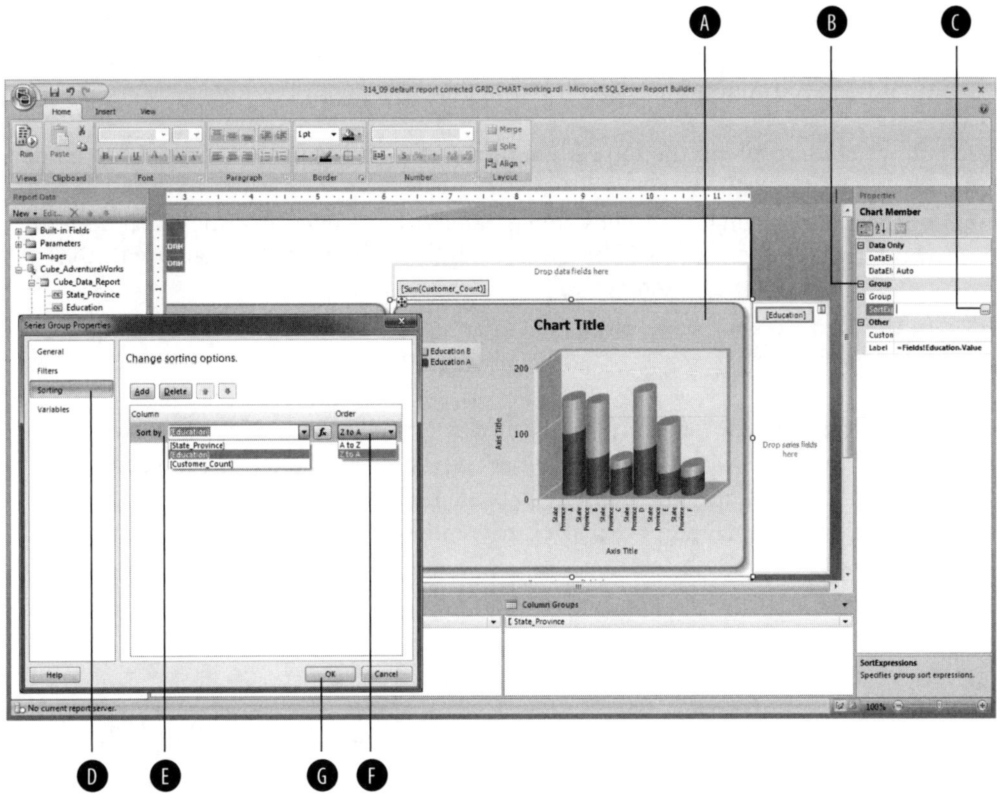

Figure 8-35 *Report Builder: working report—sorting the Chart Series data*

3. In the Series Group Properties dialog box | Sorting tab, (Step D) in the Sort By drop-down, select [Education] (Step E) to change the chart data grouping sort order to Education.
4. In the Order drop-down, select Z to A (Step F) to change the chart data grouping sort direction to descending—which will actually put the lower sort-value at the bottom of the Chart Legend.
5. Click OK (Step G) to save the Chart Series configuration.

Figure 8-35 shows that the Report Builder interface is quite detailed in supporting various data presentations, including the presentation of group data used in legends. Note that the chart Group sorting-by-Education is adjusted for the Customer Count series. Each column shows the parts and the aggregate of the Education groups of Customer Count for an individual state.

We are effectively grouping the entire chart data presentation by state along the horizontal axis, which is consistent with the matrix display of states along its horizontally arrayed column headers.

1. On the Home tab on the top ribbon menu, click the Run icon (Step A) to render the report and view the revised matrix.
2. In the Run Viewing pane, click the upper-left Parameter drop-down, and select California, Oregon, and Washington (Step B)—which are the states with the most significant order numbers.
3. In the Run Viewing pane, click the upper-right View Report button (Step C) to render the report.

Figure 8-36 shows the next version of our model report, and we've taken some care to select the states with the most data to show off the results. Again we note that something is missing—the numeric data elements need a consistent thousands separator with no decimal points, to be clearly understood.

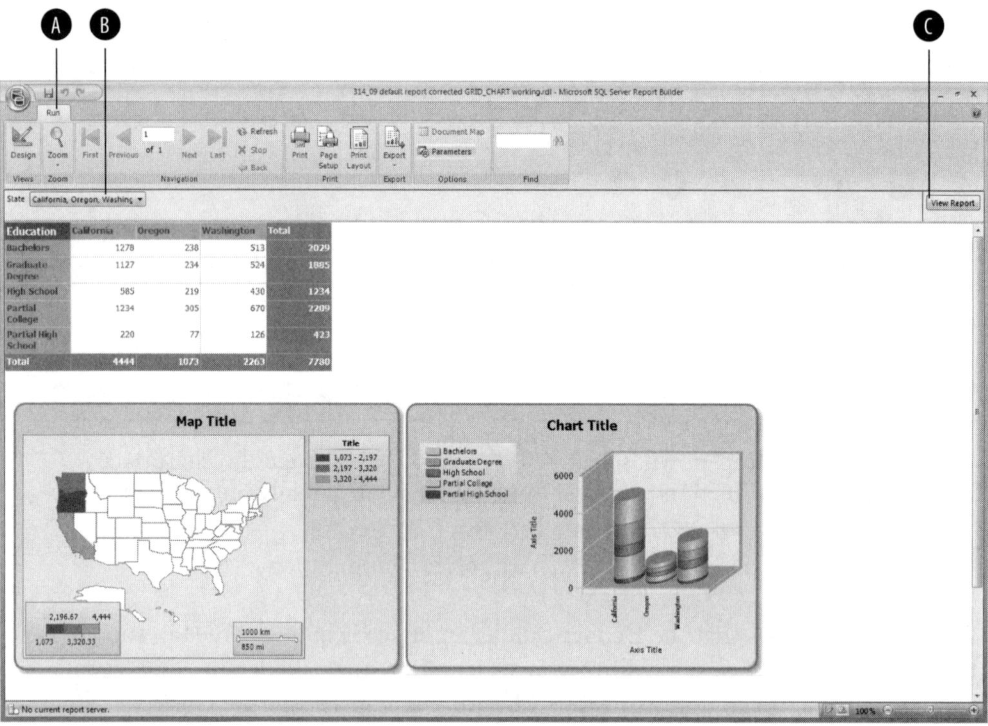

Figure 8-36 *Report Builder: working report—sorted Chart Series rendered*

BI TIP

Consistent labeling really matters in good report design. And labeling includes not only the use of easily understood headers such as Education in our working report—but also the use of consistent numeric formatting for the data displays. In this case it does not help to show decimal points, so we don't; and it helps to see thousands separators, so we apply this to all objects in the report.

1. In the main report design pane, select the chart (Step A), and click again on the vertical axis of the chart (Step B) to display the Value Axis Properties dialog box.
2. In the Value Axis Properties dialog box | Number tab (Step C), in the Category list box, select Number (Step D) to display thc number formatting choices.
3. Select the Use 1000 Separator (,) check box (Step E) to format the vertical Axis display.
4. Click OK (Step F) to save the axis configuration.

Figure 8-37 shows how we adjust the chart data display for the thousands separator. It's really amazing that the Report Builder supports an intuitive dialog box to such a level of detail, and we see this continues in Figure 8-38 as we adjust the matrix display in the same manner.

1. In the main report design pane, select the matrix (Step A), and click again on the [Sum . . .] cell of the matrix (Step B)—then right-click to choose Text Box Properties on the Text Box pop-up menu, to display the Text Box Properties dialog box.
2. In the Text Box Properties dialog box | Number tab (Step C), in the Category list box, select Number (Step D) to display the number formatting choices.
3. Select the Use 1000 Separator (,) check box (Step E) to format the cell display.
4. Repeat this procedure, selecting each of the remaining "[Sum . . .]" cells in the matrix—and choosing the Use 1000 Separator (,) check box.
5. Click OK (Step F) to save the text box configuration.

In Figure 8-38 we had to take some time to adjust the minute details of each cell in the matrix—but the result is worth it when we see the next version of our working model report in Figure 8-39.

1. On the Home tab on the top ribbon menu, click the Run icon (Step A) to render the report and view the revised matrix.
2. In the Run Viewing pane, click the upper-left Parameter drop-down, and select California, Oregon, and Washington (Step B)—which are the states with the most significant order numbers.
3. In the Run Viewing pane, click the upper-right View Report button (Step C) to render the report.

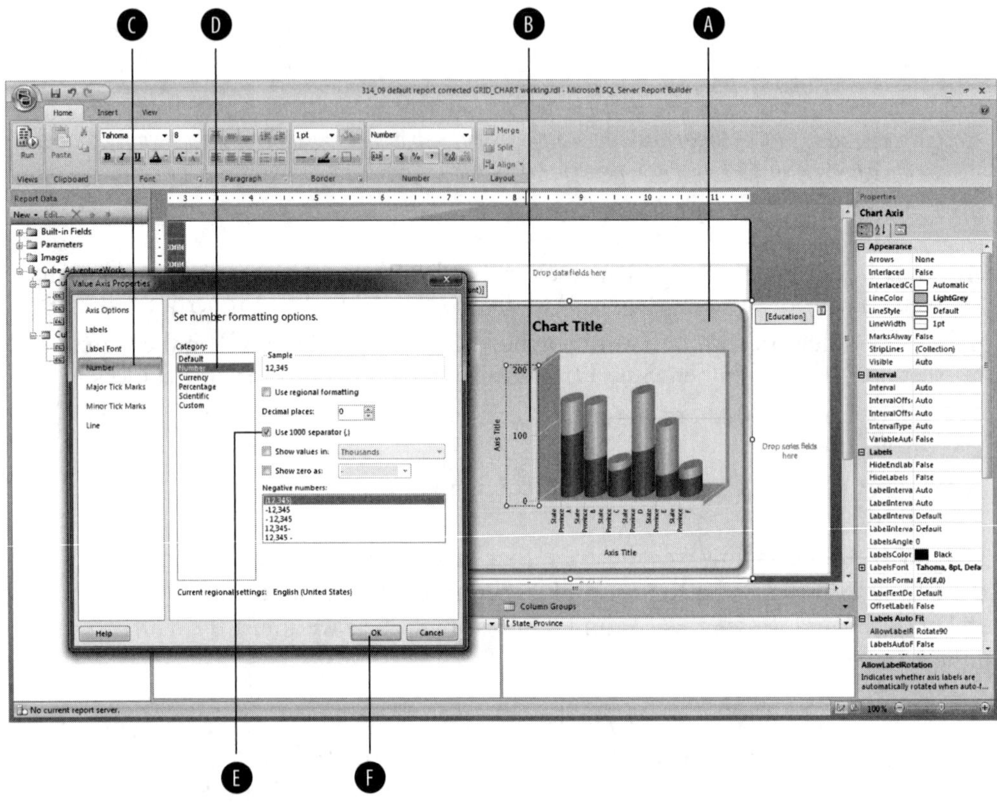

Figure 8-37 *Report Builder: working report—chart axis thousands separator*

Figure 8-39 shows a mature report design. We have three objects that portray a consistent data story, with each using a unique visualization of the same report dataset. The report consumer can grasp the "Customer Count" story at a glance and travel from the matrix detail to the map geographical display to the chart with a state-by-state relative education level display.

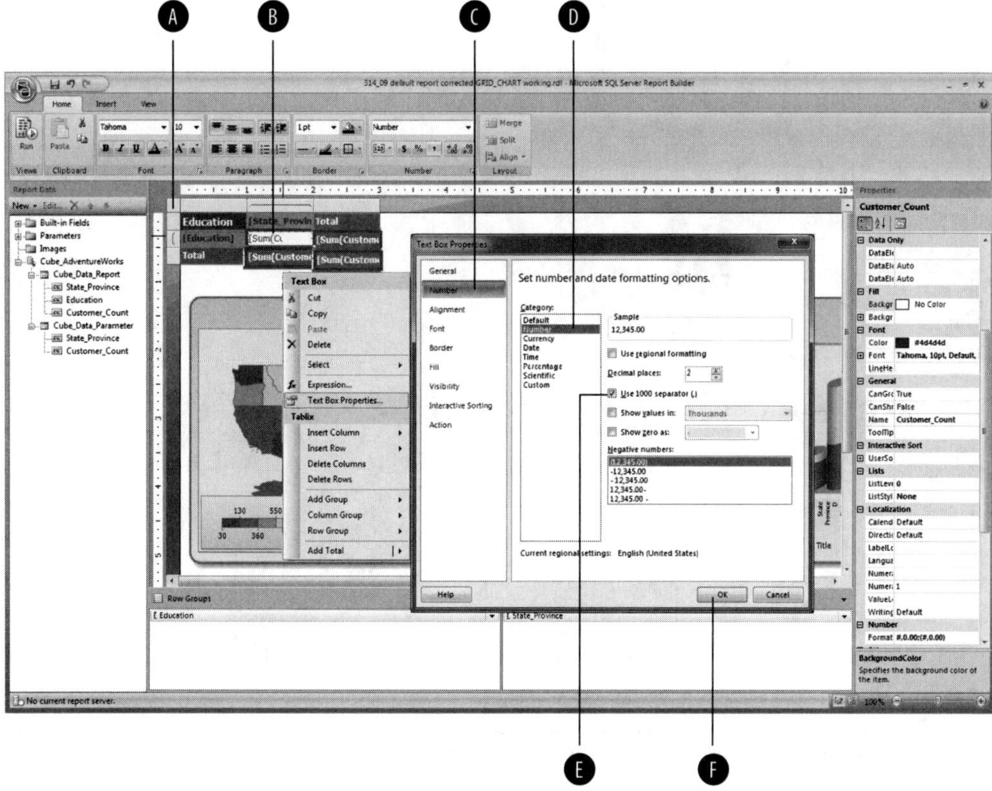

Figure 8-38 *Report Builder: working report—tablix thousands separator*

It's worth noting that the model report is driven by a parameter that allows the end user to choose one or many states and still have the report essentially fit within a single display screen on the computer. This is a good report, and yet there are still some final steps we can take to improve the display, as you'll see in the next section.

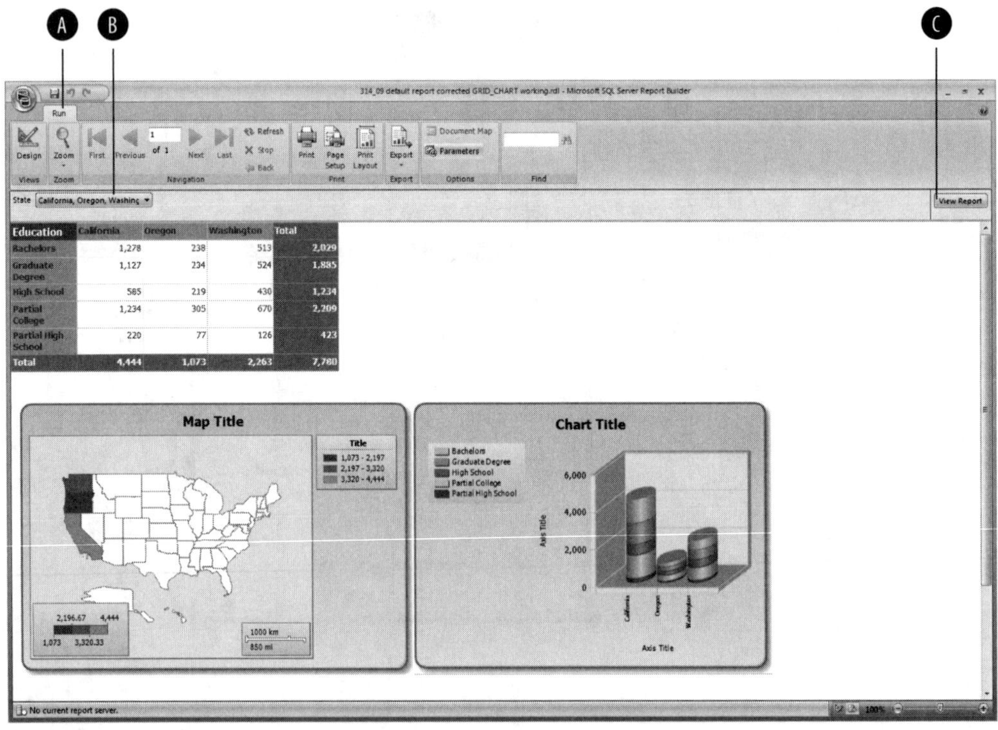

Figure 8-39 *Report Builder: working report—thousands separator rendered*

Report Element Display and Position Changes to the Model Report

As we continue to polish our model report, it makes sense to look more closely at the final formatting of our working report objects. This fine-tuning of report elements is often overlooked, but it can make a good report into a model report.

Formatting Report Objects

It's amazing to see how much control the Report Builder interface provides over the details of the map display. In Figure 8-40 we take the next steps of adjusting elements in the map object.

1. In the main report design pane, select the map (Step A), click again on the Title of the map (Step B)—and right-click to select Delete Legend (Step C) on the pop-up menu and remove the legend from the map display.

2. Click the Distance Scale of the map (Step D)—and uncheck the Show Distance Scale check box on the pop-up menu (Step E) and remove the distance scale from the map display.
3. Click the Color Scale of the map (Step F)—and right-click to select Color Scale Properties on the pop-up menu to display the Map Color Scale Properties dialog box.
4. In the Map Color Scale Properties dialog box | Number tab (Step G), select Number (Step H) to display the number formatting choices.
5. Select the Use 1000 Separator (,) check box (Step I) to format the vertical axis display.
6. Click OK (Step J) to save the color scale configuration.

In Figure 8-40 it's worth noting that we eliminated a couple items on the map display: the legend and distance scale. However, we are keeping the color scale, since it intuitively shows the relative Customer Count levels, by color, on the states of the map.

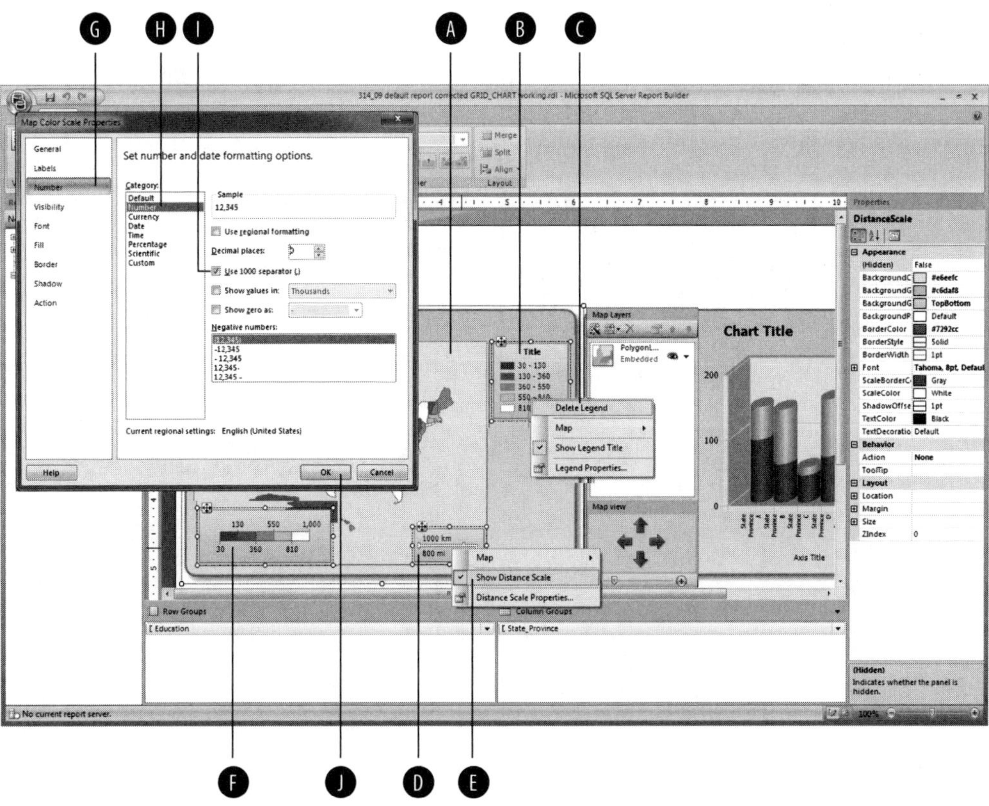

Figure 8-40 *Report Builder: working report—map formatting*

BI TIP

It's important to realize that we should not necessarily display all elements of a report object, just because we can. In most cases it's a good rule of thumb to eliminate any elements that simply tell the same "data story" for the object in a slightly different way. A good report is then left with fewer display elements that tell a straightforward story that is consistent and easily interpreted by report consumers who already understand the business process being reported.

Figure 8-41 continues our labeling exercise. The goal is to produce a consistent report with internal labels that are easy to read and make sense to the end user who is familiar with the business process being reported—who just needs a report presentation of data in a grouped manner (in this case by state and education).

1. In the main report design pane, select the matrix (Step A), and click again on the top-left cell of the matrix (Step B)—and enter **Internet Customer Count** to change the matrix title.

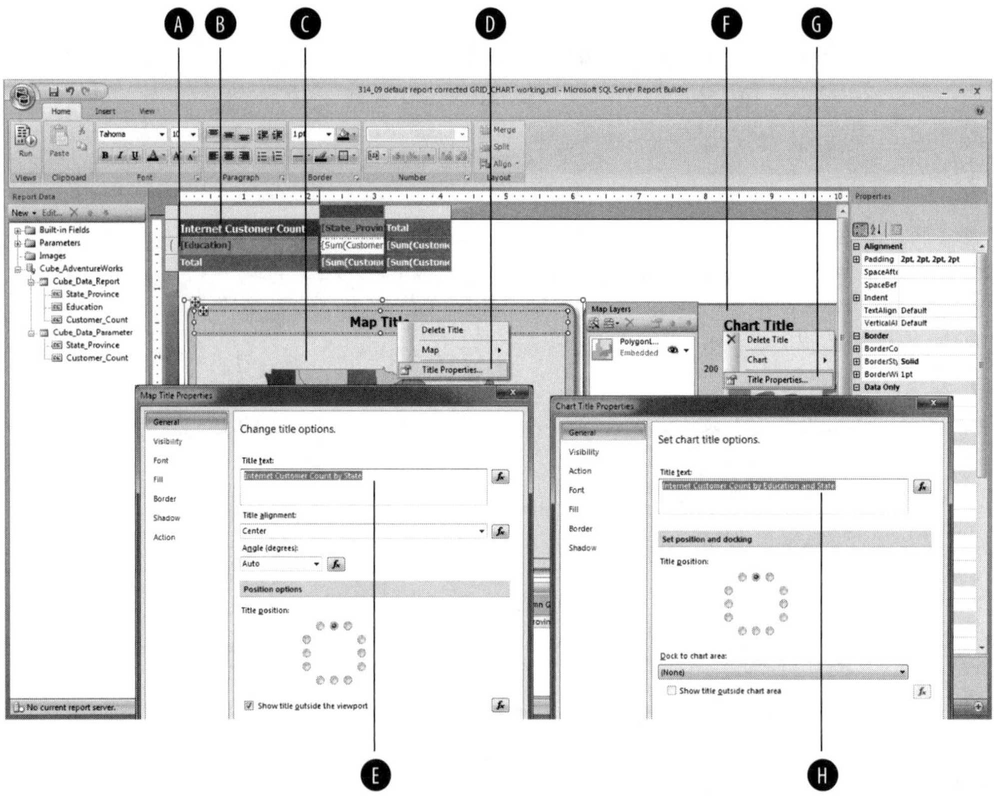

Figure 8-41 *Report Builder: working report—titles formatting*

2. In the main report design pane, select the map (Step C), and click again on the Map Title; then right-click to choose Title Properties in the pop-up menu (Step D) to display the Map Title Properties dialog box.
3. In the Map Title Properties dialog box | General tab, in the Title Text box, change the text to **Internet Customer Count by State** (Step E) for a consistent title.
4. Click OK to save the map title configuration.
5. In the main report design pane, select the chart (Step F), and click again on the Chart Title, then right-click to choose Title Properties in the pop-up menu (Step G) to display the Chart Title Properties dialog box.
6. In the Chart Title Properties dialog box | General tab, in the Title Text box, change the text to **Internet Customer Count by Education and State** for a consistent title.
7. Click OK to save the chart title configuration.

Note that in Figure 8-41 we have a nice flow to the labels of the report objects. The top matrix object has a simple label of "Internet Customer Count" that is clearly arranged by Education rows and State columns. The next object, the map, has a label of "Internet Customer Count by State" as a next variation on the data story, and the final chart object has a label of "Internet Customer Count by Education and State" (a more sophisticated display).

However, there is a problem when we run the report for all states—the matrix grows appropriately in a horizontal manner to the right, but the chart is pushed along with the right-end of the matrix to the far right end of the report! Figure 8-42 shows how we fix this aspect of the report.

1. In the main report design pane, scroll down to show a couple inches of blank space below the map and chart (Step A).
2. In the top ribbon menu, click the Insert tab (Step B), and click the Rectangle icon (Step C) to add a rectangle to the report.
3. Click at the upper-left of the blank space (Step D)—and hold the left mouse button down—while moving the mouse to the lower-right of the blank space (Step E), and thus place a rectangle on the report that is a bit wider than the map and chart combined.

Figure 8-42 uses an ingenious feature in Report Builder: the ability to keep report objects together in space relative to each other, by using a Rectangle. Some care must be used in drawing a rectangle that is a bit to the left of the leftmost margin of the map object (and positioned below the map and chart objects) and extends a bit to the right of the rightmost margin of the chart.

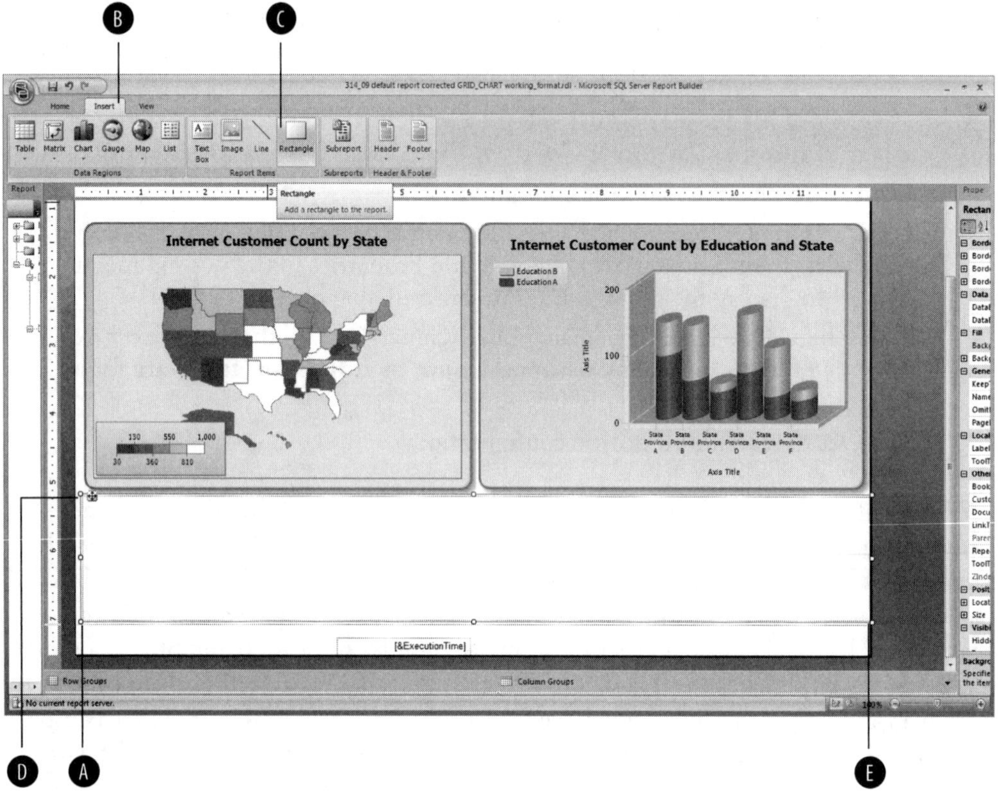

Figure 8-42 *Report Builder: Rectangle container added to report*

In Figure 8-43 you see the map and chart objects can be dragged and dropped into the rectangle below.

1. In the main report design pane, select the map—and holding the left mouse button down, drag the map into the left-side area of the rectangle (Step A).
2. In the main report design pane, select the chart (Step B)—and holding the left mouse button down, drag the chart into the right-side area of the rectangle (Step C).
3. In the main report design pane, select the rectangle (Step D), which now contains the map and chart, and drag it up to eliminate the large horizontal blank space between the matrix and rectangle-map-chart.

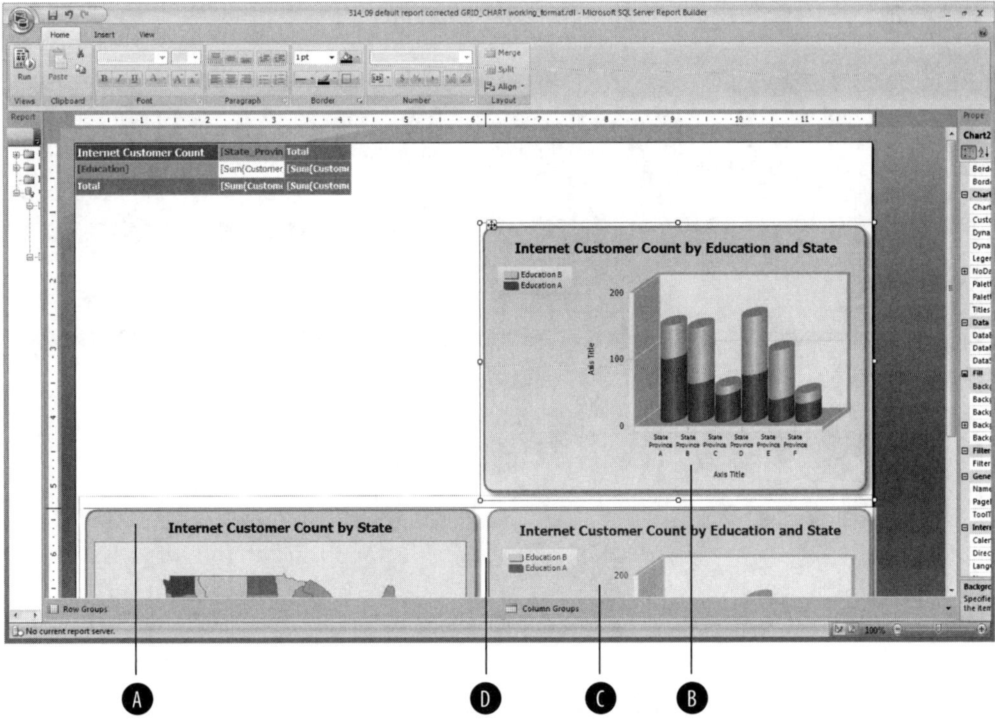

Figure 8-43 *Report Builder: Rectangle—map and chart dragged onto rectangle*

Although it may seem like we have to do some careful work to get the report objects to render in the proper configuration, it's actually pretty amazing that the Report Builder design interface supports this arrangement in a manner that works properly for browser report rendering. And with our model report we're taking report objects a step further by including three very different data presentation devices in a single interface. Figure 8-44 shows the final report as rendered with all states.

1. On the Home tab on the top ribbon menu, click the Run icon (Step A) to render the report and view the revised matrix.
2. In the Run Viewing pane, click the upper-left Parameter drop-down (Step B), and select "(Select All)" to display order numbers for all states.
3. In the Run Viewing pane, click the upper-right View Report button (Step C) to render the report.

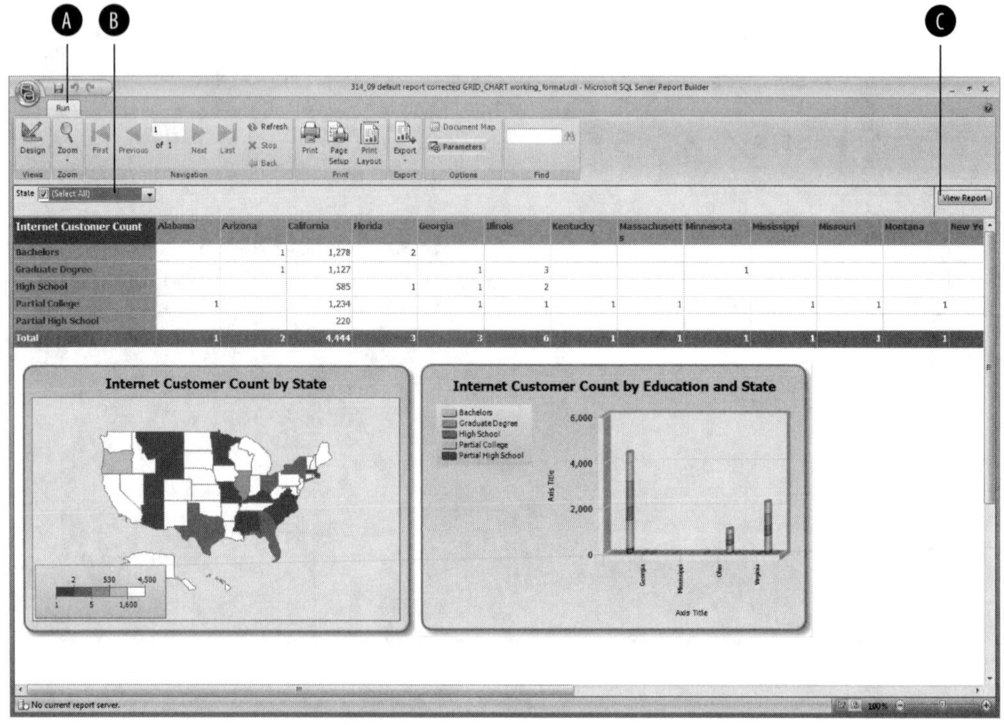

Figure 8-44 *Report Builder: Rectangle—rendered report*

Color Adjustment of the Report Objects

In this final section we'll put some final polish on our working report by homogenizing the colors of the report objects. This presents some challenges, since each object has its own color formatting configuration—each is designed to support a particular type of display object. However, it proves to be worthwhile to show Education levels, for example, with a consistent color scheme across the matrix and chart. The map is designed to support the report presentation by showing relative levels of customer counts, and so we'll adjust its color scheme accordingly.

BI TIP

Color is an important part of a report presentation, and it's used to help tell the data story. However, thought must be given to choosing colors that will display nicely on a projector screen, for example—versus a gray-scale printed page. It makes sense to choose dynamic colors for the screen-projector presentation first, and then adjust them through trial and error if the same report must also be printed to a black-and-white printer.

Figure 8-45 shows how we configure the matrix color display according to group data values.

1. On the design pane, click the "[Education]" cell of the Tablix object (Step A), and then click in the left margin of the Tablix, just to the left of the "[Education]" cell.
2. On the right-side Properties pane, click the + plus icon to expand the Fill property (Step B), click in the text box for the Fill property, and then click the drop-down icon and choose the Expression link in the color dialog box (Step C).
3. In the Expression dialog box, type the following .NET expression: **= switch(Fields!Education.Value = "Bachelors" , "Silver", Fields!Education. Value = "Graduate Degree" , "Teal", Fields!Education.Value = "High School" , "Tomato", Fields!Education.Value = "Partial College" , "Khaki", Fields!Education.Value = "Partial High School" , "Turquoise")** (Step D).
4. Click OK (Step E) to save the configuration.

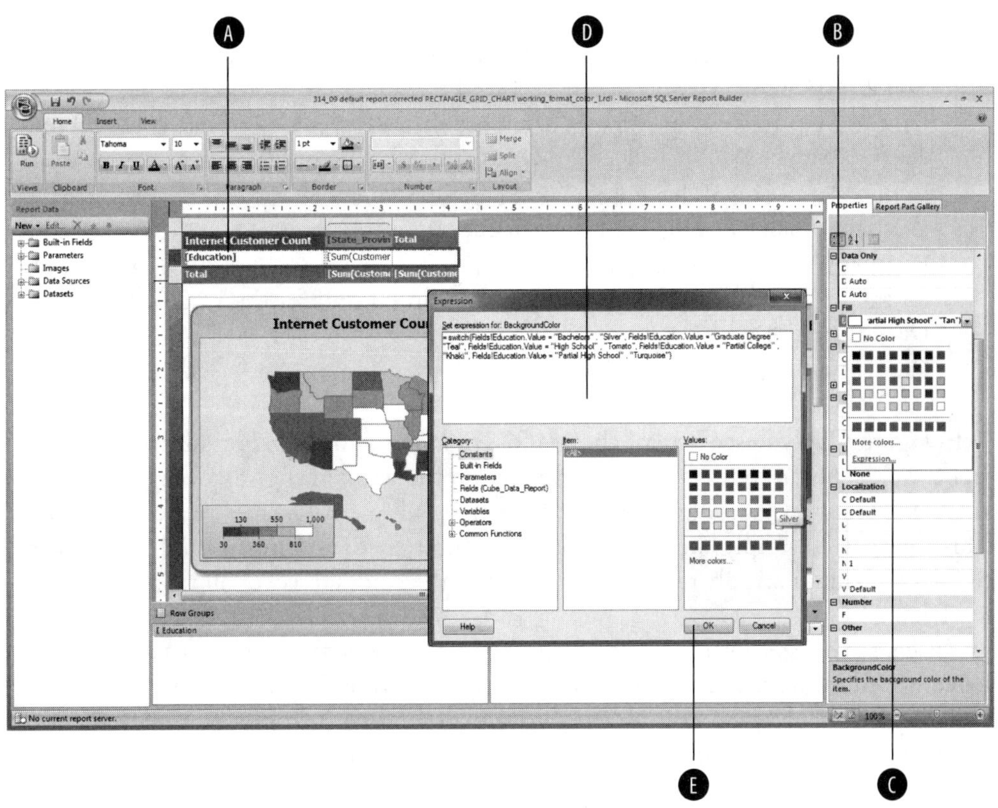

Figure 8-45 *Report Builder: tablix color expressions*

In Figure 8-45 we've become a bit more sophisticated in our report design by using .NET expressions to configure the grid colors. This is because the matrix does not have a native color configuration interface that allows us to choose or control a color scheme that changes with the Row data group values. In our working report, we would like to show different colors for each Educational group.

It's important to note that we are choosing colors that will closely complement the color scheme we'll subsequently choose for the chart object! For example, we want the "Bachelors" Education data group to be displayed in silver for both the tablix and the chart objects.

The formula we use in Figure 8-45 is actually a .NET expression syntax that can be found on any Internet search for ".Net expression syntax" examples. And while an explanation of expressions is beyond the scope of this chapter, it's important to realize that a good report designer can control almost every aspect of the report's objects with expressions where needed.

Figure 8-46 shows how we continue the color formatting design for our Map object.

1. On the design pane, click the Map object (Step A), and then click again on the Map object to display the Map Layers pop-up menu.
2. On the Map Layers pop-up menu, choose the Polygon Color Rule (Step B) to display the Map Color Rules Properties dialog box.
3. In the Map Color Rules Properties dialog box | General tab, choose the "Visualize data by using color ranges" option button (Step C).
4. For the Start Color, choose Light Green in the drop-down color pallet (Step D), for the Middle Color, choose Sea Green (Step E), and for the End Color choose Dark Green (Step F).
5. Click OK (Step G) to save the configuration.

In Figure 8-46 you see several choices for color configuration. For our working report we've chosen to let the Report Builder do the work of slightly changing the color scheme to smoothly show a gradation across the multiple color scale ranges of the map. This allows us to simply choose three colors—three shades of green—and the Report Builder will automatically produce a gradient of the colors to cover all ranges displayed on the map!

We chose the green variations because they are somewhat different from the color scheme used in the tablix and the chart—which is appropriate because the map shows a slightly different version of the data story with relative customer count levels (not the actual customer count levels by education that the tablix and the chart display).

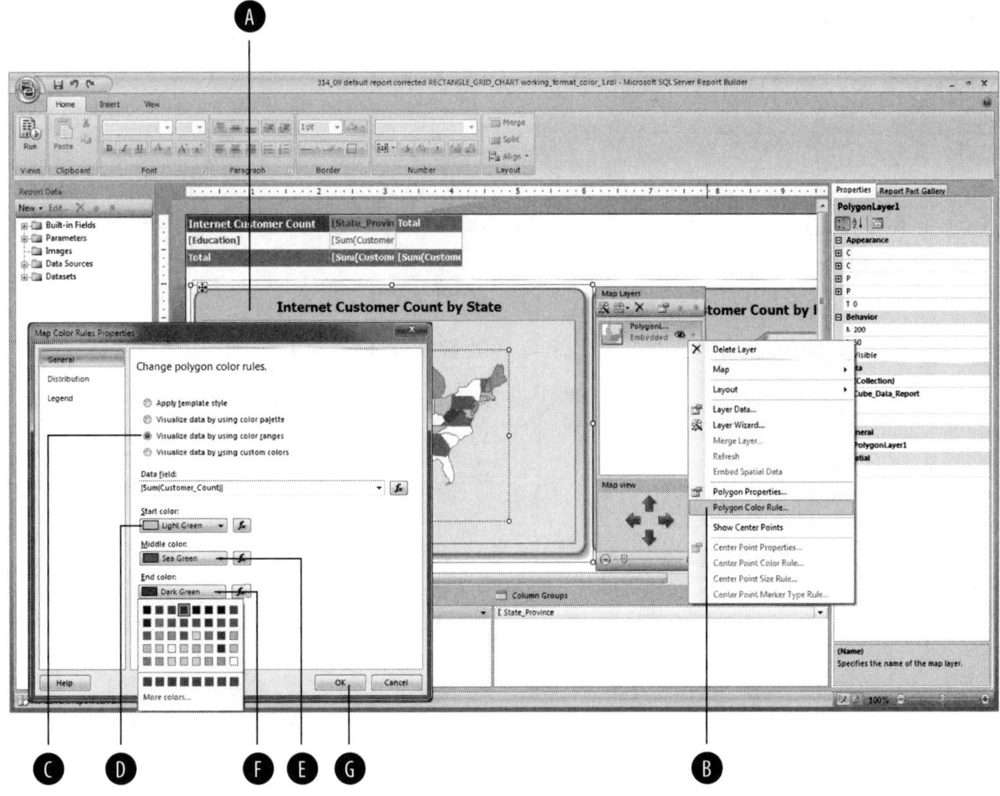

Figure 8-46 *Report Builder: map color configuration*

In Figure 8-47 we finish our color formatting exercise with the easiest configuration of all: the chart color pallet.

1. On the design pane, click the chart object (Step A), and then right-click to display the Chart Properties dialog box (Step B).
2. In the Chart Properties dialog box, choose Bright Pastel in the Color Palette drop-down box (Step C).
3. Click OK (Step D) to save the configuration.

In Figure 8-47 we see several choices for color configuration. The choice of palette affects the entire chart—and we must let the chart automatically allocate the resulting colors across the Education data groups. Given this constraint, we actually used the Bright Pastel automatic colors assigned in the chart object, to choose the colors for the expression-guided tablix in the previous steps for tablix color configuration!

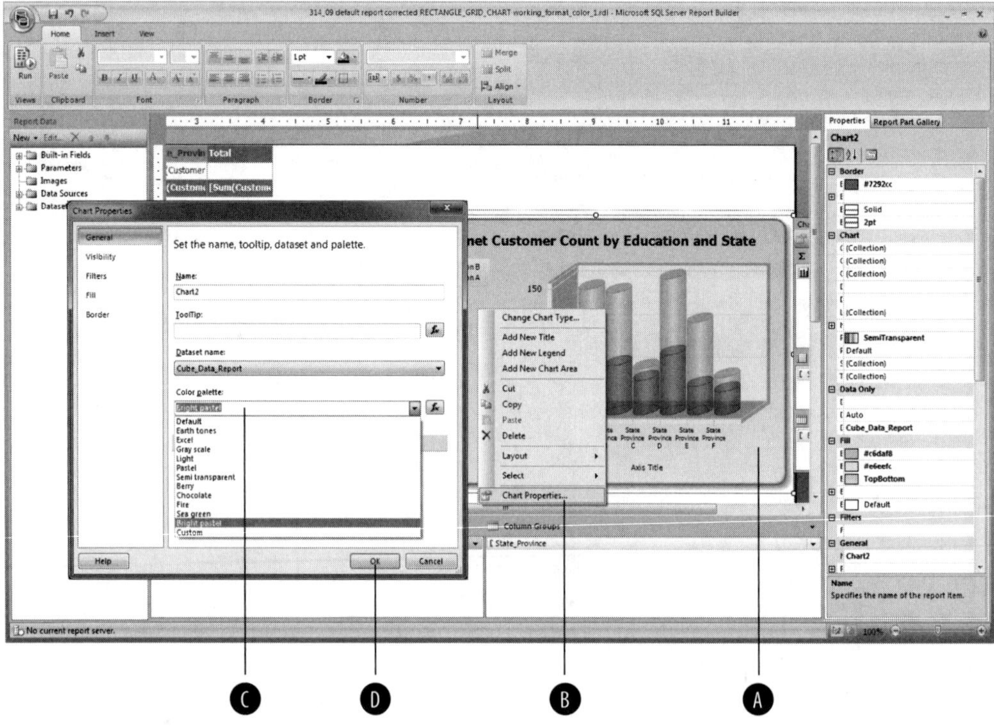

Figure 8-47 *Report Builder: chart color configuration*

Figure 8-48 shows our final working model report: a three-object single-page presentation that leads at the top with a grid of exact customer counts by state and education. Moreover, the grid has the added benefit of displaying blank cells where there are no customer counts by state and education—which in and of itself is a valuable insight.

The map shows at a glance the relative state levels of customer counts—enhancing the data story with the familiar geographic paradigm. And finally, the chart shows the graphical stacked column makeup of customer counts by state—in complement to the grid and the map.

1. On the design pane, click the Run icon (Step A).
2. On the Run screen, choose "(Select All)" on the Parameter drop-down menu (Step B).
3. In the Run Viewing pane, click the upper-right View Report button (Step C) to render the report.

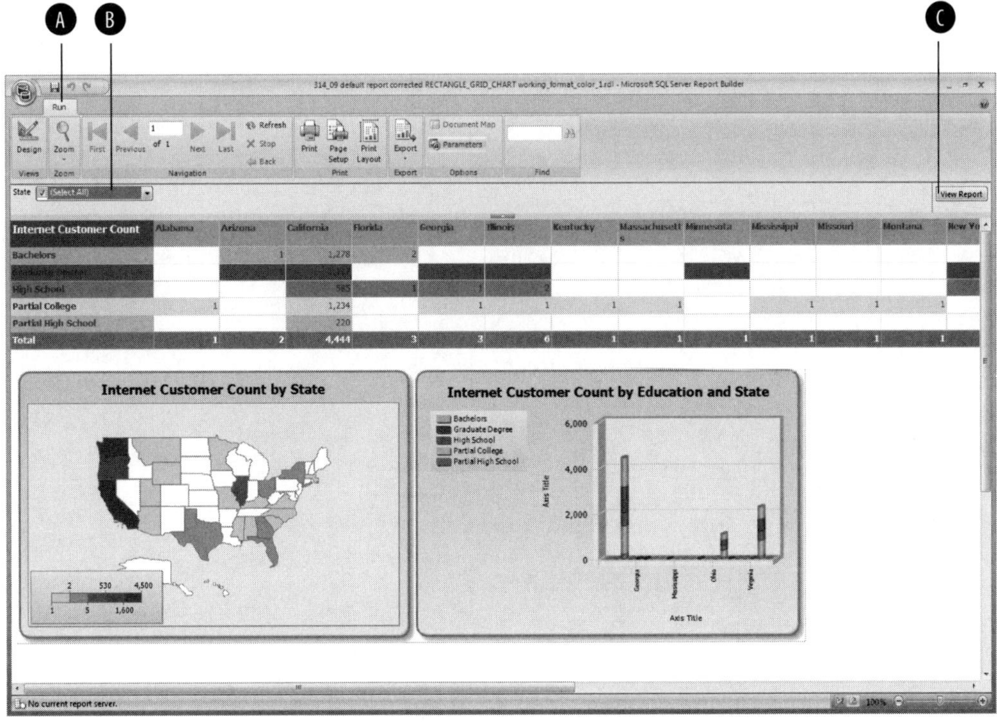

Figure 8-48 *Report Builder: color report—rendered*

Wrap-Up

This chapter has provided a fairly complete journey through the design of a complete report presentation. We worked with assumptions that a single-page display would be best for the immediate impact, and then configured three report objects to show three versions of the same "customer count" data story.

We ran down the roads of configuration for each report object, often working around the defaults to create a compelling report that really tells a story in an intuitive manner. And as we probed the configuration details, it became clear that there are many, many more configuration options available. The proper use of the configurations really depends on the business story to be explained, and will vary with each dataset and with each customer target audience. With that being said, it should be apparent that a good report designer will never stop with the default display of report objects but will instead always explore the extra options that make a report immediately consumable and understandable!

Index

Numbers

A

B

C

D

E

F

G

H

I

N

O

P

Q

R

S

V

W

Y

Z